John Brown's War Against Slavery

Drawing on both new and neglected evidence, this book reconstructs Old John Brown's aborted "war" to free the 3.8 million slaves in the American South before the Civil War. It critiques misleading sources that either exalt Brown's "heroism" and noble purpose or condemn his "monomania" and "lawlessness." McGlone explains the sources of Brown's obsession with slavery and his notorious crime at Pottawatomie Creek in "Bleeding Kansas" as well as how the Harpers Ferry raid figured into Brown's larger vision and why he was captured in the federal armory there. *John Brown's War Against Slavery* chronicles how this aged American apostle of violence on behalf of the "downtrodden," this abolitionist "fanatic" and "terroriser," ultimately rescued his cause by going to the gallows with resolution and outward calm. By embracing martyrdom, John Brown helped to spread panic in the South and persuaded Northern sympathizers that failure can be noble and political violence "righteous."

Robert E. McGlone holds a PhD in history from UCLA and is currently Associate Professor of History at the University of Hawaii at Manoa. He is the author of scholarly articles, which have appeared in the *Journal of American History* and *Civil War History*. He has also contributed to several collected volumes and encyclopedias, including *His Soul Goes Marching On*, *The Oxford Companion to African American Literature*, and the *Macmillan Encyclopedia of World Slavery*.

John Brown's War Against Slavery

ROBERT E. McGLONE

University of Hawaii, Manoa

CAMBRIDGE
UNIVERSITY PRESS

CAMBRIDGE UNIVERSITY PRESS
Cambridge, New York, Melbourne, Madrid, Cape Town, Singapore, São Paulo, Delhi

Cambridge University Press
32 Avenue of the Americas, New York, NY 10013–2473, USA

www.cambridge.org
Information on this title: www.cambridge.org/9780521514439

First published 2009

Printed in the United States of America

A catalog record for this publication is available from the British Library.

Library of Congress Cataloging in Publication data
McGlone, Robert E.
 John Brown's war against slavery / Robert E. McGlone.
  p. cm.
 Includes index.
 ISBN 978-0-521-51443-9 (hardback)
 1. Brown, John 1800–1859. 2. Abolitionists – United States – Biography.
 3. Antislavery movements – United States – History – 19th century. I. Title.
 E451.M37 2009
 973.7′116092–dc22   2008054806
 [B]

ISBN 978-0-521-51443-9 hardback

Contents

Manuscript Depositories: Abbreviations

BPL   Boston Public Library, Department of Rare Books and Manuscripts, Boston, Massachusetts
        Higginson-Brown Collection
        J. P. Quincy Papers
        Lysander Spooner Papers
        Thomas Wentworth Higginson Papers
CHS   Chicago Historical Society, Chicago, Illinois
        John Brown Collection
        Frank G. Logan Collection
        Ricks Collection
CUL   Columbia University Libraries, Butler Library, New York, New York
        The Oswald Garrison Villard Collection
HEHL   Henry E. Huntington Library and Art Gallery, San Marino, California
        James William Eldridge Collection
        Horatio N. Rust Collection
HLHS   Hudson Library and Historical Society, Hudson, Ohio
        Samuel Lyle Adair Collection
        Clark-Brown Collection
        Clarence S. Gee Collection
HU   Harvard University, Houghton Library, Cambridge, Massachusetts
        Franklin B. Sanborn Folder
KSHS   Kansas State Historical Society, Topeka, Kansas
        Samuel L. and Florella Brown Adair Collection
        John Brown Collection
        Richard J. Hinton Papers
        Huxtable Donation
        George Luther Stearns Papers
        Velma Sykes Collections
        U.S. District Court, Second Judicial District, Territory of Kansas, Journal of Judge Sterling G. Cato's court

LOC   Library of Congress, Washington, D.C.
          Henry Alexander Wise and Family Collection
MHS   Massachusetts Historical Society, Boston, Massachusetts
          John Brown Papers
          Samuel Gridley Howe Papers
NAR   National Archives and Records Service, Washington, D.C.
          Letters Received by the Office of the Adjutant General
NYPL   New York Public Library, New York, New York
          Henry W. and Albert A. Berg Collection
          John Brown Miscellaneous Papers
          Lee Kohns Memorial Collection
OHS   Ohio Historical Society, Columbus, Ohio
          John Brown, Jr., Collection
PHS   Historical Society of Pennsylvania, Philadelphia, Pennsylvania
          Ferdinand J. Dreer Collection
          Miscellaneous John Brown Papers
SUL   Syracuse University Library, George Arents Research Library,
          Syracuse, New York
          Sol Feinstone Collection
VSL   Virginia State Library, Richmond, Virginia
WRL   Western Reserve Historical Society, Cleveland, Ohio
WVDCH   West Virginia Department of Culture and History, Morgantown,
          West Virginia
          Boyd B. Stutler Collection (formerly housed at the University of
          West Virginia)
WVUL   West Virginia University Library, Morgantown, West Virginia
          Virginia v. John Brown trial documents
YUL   Yale University Library, New Haven, Connecticut
          Miscellaneous John Brown Manuscripts

Acknowledgments

I am pleased to acknowledge scholarly debts I have accumulated over many years. My interest in John Brown dates from a question that my mentor, Donald B. Meyer, asked during my comprehensive exams about John Brown's Secret Committee of Six. Meyer had inspired me to choose history as a profession by illustrating daily in his lectures that history could be a continuing adventure. But he could not then have guessed how far and how long I would later travel in pursuit of Old Osawatomie Brown.

After Meyer's departure from UCLA, Norris Hundley graciously supervised my doctoral dissertation. The seminars of Doyce B. Nunis taught me respect for the craft of history.

Colleagues at the University of Hawaii, Manoa, have shared my interest in issues raised by the Brown story. Idus A. Newby closely edited and helped me cut an earlier draft of the present study. Richard Rath and Marcus Daniel asked the right questions of it. Peter Hoffenberg and Dick Rapson encouraged my work on issues related to autobiographical memory. Craig Howes and Stan Schab of the Center for Biographical Research at the UH made the Center's resources available to me, as did its founder, George Simson, before them. Kathy Ferguson's conference papers on Emma Goldman broadened my perspective on radicalism. Former colleagues Cedric Cowing, David Farber, Louise McReynolds, and my late friend Fritz Rehbock read papers that became chapters or articles.

Over the years, historians elsewhere have contributed in various ways to the book. Jim Mohr of the University of Oregon repeatedly prodded me to return to the project with his provocative insights on conference papers. My debt to Paul Finkelman, a leading Brown scholar, and his wife, Byrgen, for their support, encouragement, and incisive editing cannot be overstated. Larry Friedman, the biographer of Erik Erikson, shared conference platforms with me, as did Catherine Clinton, Michael Fellman, Jim and Lois Horton, Leonard Richards, and Ron Walters, among others. Bertram Wyatt-Brown's astute comments on my papers were invaluable.

In four research trips across the country years ago, I incurred many debts. Park Service historian Dennis Frye gave me a personal tour of Harpers Ferry, and John Cotter showed me Brown's Adirondack home at North Elba, New York. Curator Thomas L. Vince introduced me to Hudson, Ohio, where Brown grew up, and to the essential document collections housed at the Hudson Library and Historical Society. Bob Richmond and others at the Kansas State Historical Society were equally hospitable, as were John Rhodehamel and the folks at the Huntington Library in San Marino, California, and Jim Murphy at the Ohio Historical Society in Columbus.

A computer-savvy researcher, John Barker, located and obtained electronically the maps and photos I wanted in the book and transmitted them with the permission letters for their use to the Press. Archivists Debra Basham of the West Virginia State Archives, Jill Slaight of the New York Historical Society, Melissa Cronyn of the Center for Media Services of the National Park Service, and Eva Guggemos of the Beinecke Rare Book & Manuscript Library at Yale were especially helpful and efficient in the search for images.

I am honored to add my book to the distinguished list of Cambridge University Press. My sincere thanks to Lew Bateman; his assistant, Emily Spangler; and Mark Fox at Cambridge, as well as my project manager at Newgen Imaging Systems, for their guidance in preparing the manuscript.

Family members have helped me gather information and have offered wise counsel. Ever tactful, Doris Neumann and Leslie and the late Carroll Johnson sustained their enthusiasm for the project throughout. My wife, Marion, who keeps me in touch with current realities, often traded vacations for research forays and put up with late hours to see the project to completion. A better lifeline to the present I cannot imagine.

An Exalted Defeat

The raid began well. After months of preparation and waiting, on Sunday night, October 16, 1859, John Brown and eighteen young followers abandoned their Maryland hideaway determined to free the South's four million slaves by force of arms. Bristling with Sharps breech-loading rifles, revolvers, and Bowie knives, cloaked in darkness, they trudged silently along a rain-soaked country road, then, surprising a watchman on the planked railroad bridge over the Potomac River, crossed into Virginia. Their objective was Harpers Ferry, a center of small-arms manufacturing at the confluence of the Potomac and Shenandoah Rivers and the site of a federal armory and arsenal. Brown sent men to cut the telegraph lines and others to guard the two bridges linking Harpers Ferry with the world beyond. Seizing the night watchmen at the armory, he and his men occupied the armory yard and the arsenal as well as Hall's Rifle Works a half mile upriver on Virginius Island at the bank of the Shenandoah. They halted a passenger train bound for Baltimore and held it for hours. Sending parties into the countryside, Brown "arrested" two prominent slave owners and confiscated eleven of their slaves. On Monday morning he seized dozens of armory employees as they arrived for work. Everything was going according to plan.

But during Sunday night word of the raiders' presence spread, rousing the countryside. By mid-morning Monday alarmed townsmen and militiamen began firing sporadically at Brown's sentries. Despite pleas from his men at the rifle works, Brown refused to withdraw while he still had command of the situation. That afternoon militia companies from neighboring towns recaptured the two bridges into the town and cut off Brown's men in the rifle works and the arsenal from his main force in the armory. A company from nearby Martinsburg fought its way up the armory yard from the back entrance, forcing Brown to retreat into a small brick fire engine and guard house, and closing his last avenue of escape. There Brown and his bloodied volunteers awaited their fate.

The old man had blundered badly. He had disregarded the warnings of abolitionist confidants and anxious volunteers not to launch his war against

HARPER'S FERRY, V⁴.

FIGURE 1.1. An artist's view of the busy industrial town of Harpers Ferry before the Civil War.

CREDIT: Library of Congress.

slavery in so exposed a place. He must have known that success depended on prompt evacuation of his men and the slaves who rallied to his standard. Yet he ignored the pleas from his lookouts to pull out when he might have done so unopposed. Inexplicably, he waited.[1]

Dawn of the raid's second day revealed a dozen rifle companies from as far away as Baltimore blocking every escape route. Eighty-six U.S. marines sent by train from Washington were drawn up smartly before Brown's refuge in the armory yard. Defeat was now certain. Ten of Brown's "boys," including two of his own sons, were already dead or dying, and six others were in flight. Only Brown's son Watson, his life ebbing slowly from a chest wound, and four other volunteers remained with Brown in the engine house to face the marines.

Meantime, rumors of a slave uprising created widespread apprehension. After a day of fighting and a night of whiskey swilling and waiting, nearly two thousand angry militiamen and local residents strained to hear the grim old man in the battered straw hat who spoke intently with the young army officer demanding his surrender in the doorway of the engine house. Hours before, news of the "insurrection" had flashed through the telegraph lines across the North, and by this time correspondents of several newspapers had reached the scene.

Brown was trapped. But he did not panic. He had calculated the risks of his "war" against slavery. Just as he was prepared to kill slave owners to free slaves, so he was ready to die in the attempt. He had hazarded his life repeatedly in the Kansas border war.[2] What counted now was not so much how, but why, he died. He had long been preoccupied with endings – with destroying

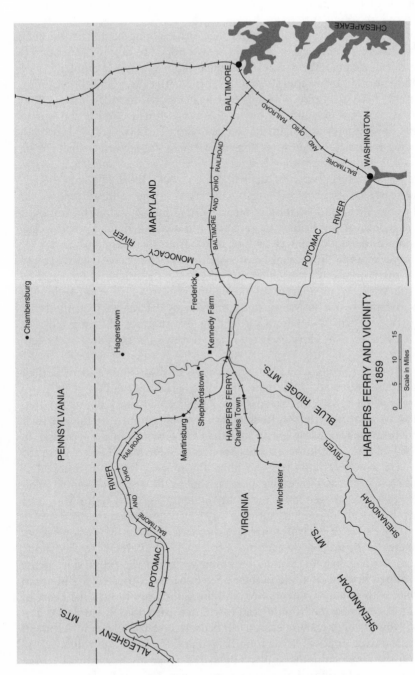

FIGURE 1.2. Surrounded by mountains, Harpers Ferry was remote from Baltimore and Washington, but accessible by river, road, and rail.

CREDIT: National Park Service.

slavery, with personal loss, with death and final states, the end of history. He was not suicidal, nor did he seek martyrdom. But if he had to die, no fate appealed to him so much as dying for the slave.

Yet as he searched the oddly familiar face of the young lieutenant bringing terms of surrender under a flag of truce, Brown hoped to talk his way out. He knew that if that failed, the marines' assault could begin at any moment.

No modern filmmaker could stage the scene better. At 7 A.M. on Tuesday, October 18, Harpers Ferry was a great theater-in-the-round. Under a low, threatening sky, wooded hills in every direction formed dark backdrops to the shafts of early morning light that eluded Maryland Heights to sketch out the closely marshaled buildings of the town below. Its factories clustered on a low shelf of land at the roiling confluence of the Potomac and Shenandoah, Harpers Ferry stretched upward against a steep, rocky bluff. Hugging the rivers' banks, two of its principal streets converged at the railroad junction at the end of the nine-hundred-foot, covered railroad bridge across the Potomac. From the mouth of the bridge, more track and a planked road carried clattering trains and wagons as well as foot traffic from the Maryland bank over the Chesapeake and Ohio Canal before vaulting the treacherous currents and eddies of the Potomac. On reaching Harpers Ferry, the tracks, shouldered by iron trestle work, swung apart along the banks of the rivers, one line following the Potomac northwest to Martinsburg and across the Alleghenies, the other running Southwest to Winchester. Wedged against the foot of Camp Hill, the narrow, stone streets of Harpers Ferry itself converged at the gates of the federal armory.

Across from the armory, on High Street, rows of shops and residences, their gray shale and red brick walls here and there plastered with a beige parging, were stacked against the steep slope. Their gabled roofs pointed redundantly toward historic Jefferson Rock and the burial ground atop the hill, their chimneys breathing wisps of smoke into the chill grayness of the morning. In two brick buildings in Old Arsenal Square across Shenandoah Street from the armory were stored perhaps 100,000 guns. Presumably Brown had hoped to equip his slave army with those weapons as well as the 950 iron-pointed pikes he had had specially forged in Connecticut and hauled secretly to his Maryland hideaway. But local militiamen, not runaway slaves descended on Brown.[3]

The armory's factories, warehouses, and offices, ordered in two long rows, were punctuated by tall, blackened smoke stacks. The buildings stretched along the Potomac River behind a stone retaining wall. On the other side of the grounds a high brick wall along Potomac Street barred intruders. Six-hundred yards long, with twenty whitewashed buildings, the armory was the heart of this small, government-built, industrial town. In busier times it employed 430 workers. Now, its high walls, elevated rail beds, steep backdrop, and turbulent rivers made escape impossible for John Brown and his desperate volunteers.[4]

Beyond the stone columns and wrought-iron fence at the entrance to the armory, Brown had gathered his five remaining men, eight of his hostages, and six of the slaves his men had "liberated." His refuge, the small, one-story, dead brick building crowned with cupola and bell that doubled as a fire engine and guard house, was freshly tattooed with the marks of musket balls and splintered wood and glass. Lifting the darkness, dawn now reached the arched windows above the heavy oak doors of the building. The light signaled the weary, frightened men inside that one way or another their ordeal would soon be over. Beyond the armory grounds, furious residents and militiamen, still baffled about the "insurrectionists," peered from doorways, windows, and rooftops. Within the compound, wearing bright blue, dress uniforms and supported by two Howitzers, a company of eighty-six marines sent by President James Buchanan readied its assault. Suggesting the haste with which the makeshift force had been assembled, the marines' commander was army brevet-Colonel Robert E. Lee of the Second Cavalry, who happened to be in Washington on leave when news of the Harpers Ferry disturbance broke. Once on the scene, Lee decided not to bargain with the "rioters" for the release of their hostages.[5] The waiting was over.

All eyes were on the double doors of the engine room, where the young army officer – Lieutenant "Jeb" Stuart of the First United States Cavalry – presented Brown with Lee's demand to surrender and his pledge to protect Brown and his men from the crowd. Stuart recognized the man. He was *Old* John Brown – Osawatomie Brown – the abolitionist firebrand who had several times eluded capture and caused "so much trouble" in Kansas. The frowning old man was thus no ordinary brigand or "incendiary." His object, Brown announced boldly, was to free Virginia's slaves.[6]

After two nights without sleep Brown looked haggard in the dim interior of the engine house, his body shielded by a heavy oak door. His deeply creased brow, heavy-lidded gray-blue eyes and close-cropped white beard were perceptible above the barrel of his carbine as he tried to bargain his way out of the hopeless situation into which his evident folly had placed him and his young followers. For several minutes, Stuart recalled, Brown spoke earnestly through the narrowly opened doors, entreating Stuart to let him take his men and hostages across the Potomac bridge, where he would release the hostages in exchange for a head start. Years later the hostages remembered snatches of his talk. "I prefer to die just here," Brown allegedly declared when Stuart rejected his proposals.[7]

Presently Stuart broke off the "parley" and, stepping aside, waved his cap to signal the assault party to charge. With spectators cheering wildly and the startled raiders firing through the doors and loopholes in the walls, a detail of twelve marines out of the line of fire rushed across the macadam street between a warehouse and the engine house. Fearing for the lives of Brown's hostages, Lee had awaited the daylight to order the assault, instructing the marines to use bayonets only. He counted on surprise. Now, failing to batter in the thick doors with sledge hammers, the marines ran at the doors three times using a heavy wooden ladder as a ram. Two marines were shot, one mortally. Scrambling through a jagged hole in one leaf of the doors with another officer, Lieutenant Israel Green thrust a light, decorative sword – his only weapon – at

Brown's belly, doubling him over. He then beat Brown unconscious with the hilt of the sword. Marines bayoneted two of Brown's men. The smoke drifted away, and the wounded were dragged in a "gory spectacle" onto the armory lawn.

Precisely what had happened during the final moments would later be hotly disputed.[8] Popular historians relying uncritically on reminiscent accounts have muddied the story. But getting it right matters. What Brown actually did and said as the marines prepared to attack is crucial to understanding both his immediate intent and his larger purpose in seizing Harpers Ferry. What he said afterward is revealing, too. Despite the blood streaking his face and beard and the utter defeat of his effort, he seemed notably talkative, even elated as Virginia authorities questioned him in the armory office. "I can hardly describe his manner," attorney Andrew Hunter, Brown's prosecutor, later told a Senate committee investigating the raid. "It struck me at the time as very singular that he should so freely enter into his plans immediately. He seemed very fond of talking."[9]

What is indisputable is that Brown not only survived his wounds to stand trial, but exploited his appearances before the Virginia court that ordered him to be hanged to win favor with northern newspaper readers. That crowded courtroom became the stage on which his failed war against slavery was reborn as a conflict of ideas, a drama of lethal potential, the very stuff of passion and myth.[10] Through the accident of his survival, the blundering insurrectionist contrived a victory of words over slavery, the "mother of all evils." Embracing martyrdom in the cause of the "downtrodden slave," Brown mesmerized the nation, infuriating supporters of slavery North and South and confirming Southerners' worst fears that abolitionists wanted to provoke servile insurrection. As Brown's most ardent champions observed, in attacking Harpers Ferry, he spread the idea of insurrection even to the slave quarters. "He translated the information into the wide-resounding dialect of civil war," the firebrand James Redpath exulted, "and compelled the telegraph, the press, the stump, the fears of the master, the hopes of the politician, the pulpit, the bar-room and the parlor to repeat it in every corner of the land."[11]

As Brown awaited the hangman in the month that followed his sentencing, he won the admiration of influential minorities in the North by picturing his failure as a deliberate sacrifice in the cause of "God's despised poor." In the end, the crucial measure of his impact as a revolutionist would be not liberated slaves but Northern converts to antislavery won during and after the most widely reported criminal trial in the republic's brief history. Brown's raid and trial also deepened the mistrust of southerners looking anxiously across the Mason-Dixon Line at what seemed an increasingly menacing North. The raid – and the abolitionists' exaltation of its defeated author – fostered intolerance toward political dissent and compromise and propelled the slavery issue to its final eruption in national politics. It changed the dynamics of sectional politics and hastened the slide into disunion. The failure of Brown's war heralded a vastly larger conflict.[12]

I

Questions about Brown bedevil historians. How had he hoped to bring down what Emerson called the South's "peculiar institution" with so small a force? Why did he not flee with his men and hostages into nearby mountains when he could have done so? Indeed, why and how had slavery become his obsession? Was he delusional? Mad? If so, how had he persuaded prominent men to finance his "mad scheme"? And how had he won martyrdom in the North even as he was convicted and hanged for treason and murder?

Brown's best biographer, Stephen B. Oates, has explained his defeat and capture by asserting that Brown was a religious fanatic who trusted God to tell him what to do after taking Harpers Ferry. A military tyro, he trapped himself waiting for slaves and "dissident whites" to rally to his standard.[13] There is some truth to the first part of this explanation. Brown was both deeply religious and a fanatic about slavery, and religion can be a powerful catalyst for violence.

But that Brown was religious is in itself no explanation for his path to Harpers Ferry. To be sure, the need for a demandingly pious vocation drove his antislavery zeal, and his belief that a just but wrathful God would punish a "guilty land" that tolerated slavery helped him justify his attack.[14] He grew up and lived his life in a family that hated slavery and loved God. His fierce sense of duty – his piety, if such it was – fused genuine compassion for the slave with, eventually, a willingness to kill for his freedom. But if evangelicals like Brown had a duty to combat sin, they also had to obey the admonition to "love thy neighbor as thyself."[15] Many of Brown's contemporaries with similar religious convictions espoused nonresistance, as Brown himself had for years.[16] His war against slavery was rooted in a lifetime of social experience and an embrace of republican ideals as much as in religious conviction.

Oates's second point is mistaken. Harpers Ferry was no act of blind faith. Brown had a plan, however flawed. The raid was the end product of long deliberation and soul searching. It was as much rooted in Brown's understanding of political realities and in hard lessons he learned in "Bleeding Kansas" as in his biblical sense of history and faith in any "call" he had to free the slaves. To dismiss the raid as deluded mistakes both the man and his times.

After Harpers Ferry, to be sure, admirers as well as critics appealed to biblical images and metaphors to describe Brown and explain Harpers Ferry. He was variously a Moses leading the slaves from Egypt, Gideon panicking slaveholding Midianites, Samson destroying the temple of slavery. These images remind us that Brown's was a time of religious awakening in which hopes for a coming millennium and fulfillment of prophecy leavened the everyday experience of the learned and the credulous alike. Christian (and sometimes classical) metaphors were templates against which people gauged outsized characters like Brown and his astonishing actions at Harpers Ferry.[17] Other contemporaries evoked similar images. To blacks, Brown's friend Harriet Tubman, a legendary "conductor" on the underground railroad, was "the Moses of her People." During the Civil War Lincoln became "Father Abraham."[18] Even white Virginians were not immune to such rhetoric. If the "Black Republican" William Seward won the presidency in 1860 because of John Brown's "blood," the Richmond *Enquirer* warned white Southerners, "the time of our exodus will have arrived, and it will produce its Moses."[19]

Brown himself contributed indirectly to his image as a religious fanatic. After his capture, his improvised persona as an antislavery martyr, broadcast in published letters to friends and well wishers from Charlestown jail and in unsolicited speeches in court, contributed to the perception that hoary wisdom and biblical examples guided his every action. Admirers compared him to the "Old Covenantor" Oliver Cromwell; detractors saw demonic fanaticism as the wellspring of his monomania.[20]

Like others who tried to understand his "war" against slavery, Brown himself saw parallels between his struggle and biblical events. He found inspiration in the deeds of Gideon and Samson, and believed his labors, like theirs, would help bring God's kingdom to earth. Writing to friends after his trial, he unhesitatingly identified himself with biblical figures and Protestant martyrs. He even compared his sacrifice to that of Paul.[21] Ultimately, he justified his recourse to violence as service to "God and humanity."[22]

But despite his public avowal after the raid that he believed himself an instrument of God, he made no claim to a revelation of his destiny. Neither did he go off by himself, as one legend builder claimed, to "wrestle with his God in secret prayer."[23] "That is all bosh," his son, Salmon Brown, said of such claims. "I never saw father with a bible or testament in Kansas. He used to ask the blessing at meal times [there] but I never heard him pray [in Kansas]. He never made a prisoner pray either." Stories to the contrary were "humbugs," Salmon added. "There is not one word of truth in any of them."[24] If Brown looked for evidence of God's Providence in events, he never said God told him to kill in Kansas or to attack Harpers Ferry. To an adherent of the New Divinity like Brown, such claims would have been blasphemy. Brown believed that we know God's will only through scripture and that sinners honor Him and discover His purpose for us in service to humanity. "What can so properly become poor, dependent, sinning, & self condemned mortals like *us*; as humility," he wrote in drafting a "sermon" on the "traits of character of the true God."[25] If Brown affirmed that shedding blood might redeem sin, as his "prophecy" implied, he cited no scriptural sanction for his war against slavery and finally confessed that God had plans for him other than to redeem the nation by the sword.[26]

The emotional roots of Brown's war against slavery were complex. His religious call was clouded by secular passions, and secular concerns largely shaped his day-to-day life. A purely religious reading of Brown thus obscures a critical dimension of Brown's imagination. He was a studied conspirator who spent long hours plotting with Kansas free-state guerrillas, persuading Eastern reformers and backers of the feasibility of his scheme, and arguing with non-resistant abolitionists, including William Lloyd Garrison himself,[27] about the justice of attacking slavery. Those colloquies and attendant "disappointments" tempered his zealotry and inhibited his actions, though they never dispelled his dream of liberating the slave. A persuasive advocate, he impressed prominent men as rational and informed, if also sometimes "imperious" and stubborn. He gave speeches to sympathetic audiences in half a dozen states, once even addressing a committee of the Massachusetts legislature on Kansas.[28] Contrary to his image then and now, he did not often act impulsively or in uncontrolled rage. John Brown was a thoughtful, often even circumspect doctrinaire.

To be sure, he continued to watch for "the language of Providence" in his quest to destroy slavery. He believed he was doing God's work. But his pilgrimage did not beguile him into delusional thinking. He knew he was no prophet nor the incarnation of a bygone martyr. Drained by chronic bouts of malaria and the constant struggle to raise money and recruit men,[29] he sometimes despaired of bringing about his "greatest and principal object." If he was dogged, he was not obsessive. Convinced of the justice of what he wanted to do, he weighed the consequences of failure against the numbing impotence of abolitionists in condemning slavery and of the federal government in arresting its spread. Even when recruiting men for his war – this "mighty & soul-satisfying" work – he asked them to enlist only "after having thoroughly counted the cost."[30] He was persuaded that the Slave Power could not be defeated through electoral politics. He was a radical abolitionist who thought deeply about the role of violence. In seizing Harpers Ferry, he acted on a considered, admittedly hazardous plan. When he struck, he had indeed "counted the cost." If Harpers Ferry was a military calamity, it was also a calculated and ultimately devastating blow against slavery.

II

The origins of Brown's war against slavery have long been disputed. Brown and his defenders claimed that he nurtured a lifelong dedication to the cause, and there is evidence for their claims, which will be noted in due course. But if he hated slavery early on in his life, nothing in his childhood or middle years foreshadowed his later turn to violence. Brown's letters from his youth and adulthood before 1855 betray no plans to attack slavery by force of arms. Critics have favored a later origin and less favorable explanations for Brown's antislavery militancy, stressing his alleged personal failures and chronic frustrations in life and positing his radical antislavery views and violence as compensating mechanisms. This interpretation is even less well supported by contemporary evidence, as will be shown in Chapter 2.

What seems indisputable is that events in Kansas transformed him. Brown was an unlikely insurrectionist. At five-feet ten inches tall and 150 pounds, in early 1855 he was an aging, spare, leathery, "rustic-looking" "gentleman" who had never fired a gun in anger or seen a man murdered. But five of his sons, now grown to manhood, had left drought-plagued Ohio in 1854 to take up homesteads in the newly opened Kansas Territory. Soon afterwards, Brown received an appeal from them for weapons to protect themselves from proslavery "Border Ruffians" from Missouri. Brown interpreted the appeal as a religious call. His decision to go promptly to Kansas changed the course of his life and the nation's history.

III

Brown's name was soon linked irrevocably to "Bleeding Kansas" – the warfare that erupted in that territory in 1856 between proslavery and free-soil forces and, by extension, the sectional strife that lingered in Kansas until the Civil War (1856–1861). On May 24, 1854, Congress had passed the Kansas-Nebraska Act opening the measureless Nebraska Territory to land-hungry settlers despite the continued presence there of Indians who occupied large areas of it. Enthusiasm for the act soon turned to dismay throughout the North. Without forewarning, the act's author and chief sponsor, Illinois Senator Stephen A. Douglas, had agreed to rewrite the bill to divide Nebraska into two territories at the 40th parallel and to omit all reference to the status of slavery in either territory. Worse, he agreed to a provision repealing the provision in the Missouri Compromise of 1820 that slavery was prohibited in all future territories carved out of the Louisiana Purchase north of 36 degrees, 30 minutes (the southern boundary of Missouri).

This meant that slavery was not prohibited in Kansas, whose eastern boundary was near the slaveholding areas of southern Missouri. New inhabitants of the territory would determine themselves whether slavery would exist there. Although the Compromise of 1850 had permitted this kind of "popular sovereignty" in what might in the distant future become the Utah and New Mexico territories, Northerners overwhelmingly saw the Kansas-Nebraska Act as a betrayal of a "sacred trust" since Kansas was north of the Missouri Compromise line. Signed into law by President Franklin Pierce, the act seemed to invite slaveholders in Missouri to seize Kansas for the South. To a man like John Brown, only the machinations of a conspiratorial Slave Power and Pierce's abuse of federal patronage could explain this diabolical development.[31]

The ensuing outrage across the North led to a rapid dissolution of old allegiances, and the birth of a new political party, the Republicans, to protest the new law. New York Senator William Seward predicted that a scramble to "win" Kansas would follow, and former Senator David R. Atchison warned his fellow Missourians that a free Kansas would threaten the survival of slavery in nearby Missouri, Arkansas, Texas, and its extension to all territories. Missourians soon founded the Kansas towns of Leavenworth and Atchison, where they and other Southerners organized secret societies and companies of riflemen committed to claiming Kansas for slavery. In the North, Massachusetts Congressman Eli Thayer and textile manufacturer Amos Lawrence, both abolitionists, founded the New England Emigrant Aid Society to colonize Kansas with free-staters. By July 1854 their efforts had resulted in the establishment of the free-state towns of Topeka and Lawrence. Henry Ward Beecher, perhaps the nation's best-known preacher, sent the free-staters in Kansas shipments of Sharps rifles, soon known everywhere as "Beecher's Bibles."

Kansas quickly became the potential prize in an eruption of long-simmering sectional rivalries. When the territorial government held an election for a territorial legislature in March 1855, perhaps 5,000 armed Border Ruffians crossed from Missouri into Kansas and voted. The resulting proslavery legislature threw out its few free-state representatives and enacted a slave code for the territory, complete with criminal penalties for speaking out against slavery or slaveholding. President Pierce recognized the proslavery government and declared illegal a rival free-state legislature that met at Topeka in the fall of 1855. In 1856 the U.S. Senate rejected the constitution that the latter body submitted in applying for statehood, despite its support by a clear majority of settlers in Kansas.

Meantime, isolated incidents of violence and the failure of the territorial government to prosecute proslavery wrongdoers created a climate of fear in free-state settlements. Amid these menacing signs of proslavery hostility, John Brown and his sons hunkered down on land claims near Osawatomie. After the bloodless Wakarusa War in December 1855, during which free-state leaders at Lawrence named him captain of a short-lived militia company composed of his sons and several neighbors, John Brown believed for some months that Kansas had been won for freedom – that the Ruffians would not stand and fight. But when a proslavery force "sacked" Lawrence the following spring, he determined to act. He accompanied a militia company led by his son, John, Jr., to the relief of Lawrence, but when the company arrived too late to punish the sackers, Brown persuaded a small party to accompany him to Pottawatomie Creek, not far from the Brown land claims.

There, on the night of May 24, 1856, Brown and his party descended on the cabins of his adversaries in what his sons later defended as a "retaliatory blow" against the proslavery party. Dragooning five men from their beds, the raiders butchered them with short, heavy, cavalry broadswords. When Brown failed to locate other intended victims, his men "confiscated" horses and disappeared into the night. The incident was remembered as the "Pottawatomie massacre."

Open warfare now broke out between proslavery "posses" composed largely of Missourians and free-state militia companies and irregulars. On June 2 Brown defeated a small force of Missourians at Black Jack. Although a settlers' meeting at Osawatomie condemned the Pottawatomie massacre, a large proslavery force burned the town on August 30 in retaliation for the killings, easily dispersing Brown's men in a firefight, and killing Brown's unarmed son Frederick. Although a new territorial governor, John W. Geary, engineered a truce before the November elections, sporadic violence resumed thereafter. On May 19, 1858, a proslavery gang killed five free-state men and wounded others on the Marais des Cygne River, not far from Osawatomie. Brown's friend, James Montgomery, retaliated by attacking Fort Scott. Led chiefly by James Henry Lane, the "Liberator of Kansas," free-state forces won battles at Franklin, Fort Saunders, Hickory Point, and Slough Creek before fighting subsided in 1859 and statehood two years later brought peace.

Bleeding Kansas destroyed popular sovereignty as a political solution to the territorial issue. It deepened distrust of the federal government in both the North and the South, breathed new life into the Republican Party, strengthened secessionist appeals, and foreshadowed the Civil War. It also gave John Brown a mission.

In 1857, his role in the Pottawatomie killings still unknown or disbelieved, Brown raised money from reformers in the East for the defense of free-state interests in Kansas. For months he led a guerrilla band in skirmishes with rival guerrillas, and briefly joined Captain James Montgomery in a free-state offensive along the Kansas-Missouri border. In December 1858, with peace restored, he led a raid into Missouri, where his men seized eleven slaves and several horses and killed a slave owner. With a price on his head, Brown boldly transported the liberated blacks by wagon and railway to freedom in Canada.

Even before peace settled over Kansas, Brown revived a plan to attack slavery in the Southern states. In May 1858 he organized a secret convention among blacks in Chatham, Ontario, which adopted a provisional constitution Brown wrote for the temporary government of a black state. The convention also declared slavery to be "a most barbarous, unprovoked, and unjustifiable war" upon an oppressed people.

Supported by contributions from a committee of reformers later dubbed the Secret Six, Brown finally gathered his force of twenty-one volunteers at a Maryland farmhouse on the Antietam or County Road across the Potomac River from Harpers Ferry. There he not only met his fate but lit a fuse that sixteen months later ignited flames that threatened not only slavery but the Union itself. The John Brown who lived out that drama was not the same man who hurried with a wagon load of weapons to Kansas four years earlier. In the struggle over Kansas, Brown witnessed proslavery "outrages" and himself committed crimes he never publicly acknowledged. Some acquaintances even then worried about his fanaticism, while others became devoted admirers. Even among his free-state neighbors, Brown was a polarizing figure.

He had long hated slavery. But in Kansas he gained a profound mistrust of proslavery government, including the federal government, which sustained "bogus" territorial law. Kansas confirmed Brown's belief that slaveholders held the federal government hostage to their interests. Brown had reached a grim assessment of the possibility of slaveholders' redemption: Their "proud hearts" would never yield to moral appeals. The nation could not be rid of slavery through moral suasion or partisan politics. The Slave Power denied both God's will and America's revolutionary heritage.

If, as I shall later argue, lifelong concerns deepened Brown's antislavery convictions, the violence in Kansas tutored him in warfare. Violence drove settlers to panicky abandonment of their claims and embittered honorable men on both sides. In the end, slavery was defeated in the territory only by the overwhelming numerical preponderance of Northern settlers. But the struggle persuaded Brown that slavery could be destroyed in the South only by creating a fear of armed interference from outside. Kansas gave Brown two powerful tools to arouse that fear: knowledge of the uses of hit-and-run warfare and an understanding of how to use the Eastern "penny" press to arouse antislavery sentiment in the North.

By making war on slavery, Brown hoped to awaken the conscience of the righteous and terrify the wicked. He thought he knew how to do that. But he brought to Harpers Ferry not only that ambition, but inner demons that boded less well for his mission. During the raid these mistaken beliefs and conflicted values played themselves out to a surprising climax. The full story of John Brown's war has yet to be told.

IV

A score of biographers has chronicled Brown's deeds and advanced our understanding of that stark, remote figure. Yet two centuries after his birth none has given us definitive explanations of his obsession with slavery or his grand scheme for ending it. Mystery still surrounds the origins of his fanaticism, his reasons for ordering the slayings at Pottawatomie Creek in Kansas, and why, at Harpers Ferry, he failed to pull his men out while he might have done so or to surrender before the marines assaulted his position. Historians are divided even about whether or not John Brown was sane. Rival groups of Brown partisans and scholars have contested his legacy since his execution. Even Brown's best biographers have failed to achieve a persuasive synthesis. In part because of the moral issues his war against slavery raises, in part because of the unreliability of witnesses to his deeds, even modern interpretations leave troubling questions unanswered. This book addresses those questions.

Admittedly, Brown is a figure of paradox. His four-year career as a firebrand and guerrilla was an odd culmination to a life devoted to raising a large family and winning respect as a citizen and neighbor. For fifty years he had toiled variously in fields, pastures, tanneries, and a counting house. A Bible-quoting Christian, in old age he became an apostle of violence. A self-styled patriot, he condemned politicians who "lick[ed] up the spittle of a southerner,"[32] and deliberately provoked sectional crisis. A believer in the rule of law, he became the first citizen hanged for treason and insurrection in the United States. Mistrustful of "mere words," he inspired adulation and hatred with oddly eloquent speeches and letters after his capture. Revered among Boston literati as a man of action, he was in a sense, as David Potter once observed, "more of an artist and man of words than any of them."[33] Brown's declaration at his sentencing that he was ready to "mingle my blood ... with the blood of millions in this slave country whose rights are disregarded by wicked, cruel, and unjust enactments" thrilled many in the North.[34] But later revelations that he had engineered the grisly assassinations at Pottawatomie disillusioned or repelled many others. When Brown is remembered today, it is, paradoxically, for both brutality and nobility of spirit.

V

In his biography of Brown, *To Purge This Land with Blood* (1970), Stephen B. Oates tried to bridge the rival biographical traditions by depicting Brown as a religious obsessive in an era of political conflict. Oates's Brown was not the Cromwellian warrior of early legend builders. Nor was he the greedy, self-deluded soldier of fortune of debunkers. He was a curious, somewhat schizoid amalgam of the legend builders' martyr and his evil doppelganger. This Brown possessed courage, energy, compassion, and indomitable faith in his call to free the slaves. He was also egotistical, inept, cruel, intolerant, and self-righteous, "always exhibit[ing] a puritanical obsession with the wrongs of others."[35]

His eccentricities grew more dangerous as he aged, Oates argued. As a youth Brown tried to master the "entire contents" of the Bible and delighted in correcting those who had not done so. "An austere, tense young man," he was "stiff as a New England deacon, utterly humorless, and so fixed in his ways that he would not bend for anybody." As manager of his father's Hudson tannery at age twenty, Oates's Brown took an "imperious attitude" toward employees. His stubbornness and arrogance grew with the years. He "never laughed" and was "uncompromising" in his convictions. Implicitly, Oates traced a growing mental instability. By 1853 Brown's moods alternated between "religious exaltation and despair." Worn down with hardship, he experienced a melancholy that left him disorganized for weeks at a time. His "excitable temperament" was much in evidence and he could become "carried away with one idea." If not "monomania," this was not rationality either.

Oates was doubtful that historians might ever persuasively identify psychosis in a subject they studied. He repudiated historian Allan Nevins's belief that Brown suffered from "reasoning insanity" and "ambitious paranoia," but he declared that Brown was not "normal," "well adjusted," or "sane" either (dismissing these terms later on as meaningless). But reference to Brown's "glittering eye" – a tell-tale mark of insanity in nineteenth-century popular culture – invited Oates's readers to conclude that Brown was touched with madness after all. Finding in Brown an "angry, messianic mind," Oates straddled the two biographical traditions.[36]

In the end, however, Oates's synthesis explained everything and nothing. In his John Brown, New Light Calvinism inspired a "nonconformist brand of abolitionism" and a belief in himself as an instrument of God's vengeance.[37] That theory clarified little. It failed to explain why the Calvinist faith of countless others produced no similar fanaticism. What was it about doctrines of foreordination and innate depravity that required John Brown to take God's vengeance?[38] Why could John Brown not satisfy his piety by rescuing slaves rather than by killing whites who owned no slaves? If the Bible taught him to serve the downtrodden, why did he become a Gideon rather than a Peter – a slayer rather than a builder? Why did he shun the path of his nonresistant missionary brother-in-law, Samuel Adair, who, almost alone among the Brown clan, remained a Kansan?[39] Oates's refusal to consider the psychological questions raised by Pottawatomie left Brown with reasons – retribution for proslavery outrages in the Territory, the hope of creating a "restraining fear" among his enemies – but no persuasive motive for the massacre. How had he chosen his victims? Neither ideology nor psychology nor the local politics analyzed by James C. Malin wholly account for the selection.[40] Thus Brown's odd yet compelling personality – his "implacable will" as well as his "messianic vision" – remained as the residual factor.[41] Consequently, Oates augmented his emphasis on Brown's reading of events by appealing to a pattern of personality traits he ambivalently associated with mental instability.

Oates's dilemma echoes the most persistent problem Brown's biographers have faced: the most compelling reasons for Pottawatomie seem insufficient to explain it. The persistence of traits formed in early life, no matter how darkly construed, also fail to persuade. There were no precedents in Brown's behavior, no agendas in his writings, that foretold Pottawatomie. That is why his son Jason and other relations drew back in horror when they learned of the murders and why some of them refused to believe that Brown ordered them. It is also why Brown's friends later said he suffered from "monomania," a form of partial "insanity" used to explain eruptions of violence in otherwise normal people. The absence of clues in Brown's early life about his potential to commit murder without remorse is in part why Allan Nevins found it necessary to theorize that Brown suffered from "paranoia." The persistence of personality traits or types could not explain Pottawatomie. Only a breakdown of personality – madness – seemed consistent with so profound a change in behavior.

Appeals to trait psychology and personality theory, I believe, have not proved adequate in coming to terms with Brown. Indeed, such an approach to explanation in biography is itself suspect. Psychologists have long argued over the validity and reliability of personality theory. In the 1970s experimental psychologists concluded that trait and type theories (those using clusters of traits to designate personality types) did not significantly predict behavior in cross-situational studies. Psychologists still committed to personality theory objected that experimenters misread the traits involved; traits could be shown to persist in novel situations, they argued, if only one measured the right traits. But whatever the merits of these rival arguments, the debate itself illustrates how subjective the identification of personality traits may be. To be sure, we all hold "implicit personality theories," preconceived notions of what traits and behaviors are interrelated.[42] We believe we can anticipate how people we know will act in novel situations. Perhaps that belief is a requisite for seeing the world as orderly and predictable. But experimental evidence suggests that an element of self-deception sustains it. In fact, experimentalists argue that we tend to distort our memory of others selectively to make their behavior consistent with our own stereotypes.[43] If that is true, traits may be "fictions," and prudence suggests that historians and biographers should not blithely attribute causative force to them.

But Oates established two points on which a fresh approach may be constructed. He argued convincingly that, however troubled and plagued by failure, Brown did indeed believe himself chosen by God to free the slaves. He was religious, though his piety was neither so benign nor so uplifting as his admirers supposed. Second, Oates's emphasis on Brown's "messianic vision" invites a focus on Brown's imagination – his self-image, his sense of mission, his perception of his own role in the course of history. Across the years, imagination was the theater in which the drama of his restless soul took place, in which his perceptions of people and events melded with his understandings, in which motives and reasons merged to shape behavior. Memory and imagination supplied the imagery and language of Brown's martyrdom as surely as for him they justified the Pottawatomie slayings. If reconciling the Gordian knot of the slayings with Brown's readiness to sacrifice himself has baffled many biographers, as it has, the central tasks of Brown scholarship are to evoke persuasively the private man and to join the gnarled cords of his inner life to his life's end.

The present study undertakes to do that. It shifts the focus away from moral issues inevitably raised by assessments of personality and character and minimizes reliance on memoirs of Brown's contemporaries and the hearsay evidence that provoked wearisome debates in the late nineteenth century. Forgetting and interference made later stories about Brown variously unreliable or far-fetched.[44] We know now that oft-told reminiscences are often bearers of unacknowledged burdens. In old age especially, memories of half-forgotten experiences serve to bolster self-esteem or protect cherished beliefs. Often the recitation of such tales tells us more about the self-image of the rememberer and the times in which he or she called the story to mind than about events remembered. Such distant memories often represent unstated aphorisms or general truths and should be read as autobiographical claims rather than faithful reports of past experience.[45]

The historical literature on John Brown is heavily burdened by uncritical acceptance of aphoristic stories as factual reports. Thus a critical reassessment of second hand stories and reminiscent testimony is in order. The resulting focus on direct evidence, especially on Brown's own words and actions whenever possible, permits a fresh reading of old conundrums and raises anew issues too long ignored.

The chapters that follow seek to resolve lingering questions:

Part I, *Inclinations of Head and Heart*, explores the experiences that shaped John Brown's imagination and informed his distinctive sense of piety. It asks why he decided to devote his life to the "service" of slaves. Why, in other words, did he become a "fanatic" for a cause?

Part II, *Rebirth*, asks why Brown went to Kansas and why he engineered the Pottawatomie killings. Was Brown a proto-terrorist seeking to effect political ends, a self-appointed "instrument of God's vengeance," or, as some claimed, a willing agent of others? When and why did he decide to make war on slavery in the South?

Part III, *Jeremiads*, considers the question whether mental disorder explains Brown's obsession with slavery, his changing moods, his willingness to kill. Was what Stephen Oates calls his "messianic vision" a paranoid delusion?

Part IV, *Strategies*, asks why Brown chose Harpers Ferry as the target of his attack on slavery. What did he hope to accomplish by taking possession of an armory and arsenal? Was it to ignite insurrection? To launch guerrilla war? Was the disparity between his limited resources and his boundless purpose evidence of "madness"? If he expected to destroy slavery throughout the South, how did the attack figure into that vision? More immediately, why did he fail to withdraw from Harpers Ferry before he was trapped? And why did he refuse Lee's terms for surrender? What happened in the final moments of the marines' assault?

Part V, *Messages*, seeks to explain Brown's apparent elation and wild claims of support after Harpers Ferry, despite the rout of his "army" and the death of two of his sons. How was he able to use his imprisonment, his performance in court, his letters from jail, and his execution to effect a symbolic victory over slavery and inspire his apotheosis among northerners opposed to or uneasy about slavery?

In short, was Harpers Ferry a historical accident – what historian C. Vann Woodward called a "private war"[46] – or a movement expressive of the political culture of antislavery? Whatever else Brown was, should he be remembered either as an early exponent of political terrorism or as an isolated, misguided zealot? What, if anything, does his example tell us of the meaning of America in the middle of the nineteenth century?

PART I

INCLINATIONS OF HEAD AND HEART

2

The Connection

Love not the world, neither the things that are in the world. If any man love the world, the love of the Father is not in him.

King James Bible, First John 2:15

John Brown is an improbable figure in American history. Hanged at age fifty-nine for inciting a slave rebellion, he personifies fanaticism. Though other abolitionists affirmed the slave's right to seize his liberty, theorized about the use of violence to free slaves, or organized slave rescues, Brown alone made war on slavery. In Kansas he captured the imagination of free-state partisans as "Old Osawatomie," an audacious, some said bloodthirsty, guerrilla leader and crusader.[1] Before he was hanged for treason, Brown defiantly hurled a prophecy of war at "this *guilty land.*"[2]

A failed insurrectionist, Brown achieved extraordinary, if polarizing fame. Surviving portrait photos of him before his desperate assault on Harpers Ferry show a sharp-featured, wiry haired, frowning old man with a firm-set mouth and intent gaze. With the long white beard he grew in 1859 to disguise himself, he looked the part of a biblical patriarch in a likeness sold widely after his death by Thaddeus Hyatt to raise money for his wife and children.[3] On the day of his execution, thousands gathered in churches and meeting halls across the North to pray for his soul. Others, across the nation, rallied in support of Virginia, projecting their hatred of abolitionists and fears of racial conflict onto him.[4]

Long before his self-described "disaster" at Harpers Ferry, his passion to destroy slavery had distanced him from old associates and "sensible" friends. He disparaged partisan politics as "talk, talk, talk!" even though he talked a good deal himself and corresponded with reformers and like-minded politicians. A devoted reader of antislavery newspapers, he belonged to no abolition society or political party.[5] Notwithstanding his later image as a fearless, even reckless warrior, he impressed acquaintances and supporters in the Northeast initially as reserved, cautious, even secretive. The wealthy reformers who

FIGURE 2.1. John Brown as a wool merchant in Springfield in 1850.
CREDIT: U.S. National Archives.

admired Brown's "manliness" and "iron will" also found him a pious, albeit strange and obstinate collaborator, a bible-quoting rebel, a Cromwell thrust into the nineteenth century to do "the work of social regeneration."[6] The "Ahab of American slavery" he has been called, and even to friends he seemed to obey some inscrutable inner dynamic. The New England literati who eulogized him as the "representative man" of his time, a "hero-saint," and an "embodiment" of the Golden Rule elevated him above ordinary mortals.[7]

Historians have pictured Brown as a grave, sharply etched zealot. Despite Richard O. Boyer's valiant, unfinished effort, *The Legend of John Brown* (1973), to plant him among reformers and philanthropists in the political landscape of his times, Brown is generally pictured by the qualities that set him apart.[8] Indeed, the debate over his "madness" stems variously from an alleged "stubborn solitariness" to the apparently suicidal nature of his raid on Harpers Ferry.[9] To many historians, as to many contemporaries, Brown exemplifies antislavery run amok, reformist idealism become delusional.[10]

But if Brown was fanatical, he was not, as one observer claimed, *sui generis*.[11] The challenge today is to understand Brown as a man shaped by his time. Put another way, it is to explain the roots of his fierce crusade against slavery.

Because the raid on Harpers Ferry heralded the Civil War, historians bracket Brown with the great figures of that fateful struggle. Legends fostered decades after his death have magnified his deeds and his iconic significance. Too often he is seen through the filters generated by the crisis of the Union in the first half of the 1860s.[12] In fact, the contours of his present historical image took shape in the late nineteenth century, when Brown himself became lost in the memory of the tragic drama his fanaticism ostensibly inspired.[13]

Consequently, in our collective memory of Brown, the four years that began with his venture into Kansas and ended in his execution after Harpers Ferry overshadow the long years he toiled in obscurity, as by turns a farmer, tanner, cattleman, horse-breeder, shepherd, and wool merchant, as well as a postmaster, surveyor, land speculator, and aspiring town builder. Brown's high-decibel heroics in the war against slavery, often using the aliases "Shubel Morgan," "Nelson Hawkins," "Isaac Smith," and "Old Hundred," obscure his life as a son, brother, husband, father, kinsman, and citizen. In biographies, his everyday life is typically represented as mere prelude to his war against slavery. Its many enduring effects on him and his "war" are scarcely mentioned.[14]

Biographers typically deal summarily with Brown's family, seeking the roots of his fanaticism in Brown the child and/or Brown the failed businessman before fast-forwarding to Brown the aging guerrilla chieftain and failed "insurrectionist." His wife and children appear in these accounts as victims of his fanaticism or co-conspirators in his outrages.[15] His puritan ancestry and his abolitionist father are duly credited as early influences, but little is said of them or other kin after Brown comes of age and finally enters his "secret service" on behalf of the slave. His lifelong tenure in the emotional universe of a large, stable, and supportive clan thus disappears into the background. Other Browns are props not players in the drama of his life.

But without the family's persisting influence – shaping his imagination, sanctioning his vision, sustaining his actions, sometimes disputing his fanaticism – the Old Hero remains an enigma. Seeing Brown in the context of his family is crucial to understanding who he was and why in his last years he became so formidable an enemy of slavery.

Even in his own family, to be sure, Brown was uniquely driven. If his father and his father's other children also hated slavery,[16] freeing the slave became a vocation and an obsession only to John. It compelled him to abandon responsibility for the day-to-day care of his home and family in favor of a perpetual, sometimes desperate search for men and money. Brown's war against slavery reordered his priorities if not his basic values. It claimed the lives of three of his sons, one in Kansas and two at Harpers Ferry, and finally, his own life. As he awaited his fate in Charlestown jail, he pronounced the sacrifice of his own life and those of his "noble boys" little enough to give for the slave.[17]

But even in his darkest hours Brown never lost his sense of responsibility. As he prepared the fateful attack on Harpers Ferry, he sent money to his wife Mary and instructions to son Salmon for the management of his farm in the Adirondack village of North Elba, New York. Just days before the attack, he asked Mary to welcome into his home his two teenaged daughters-in-law. "I want Bell, & Martha both to feel that they have a home with you untill [sic] *we* return. We shall do all in our power to provide for the wants *of the whole* as *one family*; till that time.... I expect John [Jr.] will send you some assistance soon."[18] Brown also pledged his New England supporters to provide a fund to care for his wife and young children after he was gone.[19] The day before his execution he sent a fresh will from prison to his half brother Jeremiah. It provided for the distribution of a few remaining possessions not covered in previous wills to his adult sons and daughters and for buying each of his younger children and grandchildren a bible with whatever funds were still owed him from his father's estate.[20]

In countless ways, what the Browns called their family "connection" – blood relations, in-laws, and adopted relations, the "kindred friends" – remained part of his life.[21] He had spent his early years in his father's widening family circle. Memories of cherished experiences with relatives wedded his changing image of himself to the clan. Contrary to some accounts, Brown was no drifter. At age twenty-five, he was still living in Hudson in Ohio's Western Reserve, supervising his father's tannery and brushing elbows and swapping stories with relations. He prospered there. When he moved his own family to the newly settled town of Richmond, Pennsylvania, he tried to persuade brother Frederick to follow him there and to bring "some first-rate abolitionist families" to constitute the kind of community he wanted to live in. Brown stayed in Richmond for ten years before moving again.

In later years a more traveled Brown returned repeatedly to live in Hudson or nearby Akron, areas studded with blood relations and in-laws. That growing circle remained the locus of Brown's emotional space to the end. Its ethos underwrote his antislavery convictions.

Brown's career as a guerrilla leader in the Kansas war that erupted in 1856 began with a call from his sons to join the little colony they had established there called "Brownsville" or "Browns' Station." When Brown went to the territory in 1855 with another son, a son-in-law, and a wagon load of rifles and swords, he was returning to the communion of his first family while leaving his second on his Adirondacks farm. From Brown's Station, John Brown wrote Mary: "The idea of again visiting those of my dear family at North Elba is so calculated to unman me that I seldom allow my thoughts to dwell upon it, and I do not think best to write much about it."[22]

Brown often complained of homesickness during his travels[23] and evidenced guilt about leaving Mary and the children and neglecting his family duties. "My unceaseing and anxious care for the present and everlasting wellfare of evry [member] of my family seems to be threefold as I get seperated farther and farther from them," he wrote from New York City in December 1838, during his first lengthy absence. "Forgive the many faults & foibles you have seen in me, and try to proffit by any thing good in either my example, or my council. Try and not any of you get weary of well doing. Should the older boys read and coppy my old letters as I proposed to them, I want to have them all preserved with care."[24]

Evidently, his children honored this request.[25] In his letters he begged Mary for family news. "I expected at least a few words from my [Mary] when I should get letters," he scolded during a cattle drive in 1839.[26] "I shall feel like one out of jail," he wrote from Springfield in 1846, "when I can get ready to come home again."[27] "Can it be that you have all *done* writing me," he pleaded from Iowa in 1857. "Need I say my anxiety to know of your welfare is very great."[28]

Brown invariably expressed concern for the day-to-day problems Mary and the children encountered. "I want to hear how you all do, & how you get along," he would write.[29] Even in hurried letters, he had words of affection for his children. "Say to all my little folks," he pleaded while returning from his first cattle drive to the East in 1838, "that I want much to see them, and tell Ruth [nine] and Fred [seven] not to forget the verse their father taught them last." From Erie, Pennsylvania, he added, "nothing will give me half so much pleasure as to hear that God is still granting you health and peace, & a disposition to do your duty to him and to each other."[30] The following summer he begged Mary to "read my letters to all my little folks. It is the warmest expression of a fathers heart that he can at this time afford them."[31] Eleven years later, his family now in North Elba as winter approached, he asked Mary to instruct their sons, now teenagers, to "lay up … all the stuff for wintering the stock well either in the form of feed or bedding." "I want very much to see those little girls," he wrote of Anne, age 6 and Sarah, 4, "and say to them that Father's hair needs cutting again."[32]

When at home, he dutifully reported to his grown children elsewhere the doings and state of health of every member of the local clan. "Our Oliver has been speculating for some Months past in hogs," he wrote his mature daughter Ruth in 1852. "Fredk manages the Sheep mostly; & Butchers Mutton for the Two families. Watson opperates on the Farm, & Salmon is chief Captain over the Cows, Calves, &c, (& he has them all to shine.) Jason, & Owen appear to be getting along with their Farming midling well … Anne & Sarah go to School. Anne has become a very correct reader. Sarah goes singing about as easy as an old Shoe."[33] He circulated letters from family members to all his children, often urging them to reply themselves. "Boys write your Grand Father without fail & remember his great age 80 years," Brown added at the bottom of a letter he received from his "affectionate parent," Owen.[34]

Over the years Brown relocated his family ten times but never lost touch with his closest siblings and his father. Despite differences with some of the siblings over the wisdom of his war against slavery, he remained fast friends with them. None of his family repudiated his attack on Harpers Ferry, and two of his brothers campaigned to save him from the hangman. The Browns were allies in his cause, defenders against the libels of enemies, sources of spiritual renewal and self-esteem. The principal source of his driving ambition and the fanatical energy that so baffles historians lies in the patterns of interdependence and loyalty within Brown's family of origin – his father's family.

I

Premised on implicitly egoistic psychological models, biographers' explanations of Brown's relentless hostility to slavery run a narrow gamut of possibilities. In the latter nineteenth century, the aging abolitionist writers who guarded his memory assumed that rational convictions and a "puritan" conscience motivated Brown, and heroism explained his behavior. They accepted his own memories of early experiences – such as witnessing the brutal treatment of a black playmate – as explanations of his abhorrence of slavery.[35] In fact, he related a number of such turning points. Observing as a youth the terror of a runaway slave he hid from pursuers, for example, he then and there "vowed eternal enmity to slavery."[36] Brown's children recalled other such pledges.[37] The reminiscent, self-serving character of such stories invites skepticism, but even if true, they do not explain the decisive consequences later attributed to them. They do suggest that early on he sought to ground his passion against slavery in his witness to God.

Brown's critics have identified equally unpersuasive grounds for his war against slavery. In the late nineteenth century a legion of them depicted Brown as deeply flawed, "unprincipled," a man moved by "imperial egotism" and vindictiveness.[38] Early Brown critics emphasized insanity, revenge, or "cold-blooded criminality"; later ones stressed his "enormous need and capacity for self-promotion."[39] Hostile biographers cite Brown's quarrels with neighbors, his bankruptcy and business failures, his unsuccessful law suits, and his eagerness to seize the horses and other personal possessions of slave owners as evidence of his true nature. For them, his inadequacies, not compassion or the evident cruelty of slavery, explain his zealotry.

The most influential of these explanations for Brown's transformation into an "insurrectionist" has been what I shall call the "failure" thesis. Elaborated by Robert Penn Warren in 1929 in a vitriolic biography, the thesis contends that Brown's antislavery career compensated for a life of thwarted ambition. Brown wanted to be "head of the heap," his embittered brother-in-law, Milton Lusk, once declared.[40] He failed at everything he undertook, and with each failure, Warren charges, Brown's ambition turned more and more "to meanness, to chicanery, to bitter, querulous intolerance, to dishonesty, to vindictive and ruthless brutality."[41] This thesis gained wide currency with the publication in 1950 of Allan Nevins' compelling narrative, *The Emergence of Lincoln*. Brown had endured a "peculiarly hard, failure-ridden life," Nevins believed, and increasingly "took refuge from his own deficiencies in fighting the wrongs of others."[42] That Brown turned to antislavery out of neurotic frustration over chronic failure became conventional wisdom; even sympathetic writers nod to it.[43]

But the failure thesis is rooted in outdated assumptions. Long before Nevins gave it a scholarly imprimatur, Brown's violent antislavery had been dismissed as evidence of mental illness. Brown's contemporaries called violent outbursts in otherwise rational people "monomania," a hidden, dangerous form of insanity akin to episodic possession often brought on by "overreaching" and subsequent disappointment. Brown's "ardent" or "enthusiastic" temperament predisposed him to monomania; repeated failure triggered its symptoms. That idea became widely accepted. Lincoln himself made a related argument in distancing the Republican Party from Brown's violent antislavery. Lincoln never met Brown, but likened him to "assassins" in history. "An enthusiast broods over the oppression of a people till he fancies himself commissioned by Heaven to liberate them," Lincoln told New Yorkers in his famous Cooper's Union Address in 1860.[44]

The question of Brown's mental balance is the subject of Chapters 7 and 8 of this study. The point here is that the failure-begets-fanaticism thesis has historical roots. The persistence of its facile assumption may testify to the uneasiness of scholars about Brown's sanity and to the egoistic analytical paradigm that implicitly informs their works. In Brown's own day, the theory reflected widespread acceptance of a traditional Protestant piety that called for steadiness and acquiescence in God's will. Too great an appetite for worldly success was as dangerous to salvation as to sanity. Hence chronic failure, so detractors assume, produced Brown's "monomania." A century later, Allan Nevins dressed that idea in more familiar language; Brown, he said, suffered from "paranoia."[45]

As earlier suggested, this unexamined theory misfires badly. John Brown's commitment to antislavery does not appear to have originated in pain or desperation occasioned by accumulated failures. His first documented antislavery project was based on an assumption that education would be the salvation for blacks. In 1834, when Brown persuaded his family to adopt and rear "at least one negro boy or youth" and told them of a plan he had cherished "for years" to establish a school for black children, he was a successful tanner and farmer as well as the village postmaster in Richmond, Pennsylvania, and founder of the Independent Congregational Church there. At that time his business prospects were "rather brightening" and he was conventionally successful.[46] While he was a merchant in Springfield in the firm of Perkins & Brown, wool wholesalers, in 1847, he thought of establishing "an Affrican high school" in Canada.[47] The following year he wrote his father that he wanted "to go to live with those poor despised Africans to try, and encourage them; & show them a little so far as I am capable how to manage. You kneed not be surprised if at some future day I should do so. Our business is prosperous; to all appearances. Money is becoming more easy."[48]

Until his sons wrote him from Kansas asking for weapons to defend their claims, there is no credible evidence that John Brown had conceived his anti-slavery duty in terms of taking up arms himself.[49] He was then fifty-five. Thus, the failure thesis is not sustained by any "fit" between Brown's deepening anti-slavery commitments and the rhythms of success and failure in his life. The expansiveness of his mood as he planned and embarked on projects over the years shows that Brown was doing well rather than fleeing failure or trying to cope with frustration. Even if one hypothesizes that the scars of accumulated failures finally drew him to Kansas to vent his pent up rage on proslavery innocents, it must be acknowledged that Kansas was not the scene of his first "service" to blacks. After the collapse of his partnership with Simon Perkins in 1854, Brown intended to return to North Elba to live and to teach farming to fugitives from slavery, as he had hinted he might do in 1847, rather than accompany his sons to Kansas, where fighting might erupt. When he answered his sons' call, Brown went to Kansas to help his boys and their families through the hardships of resettlement as well as to protect them from potentially dangerous neighbors. It was the later eruption of war in Kansas that occasioned Brown's own vision of a wider war against the Slave Power.

The theory that this wider war took shape in his imagination as compensation for a life of failure misfires on another count, the assumption that over the years Brown's sense of self-worth depended largely on achieving wealth and distinction.

That assumption deserves scrutiny. Of course, Brown hoped to "make it" economically. Toward that end, like many Americans in the antebellum decades, he tried his hand at a number of things, only to fall back on those he knew best. He took his knocks. But the failure thesis takes insufficient account of the fact that Brown's reversals, like his successes, occurred in the context of his closely bonded, extended family. Sympathy and support from the "connection" softened his falls. Moreover, the religious values shared by the Browns privileged his role as paterfamilias over that as businessman. As Brown's own father once told him, "I think the care of our own Famelys is the pleasent[est] and most usefull business we can be in."[50] As long as Brown could feed his children from his own crops and livestock, he remained a proper provider, however badly his business ventures went.

A further measure of self-worth was Brown's diligence in the supervision of his children and seeing to their preparation for adulthood. Evidence in his letters as well as testimony from his children attest to his success in meeting these measures.[51] With a "numerous family" dependent on him, he could not permit wounded pride from economic setbacks to embitter or immobilize him or to shatter his faith in himself. Brown's bruising encounters in the marketplace exhibit the kinds of toughness, tenacity, and canniness necessary for effective coping.

In considering the record, it is worth noting first that Brown suffered no serious business reversal until he was thirty-eight years old when he moved back to Ohio to explore opportunities in the growing town of Franklin Mills (now Kent). His reputation was at that time evidently intact and his credit good because Brown formed a partnership at Franklin Mills with a well-to-do businessman to establish another tannery. He later obtained a contract to build a leg of the Ohio and Pennsylvania Canal from Franklin Mills to Akron, Ohio, to bring water from nearby creeks and the Cuyahoga River and use "waste waters" from the existing canal. He pledged to build a flour mill on the north basin, and commissioned construction of a two-story block hotel that stood empty for years after his project failed but finally found a use with the birth of Kent village.[52] He borrowed heavily to buy lots along the proposed canal and entered a partnership with twenty-one other investors to found a new village along its path, the Brown and Thompson Addition to Franklin Mills. His brothers Frederick and Oliver were partners in the project and bought properties with him.[53] But when the canal company chose a different route, bypassing Franklin Mills, Brown and his partners were left literally high and dry. The economic contraction following the Panic of 1837 caught Brown overextended and he lost all these properties and four farms.

In the unstable world of Jacksonian America, many of Brown's friends and relations were also victims of unwise land speculation. In that context, he might have blamed his failure on the collapse of the land boom as much as his own errant judgment. His father shared John's misfortune in 1839, losing heavily during the "great speculations in Village lots" and risking his properties by backing loans at "the Banks." "I had some to pitty me but very few to help me," Owen Brown recalled. "I lernt that OUTWARD friendship and Property were almost inseparibly connected," he remembered. "I had many to inform me that I brought my troubles on myself." But Owen had recovered from making unwise purchases before, and he concluded philosophically that "loss or gain are momentary things and will look very small in Eternity."[54]

Owen survived the panic and, in 1838, asked John and two friends to sell cattle for him in the East to help his son recover. While in Connecticut that winter, John bought ten Saxony sheep and drove them back to Ohio to begin life anew. Still loaded down with debt, however, he needed a larger loan than his father could provide to avoid bankruptcy. He hoped to obtain the loan from unnamed parties in Boston, but feared he might be unable to do so. "Should that be the will of Providence," he wrote Mary, "I know of no other way but we must consider ourselves very poor; for our debts must be paid, if paid at a sacrifice.... I hope God, who is rich in mercy, will grant us grace to conform to our circumstances with cheerfulness and true resignation."[55] A week later, he asked Mary, "should I, after all my sacrifice of body and mind, be compelled to return a very poor man, how would my family receive me?" But putting aside this evident despair, he pledged to bring each of his children a Bible, "a book that has afforded me great support and comfort during my long absence."[56]

For all this apparent resiliency, the bankruptcy in 1842 wounded Brown gravely. Brown might have been prosecuted for misuse of $2,800 given him by the New England Woollen Company to purchase wool. He had used the money "imprudently...for myself," he admitted in court, to meet demands of creditors and to save his claim to a large farm. He found he could not "redeem" the debt, but hoping perhaps that he could eventually make good the missing funds, the company decided not to bring charges against him. Showing both contrition and confidence, Brown shrewdly navigated the "rules of the debtor-creditor game" in his petition to the court.[57] In his discharge agreement with the court, Brown acknowledged "the great kindness and tenderness" the company exercised "toward me in my calamity, and more particularly...the moral obligation I am under to render to all their due." He therefore pledged to pay the debt "from time to time, as Divine Providence shall enable me to do."[58]

He repeated the pledge and his gratitude to the company's agent, George Kellogg. "I have just received information of my final discharge as a bank-rupt," he wrote Kellogg, "and I ought to be grateful that no one of my credi-tors has made any opposition to such discharge being given. I shall now, if my life is continued, have an opportunity of proving the sincerity of my past professions." He was doing well this season, he continued, but in the "desti-tute condition in which the new surrender of my effects has placed me, with my numerous family," he said, he could not now make the payment he had "encouraged" Kellogg to expect.[59]

In executing the judgment against Brown, the court "set off and allowed" Brown and his family to keep their clothing, furniture, Bibles and other reli-gious books, school books, and such "necessaries" as spinning wheels, kettles, and candlesticks. The judgment also permitted Brown to keep two mares, two cows, two hogs, three lambs, nineteen hens, and seven sheep, as well as an assortment of tools.[60] Brown could survive on those remnants of his property. But he was now indeed poor.

He still felt the humiliation two years later when fortune smiled once more. In early 1844, Simon Perkins, reputedly the wealthiest man in Akron, took Brown into partnership to "carry on the sheep business extensively." Perkins would pro-vide feed and shelter for their combined flocks while Brown and his sons would do the work of caring for the sheep and marketing the wool. They would also culti-vate and harvest turnips and potatoes to feed the flock. Brown and Perkins would share equally "all other expenses" and divide the profits between them. Brown would be able to continue renting the farm operated by two of his sons while moving his second family at a nominal rent into a comfortable "frame dwelling-house" on Perkins Hill outside Akron.[61] The agreement provided for the most "comfortable" and "favorable" arrangement of his "worldly concerns" he had ever had, Brown wrote to his oldest son John, Jr., and was "no mean alliance for our family." He hoped his sons would have "the wisdom...to make the most of it. It is certainly endorsing a poor bankrupt and his family, three of whom were but recently in Akron jail [for refusing to vacate a farm lost to a creditor], in a man-ner quite unexpected, and proves that...our industrious and steady endeavors to maintain our integrity and our character have not been wholly overlooked."[62]

That was the bottom line. Despite his tangled problems, Brown was confi-dent that his pious, hardworking lifestyle had gained favorable notice in the community. He had survived an ordeal with his pride intact.

FIGURE 2.2. The big house on "Perkins Hill" in Akron owned by Col. Simon Perkins, Brown's patron and business partner.

CREDIT: West Virginia State Archives, Boyd B. Stutler Collection.

Despite the initial prosperity of the partnership, ten years later failure again overtook Brown. His success in breeding prize-winning sheep and cattle had given him a certain local fame. His skill in appraising the value of differing grades of wool and his success in working with local growers led Perkins to send him to Springfield, Massachusetts, where the partnership opened an office and warehouse in 1846. Brown was to manage and market the growing consignments of wool. In trying to get the best prices possible for the firm's wool, Brown honored the values of his Ohio neighbors. Superior grades of wool demanded higher prices, he insisted.

But the market was changing. Even before Brown began to market wool for other Ohio growers, he was publicly disputing the prices textile manufacturers were willing to pay.[63] As the manufacturers resisted Brown's asking prices, growers' demands for payment on their consignments became "incessant," as he wrote Perkins. Finding no buyers without sacrificing "our prices,"[64] he tried to outflank the manufacturers by dispatching a large shipment of wool to England for sale. The endeavor failed and Brown had to sell at ruinous losses. Perkins & Brown never fully recovered, and, after years of ensuing litigation, Brown himself dissolved the partnership in 1854.

These reverses weighed heavily on him, but he found consolation in sharing the disappointments with his family. In November 1850, he confided to John, Jr., who had clerked in the Springfield office, that he might be unable to collect $40,000 owed the firm, which would "leave me *nice & flat*."⁶⁵ John, Jr.'s reply suggests the extent to which the Browns viewed their fates as intertwined and how willing Brown's sons were to share their father's trials. John, Jr., genuinely "sympathized" with his father. Should his father be unable to pay his crushing debts, it would mean a loss of "the *plethora* [comforts] of some," John, Jr., acknowledged, "and place us back where we stood, pecuniarily, in 1837 and 8. 'What dat?'" he said cheerily. "We have our hands, heads and hearts the same, none the worse for having tasted a little experience. Suppose we were, at this moment, not worth a dollar," the son continued, "we can all emigrate to some region and stick down what roots we have, and grow. There would then be of us five pretty able-bodied men, to say nothing of Watson, Salmon etc. [Brown's younger sons]. Could we not keep ourselves out of the poor-house if we were in a healthy location?" As for his father's obligation to the firm, "Let it go, if it can't be saved without the loss of life's enjoyment. It won't pay to worry and sicken and die for a few paltry dollars."⁶⁶

Implicit in these words of encouragement was a commitment to values jointly shared. The prospect of beginning anew implied renouncing any hope of immediate wealth. However ambitious the Browns were, "money-making" was not as important as preserving the family. Bankruptcy was preferable to crippling worry. John still commanded the loyalty and affection of his sons.

He found a measure of satisfaction in John, Jr.'s proposal to start over together. "I am much pleased with the reflection that you are all three once more together," Brown replied just five days later, "& all engaged in the same calling that the old Patriarchs followed." What he feared most was Perkins' loss of confidence in him. "[Perkins] is the most noble spirited man to whom I feel most deeply indebted, & no amount of money would attone to my feelings for the loss, of a feeling of confidence, & cordiality on his part." Brown asked that his boys, who herded sheep near Perkins' hilltop home, "conduct wisely, & faithfully, & kindly, in what they have undertaken." This would "secure to themselves a full reward if they should not be the means of entirely relieving a Father of his burdens." Brown also thanked John, Jr. for his letter. "It is a source of the utmost comfort to feel that I retain a warm place in the sympathies, Affections, & confidence of my own most familiar acquaintance, my family," Brown declared. "A man can hardly get into difficulties too big to be surmounted if he has a firm foothold at home. *Remember that*."⁶⁷

Just how serious family honor was to John, Jr., however, is evident in a second letter he sent his father before receiving the reply just summarized. Mrs. Perkins had told his brother Jason's wife that Mr. Perkins should not "bear any of the loss" the firm had suffered from Brown's disastrous sales trip to England. John, Jr., was "convinced that when a *woman* gets an idea of that kind into her head, *it is very hard to get it out*." Worse still, a "*talking* woman can exert Some influence," he warned. If his father could not recover "at least a large share" of the funds owed Perkins & Brown, he should not "return to engage in this business

FIGURE 2.3. John Brown, Jr., as a student in Ohio in the 1840s. A first son, he shared his father's concern about the family's reputation.

CREDIT: West Virginia State Archives, Boyd B. Stutler Collection.

here." John, Jr., thought his father owed nothing further to Perkins and that "no blame" rested on his father because he had done "the best you could." If Brown did return, "yourself & family must suffer more humiliation and bitter taunts than *commonly* fall to the lot of poverty." John, Jr., was "convinced that the Perkins connection are, or will be disposed to throw the blame of the failure upon you – because the last failure will be known to a numerous acquaintance who are familliar with the history of a former one." Should Brown rejoin his family in Essex, he and the family there might "feel yourselves on terms of *equality* with the rest of [the] neighbors, acquaintances – to feel *less* than this is to feel a *slavery of the soul* which should not be endured at *any price*." "The Self Esteem, manliness and real dignity of the family can never be secured where a burden such as I have been describing must inevitably rest upon them."[68]

For John, Jr., the stakes in the impending contretemps were high. The "dignity" and "manliness" of the family was at issue. But his father was not ready

to panic. John, Jr.'s letter, he replied, had expressed "what has often passed
through my own mind." Were he not "a little skeptical" about the spiritualism
his son had embraced, he joked, he would "conclude you had access to some
of the knocking spirits." But Brown assured his son that Perkins had sent him a
kind letter, and "so long as he is right side up I shall by no means despond, &
indeed I think the fog clearing away from our matters a little." He wanted
John, Jr., to let him know "how 'the land lies'" and to keep him "posted up."
John, Jr., could best do that "by having every thing done up first rate, & by
becoming very familiar, & not by keeping distant. I most earnestly hope," he
said, that "should I loose *cast* my family will at least prove themselves worthy of
respect & confidence, & I am sure that my Three sons in Akron can do a great
job for themselves, & for the family if they behave themselves wisely.... Can
you not all Three effectually secure the name of good business men this Winter.
That you *are* considered honest, *& rather inteligent* I have no doubt."[69]

Brown's confidence in Perkins was not misplaced. Despite the huge losses,
Perkins "expressed a strong desire" to have Brown "continue with him at least for
another year," Brown wrote happily to his family in North Elba. Brown would
therefore return to Akron to supervise Perkins's crops and "all the stock of Cattle,
Sheep, Hogs, &c." "He seems so pleased, & anxious to have me continue," Brown
added, "that I cannot tear away from him."[70] The following spring five of his sons
decided to become homesteaders in Kansas. They urged their father to join them,
but by then Brown was committed to devoting the rest of his life to the "service"
of the "downtrodden slave," and chose to do so by teaching fugitive slaves in the
little settlement near North Elba the Browns called Timbuktu.

But his stay in North Elba was brief. Once again he joined his sons in the
struggle to survive, this time in an unknown territory. He would honor unques-
tioningly the family's claim on his skills and wisdom. The bonds with his sons
that had made possible his partnership with Perkins now drew him westward.
Brown's severest disappointments never deprived him of the affection and
respect of his "friends" in the Brown connection. For them loyalty counted. If
shame attached to failure in business, as Squire Owen's reflections on his own
past business trials suggested, older measures of self-worth still trumped what
William James would call the "bitch Goddess success."

The failure-begets-fanaticism thesis as an explanation for Brown's determination to fight slavery mistakenly assumes that he stood alone in the marketplace in which he failed. In the end, Brown not only drew support from within
the "connection," but, like other relations, he acted in its name. The failure thesis also neglects the role that religious faith played in the encounters of Brown's
family with the world. I shall discuss Brown's religion in a later chapter. Here,
the concern will be the religious history of his family.

II

Using that history as a backdrop, an alternative reading of Brown's story
becomes more promising than the failure thesis. That reading is rooted in a

recognition of the abiding influence of deep-rooted religious and moral beliefs and practices cherished by generations of Browns. During Brown's lifetime, those "habits of the heart" came into conflict with the realities of a changing world. That conflict helped birth his war on slavery.

The story begins in Puritan New England. There a fundamental conflict between communal values and individual ambition appeared even in the first generation of settlers. Social historians of village life in Puritan New England have found a precapitalist, premodern "mentalite"[71] that privileged collective values over possessive individualism. Early Puritans lived chiefly in "organic, consensual, Christian communities" in which a "general calling" to aid the unfortunate sustained traditions of neighborliness and English notions of a "moral community."

Not everyone, to be sure, agrees that Puritans altogether discountenanced worldly ambition. The dissenters contend that from the beginning, as James T. Lemon puts it, "inside the Puritan was the Yankee." Early market towns like Springfield, Massachusetts, according to Stephen Innes, defied the image of nostalgic Puritan villagers favored by his colleagues.[72] But in assessing the varied studies of Puritan communities over two centuries, historian Darrett B. Rutman concludes that for all the change driven by such factors as population pressure on limited resources, the "social milieu" of early communities persisted. These communities were small-scale, neighborly societies, little affected by ideas and events that mattered in Boston or the distant seat of empire.[73] In a remarkable study of forty rural towns in eighteenth-century Massachusetts, Gregory Nobles has shown that even county-wide politics was rooted in local ties "of friendship and kinship." As overcrowding and political instability splintered old towns, Nobles observes, new towns carved themselves out of the forests and replicated the "formal institutions and restraints of Puritan society."[74] The resulting persistence of neighborliness and mutual support within dense networks of kin characterized farming villages of western Connecticut as well. It was in that inward-looking society that John Brown's father, Owen Brown, was born in 1771 and came of age.

That society had been revitalized spiritually again and again, ever since the Great Awakening of the 1730s and 1740s. In theological terms, it was closer to John Calvin than to William Ellery Channing or Henry Ward Beecher. Leaders of the Puritan migration of the 1630s and their Congregational descendants understood Calvin much as his European acolytes did. To the latter, an omnipotent, transcendent God was the sovereign of the universe. He predestined a fallen mankind to eternal damnation, but through the sacrifice of His son Jesus Christ, arbitrarily redeemed an elect few to share eternity with Him in Heaven while banishing everyone else to Hell.

By Owen Brown's time this austere creed had already come to seem forbidding, even problematic. It came under assault by the great itinerant preacher George Whitefield (1714–70) in the religious fervor of the Great Awakening and then in the rationalist stirrings of the Enlightenment and of such radical Protestants as the Quakers. But the Awakening's perceived emotional excesses seemed to many clergymen to threaten social disorder and the survival of orthodox belief. Throughout New England, New Lights inspired by the evangelicals and Old Lights defending orthodoxy clashed over the revivals, and many congregations split to form new, rival churches. The close identification of village and church was sundered, making church affiliation increasingly a matter of choice rather than simply of place of birth.

In defending the mysterious Awakening, a young minister named Jonathan Edwards (1702–58), long a pastor at Northampton in western Massachusetts, revitalized the basic insights of Calvinism, reconciling the doctrines of predestination and free will. He did this by distinguishing natural causes from moral causes "such as habits and dispositions of the heart." Though God predestined humans to damnation or salvation, Edwards said, individuals are free to make moral choices. But because they are born sinners, they necessarily choose to be selfish and sinful rather than to please God. Despite the inevitability of sin, one should strive to live a godly life; in achieving Christian piety one could hope for signs of being chosen. "True virtue" reflected "benevolence to Being in general ... that is immediately exercised in a general good will." True religion was a matter of habitual inclinations exhibited in a pattern of godly behavior that marked a regenerate heart. Selfless conduct "should be the practice and business of life."[75]

So compelling was Edwards's work that generations of ministers clung to his teachings even as they revised and popularized them. Reflecting the changed historical conditions of the Revolutionary Era, their writings became known collectively as the New Divinity. Joseph Bellamy revised Edwards's conception of Christ's atonement: Its purpose was not to placate divine wrath, as had long been believed, but to restore moral order in the universe.[76] This reinterpretation won general acclaim among New England theologians in the early nineteenth century, and the "moral government of God" later became a shibboleth of the "biblical politics" of immediatist abolitionists.[77]

Samuel Hopkins virtually discarded the idea of original sin in favor of actual sin. Self-love, not the imputation of Adam's fall, was the root of sin. The individual was a sinner because he sinned, and could be saved only by freeing himself of self-love and professing a willingness to be "damned for the glory of God." Holiness was thus benevolence "to God and our neighbors ... or friendly affection to all intelligent beings."[78] "True holiness" or "true virtue" was "disinterested benevolence." Spiritual regeneration was an imperceptible transformation worked by the Holy Spirit in which man is passive.[79] Consistently selfless behavior was the overt evidence of a state of grace.

Unlike Edwards, Hopkins, who held a pastorate at bustling Newport, Rhode Island (1770–1803), was a social reformer and a fierce enemy of slavery. The gospel was the weapon best suited to uproot "tyranny and slavery," he wrote in *A discourse upon the Slave-Trade, and the Slavery of the Africans* (1793). Ending slavery was urgent, since its persistence threatened to bring down the "righteous judgment of God." In words that would find an echo in John Brown's own "prophecy" that "the crimes of this guilty land" would end only with the bloody destruction of slavery, Hopkins warned that Americans ought to fear that "the vengeance of heaven will fall upon us, as a people, in ways perhaps which are not now thought of, unless we repent and reform."[80] When President Lincoln suggested in his Second Inaugural Address that God might have permitted the "mighty scourge of war" to ravage the nation as retribution for the sin of slavery, he drew upon a theme familiar to followers of Samuel Hopkins.

Owen Brown was a child of the Awakening that culminated in Hopkins. All his life he sought evidence of his spiritual regeneration and held himself accountable to the Edwardsean tests of Christian practice. At the age seventy-nine, he wrote an account of his life for his daughter Sally Marian, whose family he was visiting at the time. His narrative, though no doubt an unconscious instrument of self-fashioning, was preoccupied with matters of salvation. He looked back on his life as a spiritual journey. Born in West Simsbury, Connecticut, in 1771, Owen remembered that his life began in poverty. His father, a shoemaker and farmer, died of "camp fever" (probably dysentery) only weeks after marching off to fight the British in 1776. That left Owen's mother Hannah abandoned and pregnant with her eleventh child. Though she was "the best of Mother[s] active and sensable," Owen remembered, she was unable to keep up the farm and soon lost her crops and cattle.[81]

She sent five-year-old Owen to live with his grandfather, another John Brown, in whose home he was "early brought under the influence of religious People[.] I went to meeting on the sabboth very stedely all though poorly clothed," he remembered. After a severe winter in which his family again lost "allmost all" of their livestock, Owen was sent to live with sister Asubah, who taught him to read and to think about "things belonging to my soul." While Owen was once again at home in 1782, a "great revival" swept the region. "My mother and my Older Sisters and Brother dated there hopes of Salvation from that summers revival," he remembered. Though Owen himself was unsure whether he "was a subject of the work" of the revival, he boasted that he could "now recollect most all of those [sermons] and what there texts were." The "change in our Famely was great" as a result of the revival, he remembered. "Famely worship [was] set up by Brother John, which ever after continued[.] There was a revival of singing in Canton and our Famely became singers. Conferences and meetings were kept up constantly and singing meetings all which brought our Famely into a very good association [with] a very great ade [aid] of restraining Grace."[82]

In his early teens, Owen lived "at different times" with the Rev. Jeremiah Hallock, the minister at Canton, "and received a good deal of instruction from him." After working as a shoemaker in nearby towns for several years, at the age of nineteen Owen returned home and "hired out" to Rev. Hallock for six months. With Hallock's guidance, Owen came "under some conviction of sin," but "wheather I was pardened or not God only knows." After his marriage in 1793 to Ruth Mills, "the choice of my affections ever after," he recalled, "our good minister felt all the anxiety of [a] Parent that we should begin wright."

He gave the couple "good counsel and I have no doubt with a praying spirit." In 1798 Owen and Ruth made professions of faith. This happened during two years of "memorable revivals of religion in our churches in our Town and the Towns aroun[d] us." "Perhaps," he thought, there never had been "so general a revival since the days of Edwards and Whitefield." At the height of the result-ing religious excitement in Torrington, where Owen then lived, his son John was born.

Throughout the careful recitation of the religious milestones in his life, Owen protested his own spiritual failings. His life, he testified, "has been of but little worth mostly fild up with vanity." "This I know," he moaned, "I have not lived like a Christian." Even after conversion, his faith had been "poorly manifested." He credited his accumulation of property and livestock to "the kind providence of God." He had received many blessings. His "beloved wife" Ruth had exercised a benign "ascendance" over his conduct and was respon-sible for whatever "respect" he had "in the World." His faith was tested when Ruth died in 1808 after giving birth to a child who lived only a few hours. "[A]ll my earthly prospects appeared to be blasted," Owen recalled of these "days of affliction." He and Ruth had taken in children of hard-pressed neighbors' from the start of their marriage. Now, with five small children of his own and an adopted son, his home was a "scene" that "allmost makes my heart blead now." But Owen kept his children "mostly around me," and eleven months later he married Sally Root. Owen blamed himself for permitting his "earthly cares" to become "too many for the good of my Famely and for my own Comfort in religion[.] I do not look back on my life with but little sattisfaction but must pray Lord forgive me for Christ sake or I must perish."[83]

Owen's autobiography told a second story as well. Among the blessings he counted were his children as well as his property and his progress as a shoemaker, tanner, and farmer. Though he "had great cause for thanksgiving," pride in his achievement was evident. Despite suffering from malaria ("ago," he called it), in June 1805, Owen and a neighbor piled their families onto ox-drawn wagons and trekked to the new settlement at Hudson, Ohio. There he became a "prosperious" figure while ill fortune befell a number of neighbors with whom he had grown up. They had "had rich Parents who dresed there Famelys in gay clothing [and] gave them plenty of money and good Horses to ride," he wrote. "O how enviable they appeared while my Brothers and Sisters lacked all these things." But these "smart yong Folks" turned out to be failed businessmen, "drunkards," and in three cases suicides. Owen learned not to envy such people. "God known what is best."

These cautions aside, Owen could not help boasting of his success. He and Ruth had "begun with but very little property but with industry and frugal-ity, which gave us a very comfortable seport and a small increas." Making shoes and tanning hides in several Connecticut villages, he prospered. As a new settler on the "frunteer" in Hudson, Owen "came with a determination to help to build up [the community] and be a help in the seport of religion and civil Order." "Our former poverty had kept us out of the more loos and vane

Company," he said, and soon "we appeared to be noticed by the better class of the People." At Hudson Owen came to fill "places of trust," and was proud of the "company that calld on us." His visitors included "Missinarys of the Gospel and leading men traveling through the Country." He knew "the business People and Ministers of the Gospel in all parts of the [Western] Reserve and some in Pennsylvania." He was, in short, an important man, a community builder, a founder of the town. He recognized that worldly pride had compromised his Christian practice. But the doctrines and precepts of the New Divinity that shaped his life were those upon which he raised his family.

Many years later, Owen's son, John, inspired by this family history, toured the towns of Owen's youth to raise money for the "cause of freedom" he was fighting for in Kansas. He found a warm reception. "Have just been speaking for three nights at Canton, & at Collinsville where Father & Mother were raised," he wrote to his son John, Jr., in 1857. "They gave me $80, at the two places, & have agreed that my family shall have Grand Fathers old Granite Monument sent to North Elba; on which to remember *our poor Fredk* [John's murdered son] who sleeps in Kansas...I prize *it highly*; & think the family all will."[84]

But if the Browns had not been forgotten in Western Connecticut, the religious values Owen had embraced there had begun to give way to the new evangelical culture of the age of Andrew Jackson.[85] As John Brown grew to manhood in the early nineteenth century, the Edwardsean tradition of Christian practice his father preached was challenged by the emerging culture of Jacksonian America. If the New Divinity rebuked self-love and worldliness, the new democratic America extolled individual achievement and prized wealth and fame.

The Browns were not immune to the effects of that transition. But they lived in an area only partially and unevenly affected by it. Older traditions and lifestyles could still be found in such areas in the 1830s. In the Western Reserve, families like the Browns still taught their children to live to glorify God and to expect to suffer in this world. In the Brown family, values of self-discipline, self-denial, family loyalty, and personal sacrifice held sway. The Browns still hoped their children would be "called" to uplifting vocations and lead productive lives. Disinterested benevolence was still to them the most telling mark of Christian life. Their civic views exalted personal discipline, moral stewardship, and social order.[86]

But by mid-century, as John Brown's own sons and daughters approached maturity, the communal values of the traditional piety and the individualism encouraged by the emerging capitalist economy asserted rival claims on them. If the ethos of the Brown connection still bound the younger generations to the old, dissonant notes had begun to signal its inevitable dispersal. On the eve of John Brown's war on slavery, his family straddled two worlds.

III

In 1850, John Brown's family of origin – Owen's family – was a complex web of blood, affinal, and foster relations.[87] At seventy-nine, Owen Brown was the third oldest person in Hudson Township.[88] He had outlived the two wives who bore his sixteen natural children, and married a third, "Widow Lucy" Hinsdale, a neighbor twenty-five years his junior. Lucy brought Owen five stepchildren. Her eldest daughter Abi had recently wed Owen's son Jeremiah, which made Owen Jeremiah's father-in-law as well as his father and Abi's stepfather and father-in-law. Such redundant relationships were common in the knot of neighboring families comprising the Brown connection.[89]

Generations also overlapped. Owen's first natural child, who did not survive, was born forty-two years before his last, his daughter, Martha. By mid-century, Owen's oldest surviving natural son, John, had already fathered eighteen of his eventual twenty children, seven of whom were born before Owen's last child, their "Aunt Martha." In all, Owen's living grandchildren numbered thirty-nine in 1850; another twelve had died in infancy, and a dozen more were yet to be born. Already several of his grandchildren were married, and at the time of his death in 1856, Owen had four great-grandchildren. The marriages of his progeny created a score of new families and hundreds of new in-laws. Owen was not perplexed by this. "I can follow my numerous famely, through most of there various changes in life," he wrote to his Kansas relations shortly before his death. "I think I know there dispositions and their moral caractor." He rejoiced that his "posterity" had reached the "fourth generation."[90]

The heart of this proliferating clan lay in the farm village of Hudson, twenty miles south of Lake Erie and ten miles north of Akron, already the site of forty-four "industrial establishments."[91] As one of the earliest residents of Hudson, Owen had been a steward in its formative years – an elder of the Congregational church, a trustee of its proudest institution, Western Reserve College, a justice of the peace, a county commissioner, and a substantial landowner. Between his arrival there in 1805 and 1830, when he began to suffer financial reversals, Owen purchased thirteen properties in or around Hudson averaging twenty-three acres each. In 1830 he bought 264 acres on Aurora Road from an old Connecticut friend, Benjamin Whedan, and there built the substantial, two-story house that his children and grandchildren knew as their "ancestral" or, in the phrase then becoming current, "family" home. Living abstemiously, Owen had ploughed the profits from his tannery and farms into the purchase of land. After his death the executor of his estate valued his personal property at little more than $1,000 and his real estate at $8,480.[92] Yet this was a substantial estate in that rural economy. Although not as wealthy as several of his neighbors, John Brown's father had long been known in Hudson as "Squire Owen."

The surviving children of Owen's first wife – John, two sisters, and three brothers – had grown up with the Village, and, like the children of Owen's second wife Sally Root, most of them made their homes in or around Hudson and married into local families. Even those who had moved away returned for family gatherings. Spread like the pattern of a patchwork quilt, the farms of Owen's kin created what might be called an extended family neighborhood. After his death, his old tannery, his farm, and the handsome "new"

FIGURE 2.4. Owen Brown's house on Aurora Road in Hudson, Ohio, the "family home" to his descendants. Viewed from the side in this 1959 photo.

CREDIT: West Virginia State Archives, Boyd B. Stutler Collection.

house he built in 1843 at "the Center of Hudson," probably on Owen Brown Street, as well as the Hudson homes of his sons and in-laws evoked his memory. Other familiar sights – of the town square, the Congregational church, the college, and the village cemetery where Owen lay buried between his first two wives – anchored his descendants' allegiance and gave them a sense of place.[93]

At mid-century, the number and close proximity of Owen's kin facilitated dependence within the family. For most of Owen's children the family was the basic social milieu throughout their lives, and for his grandchildren, too, though in later years they scattered far from Hudson. As farm children, most of the young Browns attended school only for short periods, but they found cousins and shirt-tail relations aplenty among their schoolmates. Sometimes the Brown women "kept a school" at home. In planting and harvesting seasons, when school was out, siblings were the children's principal playmates. Even when school was available, demands of the family economy sometimes kept children at home. In 1848, after half a year in bustling Springfield, Massachusetts, where John Brown and his family lived within sight of the railroad depot, John's school-aged sons, twelve-year-old Watson and eleven-year-old Salmon, did not attend school regularly. "We are Studing at home this winter and helping

Mother abot the house and cuting wood," Watson wrote Grandfather Owen. "Father has bought us several histories and we have read a good deal at home," Salmon added. "I work at the wool hous [sic] some of the time for Father. he has a grate [sic] deal of work to do."[94]

For adults, too, "society" was largely a family affair. Family letters and diaries report a constant round of visiting. In the biting cold of remote Essex County, New York, where Brown moved his second family in 1849, visiting was virtually the only form of amusement after dark. "What a jolly set we are," John's eldest daughter, Ruth wrote from North Elba to a sister-in-law in Ohio. "Henry [Thompson, her future husband] comes over every Saturday night and we all visit as hard as we can."[95] A "good visit" might last for several weeks and provide news for letters to relatives long after.[96]

In Ohio holiday seasons meant large family gatherings. At Christmas time in 1856, after Brown and his sons had left Kansas, Wealthy Hotchkiss Brown, the pretty, accomplished wife of John, Jr., saw nearly "all our relations" at Hudson, "making in all quite a 'shower of Browns.'" Wealthy spent Christmas day at "Uncle Jerry's," where "Abi made quite a feast, and invited her brother and sisters with their husbands & children. Father and all of his sons with the exception of Oliver were present. it really made a house full." Before Wealthy and John, Jr., returned to their home in nearby Ashtabula County, they had "grand" or "good" visits at the homes of four uncles in Hudson.[97] Visiting was more than a release from daily routines. It was an occasion to bring past and present together, to mark the chapters of life and reaffirm the sense of belonging.

IV

The Browns' efforts to preserve their family intact were informed by pride in a unique legacy. The descendants of Owen Brown were conscious of the immanence of the past to an extent difficult to grasp today. The family history reached back two hundred and thirty years – six generations – to the Great Puritan Migration. The living Browns saw themselves as heirs of their Pilgrim forbears. As successive generations of Browns came of age, they assumed its members would, in their turn, insure the future of the "line."

The Browns believed themselves to be descendants of the Peter Browne who signed the Mayflower Compact and helped found Plymouth Colony.[98] They thus saw themselves as heirs to a long tradition of religious nonconformity, moral discipline, and self-sacrifice. For Squire Owen and John what most distinguished their line was Peter Browne's pilgrimage to the New World in the service of God. But there were other prestigious relations. Owen's sister Hannah was the mother of two highly respected sons, one of them a president of Amherst College and author of a popular text on family government,[99] and the other a prominent clergyman. The Dutch ancestors of John's mother Ruth Mills included a president of Yale University and a hero of the Revolution.[100]

John Brown understood the magical effect his Separatist ancestry had upon Boston's Brahmins, and he asserted the family claim on many occasions. In the curious letter about his boyhood written in 1857, he said he was born of "poor but respectable parents: a decendant on the side of his Father of one of the company of the Mayflower who landed at Plymouth in 1620."[101] The following year, he claimed again to be "a true decendant of Peter Brown, One of the Mayflower Pilgrims." After his capture at Harpers Ferry, he wrote his reproachful cousin Luther Humphrey: "So far as my knowledge goes to our mutual kindred: I suppose *I am the first* since the landing of Peter Brown from the Mayflower that *has either been sentenced to imprisonment*; or to the Gallows." But he was not ashamed of his imprisonment or the "near prospect of *death by hanging*." He reminded his cousin that their grandfather, another John Brown, who died fighting the British in 1776, "might have perished on the scaffold had circumstances been *but very little different*."[102]

The Browns' consciousness of the past is also demonstrated by the practice of naming their children after their forbears. In general, the names of sons followed the paternal line. For five generations every first-born Brown son was named Peter or John. Owen, who was not a first-born, named his sons after ancestors or living relations. His sons – John, Frederick, Edward, Watson, and Salmon – all had forenames passed on for at least three generations. With the exception of Edward and the addition of Owen and Oliver, John Brown gave the same names to his own sons. Daughters were often named after mothers, but they might also be named for sisters, aunts, or grandmothers.

It is one measure of John Brown's standing with his children that of the six who married and had children, four named their first sons John. When John, Jr.'s wife, Wealthy, bore a son in 1852, she and John, Jr., also finally decided to call him John. This son, John Brown III, was the first son of an eldest son of an eldest son. More than a fortnight after his birth, his grandmother Brown inquired: "Do you call him John or Charles? Father will be highly pleased if you call him John."[103]

Because deciding on names often took so long, several of Owen Brown's descendants died unnamed.[104] The most convincing explanation for this delay in naming is suggested by the compromises implicit in the assignment of middle names. Since a powerful family tradition narrowed the choices, especially for first-born sons, each infant presented its parents with the problem of choosing which relations to please and to disappoint. The speculations about which of his or her kin the child most resembled may have been part of a family politics. The persistence of given names in the family encouraged the custom of giving the name of a child who died to another who survived. This practice of necronymic naming, which went back to the early colonial period, was clearly on the decline in the nineteenth century. But it persisted in the Brown family. Owen had two sons named Salmon and two daughters named Martha; John had two Fredericks, two Sarahs, and two Ellens. None of these children was named after a parent, but the names were traditional in the family. The practice suggests that the Browns sought consciously to preserve ties to forbears. Viewed across time, the Brown family was more than a string of interdependent but essentially synchronous, living generations. Before its diaspora, it was a community of kindred reaching back across generations.

Lineage as well as economic and social success, then, gave the Browns standing in Hudson. Not surprisingly, they held themselves in high regard as thrifty
and "sober-minded" if not always deeply pious people, progressive, sensible,
and "public spirited." Owen Brown had come to Hudson a half century earlier,
he remembered, "with a determination to help to build up and be a help in the
seport [sic] of religion and civil Order.[105] Whether because of or despite his
stature in 1855, the Squire warned his grandsons that in Kansas they must not
rely "on the deeds of their Parents for a good name or property." According to
Salmon Brown's recollection, Owen also admonished him and his brothers not
to show the "white feather" of cowardice.[106] Each of them had a responsibility
to protect and live up to the family name. That responsibility was keenly felt
by their father, John.

V

The Browns frequently opened their homes to dependent relations – unmarried
adult sons and daughters, widows, children attending school, the unemployed,
the handicapped, the sick, the frail, and the dying. In 1846, Squire Owen's son-
in-law, Hiram King, a widower since the death of Owen's oldest daughter, Anna
Ruth, eight years before, joined Owen's household. He brought his two children with him. A "mild and respectable man," King was "sick in the 1st stage
of consumption." By December both Hiram and Owen's seventy-three-year-old
widowed sister, Theda Merrell, had died. Tragically, Owen's eighteen-year-old
son, Lucien, who had served as his brother-in-law's chief nurse, succumbed a
year later to the same disease. Lucien had been "a very healthy, strong young
man," Owen remembered bitterly, but Lucien "took the deseas [sic] of Mr.
King."[107] Owen grieved deeply over the loss of his youngest son. Neither Owen
nor John had thought King "very warm-hearted," but they conceded he had
been a "steady friend" and a "useful" man.[108] Owen did not question his duty to
bring his unfortunate in-law into his home. In 1856, his own health at last failing at eighty-five, Owen made a similar arrangement for himself and his third
wife and reported to his Kansas relations that "we now live with Mr Clark [his
stepdaughter Lucy's husband] and form one Famely [sic]."[109]

The presence of sick and dying relations in the Brown households reminds us
that children in that era knew the face of death. Following generations of religious practice, the Browns taught their children about death and salvation at a
very early age.[110] In the nineteenth century, life was still especially perilous for
children themselves. Owen's first two wives together lost four of their sixteen
children in infancy and two in their teens; John's two wives lost four infants,
and nine of twenty children in all. In 1843 four of Mary's young children died
within weeks of one another of what Brown thought was "dysentery" and local
tradition called "black diphtheria."[111] Whatever the pathogen, its impact was
devastating. "God has seen fit to visit us with the pestilence since you left us,"
Brown wrote to John, Jr., "and Four of our number sleep in the dust." They
were all buried in a single grave,[112] he added, but the four survivors, including

Brown himself, appeared to be recovering. "This has been to us all a bitter cup indeed, and we have drunk deeply, but still the Lord reigneth and blessed be his great and holy name forever."

That conventional expression of faith in a merciful if mysterious God must have been difficult for Brown to write. But he found "some comfort in our sore affliction." "During her sickness," nine-year-old Sarah "discovered great composure of mind, and patience, together with strong assurance at times of meeting God in Paradise," Brown wrote to John, Jr. "She seemed to have no idea of recovering from the first, nor did she ever express the least desire that she might, but rather the reverse. We fondly hope," he added, "that she is not disappointed." In his grief, Brown permitted himself only one note of resentment that God had taken his little ones. "They were all children towards whom perhaps we might have felt a little partial but they all now lie in a little row together," he added.[113] From time to time, Brown knew, God saw fit to remind His children not to become too attached to things of this world. Brown's twenty-year-old son Jason understood perfectly that "These days are days of rebuke and severe trial with us."[114]

Tragic episodes such as this were all too familiar in the nineteenth century. Indeed, the fictional story of a pure, angelic child dying in serenity and sweetness had become what Lawrence Lerner has called a literary topos or a widely imitated scene in novels such as those of Charles Dickens.[115] But unlike Dickens's dying Little Nell in *The Old Curiosity Shop* (1841) or Beth in Louisa May Alcott's *Little Women* (1868), Brown's Sarah did not die slowly or painlessly. She was not wafted off in the care of angels; she lay beside her three younger siblings in a single, improvised grave. Nor did Brown assuage his grief by invoking the Victorian cliche that his children were "too good for this world." If he took comfort that, among his children Sarah, at least, may have been saved, he did not know why God had rebuked him so severely.

Whether little Sarah understood death as an earthly separation from her parents, we cannot be sure. That she knew how to be a very good girl in ways that her father respected is certain. In her last days, she monopolized Brown's attention because it was still customary to sit with the dying. If Ruth's rose-colored reminiscences of her father may be believed, moreover, "He used to hold all of his children, while they were little, at night, and sing his favorite songs, one of which was 'Blow, ye trumpets, blow!'"[116]

Three years later Brown was far from home when another infant, sixteen-month-old Amelia, had been scalded to death in a domestic accident. Writing to his "afflicted wife" and children, he professed to be "utterly unable to give any expression of my feelings" on learning the "dreadful news. I seem to be struck almost dumb," he wrote. "One more dear little feeble child I am to meet no more till the dead small & great shall stand before God." He urged Mary to be strong. "This is a bitter cup indeed, but blessed be God: a brighter day shall dawn; & let us not sorrow as those that have no hope. Divine Providence seems to lay a heavy burden on you *my dear Mary*; but I trust you will be enabled to bear it in some measure as you ought."

Brown urged that no one should place "unreasonable blame" on his daughter, Ruth, for causing the accident, since "all of us" had at times failed to take "proper care." He reproached himself severely for being away and confessed that he could not leave his post in Springfield to come home very soon despite the crisis. "If I had a right sence of my habitual neglect of my familys Eternal interests; I should probably go crazy," he protested. The only solace he could offer was his "humble" hope that "this dreadful afflictive Providence will lead us all more properly to appreciate the amazeing, unforseen, untold, consequences; that hang upon the right or wrong doing of things seemingly of trifling account."[117]

Though Brown was often absent from his family, he strove not to be emotionally distant. He often told the children how much he missed them and that he was bearing presents for them as he returned home. Writing from Springfield in 1847, for example, he expressed sorrow that he had been "away so much." His mood was dark. "I feel considerable regret by turns that I have lived so many years, & have in reality done so verry little to increase the amount of human happiness." He reproached himself for failing to be as warm as he wished. "I often regret that my manner is not more kind & affectionate to those I really love, & esteem; but I trust my friends [i.e., family] will overlook my harsh rough ways when I cease to be in their way; as an occasion of pain, & unhappiness." In a sentimental note, he told Mary, "In imagination I often see you in your room with Little Chick; & that *strange Anna*. You must say to her that Father means to come before long, & kiss someboddy." Though he had often strapped his unruly boys for misbehavior, he urged Mary to control them by a "powerful appeal to their reason" rather than by punishment.[118]

Brown's concern for his children was not a matter of guilt over his neglect of them while away from home. Over the years he showed a familiarity with their "wants" and interests as each new set of "little folk" came upon the scene. Six years after Amelia's death, in a lighter mood, he wrote, "I am gratified to learn that Anne and Sarah [another Sarah!] are trying to assist you about the housework. I am so much pleased with this that I have bought for them 'Uncle Tom's Cabin', to live in after I get home." Brown was "glad of all the good news," he said, referring to his sons' report about the health of the livestock. "I really hope the boys will be able to keep all the sheep and cattle on the top of the hill (I mean in condition)."[119] Even after he became deeply immersed in the war against slavery, Brown continued to draw his children to him emotionally. "My Dear Daughter Ellen, I will send you a short letter," he began a note to his five-year-old in May 1859. "I want very much to have you *grow* good every day: to have you learn to mind your Mother very quick: & sit very still at the table; & to mind what all older persons say to you; that is right. I hope to see you soon again; & if I should bring some little thing that will please you; it would not be very strange. I want you uncommon *good natured*."[120]

As his children came of age, Brown continued to offer moral guidance and practical advice. He taught the boys to plant and harvest crops, manage livestock, tan hides, repair the house and barn, and do countless other tasks in the farm economy. He struggled to teach the younger boys humility and respect for their "biblical" but commonplace occupation of sheep raising. He wished "his older boys could be with him" as he tried to market his wool in the East, he said in 1845, but "their turn will come." Asking that his letter be shown to his benefactor, Simon Perkins, he admonished his restless, ambitious boys: "It is impossible for them without such opportunity rightly to appreciate the advantages of our occupation, or the rich treasure we have in our poor, miserable-looking sheep. I heartily wish my whole family understood the matter as it really is. I trust they will, yet."[121] In 1847 he moved Mary, their three boys, and their two surviving little girls to Springfield where he found chores for the boys in Perkins & Brown's warehouse.

That same year he sent his eldest daughter, eighteen-year-old Ruth, to Grand River Institute in Austinburg, Ohio, to further her education and better her social standing. John, Jr., was already a student there and had met Wealthy Hotchkiss, an attractive and accomplished girl from a "good" family. Soon, John, Jr., announced plans to marry Wealthy. Brown was pleased. In July he encouraged the newlyweds to take up residence in the Akron house his family was vacating in moving to Springfield. There John, Jr., could help Jason keep the flock while John, Jr., was finding an occupation. "Say to me by return Mail if you cannot manage to come on by Stage, & bring a wife with you, & take the house, & every thing needful to make all comfortable," Brown wrote to his son, adding that he had been "trying to find some one to keep house" and was leaving an "abundance for a small family to do with."[122]

As Brown himself finally got his wife, children, and furnishings "comfortably fixed" in Springfield two months later, he related the questions that "exercised" his mind about his buxom, red-headed, "absent Daughter," Ruth, as she returned to the academy in Austinburg. "What feelings, & motives govern her?" he began. "In what manner does she spend her time? Who are her associates? How does she conduct in word, & action? Is she improveing generally? Is she provided for with such things as she needs; or is she in want? Does she enjoy herself or is she lonely, & sad? Is she amongst real friends; or is she disliked, & despised?"[123] It is noteworthy that none of these questions had to do with the course of study Ruth had chosen. Clearly, her "anxious" father hoped that Ruth would tend to business but also enjoy the "society" of proper ladies and gentlemen. He may have hoped that, like John, Jr., she would find a suitable mate at the academy. Two weeks later Brown sent Ruth money "for immediate wants" and promised more assistance when he visited her in several weeks "if life & health are spared."[124]

In March 1850, when Ruth became engaged to Henry Thompson, a North Elba neighbor from a family in modest circumstances, Brown was pleased even though Henry's father was not an abolitionist. Nor did Brown try to prevent his son Jason from marrying Ellen Sherbondy despite reservations about her family.[125] As Alexis de Tocqueville observed of American fathers generally two decades before, Brown had easily relinquished whatever traditional patriarchal prerogatives his forbears might have claimed.[126]

But when Brown learned that John, Jr., and "several" of his other grown "Children" had rejected the family's historic religious creed, his bonds with them were strained. After a lengthy debate by letter with John, Jr., Brown despaired of reversing the sons' apostasy. "One word in regard to the religious belief of yourself, & the ideas of several of my Children," he wrote in 1852. "My affections are too deep rooted to be alienated from them, but 'my Grey Hairs must go down to the grave in sorrow unless the 'true God' forgive their denyal & rejection of him.... 'A deceived *Heart* hath turned them aside,'" he concluded. "That God in infinite mercy for Christs sake may grant to you & Wealthy, & to my other Children 'Eyes to see' is the most earnest and constant prayer of Your Affectionate Father."[127]

I shall examine the points upon which Brown and his apostate sons (and his daughter Anne) disagreed in a later chapter. What I wish to note here is the strength of the family's claim to the loyalty of its members even during what was for Brown a crisis of belief.

VI

The role of wives in the Brown connection presents a paradox. In the eighteenth century, they had been expected to be dutiful helpmeets. Essential to the family economy, they did the gardening, milking, and feeding of the chickens and hogs. They built the morning fire. They prepared meals, pickled meat, put up preserves, scrubbed floors and tables, laundered clothing and bedding, and spent endless hours at their spinning wheel and knitting and sewing needles, all the while perhaps rocking an infant's trundle bed with their foot. They bathed, dressed, fed, and nursed their little ones, and, with the help of the older girls and sometimes father, taught the youngest their letters. They managed activities inside the house and directed the hired help. Excluded from their husbands' affairs, they were relatively autonomous as "head of the family."[128] Yet when widowed, they often had to become the family's provider, supervisor of their husband's farm or shop, mentor to their sons as well as their daughters, and the sole disciplinarian. When they could not remarry to create a new (blended) family, New England widows nonetheless strove to keep their children with them.

Such was the case with Owen's mother, Hannah Owen Brown, after whose family Owen, her eighth child, was named. When her husband died of "camp fever" in the Revolution, Hannah struggled yet somehow managed to raise her eleven children. Stories of "Granny Owen" were repeated in the family for generations. Squire Owen's grandchildren heard them from their mothers and aunts. Hannah's austere habits and scorn for the "sinful luxuries" that had become necessities to her grandchildren were legendary. Her example of "courage, pluck, perseverance, [and] ability to endure hardships" was her spiritual legacy to later Browns.[129]

Despite Hannah's example, however, in the mid-nineteenth century, the Brown men still dominated the hearth. They even led in the domestic practice of the art of medicine. Although Hudson had three physicians in 1850, the Browns did not always consult the doctor even for serious illnesses. They had their own remedies and treatments for everything from "ague" (malaria) to cholera and the "Bilious yellow fever."[130] When he found his son Jason in "midling health" and "low spirits" on a visit in 1858, John "prescribed...a thorough Emetic with a good Rheubarb Physic: as *I am certain* he is very bilious" (bloated with bile).[131] His daughter, Ruth, remembered her father's having nursed "ten" of his children through an epidemic of scarlet fever. "Some of his friends blamed him very much for not calling in a physician, but he brought the whole family through nicely, and without any of the terrible effects afterwards which many have."[132] John, Jr., who, after graduating from Grand River Institute, had given public lectures on phrenology, was more current in his medical thinking than his father. He, too, did not hesitate to prescribe. For his infant nephew's chest and throat infection, he urged: "First in all cases of colds, croup and the like the system is first thrown into *an Electrical* or *negative* state...the first form of disease...." To relieve the excesses of blood "thrown...upon the *internal organs,*" he recommended applications of warm water and blankets to "produce a sweating or drawing effect."[133]

Though the Brown women all had "recipes" for various diseases too, they sometimes had to establish their authority for "doctoring" the sick. In the Brown households where Grandfather Owen, John, and his brothers presided over religious worship at the supper table and routinely instructed their children in morals, their wives could not exercise the predominant influence that urban middle-class women of that period enjoyed as a consequence of the growing "separation of spheres" and the cult of domesticity.[134] They were scarcely consulted about matters such as the sale of their husbands' properties and had to ask for money to meet routine household needs. Their opportunities to shape their own and their children's lives were so circumscribed that even in establishing domestic routines their judgment did not always prevail. Thus, sometimes quarrels over how to care for the sick concealed a deeper, unstated issue – the struggle for empowerment.

This muted conflict was evident in John Brown's relationship with his dutiful second wife, Mary Ann Day Brown. The seventeen-year-old daughter of a blacksmith with a large family, in 1833 Mary had married John, a respected widower with six children, without a courtship. He was twice her age, devoutly religious, and seemingly wise in the ways of the world. For those reasons, as well as her sense of her appropriate role as a wife, she would rarely challenge his authority in making family decisions. Even on matters of treating the sick she deferred to John.

For his part, John could be condescending even when he was praising Mary. Shortly after his initial move to Springfield, he expressed relief on learning from John, Jr., who had just arrived from Akron with anxiously awaited news from home, that Mary and the children had recovered from an unnamed illness. "I hope you will not again be visited in like manner during our absence," he said. But then he chided, "Have you determined that you will never write me again yourself."[135] Five weeks later he acknowledged receiving "your very acceptable letter of the 24th August.... The very reasonable manner in which you write about my return, instead of disposing me to stay away, makes me

FIGURE 2.5. Mary Ann Brown, John's second wife, bore thirteen of his twenty children. Pictured here with Annie (left) and Sarah, c. 1851.

CREDIT: West Virginia State Archives, Boyd B. Stutler Collection.

more than ever anxious to go home."[136] In mid-October he sent her several religious "tracts" along with "fish, sugar, cloth &c."[137]

During John's absences, to be sure, Mary sometimes acted as his surrogate in business matters. In late November, a month after losing sixteen-month-old Amelia, Mary wrote to ask John how she should respond to demands from two creditors who, Brown confided to her, had "shown a disposition to take advantage of an error I committed in the mortgage I gave them (in my extreme calamity)." Brown wanted Mary "to keep your pen from all papers brought to you by any person till I can advise you further in regard to it." He told Mary not to "worry at all about the matter, even if they should try to raise a dust about it in my absence. It will be soon enough for you to sign their papers when they have proved themselves willing to do right in regard to the 10 acres which they have tried to wrong Father out of.... [Y]ou may as well keep this letter to yourself.... I am glad you had some excuse for writing to me again so soon."[138]

Despite John's sharing of confidences with her, Mary found it difficult to make her own feelings clear to him. A tall, strong woman, Mary bore John thirteen children over the course of twenty years. But the constant round of pregnancies and births, the frequent family moves that required setting up housekeeping anew each time, the burdens of caring for so large a family, and

John's preoccupation with business – all her mounting cares finally drove Mary, without informing her absent husband, to leave her family to "take the cure."

In the spring of 1849 she had lost yet another baby after an illness. She herself had been ill and "dreadfully nervous" for months. "My wife has ... been very poorly for a long time; & is yet so," John reported to Simon Perkins in 1849. "She has become quite thin & poor."[139] Yet in May, John gave up their Springfield home and bundled his wife and children off to distant North Elba while he remained behind in Springfield to try to sell a large stock of Ohio wool belonging to Perkins & Brown. Without her husband, Mary had to care for nine children in a tiny, drafty, rented farmhouse in the Adirondacks. When in desperation John left Springfield to try to sell his wool in London that summer, Mary promptly set out for the famous institute of Dr. David Ruggles at Northampton, Massachusetts, to take the "Water Cure," leaving her children in the care of Ruth, her twenty-year-old stepdaughter.

It was Mary's first act of defiance in sixteen years with John. At Northampton she heard Lucy Stone lecture – "the first time that I ever heard a Woman speak" – and "liked it very much."[140] Her sympathetic stepson, John, Jr., tried to convince his father that Mary was really ill. "Ruggles told her she had a disease called Neuralgia (which is a disease of the nerves) and that a Scrofulous humour was seated on the glands," John, Jr., explained to John in September.[141] While at the "water cure," Mary contracted dysentery and became so ill that her daughter-in-law, Wealthy, came to nurse her. Unable to eat for eight days, Mary lost weight dramatically (down to "only" 142 pounds). Complaining that her husband "never believed their was any disease about me," she now felt vindicated. When she finally returned to North Elba the following February, she had a new self-assurance. "You have no idea how large [i.e., proud] she is in her feelings since she came home from the *Cure*," Ruth confided to Wealthy.[142] A convert to "hydropathy," in the years that followed, Mary "doctored" even typhoid fever and diphtheria in her family with water and ice.[143] In 1864, when the widowed Mary and her children finally settled in California, she served her neighbors as a midwife and practical nurse, using the water cure when her patients would permit.[144] Her journey to Northampton had been her "salvation" in more ways than one. And in 1859 her newfound confidence in herself would enable her to mount a quiet revolt within the family against her husband's dangerous plan to attack slavery in the South.[145]

In the end, neither the religious apostasy of his sons nor the fears of his wife for their lives would dissuade John Brown from making war on slavery. Like belief in the "God of our fathers," antislavery was an article of faith to him; it was "in his blood." The compelling presence of the Brown connection in his early life rooted his imagination in the "inclinations of head and heart" of the Awakening that had shaped his own father. Heir to that Hopkinsian creed, he had come of age in the buzzing new world of Jacksonian America, where Squire Owen's pieties would begin to fall victim to the unfathomable cultural challenges of an open, competitive, increasingly fluid society. John Brown would long bear the marks of that discomforting confrontation.

3

First Son

The firstborn of thy sons shalt thou give unto me.

King James Bible, Exodus 22:29

Late in life, John Brown related the story of his childhood in a letter to the twelve-year-old son of one of his most generous financial supporters. The six-page letter was accompanied by a separate appeal for further assistance and was clearly written largely to please the boy's parents.[1] It was thus likely an exercise in what Paul John Eakin has called "self-invention."[2] Brown told his story in the third person, calling it the narrative of "a certain boy of my acquaintance…I will call…John." It was a story "mainly of follies & errors; which it is hoped *you may avoid*," and his telling it was "calculated to encourage any young person to persevering effort" because of John's "*success in accomplishing his objects*."[3]

Despite its problematic purpose and echoes of the didactic children's literature of the time,[4] the letter is revealing of the values Brown assigned to his public persona. This does not mean that Brown consciously misrepresented things. But he acknowledged youthful foibles in a way that enhanced implicit claims of piety and self-discipline on the one hand and betrayed pride on the other.

As a child the Brown of the letter experienced "serious doubts" about his spiritual well-being, and so became a Christian, a "firm believer in the divine authenticity of the Bible," of which he claimed that even as a child he had an "unusual memory" of its "entire contents." "From earliest childhood" John had learned to "'fear God & keep his commandments.'" And because he learned that so well, later in life he always "followed up with *tenacity* whatever he set about so long as it answered his general purpose: & hence he rarely failed…and *habitually expected to succeed* in his undertakings."[5]

As a boy, "John" scarcely attended school. But he read the "lives of great, wise & good men[,] their sayings, and writings." As a result, "he grew to a dislike of vain & frivolous *conversation, & persons*; & was often greatly obliged by the kind manner in which older & more inteligent persons treated him at their houses; & in conversation." He also "very early in life became ambitious to excel in doing anything he undertook to perform," a "kind of feeling I would recommend to all young persons both *Male & female*, as it will certainly tend to secure admission to the company of the more inteligent; & better portion of every community."[6]

What is noteworthy about this curious "autobiography" is its studied appeal to the presumed conceits of the wealthy contributor to whose son it was addressed. Equally striking is the absence of any hint at the long internal struggle through which Brown had passed before he openly avowed the worldly ambition that his "greatest or principle object" in life was the "laudable pursuit" of the destruction of slavery.

In the "autobiography," Brown attributes the birth of that pursuit to his witnessing as a child the savage beating of a kind, "very active, inteligent, & good feeling" slave boy about his own age. Brown probably included this story to emphasize the early awakening of his compassion. The brutalized slave's master, "a very gentlemanly landlord" with whom John was staying, had made John his "pet" and invited him "to table with his first company; & friends." He also flattered John for "every little smart thing" he "*said or did*," and for having by himself driven cattle more than a hundred miles from home. The "negro boy (who was fully if not more than his equal)," Brown wrote, "was badly clothed, poorly fed; *& lodged in cold weather*," and was beaten before John's eyes with "Iron Shovels or any other thing that came first to hand." The incident "brought John to reflect on the wretched, hopeless condition, of *Fatherless & Motherless* slave *children*, for such children have neither Fathers or Mothers to protect, & provide for them." Thus John "sometimes would raise the question; *is God their Father?*" The incident made John "a most *determined Abolitionist*: & led him to declare, *or swear: Eternal war*, with Slavery."[7]

It was a moving episode and has been a favorite of Brown biographers. But it does not ring true. It appears to be an instance of "aphoristic memory," a memory more notable for its moral implications than its accuracy.[8] For one thing, it lacks specificity. Where did the adolescent Brown by himself drive cattle more than a hundred miles to meet the slave boy? There were still a few slaves and slaveholders in Ohio when Brown was a boy despite the prohibition in the Northwest Ordinance.[9] But such open abuse of a slave child would have drawn criticism even in Dixie. It seems unlikely that a "gentlemanly" host could strike a slave child with "iron shovels" without inflicting serious injury or death. Brown does not say what happened to the abused slave.[10]

Aphoristic memories are marked by such contextual vagueness and carry unstated, often unrecognized messages. It seems fortuitous that Brown and the slave boy were the same age as the lad to whom Brown was writing. Like the popular Peter Parley or Gilbert Go-Ahead stories written for children in antebellum America, Brown's tale pictured a hero like its audience. The fact that slave children were often sold away from their parents was a stock abolitionist criticism; Brown had often reminded his own children over the years of the misfortunes of orphaned slaves.[11] In making his case for the cruelty of slavery, Brown pictured himself as a boy with an acute sense of injustice. The implied contrast between young John and other white boys who witnessed such outrages is obvious. Only the now grown-to-adulthood Brown was sufficiently incensed by such brutality to declare war on slavery.[12]

Just how much later experience colored Brown's account of childhood memories one cannot say. But by the time Brown wrote his "autobiography," he knew the horrors of slavery from runaways like his friends Frederick Douglass and Harriet Tubman and his reading of abolitionist tracts. He had witnessed the determination of slaveholders in the guerrilla warfare in Bleeding Kansas, and had the blood of the Pottawatomie victims on his own hands. Memory of the beating of the slave boy may have been the lynchpin of an indictment of slavery Brown nurtured over the years. It may even have been a false memory elicited to justify Brown's commitment to "forcible means" or to absolve his guilt for misdeeds in his "war against slavery."[13]

Even if the gist of the story is true, a boyhood episode can scarcely explain why, forty years later, an "old man" literally pledged his life to destroying slavery. No hint of such a commitment can be found in the records of Brown's early life. For years, in fact, Brown was a Garrisonian nonresistant committed to fighting slavery with moral suasion rather than force. In the narrative of his boyhood just discussed, he noted that because of his "disgust" at the "Military affairs" he had seen in the War of 1812, he had for years declined to serve in the militia and like a "Quaker" had paid an annual fine for his refusal. Brown the warrior – Captain John Brown, as he liked to be called after the fighting in Kansas – is anticipated in his "autobiography" only in the claim that John "was excessively fond of the *hardest & roughest*" play and liked bossing his father's tannery workers.

But when he wrote the autobiography at fifty-seven years of age, Brown was sure of who he was. He wanted his supporters to know him as a Christian warrior in the cause of liberty. The autobiography provided the moral scaffolding of that new persona.

Because of that purpose, the narrative of his childhood said little of anyone else in his life. It cited no mentors or teachers to whom he felt indebted. He mentions his mother having given him a "thorough whipping" on one occasion and tells of his pain at losing her when he was eight. But he mentions his father only incidentally, and alludes to only one of his siblings. Indeed, the young John seemed to learn best on his own. Thus on the trail at age five he "learned to think he could accomplish *smart things* in driving the Cows; & riding the horses." It was not in school or at his father's knee that he learned of the wider world, but from books and the conversation of adults. When friendly Indians taught his father to dress deer skin, John picked it up too. In doing so, he found that he "was perhaps rather observing because he ever after remembered the entire process of Deer Skin *dressing*: so that he could at any time dress his own leather such as Squirel, Raccoon, Cat, Wolf, or Dog Skins."[14]

Indeed, what is most striking about Brown's account of his boyhood is his own hubris. His "success" in managing his father's tannery as well as "the way he got along with a company of men, & boys" while still in his teens had fed his "vanity" and made him "quite a favorite with the serious & more inteligent portion of older persons." Consequently, he "came forward to manhood quite full of self conceit; & self confident: not withstanding his *extreme* bashfulness. A younger brother used sometimes to remind him of this; & to repeat to him *this expression* ... 'A King against whom there is no rising up.'" The teenage John was thus comfortable exercising authority and making decisions. This was a trajectory of life toward fame if not wealth, a story of self-creation.[15]

It was also an advertisement of Brown's readiness to command and a testament to his fitness.[16] Its odd mixture of pride and humility says something crucial about Brown's moral compass and how far in his last years that compass had swung from its early Calvinist setting.

Born on May 9, 1800, Brown grew up in a world in which narcissistic strivings were clothed in selfless Christian precepts. Self-aggrandizement had to be cloaked in disinterested benevolence. Just as vestiges of the premodern farm economy of exchange and use-value lingered in Owen Brown's family, so the moral claims of colonial village life and the New Divinity still echoed long after in the fiercely competitive, money-conscious world of Connecticut's Western Reserve in Ohio. As a child John Brown was drenched in that Edwardsean tradition as it began to assimilate the revolutionary values of civic humanism and martial valor.

Thus, in looking back in 1857, Brown had, perhaps unwittingly, projected his adult persona – his ambitions, inclinations, and values – onto his childhood. Brown may well have been as compassionate a child as the boy named John, but he surely did not as a boy conceive a career in fighting slavery. Only in reconciling the "habits of the heart" that were paramount in Owen Brown's legacy with the challenges of the world in which he had to make his way would he discover his hatred of slavery and find his calling.

I

The origins of his moral intensity and the conviction that he was called to free the slaves are buried in those religious and social matrices forged over the years by his father. To be sure, deep-rooted passions are difficult to discern in documentary records. Feelings are often unstated, perhaps unrecognized. Yet in the surviving family documents, we detect clues to Brown's ambitions, yearnings, and anxieties – habits of the heart that fired his imagination, channeled his energy, and contoured his adaptability to change.

The nexus of these clues was Squire Owen. All his life Owen remained an evangelical who saw his life as a spiritual journey through the "speck" of time allotted him on earth. Questions of his own salvation and that of his loved ones absorbed him increasingly as he grew old. His sense of things was informed by a biblical frame of reference, and his letters to his "children" revealed that fact. "The State of Religion through the civilised parts of the world seems to be very low," he warned John and his "other Children" in Kansas in 1855.

FIGURE 3.1. John Brown's father, "Squire" Owen, a founder of Hudson, the birthplace of most of his sixteen children.

CREDIT: West Virginia State Archives, Boyd B. Stutler Collection.

He hoped that "some souls [were] a saveing, but the number must be very small with [respect to] the whoule. [I]n Hudson it was never so low as in a year or two past."[17] Three months later he warned, "Gods chosen mercies are proportion[ed] to our wants.... Spiritual blessings seem to be with holden and the wicked walk on every side ... my sins are ever before me which ma[y] God pardon through the merits of Christ."[18]

Owen often sermonized in his last letters. He was particularly troubled by what he perceived around him as a growing preoccupation with wealth and extravagance. "Christ Jesus came into the world to save a world of souls that could not be numerated," Owen wrote. After his short stay on earth, Jesus had left his "work of Salvation ... to his chosen Companions as his Imbasders to carry out." It was "probable," Owen thought, that Christ's disciples were "mostly or all in low circomstances" and "not popular men." But "how many thousands have calld themselves Imbasaders of Christ who have not imatated

Christ or his apostals." Could the Christian world "expect anything but great Judgments" while controlled not only by "Infinite wisdom," but "the wrath of men."

The drama of salvation was his constant theme. Our "domestick conceirn[s] may be so aranged as to promote a usefull and Godly example, or so as to make us a mere nusence in the world and allmost sertain to shut us out of the kingdom of Heavin," Owen cautioned his "children" when he was eighty-four. "[W]here most or all of the conversation is in gitting rich there will allso be the thought and action and when we look around us we see but very few of the rich that bid fair for the kingdom of havin." "I am not a preacher," he added. "I wish to say that I beleav the Bible, is the only safe guide, for us to live by or die by." [19]

Fatherless himself since the age of five, Owen had been a dutiful, affectionate father, temperate in "measures of correction," and forgiving of his children's shortcomings. According to family tradition, when he was angry with his boys, he would grab them by both shoulders, shake them, and demand: "Will you, will you, will you be a good boy?" [20] On occasion he would spank them with a birch switch or "limber persuader," as he called his improvised instrument. Despite a pronounced stammer, he had a ready wit, loved to tell funny stories, and was, an in-law remembered, "one of the drollest of men." [21] He was generous toward all his children, who were in turn respectful of him in his role as paterfamilias.

For all his kindness and concern for his children, Owen's legacy to them was shaped largely by tradition. The most telling evidence of his patrimony was his provision for the disposition of his estate. The British system of primogeniture had given way to partible inheritance in seventeenth-century New England, where Puritan fathers sometimes used the promise of distributing land and other property by inheritance or deed of gift to maintain their influence over their sons. [22] Owen did not make his children's inheritance conditional on obedience. But he followed New England precedent in several respects. Because he lived to such a "great age," he wrote three wills – in 1816, 1821, and 1855. In each he left his wealth about equally distributed between the children of his first and second marriages. But he deeded less to his daughters – even his unmarried daughters – than to his sons. In 1855 he willed one share to his daughters for every two shares to his boys. In the earlier wills, he provided a widow's third for his second wife, Sally. Because he had made a prenuptial agreement with his third wife, Lucy Hinsdale Brown, he left her only $60.

Patriarchal practice was also reflected in his wills' provisions for the apportionment of unequal shares to his sons according to their order of birth. As the firstborn, John was to receive not only the largest share, but his father's prosperous tannery in Hudson. [23] Along with this bounty and the social standing it conferred, however, he also inherited the responsibilities of being an oldest child. Firstborn sons had long been expected to remain in the community and to preserve the family property. In that sense, they replaced their fathers. Because Owen lived so long, however, John would have to await his patrimony and his accession to his father's role in the connection all through his middle years. But he would be judged – and judge himself in some measure – by comparison with his father so long as Owen lived.

In the Brown family, where homes swarmed with children, the significance of birth order was underscored by tradition and circumstance. Children's expectations were structured by the prospect of their inheritance, the duties and chores assigned to them as they grew up, and the differing privileges each enjoyed. Named for forbears or their parents' favorite relations, as we have seen, older children especially sensed that they were part of an ongoing process – the family "line" or "house." Younger children, to be sure, were aware of their order of birth. In a memoir written at age eighty, Squire Owen, himself a younger child, carefully noted the sequence in which his own siblings were born: After the birth of four older sisters, his brothers John and Frederick preceded him, and he was followed by two more sisters and a younger brother.[24] Like Owen himself, his children and grandchildren also knew their place in the birth order as well as the family's history and its claim to *Mayflower* descent. They too were taught that their behavior affected the family's good name. But oldest sons felt a special responsibility as namesakes and presumptive family leaders.[25]

II

John Brown was not simply an oldest son. He was a special child. The circumstances and timing of his birth in 1800 enhanced his significance to Owen and his mother, Ruth Mills Brown. He would carry a disproportionate share of their hopes for the future of the family. The place ascribed to him as a first son in his father's large family carried responsibilities and burdens as well as privileges. The prospect that he himself would become the head of the clan would shape his understanding of himself and to a large extent model his stance toward the wider world. John Brown's patriarchal presumption of a duty to lead and his sense of stewardship help explain not only the intensity of his growing devotion to the slave, but the unstated terms on which he offered his succor.

Although he was their oldest surviving child, he was not the firstborn. Six years before, the Browns had had another son, Salmon, a "very thrifty forward Child" his father doted on. Two years later the boy was dead. "In the winter of 1796 [we] lost our dear Child Salmon," Owen remembered in 1850. "It was a very great Trial all though we had many to sympathise with us." Then tragedy struck again. The following November "my Wife was taken sick soon after delivered of a Babe [another son] which lived but a short time[.] my wife was very sick her life all most despeared of and [she] continued sick most of the winter of 1797."[26] Two sons lost! Ruth's illness and the couple's bereavement added greatly to their anxiety, when their daughter Anna Ruth was born in 1798. The following winter Owen moved his family to Torrington where a "powerfull awakening" was in progress. There John was born. The date was significant. As Owen noted a half century later, "In 1800 May 9th John was born one hundred years after his great Grand father."[27]

Finally Owen had a son and heir to carry forward the family name. Owen gave John the forename of his own father, grandfather, and great grandfather. Years before, when Owen's mother, Hannah, had been unable to support her eleven children after her soldier husband John died during the Revolution, Owen had lived for a time with his "Grand Father Brown." He remembered the old man fondly. Two years after John's birth, Owen would name a second child after his dead child Salmon. But in 1800 this *first* surviving child had to be John.

If Owen's son John began life with the burdens of an eldest child, he did not enjoy all the parental attention ordinarily bestowed on such an infant. From the start John had a rival. In November 1797, two and a half years before his birth, his grieving, once more childless parents had agreed to take three-year-old Levi Blakeslee, the son of their Canton friend, Rev. Matthew Blakeslee, into their home. Levi was not the first child of hard-pressed neighbors that Owen and Ruth had boarded. They had no expectation that Levi would be with them more than "a short time," but "by the earnist request of his Mother and the increas of our affection," the precocious child became "our addopted son." Levi proved to be a rugged boy and may have filled a void in Owen's affections left by the loss of his two infant sons. When Owen took his growing family on the grueling forty-five-day trek by ox-team to Hudson, he had four natural children and Levi Blakeslee in tow.[28]

John would note in his 1857 "autobiography" that he assisted ten-year-old Levi, whom he does not mention by name despite their family ties, to drive the cattle on this arduous trek.[29] The difference between the boys' ages insured that John's efforts would be overshadowed. Indeed, Levi would always outshine John. Years later Levi epitomized the successful businessman John failed to become. Surviving records mark Levi's steps toward prosperity and respect in the community. It began with Owen's generosity. In 1816 he provided in his will for Levi directly after his wife and before any of his natural sons. Levi was to receive $150 to be "paid in land at six dollars per acre" from one of Owen's lots. It was less than John would inherit, but it was a handsome sum.

Of course Levi did not receive this inheritance in his youth. But Owen provided for Levi in other ways. Levi evidently moved to the town of Wadsworth just a few miles southwest of Akron soon after Owen wrote that first will because in 1819 Levi was a charter member of the new Wadsworth Congregational Church. In 1824 Owen bought forty-one acres in Wadsworth and deeded it to Levi.[30] On this land Levi built a tannery across the road from the residence of Owen's brother, Frederick Brown, who had settled in Wadsworth on land purchased from Owen eight years earlier. Later Levi bought adjoining property from Timothy Hudson. Levi prospered, eventually married twice, and had a large family of his own. He became a prominent figure in Wadsworth, and with Frederick Brown and others in 1841 deeded the Wadsworth Congregational Church property to its trustees. In February 1858, he wrote to John's brother, Oliver Owen Brown, that sickness and "cares" had "about used me up body and mind."[31] Although his sons wanted to sell their property and move to

Illinois, Levi stayed rooted in Wadsworth, where he died on November 27, 1864, at age seventy. If the years had taken their toll, Levi's life had had many parallels with that of his adoptive father.

Owen and Levi remained fast, lifelong friends. In November 1855, when Owen sent John the cash he had raised through his son, Jeremiah, to assist the Brown homesteaders in Kansas, Owen was in ill health and staying at Levi's home in Wadsworth. "Mr. Blakeslee's [folks] send their respects," Owen wrote.[32] Although Owen visited Levi frequently over the years, John seems to have had no contact with Blakeslee even when John was trying desperately to raise money for his family. Even in his family letters, John never mentioned Blakeslee directly. Levi was his adopted brother, but not an intimate friend. Levi's successes threatened to diminish John in his father's eyes.

The story of John's childhood rivalry with Levi and his siblings has been overshadowed by the tragic death of his mother when John was just eight. Ruth Mills Brown died in childbed a few hours after giving birth to her eighth baby in just fourteen years. John's father was devastated. He remembered that "all my earthly prospects appeared to be blasted." His "beloved Wife" was buried with her deceased baby daughter in the new Hudson cemetery. In a reminiscent account written on a canal boat in 1841, Owen recalled the kind of mother John and his siblings had lost. "The law of kindness was ever on hir [sic] Tung [sic] and her countenance [H]er counsels were sweet and soft as they were mostly drawn from the word of God." Owen felt "unmand" by his wife's death.[33] "[B]eing somewhat lonesome" as he wrote, Owen may well have idealized Ruth. Within that year his second wife, Sally, had died of consumption and he was alone once again. The fresh pain may have informed his account of Ruth's passing. "These were days of affliction," he remembered. He had kept his five surviving children "mostly about me." But they had lost an affectionate and nurturing mother.

It was eleven months before Owen had married Sally Root and provided a new mother for Levi, John, and his four siblings. Sally was just twenty – eighteen years younger than Owen – when she assumed responsibility for his children. Just how this dramatic transition affected eight-year-old John is uncertain. But we have his own testimony that he mourned his mother deeply.

In the "autobiography," Brown's remarks about the loss of his mother reflect less obviously the didactic intent so evident throughout most of the letter. The loss "was complete & pearmanent," he wrote, "for notwithstanding his Father again married to a sensible, intelligent, and on many accounts a very estimable woman; yet he never *adopted her in feeling*; but continued to pine after his own Mother for years." John does not say how fond his stepmother, Sally, was of him, but he does suggest what he thought the emotional cost of losing his own mother had been. It "opperated very unfavourably uppon him; as he was both naturally fond of females; &, withall, extremely diffident; & deprived him of a suitable connecting link between the different sexes; the want of which might under some circumstances, have proved his ruin." This opaque passage has drawn the attention of Freudians.[34] But whatever its unintended significance, it may have been John's attempt to explain his "extreme bashfulness" and presumed awkwardness in "society." If he had not accepted his stepmother as his new mother – as he remembered so many years later – and if he continued to mourn his natural mother, he must indeed have been a lonely child despite his father's growing family. And with no other substitute for his mother, John must have depended more than ever on the approval and affection of his father.

But any increased dependence upon Owen's favor John may have felt added to the danger rival siblings represented. The second surviving boy whom Owen had named Salmon was two years John's junior. He proved to be a quick study. As a scholar Salmon easily outshone John, who was a mediocre student. John preferred to stay at home to work for his father rather than to study arithmetic and grammar when a school was in session at Hudson.[35] But Owen intended John, as the eldest, for the ministry. In the winter of 1816–17, Owen sent his two oldest boys, John and Salmon, east in the company of another Hudson boy, Orson Oviatt, to study at an academy. Briefly the three attended Moses Hallock's celebrated school in Plainfield, Connecticut, where John now poured himself into his studies. Moses Hallock was a close relation to the Reverend Jeremiah Hallock who had mentored Owen himself as a boy. Later schoolmaster Hallock remembered sixteen-year-old John as a "tall, sedate, dignified young man."

After several months at Plainfield, the three boys transferred to Morris Academy in Litchfield. There John's brief career as a scholar ended. He developed an "inflammation of the eyes" that made prolonged study impossible. He abandoned school and returned home to work in his father's tannery. Since in later years John did not require glasses to read as he poured over the books of Perkins & Brown, it is tempting to speculate that his failure at Litchfield may have been a response to his inability to compete with Salmon. Clearly, he was no match for Salmon as a scholar. Salmon would later become a prominent lawyer in New Orleans and an editor of the New Orleans *Bee*. But John's eye problem may not have been psychosomatic. He did occasionally have similar problems of eye irritation later in life. He may simply have had conjunctivitis or a convergence weakness that made reading difficult despite the initial clarity of a printed or handwritten page. Whatever the reason for his abrupt abandonment of his studies, he seems to have been relieved to turn to other challenges.

John openly disapproved of his precocious brother. One of John's early biographers relates the story that when Salmon's instructor failed to punish him for some infraction of school rules, John admonished the teacher and later, ostensibly "in sorrow more than in anger," gave his brother "a severe flogging" – all because "father would have punished him."[36]

But John's failure as a scholar was a blow to his father. One of John's closest associates in those years, James Foreman, remembered that John "as I have always understood was designed for the ministry.... Necessity compelled him and his father to give up the original design."[37] Owen's disappointment with John may not have been acute, but John's failure to enter the ministry added urgency to his need somehow to shine in his father's eyes. Ironically, it also gave him the opportunity to do just that.

Years before, his father had sent John's older sister, thirteen-year-old Anna Ruth, to live with relatives in the East. She was not in any sense banished, we may infer, since her father visited her in Connecticut six months later. But she was gone. By 1816 Levi Blakeslee had left Owen's tannery and moved to Wadsworth. For a time Salmon remained in school in Connecticut. John's industry now attracted his father's notice and he soon became foreman of Owen's tannery. John was now unchallenged in his father's favor. In his "autobiography," he acknowledged that "the habit so early formed of being obeyed" as his father's foreman had "too much disposed him to speak in an imperious and dictatorial way."[38] But perhaps this confession was an unacknowledged boast about his ability to discipline men; after all, he was representing himself to his backers as a military leader in Kansas. Yet that boast was also a manifestation of Brown's pride in having been his father's choice to manage the tannery.

If John was not close to his brother Salmon, neither in the end was his father. When Salmon decided to study law in 1823, Owen had given him $500. But Owen later remembered having "great anxiety" about Salmon during these years "and many fears came upon me."[39] Owen did not approve of Salmon's display of learning and worldliness. It suggested vanity and impiety. Owen criticized a "circumlocution of 'compliments'" in Salmon's elegant personal letters to him, and Salmon agreed ruefully that such professions were "one of the defects of my letters in general."[40] If Owen loved Salmon, he did not always show it. For four months in 1827 he (and John) neglected to answer Salmon's letters asking for a favor. Salmon was reproachful. "It was an almost total derangement of my calculations to be kept so long in suspense," he wrote from Washington during a speaking tour. "I have since written twice to John, but I can get no answer from him."[41] Salmon died unexpectedly during a yellow fever epidemic at New Orleans in 1833, where he had briefly been the editor of the *Bee*. Owen, preoccupied with the question of his own salvation, remarked coldly of Salmon in his 1850 autobiography that "He was of some note as a gentleman but I never knew that he gave any evidence of being a Christian."[42]

This psychological distance between Owen and Salmon was repeated in other relationships. The Squire was closer to John than to any of the other sons of his first marriage, just as John himself would confide in and rely chiefly upon his own first-born, John, Jr. Owen's third son, Oliver Owen, occasionally shamed the family because of his ill temper and reputed cruelty to his apprentices. Once the irate man allegedly shot a rifle ball through the hat of a neighbor with whom he had quarreled about the direction of a surface sewer line that was backing sewage water onto Oliver Owen's property. Over the years Oliver Owen and his father had numerous business dealings, but not without rancor. In 1853 the son asked his father to "buy" a judgment against him and "have it assigned to you" in exchange for two parcels of land. "I would not trouble you with this business if I did not suppose you could do it better than any other one," he urged.[43] But in 1855 Oliver Owen fought with his father and became disrespectful. In a quarrel over a court verdict in Oliver Owen's favor against a man with whom Owen was in business, the son insisted the award was "justly" his due. "But owing to some strange infatuation you think otherwise," he protested to his father. "Now considering your age and the great anxiety you manifest in the matter," Oliver Owen said archly, he had "concluded to say" that Owen might pay only a portion of Owen's share of the $1,500 due to him. "[If] I held [the claim] against any other man living who was able to pay I would under all circumstances collect the whole amount, principle & interest," he emphasized.[44] After Owen died in 1856, Oliver Owen received only one dollar of the estate because the executor had already paid out $1,800 from his share.[45]

Oliver Owen's relations with John were better. Both Oliver Owen and Frederick bought lots in John's ill-fated Franklin Mills development and backed him by putting up properties of their own when John appealed a ruling in a lawsuit against him in 1839.[46] And, like all his brothers except Salmon, Oliver Owen was a rabid abolitionist. Once, finding that a church on property he owned was closed to an antislavery meeting he had scheduled, he reputedly ripped out its pulpit and burned it on the front lawn before throwing the church open to "a most rousing anti-slavery meeting."[47] In 1858 he wrote his children that he had "taken a great intrest in my brother Johns children since they went to Kansas although I have not been able to render them any assistance." But John had warned his own sons to keep their distance from their volatile uncle in seeking temporary employment after fleeing from Kansas. "Father was very anxious that I should not go to Uncle Olivers," Salmon wrote to his mother and siblings from Newburg, Ohio. "But you may tell him that there is no danger for I do not like him well anough. He is one of the worst men that I ever saw and one of the meanest."[48]

Oliver Owen's temper made him something of a misfit. And for all his passion against slavery, he differed from John in his antislavery philosophy. Like William Lloyd Garrison and his followers, Oliver Owen wished fervently for the collapse of the "manstealing" slaveholder-dominated U.S. government. "I am more & more satisfied there is no hope for the slave but in the disolution of the American Union," he insisted in a letter to his children in February 1858.[49] Of course John did not wish to see the South expelled from the Union if it meant the perpetuation of slavery. Indeed, he was himself by then raising a force to invade the South and free its slaves.

The father of eight children by two wives (sisters), Oliver Owen had "overreached my means in trying to help my children" during the hard times and was heavily in debt in 1858. Shortly before Oliver Owen's unexplained death that year, he complained: "It is a long time since I saw any of you or heard from you."[50] But he was not forgotten. John's sons remembered him as a staunch ally in the war against slavery. Writing to a family friend in 1884, John Brown, Jr., declared, "I say, all honor to Uncle Oliver O. Brown, who, had he lived at a later period, would have been found among those who fought slavery to the end!"[51]

John's relations with his younger brothers were warmer. If familial relations tend to be triangular, as family systems theorists have suggested, John and his brother Frederick were closest to their father. Six years younger than John, Frederick was less a threat to his primacy in the family than Salmon and Oliver Owen. John and Frederick were close friends in childhood and remained so. They frequently lent each other money and on occasion lent mounts when one had to travel by horseback.[52] In 1834, as noted earlier, John tried to persuade Frederick to move to Randolph, Pennsylvania, to help him launch a school for blacks.

John was also fond of his half brother, Jeremiah Root Brown, who was just two years older than John's first son. Before the Harpers Ferry raid, Jeremiah stored weapons in his Hudson home for John, and during John's trial in Virginia, Jeremiah gathered affidavits to help prove John sufficiently unbalanced to win an insanity plea.[53] The trust and affection between John and Frederick and Jeremiah proved valuable when, after Squire Owen's death, the younger men lent money to help John and the Kansas connection survive. "I take the first opportunity to acknowledge the kindness of you both," John wrote in October 1856. The relief you sent us was very timely."[54]

On the eve of John's execution, Frederick gave a public lecture in Cleveland in tribute to his brother's life and "deadly hostility to slavery."[55] It attracted a good deal of public attention. For several months Eastern abolitionists eager to canonize John sponsored Frederick in a series of talks.[56] His tour overshadowed Jeremiah's quiet work in gathering petitions addressed to Virginia authorities to save John from the scaffold and seems to have occasioned a breach between the two. They had been close. Jeremiah had helped care for Frederick's children when his wife, Julia, was repeatedly sent to an insane asylum for treatment.[57] But in 1873, learning that Jeremiah had tuberculosis and had gone to California in desperation to seek a cure, Frederick tried to heal the wound that had driven them apart. He denied that he had ever said that he was John Brown's only living brother or that he had "lost my property in a[i]ding him in Kansas." As "Jerry's" "day" was "well nigh spent," Frederick "thought it fit and propper that I say to you that what ever that has past in our history wheather real or imm[ag]inary that was rong in the sight of God or man I wish by this act to bury in the land of forgetfulness and humbly pray God that it may be like watter spilt on the ground." At sixty-six, Frederick himself was unable to find work, had moved to Necedah, Wisconsin, and was trying to raise a fatherless grandson (Boyd O. Brown) with the help of his daughter, Julia. Frederick concluded that he sometimes thought Jerry's "situation" more enviable than his own.[58]

John's ambivalence toward Levi, Salmon, and Oliver Owen contrasts with the warmth with which he accepted Frederick and Jeremiah. This was partly because John's father gave him authority over the younger boys. As his father' surrogate, he was not in competition with them for primacy in the family. In a sense, John's wayward half brother, Edward, twenty-two years his junior, even became a project for him. At fifteen Edward accompanied John on a cattle drive to New York state. John assured Owen that the boy would grow from the experience. "I am not without hopes that Edward will proffit [sic] by the many different kinds of company, and Examples he will of necessity meet with," John wrote from Allegheny County. "I mean to give him the same kind, & useful hints so far as he will receive them, & I am capable, that I would one of my own dear Sons," John added. "I well know your feelings on his account."⁵⁹

Edward had no settled occupation eleven years later when he married Samantha Perkins, one of eleven children of Col. Simon Perkins, John's business partner, on March 15, 1850. Since Perkins was "just about the most important man in the Western Reserve," the marriage was a stunning triumph for the Brown family and perhaps one reason for Perkins' continued loyalty to his bungling partner. But almost immediately after the wedding, perhaps feeling compromised by his uncertain prospects, Edward left for the California gold fields to make his fortune.⁶⁰ Everyone was stunned. Owen wrote to John in December that Edward was in good health but had not been "very prosperious in gitting gold[.] if he gets wisdom we will all be contented."⁶¹ Edward returned in 1854 but soon went west again. In October 1855 he was back in Ohio working for his father and trying to piece his life together. "Edward does not please Father...and Father is very discouraged about him," Jeremiah reported to a cousin in Kansas. "They can't work together at all and realy I don't know what Edward will do." Edward "would not take advice," Jeremiah added, "and his breath sometmes indicates a wrong spirit within." Jeremiah had put some money in a Savings Bank for Edward, but thought the "poor fellow" might be better off without money than with it.⁶²

In 1856, when Edward told his father that he was thinking of joining the Kansas Browns as a homesteader, John still had hope for his now thirty-three-year-old half brother. "If Edward would stay at home; & would associate with none but good company I would not hesitate to encourage his coming here if he feels inclined to do so," John wrote his father. "Perhaps Edward might do something to strengthen the Free State cause here; he doubtless *would*: if he will only respect himself."⁶³ That Christmas Edward attended the family gathering at Jeremiah's home in Hudson. "[Edward] had just returned from the west," John, Jr.'s wife Wealthy reported to her sister-in-law Ruth. "He did not say what he intended to do." Whether or not Edward was an alcoholic or simply lacked direction, he was a sad story to the family. "Jerrys [sic] folks and others seem to have given him over as a hard case," Wealthy ventured. "I am afraid it is too true."⁶⁴ But the following spring, Owen's "head strong" youngest son appeared to Jeremiah "reasonably steady" if deeply in debt and unwilling to share his plans for the future.⁶⁵

It is at least ironic that John Brown, who had moved his wives and children fourteen times since 1825 and tried his hand at so many occupations, should lament the restlessness of his half brother. Owen himself had moved several times before migrating to Hudson so long ago. But the standard for Browns had been set by Owen's half century of prosperity and preeminence in the civic affairs of Hudson. Edward was the last of Owen's sons to reach manhood.⁶⁶

John's paternalistic attitude toward him reflected not only John's close identification with his father, but his own growing sense of stewardship.

III

As Owen Brown lay dying in the spring of 1856, John was throwing himself into the struggle to save Kansas for freedom. At fifty-six, he still had something to prove to his father and time was running short. His whole life he had sought his father's approval and respect. It had not been easy. For John, reading his father's thoughts and sensing his father's moods had always been part of a strategy for survival and preferment. His mind resonated with Owen's in ways that his siblings' did not. Unlike Salmon and Oliver Owen, for example, John never quarreled with his father. His religious beliefs and practice conformed closely with his father's. His relish for hard work and exacting routines evidenced the "sober-minded," "steady" spirit his father took as a mark of piety. Despite the formal language in which John and Owen addressed each another, after John reached manhood, they shared their fears and troubles freely.[67]

Owen was never far from John's thoughts. In fact, John's life revealed a striking identification with his father. From his youth, John's antislavery activities paralleled Owen's. Owen's home in Hudson, where John grew up, was reputedly a "station" on the "underground railroad." There he helped his father hide runaways and aid their flight to freedom.[68] He even turned the Perkins & Brown warehouse in Springfield into a refuge for harried free blacks as well as fugitive slaves. If Brown's friend Frederick Douglass remembered correctly, Brown's Harpers Ferry plan grew out of an earlier scheme to set up a new and larger "Subterranean Railway" to rescue slaves. An avid reader of antislavery newspapers, Owen Brown plied John with a steady stream of abolitionist propaganda. John in turn commended those papers to his own sons. In 1832 John organized an Independent Congregational Church in Richmond, Pennsylvania. Ten years later Owen left the First Calvinistic Congregational Society in Hudson, to which he had belonged since 1808, as insufficiently radical, and helped to found the Free Congregational Church of Hudson.[69] Neither John nor Owen tolerated racial discrimination. John defied the deacons of his church in Franklin Mills by seating black worshipers in his family pew. When the deacons "cut him off" in 1839, Brown cried "proslavery diabolism," and his sons determined never to rejoin a church.[70] Similarly, when Western Reserve College refused to admit a black student applicant, Owen transferred his patronage to Oberlin College, where he became a trustee.

For years father and son placed their hopes for ending slavery in education. In 1834 John talked of opening a school in Randolph for black children, and later of founding an "African high school" in Canada. In April 1837 Owen submitted resolutions to the Ohio Anti-Slavery Society calling for the creation of education societies to "elevate the colored people."[71] Both men respected the right of fugitives to protect themselves. Only after he reached Kansas did John take up arms in the cause. Even then Owen cautioned only that "defensive" measures might lead to "offensive" ones. He did not rule out the use of force.[72]

An event of significance for both men occurred in 1837, when a mob from Missouri crossed the Mississippi River to Alton, Illinois, and killed Elijah Lovejoy, an abolitionist printer. Across the North protest meetings ensued.[73] Owen and John attended and reputedly spoke to a prayer meeting at the Hudson Congregational Church protesting the murder. According to a much later reminiscence of the meeting by a lifelong friend of John's, Owen, who had stuttered badly all his life, offered a prayer and made a brief call to action. Then John "arose and in his calm, emphatic way says: 'I pledge myself with God's help that I will devote my life to increasing hostility towards slavery.'" That was apparently Brown's first public declaration against slavery.[74]

The story that Brown offered such a pledge is certainly plausible, though it cannot be documented by contemporary sources. Brown was living in Hudson at the time and would hardly have missed so important a meeting. Nor was he one to let such a moment pass in silence. Like other abolitionists, he later referred to Lovejoy's martyrdom as evidence of proslavery lawlessness,[75] and he credited his aged father with having dedicated himself to the cause of the slave. In his last letter to Owen from Kansas in 1856, John concluded with the wish that "you may be continued to witness the triumph of that cause you have laboured to promote."[76]

The most striking affinity between John and Owen is the rhetoric they used in expressing their piety.[77] Each voiced regret that he had not spent his life to better purpose; each bemoaned his neglect of his family; each called upon his wife and children, in John's words, to meet adversity with "cheerfulness and true resignation," and to "cease not to ask God's blessing on yourselves and me."[78]

Both Owen and John believed that to live as a true Christian required "hard application." All mankind were sinners in need of God's grace. Man's brief "passage" on earth was a trial of faith, a preparation for death and eternity, an ordeal that required a careful balancing of legitimate everyday interests with higher spiritual concerns and disinterested benevolence. Both men were concerned with the morals of the wider community, which to both were variously "not improving," or "in the decline."[79] People in high places could not be trusted; "slavish tyranny" if not the Slave Power itself might yet prevail. God would surely one day punish the country for its "wickedness." Or in words echoing Owen's Jeremiads that John would write on his way to the gallows, the "crimes of this guilty land" could never be washed away "but with blood."[80]

IV

This convergence of Owen's and John's views betrayed John's emotional and intellectual dependence on his father. John's world was in many ways bounded by Owen's. To question the precepts, judgments, and habits of mind and heart he shared with his pious father was unimaginable to him. Yet John's eager compliance with his father's wishes as a child and his reaffirmations of his

father's faith as an adult did not protect him altogether from Owen's sometimes harsh criticism. John learned that Owen's candor spared no one and that
his words could hurt. Though he never rebuked Owen for such words, he evidently thought it necessary to ask his father to go easy on his deeply troubled
son Frederick: "I want to request as a particular favour," John wrote his father
in 1850, "that should my Frederick be with you any; that you be exceedingly
patient with him, & get along by encouragement as much as possible."[81]

Like John himself at times, Owen could be censorious, even unintentionally
cruel. Though John came to recognize his own "rough harsh ways" as a failing,
he never outgrew his fear of Owen's disapproval. That fear fostered in John a
need for self-justification and a sense of urgency in placating his father. It is a
key to understanding eruptions on sensitive matters of his "ardent," sometimes
"excitable" temperament. To be sure, Owen's exacting moral standards were
difficult for all his children. But more was expected of John, his first son and
the primary guardian of the family name. The profound ambivalence Owen
regularly betrayed about money and worldly success especially created ten-
sions in John. Owen took pride in knowing "the business People and Ministers
of the Gospel" over a wide area, and himself aspired to be one of those "leading men."[82] John shared that admiration for the important men in the community – businessmen and ministers, men of the world and men of the cloth.
His admiration was mirrored in John's own claim in his autobiography that
when he was an adolescent "intelligent" and influential men had shown him
respect.[83] As we shall see, his lifelong deference to such men would play itself
out in mistaken decisions during the Harpers Ferry raid.

Owen admired ministers for their piety and businessmen for their acuity.
But to some extent these classes of "leading men" exemplified different sets of
values. Owen's didactic point was that Christian virtue and self-denial would
triumph in the end. But the lesson was less clear in his own behavior. Owen had
worked hard to become a man of property and standing. He cared very much
about the opinions of others. Material things, even trifling things, mattered to
him. When he built his big white house on Hudson-Aurora Road, he kept the
furniture in the parlor covered to protect it against soiling.[84] If Owen asked for
God's grace and worried perpetually about his salvation, he was also proud
of his business acumen. He accepted deaths in the family as God's inscrutable
will, but he took business reversals as evidence of human wickedness abroad in
the land. John's son Jason, who, like his brothers, had become a religious skep-
tic, reported in 1853 with evident amusement, Owen "says in a letter to Father,
'I find E. Shuman to be a hard case; Morality seems to be withdrawn from the
human race, in a great measure, and wickedness taking its place, even in high
places.'"[85] Everyone in Owen's family understood that the old Squire was proud
of both his piety and his wealth.

Owen lived well but preached simplicity. He wished his children to be successful but not to forget God. He was proud of their "prosperity," but admonished them not to care for money or comforts. As standards for a worthy
life, these tests could be painfully at odds. For John they created, in Gregory

Bateson's apt term, a classic "double bind."[86] To please Owen, John would have to pursue the prosperity his father respected while condemning the greediness his father consciously despised. That challenge proved to be a source of frequent irritation to John.

In 1847, while John was living in Springfield, Owen detected an excessive concern in John's letters about the hardships his wife and children were enduring there. Owen implied that John was permitting worldly concerns to lead him away from God. John replied that he had not forgotten how brief our time on earth is compared to eternity. "I am quite sensible of the truth of your remark that my family are quite as well off as though we possessed millions. I hope we may not be left to a feeling of ingratitude or greediness of gain," he assured his father, "& I feel unconcious of a desire to become rich. I hope my motive for exerting myself is higher." He declared that he was not attached to his "present business," and he thanked his father for "such kind & seasonable [advice] pointing me to the absolute vanity of this world's treasures; as well as the sollemn future, which is before me." John promised to preserve his father's letter "carefully."[87]

Six months later Owen again expressed fear that John was "too much engrossed in money making." John's reply was stiffer this time. "I trust that getting, or looseing money does not entirely engross our attention; but I am sensible that it occupies quite too large a share in it," John admitted. Then he reaffirmed his father's principle while minimizing the accuracy of his suspicions. "To get a little property together to leave; as the world have done, is really a low mark to be fireing at through life," John wrote. "'A nobler toil may I sustaine, A nobler satisfaction gain.'" John then expressed the hope that a friend in failing health might live long enough "that the little of duty to God, & mankind it may yet be in his power to do, may be done with his might; & that the Lord Jesus Christ will be the end of the law for righteousness for that which must be left undone." John closed with a metaphor whose significance his father may have missed. "This is the only hope for us; Bankrupts, as we may see at once; if we will but look at our account." His reference to a common danger of spiritual "bankruptcy" in this life might have served – deliberately or not – as a reminder to Owen that John had suffered financial bankruptcy. Implicitly, it was a reproof to his father. Surely John was entitled to "get a little property together" for his family.[88]

This defensiveness about worldly success appears with regularity in John's letters to his father. Often John sandwiched news of his success between expressions of religious commitment, as if to guard himself against the appearance of worldliness. As early as 1830, John reported from Randolph: "Business not brisk but perhaps as good as is best. Our stupidity ingratitude & disobedience we have great reason to mourn & repent of. I feel that I ought to expect Gods judgments when his mercies do not awaken more of my love & gratitude, & zeal for his honor."[89] In December 1838, during a cattle drive, John wrote Owen from West Hartford, Connecticut, to ask Owen if $41 "could some way be obtained for me" and paid "as the balance due the estate" of the late David

Hudson and his wife on a deed John had purchased. Despite his obvious anxiety about his financial situation, however, John expressed resignation about his prospects. "Whether final success will attend my exertions or not, is for a wise, just and merciful God to determine, and I think I am in some measure willing to abide his holy will in regard to it."[90]

John understood at some level that he must not be too proud of his successes. In 1850 John urged his father to hold onto one of his properties because railroad builders would want it. Then he added what had become a compulsory denial of greed. "I think I feel from time to time something more the *great* importance of our proveing [sic] by an every day consistent disposition, & conduct, before our families: that we really do not consider gain to be Godliness." He had just left his wife and ten children on a bleak farm in remote Essex County, where a colony of blacks was settled on land donated by Gerrit Smith. It would not be long before John was prepared finally to renounce worldly gain himself and serve those refugees as a teacher and friend in "Timbucto."

That decision was a turning point. Through the years, he had been locked tightly in the "double bind" of Owen's mixed signals about piety and worldliness from which he could find no resolution. By finally removing to North Elba, he could satisfy his need to devote himself to others by helping fugitives learn to farm and manifest the disinterested benevolence that marked God's chosen. But to do so he had to forswear his unacknowledged wish to achieve wealth and respect as a businessman. Thus he would become a virtual ex-patriot from his father's world even as he lived out the creed of "our fathers" that he shared with Owen. He might embrace a devotional life serving his poor black neighbors, but he would not achieve the prominence in the world he knew his father admired and perhaps expected of him. North Elba was a refuge not from failure, but from internal conflict. At age fifty-four John Brown still yearned to be somebody his father would admire. In retreating from the world after a string of ultimately failed enterprises, he was now risking irrelevance in his father's eyes.

But he would soon receive a "call" to go to Kansas where "service to the cause" took on another, more redemptive, and far more conspicuous meaning. There, in the whirlwind of Bleeding Kansas, Owen Brown's eldest son, the defender of ancient pieties, would become a revolutionary.[91]

PART II

REBIRTH

4

Pilgrim

These all died in faith, not having received the promises ... and confessed that they were strangers and pilgrims on the earth.

King James Bible, Hebrews 11:13

To know John Brown is to fathom his darkest secret – his purpose at "Bloody Pottawatomie." For if Brown achieved lasting fame by failing spectacularly at Harpers Ferry, he won posthumous infamy for clandestine assassinations in Kansas that he never publicly confessed to be his doing.[1] At Pottawatomie Creek, on a still summer night in 1856, he and seven other free-staters dragooned from their cabins six adherents of the proslavery territorial government, one or two at a time, questioned them briefly in the darkness, let one of them go, and hacked the others to death with finely honed broadswords. Deciphering Brown's motives in instigating and directing these slayings is crucial to understanding the origins of his war against slavery. It is also crucial to understanding who he was and how a professed Christian, living, as he often claimed, by the Golden Rule, could commit such an act. That assessment promises to make sense of an antislavery fanatic – a man for whom the embrace of "forcible means" became in Kansas a sanction for remorseless killing.

I

Brown's responsibility for the killings was soon suspected but for a long time unproven. Within three weeks after the events at Pottawatomie, two eyewitnesses told a Congressional committee investigating the "troubles" in Kansas[2] that Brown had led the self-styled "Northern Army" that committed the murders. A territorial court thereupon indicted Brown and several of his sons, but local authorities could not arrest them in the ensuing months during which clashes between guerrilla bands supplanted law and order. For a while, federal posses hunted him,[3] but Brown's crime vanished into the vortex of the civil war in Kansas until his capture at Harpers Ferry resurrected memories of it.

In 1860 Brown's first biographer, an abolitionist devoted to his memory, flatly rejected the charges against the "Old Hero,"[4] and for years thereafter Brown's sons and other relations did the same, or remained silent.[5] Brown's guilt was therefore not widely accepted for a quarter century. During that time, Northerners celebrated Brown as the martyred hero of Harpers Ferry, a selfless champion of the slave. During the Civil War, Union forces marched to the strains of "John Brown's Body," though the memory of Brown inspired revulsion and hatred among white Southerners long after Confederate defeat. The "confession" of James Townsley, a house painter from Maryland who had settled on Pottawatomie Creek in 1855 and carried Brown's party to the scene of the "massacre" in his lumber wagon, established Brown's responsibility for the crime. Published in a Kansas newspaper in 1879, Townsley's story compromised Brown's memory even among his apologists and presented historians with sobering new questions.[6]

Pottawatomie was no mere episode of frontier violence in the settling of the American West. Neither its perpetrators nor its victims were outlaws or rivals for land, timber, or water rights. None of Brown's men had killed before. Nor were the slayings committed impulsively. Brown struck thirty-six hours after ostentatiously ordering his two-sided broadswords ground to fine edges in the presence of three companies of cheering free-state militiamen, though they knew nothing of his plan. Although he had never met his victims, he knew whom he was after and, with Townsley's aid, where to find them. Afterwards, when others in his party recoiled from the butchery they had committed, Brown stiffened their resolve.

If the "massacre" was not typical frontier violence, neither was it a simple descent into madness. To be sure, no other abolitionist, even in Kansas, directed a comparable bloodletting.[7] But if Brown increasingly thought of himself as God's "instrument" to free the slaves,[8] no voices told him to kill and no one before the attack thought him delusional. The claim that mental instability accounts for the tragedy – a claim favored, as earlier noted, by a number of recent scholars[9] – fails to explain how Brown picked his victims or why he chose to kill at all. Nor does it explain why other free-staters soon rallied to his side and Eastern reformers gave him financial and material support. If Brown was outraged by proslavery lawlessness, we must nonetheless dismiss as erroneous the familiar story that he and his sons "went crazy – crazy" when a messenger reaching their camp on Ottawa Creek near Prairie City brought news that a southern Congressman had assaulted Massachusetts Senator Charles Sumner on the floor of the Senate.[10] In 1856 news from the East still reached Kansas City by river steamer, not by telegraph.[11] Some of Brown's contemporaries later saw him as a "monomaniac" – a sane person "insane" on a single subject. But this conclusion only labeled their bafflement at his fierce hatred of slavery. I will examine the question of Brown's alleged "madness" in Chapters 6 and 7.

Brown was deeply religious and ready to hang for "God's despised poor." But Bloody Pottawatomie was premeditated murder, a blatant flouting of the first commandment. Nothing in his religion encouraged such an act. Religious conviction as intense as Brown's may lead to quietism and withdrawal from the sinful world, and religiously inspired militance may be expressed, as it was for Garrisonians, through nonresistance. Brown was an evangelical, and many evangelicals expected God to punish America for the sin of slavery. They did not, however, believe God had appointed them personal instruments of His vengeance. To say that Brown was a *religious* fanatic does no more than identify the idiom in which his violence found public expression.

Historians must wrestle with deeper mysteries. To people who knew Brown well, murder was radically out of character for him. He had been a dutiful son and husband as well as a responsible father. His neighbors acknowledged him as a "steady," if sometimes contentious, citizen. Though often a litigant, he was no troublemaker and certainly no brawler. A self-proclaimed radical abolitionist and advocate of free-state causes, he had never raised a hand in anger against a supporter of slavery.

Following the Kansas slayings, this reputable John Brown became the fanatical Osawatomie Brown. For months he led a guerrilla band in skirmishes with proslavery militia. Accompanied by admiring correspondents from Eastern newspapers, Brown terrorized proslavery Kansans and gained a national reputation as a free-state chieftain.[12] Calling himself variously Shubel Morgan, Nelson Hawkins, and Isaac Smith, he eluded federal authorities and fled to Ohio and then to the East, where he raised money and enlisted volunteers. Then, in 1857, he returned to Kansas, ostensibly to protect free-state emigrants, perhaps hoping to renew the war. To his Eastern financial supporters, he personified the cause of "freedom." To those who saw him in the field, he was a stark figure, frowning, hatchet-faced, bowed by age but lean and sinewy. Shrouded in a white linen duster that covered his coat, bristling with weapons, and peering restlessly from under a shapeless straw hat, he looked like vengeance incarnate. Antislavery became his vocation and his calling, invested with every ounce of energy he possessed.

Pottawatomie transformed him. It constituted a moral fault line in his life, separating states of self-consciousness as clearly as it transformed his public careers. If on its face Pottawatomie was plainly a betrayal of Christian doctrine, then it is essential to know how Brown justified the killings to himself. Terms such as "fanatic" or "depressive" do not lessen their horror. To grasp the meaning of Pottawatomie, one must see it first through Brown's eyes. One must discover, in the language of cognitive psychology, the privileged schemata – the patterns of predispositions and representations of self – that shaped his sense of social reality.

Brown came to Kansas bearing not only rifles and swords, but moral baggage as well: convictions about the struggle in Kansas and its significance in the eternal war between good and evil, and a consciousness of his own unmet responsibilities in that struggle and his own private, unfulfilled ambitions. He was a charge ready to fire. In Kansas the "outrages" of hostile proslavery elements aroused in him the volatile chemistry of tribal politics, personal crisis, and private apocalypse. At Pottawatomie, Brown struck in part out of a conviction of imminent danger to his clan – a perception indebted as much to

FIGURE 4.1. This 1857 daguerreotype reflects Brown's transformation in Kansas.
CREDIT: West Virginia State Archives, Boyd B. Stutler Collection.

inner turmoil as to "proslavery diabolism." He struck also in response to a
sense of imminent personal loss and of the precariousness of his own soul. If
the Pottawatomie killings spread panic and confusion in southeastern Kansas,
for Brown they resolved inner conflicts of which he was largely unaware but
whose resolution helped him create a new persona.

II

If Pottawatomie has too long remained a mystery, that was not for lack of
interest. Questions about Brown's motives and the criminality of the killings
have been focuses of bitter controversy, and have nurtured rival, partisan

historiographical traditions. Brown's partisans have relied chiefly on the later testimony of his family and friends to justify the slayings as "executions" in a moral cause. Townsley's "confession," published in the Lawrence *Daily Journal* more than two decades after Pottawatomie, elicited several responses from Brown's sons and close associates, which his scholarly defenders use to make their case.

The pro-Brown witnesses called the killings defensive: Brown intended Pottawatomie, they say, to inspire terror among "ruffians" who threatened the Browns and their free-state neighbors. It would create, Brown hoped, a "restraining fear." Beyond that, it was an act of "retributive justice" for the recent "cold-blooded murders" of five free-state men. An eye for an eye. Brown's victims were, in any case, notoriously bad men, his defenders insisted, troublemakers, and allies of Border Ruffians and of Major Jefferson Buford of Alabama, whose military force of four hundred encamped on nearby Ottawa tribal land and menaced free-state settlers. Some Brown adherents insisted that the free-state leaders at Lawrence had given Brown the names of men to be killed, while others declared that a "council" of Pottawatomie and Osawatomie militiamen had endorsed his plan.[13] In these scenarios, the killings were equally a blow for a free Kansas and a preemptive strike to protect the Browns and their neighbors.[14]

All of these stories depended on the credibility of the Browns, who for many years had denied involvement in the massacre. Brown's detractors told very different stories of what they saw as heinous murders. Their accounts attacked Brown's character, citing as their authority one of his own volunteers who found the Old Man "imperious," "self-centered," and "cruel."[15] If Brown had defenders among old Kansas free-staters, he also had enemies. Their insistence on his guilt had finally helped to elicit Townsley's confession.[16] Brown's scholarly enemies dismissed the stories of threats to the Brown women or neighbors as fabrications unsupported by contemporary evidence and intended to justify an indefensible crime.[17] They denied that the slain men were plotting to burn the Browns out or to assault their women. Brown's victims were decent, blameless settlers, they argued, not agents of a proslavery conspiracy.

Citing remarks of Brown's sons, James C. Malin, the foremost critic of the Brown "legend," suggested in 1942 that the Pottawatomie killings were political assassinations. All but one of the victims, he noted, were members of the territorial court for the southern district, an arm of the proslavery government at Leavenworth that was indicting free-state men associated with the rival Topeka government for treason.[18] Brown killed at Pottawatomie, Malin wrote, to avoid his and his sons' prosecution. Rejecting as myths all plausible "excuses" for the "massacre," Malin suggested that the Old Man determined upon the killings as a means of reasserting his authority over his sons.[19] At Pottawatomie, Malin and others insisted, Brown actually brought violence to a neighborhood in which no man had been killed and no woman assaulted, despite rumors and threats. And by killing supposed adversaries when they were unarmed and unable to protect themselves or their families, historian David Potter has noted, the Old Man opened a new phase in the Border War.[20]

Despite such differences of interpretation, scholars have agreed upon a rough chronology of events preceding the Pottawatomie slayings.[21] The killings, they generally acknowledge, were part of the twister of anarchy and murder that began sweeping across the Territory months before and left the legacy historians know as Bleeding Kansas. For two years migrants had quarreled over land claims that fanned out across nearly fifty million acres not yet legally open to settlement because federal land surveys no less than Indian cessions lagged far behind the demands of impatient settlers. Cultural differences between New Englanders and Southerners aggravated the disputes prompted by these delays. And those differences as well as the disputes found immediate, widespread expression in territorial newspapers and politics.

Conflict between pro- and antislavery settlers soon became institutionalized. A proslavery legislature, elected by the votes of nearly five thousand Missourians who swarmed into Kansas on election day, had met at Shawnee Mission in July 1855. It promptly purged its few free-state members, adopted a slave code, and outlawed antislavery activity. Three months later delegates elected to a free-state constitutional convention held at Topeka repudiated the Shawnee legislature and its "bogus" laws protecting slavery. They drafted a frame of government forbidding slavery and authorizing the election of a free-state government. Kansas now had two separate political communities, a proslavery community clustered around the border towns of Leavenworth and Atchison on the banks of the Missouri and a free-state community to the west around Topeka and Lawrence on the Kansas River. The creation of the Topeka government prompted the formation of the proslavery Law and Order Party. One of its leaders, the territorial governor, Wilson Shannon, issued a call, answered by 1,200 Missourians, to help enforce proslavery territorial law in the free-state town of Lawrence. Named after the Boston philanthropist and reformer, Amos Lawrence, who had sent rifles to free-state settlers without charge, the town had become a symbol of northern resistance and a flashpoint of conflict. Only a last-minute "treaty" between Shannon and free-state leaders Charles Robinson and James Lane averted open warfare at Lawrence.

A severe winter and swollen rivers enforced the truce, but isolated shootings of five free-staters fed suspicions of a proslavery conspiracy. An unsuccessful attempt to kill Sheriff Samuel J. Jones of Westport, Missouri, a leader of the Border Ruffians, as he tried to arrest free-state leaders in Lawrence on April 23, 1856, precipitated a second crisis in the town. Following Jones's attempt, the U.S. marshal for Kansas issued a proclamation calling on citizens to assist him in serving arrest warrants in Lawrence, the "abolitionist" town. Thus it happened that in the helter-skelter of territorial strife, a federal posse of some 750 Missourians and recent migrants from the South, led by the recently wounded Sheriff Jones himself, encamped near Lawrence. The resulting call for help reached Brown and his free-state neighbors at Brown's Station on May 21.

The result was the bloody but unexpected climax for which John Brown is chiefly remembered in Kansas history. In response to the appeal from Lawrence, John's oldest son, John, Jr., who had been a leader in the Topeka movement, rallied his militia company, the Pottawatomie Rifles. At dusk on May 21, thirty-four "Pottawatomies" began a rapid march to save Lawrence. Although "Old Brown" himself was not a member of the Rifles, he and six other irregulars accompanied them. Joined at Prairie City by two militia companies from Osawatomie, the Browns soon learned they had come too late. Jones's posse had "sacked" Lawrence and burned the Free State Hotel and the offices of the town's two newspapers. The Missourians then withdrew from Lawrence but were still in Kansas. The angry free-staters, camped at Prairie City, quarreled among themselves about what to do next, and as rumors inspired conflicting plans, they waited.

Brown himself left camp shortly after noon on May 23. The following night, after resting in a wood near the Creek, he directed his small party – four of his sons, a son-in-law, and two neighbors, Townsley and a storekeeper named Theodore Weiner – to the scattered split-log cabins of proslavery settlers near Dutch Henry's Crossing (later Shermanville), forty miles south of Lawrence. After enquiring about the men they sought and questioning several terrified residents, Brown's "Northern Army" took five proslavery men, one at a time, from their families and silently hacked them to death. Distraught relatives and neighbors found the men's bodies the next morning strewn about the open prairie, as if spewed from a satanic funnel cloud. Four of the slain men – James P. Doyle and two of his sons, aged twenty and twenty-two, and Allen Wilkinson, a member of the Shawnee legislature – were from Tennessee. The fifth, a German immigrant, William "Dutch Bill" Sherman, was a brother of "Dutch Henry" Sherman for whom the crossing was named. All of the murdered men were horribly gashed – some later reports said mutilated – and James Doyle had been shot in the forehead. This grisly work by the Brown party was soon known as the Pottawatomie Massacre.

In so skeletal an outline of events, Brown's motives necessarily remain a matter of speculation. The story's connective tissues are spare for several reasons. First, contemporary and reminiscent sources are variously unreliable, incomplete, contradictory, and/or fiercely partisan. They must be used with caution. Second, modern researchers have focused so narrowly on the politics of what happened that they have neglected the social and cultural context of the crisis they describe. Third, Pottawatomie remains a mystery because Brown's biographers have been committed implicitly to narrowly egoistic frames of reference or psychological models. As a result, they have catalogued his alleged defects of character or personality to explain his antislavery fanaticism.

As we have seen in Chapter 3, even sympathetic historians have accepted with little question the thesis that Brown's violence in Kansas expressed deep frustration over a life of persistent failure. His war against slavery was, they imply, compensatory and irrational, failure presumably begetting fanaticism. The implicit premise of this argument is that Brown's self-esteem depended chiefly upon fulfillment as a businessman or a gentleman of means. As we have seen in Chapter 2, however, that notion is a presentist misreading of Brown's ideological and emotional universe. He was, to be sure, ambitious, and hoped

for worldly success and respect. He likewise feared the loss of status that economic failure implied. But though he had his failures and hardships, he also
had successes, first as a tanner, then as a livestock grower, and, for a time, as
a speculator and wool merchant. The problem was that these occupations did
not constitute a career that in his own estimation measured his life's progress or
constituted his life's work. None was a calling. Brown's self-respect rested only
in part on whatever recognition he gained for achieving prosperity and providing his family with "worldly comforts." To a disciple of the New Divinity, these
goals represented a "low mark" to shoot at. Brown's sense of self also rested on
ascriptive, largely familial statuses, and on his own sense of his civic persona.
Brown saw himself as head of a large family, a respected member of a prosperous clan and community – as one whose opinions counted, who had to be
reckoned with. He did not think himself a failure, chronic or otherwise.

The historian's task is to get inside Brown's mental world to see the struggle
in Kansas as he saw it. To do so it is necessary to shift the focus from public
to private events. The largely unexploited correspondence between the Brown
pioneers in Kansas and their relations back home permits a fresh reading of
Brown's view of the Kansas strife. Before Brown arrived in the territory, his
understanding of the turmoil there rested largely on accounts in his sons' letters
and reports in antislavery newspapers. Once in Kansas, he found his actions
both facilitated and constrained by the interdependence of a widening circle
of kin there. His kinsmen's concerns and ambitions soon became his. Their
struggles to become homesteaders in a free state provide a crucial context in
which to understand Brown's new public career as a warrior for the Lord.

In short, the secret of Bloody Pottawatomie lies in recognizing that Brown
was a protagonist in an ongoing family drama that imposed private meanings
on the conflict in Kansas. To get at the secret, one must reconstruct the ethos
and emotional dynamic of Brown's clan and see Brown's story as a subplot
in the drama of his kinsmen's settlement and their widening role in the local
politics of southeastern Kansas. Seeing Brown in this way permits a fresh reading of evidence about old threats and local rivalries and illuminates neglected
and newly available sources. This in turn clarifies the pattern of incentives and
predispositions pressing Brown to bring events in the territory to a head and
suggests how those factors shaped his perceptions of the sequence of events
that climaxed in his fateful decision to return to the Pottawatomie.

III

John Brown's antislavery stance drew strength from a compelling vision of the
American republic as an instrument facilitating the coming of the kingdom of
Christ to earth. That vision was a legacy of his formative years in Hudson. The
taproot of his antislavery convictions and one source of his predisposition to
find "proslavery diabolism" in Kansas was the ethos of his father's ardently
antislavery family. Eighty-four years of age when John went to Kansas, Owen
was the only surviving member of Hudson's founding generation. Before the

opening of Kansas, most of his fifty-one grandchildren lived within a few miles of what they called his "ancestral home." Within the Brown "connection," the old squire had become a benevolent paterfamilias, who saw mentoring his "numerous progeny" as a spiritual challenge he felt duty-bound to accept.

Shaped by the ferment of the Great Awakening, Owen had communicated his deep religious convictions to his offspring by precept, persuasion, and example. Owen embraced the "moral government of God," the republican successor to the Puritan idea of the covenant, and believed explicitly that God rewards and punishes nations according to their obedience to His law. Christians had a solemn duty to overcome their corrupt hearts to achieve "disinterested benevolence" and to be concerned about the moral transgressions of others. Samuel Hopkins's postmillenialism remained for Owen a lifelong incentive to support Sabbath reform, temperance, and antislavery – all harbingers of the advent of the great, if still distant millenial age preceding the return of Christ.[22]

Owen brooded over the Church's struggle to purge itself of moral inconsistencies so that its members might bear witness more effectively to the power of the Gospel over men's lives. Reformed assemblies adopted annual "narratives of religion," which pronounced the morals of the world to be rising or declining. In his own regular assessments of the subject, as previously noted, Owen often warned his children of decline, citing current events in Hudson and the nation in support of his judgments.[23] Owen invited his children to reflect especially on the apostasy of slaveowners and on their resistance to the kingdom of God. Such admonitions resonated with the warnings of "counter-subversive" alarmists who were convinced that the Slave Power Conspiracy was undermining free society and inviting the retributive justice of the Lord.[24]

"I am an abolitionist," Owen declared in 1850. "I know we are not loved by many." He liked to relate that he became fond of blacks when, during the Revolution, his father was away with his militia unit and a neighbor lent his mother a slave named Sam to work the Browns' fields. Sam often carried Owen on his shoulders and, so Owen recalled sixty years later, "I fell in love with him." In 1790, while a guest in his minister's home, Owen listened to Samuel Hopkins himself condemn slavery "as a great sin." Owen was further inspired by a pamphlet in which Jonathan Edwards, Jr., denounced slavery unsparingly. Those powerful testimonies were convincing, he remembered, and however accurate the memories, they represented an essential theme in Owen's understanding of his life. His opposition to slavery only deepened as sectional strife worsened in his later years. When the colonization issue split the Hudson church in 1842, he was among the angry seceders who promptly founded the Free Congregational, or "Oberlin," Church. Proud of his stance against slavery, Owen boasted, "I think I shall die an Abolitionist."[25]

Within his great family, "Father Brown" commanded unfailing filial devotion. He set high moral standards, discouraging "frivolous talk" and punishing his children for selfishness, idleness, lying, and "tattling," sometimes with admonitions but sometimes too with a switch or "limber persuader." To his children Owen thus stood between worlds. His stature as a founder of Hudson and a large landholder lent his words authority, while his great age permitted him to speak for and about the family's past. In Owen's demeanor, then, tradition fused with the present. Indeed, in the fluid, multigenerational households of Brown kinfolk, all of the older members embodied a heroic past for the young. To every Brown, the family embraced not only the entire "connection," but the dead and the yet unborn as well. The family thus transcended individual lives and immediate personal concerns. All of Owen's children had to come to terms with his understanding of these things and with the expectations that understanding carried for him. As the eldest son and the namesake of Owen's grandfather and idolized father, as I have noted, John bore a special responsibility to represent the family and uphold Owen's expectations for it.

During the later years of John's childhood, Owen's rule was untempered by maternal tenderness. John was eight when his mother died after giving birth to her eighth infant. By John's later account, he never felt close to his stepmother[26] and continued to "pine after his own Mother for years." Unquestionably, Brown saw himself as having had a tragic childhood, which God used to teach him "hard lessons" about attachment to worldly things.[27] To Calvinists like Brown, God, through death, took loved ones from them to remind them that eternity was all that really mattered. As a youth John's sense of the tragic had been deepened by Owen's religious teachings as well as his pious reserve toward John.

Indeed, a recurring theme through Brown's changing images of his life was the inevitability of loss. In his later years, John exhibited a persistent though subtle mistrust of the world that probably had its genesis in his mother's death. Death stalked his life. "Sometimes my imagination follows those of my family who have passed behind the scenes; and I would almost rejoice to be permitted to make them a personal visit," he wrote his daughter Ruth, then seventeen, in 1847. "I have outlived nearly half of all my numerous family, and I ought to realize that in any event a large proportion of my journey is travelled over."[28]

His mother's death had made John at once more dependent on his father and more uncertain of his place in life. He looked to Owen to show him that place. He never rejected his father's moral authority or acted decisively to escape his influence. Owen was John's mentor. But despite their shared convictions, the two men were different in temperament. Unlike the squire, John was not a joiner when he could not lead, and he had little tolerance for views contrary to his own. Whenever he saw principle at issue, John acted swiftly to affirm it. By contrast, Owen recognized "our duty to others that we see rong in prinsiples and practice"; yet after reviewing the lives of "old Saints" in the Bible, he concluded that patience and faith might yet bring a "reformation both in Church and State." Owen fulfilled his sense of duty by working for reform; John pursued more insistent initiatives of his own.

Despite differences in disposition, John shared Owen's theology and sense of religious purpose. On many questions his views and Owen's were indistinguishable. He taught his own sons the values Owen had taught him, and, like his father, habitually warned them against worldliness. "We get along in our business as well as we ever have done, I think," he reported to John, Jr., in

1845. The family's "worldly prospects are as good as we can bear. I hope entire leanness of soul may not attend any little success in business."[29] John also admonished his children to revere their "aged grandfather." When his oldest sons abandoned the family's creed for spiritualism or skepticism, John began an enduring campaign to reclaim them for the faith of "our fathers." As Owen routinely peppered his letters with religious entreaties and admonitions, so did John. Both men evangelized out of habit. When John's son Jason lost a child to cholera, John wrote Owen of his hope that "the affliction of Jason & Wife will not be wholly lost on them."[30] God's lessons were hard indeed.

Yet for all his serious-mindedness, John never quite satisfied Owen that he was sufficiently concerned with spiritual ends. It was Owen's lifelong habit to admonish his "progeny" against moral delinquency. Over the years, Owen's letters to John, as we have seen in Chapter 3, were leavened with well-intended but biting warnings.[31] Although Owen and John remained close, John's deference to his father and Owen's watchful reserve toward his son fostered in John a pattern of implicit boasting coupled with affirmations of piety and faith. When John, at age fifty-four, left the Adirondacks for Kansas, collecting arms enroute, he stopped in Hudson to secure Owen's blessings for his mission. His self-esteem still rose and fell according to the old squire's appraisals of him.

That emotional dependency persisted until Owen's death in 1856. John's sons recognized his eagerness for his father's admiration, and in their own ways sustained it. Despite his own prominence as vice-president of the Topeka convention and then as a free-state legislator, John, Jr., dutifully reported his father's doings and movements to Squire Owen. "Father ever since he came on has devoted his whole time and means" to rescuing the family from the "destitution" threatened by the spread among them of "chill fever and ague." "Father has undergone extreme hardships and especially deserves from us an expression of warmest gratitude," John, Jr., added. "As an earnest and efficient supporter of the good cause here he has gained a wide reputation."[32] Not to be outdone in singing "father's" praises, John, Jr.'s wife, Wealthy, added admiringly, "Father seems to be as rugged as I ever saw him."[33]

Owen's spiritual sway over John was not absolute. John's ten-year partnership with Simon Perkins gave John a powerful ally and mentor,[34] as well as the kind of recognition he prized and a friendship that grew over the years. John and his family had been "poor bankrupts" when Perkins picked him to raise sheep and then to open their commission house in Springfield, Massachusetts, to sell wool. John considered the opportunity "no mean alliance for our family," and was humbled by Perkins's help. Discovering that his sons had played a prank on one of Perkins's hired girls, Brown was so chagrined that he bought his wife a new dress to wear to deliver an apology for the prank to Mrs. Perkins in the Big House on "the Hill."[35]

The prospect of losing Perkins's respect was more to be feared than losing his investment in the firm. Faced in April 1850 with heavy losses due in part to Brown's mismanagement of sales, Perkins nonetheless gave an anxious Brown only "words of comfort & encouragement" and his "fullest assurance of his undiminished confidence, & personal regard." Such assurances, Brown reported to John, Jr., "I had not dared to expect."³⁶ The following December John confided again that Perkins is "a most noble-spirited man, to whom I feel most deeply indebted; and no amount of money would atone to my feelings for the loss of confidence and cordiality on his part."³⁷ After the dissolution of their partnership and years of litigation with their creditors, Perkins entrusted Brown with the task of again raising sheep for him. It was Brown who chose to end the collaboration. In the spring of 1854, he and Perkins reached what Brown considered a "perfectly comfortable" division of their joint property. In Brown's estimation, Perkins was "every inch a gentleman" even though no opponent of slavery. The two ended their partnership with Brown's pride intact.³⁸

IV

The collaboration with Perkins permitted John Brown to achieve a measure of autonomy from his father. It broadened John's understanding of business and gave him a chance to meet antislavery reformers in the East. But the ultimate failure of the collaboration not only compromised that measure of autonomy but left Brown, at age fifty-four, uncertain of what to do with his life. He saw two choices. He might join his sons, who, facing drought and hard times in Ohio, had decided to start over in Kansas. Or he might return to Essex County in the Adirondacks, where he had lived briefly before returning to Akron in 1851. When his association with Perkins ended, the latter had been his plan. But the opening of Kansas created new circumstances. In August 1854 he wrote to John, Jr., "If you or any of my family are disposed to go to Kansas or Nebraska, with a view to help defeat *Satan* and his legions in that direction, I have not a word to say; *but I feel committed to operate in another part of the field*. If I were not so committed, I would be on my way this fall."³⁹

A month later, John clarified his position to daughter Ruth, who had married Henry Thompson, an Essex County neighbor. His sons in Ohio were "pressing" him to go with them to Kansas on grounds that to do so would be "more likely to benefit the colored people on the whole." John had "consented to ask" Ruth and Henry their "advice and feeling in the matter," but he also wanted to know what blacks in the neighboring settlement of "Timbucto" wanted him to do, for he had "volunteered in their service." Brown also consulted prominent abolitionists he counted as friends, including Gerrit Smith and Frederick Douglass, before deciding the matter.⁴⁰

In the end he deferred to the wishes of his wife Mary, who still had the care of three of their children and desperately wanted to settle in a permanent home. She had recently been ill and saw in Essex a refuge where she could have Ruth and others to help her and provide "society." Brown therefore decided to return to North Elba, where he could work for the cause by teaching fugitive slaves to farm on properties donated by Gerrit Smith while working his own land. Brown eventually secured title to three farms at North Elba, though he never paid fully for them or settled all of his debts in Ohio. In November 1854 Ruth wrote Mary that she "rejoiced to hear" that her father had "given up the idea of going to Kansas, but will move here this winter... as soon as he can go home and get all things ready."[41] Brown was still working three rented farms near Akron that winter to pay for the move to North Elba, and it was not until June 1855 that he was able to sell his prize Devon cattle in preparation for the move. By then his older sons had established land claims in Kansas near the free-state settlement of Osawatomie.

It is important to note that in the summer of 1854 Brown was still undecided about going to Kansas, though not about his commitment to antislavery. Some scholars have lost sight of the distinction between these things and have consequently discounted Brown's decision to return to Essex County. Eager to debunk the "legend" of John Brown, James C. Malin argued that Brown went to Kansas hoping to make a killing in business.[42] On the other hand, Oswald Garrison Villard, whose detailed biography was long the standard, concluded that Brown's "only purpose" in going to Kansas was "to test himself as a guerrilla-leader."[43]

These conclusions are erroneous. The first discounts much contrary evidence and ignores Brown's sense of himself as a religious man dedicated to a life of sacrifice. It is true that in February 1855, as Brown was struggling to raise money for the overland move to North Elba, he briefly considered a project "to direct the opperations of a Surveying, & exploring party, to be employed in Kansas for a considerable time perhaps for some Two or Three years."[44] But nothing came of that plan, and Brown never staked a claim or determined to stay in the territory himself after he reached Brown's Station. The contention that Brown went to stir "troubled waters" mistakenly credits later claims that he had planned since 1839 to attack slavery by force of arms.[45] As late as September 1854, as I shall argue in Chapter 9, Brown had no "great plan" and no very clear idea how he might advance the cause. Nor did Brown become a guerrilla leader until after the "sack" of Lawrence, when Pottawatomie unleashed the dogs of war.

The prospect of laboring in so remote a theater as North Elba while Kansas became the focus of national attention might soon have proved unsatisfying. But as Brown worked to have his worldly possessions hauled to the Adirondacks, he remained ambivalent. Frustrated at being "money-bound" while trying to sell his livestock to pay for the move, he became increasingly bitter at the machinations of the Slave Power. "Should God send famin, pestilence, & war; uppon this guilty hypocritical nation to destroy it; we need not be surprised," he wrote Ruth and Henry in January 1855. "Never before did a people so mock, & despise him. There seems to be no sign of repentance amongst us."[46] The words echoed those of Owen's jeremiads, but they bespoke as well John's accelerating tendency to see himself engaged in a struggle larger than the well-being of his family. Despite his rising anger at the Slave Power, he went to Kansas himself only after he became convinced that his sons there were in peril.

v

The Browns' migration to Kansas began under Owen's aegis. The first party took its leave from Ohio in a ceremonial visit to Hudson, where the frail patriarch sent the migrants off to the wilderness with his blessing. The "pioneers" thought of themselves as Squire Owen's descendants and thus carriers of the Brown "connection" from the Western Reserve. They saw their overland journey as reenacting Owen's trek from Connecticut to the Ohio frontier half a century earlier. Although most of John's siblings and his own children had long since moved from Hudson, for the migrants "Grandfather Owen" once more became a central figure in their lives.

The first of the Ohio clan to move to Kansas – and the only one who remained after the Border War – was Owen's son-in-law, Samuel Lyle Adair. Though he had begun studying for the ministry at Western Reserve College in 1834, Adair finished his degree at Oberlin, where he met and later married Owen's daughter Florella.[47] For more than a decade thereafter, Adair held Congregational pastorates in Ohio towns around Hudson so Florella could be close to her family. But early in 1854 he felt a call to go to the territory. In May the American Missionary Association agreed to support his mission, and Adair with his reluctant wife and children went to Kansas. After several months spent "cooped up" with sickness in Kansas City, Adair explored the territory and decided to settle in Osawatomie, fifty miles southwest of Kansas City. His cabin on the edge of the town became the end of the trail for the Browns who came later, and a frequent meeting place for John Brown and his sons.

A free-state settlement founded with assistance from the New England Emigrant Aid Society, Osawatomie was congenial to Adair's beliefs as well as his antislavery politics. In April 1856, he organized the First Congregational Church of Osawatomie with one male and six female members who boldly committed themselves to raising the "character of the entire pastoral district." Five weeks later the Pottawatomie tragedy made Osawatomie, a town Missourians thought of as John Brown's headquarters, the target of proslavery reprisals. On August 30 Adair hid in the brush as an army of Missourians, claiming authority under a proclamation of the proslavery territorial governor, burned Osawatomie to the ground. Following a desperate but unsuccessful fight to save the town, Brown gained the sobriquet "Old Osawatomie."

Like the Adairs, the five sons of John Brown who went to Kansas met hardship and illness en route. Three of them – Owen, Frederick, and Salmon – left for Kansas in October 1854, taking eleven head of cattle and three horses, their joint property, by boat across "the lakes" to Chicago. They then drove the stock across Illinois to the banks of the Missouri near the home of an aunt, where they wintered. By late April they had reached Kansas. The others – John, Jr., and Jason, Brown's oldest sons, and their wives and children – took passage on a steamer down the Ohio to St. Louis, then up the Missouri to Kansas. They brought crates of fruit tree saplings and grape vines, a plow, a few farm implements, and their

FIGURE 4.2. The Osawatomie cabin of Rev. Samuel Adair, Brown's brother-in-law, built with the Browns' help.

CREDIT: West Virginia State Archives, Boyd B. Stutler Collection.

father's old surveying equipment. When Jason's four-year-old son, Austin, died of cholera en route, his parents buried him at Waverly while the boat's rudder was repaired. Although the Browns had paid full fare, the captain, perhaps fearful of spreading the cholera, cast off while they were still ashore, leaving them to make their way to Kansas City by stage. Along the way hostile Missourians refused to sell them food. They reached Osawatomie on May 7.

The five Brown men promptly established claims to land with timber and water eight miles from Osawatomie. They were "sanguine" that they had found a healthful climate and fertile land; but their letters to John and Owen included ominous reports of proslavery hostility. John, Jr., was "fully convinced" that proslavery men in western Missouri and eastern Kansas had organized "'Annoyance Associations' whose object is to make Free-State folks all the trouble they can ... driving off their stock, injuring their crops, and in every mean way do[ing] all they can to impede their prosperity."[48] The Browns had come to Kansas armed only with two "squirrel rifles" and a revolver among them. But two weeks after arriving they concluded they needed more arms. "The interest of despotism" – the Slave Power – had organized thousands of the "meanest and most desperate of men, armed to the teeth with Revolvers,

Bowie Knives, Rifles & Cannon," John, Jr., declared. "Every Slaveholding State from Virginia to Texas is furnishing men and money to fasten Slavery upon this glorious land, by means no matter how foul." Free-state men, on the other hand, were unorganized and unarmed, and showed only a "most abject and cowardly spirit" in the face of the "foreign Scoundrels." The Missourians boasted that they would control the upcoming Kansas elections without firing a shot.[49]

Brown's sons proposed to organize free-soilers into military companies. Citing a memorial to Congress recently adopted at Osawatomie, John, Jr., told his father that the issue was no longer a question of the slavery of blacks but of "the enslavement of ourselves." He then listed weapons he asked his father to obtain, promising to repay the contributors as soon as Kansas was safely free. Since his father was then presumably already on the way to North Elba, he sent the appeal to Ruth and Henry Thompson to forward to John. The sons thought John might bring the weapons himself, but John, Jr., included instructions for addressing them to Osawatomie in case "father *sends* the arms."[50] If Brown had intended to go to Kansas all along, as Sanborn alleged, clearly he had not told his sons when they might expect him to arrive.[51]

Living in tents and a wagon until they ploughed and planted their land, Brown's sons were nonetheless prepared to fight. "Here are 5 men of us who are not only anxious to fully prepare, but are thoroughly determined to fight. We can see no other way to meet the case," Salmon wrote his father. "The boys have their feelings well worked up, so that I think that they will fight. There is a great lack of arms here in Brownsville. I feel more like [a] fight now, than I ever did before."[52] Five weeks later, John, Jr., represented the "Brownsville" district at a free-state convention at Lawrence, where he introduced successful resolutions authorizing the organization and arming of militia companies in sympathetic precincts. The convention also repudiated the Shawnee legislature and its laws. "The storm every day thickens," John, Jr., wrote his father. "I am convinced now more than ever that...the great struggle in arms of Freedom and Despotism" will begin in Kansas.[53]

VI

His sons' appeal for arms reached John Brown in early June 1855, an especially vulnerable moment. With no fulfilling occupation and a compelling need to do significant work to demonstrate his piety, he read John, Jr.'s letter as a call. He decided at once to go to Kansas, arm his sons, and help save the territory from "despotism." The prospect immediately captured his imagination. "I think could I hope in any other way to answer the end of my being," he wrote to his unhappy wife later from Iowa, "I would be quite content to be at North Elba."[54]

The suggestion of some scholars that Brown saw Kansas as a means of launching a general war against slavery – that Kansas was a calculated prelude to Harpers Ferry – owes too much to hindsight.[55] Brown went not so much to make war as to defend his sons and help them make new homes. As August Wattles, a close Kansas friend with whom Brown often stayed, later told a congressional committee, Brown came to "assist his sons in their settlement and to defend them, if necessary, in a peaceable exercise of their political rights." But Brown also felt a "deep solicitude" for his wife, Wattles continued, and expected in due time to return to North Elba.[56] Brown knew his sons needed his skills to build their cabins and fence their fields. Even as he read John, Jr.'s letters to a conference of Radical Abolitionists at Syracuse on June 28 and gathered weapons in New York, Massachusetts, and Ohio, he had still not ruled out the possibility of staking a claim himself and bringing Mary to Kansas. "Father and I are thinking of taking each of us a claim & make some improvement on them this winter," Brown's son-in-law, Henry Thompson, wrote to his wife Ruth two weeks after he and Brown arrived at Brown's Station. Henry had accompanied Brown to Kansas in part because he was a carpenter. "We intend first to help the boys get up some houses to live in .... I should have thought they might have got up one house among them all."[57] But the possibility that John himself might settle in Kansas was an afterthought. Brown went to Kansas not to make a killing in "business" or to start a war, but to help his sons.

VII

As Brown threw himself into the task of finding arms for his sons, his spirits lifted. By late summer he was back in Hudson, where he made his father's home a base of operations for his efforts. On August 8, at Edward's place in Munroe Falls, Owen noticed John's zeal. "He has something of a warlike spirit," Owen wrote the Adairs. "I think as much as necessary for defence. I will hope nothing more." Owen himself believed that Kansas might soon be ablaze. "I have thought for some time that Kenses would be the next seat of war," he lamented, "but did not think of it falling so heavy as I fear it will on my Famely."[58] But Owen had no notion that John was going to Kansas to ignite a war or to stay until Kansas was free. He thought of John's journey as a rescue mission. Less than a month after John arrived at Osawatomie, Owen wrote asking "when you will be on your way back."[59]

Even while John was still driving his wagon through Missouri, Owen was offering advice and support to his "children" in Kansas. In long, closely written letters, he assured them, "All my dear children in your parts have a shair in my affections." He urged them to seek counsel in the "law and testimonyes of God" and to make the Bible their "guide to live or die by." They might keep moral order, he urged once more, by regular family prayer and by observing the Sabbath.[60]

He warned especially against divisiveness. A "large circut of kindred Friends," he cautioned, "must necessarely be dependant on each other." To avoid any "falling out," he urged them to "plant no seeds of bitter frute," which, he insisted, usually "take there deep root in the W I L L s (wills)."[61]

They should also guard against jealousy and bearing tales. Indeed, his letters were sermons aimed at the religious heterodoxy of John's sons. "Now hear the conclusion of the whole matter," he wrote at the end of one meditation. "Fear God and keep his commandments." Referring to John's sons, he admonished in closing another letter to John, "I want to hear that they all believe in the Lord Jesus Christ as ther only hope."[62] "In your letters you will embrace all my descendants in Kansas as one family," he advised in another letter, as if "they might all belong to one household of faith."[63]

Owen urged his kin to "submit" to duty, "beleaving that god will do wright." He expected them to stand up against slavery and for the moral government of God. "Begin right," he admonished the pioneers. "If you have any public spirit don't suppress it: make good provision for all civil and religious privileges, schools and meetings; if you take the lead in this, you will keep it a great number of years." Owen avidly read the Kansas newspapers they sent him and he bought subscriptions to antislavery papers for them. He saw them as committed to a cause from which there could be no backing down. "I have always favored defensive measures, but guarding against offiensive, as the one sometimes runs into the other," he cautioned.[64] Late in life grandson Salmon thought he remembered that Owen had seen John's sons off to Kansas with the admonition never to show the "white feather in the coming conflict." The recollection is much colored by later events, and Owen probably did not anticipate war at so early a date. But the idea that he issued such a warning is consistent with Owen's sense of manhood and family tradition. Evangelicals were ready to battle for the Lord.[65]

As winter approached, Owen became the eastern lifeline of the Browns in Kansas. He had sent $40 with John to be divided between the Adairs and John's destitute son, Jason. But John had spent the money on the road, in part to buy Jason a stove. Unaware that his family at North Elba had appealed to Owen for help, John himself now reluctantly did so. He expected to replace the $40 by selling his horse, but he had arrived to find "so much sickness among the men folks of the company that I have been obliged to give my whole strength to providing some way of keeping the families from present: & future suffering." Hence he had not been able to "look about for a market for [my] Horse or any thing else." Seeing no end to his labors and protesting that all of the families "really need some comforts," John "concluded to ask you in some way to help me to Fifty Dollars ... if you can without too much inconvenience to yourself.... I will replace it as soon as I can."[66] Owen sent the money.

It must have been difficult for John Brown to write such a letter. He knew that any money he was unable to repay his father would be charged against his share of Owen's estate. But Owen was cash poor, and he would have to find the money for John among his sons in Ohio or sell a piece of property. Moreover, he was still weak from a recent illness, and too much exertion would not be good for him. Compromised in any case by having to ask his father for help, John was careful to frame his request as part of his effort to save the others and to note that the money was for them. Their desperate situation was owing to no failing of his.

John did not learn until later that that very week his father had sold property in Monroe at a considerable loss to raise money for John's family in North Elba. "I am very glad your family had confidence enough in me to make known their wants, and more, that the means were so soon provided," Owen wrote him on November 16.[67] John was distressed to hear that Mary had asked their son Watson, who was managing the farm, to ask Owen for money. John knew the appeal would remind his father of the bitter times when John himself had suffered bankruptcy. John thought Watson's request implied that he, John, had not provided for his wife for the winter. Before he had left North Elba, he had spent a month trying to get his fields in order and readying for the winter the still unplastered house Henry had built for him. He left feeling ill-at-ease about not finishing those tasks. A week after reaching Osawatomie he wrote Mary to express his concerns. "I notice in your letter to Salmon your trouble about the means of having the house made more comfortable for winter," he said. Funds owed him from the sale of cattle in Connecticut should have come, he reminded her, adding that he would find other means if they did not reach her. He urged Mary to be "cheerful" and "always 'hope in God,' who will not leave nor forsake them that trust in him.... You are all very dear to me," he concluded, "and I humbly trust we may be kept and spared to meet again on earth."[68] He was not ready to return.

FIGURE 4.3. The Adirondack farmhouse at North Elba where Brown's wife and younger children remained when he went to Kansas. Brown's gravesite is in the foreground.

CREDIT: West Virginia State Archives, Boyd B. Stutler Collection.

On the day that he wrote Owen for money, John again counseled Mary to have patience. "I do not send you this account to render you more unhappy but merely to let you know that those here are not altogether in Paradise, while you stay in that miserable Frosty region." He emphasized his "anxiety about your being made in some measure comfortable for the winter," but he had no money to send.[69] It was not until Spring that he was able send a draft to pay Mary's debts, and he took the occasion to criticize her for writing his father for help. Her response was in turn reproachful. "You blamed me for not writing to you our situation," she wrote on May 20. "[W]e was expecting something from Conn every week by what you was a writing untill we got on our last loaf & I did not know what to do. When Watson wrote to your father for help he expected to get some to pay him before this time from Conn. What is to be done about it. [W]e had 35 dollars. [N]o more now."[70]

For all John's good intentions, Mary felt deserted. Filled with "anxious forebodings,"[71] she "despaired" of her two youngest sons "ever returning home."[72] With his half-brothers, eighteen-year-old Salmon had staked a claim at "Brownsville," and sixteen-year-old Oliver, who had joined John en route to Kansas, was not altogether reassuring about coming home. "Unless father concludes to move here," he wrote Mary, "I shall return provided I shall live through the times as I have no inclination to shrink from the duty of serving out my time."[73] As John Brown and Henry Thompson threw up cabins to protect the ailing men and their families against what proved to be the severest winter in Kansas history, John's concern about Mary added to his eagerness to finish his mission in Kansas as quickly as possible. As Adair wrote to Owen, John seemed "anxious to have the crisis come so that if he lives through it he may soon return to his family again."[74]

VIII

Other pressures also encouraged prompt action. During the merciless winter of 1855–6, John's apprehensions grew that Owen's life was slipping away. Owen had long expected the end. For decades he had been ordering his affairs, having produced over the years three wills, and two reminiscences of his life.[75] In the second of these narratives, probably written in 1850, Owen evidenced his growing preoccupation with death by speculating whether each of his deceased wives and children had been a true "Christian" and might thus be enjoying eternal salvation.[76] As he saw death approaching, his "sins" were "ever before" him, he wrote, and he felt "great guilt" that his life had not always been exemplary.[77]

Facing eternity, he looked not only back upon his journey, but ahead with increasing concern to the fate of his "posterity," expressing "great anxiety for [his] Children even to the fourth generation." "I can follow my numerous famely, through most of there various changes in life," he wrote the Kansas Browns. "I think I know there dispositions and their moral caractor."[78] As John's half-brother, Jeremiah, later reported, Owen's family was his principal concern in his final days.[79] Through the winter he visited his sons in and about Hudson, and he and his third wife Lucy, moved in with in-laws to ease the burden he caused her. But he never lost interest in the news from Kansas and followed events there through an assortment of newspapers.

In September, not long after John's departure for Kansas, Owen suffered a "severe fitt of sickness," aggravated, he thought, by taking too much "fisick," – he could not remember having taken medicine in fifty years. His sons in Hudson feared he would "shortly die." This illness was the first of a series of warnings. Plagued by what his doctor diagnosed as heart disease, he experienced prolonged episodes of lung congestion. The end seemed near. Writing in February to a twelve-year-old grandson in Kansas, Owen expressed pleasure at receiving the boy's letter and promised to "lay it away with care." The grandson might "do the saim with mine," he added, "as it may be my last."[80] In March, as his spirit sank, he wrote John that he felt "as though death was at the door"[81] and the following month Jeremiah reported that Owen "could not lay down…and did not sleep in any position but a few moments at a time." A circle of friends prayed for his soul during the last days as terror gripped him. "I am sorry to say," Jeremiah related, "that his mind was gloomy and the prospect of death was dreadfull to him.… [He] did not seem ready to leave the world."[82]

John's mood darkened as his father's hold on life ebbed. His letters became increasingly solicitous. After reaching Kansas in October, he excused his failure to write promptly by saying he could find no place sheltered from the "cold chilling Winds." "We hear that you have been very sick; & not expected to live but that you had got about a little," John wrote Owen. "We shall all be looking anxiously to hear from you again."[83] Two days later John wrote thanking Owen for a long letter of advice. "We bless God that your life has been prolonged; & that your health is in any measure restored," he penned. "We really hope you may enjoy the few days at the close of your journey (as regards all things both spiritual & temporal) much more than any preceding ones."[84]

In these last letters, John repeatedly thanked Owen for his lifetime of help. "We are all fully sensible of your care for us & wish it was in our power to make a better return," he wrote on March 20, adding reassuringly, "I think there is a general disposition on the part of the connection here to help one another." John urged Owen not to "give yourself unreasonable trouble or anxiety on our account," and closed the letter by wishing that his father's life "may be continued to witness the triumph of that cause you have laboured to promote."[85] On May 8 John pledged "to write you often even when I have but little to write."[86] No more letters were necessary; Owen had already died.[87]

Word of Owen's passing had evidently not reached Brown's Station more than two weeks later, when John and his sons left to save Lawrence from the Missourians. For months the winter's "deep snows," drifting to six feet, had stopped the mail; then high waters delayed it, often up to three weeks.[88] Although service was more regular now, Adair had heard nothing of Owen's death on May 16 when he wrote his father-in-law a long, troubled letter about the "growing alarm" that nearby proslavery forces were creating among his neighbors.[89] The final leg of the mail's journey to the Browns in Kansas was a weekly stage that left Kansas City, fifty miles away, on Wednesday mornings in the direction of Osawatomie.[90] Word had finally reached Osawatomie by the 19th when Florella began a letter to a sister in Ohio, asking for details about their father's last days.[91] But word had not yet reached Brown's Station. It was customary for one of the men at Brown's Station to ride or hike the eight miles to Osawatomie on Saturdays "to carry & get Letters."[92] Thus neither Jeremiah's letter of the fourteenth[93] nor apparently Sally's earlier letter bearing what Adair called the "heavy tidings of a beloved father's death"[94] had arrived before Saturday, May 17, when someone presumably retrieved the mail for Brown's Station.

By the twenty-first a messenger bearing news of the Lawrence crisis had reached Brown's Station and, later that day or the next morning, the Brown women went – not to Osawatomie, as has long been supposed – but to the cabin of Orson Day, two miles distant, for protection. Thus, as John Brown trudged grimly toward Lawrence with the Pottawatomie Rifles on the night of the twenty-second, he probably knew only that his father might die before he could learn that free-state men in Kansas had taken up arms to defend themselves.

For John Brown, his father's final illness was an added incentive to act decisively, dramatically, for the cause. The Jeremiads that were Owen's last letters fueled John's determination. Owen's warnings heightened John's own fears about the course of events in the territory. The kingdom of Christ seemed farther away than ever as Missourians menaced Lawrence and proslavery barbarism triumphed over antislavery righteousness. At the same time, his awareness of Owen's imminent death kindled John's sense of impending loss. It raised the prospect of being cast adrift in a world of sorrows. It heightened John's awareness of his own mortality and his estrangement from God's grace. Were we not all "strangers and pilgrims on the earth"?[95] To demonstrate his dedication to the cause into which Owen had inducted him so long ago, to show his readiness to lay down his life as he had pledged at the Lovejoy meeting in Hudson, and to claim Owen's unqualified love and respect – he had to act boldly and soon.

IX

Owen's death was a public event in Hudson. "There was never so large a funeral procession," Jeremiah assured his Kansas relations, "and all seemed to feel they had lost a respected friend and neighbor." At Owen's funeral all of Hudson's ministers praised his piety. But in Kansas Owen's passing received no notice beyond the circle of the Browns themselves. The news was lost in the excitement over the attack on Lawrence and the Pottawatomie killings. Yet Owen's presence hovered over his children's thoughts as they endured the harsh winter of 1855–6. Awaiting news of his death as well as the return of the Missourians, Owen's Kansas progeny knew that his moral and financial support was ending. While Owen lived, there was always the possibility of returning to the "ancestral home" in Hudson. His death ended that prospect and hence an epoch in the family's history. So long as they sought Owen's approval and honored his wishes, the pioneers found it possible to suppress quarrels and monetary problems. Owen's passing removed that force for cohesion and sacrifice within the Kansas clan. The family now lacked a center, in part because Owen's heir apparent had become a fugitive guerrilla chief accused of multiple murders.

5

Steward

With the exposures, privations, hardships, & wants of pioneer life [the elder Brown] was familiar; & thought he could benefit his Children, & the new beginners from the older parts of the country.

John Brown[1]

Tormented as he often was by doubts about the state of his immortal soul, John Brown hoped "to answer the end of my being" in Kansas.[2] Anxiety about Owen's failing health and the welfare of Mary and the children in North Elba preyed upon him as winter scourged the plains and slowed his efforts to rescue his sons' families from privation. Events in the widening struggle over slavery in Kansas competed with these private concerns for his attention. Memories of a lifetime of "hard lessons" became lenses darkening his perceptions and fusing together his sense of the dangers to his family at Brown's Station and his apprehension over the "cause of freedom." The appeal for weapons that brought him to his sons and to Kansas would twice be echoed by free-state leaders' calls to arms. His hopes to serve the cause of his "fathers" intensified with each summons, and in the threatening cataclysm he found his higher call.

In the six months after John Brown's arrival in Kansas on October 7, 1855, the Brown connection continued to grow and make alliances and friendships with antislavery neighbors. Like a radio antenna, this widening circle of kin gathered rumors from the air and transmitted them by word-of-mouth to every household and neighborhood. The Browns' involvement in local affairs magnified the meaning of political signals from Lawrence, Topeka, and Leavenworth. Received over partisan frequencies, news reports from Kansas and Missouri raised cultural as well as political antennae, whetting sectional differences with the language of violence. Threats of war in the Missouri papers were especially resonant along the Pottawatomie, as vibrations of the national struggle over Kansas flashed across the ocean of grasslands to the scattered cabins at Osawatomie and Brown's Station.[3] John Brown's reading of these signals and his anxiety about his family's circumstances in Kansas served to remind him of lifelong convictions and his oft-deferred commitment to the cause of antislavery. It was a volatile mixture.

As all of the Browns searched these signals for meaning, isolated events increasingly seemed to pattern themselves. Distant proslavery "outrages" appeared to threaten free-staters everywhere. Efforts of the territorial government to protect slavery by statute and to punish dissent through the courts reinforced the Browns' Manichaean disposition to see evil and depravity in every adversary. The open alignment of the Pierce administration with the proslavery legislature confirmed their fears of a conspiracy of proslavery forces.[4] By spring the presence of hundreds of armed Southerners on Ottawa tribal land near Osawatomie emboldened proslavery settlers on Pottawatomie Creek to threaten to drive the abolitionists out. Fear and rumor fed each other. By the eve of the Missourians' attack on Lawrence in May, a siege mentality gripped the Brown connection. With a growing sense of apprehension, Brown himself witnessed the course of events as bound up with the ultimate meaning of his life.

I

When John Brown reached his sons' claims on October 7, not long after Oliver and Henry Thompson had arrived, he realized that winter was his immediate adversary. "We found all more or less sick, or feeble, but [John, Jr.'s wife] Wealthy.... Fever and ague and chill fevers seem to be very general." Living in tents and a makeshift shed, their crops unharvested, their cattle and oxen wandering across unfenced prairie, Brown's sons were a desperate crew. Brown found them "shivering over their little fires all exposed to the dreadfully cutting winds morning and evening and stormy days." Other dangers besieged them too. Wolves stalked their livestock. Fires rode the fierce winds. "We were all out a good part of the night last helping to keep the prairies fires [sic] from destroying everything," John wrote to his wife in mid-October.[5] Three weeks later John could tell Owen, "We have just got a Shanty 12 by 16 Feet fixed for Jason that will protect his company from cold & storms." But Oliver and Henry had fallen ill with what the younger Browns were calling "malarial fever." The construction of permanent cabins thus had to be delayed. "I never witnessed in Ohio such severe storms so early in the season nor harder freezing," John reported.[6]

But winter had just begun. The men's feet and noses froze as did the cows' teats. Ice was ten inches thick on the Osage River and the temperature reached 28 below. During weeks of "hard freezing" the snow kept blowing into drifts, as Brown crossed into Missouri to buy provisions at better prices.

Despite the paralyzing cold and persisting sickness, John, Jr., and his family had a comfortable cabin by mid-March, at which John, Sr., and Oliver stayed. With Henry's aid, John and his healthy sons helped Jason build a shelter, and in the spring John and Henry put up a new house for Samuel Adair, who feared his first cabin was not on his still unsurveyed claim. The Browns also raised another cabin, for John's brother-in-law, Orson Day, who arrived with his wife and son in April.

Although the clan survived the winter, the continued sickness served to remind everyone of the fragility of life, and, John, at least, of their dependence on God. While traveling up the Missouri River on his way to Kansas, John had disinterred the body of Jason's four-year-old son, Austin, and brought it for reburial at the settlement. The death of his son and the hardships of the winter caused Jason, who rejected John's austere creed, to affirm that if he and his wife did not believe that "God rules in mercy, we could not bear up under this dreadfull stroke."[7] But by this time, in June, Jason was "taking hold." He and the other boys were back on their feet. John's mood was buoyant as the work at the settlement progressed, and his sons and their wives sang his praises in letters to Owen.[8]

Within days after reaching Brown's Station, John had been drawn into political conflict. On October 9, the Brown men, heavily armed, hiked to Osawatomie to vote for delegates to the free-state constitutional convention. The news next day was good. No "enemy" had appeared at the polls, and the election elsewhere in the territory had proceeded without disruption. Better yet, John, Jr., was elected to represent the Pottawatomie district at the Topeka convention. His father was optimistic. "I believe Missouri is fast becoming discouraged about making Kansas a slave state," John wrote to North Elba, "and think the prospect of its becoming free is brightening every day."[9]

This optimism persisted in the face of evidence that the proslavery faction had by no means given up on Kansas. On November 14, two days after the Topeka convention adjourned, proslavery delegates met in Leavenworth to found the Law and Order or States Rights Party. In an act of open partisanship, the newly arrived territorial governor, Wilson Shannon, a former governor of Ohio, attended the Leavenworth convention as a delegate from Douglas County and accepted the chair. In a speech to delegates, he affirmed the legality of the Shawnee legislature and branded the Topeka movement illegal and revolutionary.[10] Shannon's proslavery stance fueled belief among the Browns and others that the Slave Power would use federal authority to win Kansas.

Two weeks later, a shooting triggered the "Wakarusa War" – misnamed since no actual fighting occurred. This crisis brought armed free-state men to Lawrence from great distances to muster into an improvised Northern Army. There, they faced a proslavery militia of perhaps 1,200 men, nearly all of them Missourians, led by Samuel J. Jones, the postmaster of Westport, Missouri, who was also sheriff of Douglas County, Kansas. In the Wakarusa War, John Brown first drew public attention as a militant in the free-state cause.

The crisis grew out of a private quarrel. A settler from Virginia had shot and killed Charles Dow, a young free-state man from Ohio, in a dispute over a land claim. When the Virginian was not arrested, Dow's free-soil neighbors organized a posse to apprehend him. Sheriff Jones thereupon arrested Jacob Branson, the free-state man with whom Dow had been living, on charges of breaching the peace. On a road outside town that night a party of free-state men led by Samuel N. Wood of Lawrence intercepted Jones's posse, denied

Jones's claim to authority in Kansas, and took Branson from Jones at gun-point. The triumphant return of the rescue party to Lawrence raised fears that Jones would use Wood's intervention as an excuse to attack the town. Denying responsibility for Branson's rescue, leading residents of Lawrence formed a Committee of Safety and prepared to defend the free-state stronghold.

Meanwhile Jones sent back to Missouri for help, and after free-staters burned the cabins of Dow's absent killer and two of his proslavery neighbors, Jones told Shannon that "open rebellion" had begun. Without investigating Jones's tale, Shannon dispatched units of the Kansas militia to help the beleaguered sheriff. To Shannon's dismay the force that soon rendezvoused, just south of Lawrence on the Wakarusa River, consisted largely of Missourians spoiling for a chance to destroy the "abolitionist" town. Once he grasped the danger, however, Shannon pleaded with U.S. army officers at Fort Leavenworth to intercede. They refused, protesting that they had no authority in local affairs. Fearing the repercussions that an attack on the free-state town might have on the national Democratic Party and on his own reputation, Shannon negotiated a "treaty" with Dr. Charles Robinson, agent of the New England Emigrant Aid Society, and the firebrand, James T. Lane, a recent convert to antislavery. The settlement averted violence.

The call for free-state men to rescue Lawrence reached the Browns on December 6 and produced a flurry of hasty preparations. Armed with rifles, revolvers, and swords, and with additional weapons stacked in a lumber wagon, the five Browns who were well enough to hike the nearly forty miles to Lawrence made an overnight march, in the course of which they passed through a line of armed Missourians and reached the town late the next morning. There they found five hundred men, many armed with Sharps rifles or "Beecher's Bibles," building earthworks and drilling in the streets. The negotiations with Shannon had already begun. But G. W. Brown, editor of the *Herald of Freedom*, intro-duced himself to the new arrivals and took them into the Free State Hotel to meet Robinson and Lane. Robinson commissioned John Brown – the "aged gentleman" who seemed to be in command of the new group – a captain in the First Brigade of Kansas Volunteers and formed a company of Brown's sons and fifteen others, several of them from Pottawatomie.

Although the Liberty Guards were disbanded December 12 after five days of actual service and no action, Brown was jubilant when the crisis ended. Several years later G. W. Brown launched a campaign to destroy John Brown's reputation and overturn his "canonization" by claiming that from the very "hour" Brown received his commission, he began making trouble, and when his "wild schemes" won no support, he *"retired in disgust."* Much later, in 1879, G. W. Brown further charged that even after Shannon and Robinson completed their "peace treaty," John Brown "harangued" the crowd and appealed for volunteers to follow him in an attack on the Missourians, declaring that "'without the shedding of blood there is no remission.'" Editor Brown also claimed that he had informed the Committee of Public Safety that Brown was "trying to excite insubordination," and that the committee dispatched Col. G. W. Smith to "arrest" him.[11]

Another version of the story of Brown's alleged opposition to the Wakarusa settlement is illustrative of memory distortion created by what memory experts call interference. Simply put, witnesses' memories of events may be altered by hearing different versions of the same events later. Over time, mistaken memories may supplant original impressions.[12] As historian James C. Malin recognized long ago, reminiscent accounts of much that happened in Kansas are replete with errors and distortions.[13] The "crop" of stories about the Wakarusa War underscores his point. Fifty-seven years after the confrontation between Shannon and Robinson, in 1913, Brown's son Salmon, who spun a good many yarns about his youthful militance in Kansas, first recounted his own experience during the crisis. Embellishing G. W. Brown's tale of John Brown's supposed opposition to the peace settlement, Salmon dictated a long letter to a supporter giving a lurid account of his father's impetuous behavior during the peace negotiations. As in most of Salmon's reminiscences, he gave himself a prominent role. "My brother [John] placed me at the door to watch my father for fear that he would shoot Sheriff Jones if he came in," Salmon claimed. "My father, who wanted to make a night attack on the ruffians...was so put out by the ruffians that when Shannon finished his speech he got upon the same planks and said, 'We here have been betrayed by this compromise.' Robinson caught hold of him and pulled him down off the planks."[14]

So runs Salmon's account. But no contemporary evidence supports any version of the story or offers any hint that John Brown opposed the treaty. Only days after returning to Brown's Station, in fact, Brown boasted that the free-state leaders had exploited Shannon's "Cowardice, & Folly; & by means of that & the free use of Whiskey; & some Trickery; succeeded in getting a written arangement with him much to their own liking."[15] On December 14 he wrote a brother-in-law, Orson Day, who hoped to migrate from New York to Kansas, that the territory was now "entirely in the power of the Free-State men...and I believe the Missourians will give up all further hope of making Kansas a slave state." As late as February, Brown assured Day that the Missourians would not interfere with his family on their journey. "I think the Free State people who go quietly along their way will not now meet with any difficulty. I have been a number of times of late into the State," he added, "& though *I always* (when asked) frankly avow myself a Free State man; have met with no trouble."[16]

In fact, Brown was elated at what seemed a free-state victory. Shannon had given up "all pretension of further attemp[ts] to enforce the enactments of the Bogus Legislature," he wrote Mary and Watson, "& retired subject to the derision & scoffs of the Free-State men...and to the pity of some; & curses of others of the invading force." The "last Kansas invasion" had thus ended with the Missourians "suffering great exposure, hardships, & privations, not having fought any Battles, Burned or destroyed any infant towns or Abolition Presses; leaving the Free-State men *organized & armed* , & in *full possession* of the Territory.... Free-State men have only hereafter to retain the footing they have gained; *and Kansas is free*," he exulted. Brown also boasted of the determination of his sons, each of them armed with a rifle and three "large revolvers," as they passed without incident over a bridge guarded by a larger force of Missourians. Throughout the siege, Brown related, "I did not see the least sign of cowardice or want of self-possession" in any of the hundreds of free-state volunteers. He added, "I never expect again to see an equal number of such well-behaved, cool, determined men; fully as I believe sustaining the high character of the Revolutionary Fathers."[17] Only the day before, he continued, the "people passed uppon [sic] the Free-State constitution." Freedom in Kansas was assured.

To be sure, this enthusiasm later faded. But Shannon had indeed made concessions. He agreed that the residents of Lawrence had broken no laws, denied he had summoned the Missourians, and pledged to disband the drunken, disorganized force on the Wakarusa and order the men out of the territory. (A sudden blizzard may have been more responsible than the governor for their compliance with the latter order.) Implicitly, Shannon had also acknowledged free-state volunteers as legitimate Kansas militiamen. Of course Lane and Robinson made concessions too. They denied responsibility for the rescue of Branson, assured Shannon they knew of no secret organizations pledged to resist territorial laws, and pledged to assist in the execution of the law whenever the "proper authority" called upon them to do so. To make it clear that they had not endorsed the "bogus laws" of the Shawnee legislature, however, Robinson and Lane added a disclaimer to the treaty: "We wish it understood," they wrote, "that we do not herein express any opinion as to the validity of the enactments of the Territorial Legislature."[18]

Months later John Brown repudiated the Wakarusa settlement. But it is worth noting that he believed the free-staters had won the Wakarusa War. He was proud that "the disposition of both our camps [at Brown's Station and Osawatomie] *to turn out* was uniform."[19] For all his martial ardor, he had been satisfied that the demonstration of manhood and character had assured the triumph of the Godly. If during the negotiations he called for an attack on the Missourians, as some later alleged, clearly he did not feel for some time after the Wakarusa War that fighting or bloodshed was required in order to stand up for the Lord. Conviction was what counted. His own and his family's show of determination was itself a victory.

Indeed, Brown seems to have been genuinely moved by the sight of the one casualty of the Wakarusa War. Because of Brown's role in the bitter fighting that broke out the following May, scholars have too easily forgotten that Brown himself was not inured to the sight of death. Until the moment that he went to "war," he had never witnessed a shooting or seen the corpse of anyone who died of anything but natural causes. In his letter home, John reported the one slaying even before he discussed the treaty or described his sons' performance in the "war." A small party of "invaders" had killed a "wholly unarmed" free-state man from Ohio, Thomas Barber. Barber's body lay for days in a room in which a part of Brown's company was quartered, and many of the men had "witnessed the scene of bringing in the Wife & other friends of the murdered man." The sight, in Brown's words, was "Heart-rending; & calculated to exasperate the men exceedingly; & one of the sure results of Civil War."[20] Brown had been angered when he learned earlier of the death of Dow; the sight of Barber's body and of his weeping wife struck a much deeper chord in the old man, who had himself so often mourned the passing of a loved one.

As late as mid-January, on the eve of elections for the Topeka Legislature, Brown was still optimistic that Kansas was secure for freedom. He did not regard the Southerners in his neighborhood or elsewhere in the territory as enemies. Even the predominance among his neighbors of "free-white-state" men, who not only opposed slavery but also favored excluding free blacks from Kansas, did not discourage Brown. "We have in the Territory a great many Southern men who are as yet but half right in regard to Slavery; and go for Negro, & Mullatto exclusion," he wrote to his father. "Some of them are very earnest Free State Men. They probably outnumber the real Anti-Slavery men here."[21] By this time – early 1856 – Brown had made several trips to Missouri and had found the people there friendly and even tolerant of his free-state opinions. If he anticipated war at this time, he gave no hint of it in his letters. "Since the Kansas invasion [in November]," he wrote his wife on January 9, "we have no news to send you scarcely; & we get no News from the States of account to satisfy our hunger which is very great."[22] It was a time of watchful waiting.

II

The vortex of Bleeding Kansas soon drained away all hopes for peace. The murder of Captain Reese P. Brown (no relation to John), a free-state leader in proslavery Leavenworth, revived fears of proslavery attacks and another "Ruffian invasion." The new tragedy grew out of the elections on January 15 to choose legislators and territorial officials under the free-state Topeka constitution. The elections generally went smoothly, but in Leavenworth the proslavery mayor forbade the balloting as unlawful. An attempt by free-staters there to hold a secret election in their homes was unsuccessful, so they made a second attempt three days later at Easton, twelve miles away, despite the efforts of proslavery men to block the voting. At dusk on the day of the voting a force of proslavery men failed in an effort to take the ballot box from the free-state men guarding it. But shortly thereafter, the same proslavery band seized a free-state settler named Steven Sparks on his way home from voting. Reese Brown led the party of free-staters sent to free his friend Sparks. As the proslavery men rode away after surrendering Sparks, a sudden outburst of gunfire left Sparks and a proslavery man named Cook wounded.

The next day a proslavery militia, the Kikapoo Rangers, seized Reese Brown and his men on their way back to Leavenworth. Word that the Rangers had killed Brown, reportedly by one or more blows from a hatchet, spread throughout the territory. Especially shocking was a story that the badly mutilated, but still breathing Brown had been dropped at his doorstep in front of his hysterical wife. The weekly free-state newspaper, *Herald of Freedom*, which was owned by the New England Emigrant Aid Society and edited by George W. Brown in Lawrence, reported that Reese Brown had been "chopped...in pieces" in the mistaken belief that he was the hated abolitionist editor himself. "Poor Brown" thus joined the list of free-state martyrs "whose blood cries aloud from the earth for redress."[23] The story grew grislier as it spread. "These men, or rather demons," the correspondent of Horace Greeley's New York *Tribune* said of the murderers, "rushed around Brown and literally hacked him to death with their hatchets." The proslavery Leavenworth *Herald* deepened the sense of outrage among free-staters by seeming to defend the killing. The *Herald* served notice to abolitionists: "These higher-law men will not be permitted longer to carry on their illegal and high-handed proceedings. The good sense of the people will frown it down. And if it cannot be in one way it will in another." Some Missouri papers were now calling openly for war.[24]

Four months later, when a parade of witnesses testified about the killing before a Congressional committee sent to investigate the troubles in Kansas, a different story emerged. The Kikapoo Rangers had captured Brown and his men, it seems, to determine whether they were responsible for shooting the proslavery man, Cook, the previous night. Regrouping at Dawson's grocery nearby, the Rangers planned to hang their captives on the spot. Hearing of the incident, other proslavery men joined the Rangers, bringing the total at Dawson's grocery to more than a hundred.[25] While the prisoners were being interrogated, the rangers imbibed freely and a drunken Ranger named Bob Gibson challenged the unarmed Reese Brown to a fight, and Brown apparently accepted the challenge. After knocking Brown to the floor, Gibson struck him on the forehead with a lath hatchet. At that point, other Rangers intervened, but not before Gibson narrowly missed striking a second prisoner with his hatchet. Bleeding profusely from the hatchet blow, Brown managed briefly in the confusion to escape from his captors, only to be retaken. Hours later, a ranger captain, Charles Dunn, himself intoxicated, spirited Reese Brown away and took him to Brown's home.[26] A neighbor summoned immediately by Brown's wife had arrived while Brown was still conscious and found no wounds other than a bruise on Brown's forehead, where he had been kicked, and a single deep cut in his left temple, from which Brown died.[27] Local authorities declined to hold an inquest into the cause of death, but, at the request of Brown's brother, three Leavenworth physicians exhumed the body, frozen stiff and still well preserved, and agreed that death had resulted from a single blow to the temple, which drove fragments of skull nearly two inches into the brain cavity.[28]

This testimony was shocking enough. It assuredly did little to exonerate the Rangers of vigilante behavior and criminal negligence. But it was not covered in the press, and had little impact on larger events. Nor did it support the allegation in the *Tribune* that a circle of hatchet-wielding "demons" had hewn the helpless Brown to pieces, although it is not surprising that the story grew more terrifying in the retelling. Kansas papers, as David Potter reminded us, were partisan instruments, and correspondents for eastern papers vied with one another in sensationalizing the events they reported.[29] By this time, in any case, regional and other loyalties effectively shaped the meaning of any news that circulated by whatever means through the tiny prairie settlements scattered across eastern Kansas.

The hatchet slaying of Reese Brown inspired a sense of peril among free-staters throughout the territory. Imagination filled gaps in the story as related and fed conspiratorial imagery. In the Browns' eyes, it was not merely the Kikapoo Rangers, but "Missourians" generally who had committed the murder. The seeming danger to everyone grew as news of the incident spread. Echoing the *Herald of Freedom*, Adair exclaimed, "Missourians have been committing murder again. Many [free-state settlers] have left the vicinity and gone to Lawrence for safety." But to Adair, G. W. Brown's warning that a large "guerrilla party," a "regular army" of Missouri Ruffians, might fan across the territory at any time was now confirmed.[30] Adair believed that Reese Brown's killing was part of a larger, concerted effort. "Missourians at some of the towns on the border are forming companies of armed and mounted rifle men to rush in and make onslaught and then retire across the line before a sufficient force can be collected to repel them," Adair told Owen Brown. Two such scouting parties have already entered the territory, he wrote. "The first destroyed a printing press – threw it into the river at Leavenworth. The second killed one man [Reese Brown] in a most terrible manner – choped him with hatches, and stabbed him with bowie knives. Wounded some others." Taking a cue once more from G. W. Brown, Adair suggested that Missourians were preparing "another invasion." If the free states in the East did not send help soon, the Kansas Browns and their neighbors could expect a "bloody onslaught."[31]

John and his son Salmon had been in Missouri buying provisions, their return delayed by a blizzard, while these events happened. They heard of the murder of Reese Brown only on reaching the Adairs' cabin. "We have just learned of some *new*; and shocking outrages at Leavenworth and that the free-state people there have fled to Lawrence," John wrote Mary and Watson. If the threatened attack on Lawrence took place, he added, "we may soon again be called upon to 'buckle on our armor,' which by the help of God we will do.... My judgment is that we shall have no general disturbance until warmer weather."[32]

The "martyrdom" of Reese Brown made a deep impression on the Browns and on free state men throughout the territory. In March Representative John Brown, Jr., was one of three members of the Topeka Legislature who drafted resolutions condemning the killing and demanding prosecution of the perpetrators.[33] Stories of the attack and images of Reese Brown's mutilated body reinforced predispositions of free-staters to see Missourians variously as "savages," whiskey-soaked illiterates, and subhuman "Pukes" wielding Bowie knives and hatchets. At the same time, the stories strengthened free-staters' image of themselves as godly emissaries of civilization and Yankee enterprise and manly defenders of the freedom that constituted the essence of the American heritage. Events such as the slaying of Brown did much to brutalize free-staters' perceptions of Southerners as the Other. The growing list of "martyrs" to the cause increased free-state demands not so much for redress as for vengeance.[34]

The Brown clan still hoped for protection from Congress. The efforts of President Pierce to resolve the crisis served only to strengthen the Browns' feeling that the Slave Power was forcing their hand. Following the free-state elections, Governor Shannon had gone to Washington to seek federal support for his efforts to suppress the free-state movement. He and Secretary of War Jefferson Davis of Mississippi persuaded Pierce to take a public stand. In a special message to Congress on January 24, Pierce declared the Shawnee Legislature legal and denounced its free-state counterpart as illegal and revolutionary, "avowedly so in motive." Free-staters who went so far as "organized resistance by force to the fundamental or any other Federal law, and to the authority of the general government," the President warned, would be guilty of "treasonable insurrection." On February 11 Pierce followed up on this declaration by issuing a proclamation placing the federal troops at Forts Riley and Leavenworth at Governor Shannon's disposal to enforce the law and keep the peace. To free-staters, this proclamation placed the authority and power of the United States on the side of proslavery, and by implication denied the Topeka government and its adherents any protection from "Border Ruffians."³⁵

Shannon's mission to Washington had not gone unnoticed. As Jason wrote his grandfather on January 23, "We hear...Shannon has gone to Washington to get authority from Esqr. Pierce to call on the U.S. troops at any time he may think best – Pierce says the people of Kansas must be protected. Of course the proslavery settlers and Missourians will be. They still are committing outrages near the Missouri line."³⁶ By February federal troops had been deployed near Osawatomie, as John Brown told Ohio Congressman Joshua Giddings, an old acquaintance, "for the ostensible purpose of removing *intruders* from certain Indian Lands." But Brown feared that "the real object is to have these men in readiness to act in the enforcement of those *Hellish enactments* of the (so called) Kansas Legislature.... I confidently believe," he predicted, "that the next movement on the part of the Administration and its Proslavery masters will be to drive the people here, either to submit to those Infernal enactments; or to assume what will be termed *treasonable grounds* by shooting down the poor soldiers of the country with whom they have no quarrel whatever." Brown invoked the "name of Almighty God;...our venerated fore-fathers...[and] all that good and true men ever held dear" in asking Giddings whether Congress would "suffer us to be driven to such 'dire extremities'? *Will anything be done?*"³⁷

Delayed by storms, Giddings's reply to Brown's letter reached Osawatomie on March 17. "The President will never *dare* employ the troops of the United States to shoot the citizens of Kansas," Giddings assured Brown. Such an act would "light up the fires of civil war throughout the North" and "bring the President so deep in infamy that the hand of political resurrection will never reach him."³⁸

By this time, John believed that only statehood could insure the "cause of liberty" in Kansas. "There is great anxiety felt here about the action of Congress," he wrote his father on that subject on March 26. "If Congress do[es] not recognize the action of the Free State people here there is every reason to expect trouble: as the Missourians will take new courage in that event."³⁹ Adair had told Owen three weeks earlier that John now "seems to think matters in Kansas indicate war more than at any previous period." John was anxious for the "crisis" to come so that he could "return to his family again," Adair wrote. "He regrets more and more the way things were managed at Lawrence" during the Wakarusa War. Had the leaders there "maintained an independeant and upright course with the Governor," Adair observed, "I have no doubt that it would have resulted much better than it had."[40]

John, Jr., returned from the March session of the Topeka Legislature with enhanced prestige. He had been one of three members selected to draft a memorial asking Congress to organize Kansas as a free-state under the Topeka constitution, and also one of the committee assigned to prepare a code of laws to be adopted at the July session. He was thus in high spirits when he reached Brown's Station on March 20. Missourians at Lexington had seized a shipment of 100 Sharps rifles and two "breech loading Cannon" intended for free-state forces, he told his grandfather, but the "better class of people in Missouri" condemned such robbery and feared the loss of trade that would result from migrants choosing to come to Kansas through Iowa rather than Missouri. He was also impressed by the "spirit of 76" evidenced by the Northern settlers bringing "free labor and free institutions" to Kansas, despite the "wars and rumors of war." The bravery of his fellow legislators, facing possible arrest for "High Treason," was likewise "a source of encouragement."[41]

But like his father, John, Jr., believed events were drifting out of control. The newly elected free-state governor, Charles Robinson, had urged the legislature to adopt a "Fabian" policy of avoiding actions that might provoke proslavery authorities, and called upon legislators to renounce the "spirit of retaliation." Robinson hoped thereby to keep the moral high ground and win the battle of public opinion in the nation.[42] John, Jr., had supported Robinson's call to memorialize Congress on the issue of statehood, but he told Owen that he now believed proslavery forces were trying to "drive us to forcible resistance, and thereby involve us in a quarrel with the General Government." Adair agreed. In President Pierce's actions, Adair saw a plot to back up the "bogus" Shawnee Legislature and then "accuse us of treason."[43] For his part, John, Jr., was prepared for death, he declared in a letter written on April 4 for *Frederick Douglass' Paper*, but "chains never." The policy of moderation favored by Robinson, he added, "is fast drawing to [a] close," and "shadows … upon our pathway" forecast "revolution."[44]

III

Events nearer home now claimed the Browns' attention. The territorial court of the second district was scheduled to open its spring term April 21 at Dutch Henry Sherman's tavern, where the California Road crossed Pottawatomie Creek. Federal Judge Sterling G. Cato of Alabama, ardently proslavery, would preside. The Kansas-Nebraska Act required Cato to apportion the term of his court between cases arising under U.S. law and those arising under territorial law. Thus he could impanel a grand jury, or so the Browns thought, and ask it to indict them and their antislavery neighbors for support of the Topeka government or resistance to territorial law.

Free-state men had a long list of grievances against the territorial courts. The courts had refused to indict the accused killers of Dow, Barber, Reese Brown, and other victims of proslavery violence. But they had tried to prosecute a free-soiler, Cole McRea, who had acted in self-defense, free-staters believed, when he killed a proslavery man at Leavenworth in April 1855.[45] Given Pierce's mandate to Shannon to regard the Topeka government as "revolutionary," free-state officials throughout the territory now feared indictment. When a federal court convened in Jefferson County on March 27, a company of armed free-state men drilled nearby, threatening to break up the court and to resist all processes issued against free-staters. In April former governor Andrew Reeder refused to obey a federal subpoena to appear as a witness and dared authorities to arrest him. In Douglas County, the chief justice of the territorial courts, Samuel D. Lecompte, formerly of Maryland, charged a grand jury to take into consideration the "treasonable" attempt to create an illegal free-state when acting on cases brought before it. Soon thereafter the jury indicted Charles Robinson and four other free-state officials for treason.

Meantime, the prospect that Judge Cato's court might prosecute Franklin County men who refused to pay taxes to the territorial government prompted twenty-three residents of Osawatomie and Pottawatomie to call a settler's meeting. The meeting, at Osawatomie April 16, revealed a deep division between those prepared to obey the law and those prepared to defy it. An angry exchange between John Brown, who was ready to fight, and the Rev. Martin White, a "free-white-state" man from Illinois who had a claim two miles east of the Browns, disrupted the meeting. White led a walkout of those opposed to Brown's militancy and soon after joined the proslavery faction. Those remaining, including John, Jr., and Adair, denounced the Shawnee legislature as the illegal product of a "foreign vote" and denied the authority of its officers in the territory. They also pledged each other mutual aid if "forcible resistance" became necessary and warned tax assessors and sheriffs that they would discharge their duties at their "peril." These defiant resolutions and the minutes recording them were ordered to be published in Kansas newspapers and copies sent to local officials.[46]

Thus when Cato's court opened on April 21, a confrontation seemed unavoidable. Legend has it that the Browns intimidated the court with a show of force and Cato fled the second night never to return. Witnesses, however, disagreed about what happened. Several conflicting versions of the encounter soon appeared, beginning with an anonymous letter from a proslavery witness in the Leavenworth *Herald* on May 5 and John, Jr.'s, narrative in the *Herald of Freedom* on May 10.[47] Over the years sympathetic local historians like James Hanway, a free-state settler, and John Brown's sons, added subplots and details to the story like ornaments to a Christmas tree. Salmon Brown insisted in several interviews nearly fifty years after the incident that his father had sent him and Henry Thompson to the court to see whether Cato would have them arrested.

The plan was that his father and John, Jr.'s Pottawatomie Rifles would rescue them the following day.[48] In another version, James P. Doyle, later a victim of the Pottawatomie Massacre, allegedly swore out a warrant against Henry Thompson, with whom he had quarreled over slavery. The Browns then reportedly held a "council" and decided that Thompson should go to the court accompanied by Salmon, to give himself up. Then on Salmon's signal the others at the council would enter the court and hand two revolvers to Thompson, who would force the court to adjourn and destroy its prestige.[49] But Court records reveal no warrant for Thompson's arrest. Nor does any contemporary evidence hint that the others sent Salmon Brown and Henry Thompson to the court. Both stories were premised on the assumption that John Brown wished to force the issue and perhaps precipitate civil war, a thesis Brown's admirers favored in later years.

What we can verify from contemporary sources is less spectacular and even leaves unclear whether Brown himself played an active role in the affair of Cato's court. On April 22, the second day after the court's session, Brown himself wrote an account of the incident to Adair. "Yesterday I went to Dutch Henrys to see how things were going at Court; & my boys turned out to train at a house near by," he began. The phrase "my boys" evidently refers to John's sons, not the Rifles, since he immediately noted that "many of the Volunteer Co." under John, Jr.'s command entered the court "without show of arms" to hear Cato charge the grand jury. "The Court is *thoroughly Bogus*," Brown continued, "but the Judge had not the nerve to avow it openly. He was questioned on the bench in writing civilly but plainly whether he intended to enforce the Bogus Laws or not; but would give no answer," Brown reported. "He did not even mention the so called Kansas *Legislature or name their acts* but talked of *our* laws, & it was easy for any one conversant with law matters to discover what code he was charging the Jury under."[50]

Brown seemed to hold Cato in contempt, but the judge had not been intimidated.[51] The court had proceeded despite the presence of the menacing free-state militia. Judge Cato "evidently felt much agitated but talked a good deal about having criminals punished, &c.," Brown wrote. At that point John, Jr., left the courtroom and in a voice loud enough for the judge to hear called a meeting of his rifle company outside. "After hearing the charge & witnessing the refusal of the judge to answer," John Brown went on, "the volunteers met under arms [and] passed the Osawatomie Preamble & Resolutions every man voting aye." They then appointed a committee to "wait on the Judge at once with a coppy in full; which was immediately done."[52] Some of the later stories have Brown himself delivering these resolutions to the court, sometimes accompanied by Henry H. Williams, a member of the Rifles.[53] But if he did so, he was uncharacteristically modest in reporting the incident to Owen. "One of Frank Pierce's judges" had made "an attempt at holding a Bogus Court," he wrote. "The Court however broke up on the second day without doing anything."[54] No contemporary account names Brown, who was not a member of his son's rifle company, as one of the "committee."[55] What is clear is that John, Jr., not his father, held center stage in the incident.

FIGURE 5.1. Three sons of John Brown, left to right, Jason, Frederick, and John, Jr., in free-state militia uniforms, spring 1856.

CREDIT: Ohio Historical Society.

Although John Brown had not yet heard how Cato responded to the defiant Osawatomie resolutions, he told Adair the following day that "matters are in a fair way of comming to a head."[56] Just what he meant by this is uncertain; some writers have seen it as a portent of war. But if so, it was not a reference to any disturbance at the court, for as Brown told Adair, the court was to sit again that very day. Clearly, Brown did not expect violence, and apparently did not even plan to attend. Neither did John, Jr. The assumption that Brown hoped to precipitate war by disrupting the court makes little sense, in any case. Large-scale resistance at Lawrence might have had that effect, but sparsely settled Franklin County was too small and too remote for an incident there to have done so. Legend notwithstanding, John Brown and his sons had not routed the court or even forced it to suspend its proceedings. They had not actually even denied the authority of the court under *federal* law. The issue they raised was the pragmatic one of whether Cato would try to enforce the hated "bogus" territorial laws in Franklin County. Brown was evidently uncertain whether Cato would try to do that. What is clear is that Brown and his allies had made an effort to intimidate the court. But like the Jefferson county free-state men before them, they made a show of force and stopped well short of violence.

After a careful examination of the records of the court, historian James C. Malin determined that the only business Cato conducted on April 22 was to indict three men for minor offenses and to issue warrants ordering two of the offenders to appear at the fall term of the court.[57] The court then adjourned at noon on the twenty-second and moved to Anderson county as required by territorial law. Apparently, Cato had not been prepared to challenge the organized antislavery forces in Franklin County or officials of the Topeka government. Nor was he willing to test the infamous "black laws" proscribing antislavery opinion. Nothing in the court records, as Malin says, suggests that he intended to test any "bogus" law.[58] But Cato had stood his ground, and in so doing had affirmed territorial law in principle. When presented with the Osawatomie resolutions, he simply shrugged them off. They did not deny the authority of federal judges to hold court. But at a later sitting and under different circumstances, Cato issued indictments against the Browns and others for conspiracy to resist the tax laws of the territorial government.[59]

To the Browns, Cato's court symbolized the moral corruption of territorial law. All the grand jurors, trial jurors, and witnesses sworn in the first day, including several men who had voted in the free-state elections, swore an oath affirming the right of Kansans to own slaves. The selection of officers of the court was equally disturbing; all of them were proslavery zealots, including Allen Wilkinson, a Shawnee legislator, who became district attorney pro tem, and Thomas McMinn, foreman of the grand jury. The jury included James P. Doyle, a member of the Law and Order Party who had quarreled frequently with his free-state neighbors. His son William P. Doyle, age twenty-two, was bailiff for the grand jury, while James Harris, who worked for the ardently proslavery Dutch Henry Sherman, was a juror.

Late in his life Salmon Brown contended that his father decided to kill the "dirty curs" Cato had appointed "officers to enforce the [bogus?] laws," and that his father told members of the Rifles that he and his party were "going back to Pottawatomie to break up Cato's court."[60] As Malin noted, several men associated with the court were hacked to death in the Pottawatomie Massacre,[61] which led him to conclude that the Pottawatomie killings were political assassinations aimed at Cato's court. But, as Malin himself conceded, the Browns had called out, questioned, and released James Harris, a juror. They also failed to seek out other court officials then living on Pottawatomie Creek, but killed James Doyle's second son, eighteen-year-old Drury Doyle, who had no connection with the court. The questions John Brown put to Harris during his interrogation suggest that support for the Law and Order Party or aid to the

Missourians was sufficient to warrant "execution," while service on the local jury was not.[62] Malin's scenario does not explain, furthermore, why Brown would kill local members of the court when Cato would not return until the fall. At that session, after all, Cato could appoint new officers and jurors. As historian Stephen B. Oates asks, why should Brown fear indictment when none of the men indicted on April 22 had been arrested?[63]

Malin might have answered that the courts could now call upon military force to uphold territorial law. Sheriff Jones had brought ten dragoons with him to Lawrence just before Cato opened court at Dutch Henry's Crossing. But if Brown had feared indictment, as Malin implies, adding murder to the charges against him would scarcely have increased his chances of evading prosecution.

To be sure, the Browns had been distraught at the coming of Cato's court. But it was what they saw as the perversion of law to wicked purposes rather than fear of indictment that led them to make a demonstration of defiance. Free-staters were irate that the territorial courts had not prosecuted proslavery murderers. "Not an instance has yet come to my knowledge where any attempt has been made by either the United States authorities or the officials of the bogus legislature to arrest a pro-slavery murderer," Adair wrote three weeks after the court session. "Such a state of things as this maddens men, and throws them back upon their own resources for redress. And it is dreadful to see how all the evil passions rise and rage at the oft recital of these terrible outrages so near home.... O the depth of revenge in the human heart when the powers that should execute justice, not only connive at the wrong, but abet, and help it on, and screen the offender. May heaven grant us deliverance soon."[64] To men like Brown and Adair, the law of necessity had to reflect the harmony of God's creation. Courts that perpetuated or tolerated slavery and other injustice defied God and opened the nation to divine retribution.

This had long been a basic tenet of Brown's political thinking. In an 1854 letter intended for publication in the newspaper of his friend and ally, Frederick Douglass, Brown outlined an apocalyptic view of the situation created by the passage of the Fugitive Slave Law of 1850. To Brown, republican institutions, especially the courts, were all that held in check the "passions of fallen men." Without moral law and order, Brown wrote Douglass, sinful men "would give the world a constant succession of murder, revenge, robbery, fire and famine; or, first, of anarchy in all its horrid forms; and then of the most bloody despotisms" in repeated cycles of anarchy and despotism. "What punishment ever inflicted by man or even threatened of God, can be too severe," Brown asked, for those who "hate the right and the Most High." Passage of the Fugitive Slave Law at the bidding of iniquitous slaveholders was a dangerous perversion of law itself. Proslavery men in Congress and even in some Northern legislatures, Brown complained, passed "unjust and wicked enactments, and call them laws." Similarly, presidents and governors who signed such enactments, like the judges who upheld them and the marshals, sheriffs, constables and policemen who enforced them were all members of the "same horde." Brown added to his list of fallen men "Doctors of Divinity" who "defiled the priest-hood" by ignoring the Golden Rule and counseling the return of fugitive slaves, thereby "trampling underfoot the laws of our final Judge." Editors of proslavery newspapers and periodicals who similarly stifled conscience and insulted God by encouraging the passage of "abominably wicked and unjust" laws were likewise guilty.[65] The old New England idea of moral declension, so evident in Owen's commentaries, had begun to obsess John Brown's imagination.

IV

In Brown's mind, as we shall see, a more immediate reason for action was a growing sense of peril to his family. Events at Lawrence had for a time over-shadowed the danger on the Pottawatomie. The crisis at Lawrence began on April 19, when Sheriff Jones returned to town with warrants to arrest S. N. Wood, leader of the Branson rescuers, and others. Unable to deputize men in the street to effect the arrests, Jones left only to reappear on the twenty-third with a detachment of troops from Fort Leavenworth, who enabled him to arrest the indictees. That night, as Jones watched over his prisoners in his tent, a young New Yorker shot and wounded him from outside the tent. Although a town meeting promptly denounced the shooting and the *Herald of Freedom* insisted that "public sentiment...condemns, in unmeasured terms, the assassination" attempt, Missouri newspapers called for vengeance.[66] While Governor Shannon mustered hundreds of volunteers into the Territorial Militia, the *Herald of Freedom* declared an "invasion" seemed imminent and that "stealthy assassins" threatened the "liberty-loving" citizens of Kansas.[67]

On May 5 Chief Justice S. D. Lecompte, presiding over the first district court, issued warrants for the arrest of prominent leaders of the Topeka government, including Robinson and Lane, for "constructive treason." Warned of his indict-ment, Robinson fled the territory, only to be captured by a mob in Lexington, Missouri, and returned to Lecompton for trial. Former Territorial Governor Andrew H. Reeder, recently chosen by free-staters as a delegate to Congress, escaped arrest by fleeing Kansas disguised as a riverboat deckhand. By early May, free-staters were thus leaderless, and Jones, recovered from his wound, announced himself prepared to lead a "posse" against Lawrence, where panic began to take hold.[68]

Closer to Osawatomie, Southern strength in Kansas increased notably when Major Jefferson Buford of Alabama led a force of 400 armed men across the border on May 2. Many of Buford's "immigrants" actually sought land for claims, but they rode in companies and bivouacked on Ottawa land not far from Osawatomie, and about two miles below Dutch Henry's Crossing on Pottawatomie Creek. "The Alibamians and Georgians are most of them hard cases," Adair wrote of the armed men. "Drunken, profane, wreckless.... They are encamped about in different places in companies of from 50 to 150, threat-ening to drive off free state men from their claims and take possession of them. In some places great insecurity is felt, and much alarm."[69]

Some historians have discounted as irrational the panic these developments created among free-staters. No violence had occurred in Franklin County, they note, and inflammatory stories in Missouri newspapers should have been discounted. More specific threats against the Browns and their friends, these writers contend, were only rumors or meaningless "bombast."[70] Relying on reminiscent accounts, these scholars fail to consider the perceptual world of the Browns and their friends who were hunkered down in isolated cabins across a patchwork of claims spread across miles of open prairie. They knew that if attacked, no officers of the law would come to their aid. Their assailants, on the other hand, would have to fear neither prosecution nor punishment. Once the fierce winter relented and the swollen streams no longer afforded barriers against invasion from Missouri, the hatchet-wielding Kikapoo Rangers as well as Buford's hard-faced ruffians might ride into their neighborhoods at any time, and force entry into their homes. If it was also true that Missourians feared free-state militias, that fact did not make families at Osawatomie feel more secure. "We are constantly exposed and we have almost no protection," John Brown's sister Florella wrote to her sister Martha on May 16. "A few have their guns and revolvers, but as a people and place we are without even these and the place is known and called an '*abolitionist nest*.'"[71] As renewed threats to Lawrence raised apprehension among the Browns and their neighbors of a general invasion, proslavery groups on the Pottawatomie seemed bent on driving abolitionists out of the district.[72]

6

Terroriser

> This day will I begin to put the dread of thee and the fear of thee upon the nations...who shall hear report of thee, and shall tremble, and be in anguish because of thee.
>
> King James Bible, Deuteronomy 2:25
>
> I looked at the traitor and terroriser...with unlimited, undeniable contempt.
>
> John Wilkes Booth[1]

The manifest sense of peril in the Brown camp does not by itself explain the Pottawatomie killings. Crucial questions remain. Why did killing seem necessary or justifiable to Brown? Might not defensive measures alone have reassured the Brown women? What did Brown hope to accomplish in killing just five of his family's enemies? Doing that surely invited retaliation, especially if relatives or friends of the victims sought help from the Law and Order party, of which James Doyle was a member, or from Buford's men, with whom the victims had had contact. At the very least, the killings would draw the attention of proslavery leaders to Brown's Station as a locus of opposition. And how did Brown choose his victims – Wilkinson, Dutch Bill Sherman, and the three Doyles? In that selection, as James C. Malin perceived, can be found the immediate reasons for the bloodletting as well as clues to John Brown's deeper motives.

Malin dismissed later accounts of the incident by Brown's allies, and rightly so. Memories fade; sequences of events become confused. Moreover, such accounts evince a considerable "rescripting" of the past. We know from recent work in the psychology of memory that stories repeated over time become interlaced with plausible but inaccurate information. Psychologists theorize that gaps in memory are filled by "default" data from "scripts" or standardized expectations about how everyday activities are structured. In using the term "rescripting", I mean to characterize a process authenticated in the literature of experimental psychology in which general knowledge of everyday life alters or supplants detail in personal, or autobiographical memories.[2]

To be sure, James Townsley insisted in his 1879 memoir of Pottawatomie that the murders were "vividly fixed in my memory." But the more salient point was that he had "thought of them many times since."[3] Repeated musings over that horrifying night permitted Townsley unwittingly to rescript the events in subtle ways, giving his story new meanings consistent with his changing understandings of the world and his evolving image of himself in the world. Arguably, his misnamed "confession," repeated to Johnson Clark a "dozen times" in 1879 in the presence of Judge James Hanway,[4] sought to establish his own innocence of the crimes.

The circumstances in which memories are retrieved also tend to alter them. The solicitations of prominent men like Clark, Hanway, and the editor of the Lawrence *Daily Journal* also gave Townsley a brief celebrity as a man able to unlock a dark secret. They offered him an opportunity to unburden himself without risking prosecution. Thus Townsley's confession is self-serving as well as heavily rescripted. Similarly, reminiscent accounts of Brown's son Owen and his son-in-law Henry Thompson and still later narratives by Salmon Brown were unconsciously rescripted, and sometimes deliberately written, to refute the accounts of Townsley and other "enemies" of the Brown family. Details in all these accounts are often badly muddled. Obvious, if perhaps unintended, inventions mar every version. In these reminiscences, memory is the servant of self-esteem, and old quarrels find new public venues.

Fortunately, contemporary evidence, including newly available family letters and documents, provides clues to Brown's thinking at the time. A letter the Rev. Samuel Adair wrote four days after Pottawatomie to his sister-in-law, Sally Marian Hand, and her husband, Titus, is especially instructive. John Brown and his sons, who had recently built a new cabin for Adair, had "made their home much of late at our house," Adair wrote. Of course Adair was not privy to Brown's plans. Evidently he did not know when Brown left for Lawrence with the Pottawatomie Rifles that Brown might kill anyone in their own neighborhood. Probably John himself had no plan to do so at the time. But Brown and Adair shared many confidences and fundamental beliefs. Both reacted to proslavery "outrages" with passion, and the two talked much about the wrongs suffered by free-state men.

Though at the time Adair wrote the letter to the Hands, he could only surmise that John and several of his sons were with the Pottawatomie party, but he was pretty sure whose work the killings were. Indeed, Adair's rambling, emotional letter is partly perhaps an unconscious justification of the killings. In trying to make sense of the panic that seized people on both sides of the slavery question after Pottawatomie – in trying to comprehend the madness his life had suddenly become – Samuel Adair did what he often had before: He echoed Brown's opinions in his own, thus providing a point of departure for an effort to tap into Brown's imagination.

Adair began by listing the crimes of the proslavery faction that his wife Florella had related to the Hands (John's half sister and her husband) only a week before: "the murder of two Free State men, the taking of Lawrence by a posse under U.S. authority, the destruction of the American hotel, two printing presses, burning of other buildings, together with the marshalling of forces." Then he told of "guerrilla parties" of Border Ruffians who forced their way into homes and took money, arms, goods, and livestock "at the peril of life," not only in Lawrence but throughout the countryside. Now free-state men were no longer willing to stay their hands. The metaphorical "gun" Missourians had been firing was "beginning to kick," Adair said in an allusion to Pottawatomie, and was doing as much damage at the breech as it had at the muzzle. "You will recollect the murder of Dow last November – of Barber in December of Brown in January of Jones & Steward, last week; or a thousand other outrages. Five Free State men shot or butchered: not only did … bogus authority refuse to lift a finger to bring to justice these murderers, but has shielded them. The U.S. territorial officers have done the same."[5]

"Now what is the result?" Adair asked perhaps rhetorically but perhaps also to enable him to begin rationalizing what he feared John Brown and his sons had done. Free-state "guerrilla parties" and militia units, he answered, were mobilizing throughout the territory in response to the "sack" of Lawrence and to the presence of an uncontrolled mob-militia of thousands of armed Missourians. Adair then came to the source of his evident anxiety. "One party," he wrote with a certain abstractness, had made a descent "on Saturday night last & five pro-slavery men were shot or butchered in one night. Some of them," he said of the victims, "had made threats, had threatened the lives of Free-State men – had acted most outrageously for some time past – they were probably dreaming of no danger to themselves. Some of them were taken from their beds and almost literally heived to pieces with broad swords." "The scene of these desperate deeds, is only about eight miles from us."

The aftermath of the grisly affair was dramatic. "Some pro-slavery men took alarm & fled," Adair related, while some free-state men "also left their houses for a few nights." But the larger effect was on the advocates of slavery. "Runners were sent to Missouri, for help," Adair said, "And pro-slavery men in different localities gathered together or stood in fear of their lives." The killings might therefore be efficacious; they might prompt would-be proslavery assassins henceforth to think twice about the consequences of their deeds.

After summarizing the panic that followed news of the Pottawatomie killings, Adair returned to his meditation on the larger madness gripping Kansas. The killings made sense to him only in Old Testament terms. "As many pro-slavery men must die," he said, "as free state men are killed by them, and they will not be particular who [their victim] is, so [long as] he is one who has made himself officious in Kansas matters. 'Eye for eye, tooth for tooth' – dollar for dollar & compound interest in some cases may be demanded." Adair expected the Missourians to retaliate. If they come, he added flintily, "they may expect to find one of their party dead when they return, a house burnt, a horse stolen, as the case may be when they return." But "an eye for an eye" worked both ways. No one now slept without fear. "You cannot easily imagine our situation when it [is] known all abroad that our relatives have had a hand in this affair."

In Adair's troubled view the Pottawatomie massacre was clearly no isolated, meaningless act. It was retributive, even biblical justice, a warning that murder would not go unpunished. The victims paid with their lives for those of Dow, Barber, Reese Brown, and two other free-state men murdered in the preceding week. They were targets because they had been aggressive proslavery advocates who repeatedly threatened their free-state neighbors. The killings were thus intended to strike terror among proslavery people and to persuade ruffians they could no longer kill with impunity. In advancing these arguments, Adair anticipated later arguments Brown's sons and their allies would make in defense of the "executions." But Adair emphatically rejected one claim Brown hagiographers later advanced: that the massacre would bring peace to the Pottawatomie.

It is evident also that if Adair thought he knew John Brown's reasons for the killings, he did not approve of them. Had he been consulted beforehand, Adair would certainly have rejected murder as a political weapon. He was as committed as Brown to resistance to "bogus law" and, like Brown, was furious at the efforts of proslavery partisans to use the courts to suppress the free-state movement. He had repeatedly warned correspondents in Ohio that war would break out if the Shawnee government attempted to impose its will on free-state men. Indeed, he even boasted of his own militance in the antislavery cause. A week before Pottawatomie, by his own account, Adair had told a "bogus [tax] assessor" that he had nothing but contempt for the man and for any officer of the "mob-elected Legislature" at Shawnee. Adair had even given a tax assessor "some pretty plain talk." "They threaten us," he continued, "but if they get any thing from many, they will get it as the highway robber gets it, and run similar risks."[6] Adair was not a nonresistant.

But scruples forbad Adair's joining the Rifles or openly embracing forcible means. In truth, Adair was terrified of violence and feared that his family was overly exposed to retaliation. When John's son Owen sought refuge at Adair's cabin after Pottawatomie, Adair sent him away saying that the killings were a "terrible calamity" to "your friends," and calling Owen a "marked man." Owen never spoke to Adair again.[7] Thus Adair's letter to the Hands was not a conscious apology for John; but if his reflections fail to fit all of the available facts, they do advance our understanding of Brown's motives as one of his sympathetic kinsmen set them forth.

I

Consider first Adair's suggestion that the killings be seen as Old Testament-type acts of retribution. This scenario goes awry when we consider those Brown chose – or might have chosen – to kill. Like the political assassination theory, this scenario is too neat by half. If Brown had set out to take the lives of five men, the number of murdered free-state men by Adair's count,[8] he seemed to blunder early on. Townsley and Salmon Brown both remembered details that conflict with the eye-for-an-eye scenario. The "whole company" had crossed

Mosquito Creek above the Doyles' cabin when one of them knocked at the door of another cabin and got no answer.[9] In Salmon's version, they "scattered" when an inhabitant thrust a rifle barrel through a chink in the wall.[10] Why had the assassins stopped at this cabin? Were they planning to kill the resident? If so, in Salmon's version, they were easily deterred from the task. And if they had killed at the first cabin, would they have gone on to kill the Doyles, Allen Wilkinson, and William Sherman? Or would they have spared one of the later victims to keep the total at five?[11] The aborted first stop suggests a more random process than Adair's scenario supposes.

There is another difficulty with the eye-for-an-eye thesis. According to that thesis, by killing Doyle and his two oldest sons – the first of the murders – Brown precluded the possibility of killing Wilkinson and both Shermans. Mrs. Doyle testified on June 7 that the Browns prepared to kill her third son, sixteen-year-old John, after killing her husband and two older sons, but spared him because of her tearful pleadings.[12] After completing their gruesome task at the Doyles's, which began about 11 P.M., the assassins – or some of them[13] – next dispatched Wilkinson, presumably according to plan. Yet while at the Doyles's none of them knew that Henry Sherman would be away from home and from the cabin James Harris occupied on Sherman's property, where either the Browns or Henry Thompson and Weiner finally found William and two other men. By chance Henry Sherman was out on the prairie looking for stray cattle that night. Suppose he and William had both been in bed. The assassins had already killed four people. Would Brown have killed one Sherman brother and left the other alive to seek revenge?

Moreover, the Browns apparently intended to kill others. Louisa Jane Wilkinson, the wife of Allen Wilkinson, remembered that they asked her whether Thomas McMinn, who had been the foreman of Cato's jury, lived nearby.[14] From Harris's affidavit we also know that Brown was looking for Henry Sherman. Brown questioned Harris outside in the dark. Had Harris confessed to aiding proslavery men or participating in the sack of Lawrence, he would no doubt have been killed. Only after releasing Harris did Brown take William Sherman outside. Sherman did not return; the next morning Harris found him with his skull split in two places, a "large hole in his left breast, and his left hand cut off."[15]

If Brown had no plan to limit his killing to the symbolic five, how many did he plan to kill? Clearly, he did not intend to "sweep the creek … of all the pro-slavery men living on it," as Townsley recalled. Townsley quotes Brown as demanding that Townsley "pilot the party into the neighborhood where I lived, and point out all the pro-slavery men in it, whom he proposed to put to death." That claim is clearly too sweeping, for if merely supporting slavery were sufficient grounds for execution, Harris should have been slain.

Nonetheless, Adair's argument for retribution is closer to the mark than Townsley's version of indiscriminate slaughter. Throughout his narrative, Townsley insisted that he wished to have no part in the killings. His familiarity with the neighborhood was ostensibly the reason Brown refused to let him go home. But Townsley's claims at this point are at best dubious. Weiner, a grocer whose store was a short walk from Dutch Henry's Crossing, knew the neighborhood well, and was eager for revenge against the proslavery men who had menaced his business. Townsley is also unclear or self-servingly silent on several relevant points. He claims Brown intended to kill George Wilson, Probate Judge of Anderson County, who had a claim eight miles south of Dutch Henry's Crossing and had been "notifying Free-State men to leave the Territory. I had received such a notice from him myself," Townsley recalled; but he failed to explain why Brown expected to find Wilson at Dutch Henry's. More important, Townsley gives no reason why Brown called his men together after William Sherman was slain, or why Brown returned with them to camp, leaving most of the proslavery men on the Pottawatomie asleep in their beds.

If Adair's "five-for-five" theory is doubtful, nonetheless his suggestion that Brown saw himself as an avenging angel for the free-state cause is close to the mark. The affidavits of survivors of the Pottawatomie massacre agree that Brown introduced his men as an agent of the "northern army." When Brown and his party questioned Harris outside the cabin he rented from Henry Sherman, they asked whether he had helped bring proslavery men to the territory, had taken part in the "troubles at Lawrence," or had ever done the free-state party any "harm." Harris said "no" to each of these queries. Harris had moved into the area only two months before, and the Browns asked him why he chose to "live at such a place." Although Harris recognized "old man Brown" and his son Owen, the intruders accepted his answers and released him. When they reached Wilkinson's cabin a short time later, the Browns demanded to know whether Wilkinson was a "northern armist" – an opponent of the free-state party. When he answered in the affirmative, they demanded that he surrender and open the door. After he did so, they took Wilkinson outside, where they cut him in the head and on the side of the torso, and slit his throat.[16]

Why might Brown have chosen so gruesome a manner to act as God's "instrument" of free-state vengeance? In later years Brown's defenders claimed that the free-state leaders at Lawrence had authorized the killings and even given Brown a list of those deserving execution. But if so, it was curious that Robinson, Lane, or other leaders should have chosen so obscure a set of victims as the Doyles, the Shermans, and Allen Wilkinson. No credible evidence implicates anyone in Lawrence in the murders or even shows that Brown met with any free-state leader there. If local militia leaders like Henry H. Williams had authorized the killings, as Salmon Brown later claimed,[17] it is clear that John Brown selected his own victims. No credible evidence supports the claim that the attack was anyone's idea but Brown's.

By the time of the attack, Brown was peculiarly susceptible to the idea that he was God's chosen instrument for avenging the martyrs to His cause. When Kansas was opened for settlement, Brown was in the midst of a protracted search within himself for signs of God's plan for him. He had consecrated his life and being to the cause the "poor slave," but he had no conspicuous way of satisfying his need to demonstrate his piety through "service." The calls for help from free-state forces in Lawrence on the eve of Pottawatomie echoed his sons' earlier summons to help them defend freedom in Kansas. Robinson's appointment of Brown as a captain in the free-state army during the Wakarusa War might for a time have assuaged his need for service and recognition. Convinced of the triumph of the free-state cause, Brown threw himself into the effort to establish his family's claims and comfort. But the shooting of Sheriff Jones had once again agitated Lawrence, and the ensuing month of crisis focused attention in free-state camps throughout the territory on "outrages" committed by proslavery men. Brown read the "heart-rending" stories of martyrs that appeared regularly in the *Herald of Freedom* as tragic consequences of tolerating proslavery lawlessness.

Brown's preoccupation with "proslavery diabolism" grew apace with the emergence of a second Lawrence crisis, reports of which Brown received with special poignancy. In early April, G. W. Brown visited an editor in Alton, Illinois, whom he convinced to publish a series of articles on the 1837 murder of Elijah P. Lovejoy, the abolitionist printer whose death had deeply affected John Brown and his father. Now, as a new threat to freedom seemed imminent in Kansas, G. W. Brown stood at Lovejoy's grave and reflected on the "curse" his murder had inflicted on Alton.[18] While G. W. Brown was absent from Lawrence, his negrophobic associate editor, J. H. Greene, ran an article from an Alton paper – doubtless sent by G. W. Brown – claiming that one of Lovejoy's assailants was later "chopped to pieces" by Indians while another had been "cut to pieces with a bowie-knife" in an "affray" in a New Orleans gambling house. Crimes must eventually be punished, Greene (or G. W. Brown) was saying. "The murderers of Dow, Barber, and [Reese] Brown will some day meet a fate commensurate with their guilt.... But if man never punishes them," Greene insisted, "God and nature will. No crime of any grade can be committed with impunity. Suffering follows guilt.... It is a law ordained by God, and no man can escape it."[19]

The *Herald of Freedom* stories must have awakened in John Brown memory of the 1837 Lovejoy prayer meeting in Hudson at which he and his father had pledged their lives to the fight against slavery. Now, as his father lay dying, John knew that he himself had not fulfilled that pledge. He must also have known that Owen might not live to see, as John put it in a letter to Owen dated March 26, "the triumph of that cause you have laboured to promote." The idea that God punished evil was an article of John's faith, and Owen's jeremiads were painful reminders that God's punishment was impending. Now, the Missourians menacing Lawrence were also threatening the moral order of God. The long arm of the Slave Power had reached not only into Kansas, but into John Brown's tortured imagination. Arriving with the Pottawatomie Rifles too late to save Lawrence, he looked around urgently for a way to redeem his pledge.

II

If the signals from Lawrence stirred Brown, dangers nearer home played a part in his decision to strike. The second point in Adair's account was that the slain men threatened the Browns and their free-state neighbors. The threats presumably explain why Brown marked for death the Doyles, the Sherman brothers, Wilkinson, and perhaps two or three others who escaped his anger. Brown's purpose was not merely to hit adversaries before they hit him. It was to create a "restraining fear" among all of their kind who harbored plans against antislavery men in Franklin County. In this version, Brown's foray was a preemptive strike.

Certainly rumored threats abounded in 1856, though historians have not credited the claim that the Browns and their families were in imminent danger. Even Brown's admiring biographer, Oswald Garrison Villard, who examined "fully 55 narratives" of old Kansas settlers, could not "justify" Pottawatomie as "lynch law" or credit the contention that the Browns were in danger, and he dismissed it as a "fabrication" of Brown's defenders.[20] But in his eagerness to vindicate the view of his grandfather William Lloyd Garrison that moral suasion alone was permissible in the cause of social reform, Villard lost sight of the question whether the threats seemed credible to the Browns in 1856. With that question in mind, a modern biographer, Stephen B. Oates, finds "quite convincing" the evidence that the "Wilkinson-Sherman-Doyle faction" threatened their free-state rivals. But he also believes that the free-state majority dismissed the threats as bluff. Oates observes that the thirty-four men who left the Browns' neighborhood to defend Lawrence against the Missourians would not have done so had they felt their families threatened.[21]

New evidence invites a different assessment of these judgments. Brown's sons and his Kansas allies rested their later defense of Brown chiefly on threats against the family and its free-state neighbors. In so doing, they focused largely on three stories.

The first story was that of the "Surveying Spies." On different occasions years after the event, Salmon and John Brown, Jr., and one of Brown's Kansas friends, E. A. Coleman, each told this tale of daring detective work in the camp of the enemy. On May 2, 1856, as already noted, Major Jefferson Buford of Alabama rode into the Territory at the head of an armed force of 400 prospective settlers from Georgia and Alabama, and camped on Indian lands near Pottawatomie. Although Buford's men soon dispersed to find claims, they routinely assembled in shows of force near the homes of free-state settlers. In that atmosphere rumors spread that they intended to kill or burn out free-soilers. A few days before the raid on Lawrence, so the story goes, John Brown and three of his sons, including Salmon, "disguised" themselves as government surveyors and audaciously ran a line through Buford's encampment in order to learn the Southerners' plans. At the time the proslavery legislature appointed government surveyors, and Buford's men presumably assumed that the surveyors were proslavery despite their Yankee accents. In fact, some of the Georgians freely boasted to them of their determination to make Kansas a slave state. "One thing we will do before we leave," Salmon recalled one of them saying, "we'll clear out the damned Brown crowd."[22] They would "whip, drive out, or kill" all abolitionists, including "them damned Browns," another declared. In

Coleman's version, Brown carefully ran his line past the cabins of his enemies and got them to betray their plans by himself complaining about the abolitionists in the area. Then, peering through his surveyor's compass and waving to his flagman, he wrote down precisely what each of the settlers had threatened to do. Since the bullies had "committed murder in their hearts," Brown supposedly told Coleman, "I felt justified in having them killed."[23]

Even if this story were credible, it loses some of its punch when one recalls that the men slain at Pottawatomie were not Buford's newcomers. The Browns who told this tale insisted that the Doyles, Sherman, and Wilkinson had aided the Georgians, just as they had earlier helped Missourians bent on driving free-soilers from the territory. In effect, the slain men were allies of Buford and guilty by association.

This tale is the most direct "evidence" that the Browns themselves were about to be attacked. "We had ... abundant and satisfactory evidence that our family were marked for destruction," John, Jr., told Franklin Sanborn years after the event in the earliest version of the Surveying Spies story. Perhaps sensing the lack of moral weight in the argument that the Browns had merely struck first, and eager to refute the charge that the Browns had acted out of vengeance, John, Jr., added, "The blow struck was for Kansas and the slave"; it was not a mere "settlement of accounts with a few proslavery desperadoes."[24] The dilemma these statements reveal was ethical. To claim Pottawatomie as a blow for the cause, John, Jr., could not let it be seen as clan warfare; but to justify the choice of victims, he needed concrete grounds for what his father did.

The second story about Brown's motivation better satisfies this moral dilemma. It concerns a Michigan settler, Old Squire Morse, who lived with his two young sons on a claim a short walk from Dutch Henry's Crossing. In 1860 James Hanway, an Ohio emigrant who had served in the Rifles and was later one of Brown's chief defenders, first mentioned threats Brown's victims had made against John G. Morse and others. He did so in a letter to Redpath protesting untruths and inaccuracies in Redpath's biography of Brown.[25] But the Squire Morse story was not detailed publicly until 1879, when a Lawrence newspaper reporter interviewed another old free-state settler, George Grant. At the time Grant had been a youth living with his father, John T. Grant, on land near Squire Morse's claim, and he knew Morse well.

When news that Missourians were threatening Lawrence reached Franklin County in May 1856, free-state men in Osawatomie and along the Pottawatomie began arming themselves. Morse sold the Grants several bars of lead for making bullets. When Frederick Brown carried this lead to the Grants' cabin, he had passed Dutch Henry's house. There, the Doyles and William Sherman became incensed when he answered their queries by telling them that the lead was to be used for free-state bullets.[26] The morning after the Pottawatomie Rifles left for Lawrence, Wilkinson, James Doyle, Doyle's two oldest sons, and Dutch Bill Sherman showed up in front of Morse's house, displayed a hangman's rope, and threatened to hang him for helping their enemies. They further demanded that Morse leave the territory before eleven o'clock that morning. At that hour, several of them returned, half drunk, threatening this time to kill Morse with an axe. The tears and pleas of Morse's young sons saved him, but the intruders again warned Morse to leave the territory, this time by sundown. Terrified, he fled to the Grants' house for protection, where Henry Sherman soon appeared and threatened not only Morse but the Grants as well. To escape his tormenters, Morse hid for several nights in the high prairie grass, but soon after, according to George Grant's recollection, died of a "violent illness" caused by the ordeal.[27] Thus, when Brown killed at Pottawatomie, he was avenging John Morse as well as others.

Like the Morse Story, tales of the offenses of proslavery men against free-state women also appeared early in Brown's defense. In December 1859 Richard J. Hinton, a young follower and later a biographer of Brown, told the first such tale, citing in a Boston newspaper a "fiendish attempt [by James Doyle and others] to outrage the persons of Capt. Brown's daughter and daughter-in-law."[28] Redpath picked up the story and repeated it in his celebratory 1860 biography, embellishing it with references to the "grossest indignities" suffered by Brown's daughter and daughter-in-law. In so doing, he evidently confused, as had Hinton, one of John's daughters-in-law with his daughter, Ruth Brown Thompson, who was never in Kansas.[29]

Another story with sexual overtones concerned the daughter of John T. Grant, who helped run bullets for free-state men. Franklin Sanborn first printed this story, involving Mary Grant, in his 1885 biography of Brown. One of Sanborn's correspondents implicated "Dutch Bill" Sherman, one of the Pottawatomie victims, in threats against the Browns. The tale is noteworthy because it links Mary Grant with Brown's ill-fated son, Frederick, a handsome, emotionally unstable six-footer then twenty-five years old. Rumored imbecilic, Frederick Brown was actually a bright, conscientious youth who won election to the free-state legislature only to be murdered before assuming his seat. Quoting an aged Kansas settler, Sanborn reported that Dutch Bill had been spurned by "the daughter of one of his Free-State neighbors" – in context, an obvious reference to Mary Grant – and then used "vile and insulting language" toward her because of the rejection. Mary had then allegedly asked Frederick for protection when the two of them confronted Dutch Bill brandishing a knife and demanding "You shall marry me or I'll drive this knife to the hilt until I find your life."[30]

Another version of this story has Dutch Bill forcing his way into the Grant home after the Rifles had left to defend Lawrence and attempting to assault Mary. In this account, the Grants sent a messenger – one of Mary's brothers – to the Rifles' encampment near Prairie City to urge the men to return to protect the women. In 1908 Mary Grant herself told a less melodramatic story at her home in San Jose, California. As she recalled, "Dutch Bill arrived at our house, one day, horribly drunk, with a whiskey bottle with a corncob stopper, and an immense butcher knife in his belt." Mary's father, John T. Grant, who was sick in bed, had his shotgun at his bedside and an armed neighbor present to guard him. "'Old woman,' said Bill Sherman to my mother, [Mary Grant recalled] 'you and I are pretty good friends, but damn your daughter. I'll drink her heart's blood.'" Mary's "little brother, Charley, a mere boy of twelve or fourteen," defused the potential confrontation when he persuaded Sherman to go home. Frederick Brown had had nothing to do with the incident. But Mary did remember that Frederick had asked her repeatedly about the incident before the Rifles left for Lawrence.[31] Whether young Brown was engaged to Mary Grant, as his half-sister Annie Brown Adams later claimed, is uncertain. But it is clear that Frederick had more than a passing interest in her.

John Brown's defenders cited other "outrages" in justifying Pottawatomie. But these three stories just noted were the principal ones they used to explain the timing and defensive nature of the killings. The validity of all three stories, however, depends almost entirely on the accuracy of memories gathered more than a quarter century after the events they describe. The first of the stories, the Surveying Spies story, relied ultimately on the word of the Browns themselves, and was persuasive only to the persuaded.[32] Those who remembered how long the family suppressed information about John's responsibility for the slayings were unpersuaded. The credibility of the Squire Morse and Mary Grant Stories demands a precision lost in the disparities of their tellings. The several versions of them disagree on vital details, including how word of the alleged proslavery offenses reached Brown and his men at Prairie City. There had to be a messenger or messengers.

Henry H. Williams, James Hanway, and others remembered just such a messenger arriving; even Townsley recalled hearing about a messenger, though he saw no messenger himself. Some of the Rifles later thought the messenger was George Grant, but he had marched with the Rifles on May 22, while others offered different names.[33] Salmon Brown, on the other hand, insisted that no one summoned the Browns to return to their families. For the stories of the dangers to Squire Morse and the Brown women to be convincing, moreover, the messenger had to arrive before noon on Friday, May 23, the day after the Rifles' departure and the day John decided to return. The "outrages" had to have occurred after the Rifles had marched off to war; otherwise, Brown and the others would not have left their women and neighbors defenseless. The messenger therefore had a narrow time frame during which to act. The sinews of the stories thus seem frail indeed.

Such reminiscences are likely to be heavily rescripted. They may be mistaken in crucial details even when their gists are true. That is the case here. There is a contemporary document that lends credence to the Squire Morse and Mary Grant stories. Less than three weeks after Pottawatomie, while witnesses swore affidavits against Brown before a Congressional committee, Dr. Lucius Mills, a cousin of John Brown, was gathering evidence against Brown's victims. Brown later listed Mills as a "worthy Free State man" who deserved financial compensation for "sacrifices" on behalf of the cause in Kansas, even though Mills had refused to fight. In an undated memo to the agent of the Massachusetts Kansas Committee, probably written in 1857, Brown observed that Mills "devoted some months to the Free State cause collecting & giving information" as well as "prescribing for & nursing the sick & wounded at his own cost."[34] Among Mills's services, apparently, was interviewing Francis Morse, one of the Squire's sons, as well as John T. Grant and his son William, and Mrs. Orson Day, Brown's sister-in-law. A copy of the dated and signed interviews, in Mills's hand, is in the Adair Papers recently donated to the Kansas State Historical Society. Whether Brown sent Mills to collect evidence against his victims in order to justify the killings is an open question. It is also unclear in just what venue such testimony might have been useful. What is apparent is that the Browns' later charges against the Doyles, the Shermans, and Wilkinson find a degree of support in Mills's statements.[35]

On June 12, 1856, Squire Morse's son Francis told Mills that James Doyle, Thomas McMinn, and Henry Sherman had come to Morse's house about noon three or four days before Pottawatomie. "They called themselves a committee and they told him if he did not leave that day before sundown they would burn his house. They [also] called him hard names," the boy continued. "Doyle said they would burn the house as sure as he had an axe in his hand, which he did." During the encounter, Sherman declared that Morse "wasn't a law-abiding man to give lead away to kill folks with."

Assuming its authenticity, this statement confirms that Squire Morse was threatened because of his aid to the Grants and the Browns. It also explains why during the massacre Brown and his party asked the whereabouts of McMinn. If the threat to Morse had occurred three or four days before Pottawatomie, as the boy remembered, the Browns may have known of it before they went to the relief of Lawrence. The timing here is crucial; if Brown knew about the threat to Morse before he left for Lawrence, no messenger was necessary to inform them of the danger. Brown might have talked up the incident in camp after he learned that the Rifles had arrived too late to save Lawrence and the company was debating what to do next. But if the danger to Morse was unknown to Brown when the Rifles moved out, both Francis Morse and William Grant, previously unmentioned in accounts of the incident, were old enough to have ridden to the Rifles to get help.

John T. Grant, the father of William Grant, had lived with the Shermans when he came to the territory, but his allegiances were clearly those of a free-stater. On June 12 he told Dr. Mills that William and Henry Sherman were heavy drinkers, and that William especially often got into drunken brawls. Allen Wilkinson, who lived a few rods distant from the Shermans, Grant added, was a "man of bad disposition and evil temper." In Grant's presence Wilkinson said to "a man named Morse," concerning an apparent insult, "If you have said so I'll be damned if I don't rip you!" "At a settlers meeting last summer," Grant went on, "Wilkinson drew his pocket knife evidently intending to use it in a trifling quarrel." In this signed statement Grant not only blackened the names of the murdered men, but refuted the testimony of Mrs. Harris who had "told me and my family the next day [after Pottawatomie] that she did not know any of the men concerned in the murder and had no suspicion of any particular person or persons. The next day after the murder of Allen Wilkinson," Grant continued, "I heard Mrs. Wilkinson, his widow, say that she did not know any of the men concerned in the affair." Apparently Grant was trying to discredit Brown's accusers.

Grant's youngest son, William, told of frightening experiences with William and Henry Sherman:

Early in the last Spring William Sherman called at my father's house a good deal intoxi-cated with a bottle in his pocket and a bowie knife in his belt and threatened that he would cut out the damned black hearts of my father my oldest brother and sister [Mary]. The next morning I called on an errand at the Shermans; William was on the roof of an outhouse he called to me swinging his bowie knife and threatening to cut my damned throat before I got out of the yard. Henry came up to me and declared he would whip my father brother and sister like hell.

Mills evidently gathered these statements to prove that the slain men had threat-ened free-state families. What lends a measure of credibility to the statements already quoted is the statement of Mary Day, the wife of Brown's brother-in-law, Orson Day. Mrs. Day's statement is so circumspect that it could hardly have helped exonerate her kinsmen. The day after Pottawatomie, she said, eight men had stopped at her house and stayed for supper. Mrs. Day did not say who they were or whence they came, although she acknowledged that later "they had gone to Browns Station." She had no knowledge of the "murderers," she said.

This curiously opaque statement suggests either that Mary Day did not know the man who questioned her – her in-law, Dr. Mills – which is very unlikely – or that she was eager not to become involved in the turmoil Pottawatomie had created. If the eight men had been Brown's Pottawatomie party, as surely they were, they included several who had finished construction of the cabin into which she had recently moved, among them Henry Thompson and John Brown himself.[36] If Mills or Adair had hoped Mrs. Day would provide an alibi for John and his sons, they must have been disappointed.

Ironically, Mrs. Day's statement does refute the premise of those writers who have questioned the sons' claims that they had feared for their families. Those writers have alleged that Brown and his men made no effort to determine the safety of their women either before or after the killings.[37] On the morning after Pottawatomie, their accounts allege, the Browns rested in a wooded ravine from which they went directly to rejoin the Rifles encamped at Ottawa Jones's. But Mrs. Day's statement suggests, to the contrary, that not only did Brown and his men appear at her home at midday, but that the wives and children of John, Jr., and Jason had been sent there during the absence of the men. Only after checking on their wives and children had the Brown party proceeded to Brown's Station.

In a neglected reminiscence of those crucial days, Brown's son Owen may have confirmed Mary Day's statement. "The day before the Potawatomie executions the party left John [Jr.'s] camp in the forenoon... and they got to the Brown settlement, perhaps to Pottawatomie." After the killings, Owen remembered, they "rested all that day near Morse's house" and on the following day went into camp "not far from Orson Day's house."[38] Owen's memory may have reversed the sequence of these movements, but the absence of references to either of the Browns' visits to their families before and after Pottawatomie in Townsley's "confession" may reflect nothing more than that the stops seemed unrelated to the killings. Only in the twentieth century did this question gain significance.[39]

What can we conclude from the disjointed statements recorded by Mills? First, it must be acknowledged that the statements themselves are tainted by Mills's relationship to Brown. There is no record of what Mills asked those he interviewed or of who may have been present at the time or in what circumstances Mills conducted the interviews. There is therefore no way of knowing whether the interviewees were truthful and forthcoming or told Mills what his leading questions implied they should tell him. In any case, Mills and perhaps all of his witnesses were clearly friendly to Brown. The very disconnected quality of the statements in the Mills interviews, on the other hand, suggests that the interviewees were unrehearsed. The statements appear authentic, however they were obtained. Since Mills left the territory soon after Pottawatomie, moreover, we may conclude that he gathered them not long after the killings; indeed, the June 12 written on the copy dates them just three weeks after the incident. Finally, the recollections of Francis Morse and William Grant corroborate aspects of the stories discussed earlier about Squire Morse and Mary Grant.

Even if true, however, the stories of Morse and Grant hardly added up to the "base conspiracy ... to drive out, burn, and kill" free-staters Hanway wrote of four years later.[40] In the days before Pottawatomie, the Doyles, Shermans, and Wilkinson had burned Weiner's store and driven Morse into the brush. Did Brown believe they would go further, even strike at Brown's Station itself? Adair's letters again provide a clue. On May 16, a week before the killings, with Lawrence menaced and John, Jr.'s men preparing to march to its defense, Adair sent "Father Brown" a summary of the course of recent affairs, unaware that Owen had recently died. "Some think we are as much in danger here as they are at Lawrence," Adair wrote. "John is of the number, and is unwilling to go without more reliable information.... Rumor says that a company of armed men were seen yesterday in a grove on Indian lands, a few miles from here. Some are alarmed and much excited."[41] That at least some of the Browns feared that proslavery men might attack free-state women is suggested by a remark of Jason's in a letter to North Elba a month after Pottawatomie. "No women have been injured yet; so far as I know," Jason began. "Some of the five pro-slavery men who were killed had threatened the lives of Free State men near them; and also to cut the throat of a young woman, a neighbor."[42]

When John Brown decided to leave the settlement and march with the Rifles to save Lawrence, he took Henry Thompson and his unmarried sons with him, putting the women and children under the protection of Orson Day, whose cabin was two or three miles closer to Osawatomie than Brown's Station.

Jason later testified that the women and children were sent to Osawatomie for safety, though he might well have confused Orson Day's with Adair's cabin.[43] But he was doubtless correct in remembering that the Browns had protected their familial flank.

The testimonies of Francis Morse and John and William Grant thus support Adair's thesis that John Brown struck at enemies of his family and his free-state friends. Indeed, the implication of these testimonies is that the killings reflected a kind of tribalism. We may thus surmise why the list of Brown's intended victims at Pottawatomie included McMinn and Henry Sherman, both of whom the Brown party tried to find. They too had made threats. Indeed, the thesis that the killings were reprisals for threats accounts for all the men marked for death.[44] It is true that Francis Morse did not mention John and Drury Doyle by name as among his father's tormenters. But if they were not parties to the intimidation of the elder Morse, Brown may have killed them to prevent retaliation. Had Brown found Henry Sherman or Thomas McMinn during the foray, he would surely have killed them too. Thus if Pottawatomie was a retaliatory blow in behalf of the free-state cause, it was also the climax of local quarrels, a preemptive strike in a clan vendetta.

III

Pottawatomie was also a "Family Massacre," a characterization meant to suggest that a sense of shame for the crime followed the conspirators to their graves.[45] But the killings were a family affair in a profounder sense. Four of John's sons and his son-in-law Henry Thompson were with him on the fatal night, and all shared his guilt as assassins or accomplices. Although Jason Brown, who was not there and who knew nothing of the plan, later told his father that Pottawatomie was a "wicked" act, he soon changed his mind, and like the other Browns defended the "necessity" of the killings.[46] After Jason's initial rebuke, none of the Browns ever publicly repudiated "father" or acknowledged his deed was wrong. The surviving sons later helped the family rationalize the killings as vital to saving Kansas for "freedom."[47] In old age Henry Thompson still insisted, his face flushed and his eyes filled with tears, "It was the best act that was ever done for Kansas."[48] But the family's long silence about the crime attested to a sense of complicity as well as a fear of public disapproval.

One of the little-recognized problems in fathoming Pottawatomie is to explain the participation of four of Brown's sons. Together with Henry Thompson and perhaps also the storekeeper Weiner, two or three of Brown's sons struck the lethal blows. If John Brown's fanaticism or "madness" inspired the act – the view of many historians[49] – why did his sons and son-in-law carry it out?

The two oldest sons did not participate. Neither of them knew what their father intended to do when he left the camp of the Pottawatomie Rifles. The first son, John, Jr., thirty-four, was in command of the Rifles when his father's men piled into Townsley's wagon and headed back to the Pottawatomie, with Weiner following on his pony. Brown's second son, Jason, thirty-three, who was too "tenderhearted" to kill even small game animals, also remained at the Prairie City camp. Later accounts suggest that John, Jr., did not want his father to detach members of the militia from Prairie City when the men might yet be needed to fight the "ruffians." But it may have been fear for the safety of his wife and little boy that led John, Jr., to warn his father to do nothing "rash" as the Old Man left the Pottawatomies' camp.[50]

The actual killings were the work of John's red-bearded third son, Owen, thirty-one, a sometimes solitary "eccentric" with a "crippled" right arm; another son, Salmon, a pugnacious nineteen-year-old; son-in-law Henry Thompson; and probably Weiner.[51] Frederick Brown, a sensitive, handsome twenty-five-year-old who suffered brief, recurrent episodes of disturbed behavior,[52] stood watch with Townsley during the attack. Although accounts differ, Brown's strapping youngest son, Oliver, also probably killed no one. By the sons' later testimony, Brown himself took no part in the killing, firing his revolver only once – into the forehead of the already dead James Doyle.[53]

If Brown himself was "crazy," as some have alleged, what were the motives of his sons? Must they have been disturbed or unbalanced to butcher their victims? Is "madness" the most plausible explanation for so shocking a crime when committed by hitherto peaceable men? Clearly, that idea fails in this instance. No one has argued plausibly that Owen, Salmon, and Henry Thompson – or Weiner, for that matter – were mad.[54] Nor has anyone claimed they were religious fanatics. In fact, all of Brown's sons rejected his evangelical faith. Owen, the most loyal of them, was estranged from his stepmother precisely because of his avowed skepticism. He had in fact left his father's home – and his stepmother's presence – for that reason. The apostasy of his sons had been a "sore disappointment" to Brown for years. In 1853 he had complained bitterly that "my younger sons" had recently discovered that the Bible was "*all* – a fiction." John, Jr.'s apostasy was a special cause of "pain and sorrow,"[55] and Brown could only hope that "my sons will give up their miserable delusions and believe in God and in his Son our Savior."[56] He was to be disappointed in this hope; only his oldest daughter, Ruth, embraced his faith during his lifetime. In his last days, as a prisoner awaiting the hangman after Harpers Ferry, Brown was still urging his sons to surrender to Jesus.

Despite the religious independence of the sons, some historians have explained their complicity in Pottawatomie by suggesting that Brown dominated them so completely that in the turbulent politics of Kansas he nerved them to kill in spite of themselves. Following Oswald Garrison Villard, Stephen B. Oates elaborates this thesis in his influential biography, *To Purge This Land with Blood*.[57] By the time Brown proposed the strike at Pottawatomie, Oates says, his "hold" over Henry Thompson and his unmarried sons "had become unbreakable, like a spell. Even Oliver and Frederick, who did not relish the grisly work ahead, obeyed the old man without question," while Owen and Salmon, who were more willing to fight, easily succumbed to his "thrilling pronouncements" about defending the cause. When Frederick and Oliver "balked" at the butchery the assassinations would require, their father, "his eyes shining obstinately, forced them all back to his side with his implacable and domi-neering will." Brown spent the rest of the evening of the twenty-third and the whole of the following day, Oates claims, exhorting the men to "strike terror in the hearts of the proslavery people." By that evening Weiner, Owen, Salmon, and Henry were "as worked up as [John] was and anxious to get on with the mission."[58]

This argument fails on two counts. First, the sources do not support it. There are reminiscent accounts by four participants – James Townsley, Owen and Salmon Brown, and Henry Thompson – each of which must be used cau-tiously. All of them were heavily rescripted – altered by time and retelling – when they surfaced publicly decades after Pottawatomie. Those of Thompson and the two Browns, for example, dispute that of Townsley on key points. In any event, these narratives, separately or collectively, do not provide sufficient evidence to sustain Oates's melodramatic argument. Townsley's "confession" suggests that he at least was not under Brown's spell. In fact, Townsley claimed that the attack was postponed a whole day because he had been unwilling to lead Brown to the cabins of his victims, who were Townsley's neighbors. But as Villard pointed out long ago, Weiner, the local storekeeper at Dutch Henry's Crossing, knew the neighborhood much better than Townsley knew it. Thus, Brown did not have to wait for Townsley to get on with the raid.

The delay Townsley spoke of did occur. Perhaps the men rested Friday night because they were exhausted from the overnight march with the Rifles two nights before, or perhaps they needed time to get their bearings or to work out details of the raid. Perhaps they had to wait until their victims were at home, as Salmon later stated.[59] In any case, they delayed until it was dark in order to conceal their movements from the men they intended to kill. Their purpose, after all, was to kill by stealth, not to provoke an open fight. Townsley does not claim that he challenged Brown for long; he says only that Brown "refused" to let him take his team and "go home." Townsley may have had his differ-ences with Brown, but he was surely no prisoner of the Browns, as his account implied. During the attack, by his own account, he dispatched one of James Doyle's dogs "with my sabre."[60] If Brown had been suspicious of him, he need not have entrusted Townsley with one of the swords.

In evidence of dissension among Brown's sons at the time of the raid, Oates cites the statement of an "unnamed member of the party" reprinted in Franklin Sanborn's admiring biography of Brown. The source of this statement is unmis-takably Owen, the text of whose interview with Sanborn, in Sanborn's own hand, is in the Houghton Library at Harvard. Evidently to conceal the source of the statement, Sanborn altered it slightly in his biography. Even in the altered version, however, it lends little support to Oates's interpretation. From the out-set Owen agreed with his father that killing was "a matter of duty," though he was at first "opposed to doing it myself." He recognized the "inconsistency" in this position, he recalled, and "afterwards acted consistently."[61] Owen also conceded that Frederick was opposed to the killing, but said nothing about further discussion between the sons and their father. In two separate versions of the raid, Salmon mentioned no discussions before the strike and gave no indication that any of the sons except Frederick ever had any doubts about the justice of the killings.

The Browns thus returned to the Pottawatomie to "protect our people" from the Doyles and their ilk, who were "as low down dogs as men ever get to be," in Salmon words.[62] Salmon made no apologies for Bloody Pottawatomie. Henry Tompson also remembered no debate before the massacre. Townsley was a "southerner" who had volunteered for the mission but "chickened out" on the way, Henry claimed.[63] The surviving Browns dismissed Townsley's statement, made in 1879, as self-serving and even cowardly. Throughout their later years, Owen and Salmon Brown as well as Henry Thompson affirmed the terrifying deed as their own.

A second reason for dismissing the idea that Brown had some kind of unnatural hold over his sons and son-in-law is the manifest independence all of Brown's sons had displayed at one time or another. Of the sons in Kansas, only Oliver, who apparently declined to kill at Pottawatomie, still made his home with "father." Brown had long since acknowledged his sons' freedom from filial obligation. Though several of them aided him in his business venture with Simon Perkins, he expected them to make their own decisions. In 1854, when John, Jr., raised the possibility of moving from Ohio to Essex County to be near his father, Brown cautioned: "I would like to have all my children settle within a few Miles of *each other; & of me* but I cannot take the responsibility of advising you to make any *forced* move to change your location. Thousands have to regret that they did not let *midling* 'well alone.'"[64] Soon thereafter, Brown advised John, Jr., against moving to Kansas, fearing, the latter recalled, "the debilitating influence of milder climates, [and] of the comparatively easy methods by which treasures could be laid up on earth."[65] The decision in 1854 of his older sons to migrate to Kansas was taken without his consent or his serious objection. Although they asked Brown's assistance after they got there and fell on hard times, the sons who moved to Kansas were their own men.

Salmon and Oliver, sons of Brown's second wife, Mary Day Brown, had been defiant even while growing up and were always willing to stand up to their father.[66] Fearless and impetuous, Brown's youngest son, Oliver, was occasionally verbally abusive even to his mother and siblings.[67] Just sixteen when he went to Kansas, Oliver had "rebelled against his father's authority, outright, so that Brown had to recognize him as a man with a man's individuality," his sister Sarah remembered.[68] "Oliver and father generally agreed," Salmon told an interviewer in 1908, "but Oliver was pretty hard to control. He was a great, stout, strapping fellow" who "felt his father could not run over him." As Brown and his younger sons left Kansas ten weeks after Pottawatomie, Oliver and his father had "an open battle," Salmon recalled. The quarrel was over a pistol Oliver wished to give to Lucius Mills, who had treated the gunshot wounds of Owen and Henry Thompson. Brown "did not like Lucien [sic] because he … would not fight," Salmon recalled, and, if Salmon may be believed, after a scuffle Oliver pinned his father against the side of a wagon and scolded him "to behave yourself" until Brown gave in.[69]

It is not clear, moreover, why John Brown was able to mesmerize Henry Thompson and his four sons, as Oates claims he did, either when encamped with the Rifles near Prairie City where he first revealed his plan to them or as they waited in the timber not far from Pottawatomie Creek for the moment to strike.[70] Brown had no formal command of his own and the free-state men had never heeded his advice. Indeed, on every point he disputed with his father before the company, John, Jr., had prevailed.[71] Why or how such defeats enhanced Brown's "spell" over four of his sons and his son-in-law is unclear unless they shared his wish to act against their proslavery "enemies."

The implicit premise of Oates's explanation is that the members of the party wielded their swords against their wills. Contemporary evidence suggests a simpler hypothesis: Brown's sons and son-in-law felt they had sufficient reasons to be at Pottawatomie, inasmuch as all of them shared a wish to punish the clan's proslavery enemies, though Frederick and Oliver Brown quarreled with their father over the morality of killing unarmed men. But if the two refused to wield their swords, they evidently did nothing to prevent the killings and certainly never repudiated Pottawatomie or expressed remorse for the suffering it caused. During the day before the massacre, they were four or five miles from their own claims and might have walked away to their homes had they wished to do so.

To be sure, some of Brown's sons were unnerved by Pottawatomie and its aftermath. Owen was "conscience-smitten" over his part in the killings and wept openly.[72] Years later he still acknowledged that "the antislavery people in the Territory disapproved of the killing, – Mr. Adair among them." But he also still defended the killings as essential to the survival of liberty.[73] John, Jr., and Jason had been dismayed at the news of the killings and at seeing their father and Salmon ride into the Rifles' camp on horses they knew belonged to the victims.[74] Some months later, after the Browns fled Kansas, all the boys renounced "warfare" altogether, declining even to support an effort to carry the war against slavery into "Africa."[75]

Before the killings, as they awaited the moment to strike, Brown's sons and son-in-law were persuaded of the necessity of their task. They had discussed it among themselves and they, like Frederick and Oliver, might well have refused to "execute" their enemies. Brown had not mesmerized them. On the contrary, Owen and Salmon Brown and Henry Thompson killed for the same calculated reasons that led Brown to urge them to. Their concern was not merely to placate Brown or win his approval. Rather they shared not only Brown's antislavery convictions but his family's imperatives to fight the institution. Above all, like Brown, they harbored a deep mistrust of their proslavery neighbors and a clear sense of imminent danger. Like other free-staters in the territory, they were enraged by the "sack" of Lawrence and the refusal of the territorial courts to punish the murderers of the free-state "martyrs."

Even before their father had come to Kansas, they had publicly repudiated the "bogus" laws of the proslavery territorial legislature and defied officials to

enforce them. Feeling threatened and spoiling for a fight, they organized themselves and their neighbors into military companies. Their experience established the terms of the family's relations with proslavery neighbors. When the
Old Man arrived in October 1855, John, Jr., was already a free-state legislator.
John Brown, Sr., brought with him his youngest son, Oliver, sixteen, and Henry
Thompson, a carpenter, thus adding skill as well as direction to the struggling
families at Osawatomie and Brown's Station. The first Brown migrants had
become so absorbed in the struggle against slavery that they had failed to provide their families with adequate shelter.

Evidence of the extremism of the younger Browns should not be overlooked.
Pottawatomie is their story too. "The boys have their feelings well worked up,
so that I think that they will fight," Salmon wrote his father in the spring of
1855. "I feel more like [a] fight now, than I ever did before."[76] That summer,
still before his father had reached Kansas, Salmon was angry that a free-state
man being held for a killing Salmon believed was committed in self-defense
could not get a fair trial. Salmon was "anxious" to rescue the man from jail.[77]
A month before John Brown reached Brown's Station, John, Jr., wrote his stepmother expressing his indignation that the Shawnee legislature had made it a
felony, punishable by "not less than two years" imprisonment, to speak, write,
or print opinions against slavery. "Yesterday I told a man who, I since learn,
has a slave here," John, Jr., boasted, "that no man had a right to hold a slave
in Kansas, that I called on him to witness that I had broken this law, and that I
still intend to do so at all times and at all places, and further that if any officer
should attempt to arrest me, for a violation of this law, and should put his villainous hands on me, I would surely kill him, so help me God."[78]

Soon after Brown's arrival, Frederick wrote his brother Watson that he saw
no immediate danger of fighting between proslavery and antislavery factions.
"There has been too many threats that have not been carried out for want of
grit," he said. "The fact is the Missourians will not stand fire."[79] Oliver Brown
was contemptuous of the "peace men, money lovers, fence riders and proslavery men" in the territory. By early 1856, he was as critical of the Wakarusa
settlement as his father had become: "Well you have undoubtedly heard of
the winding up of that blessed farce how it was settled by Lane & Robinson
without the least allusion to the bogus laws," Oliver wrote his mother and the
others at North Elba. "This was a half way done thing and never will answer
the purpose for which made. War again threatens Kansas and we expect every
day to be warned out to meet its call.... Though we are few in number it is
enough with our advantages to whip out all the men Misoura can Spare."[80] If
Brown's sons were less certain than he was of the manliness of their venture on
the Pottawatomie, they had been ready to fight for the cause months before the
"sack" of Lawrence.

The thesis that Brown mesmerized his sons into taking up his fight also fails
to account for the presence of Henry Thompson at Pottawatomie. Brown had
no hypnotic control over his son-in-law, who later declined to join him in carrying the war against slavery into Virginia. But like Brown's sons, Thompson was

committed to the cause. In April, five weeks before Pottawatomie, he received a letter from his wife begging him to return to Essex County. "It is a great trial to me to stay away from you," Thompson responded. "But I am here and I feel I have a sacrifice to make, a duty to perform. Can I leave that undone, and have a conscience void of offence. Should I ever feel that I had not put my hand to the plough and looked back?"[81]

At Pottawatomie, Thompson was prepared to use his broadsword, and apparently did. Salmon recalled years later that Thompson and his friend, Theodore Weiner, had cut down both William Sherman and Allen Wilkinson, though Townsley claimed that the "younger Browns" had slain both men. Salmon implicitly acknowledged killing James Doyle and one of his sons; thus it is difficult to believe he wanted to deflect responsibility for killing others onto Thompson. Still, if the party divided after slaying the Doyles, as Salmon contended, Thompson could hardly have killed both of the other victims. In old age, Thompson himself finally wrote a full account of the killings for a trusted friend, but his daughter Mary, then a schoolteacher in Pasadena, California, fearing for her family's reputation, destroyed it.[82] In 1908 Thompson gave a guarded interview to Villard's research assistant, reaffirming his conviction that Pottawatomie had saved Kansas.[83] That he had bloody hands there seems likely, but the fact cannot be certainly established.

What is certain is that Thompson was at Pottawatomie for his own reasons. Soon after he arrived in the territory, Thompson found a job at the store owned jointly by Weiner and two other Austrian Jews, August Bondi and Jacob Benjamin. For $20 a month he cooked, cut wood, and did other chores for Weiner while he lived alone in a cabin about twenty rods behind the store, where he slept with a six-shooter and a squirrel rifle at his side. The friendship between Thompson and his employers became stronger when, on January 24, 1856, local residents held a "settler's meeting" to discuss the case of a "claim-jumper" who had taken up residence on land Jacob Benjamin claimed. The settlers decided to evict the intruder, and the following day Thompson, John, Jr., Oliver, and Frederick Brown went to the man's cabin, knocked in his door, and "turned him out." Thompson stood by, revolver in hand, "ready to shoot if necessary." The claim-jumper, he reported to his wife, "went off threatening vengeance."[84] In later years, Thompson contended that the squatter was "old man White,"[85] the same Rev. Martin White who led the posse that burned Osawatomie to the ground on August 30, 1856. Whoever the evicted man was and whatever the merits of his claim, Thompson had linked the Browns irrevocably with Weiner and his partners. When the Shermans burned Weiner's store, they invoked this implicit compact.

IV

Adair's third suggestion – that John Brown intended the slayings to terrify the proslavery faction – is consistent with the evidence. In fact, in some respects the slayings anticipated latter-day terrorism – acts of violence designed to produce political change by inspiring widespread fear.[86] In Adair's view, Brown had done just that in his Sabbath eve attack, committing an act unprecedented in character as well as impact. The earlier murders of free-state men had been disturbing enough, but the "murderers" had killed one settler at a time and none of them struck by stealth. As terrifying as were the images of Kikapoo Rangers allegedly dancing wildly around Captain Reese Brown brandishing their hatchets, R. P. Brown had been an obvious target of their wrath. The day before his capture, he had commanded a party that exchanged fire with pro-slavery men, killing one of them. Pottawatomie was much more chilling and it was calculated for effect. "Five pro-slavery men were shot or butchered in one night," Adair told the family in Hudson, "taken from their beds and almost literally heived to pieces with broad swords." They "were probably dreaming of no danger to themselves," Adair suggested; they had had no public quarrel with Brown, indeed they knew their assailant only by reputation. No familiar explanation made their deaths comprehensible.

Adair realized that Pottawatomie was likely to inspire widespread fear because of the apparent randomness of the killings. He believed that proslavery men now "took alarm & fled" or "gathered together or stood in fear of their lives." He understood therefore that Pottawatomie might be but the first such episode, and in the fight free-state men would not be "particular" whom they kill so long as the victim "has made himself officious in Kansas matters." Like Adair himself, many free-state residents had taken to the bush at night after Pottawatomie, watching for approaching raiding parties. Pottawatomie threatened to let loose the dogs of war.[87]

In later years the Browns claimed explicitly that they intended Pottawatomie to generate a "restraining fear" in the proslavery faction. Townsley recalled that they meant the killings not merely to remove dangerous individuals. When he told Brown that he objected to what they were about to do, Brown replied, in Townsley's account, that "it must be done for the protection of the Free State settlers; that the pro-slavery party must be terrified, and that it was better that a score of bad men should die than that one man who came here to make Kansas a free State should be driven out."[88] Such vivid recollections are notoriously subject to error, and Townsley's reported exchange with Brown may have been a false memory. By the time he made that recollection public, twenty-three years after Pottawatomie, the claim that the killings were intended to create terror in the proslavery camp was hardly new, and Townsley's recollections may well have been influenced by restatements of that idea.

But the method and timing of Pottawatomie lend credibility to the essentials of Townsley's account. Brown had long known that fear itself was a political weapon. In this as in other things, his thinking was inspired by biblical accounts. Brown relished the story of Gideon's rout of the Midianites, which was accomplished at night by terrorizing the sleeping enemy with trumpet blasts, shattering pitchers, and flashing lamps.[89] The influence of this story on Brown was evident as early as 1851, when he organized the United States League of Gileadites, a group of Springfield African Americans concerned about the Fugitive Slave

Act. Brown urged blacks to surprise the authorities when rescuing accused runaways, to conceal their weapons, and to make "clean work with your enemies,"
insisting that "all with them will be confusion and terror."[90]

In our own time, when terrorist incidents are commonplace, the idea that
Brown intended the Pottawatomie massacre to intimidate his foes seems plausible. But it is anachronistic to speak of "terrorism" in antebellum America.
Despite mob attacks on abolitionists, Mormons, or Irish "Papists," the frontier
tradition of vigilantism, and the terror implicit in the perpetuation of slavery,
no doctrine – or rationalization – equivalent to that undergirding modern terrorism had been articulated.[91] Yet if terrorists are individuals or groups who
use clandestine violence to gain political objectives, then Brown and others
who followed his example in Kansas may be seen as among their precursors.

To be sure, Brown was no modern terrorist. His mission on the Pottawatomie
grew spontaneously out of the Lawrence crisis and at the time he apparently
then had no articulated, long-term objectives. Nor did Brown and his party
have a high degree of organization. The improvised band had no formal command structure and no political wing. Brown identified his men as they forced
their way into the cabins of the Doyles and Shermans as the "northern army."
After Pottawatomie, Brown's men became a guerrilla band fighting openly
against proslavery militias and federal posses, whereas terrorists by definition
avoid direct military confrontation. The line between terrorism, political violence, and guerrilla warfare is not easily drawn even in our own times, and the
conflict in Kansas presents a bewildering mosaic of violence that defies precise
labeling.[92]

During the Pottawatomie foray, Brown behaved in ways that readily distinguish him from modern terrorists. He and his men wore no masks, yet he
questioned and released two men and two women who might later identify
him. One of these, James Harris, recognized Brown and his son Owen, both of
whom had seen the Doyles on several occasions and were likely to be recognized by Doyle's widow and surviving children. In deference to Mahala Doyle's
pleading, Brown spared sixteen-year-old John Doyle, who soon testified about
Pottawatomie before a Congressional investigating committee. Mrs. Louisa
Jane Wilkinson also recognized the voice of one of Brown's sons, yet Brown
not only spared her but on learning that she was sick, inquired whether she had
neighbors to help her now that her husband was dead.[93] Although remorseless
in the killings, Brown evidently saw himself – or wished to be seen – as chivalrous toward women and, in his own bizarre way, a just man. He questioned his
victims briefly and killed only the "guilty."

After the raid, Brown was equally careless about concealing his responsibility for it. Late the following day he and Owen boldly rode into the Rifles' camp
on horses they had taken in the raid and that they knew would be recognized.
Although Brown admitted to no one that he was responsible for Pottawatomie,
he let free-state men draw their own conclusions. Evidently he wished not
merely to strike terror, but to be known and feared as the agent of free-state
vengeance.

V

This brings us back to the question of how a deeply religious man like Brown could silence his conscience sufficiently to order murder. How could he believe himself chivalrous or just while taking men from their homes and families in the dead of night and butchering them? It defies moral sense that Brown could summarily order the deaths of three Doyles and spare a fourth. For if she needed her sixteen-year-old, the impoverished and uneducated Mrs. Doyle needed her husband and her other two sons even more. And that Brown should inquire about the welfare of the ailing Mrs. Wilkinson while seeing to the murder of her husband is just as bizarre.

Questions like these have intrigued scholars of twentieth-century terrorism, among them social psychologist Albert Bandura,[94] whose analysis of the issues they raise is especially instructive for the student of Pottawatomie. Terrorists make culpable acts honorable to themselves and their sympathizers through cognitive restructuring of the moral prohibition against killing, Bandura says, not by changing or trying to change their own or their fellow terrorists' personalities, drives, or fundamental beliefs. Bandura identifies six psychosocial "mechanisms of moral disengagement" that terrorists use to silence their own "self-sanctions" and placate the scruples of their supporters against committing destructive acts.

First, terrorists rationalize violence by putting it in the service of religious creeds, righteous ideologies, or national imperatives. Second, they try to compare their acts advantageously to allegedly more heinous acts or plots sponsored by an oppressive enemy. Thus, they may picture assassinations and bombings as the only measures available to oppressed people. Third, they may deflect or mitigate their sense of responsibility for the violence they commit by seeing themselves as instruments of impersonal forces over which they have no control. Fourth, they may blame their actions on the provocations of a third party, as when terrorists strike at Americans on grounds that the American government is complicit in the victimization of the terrorists' people. By blaming others or oppressive circumstances, terrorists not only absolve themselves from responsibility for their actions but feel self-righteous for having committed them. Fifth, through selective inattention to consequences, terrorists may disregard or distort the effects of their deeds. Finally, they dehumanize their victims by objectifying them into "savages" or "satanic fiends," or assigning them to other categories that render them incapable of suffering or responsive only to brute force. These "mechanisms" of moral disengagement are often interrelated and mutually reinforcing. Even for terrorists moral callousness may come only slowly and through a process of inculcating "revolutionary morality" to neutralize residual self-censure.[95]

All these devices may seem to be mere rationalizations, forms of lying to oneself. But Bandura insists that an individual cannot literally be at once deceiver and deceived. Rather, terrorists appease conscience by ignoring evidence inconsistent with their larger beliefs. True believers, they scrutinize their own arguments no more than those of their enemies; they know the truth.[96] Confronted with evidence that disputes their truth, they question its credibility, dismiss its relevance, or otherwise twist it to fit their worldview. Studies of self-deception show that people can be exceedingly resourceful in finding ways to keep themselves uninformed about unwelcome information. Thus, Bandura concludes, terrorist acts are better understood as deliberated applications of principle than as unrestrained actions against targets of opportunity.[97]

These insights help explain Brown's puzzling behavior at Pottawatomie. All of Bandura's "mechanisms of moral disengagement" appear to have been at work there. Like his sons, Brown had come to see the struggle in Kansas as a confrontation between freedom and proslavery "diabolism." For him nothing less than the fate of the republic and moral government under God was at stake, as his father's jeremiads kept reminding him. Similarly, Brown blamed the Missourians and their allies in Kansas for a pattern of oppression that had come to obsess him. He had "no desire ... to have the slave power cease from its acts of aggression," he had said in April. Quoting Deuteronomy, he declared, "Their foot shall slide in due time."[98] The attack on Lawrence and the roving bands of armed men he believed were killing, stealing cattle, and burning settlers' homes had inaugurated what G. W. Brown called a "reign of terror." For John Brown, "civil war" had erupted, and the responsibility for it lay with the "ruffians." The men he killed at Pottawatomie had menaced his friends, threatened Morse, burned out Weiner, and threatened to "cut out the heart" of Mary Grant and others in her family. By showing concern for Mahala Doyle and Jane Wilkinson, Brown distanced himself from such unspeakable acts.

In presenting himself as a representative of the "northern army," Brown implied that he was an agent of larger structural forces. After the raid, he told friends, as he later told his Virginia captors at Harpers Ferry, that he saw himself as an "instrument in the hands of God."[99] Brown also blamed circumstances for forcing his hand. He had seen the federal government and the territorial courts try to enforce "bogus laws" and arrest free-state legislators. He was persuaded that Buford's men intended to drive free-state men from the territory.[100] The "invasion" from Missouri in May confirmed his belief that his own family was "as much in danger" as the residents of Lawrence. For that reason, he averted his eyes from the consequences of the killings for the families of his victims. Inquiring whether a neighbor was available to nurse Louisa Jane Wilkinson through her illness hardly acknowledged the problems widowhood would bring her. The Browns' later insistence that Allen Wilkinson beat his wife implied that Louisa was well rid of him, but no one was bold enough to claim that she welcomed his death. Finally, Brown viewed his victims as brutal and depraved, thus dehumanizing them and exculpating himself and his sons from blame for their deaths by insisting that the Doyles and the Shermans of this world understand only "war to the knife." The perceived threat to the Brown clan of Southern migrants camped on Ottawa lands just to the north of their claims and at "Little Georgia" just below Dutch Henry's Crossing encouraged insecurity, bred rumors, fostered stereotyping, and invited projection.

Bandura's theoretical mechanisms of moral disengagement thus illuminate the moral blindness that sanctioned Pottawatomie for Brown and his sons. Yet Brown's refuge from his bloody deed was not entirely psychological. In firing a bullet into the brain of the dead James Doyle, he joined in the bloodletting himself. Controversy long raged over when and why Brown shot Doyle, and whether Doyle was dead when Brown did so. "Old John Brown drew his revolver and shot the old man Doyle in the forehead," Townsley claimed in 1879, "and Brown's two youngest sons fell upon the younger Doyles with their short two-edged swords."[101] This testimony does not account for the deep stab wound in Doyle's breast, which would not have been inflicted if Doyle had fallen instantly from Brown's ball, and it is inconsistent with other accounts. Townsley, moreover, was some distance away, guarding the horses during the slayings. Salmon Brown insisted years later that "father never raised a hand in slaying the men. He shot a bullet into the head of old man Doyle about a half hour after he was dead, but what for I do not know. Perhaps it was to call Thompson and Winer so that they could locate us and we could all get together and return to our camp."[102]

In 1880, Owen Brown told Franklin Sanborn that his father had ordered that no shots be fired, since a shot might alarm the neighborhood and betray the raiders' presence. Owen had heard only one shot – fired "at least a mile away" – while he stood guard at Harris's cabin after the last victim was marched into the night. But Owen learned later that his father "fired a revolver to make sure that one of the party was dead – not one of the Doyles." Owen had not personally seen his father fire[103]; and his reminiscence clarifies little, since only James Doyle suffered a bullet wound during the "massacre."

Contemporary testimony again helps resolve the welter of contradictory evidence. Doyle's widow, Mahala, testified on June 7, 1856, that the armed intruders "first took my husband out of the house, then they took two of my sons." A "short time afterwards" the terrified woman thought she had heard two gunshots followed by moaning and a "wild whoop."[104] But how long was this "short" time?

The answer is provided by James Harris, the most credible of the contemporary witnesses. Like Brown's sons and Townsley, Harris in his home heard only a single shot. His testimony, given ten days after the massacre, establishes that the shot was fired a considerable time after the Doyles had been slain. Harris occupied a house owned by his employer, Henry Sherman, whose quarter section of land on Pottawatomie Creek was a mile from the Doyle claim on Mosquito Creek. Allen Wilkinson's claim and that of another settler separated the Doyle and Sherman properties. Assuming that the raiding party divided after killing the Doyles and that Brown himself jogged or walked briskly in the moonlight with Owen and others to Harris's cabin, crossing Mosquito Creek and abandoning the dirt road, they would have needed ten to fifteen minutes to reach Harris's cabin, where they lingered for some time. William Sherman and two men were spending the night at Harris's house when Brown's men, with "sabres" and revolvers drawn, burst into the room where Harris and his wife and child were sleeping. The intruders "ransacked" Harris's house in search of ammunition for two rifles they found and confiscated. Then they took one of Harris's "guests" outside for questioning. The Brown party searched the place a second time, still hoping to find Henry Sherman, who was still out on the prairie looking for stray cattle. Only then did they force Harris himself into the night to determine whether he had aided the Missourians. Satisfied that he had not, Brown returned Harris to the cabin and took William Sherman out, leaving two men to guard Harris and his two guests. "I heard nothing more for about fifteen minutes," Harris recalled. Brown's guards left when "we heard a cap burst."[105]

The next morning Harris found Sherman with his skull split in two places, "a large hole ... in his breast," and his left hand cut off, suggesting that Sherman tried to fend off his assailants. Like Wilkinson, he had no bullet wound. Thus, Harris's account suggests that Brown left Dutch Henry's property just as, or just after, his men hacked "Dutch Bill" to death, at which time he returned to Doyle's claim where he shot the dead man in the head. Given the distance of more than a mile between the cabins, the fifteen minutes Harris thought elapsed after Brown left his place would have been sufficient to accomplish the grisly "execution" of William Sherman and hike back to Doyle's. As Salmon remembered, then, his father must have shot Doyle at least half an hour after Doyle was originally stabbed in the chest. The shooting of the deceased man was the final act of an hour of macabre terror.

Why did Brown shoot Doyle? Stephen Oates echoes Owen Brown in suggesting that John Brown shot someone – Oates says Doyle – "to make sure work of it." Misled by Townsley's faulty memory, Oates mistakenly assumes that Brown shot Doyle at the beginning of the massacre.[106] In fact, Brown shot Doyle when he returned to the rendezvous point perhaps half an hour later, when Doyle was probably quite dead, as Salmon recalled. It seems unlikely that Brown and his men left Doyle alive and alone for half an hour. If Doyle was still breathing, in any event, Brown himself did not have to shoot him. Salmon was there and by his own account had already stabbed Doyle and one of his sons. Brown could have directed Salmon to finish the job if Doyle was still alive.[107] On the question of whether Doyle was dead, Salmon's testimony must be preferred.

Hence the mystery: Why shoot a dead man? If Brown fired to signal the recall of his scattered force, he might have shot into the air or the brush. It cannot be known whether Brown reflected before defiling further Doyle's bloody body, but it had to be a deliberate act. Looking into Doyle's face as he fired, Brown must have been aware at some level of consciousness that he was affirming his own responsibility for the killings. The act of shooting Doyle collapsed whatever psychological distance Brown might otherwise have maintained from the slayings by claiming to himself and his men that he took no satisfaction in directing the strike. This final insult to Doyle's body was evidence not of the "trance" Oates imagines Brown was in during the raid, but of self-possession. Indeed, Brown had been cool and deliberate throughout the foray, questioning sharply, giving "quick" orders,[108] making swift decisions. At midnight, at the end, Brown affirmed his authorship of the raid, claiming the massacre as his own work.

VI

For Brown Pottawatomie was thus an act of self-definition. He had come to the territory the previous fall with a wagon load of weapons intending to defend his family and had promptly assumed a kind of stewardship over the family settlement. He was a latecomer to the political scene, in which John, Jr., played a larger role. Uncertain what God planned for his last years, Brown expected to return to his wife and children in Essex County once Kansas was secure for freedom. His apparent destiny was to labor in the rock-strewn fields around his wintry mountain home teaching black fugitives how to farm. At fifty-five he had volunteered in "service" to blacks, but had never found his calling – work that satisfied at once his sense of piety and his thirst for recognition.

Brown still craved the admiration of his land-rich and pious father that he had for years purchased by public renunciations of his unacknowledged wish for worldly gain and affirmations of his father's Edwardsean faith. For all of his adult life, the ebbs and flows of his fortunes had found their counterpoints in Owen's admonitions; invariably the old squire saw hubris in his son's successes and avarice or failure in his complaints of poverty. John knew that Owen respected ministers of the gospel and men of commerce, but John early failed in his studies for the ministry and had only recently failed again as a wool merchant. Although himself the father of a large family, John came to Kansas still the pilgrim son of Squire Owen – still uncertain who he was in his own right and what his standing was with the God of "my fathers." In rescuing his sons from the Kansas winter and defending the "cause of freedom," John at last found a theater in which to win his father's unconditional approbation for his piety as well as his worldly success. Not the prospect of wealth but hope for Owen's esteem and for wider renown spurred his labors.

John's darkening mood reflected Owen's despair as Owen's life ebbed away quite as much as it reflected the drift of Kansas toward anarchy. Owen's embittered jeremiads resonated with special effect in the territorial crises in which the ruffians and the Slave Power seemed about to triumph. Owen's portents of calamity led John to brood over his unfulfilled pledge to fight slavery. At the same time, Owen's homilies of faith and selflessness, like his loans to his "progeny" in Kansas, reproached John for his dependence, while the prospect of his father's imminent passing evoked John's childhood fears of being cast adrift in the world. As matters stood before Pottawatomie, Owen's death portended John's personal disintegration.

John Brown read these unnamed fears into local events, thereby transforming them into omens of danger to his family. The laws of the "bogus legislature," the perversion of the courts, the failure to punish proslavery murderers, the "ruffian invasion," the "sack" of Lawrence, the swarms of heavily armed Missourians and Georgians taking up homesteads across the prairie – this litany of disasters challenged Brown's sense of self as they tortured his conscience. As this crisis of "law and order" yielded to "civil war," and as his father drew his last painful breaths in Ohio, John became obsessed with the need to strike back. The Pottawatomie massacre was the poisoned fruit of this coincidence of Brown's personal crisis with the growing political violence. That splicing of inner and outer turmoil made it imperative that he act, that he live out his commitment to the cause and testify to his faith. Brown's spiritual craving gave him permission to act as God's instrument.

His imagination had constructed a perceptual world in which events had larger, hidden meanings.[109] The Old Testament lessons he learned from Owen now informed his sense of reality. He drew on biblical analogies and imagined himself as living in prophesied times, a latter-day Gideon in a camp of Midianites. Jason told a story years later of his father proposing in the streets of Lawrence during the Wakarusa War to lead a surprise predawn attack by just ten free-state volunteers flashing "policeman's dark lanterns" and firing their Sharps rifles to panic the sleeping army of besieging Missourians. The story may be an invention.[110] So probably are the later claims of his adversaries that Brown preached that "'without the shedding of blood there is no remission.'" After all, Brown often affirmed that the crucifixion of Jesus had atoned for the sins of man.[111] But the seriousness with which his sons as well as his enemies offered such tales of his militance affirmed the common belief in his stern, some said "cranky" piety.[112]

Although Brown did not believe bloodshed was necessary for redemption, he himself ironically achieved a kind of redemption at Pottawatomie. That night of savagery, an act of perverted principle, signaled in Brown the emergence of a new strength of purpose. Pottawatomie was a metamorphosis for him. In directing the slayings he abandoned his allegiance to his father's style of antislavery. He ceased to be Owen's disciple. He declared open war against the "sum of all villainies." His identity was now grounded in allegiance not so much to his father as to his grandfather and namesake, "a Revolutionary Captain." In March 1857 John even arranged for the granite headstone on his grandfather's grave in Connecticut to be brought to his farm in Essex County where his own name was to be carved onto it.[113]

In the aftermath of Pottawatomie, Brown gained a new sense of vocation that he would not afterward relinquish. He became a guerrilla leader, a holy warrior, "Captain John Brown," and after his spirited but futile defense of Osawatomie, "Old Osawatomie Brown."[114] Soon back in the East and dressed in his favorite Kansas four-piece suit and black cravat, a bowie knife and revolver stuffed prominently in his belt, the now famous Brown began to haunt the parlors of wealthy patrons. Delighted to have "U.S. Hounds" on his trail,[115] he was soon sending furtive messages to co-conspirators under aliases.[116] He found a new joy in life. And when peace finally came to Kansas, he determined to carry the "war" into "Africa." John Brown had found his calling.

PART III

JEREMIADS

7

Monomaniac

> Lincoln's bodyguard, Ward Hill Lamon, was "a monomaniac on the subject of my safety [Lincoln said]. He thinks I shall be killed, and we think he is going crazy."[1]

Brown's motives for directing the Pottawatomie slayings are best understood, as we have seen, in the context of sectional crisis, clan enmity, and his own spiritual unease. But for his contemporaries as well as posterity, the sheer savagery of the murders called his "sanity" into question. His astonishing seizure of Harpers Ferry three years later with a tiny "army" of twenty-one men revived that question even among his friends and supporters. Ultimately, Brown had to defend his sanity in order to defend his cause. Thus a close look at the question promises to shed additional light on the genesis of his war against slavery. A facile assumption that Brown was mad has short-circuited studies of the Harpers Ferry raid. Any effort to reassess it must ask whether it was born of a plausible vision or delusional thinking.

Brown himself could not escape that question. After the debacle at Harpers Ferry, his deepest convictions about the meaning of his life were tested by public charges that he was mad. He went to his death protesting that such charges mocked him and his cause. After his capture, he defended the raid as "perfectly justifiable" and warned that the South must prepare to give up its slaves. When an onlooker called him "fanatical," he shot back: "I think you are fanatical. 'Whom the Gods would destroy they first make mad.'"[2]

At his trial he emphatically rejected an insanity plea as a possible means of saving his life. When an Akron newspaperman telegraphed Brown's attorneys that insanity was prevalent in Brown's family, he acknowledged the truth of the report on his mother's side, but insisted that no one in his father's family had ever been mad. Still weak from his wounds, Brown declared in court that he was "perfectly unconscious of insanity" in himself, and denounced as a "miserable artifice and pretext" attempts by sympathizers to portray him as insane to save him from hanging.[3] After his conviction he repudiated similar efforts of old friends and relations to have his sentence commuted on grounds that he was a "monomaniac."

FIGURE 7.1. The 1857 photo of Brown in Boston reputed to show his "madness."
CREDIT: West Virginia State Archives, Boyd B. Stutler Collection.

the issues of morality involved in Brown's war against slavery from others
such as his grasp of reality. Should one credit his claim to have acted out
of noble purpose? Is an individual morally justified in taking life to free the
oppressed? Is the commandment not to kill inoperative in a self-proclaimed
war like Brown's? Under what, if any, circumstance is heroic self-destruction
rational?

Epistemological questions about Brown's mental balance and mental illness
generally have long perplexed biographers and other students of abnormal
behavior. Scholars have been uncertain about the usefulness of modern concepts and theories in assessing mental disorders attributed to people in the past.
Some historians question their own qualifications to make such assessments or
to know what constitutes valid evidence of mental illness. Since change is the
fundamental concern of historians, they must ask whether "madness" itself – as
well as the perception of madness – has changed over time. Are mental illnesses

emergent? universal? culturally constructed? Would we always recognize mental illness even if we had evidence sufficient to identify it?

In this chapter I will assess assumptions about madness that informed the perceptions of Brown's contemporaries, introduce new evidence about Brown's mental state, and make a fresh assessment of what critics and some sympathizers called Brown's "monomania."[11] In chapter 8 I will consider whether Brown's behavior was sufficiently aberrant to meet criteria for mental illness as understood by modern psychiatry.

I

Whatever their views of Brown's rationality, historians have had to evaluate the extraordinary outpouring of statements and affidavits sent to the court attesting to his madness.[12] Although scholars differ sharply about the value of these and other claims that Brown was mentally ill, their arguments involve issues that must be addressed in any reappraisal of Brown.

Foremost among those who have argued that Brown suffered from a major mental illness – a psychosis – was Allan Nevins, whose argument helped to shape opinion for a generation after 1950. Brown had endured a "peculiarly hard, failure-ridden life," Nevins wrote, and increasingly "took refuge from his own deficiencies in fighting the wrongs of others." Contradictions in his personality, especially his "self-righteous stubbornness and utter intractability," betrayed "some psychogenic malady." A believer in the harsh, implacable Jehovah of the Old Testament, lacking compassion and mercy, Brown suffered from a "mental disease marked by systematized delusions" properly termed "reasoning insanity, a branch of paranoia." Affidavits from Brown's friends and relations, his "inordinate preoccupation with one topic after another," his "extravagant religious fixations," his "feverish absorption" with the idea of a guerrilla warfare against slavery, his "wild scheme" to incite a bloody slave insurrection, his "consuming inner fire" – all proved to Nevins that the Old Man was psychotic.[13]

Nevins began his study of the Civil War Era when revisionist scholarship on the "needless war" was ascendant. Revisionists argued that the War Between the States, as they termed it, might and should have been averted if responsible and temperate leadership had prevailed. But fanatical secessionists and abolitionists had poisoned the political atmosphere, and Presidents Pierce and Buchanan lacked the wisdom and fortitude to neutralize extremists and effect a compromise. The slavery question was artificial, a false issue: Given time, the South's archaic labor system would have died of its own inefficiency.

After the firestorm ignited by John Brown's raid, Southern "fire eaters" added to the resulting hysteria with tales of phantom abolitionist armies and imaginary spies ordered by Brown to spread discontent among slaves across the South. Northern praise for Brown fed Southern fears of slave insurrection. Brown's raid thus abetted the cause of extremists in both sections.

To revisionists, then, the war had been unnecessary, and it came in substantial part because of "wild fanatics" like Brown. Although Nevins broke

ranks with revisionists on important issues, he echoed their logic in assessing Brown: "John Brown's raid, so malign in its effect on opinion, North and
South, might justly be termed an accident," he declared. "Nothing in the logic
of forces required so crazy an act."[14]

Nevins' portrait of Brown found sympathetic readers in the 1950s as the
specter of nuclear war made fanaticism especially dangerous. Nevins seemed
to confirm that not slavery but Brown's tormented mind was responsible for
Harpers Ferry and in some measure for the Civil War. Other historians offered
variations of Nevins' theme,[15] and "Crazy John Brown" became a standard
figure in history texts.[16]

The emergence of the Civil Rights movement in the late 1950s and early
1960s coincided with the commencement of a scholarly reassessment of the
nature of slavery and of those who opposed it. Many scholars who witnessed
in person or on television assaults on civil rights demonstrators began sec-
onding the demands of blacks that the nation fulfill the promise of equality
for everyone. The 1960s became a Second Reconstruction. The slavery issue
returned to center stage in the history of the drama that Union men had called
the War of the Rebellion, and historians began looking back at antislavery
activists with renewed sympathy.

Admiring popular biographies soon appeared presenting Brown as a racial
egalitarian and would-be revolutionary. Black historians, whose forbears had
honored Brown's memory by memorializing his death as Martyr's Day and hon-
oring him as instrumental in the coming of freedom, challenged the revisionist
images of their icon. They reminded readers of Frederick Douglass's question:
were heroism and insanity synonymous in the American dictionary?[17] At the
height of the black power movement, radicals began dismissing Lincoln as a
reluctant emancipator and white supremacist, and cited Brown as a standard
of self-sacrifice against which advocates of racial change and equality must be
judged.

Brown's new champions rejected the affidavits attesting his insanity as
larded with "hearsay" and "loose and unsubstantiated" allegations inadmis-
sible as legal evidence and lacking even "journalistic merit." Since the affiants'
purpose was to save Brown's life, the documents were "highly suspect as valid
evidence."[18] Jules Abels observed that much of the affiants' testimony demonstrated little more than disapproval of his opinions about the urgency of the
slavery question and the role of "forcible means" in addressing it.[19] As James
Redpath commented in 1860, "political monomaniacs" in the North began
urging Brown to plead insanity even before the matter arose in court, because
they "could not understand a heroic action" yet were "unwilling to denounce
John Brown."[20]

The sympathetic affiant-analysts took their cue from Emerson who scorned
"a public opinion changing every day" and "soften[ing] every hour its first
harsh judgment of [Brown]." A "pure idealist," Emerson's Brown was "precisely what lawyers call crazy, being governed by ideas, and not by external
circumstances."[21] In 1959 Louis Ruchames reminded everyone that William

Lloyd Garrison and other nonresistant abolitionists were similarly described as fanatics "insane on the subject of slavery." The point, Ruchames suggested, is that anyone who is "deeply sensitive to injustice" and devotes his or her life to end the suffering of others is likely to be called crazy by "the smug, the callous and the well-placed."[22]

Brown's eloquent speech at his sentencing and the "elevated and high-minded" letters he wrote from prison were not the ravings of a "lunatic," his admirers insisted.[23] If Brown was mad, they asked, why had responsible, upstanding people given him material and moral support? Why had his family supported his "war" against slavery? His plan to seize Harpers Ferry was no more crack-brained than other audacious efforts to awaken antislavery sentiment in the North or antiabolitionist fire-eating in the South. Many abolitionists shared Brown's "delusion" that the slaves would rise if and when the occasion presented itself – the "spartacus complex," one writer has called it.[24] For Brown this conviction was reinforced by reports he received from John Cook, the spy he planted in Harpers Ferry a year before the raid. It was also not unreasonable for Brown to expect support among antislavery whites in and around Harpers Ferry, as he told Governor Wise after the raid. Clearly, he knew his actions were criminal and that he would hang if captured. "He was not psychotic," as Jules Abels wrote in 1971, "since he did not have and was not guided by visions and was acutely aware of reality. He was sane in the sense that his actions were rationally and purposively directed to his end." His hesitation at Harpers Ferry resulted from exhaustion and the ravages of malaria. At worst, Abels concluded, John Brown was only a "garden variety fanatic."[25]

Several historians have been more cautious, warning that any effort to diagnose Brown is fraught with hazards. Insanity is a "clear-cut legal concept concerning a mental condition which is seldom clear-cut," David Potter noted in 1968. "The insanity explanation has been invoked too much by people with ulterior purposes – first by those who hoped to save Brown's life, then by Republicans who wanted to disclaim his act without condemning him morally, and finally by adverse critics who hoped to discredit his deeds by calling them the acts of a madman." Potter assessed Brown in other terms. He admired Brown's composure and manliness in facing death, but saw the Old Man as deluded by the false image he had created of himself to avoid the truth that he had "failed at every enterprise to which he set his hand and had repeatedly violated his own principles." Brown was thus compensating for inner weaknesses – "flawed judgment, homicidal impulse, and simple incompetence."[26] If Potter's Brown was not crazy, he was not mentally stable either.

Brown's best scholarly biographer, Stephen B. Oates, was also wary of drawing conclusions about his mental balance. The "evidence regarding Brown's alleged 'insanity' is too partisan and controversial for use in clinical analysis," Oates contended in 1970. "Insanity" is a "vague, emotion-charged, and clinically meaningless" word, a "catchall term" that might describe "a wide range of odd or unacceptable behavior, including epilepsy and multiple sclerosis."

As for mental illness in Brown's maternal family, Oates showed, much of the evidence is hopelessly vague or mistaken; he found no convincing evidence that any of Brown's sons suffered from mental illness. Since psychologists still debated whether hereditary or environmental factors account for mental disorders, Oates reasoned, evidence on that point was "moot." He questioned whether "psychoanalysis" is even a "valid approach" for biography. "Any biographer or historian who argues that 'insanity' is hereditary intrudes upon his craft the controversies and disagreements of what is still an imprecise science." Although refuting much of Nevins's evidence, Oates stopped short of denying that Brown was mentally unbalanced. He conceded that Brown had been reckless in business, as well as "negligent, careless, and inept." But Brown failed at Harpers Ferry through a series of tactical blunders and bad judgments, not because he was mad. Oates's assessment nonetheless raised the issue again in remarks on Brown's alternating moods of "exaltation and despair," his "glittering eye," and his "implacable and domineering will." Oates's Brown remained a "messianic, paradoxical, and essentially tragic" enigma.[27]

He may have been an enigma, but to describe Brown as "messianic" is to raise the very questions Oates forswears. After all, many zealots endorsed nonresistance, but no other advocate of "forcible means" nor even the boldest slave rescuer attacked slavery by force or in so formidable a stronghold as Harpers Ferry. Yet as Woodward admonished, historians should no longer "blink" at the issue. For as Brown believed so fervently and Nevins' reading showed more soberly, whether or not Brown was sane made – and still makes – all the difference.[28]

Scholars have tabled the question of Brown's sanity without exploiting their own sometimes striking insights. Even those convinced of Brown's rationality have observed dramatic alterations in his personality, vision, and moods. Periods of remarkable stamina and enthusiasm gave way repeatedly to periods of relative inaction or brooding. As noted in Chapter 1, Brown's mood during his interrogation after the raid seemed oddly expansive and grandiose and some of his responses to questions farfetched. Bertram Wyatt-Brown recently argued that Brown was a "depressive" for whom the "idea of war and death in battle" had special significance.[29]

But Brown seemed neither depressed nor excited as he awaited the hangman. His widely praised prison letters suggest a surprising serenity, especially in one who not long before had ordered the "executions" at Pottawatomie. If, as he claimed, life in the shadow of death was "very like a pleasant dream" and he "scarce realized" he was in prison, the Christian "martyr" was buoyed by a mood unknown to most condemned men. And if Brown was sure of his sanity, his understanding of that term was different from ours. Making a psychiatric assessment of anyone in the past is hazardous, but biographers cannot ignore such paradoxes or arbitrarily rule out mental illness if they are to probe the vanished world of a man like John Brown.

To be sure, historians cannot submit Brown's blood to lab tests, order EEGs or MRIs of his brain, or administer personality inventories.[30] But their task is facilitated ironically by the fact that Brown lived in the nineteenth century. An abundance of surviving letters and documents provides countless details of his everyday life that would not be accessible for patients today. In addition, any illness he may have had was not masked by drugs, alcohol, or medical intervention, and the natural course of an illness must have become manifest over time. Such an unabridged story can be revealing. Yet historians have not retraced Brown's medical history, a task I reserve for Chapter 8, or closely analyzed what his contemporaries meant when they spoke deploringly of his "monomania." Did mental illness color Brown's moods and imagination? Did madness guide his strange odyssey or destine it to end on the gallows?

II

Despite several more recent studies of Brown's iconic significance, Oates's 1970 biography remains the standard account. His cautions are still warranted. Could Brown's friends and relations have had correct or useful notions of mental illness before such diseases as schizophrenia and manic-depression had been identified?[31] Historians of psychiatry recount a paradigm shift in the discipline that occurred in the late nineteenth century in the perception of mental illness. After that shift, earlier systems of classification seemed to obscure rather than clarify patterns of mental illness. Should the testimony of Brown's madness be discounted as evidence of mental illness if the illness attributed to Brown has no hereditary basis or modern analogue? "Monomania" is not a modern diagnostic category, but the loosely defined "clinical" picture it presented was a potent social fact and heralded the discovery of several recognized psychiatric illnesses.

Oates's cautions notwithstanding, I believe that advances in psychiatry during the past quarter century make diagnosis, or what I shall call a preliminary assessment, far less problematic than it was when Oates urged historians to stay clear of it. New subfields such as comparative and epidemiological psychiatry, molecular genetics, and neurobiology have contributed vitally to the understanding of mental illness. Behaviorism and pharmacology have supplanted psychoanalysis as primary clinical resources in the field. Professional systems of classification such as the *Diagnostic and Statistical Manual of Mental Disorders* of the American Psychiatric Association, now in its fourth major revision, provide clinicians and researchers with increasingly clear and concrete diagnostic criteria. A task force of specialists numbering more than 1,000 contributed to the latest edition. *DSM–IV* (as the manual is known) makes diagnosis and assessment accessible to a wide range of health workers and mental health professionals. Freed from theoretical baggage, diagnostic categories are now descriptive and supported by an "extensive empirical foundation."[32] The task of diagnosis is thus logically separable from that of analyzing the origins (etiology) of an illness. We do not have to "psychoanalyze" Brown, as Oates feared, to determine whether he was mad.

Oates's concern over the nature-versus-nurture debate is also no barrier. A generation and more ago, as Oates recognized, few authorities believed that inherited vulnerabilities could be fundamental to the development of mental illness. Lest such a conclusion cast a stigma on patients and lead to "therapeutic nihilism," Elliot Gershon has written, "many clinical observers found social and developmental reasons to explain the inescapable fact that mental illness runs in families." But studies of identical twins raised in separate families and of family genetic "pedigrees" over generations have produced evidence of the heritability of mental illnesses too powerful to ignore. Recent discoveries in the molecular genetics of several neuropsychiatric diseases, notably the discovery of chromosomal "linkage markers" for manic-depressive illness in family pedigrees, promise greater understanding of the physiological mechanisms for the inheritance of vulnerability to such diseases.[33] Indeed, since the Ohio Historical Society has an envelope of John Brown's hair, in principle DNA testing might one day reveal whether he was predisposed to affective illness.[34]

Some diseases, moreover, leave historical signatures, and scholars in several fields now routinely classify historical figures in broadly clinical terms, making in effect the kind of "preliminary diagnosis" or "assessment" I referred to earlier.[35] What I wish to do is not so much to give a name to any illness Brown might have had but to determine whether and to what extent illness per se informed or distorted his thinking, mood, and vision. In light of recent advances, taking a family history of mental illness has become standard procedure in clinical practice. If, to be sure, we cannot determine whether Brown suffered from mental illness simply by studying his family history, we may surmise that he carried either a dominant, codominant, or recessive genetic vulnerability to whatever disease his mother's relations may have transmitted through the generations. If hereditary disease is established in his maternal pedigree, determining what that illness was might provide perspective on Brown. The question then becomes whether stresses in his environment triggered similar symptoms in him.

In this chapter, accordingly, I consider several questions: What was the illness, if any, in Brown's family of origin? Did Brown show signs of any illness evident in his mother's family? What sort of madness did the court's petitioners ascribe to Brown in labeling him a "monomaniac"? Did Brown really exhibit symptoms and behaviors associated with that label?

III

Though the affidavits attesting to Brown's "insanity" were appeals for clemency, they contained compelling evidence of mental illness in his maternal family. Five of Brown's close relations swore to court officials in Ohio that "insanity" was hereditary in the family of his mother, Ruth Mills Brown. Given the shame and fear that insanity then inspired, its presence was a dark family secret. In 1843 the reformer Dorothea Dix publicly decried "the state of insane persons" in asylums "confined ... in cages, closets, cellars, stalls, pens, chained, naked, beaten with rods, and lashed into obedience."[36] Many Americans considered asylums "madhouses" and commitment a form of imprisonment.[37] The eighteenth-century custom of permitting the public to gape at asylum "lunatics" for a fee had been discontinued, but "mad people" were still subjects of morbid curiosity.[38] Families preferred if possible to care for mad relations at home; commitment to an asylum was admission that a family member was uncontrollable, that "insanity" ran in the family and thus might have tainted everyone. Brown's kinsmen's disclosures must therefore have been painful. They attest the strength of family loyalties to the imprisoned man.

Gideon Mills, a maternal uncle,[39] swore in one of the affidavits that his own mother had been "insane for a number of years before her death and died insane." Three of his children, Mills added, had been institutionalized, one repeatedly. Superintendent O. C. Kendrick of the Northern Ohio Lunatic Asylum at Newburgh, who apparently did not know Brown, confirmed these statements from records of the asylum. Mills's son George was currently in the third year of his third confinement, and another son, Andrew, also an inmate, was "insane." Although Kendrick knew from his own acquaintance with the Mills family while he had lived in Hudson that their "disease" was hereditary, he did not label it or describe the symptoms of Gideon Mills's children.[40]

Two of Brown's first cousins, Sylvester and Mills Thompson, whose mother was Ruth Mills's sister, swore that their mother too had been "more or less insane for six years and died insane." Their maternal grandmother, two Mills aunts, an uncle, a sister, and five cousins were also affected in varying degrees. The sister had been sent home from the asylum as "incurably insane." The father of these affiants, Salmon Thompson, confirmed their statements and added that John Brown's only full sister, Anna Ruth King, who died in 1838, had occasionally been insane; and John's younger brother, also named Salmon, had often "showed evidence of insanity." Thompson added that Oliver Mills, Brown's first cousin, had recently betrayed "a very strange condition of mind.... He excludes himself from our society and is gloomy and despairing," though Thompson was not prepared to call Oliver "insane."[41]

Mental disease exacted a fearful toll of Millses. But a caveat is in order. We know too little of the symptoms of their illness to identify it. Not everyone sent to an asylum in the middle decades of the nineteenth century had what a psychiatrist today would call a mental disorder. Epileptics and the severely retarded were often institutionalized as insane. Indeed the Newburgh asylum admitted people suffering from consumption. By the 1850s public asylum inmates were increasingly poor people, and asylums were places where difficult individuals who became too burdensome for their families could be dumped.[42] Confinement was based chiefly on declarations of relatives, supported by a physician, that a person was mad or dangerous. Not until the 1860s did states begin to require the verdict of a jury in a sanity trial before confinement.[43] Nor was the duration of confinement limited by law.[44]

Determining the disease that ravaged the Millses is confounded by fuzziness in the affidavits filed on Brown's behalf. Salmon Thompson's claim that as a youth John's brother Salmon had "many times" seemed insane, for example, may have reflected nothing more than dismay at the behavior of a precocious or irritable adolescent. As a youth Salmon outshone his brother John in scholarship despite being two years younger, as noted in Chapter 3, but Salmon had to be disciplined for his behavior at school. As an adult, Salmon became the most accomplished and influential member of Owen Brown's large family despite his father's anxiety about his spiritual state.[45]

Salmon Brown showed no signs of any illness involving either mental deterioration (dementia) or irrationality. But at age twenty-eight he worried about a growing palsy or tremor in his hands. Despite generally good health, he wrote his father, "An infirmity in my nerves, proceeding from an unknown cause, makes it difficult to write legibly. I have been conscious this was growing upon me for years, without being able to apply any remedy."[46] Three years later he died of yellow fever, the cause of his chronic tremor still a mystery.[47]

The evidence of mental illness in Brown's children is more revealing. One son suffered from a serious disorder that required periodic confinement at home. Another experienced a psychotic episode in Kansas followed by a long period of despondency. And late in her life Brown's eldest daughter had a disabling "nervous" disorder that lasted for years. Despite the differences in the symptoms of these illnesses, they suggest a common genetic vulnerability.

In the first of the three instances just noted, Brown's fourth son, Frederick, suffered from a severe, chronic, episodic mental illness that first appeared when he was sixteen. At the onset in 1847, three months before Frederick's seventeenth birthday, the symptoms became so severe that his father took him to an alienist in Springfield, Massachusetts. "Frederick has been under the treatment of one of the most celebrated Physicians in Mass & for some part of the time has appeared to be as well as ever," Brown reported, "but has not appeared so well for a few days past." Frederick's malady troubled the family so often that for extended periods we can track the frequency and duration of his "attacks." In 1850 he and his brother Jason were working a farm together when he became ill. As a result, on July 30 he had to move into his Grandfather Owen's house, leaving Jason short-handed in the field. According to Jason, Frederick "has not been very well since Father came here, but has got a good deal better." The episode was not over, however. On August 6 Frederick was "a little flighty again," but on August 22 Brown reported that "Frederick seems to be a little better." The episode had lasted more than a month.[48]

Another "spell" is noted in December 1851, when Frederick was "very wild again." At that time, Brown told John, Jr., "*He is again* however to all appearances nearly recovered from it, by the return to an abstemious course of living; as *almost* if not *quite* the only means used. He had gradually slid back into his old habit of indulgence, the effect of which I consider as being now fully demonstrated." But no cure resulted. Frederick's attacks persisted, sometimes in greater severity. In March 1852 he had "one of his poor turns again," but we do not know how long it lasted. In January 1854, Frederick, though once more on the mend, "has had some hard spells (what he calls quite fevery) within a couple of weeks."[49]

In 1856 any hope that he might outgrow the malady was crushed: "Fred" had an episode that lasted three months or more. The onset was less dramatic than earlier episodes. Frederick "has had a little return of his old difficulty," his father wrote home from Kansas, "but he seems to be getting nearly over it." But three weeks later Frederick's uncle Adair observed that the young man "has had rather a bad spell – plethory – but not near so bad as he has been on some occasions." To reduce pressure from "blood" believed to be on his brain and to ease his "blinding" headaches, Frederick was "bled freely a[nd] dieted a[nd] has pretty much recovered," Adair reported. By May 16, however, Adair confessed that "Frederick has been very bad this Spring – for a short time very much beside himself." The attack had at last subsided and Frederick was "able to work again." Ironically, he recovered just in time to accompany his father and brothers into the madness of the border war; and in the summer his symptoms returned.[50]

During this thirteen-year period of recurring mental illness, Frederick seems to have suffered no lasting intellectual impairment. Everyone considered him bright, and Samuel Adair, who saw him frequently, denied that he was "half witted."[51] During intervals between the episodes, Frederick's letters reveal a sensitive, affectionate, surprisingly cheerful youth who enjoyed kidding his brothers and sisters. When his brother Owen failed to write to Ruth, Frederick joked: "I will punch his ribs 'till he du so I will.'" He chided his younger half-brother Watson, at home in North Elba running the farm while the others were in Kansas, about running after girls, but added, "I have no doubt you do a good business at it and I dont blame you after all."[52]

A handsome, broad-shouldered six-footer, Frederick himself had several romances. After a disappointment in 1853, he wrote to his brother John: "I think I acted the fool most completely last Spring, and by looking the matter over I cannot blame her a bit for giving me the slip on the night of the sugar party, it was the result of a misunderstanding alltogether." While still in Ohio, he apparently became informally engaged to a girl his sister thought too young for him. In Kansas he kept company with the "very pretty" Mary Grant, who seems to have returned his affection. Even during "the wildest moments of his malady," his half-sister Annie remembered, "poor Fred" never forgot to be "tender and kind to his little sister."[53]

Despite his episodes of mania, Frederick won the respect of family and neighbors. Brown's friend, James Hanway, thought Frederick "excitable in debate" but of "good argumentative powers." Frederick was even elected as a delegate to the free-state constitutional convention, although a bout of his illness prevented him from attending. A "true blue" antislavery and temperance man, he shared his brothers' disdain for the "old hunker rumies of both the old parties." He joined his father's company during the border war. Left to guard the horses during the battle of Black Jack Creek because he was having a "spell," Frederick, according to a later recollection of his brother Owen, frightened the proslavery men into surrendering by galloping the horses around them waving his sword and shouting, "We've got them surrounded and have cut off their communications."[54]

During the Pottawatomie raid, Frederick refused to take a hand in the killing. Stories differ about his reaction to the slayings: Jason remembered that

Frederick wept, and Henry Thompson believed he joined Jim Lane's free-state force in August as "atonement" for Pottawatomie. But his half-brother Salmon remembered him as "wild with enthusiasm" to get back to the fighting. Indeed, Frederick may have signed up with Lane during an episode of his mania.[55]

For all his sternness about how to treat his son's illness, Brown was an affectionate and sympathetic father to Frederick. "I want to request as a particular favour that should my Frederick be with you any," Brown wrote his own father, "that you be exceedingly patient with him, & get along by encouragement as much as possible." When in the summer of 1854 the young man "subjected himself to a most dreadful Surgical opperation" to remove an unnamed portion of his anatomy, for more than two weeks John "did not take off my clothes (except for washing) on his account." "I will say of Frederick that such was the *nature* of his difficulty as to render it *impossible* to relieve him but by an opperation; that he is now doing well & appears to have a radical cure," Brown wrote seven weeks later. Frederick accompanied his father to Kansas in 1855 still weak from this ordeal.[56]

In a retaliatory raid on Osawatomie in August 1856, a posse of Border Ruffians chanced upon Frederick in the road and shot him dead. Brown was enraged and bitter. Pocked with bullet wounds, Frederick's body "had lain on the ground to be worked at by flies for some 18 Hours," John mistakenly believed.[57] The Old Man sat for an hour alone with the body before rallying his scattered men once more. Brown later denied that his crusade against slavery in Virginia was inspired by vengeance, but he felt the loss of Frederick deeply.

In Frederick's tragic life we have evidence of what Brown himself called an "illness attended with insanity." But what illness? Frederick's episodes were marked by severe headaches, sleeplessness, "fevery" or delirious thought, "wild" and impulsive behavior, and temporary disruptions of his occupational and social functions. For periods of a month or more he could not work and had to be confined to a room at home. The pain, distress, and disability that Frederick's moods cost him mark his condition as, in modern terms, clinically significant. Yet he was never uncontrollable and his family felt no obligation to commit him to an asylum. Nor did Frederick finally give way to despair or forget who he was. In the intervals between his "turns," his mind was intact.

Some of Frederick's symptoms may be explained by any of a number of organic disorders that affect mood, but the episodic character and long duration of his elevated and expansive moods suggest other pathologies. Nor was Frederick schizophrenic. Although his age at the onset of his illness and its disruption of his social and occupational functioning are characteristic of schizophrenia, Frederick did not exhibit a *continuing* lower level of functioning in such areas as work, social relations, and self-care. His father had found him at sixteen "disposed to reading & some thought."[58] Frederick returned to work promptly after his bouts of "insanity," maintained his friendships, and even assumed new responsibilities in Kansas. He was not noticeably demented and his emotions were not "flat" or inappropriate during normal intervals. On the contrary, he was positive about the future, hoping to become a "correct writer" and to improve himself in other ways. Though his highs erupted unpredictably, his impairment was noticeable only during "wild" episodes and in less frequent periods of dejection. His illness was cyclical; in the final weeks of his life, he was "rapid cycling."

This evidence suggests strongly that Frederick Brown suffered from manic episodes. His decreased need for sleep, racing thoughts, impulsiveness, and excessive risk-taking satisfy several *DSM–IV* threshold criteria for a diagnosis of manic-depressive disorder. But he fails in other respects to qualify, since some criteria are inapplicable to his situation. His illness did not lead to buying sprees, foolish investments, loss of occupational roles, or rejections from loved ones – all noted currently as measures of the presence of manic-depressive illness. He could not suffer serious financial losses in that cash-poor economy or lose his employment in that extended farming family. If his relations with young women were sometimes awkward and unlikely to lead to marriage, he nonetheless found romantic partners among women who knew him. He always had a home with his brothers and their families, who loved him enough to tolerate his episodes and look after him. In short, Frederick does not meet all the threshold tests for a diagnosis of manic-depressive illness at least in part because he lived in a social environment and economy in which he could function even with occasional full-blown symptoms of psychosis.[59]

The second of Brown's offspring who suffered from mental illness was his oldest son John, Jr. In Kansas, John, Jr., endured a period of mental distress so severe that he experienced delusions and behaved irrationally for days, and he felt the episode's effects long after. His symptoms first appeared suddenly the night after learning that his father was responsible for the murders at Pottawatomie. A rider galloped into the camp of the Pottawatomie Rifles on the afternoon of May 26, 1856, shouting that five men had been "butchered and brutally mangled, and old John Brown has done it." The men in John, Jr.'s command were so shocked at the news, John, Jr., and brother Jason remembered, that they promptly deserted, even though neither of the brothers knew anything of the killings. Earlier the same day, the Rifles had removed John, Jr., as their captain for liberating two slaves, and then returned the slaves to their master. John, Jr., felt "betrayed" by these actions. Whether the shock of the Pottawatomie killings, his loss of command, or fear of arrest, or some combination of the three, triggered John, Jr.'s derangement is uncertain. But as he and Jason hid in the Adair cabin that night, he told his aunt Florella he felt as if he was "going insane." Soon after, he became a "raving maniac." During the night he fled to a nearby ravine, convinced that a mob was pursuing him. Several days later a proslavery posse arrested him on a charge of treason for his service in the free-state legislature and took him to a prison camp not far from Osawatomie.[60]

A month later he was still in custody when Jason described his "insanity" in a letter to North Elba. At first John had "appeared much excited. After that he became more and more confused in mind, till the 26th [of May] at evening, when he was quite insane." In prison, he was "knocked and kicked" for allegedly "feigning" insanity, Jason remembered years later. But John "actually fancied himself commander of the [prison] camp...shrieking military orders, jumping up and down and casting himself about." Soon afterward, he was hustled off to a camp at Paola, his arms tightly bound and a rope halter attached to them; later, his ankles chained, he was marched miles to Tecumseh for questioning. When the authorities released Jason in late June, John, Jr., still a prisoner awaiting charges, was "becoming quite rational" and "seemed to be in good spirits." His psychotic episode was over.[61]

In mid-August, John, Jr., while still a prisoner on "trumped up charges" in Lecompton, wrote to his brother Frederick warning of an impending attack on Osawatomie, and wondering if the purpose of his father's rumored return to Kansas was to rescue him. He was now "fully convinced," he told Frederick, "that you and I cannot remain in Kansas...with any degree of safety." A storm was brewing. He cautioned Frederick not to trust Lane's men "in the hour of adversity," adding, "My name will be X. Y. Z. until further notice." Whether these fears and suspicions were rational or delusional is uncertain.[62]

Finally freed in early September, John, Jr., returned to Brown's Station to find his home and books burned, his stock scattered, and Frederick dead. In October, with his father and brothers, he abandoned Kansas abruptly because his "symptoms of mental abberation [sic] were again manifest." At Tabor, Iowa, his father found him still "very much broken down and altered by his toubles." Eighteen months later, back in Ohio, John, Jr., explained his flight from the territory on grounds that in such painful circumstances he feared he might "again lose my balance entirely." He was still suffering from "foreboding apprehensions of trouble to myself and family," "constant wakefulness by day and night," and "absolute inability to prevent shedding tears no matter how trivial the cause." In June 1858 his father found him much improved but still complaining of "gloomy turns."[63]

Had the Mills family taint destroyed John, Jr.'s reason for a while and left him anxious and depressed for two years? Without naming John, Jr., his father conceded as much to the Virginia court. Many years later Adair told Franklin B. Sanborn that he believed John, Jr., had been without sleep for several nights and was disturbed by the Pottawatomie killings when he became "beside himself." Adair remembered insisting that for safety John, Jr., surrender his weapons while he was in Adair's house and that friends arranged to hand him over to United States troops for "safe keeping." Although John, Jr.'s recollection on these points was quite different, he conceded that "for a time" his reason "finally gave way under a strain that would have broken a Sioux Indian."[64]

In his own assessment, then, his psychotic episode was an aberration not to be confused with the illness that plagued Frederick. That was a plausible assessment. At least initially, John, Jr.'s "mania" was neither expansive nor grandiose; his impulse had been to hide, not to rally free-state forces. The delusion that he was in command of the camp in which he was first imprisoned, if not feigned, suggests a mood closer to Frederick's mania. But John, Jr., never suffered another such episode. If he carried a genetic vulnerability to depression, he proved resilient enough to fight it off. Indeed, he soon resumed his work for the cause. When the Civil War broke out, he was deeply involved with James Redpath in effecting the migration of fugitive blacks in Canada to Haiti. In the fall of 1861 he raised a company of "antislavery men" to serve under free-state guerrilla leaders he had known by reputation in Kansas. That winter he wrote Jason from Kansas that his regiment had freed 1700 slaves and he promised Jason to visit Osawatomie, where he had seen so much tragedy.[65] Crippled by arthritis, he left the service in April 1862, and in October moved to an island in Lake Erie, where he lived supporting reform causes till his death in 1895 at seventy-three. There is no evidence that he suffered any recurrence of his depression.

Whatever triggered John, Jr.'s psychotic episode in 1856, its aftermath suggests the possibility that he suffered from what soldiers in the Civil War called "soldier's heart" or "irritable heart," a syndrome that anticipated later diagnostic descriptions of posttraumatic stress disorder. John, Jr.'s sleeplessness, anxiety, depression, and fear of familiar scenes all fit that profile. So too did the recurrence of the symptoms when his father asked him to join his Virginia campaign. Limiting himself to forwarding supplies and recruiting volunteers for that campaign, John, Jr., avoided a repetition of the horrors he experienced in Kansas.[66]

The examples of Frederick and John, Jr., heightened fear of "insanity" in their brother Jason and sister Ruth. After Jason returned to Hudson with his wife and infant son, his half brother Salmon reported that Jason had "had the blues very bad since he got home.... He thinks that he must settle down soon or he will have a crazy spell." Jason did stay put for years. Though he stored a cache of arms for his father, he refused to join the Harpers Ferry expedition. In his later years, he gained a reputation for eccentricity and lived for some time with brother Owen in the mountains above Pasadena, California, but his fears of going "crazy" proved unwarranted.[67]

Brown's daughter Ruth was dogged through her life by fears of mental illness, and long after her father's hanging, when she was in her fifties, she experienced a prolonged period of "nervous prostration" that "held me down like a nightmare." It was so severe, she told a family friend in 1899, "I could not write to any one not even my children." For seven or eight years Ruth's husband Henry Thompson had had to stay home and "do the housework and take care of me," she wrote. Ruth was at last recovering but even now was "never strong or free from pain." She was "happy and grateful" that the terror had passed and she enjoyed life "wonderfully."[68] The symptoms she evidenced during her long confinement meet several diagnostic criteria for a major depressive episode.

Thus three of Brown's children – Frederick, John, Jr., and Ruth – may all have suffered from an inherited susceptibility to manic-depressive illness. But if that was part of their genetic legacy, did it pass down to them through their father's genes or those of their mother Dianthe Lusk Brown? Mental illness had stalked the Lusks too.

Dianthe Lusk, who married Brown at nineteen, bore him seven children in twelve years and died of heart failure in 1832 after giving birth to a still-born boy. The question of her "insanity" is clouded by later controversies over Brown's character, including his children's efforts to deny that Brown was mentally ill. If the malady that afflicted Frederick was traceable to the Lusks, Brown's defenders implied, Brown himself had a clean bill of health.

The Lusks were a proud family, claiming descent through Dianthe's mother from the line that gave the nation John and Samuel Adams. Their response to the suggestion that Dianthe was mad was to blame Brown for her emotional troubles. Old Hudson neighbors even maintained that Brown's mistreatment of Dianthe precipitated her "insanity." But no one who repeated such stories was quite sure in what way the "tyrant" Brown had allegedly tormented the frail Dianthe.[69]

Despite these stories, it is apparent from family letters that Milton Lusk, Dianthe's brother, enjoyed cordial relations with Brown's sons and half-brother Jeremiah after Dianthe's death.[70] Brown's children insisted that their father had always been a tender and considerate husband. Daughter Annie, born eleven years after Dianthe's death, claimed her father had nursed Dianthe through "attacks of insanity." Annie also told Franklin B. Sanborn that Dianthe was a "partially deranged women" when Annie's father married her, and "at times afterward she was maniacal." She thought Dianthe's children had all evidenced her "malady" at times.[71]

Sifting facts from such reports is difficult if not impossible. Most surviving statements about Dianthe are little more than family gossip recorded years later. But it is noteworthy that none of Brown's latter-day critics denied that Dianthe had been irrational at times. The scant contemporary evidence tends to confirm that implicit concession, though when she died, Brown assured Owen that "Her reason was unimpaired & her mind composed with the Peace of God."[72]

Two of Dianthe's nine siblings, Minerva and Julia, reputedly died "insane." Julia was supposedly at times "violently insane" and was in an asylum "several times." A companion of Julia's daughter remembered that Julia, "feeling her terms of mania approaching, used to ask to be taken there." Of course, any of a number of complaints might have driven Julia to the asylum, but we have a possible clue to the nature of her illness. Julia's daughter and namesake, Julia Pitkin Caldwell, died of "paresis" in 1908.[73]

General paresis is a syphilitic infection that modern medicine no longer treats as a psychiatric illness. But before the advent of penicillin, it was known as the "great imitator" because it mimicked psychiatric disorders, often presenting as "a classic affective psychosis." In the third stage of the disease, from five to twenty years after infection, syphilis attacks the cardiovascular and central nervous systems, impairing judgment, speech, and memory. It deranges behavior and may produce a manic syndrome with euphoria and grandiose delusions as well as depression and delusions of persecution. In short, it may resemble manic-depressive illness.

Since syphilis may be transmitted to a fetus during pregnancy, Julia Pitkin Caldwell's diagnosis would seem to raise the possibility that her mother, Dianthe's sister, might also have died of neurosyphilis (general paresis). But it is highly unlikely that Dianthe's mother passed such an infection to her daughters. The fetal damage from congenital syphilis is likely to be so severe that an infant born infected would have little chance to grow to maturity and reproduce. The chance that the granddaughter of a syphilitic woman contracted congenital neurosyphilis through her mother is indeed remote.[74]

The symptoms of mental disorder for which Dianthe's sister Julia was hospitalized a number of times were thus probably unrelated to syphilis. And if Julia's daughter, who lived into old age, died of general paresis, it was not congenital. If misdiagnosed, she may nonetheless have had the same illness her mother had experienced. Since paresis masquerades as manic-depressive illness, Julia's daughter may actually have carried a genetic vulnerability to the same scourge that preyed on Dianthe's children. They may all have been bipolar. And if Dianthe was its victim too, then she, not Brown, may have transmitted it to her children.

All this is speculation. But the evidence of the presence of *some* form of mental illness in the Lusk pedigree compels us to conclude that Brown's "close association" with madness proves nothing about Brown himself. We cannot be sure that he was the carrier of the genetic marker(s) that formed the biological substrate of the illness that afflicted Frederick and perhaps John, Jr., and Ruth. And if, as Brown's surviving children believed, Frederick did suffer from his mother's malady, perhaps Brown himself recognized in his unfortunate son the fires that from time to time had consumed her tormented mind.

IV

The issue, of course, is whether Brown himself shared the genetic vulnerability to mental illness of his mother's relations or experienced the symptoms of manic-depressive illness apparent in Frederick. Did mood swings or psychotic delusions so distort his reality that his quest to discover God's will for him was a fool's quest?

We begin by examining the affidavits and petitions urging Governor Wise to spare Brown's life. What symptoms did petitioners attribute to Brown and what type of "insanity" did they see in him? Caution is warranted. The impressions of Brown presented by nineteen affiants and other petitioners rested chiefly on memories of events long past, memories which may have been altered by knowledge that his raid had failed and by reports of what he said before and during his trial. Many of the letters Brown wrote in prison appeared in the newspapers,[75] and later experiences or information about a remembered event may blur or supplant memories of the event.[76] Furthermore, portions of the affiants' testimony were hearsay, and affiants were not always careful to acknowledge it as such. Although most of them had known Brown for years, they had seen little of him since his return from Kansas. Those who had seen him were irritated and fatigued at his obsessive talk of Kansas and slavery.

Of course none of the affiants had witnessed or knew much about what Brown had experienced in Kansas. Some of them sympathized with Brown's "sufferings," but none approved of his course in 1856–7, and most disavowed any support for his militant antislavery. Most had had business dealings with Brown. In fact, beyond Brown's own kin, the affiants were "gentlemen of high standing" – businessmen, cattle growers, landowners, professionals – men obviously chosen to make an impression on Wise. Many of their depositions were endorsed by still other "reputable citizens."[77] Perhaps in part because of their shared positions and preconceptions, their recollections revealed a generally consistent picture of Brown's "madness."

The affiants' argument was simple. They praised Brown's past character but insisted on his present insanity. Hoping to save his life, they portrayed a good man driven – or predisposed – to madness. Most stated that before his "crazy" adventure in Virginia, Brown had been an honorable, conscientious man, and by implication one deserving of clemency. Edwin Wetmore, for example, had known Brown since childhood to be "strictly honest and upright" and a man "of a gentle and mild disposition." But Wetmore had recently found his friend "frantic and furious and incapable of reasoning or of listening to reason." Ethan Alling, an early business associate, remembered that Brown had had a "peculiarly kind & mild disposition & character," that he had been "upright & honest... energetic & persevering, scrupulous & conscientious." Alling had not seen Brown recently but related that he was "reputed to be partially or wholly insane." Even S. N. Goodale, who had quarreled publicly with Brown and thought him undeniably insane, confessed that Brown had maintained a "kind benevolent & humane disposition" toward him personally and was a "man of strict integrity and moral & religious worth." Harvey Baldwin, who had known Brown "intimately" since 1814, put the affiants' case concisely: Brown was "a man of rigid integrity & of ardent temperament."[78] But when his mind "fastened" on a single subject, it showed signs of "aberration."[79]

With few exceptions, the affiants stated or implied that Brown was a monomaniac. He was not a "lunatic," one completely "deranged." Instead, he was "insane" about slavery, and, some added, about Kansas and a few related matters as well. He habitually focused upon one subject, about which he was wholly irrational, and yet was rational about other things. Brown was not merely preoccupied or obsessed with slavery, he was "insane" about it, unable to see how anyone could honorably hold views different from his own. He was variously "enthusiastic," "agitated," and "excited" when speaking about slavery.

In antebellum America these terms carried shades of meaning they may no longer have. They implied a degree of vehemence in speech and intensity in feeling far beyond that expected in normal discourse. The affiants were saying that Brown was frenzied, "furious," or violently agitated when he harangued them about the sin of slavery or recalled the evils of the Slave Power in Kansas. His conversation skewed off into diatribe. He ranted. His whole life, some affiants observed, had been given over to what he called the "service." He had abandoned his family and occupation and was willing to sacrifice his sons to free the bondsman. Of course the affiants did not mention what was apparent to Governor Wise: Brown was equally ready to sacrifice anyone else who stood in his way.

Beyond the broad outlines of this image, however, the affiants agreed on little else. They differed sharply about when and why Brown became "insane." Several affiants saw madness in Brown as a youth. His cousin and boyhood playmate, Salmon Thompson, who had testified about insanity in the Mills family, believed that since adolescence Brown had labored "occasionally under hereditary insanity." When young, Brown became so "strongly excited upon a particular subject" that Thompson had often been "compelled to...restrain him." Thompson's Brown had always been of an "ardent" and "excitable" temperament. Events in Kansas had concentrated Brown's focus on the slavery issue.

Brown's uncle Gideon Mills thought him "honest and upright" though for twenty years "subject to periods of insanity." Brown's brother-in-law Milton Lusk identified Dianthe's death a quarter century before as the moment Brown began to show "strange peculiarities in his conduct and conversation." Lusk and his family had concluded soon thereafter that Brown was "not of sound mind," and had considered him "more or less insane" ever since. He was "disposed to enter upon wild and desperate projects and adventures and [was] incapable of deliberation or reasoning in regard to them," Lusk said. Lusk had seen Brown when he left for Kansas in 1855 "armed to the teeth" and had tried to talk him out of going because it was "insane" and because he had "no sympathy" with it.

Others saw Brown's madness as a result of his family's ordeal in Kansas. James W. Weld, a longtime friend, had seen Brown en route to Kansas in 1855 and saw "no appearance of insanity." He had also at that time "never heard" that anyone thought Brown mentally unbalanced. But in 1859, when Brown came to Weld's farm with some of his followers, Weld found his "whole manner" changed. Brown could not be dissuaded from talking about the "difficulties" in Kansas, "the deaths of his sons [sic] and slavery." Weld tried to persuade Brown that "they must rely upon the ballot box," but found him "altogether insane" on the slavery question. Cousins Sylvester and Mills Thompson could remember nothing strange about Brown in his early years, though his judgment as an investor had been "erratic" back in the thirties. But after his return from Kansas it was "apparent" that on "matters growing out of the difficulties in that Territory his mind had become deranged." Brown's closest relation in Hudson, half-brother Jeremiah, concurred: Since the "troubles" resulting from the settlement of Kansas, he said in his affidavit, "I have observed a marked change in my brother John." He had "abandoned all business and...become wholly absorbed by the subject of slavery."

Affiants differed too about whether Brown's insanity was hereditary or the tragic consequence of experience. At one extreme, E. N. Sill thought all the

Browns a little unbalanced. Squire Owen had been a "most excellent but peculiar man," and several of Brown's brothers, though "possessed of more than ordinary character," had "very striking idiosyncracies." Sill admired Brown's "courage" and "devotion to his beliefs," but thought him "as surely a monomaniac as any inmate of any Lunatic Asylum in the country." William Otis, an attorney who had represented Brown more than once and whose Bible class Brown had attended a quarter century before, struck a typical balance on the heredity-versus-experience question. Otis believed Brown had "more than ordinary" intelligence and unblemished moral character, but also an "ardent and excitable temperament." Otis long ago realized that a "hereditary predisposition to insanity" accounted for the "fits of insanity" of Brown's sons, and concluded now that Brown would be likely to become insane under "strong excitement," especially from "absorbing attention to...what he might regard as religious or philanthropic subjects." Otis attributed Brown's monomania to the "trials and sufferings which he and his family had undergone in Kansas."

Despite these differences, the affiants agreed in striking ways about Brown's temperament and behavior. This was due in considerable part to the context of their recent contacts with Brown. Many had seen Brown only once or twice since his return from Kansas, either in chance encounters or at home when Brown came to solicit funds. Brown's insistence on talking about Kansas and slavery and asking them for money for his cause shaped their impressions of him. In fact, he was campaigning, giving speeches where invited,[80] and calling on friends, often accompanied by several of his well-armed Kansas volunteers, whom he may have brought along to strengthen his credentials as a military leader.

Running across William Otis on a train, Brown talked at length about fundraising in the East before Otis realized that Brown planned to make new "incursions" from Kansas into Missouri "in order to run off slaves." In the spring of 1858, Brown and two "followers," all three bristling with weapons, bummed a ride into Akron with David L. King. "Passing the time in conversation" with him as he drove his wagon, King became convinced that Brown was "crazy" on the subject of slavery. When King asked Brown's companions who they were, they told him they were "Sons of Liberty" on their way to Kansas to join in the "good work." They always went armed, they said, and would never be taken alive.

Of course King did not consider these men monomaniacs; but he implied that men of Brown's age and family responsibilities should know better than to pursue such quixotic projects. In the summer of 1857, S. N. Goodale, like Otis, ran into Brown "in the cars." Brown was about to return to Kansas, and soon began to talk "with great earnestness of the evils of Slavery." He insisted that "stealing or coaxing niggers to run away from their masters was honorable." Goodale proposed a "more conservative course," suggesting that Kentucky might already be a free state had it not been for the "excitement and prejudice engendered by ultra abolitionists of Ohio." At this Brown "sprang to his feet with clenched fist and eyes rolling like an insane man (as he most assuredly was)," insisting that the South would soon be free but for "scoundrels" like Goodale. After this exchange, reported Goodale, everyone on the train agreed with him that Brown was insane.

There was, of course, another side to these stories. Brown's moral outrage did not seem bizarre to his Kansas allies, his volunteers, his Eastern financial supporters, or brothers Oliver Owen and Frederick, all of whom agreed with him. They saw in him a rational but deeply committed abolitionist. A strong abolitionist himself, Oliver Owen was a passionate critic of the "manstealing" national government, a disunionist who supported antislavery and was ready to endorse violence, but who died in 1858 before Brown's plans matured. John Brown, Jr., later declared that Uncle Oliver Owen was "true blue" and, had he lived longer, would have fought slavery to the end.[81] Frederick Brown made a speech in Cleveland praising Brown on the day of his execution, and within a month thereafter began a lecture tour in New England under abolitionist sponsorship.[82]

By initiating the clemency drive, in contrast, half-brother Jeremiah and others chose to save the condemned man rather than affirm his cause. Jeremiah saw no betrayal in this and helped to pay John's legal costs with money from their father's estate. When his petition drive failed to save Brown from the hangman, Jeremiah planned a public demonstration should Governor Wise refuse to give Brown's body to the family.[83] In later years Jeremiah and Frederick feuded over who had the better claim to glory as John's brother and champion.[84]

There is no way of knowing how many friends or acquaintances declined to swear they believed Brown to be insane. But the same Brown who in 1857 unsuccessfully solicited funds from the Ohio affiants had made a quite different impression on New England reformers, whose contributions enabled him to feed and arm his men. In January he won the support of the Secret Committee of Six and later addressed the Massachusetts legislature with an appeal for Kansas.[85] Privately, Thomas Wentworth Higginson, Samuel Gridley Howe, and George Luther Stearns, all reformers and members of the Secret Six, were as convinced as Brown that the time to use force against slaveholders had arrived, and were even prepared to underwrite a slave insurrection. Brown seemed temperate, disciplined, and self-controlled as he pleaded his cause in meetings with such men.[86] Unlike the Ohio affiants, these men were involved in the struggle for Kansas and had emotional stakes in its outcome. They saw Brown as a hero of the fighting there. Frederick Douglass, at whose Rochester home Brown had stayed for three weeks in 1858, remembered his friend years later as "an even-tempered man, neither morose, malicious nor misanthropic, but kind, amiable, courteous, and gentle." It was his "hatred of oppression," Douglass said, that roused him to "walk the room in agitation" at the mention of slavery.[87]

Amos Lawrence, director of the New England Emigrant Aid Society and the man for whom Lawrence, Kansas, was named, was favorably impressed with Brown when the two first met and talked in Boston about saving Kansas for freedom. In his journal in January 1857, Lawrence described Brown as a "calm, temperate, and pious man, but when roused ... a dreadful foe." Brown's "severe simplicity of habits, his determined energy, his heroic courage in time of trial, all based upon a deep religious faith, make him a true representative of the Puritan warrior." Lawrence gave Brown money for his personal use. Later he wrote to Brown, "You may be assured that your wife and children shall be cared for more liberally than you now propose." True to his word, Lawrence raised a fund to support Mary Brown and her children after Brown's death.[88]

Lawrence recognized that Brown was headstrong. He wrote to his friend Charles Robinson, governor of the outlawed free-state territorial government, that Brown "requires some coaxing as well as some controlling power near him." Brown himself recognized that he had made his appeals to Lawrence for money to support his family "with a tenacity that disgusted him and completely exhausted his patience." Only after Brown had made his widely publicized raid into Missouri, fifteen months after their first meeting, did Lawrence begin to see the "Puritan warrior" in a harsher light. "Captain John Brown of Osawatomie called to see me with one of his rangers," Lawrence wrote in his journal in May 1859. "He has been stealing negroes and running them off from Missouri. He is a monomaniac on that subject, I think, and would be hanged if he were taken in a slave State." After learning of the Harpers Ferry raid, Lawrence wrote in his journal: "The old man has become a desperate abolitionist, and hates the slaveholders the more because he believes that they are responsible as a class for the death of one of his sons and the imprisonment and insanity of another."[89]

Context thus mattered in perceptions of Brown. If New England reformers saw Brown as a Puritan warrior, the affiants found in monomania a frame of reference to explain his behavior. Their realities and Brown's had become incommensurable. Brown had abandoned their world and its norms of civic behavior. They feared and disliked what he had become. Their charge of monomania was a way to discount his passion about slavery and dismiss as irrational his indignation at their own "temperate" attitudes.

Despite the Ohio affiants' purposes, it does not follow that their reports of his behavior were concocted. Certainly Jeremiah was truthful in swearing to his own reservations about Brown's war against slavery. Within a month of Brown's return to Hudson in October 1856, Jeremiah expressed his concern. "Judging from what [his] Boys say I am affraid that Capt Brown" has got the war spirit so strong that he will carry the thing farther than is best but hope not," he warned Adair. "I think that none of the Boys will follow fighting altho their Father seems determined to raise men and money to fight with in Kansas and I think does not intend to be confined to Kansas. I greatly fear that this is not the best way."[90]

Of course Jeremiah knew that John was not alone in the Brown connection in embracing "forcible means" against slavery in principle. For a time Adair himself thought a defensive war might be necessary to save Kansas. Like John and Squire Owen, Jeremiah privately hurled jeremiads against the indifference of the nation toward slavery. "I am beginning to think that God has great judgments to pour out on this nation and that all that can be done to stop the aggression of the slave power will avail nothing but that it will go on until it dashes this republic to attoms," Jeremiah wrote Adair in November 1856. "[N]othing else will wake up a time serving church."[91] John's monomania, Jeremiah fretted, was not evidenced in his outrage, which Jeremiah shared, but his claim to possess a special commission to disobey the law. That, to him and many others, was a sure sign of madness.[92] It was John's insistence that he was, as David King recalled Brown's words, "an instrument in the hands of God to free the slaves" that was the problem.[93]

Jeremiah recalled Brown making much the same declaration. According to Jeremiah's affidavit, two years earlier he had challenged Brown to justify his determination to continue the war, warning him that his present course would "prove his own destruction and that of his boys." To this Brown replied that he knew his "duty" and had to pursue it "though it should destroy him and his family. He told me," Jeremiah swore, "that he was satisfied that he was a chosen instrument in the hands of God to war against slavery." Brown had "taken offense" at Jeremiah's remark that he was "insane" about slavery, and the two had not spoken of it since.[94] Jeremiah did not abandon his support for his half-brother altogether after their quarrel; they continued friends.[95] Stricken with malaria en route to Tabor, Iowa, where he was assembling a force to reenter Kansas if fighting should erupt, Brown had stayed with Jeremiah from May 27 to June 12, 1857.

Thus to Jeremiah as well as other affiants, Brown's conviction that he was God's agent was evidence not just of aberrant thinking but of pathology. In monomaniacs, delusional ideas betrayed misreadings of reality, especially inflated views of their own powers. Brown's boast to one Ohio affiant, James Weld, who tried to talk him out of his war against slavery, seems to bear out that grandiosity. Brown asserted that he already had a hundred men ready to "march to Kansas," and that "with a hundred men he could free Kansas and Missouri too, and could then march to Washington and turn the President and his Cabinet out of doors."[96]

Brown made equally wild claims to both Senator Mason and Governor Wise after his capture at Harpers Ferry. Were such boasts delusional? Brown did not then – or ever – have a hundred men under his command. But his experience as a captain in the free-state army and his company's skirmishes with proslavery units in Kansas, where at one point he had forty men, validated his sense of being a warrior. After the fight at Osawatomie, Brown had entered Lawrence to the cheers of hundreds of free-staters. In the summer of 1857, Lane sent "Genl" Brown $50 and told him that it was "all important to Kansas" to get his wagonloads of weapons and men to the territory to protect free-state voters from intimidation.[97] In 1858 Brown joined forces with James Montgomery in renewed skirmishes with proslavery troops in Kansas. Such events fed Brown's hubris. With sufficient weapons and cash to feed them, he might reasonably have supposed he could raise a hundred "regulars" should war in Kansas erupt again.

And if Brown was blustering, so were many others. It was an age of filibusters and amateur soldiering. The ideal of the citizen-soldier and the "grey champion" as a military leader still claimed respect. (Brown himself assumed command of the volunteers at Black Jack over Captain Samuel T. Shore because Brown was, as he explained, "much older.") Sectional antagonism boiled over wherever Northerners and Southerners met. Fistfights had broken out in Congress and legislators flaunted sidearms. Braggadocio was common coin in national politics. Wise himself declared that if the Republicans won the presidential election of 1860, he could "arm and equip 50,000 men … ready for revolution." Amidst such political rhetoric, Brown's bombast was unexceptional.[98]

By April 1859, Brown was looking South, not West, planning to carry the war into "Africa." And as Harpers Ferry would prove, Brown's seeming confidence that the federal government would stand by in the face of a violent assault against slavery was mistaken. But if Brown's inflated assessment of his own prowess as a soldier seemed "insane," Brown's Kansas experience suggests it was not altogether bizarre. The Border War had fed not only his appetite for war and his sense of mission, but his belief that he was a soldier of God. If some of the affiants understood that Kansas had inspired Brown's bellicosity, they could not conceive a war against so deeply rooted an institution as slavery to be sane. What made Brown frightening to them was their belief that, crazed by delusions, a monomaniac might suddenly erupt into violence at any time.

V

How weighty were the affiants' charges of monomania? If Brown had entered a plea of partial madness at his trial, would a jury have considered sparing his life? Would his alleged monomania have afforded grounds for Wise to commute his death sentence?[99] And how might Brown's monomania have affected the raid itself?

In the mid-nineteenth century, monomania was a frightening, rather faddish "disease." For centuries physicians in Europe and America had recognized four general types of madness: *mania*, which was characterized by uncontrolled, racing thoughts, expansive or irritated moods, and wild behavior; *melancholia*, which connoted despair, passivity, and loss of self-esteem; *dementia*, the deterioration of mental abilities, especially memory, usually because of organic injury or disease; and *delirium*, in which disorientation, dreamlike hallucinations, fleeting delusions, restlessness, and sometimes fever predominated. But by mid-century these ancient classifications had become hopelessly vague and inclusive, and dozens of subcategories were gradually being added under each head in the medical lexicon as a growing awareness of the presence of the mentally ill inspired closer attention to their diagnosis and treatment. Although psychiatry was not yet a recognized specialty in the United States, the asylum movement provided patient populations for systematic, long-term study. But in the 1850s diagnostic classification remained of little value in treating madness.

American medical writers contributed to the conceptual bedlam by intro-ducing their own terms and distinguishing subtypes of the traditional diseases. The publication in 1838 of Isaac Ray's *Treatise on the Medical Jurisprudence of Insanity*,[100] however, helped to standardize the evolving system of clas-sification of psychiatric disorders in the United States. It quickly became a classic in forensic psychiatry.[101] Ray distinguished general from partial mania and intellectual from moral mania. *Partial intellectual mania* identified a class of illnesses for which the term monomania was "now in general use," Ray explained. Its symptoms included a preoccupation with delusional bodily states accompanied by misleading sensations, and it probably served as a label for many patients that psychiatrists would today diagnose as schizophrenic. "Thousands have believed their legs were made of glass, or that snakes, fish, or eels had taken up their abode in their stomach or bowels," Ray said. In another set of monomaniacs, a single "predominant idea" or a "train" of delusional ideas might evolve rapidly, one "insane notion" giving way to "another and another." Monomaniacs retained the "acuteness" of their reason and would conceal their delusional ideas if they feared ridicule or personal inconvenience. But their "understanding," Ray warned, "is more extensively deranged" than was "generally suspected."[102]

Following the taxonomy of the English physician and anthropologist, James C. Prichard,[103] Ray identified a second broad class of monomanias. These disorders affected the "sentiments," disposition, and habits of the victim, distorting his or her moral sense. These *moral manias* included the numer-ous cases in which the emotional "faculties" became deranged "independently of any appreciable lesion of the intellect." In "true mania" the patient could assess the consequences of his actions correctly without "being in a condition to repress his passions, and to abstain from acts of violence to which they impel him." In "*partial* moral mania" the "derangement" was confined to "one or a few of the affective faculties, the rest of the moral and intellectual constitution preserving its ordinary integrity." He listed several varieties of partial affective monomania, including pyromania, and the unnamed "irresistible propensity to steal" that we now call kleptomania. More ominous was *homicidal or instinc-tive monomania* in which a seemingly normal person committed a crime with-out motive or remorse from "blind, irresistible impulse."[104]

In the 1850s the presumed causes of monomania and madness in general reflected changes in culture as well as a growing effort to find empirical evi-dence. Ray noted that the violent acts of the monomaniac were still some-times popularly attributed to God's chastisement or the mysterious workings of His providence. Ray deplored the "air of mystery" perpetuated by "igno-rance and superstition" still surrounding the disease. Many people believed the devil might drive or tempt the unwary into acts of madness, and the notion of demonic possession still muddied the picture. Ray pleaded for the "scientific" view that lesions of the brain accounted for madness.[105]

That view was gaining ground. Since the late eighteenth century, the religious context for explaining mental illness had been fading. Influenced by Locke and later by phrenology and Scottish commonsense philosophy, leading physicians now identified a combination of physical injury to the brain and personal failings as the proximate causes of insanity.[106] At mid-century Edward Jarvis, a noted statistician and alienist, summarized those causes in an influential report. He distinguished physical from "moral" or emotional causes. Physical causes affected the structure of the brain or another organ and indirectly disordered the mind while moral causes acted directly upon it.[107]

In an 1859 summary of admissions to eighteen American hospitals for the insane, Jarvis elaborated and documented his analysis. Assuming that a limited if variable amount of energy was a biological given for everyone, Jarvis found "undue" and "inappropriate" uses of the mind in most inmate case summaries. Immediate sources of insanity were "excessive study" – especially the study of metaphysics, phrenology, Fourierism, animal magnetism, Spiritualism, and the Scriptures – and "great mental excitement from intense attention to business, care and anxiety." In his summary of the annual reports, he counted 174 "kinds of events, habits, or circumstances connected with the misuse of the mind." Stimulating or depressing emotions were themselves causes of most "maladies."[108] Implicitly, Jarvis's clinical assessment of the precipitating causes of mental illness reflected the dominant middle-class values, New England ancestry, and traditional, restrained Protestant religious piety of the superintendents. These pioneer psychiatrists conceived mental disorders, Gerald Grob has observed, as "the inevitable consequence of behavior that represented a departure from their own normative model."[109]

In theory monomania could thus be triggered by a host of stressful experiences and unseen injuries. As the Brown affiants feared, it might appear in anyone in a sudden act of "abstract fury." Medical journals and popular magazines were cluttered with cases of refined women who smothered their babies, gentlemen who murdered their beloved wives and children, and emotionally "exalted" and cunning men leading secret lives. At least to American physicians, monomania signaled much more than just an obsession about one irrational idea. Under that rubric, medical writers included a number of disorders we would today consider psychotic. Monomaniacs were especially dangerous because their delusional ideas could be discovered only with patience and deliberation. The "confirmed monomaniac," as Ray put it, "by carefully abstaining from the mention of his hallucinations, has the semblance of a perfectly rational man."[110]

But by mid-century the concept was already under attack in medical circles. In Paris a vigorous controversy had broken out among "eminent physicians for the insane." Following the reformer Philippe Pinel, one party maintained that the faculties of the mind are distinct and thus it is possible to have insanity that affects only one or a few faculties and leaves the others intact. To them partial or limited insanity was quite possible. Their opponents insisted that the mind works as an integrated whole and that healthy faculties cannot exist in isolation from diseased ones. In our time – and in another vocabulary – that debate continues in psychology and neurobiology. But in the mid-nineteenth century,

the leading American physicians supported Pinel.[111] The new science of phrenology, which mapped brain faculties and asserted that each could be stimu-
lated separately, strengthened those arguing for the localization of functions.

The legal implications of the issue were far-reaching. Advocates of the concept of moral mania and monomania such as Ray asked the courts to accept
that an accused person, although "alleged or admitted to possess perfectly
sound intellect and exercising perfectly free volition, is an irresponsible moral
agent." Their opponents denied the possibility of "moral insanity." They could
not accept the premise that emotions or sentiments could be deranged without
any impairment of reason. Thus if an accused murderer's intellect was not
disordered, however depressed, obsessed, or grandiose he might be, he was fit
to hang.[112]

In Anglo-American jurisprudence the principle had long been established, as
James Mohr has shown, that no person should be held accountable for "actions
he or she could neither willfully control nor consciously understand."[113] As
early as the seventeenth century, English legal authorities had discussed the
complex issue of "lucid intervals" and the difficulty of determining appropriate
punishments for crimes committed under varying degrees of sanity. Following
English precedents, American courts also held that guilt required both criminal intent and comprehension of the significance of one's acts. The concept of
monomania invited a wider application of these principles and hence potentially more acquittals on grounds of insanity. In 1844 the champions of the
new, broader idea of insanity won a crucial victory in the Supreme Judicial
Court of Massachusetts, where Chief Justice Lemuel Shaw upheld an appeal
on grounds of a monomania. In *Commonwealth v. Rogers* he held that in cases
involving monomania, "The conduct may be in many respects regular, the
mind acute, and the conduct apparently governed by rules of propriety, and at
the same time there may be insane delusion, by which the mind is perverted."
When that happened, "the mind broods over *one idea* and cannot be reasoned
out of it."[114]

But jurors and judges found it difficult to decide whether accused persons
were monomaniacs or simply depraved. As the medical profession backed away
from the positions advocated by Ray, public opposition mounted to acquitting
violent criminals on grounds of partial insanity. Lawyers discovered that they
could find physicians willing to testify to any conclusions. The "experts" were
soon discredited. By the 1850s physicians were backing off from claims to
be able to identify insanity in accused persons and were abandoning moral
insanity.[115]

To many of America's 40,000 ordinary physicians, in fact, the idea of a "partial" mania was an oxymoron. They could not reconcile monomania – insanity
bounded by sanity – with their notion of the moral sentiments or conceive of
an essentially sane or good person committing a violent crime. For them mind
was synonymous with rationality. To become insane was to "overthrow the
mind," "lose one's mind," or be "out of one's mind." Since the intellect was wedded mysteriously to the immortal soul, furthermore, insanity might endanger

salvation.[116] Ordinary physicians believed, like Thomas Jefferson before them, that the moral sense was inborn. Thus "instinctive fury" could arise only from outside the ordered and balanced sphere of the human mind. The terrible acts of "monomaniacs" had to be explained by reference to physical injury to the brain, not by fractured consciousness. Only with the discovery or invention of the unconscious a generation later would the existence of affective (emotional) psychoses and personality disorders such as psychopathy or antisocial personality gain general if still problematic professional acceptance. Only then would the concepts of moral mania and monomania, which had served as conceptual hosts for such maladies, be discarded. So serviceable had the notion of monomania been that scholars today trace the historical origins of concepts such as paranoia (delusional disorder), manic-depressive illness, obsessive-compulsive disorder, antisocial personality disorder and other modern diagnostic categories to monomania.[117] Monomania had become a medical catchall.

VI

Through their writings and in their sometimes controversial management of asylums, the superintendents helped to popularize the new ideas about madness. Like other educated men of the time, they were well read in literature, especially British classics. They found practical illustrations of the principal forms of madness in the works of Shakespeare, whose plays were then enjoying great popularity in many American cities. King Lear's rages identified him as suffering from mania, while Hamlet's brooding revealed his melancholia. Amariah Brigham doubtless exaggerated when he claimed that he had seen all the characters of Shakespeare in the New York State Lunatic Asylum, but during his two decades as editor of the *American Journal of Insanity,* he accepted a dozen articles from colleagues "diagnosing" leading characters in Shakespeare's plays.[118]

In fact, the stage was a principal means of popularizing images of insanity in antebellum America, and playbills, newspaper ads, and scandals affecting leading tragedians gave their performances publicity among those who did not attend the theater. In the 1840s Junius Brutus Booth, the famous father of actors Edwin and John Wilkes Booth, played Richard III and King Lear in Pittsburgh, Cincinnati, and many smaller cities throughout the Midwest and South.[119] An alcoholic reputed to have "fits" of madness himself, Junius imbued Richard III with all the ruthlessness and obsessive ambition of a monomaniac. Edwin Booth's famous Hamlet and Edwin Forrest's Lear undoubtedly did much to shape the appetite for melodrama as well as the image of madness among genteel audiences. For nearly three decades Forrest made Spartacus, the fanatical leader of the slave revolt against ancient Rome, in the American play, *The Gladiator,* one of his greatest roles. The eagerness with which some abolitionists imagined a slave uprising in the South probably owed something to such dramatizations.[120]

If American medical psychologists had readily added monomania to their taxonomies, educated Americans generally were equally enthusiastic.

FIGURE 7.2. The earliest photo of Brown, showing him taking an oath, perhaps in support of his scheme to rescue slaves through a Subterranean Pass Way. Brown's self-dramatization and his growing obsession with slavery evidenced to some a "monomania." Photo by Augustus Washington, c. 1846.

CREDIT: West Virginia State Archives, Boyd B. Stutler Collection.

The term crossed the Atlantic even before E. K. Hunt had translated Jean Esquirol's *Mental Maladies* into English in 1845 or Brigham, the editor of the new *American Journal of Insanity*, had published an article on it in the first issue in 1844.[121] The idea quickly found wide acceptance. In 1838 a New York physician, for example, warned the public that a preoccupation with reform could overthrow the "balance of the mind" and result in monomania. A monomaniac is "prepared to labour, to suffer, or to die for his cause," and would "glory in martyrdom itself" to gain its triumph, the doctor cautioned. Among the "humbugs" he sought to discredit, "ultra-abolitionism" ranked high.[122]

Stories of monomania and "confessions" of its victims spiced genteel magazines and popular journals with a touch of the bizarre. Some pieces were didactic. Parents who were too busy with "business and enjoyments" and "laughed away" their child-rearing duties invited disaster, scolded a self-proclaimed monomaniac.[123] The legal and moral implications of monomania were widely discussed. "Most of those confined in our asylums," wrote an observer (mistakenly) in the *American Whig Review* in 1848, "are what we call monomaniacs.... They are insane on religious questions, on money matters, love affairs, and schemes of speculation; from sickness, disease on the brain, loss of friends, and a thousand other causes." Since it was difficult to draw the line between those who were partially and totally insane, current law was "extremely diffi-cult" to administer, he said. The courts generally found that on the "immediate subject" of the particular delusions of monomaniacs, they were "not consid-ered moral agents," while on all others they were "held to a strict account-ability." The author argued that the insane should be treated like children who understand right from wrong long before we hold them responsible.[124]

Like Freudian terms in the 1920s, the jargon of medical psychologists soon became fashionable. It passed into everyday discourse. Monomania became a catchall term for the single-minded pursuit of a chimerical goal, the cliche mal-ady of the ambitious or obsessional, and a facile explanation for isolated acts of violence. It gave bite to humorous stories. In a sometimes acerbic account of a tour of the Old South, Frederick Law Olmsted (remembered as the designer of New York's Central Park) complained of the hotel service at Vicksburg: "If a disposition to enjoy occasional privacy...were a sure symptom of a monomania for incendiarism," he complained in 1854, "it could not be more carefully thwarted than it is at all public houses in this part of the world."[125] Any unhealthy preoccupation might be termed a monomania. Lincoln told a cabinet member (perhaps in jest) that his old friend and bodyguard, Ward Hill Lamon, who on occasion insisted on sleeping on the floor outside Lincoln's bedchamber, was "a monomaniac on the subject of my safety.... He thinks I shall be killed, and we think he is going crazy."[126] Unknown to the president, the popular young actor, John Wilkes Booth, had a seeming "monomania" about Lincoln and would soon be declared a "maniacal assassin."[127]

The most sensitive writers of American fiction saw something deeper in the discovery of monomania. It became a vehicle for developing what Melville called "the power of blackness." Torment, melancholy, and madness, as Harry Levin observed, is a recurring theme in Hawthorne, Poe, and Melville.[128] In "The Tell-Tale Heart," Poe recreates the mind – say rather the disease – of a monomaniac whose hallucinations of the beating of his victim's "hideous heart" betray him to the police. In "The Murders in the Rue Morgue," "William Wilson," "The Fall of the House of Usher," and several other stories, as George Stade has noted, Poe depicts multiple personalities – "bi-, tri-, and poly- part souls at all angles of attraction and repulsion to each other." In Poe's horror stories "the self is full of flaws; along these it splits, fractures, and falls apart into independent agents that haunt, menace, and possess each other, unto mad-ness or death," Stade writes. In "The Fall of the House of Usher," a story of multiple dissociation, Roderick Usher is driven to madness and death by a nameless horror. The sustained terror of these tales, Stade suggests, is akin to the experience of a paranoid schizophrenic.[129]

The greatest novel of the period, *Moby-Dick*, can be viewed on one level as a portrait of a monomaniac.[130] Melville refers repeatedly to Ahab's secret "mad-ness" and "monomania." In this interpretation, Moby Dick is the objectification or projection of Ahab's illness, and Ahab's mad quest for the great sperm whale becomes a "self-assumed, independent being of its own." Melville's evocation of Ahab parallels the medical literature of the time down to its belief that "physiognomy" reveals madness. Ahab's obsession is manifest in his features and especially in his "glaring eye." He sleeps little and is awakened by terrifying dreams. He has furious energy in his quest. His manner betrays his obsession. "There was an infinity of firmest fortitude, a determinate, unsurrenderable wilfulness, in the fixed and fearless, forward dedication of that glance." His monomania has a visible symbol. Although "wild Ahab" bears "no sign of common bodily illness about him," Melville reveals, Ahab carried a white, "rod-like" scar from his forehead "down one side of his tawny scorched face and neck." As with the monomaniac depicted by medical psychologists, Ahab senses that his quest is mad. "Now, in his heart, Ahab had some glimpse of this, namely: all my means are sane, my motive and my object mad." If his judgment was twisted, his intelligence was unimpaired. "But, as in his narrow-flowing monomania, not one jot of Ahab's broad madness had been left behind," the narrator says, "so in that broad madness, not one jot of his great natural intellect had perished." If Ahab is a symbol of humankind, Melville has identified his humanity not in his reason but in his disease.[131]

VII

Amidst the spiritual uncertainty and social turbulence of the mid-nineteenth century, the concept of monomania filled a conceptual void. It provided a name and an explanation for episodic and limited aberrant behavior in otherwise rational people. At mid-century authorities routinely attributed notorious and sensational crimes to "monomaniacs." Like demon possession in former times, monomania was seen as a kind of possession by disease and obsession. In an age of evangelical optimism and millennial expectations, monomania accounted for acts of willful evil and the darkest, least controllable impulses of the mind. Socially constructed, it reified erratic, reckless, self-aggrandizing, violent behavior.

Second, in medical writings like those of Edward Jarvis, it also implicitly vindicated conservative values. Presumably monomania was caused in part by immoderate and immoral behavior, overreaching, and excessive ambition. Its sufferers required treatment, especially when it possessed those who, like John Brown, seemed both unduly stubborn, obsessive, and unresponsive to "reason," and were guided by an inner compass that knew only one direction.

Third, as a popular idea, monomania objectified those who adopted excessive, radical, or outlandish stances or failed to perform rationally in business. An epithet often hurled at abolitionists and other reformers, the label monomaniac banished those who were so alienated from or incensed by the indifference or depravity of society as to abandon a settled vocation and inflict their madness on the world.

Whatever demons drove John Brown, for the Ohio affiants he was a monomaniac in these senses. Monomania had turned him to violence and estranged him from everyday life and old acquaintances. It had led him to renounce law and order and usurp God's judgment. Brown's implicit repudiation in 1854 of his ambitions as a businessman in pledging himself to the "service" of the blacks thus carried subversive implications. Just as his seventeenth-century for-bears had renounced England as a "dunghill" of sin and corruption, Brown condemned with increasing vehemence the machinations of the Slave Power as a pervasive evil and slavery itself as the "sum of all villainies."

But like Melville's story of Ahab, the John Brown story was finally about spiritual quest. Like Ahab, Brown manifested his humanity in his monomania. But unlike Ahab's disease, Brown's destructive purpose gave him a measure of fulfillment. The aim of his monomania was to free others. His "madness" freed up his energy and buoyed his faith. If his monomania ended in his destruc-tion, it also permitted him to preach to a vast congregation. In his biblical Christianity he found injunctions to purge American society of a great evil and, in Bleeding Kansas, God's presumed sanction for making war on it. To the end Brown defended that war in religious, apocalyptic, monomaniacal terms.

VIII

Despite the accusations that he suffered from a monomania, Brown ignored the term in pleading his sanity. He appealed to older, more familiar cultural arche-types of madness in insisting he was sane. Declaring that he had experienced no "ravings" or "terrible visions," he implied he was not, like King Lear, a maniac. His repeated claims that, despite his "peculiar circumstances," he was "remark-ably cheerful," had never been more "happy" in his life, and slept like a "joy-ous little infant" implied that neither was he a melancholic. His serenity also hinted that he was in a state of grace. But even had he wished to deny explicitly that he was a monomaniac, he could convince no one with logic. He could not deny that he was preoccupied with slavery and still affirm it a great evil he was sworn to destroy. Nor could he repudiate his claim that he was God's instrument without abandoning both his hard-won new identity and his claim to martyrdom. Since monomaniacs were believed to obey a secret "system" of delusions, moreover, such seemingly grandiose claims only proved he was self-deceived. And since monomaniacs were notoriously cunning in concealing their madness, Brown's very denials could be taken as evidence of his derange-ment. If Brown was indeed sane, he could find no words to prove it.

In Chapter 8 I consider whether Brown's thinking and behavior were warped by some mental illness we might identify today. Was he suffering from dementia or a major mood disorder? Was he delusional? Was Harpers Ferry the blighted harvest of madness?

8

God's Reaper

I felt for a number of years in earlier life: a steady, strong, desire: to die: but since I saw my prospect of becoming a 'reaper' in the great harvest I have not only felt quite willing to live: but have enjoyed life much & am now rather anxious to live for a few years more.

John Brown[1]

If to some John Brown was arguably a "monomaniac," was he suffering from mental illness – from what psychiatrists today call a psychosis or a severe personality disorder? Brown defies easy labeling. To his Virginia captors he seemed self-possessed and manly as he answered questions after the raid on Harpers Ferry. Similarly, the "perfect words" he wrote to relatives and admirers from Charlestown jail suggest no hint of a "frenzied fanatic." In the six weeks between his "disaster" at Harpers Ferry and his hanging, Brown succeeded in winning back what he called "lost capital" by accepting his fate with courage and outward calm. George H. Hoyt, a young attorney sent to Charlestown by Boston abolitionists to defend Brown and to keep them informed, noted that Brown was determined to go to the gallows with "great serenity and firmness." He was "calm, apparently happy & inspired with a most Godlike resignation," Hoyt assured Mary, although Brown feared that a visit from her might "unman" him.[2] He seemed anything but a maniac.

Even before his sentencing on November 2, Brown embraced his "public murder" as capital to spend in his cause. On November 10 a newspaper correspondent asked him to comment on Rev. Henry Ward Beecher's sermon declaring "Let no man pray that Brown be spared. Let Virginia make him a martyr." Brown had failed, Beecher declared, but "a cord and gibbet would redeem all that." Brown wrote "good" in the margin of Beecher's text.[3]

But Beecher also said that the shot that killed Brown's son Frederick in Kansas had "crazed" Brown. Taking his text from *Jeremiah*, Beecher claimed that Brown had brooded over his "wrongs" and nursed "his hatred of that deadly system" until finally his "phantoms" had gained "a slender reality" and inspired "such an enterprise as one might expect from a man whom grief had bereft of good judgment." In short, brooding had made Brown delusional.

To this Brown responded only that Beecher was "not well posted" and did not know his "subject."[4] From the day Brown was captured he insisted that seeking vengeance had no part in his decision to seize Harpers Ferry. In his interview with Senator Mason after the raid, Brown justified his actions by the Golden Rule. "I pity the poor in bondage. That is why I am here. It is not to gratify any personal animosity, or feeling of revenge or of a vindictive spirit."[5] Throughout his final ordeal, moreover, Brown remained self-possessed and apparently rational. He played the martyr to perfection.

But mood disorders may profoundly affect a sufferer's judgment, even creating delusions and hallucinations, without revealing cognitive impairment to casual observers.[6] Thus historians cannot disregard the possibility that Brown's campaign to free the slaves was itself a symptom of mental disorder as some critics believed. Despite his denials, might he nonetheless have been driven by grief and hatred as Beecher surmised? Might his unflagging efforts to assault slavery have been buoyed by manic rage? Did his baffling performance during the raid itself reflect depression or what Allan Nevins called "systematized delusion" or "religious hallucination"?[7]

I

To assess John Brown's mental health, it is helpful to sift through the evidence afforded by his medical history. Doing so may reveal any signs of mental disorder he exhibited to observers or symptoms of which he complained in his last years.[8] That information may then be weighed against criteria for mental illness. Of course the task is not to attempt a differential diagnosis. It is to determine whether Brown exhibited symptoms of sufficient intensity and duration to betray some disease process or organic impairment. Did he have a history of disturbed behavior or thinking? His scores of surviving letters and other writings reveal patterns of thought that might evidence mental disorder. To understand the meaning of Harpers Ferry, we must know whether or not it was born of madness.

As many writers have noted, John Brown was often ill from infectious disease. Although he seems to have been hardy and active as a young working man, in his later years disease laid him low with increasing frequency and severity. Like others in his family he had "hard colds," ear and eye infections, "bowel complaints" that suggest dysentery, and especially "chill fever and ague," then a common name for malaria. No picture of Brown's crusade against slavery would be complete without acknowledging his waning physical fitness in his last years.[9]

In the nineteenth century malaria was endemic in the Mississippi Valley. Caused by the bite of an Anopheles mosquito, it infected the bloodstream and liver producing bouts of shivering, sweating, and anemia that left its victim listless, easily fatigued, sallow in appearance, and with reduced resistance to other infections. Typically, paroxysm began with a severe chill or "shake," accompanied and followed by fever and weakness and sometimes by vomiting and diarrhea, and ended with profuse sweating. Chronic malaria might develop after repeated attacks of an acute form and was characterized by emaciation, sallow complexion, edema, poor digestion, weakness, and depression.

Brown had malaria so often in the 1850s that by 1857 he may have had a chronic, debilitating form. A bout in the late summer of 1852 left him "pretty much laid up, & not good for much any way." A year later his health had been "poor" for more than three months. When he reached Browns Station in October 1855, he was for a time as "rugged" as his sons there had ever seen him, but his use of quinine to "break up" attacks seems to have helped little in the "sickly season" the following summer and autumn.[10]

In 1857 he was felled again by repeated infections that drained his energy and spirits. From May 11, when he left North Elba planning to return to Kansas with an armed force, he was desperately ill much of the time until late October. Soon after this episode began he confessed he was "much confused in mind & cannot remember what I wish to write," a statement some writers have taken as evidence of mental disorder. But when he wrote it, he was "still troubled with the Ague" and running a fever. His "confusion" did not prevent him from giving directions about things to be done at North Elba during his absence. Bedridden at Hudson from May 27 to June 12, in August he joined his men in Iowa still "quite lame" in his back, and uncertain of his next move in the struggle for Kansas. In October he was still sick.[11]

In 1858 Brown was again "down with the Ague" from late July through much of December, and so weak that at times he could answer letters only "with great labor." He had been "entirely laid up" for six weeks, he reported on September 9, and had never been sicker. He remained ill at Osawatomie for a month attended by his loyal lieutenant, John Henry Kagi. Still at Osawatomie in October, he had long been "very feeble" and too weak to travel. In early December he was still getting "a Shake pretty often," but had evaded capture and was soon in the thick of renewed hostilities. On December 20 he led a raid into Missouri, freed eleven slaves, and soon after went into hiding in Lawrence. In February he crossed into Iowa with his rescued slaves, but on March 2, 1859, was again too sick with "ague" to travel. Intermittent attacks continued through the spring and summer.[12]

During this period Brown experienced a "difficulty in the head" that some writers have mistaken for a symptom of psychiatric disorder. In fact, the problem was a persisting infection in his sinuses and right ear. "Have been quite prostrated almost the whole time since you *left* me at Johns," he wrote Kagi from the East in April, "with the difficulty in my head, & ear: & with Ague, *in consequence.*" But "Am some better now.... I shall not be idle." As his fundraising succeeded slowly, Brown remained upbeat despite his illness. Edwin Morton, a staunch supporter, wrote Sanborn, "Brown left on Thursday.... From here he went in good spirits, and appeared better than ever to us, barring an affection of the right side of his head." But a week later Brown wrote Kagi,

"I have again been entirely prostrated with the difficulty in my head and with Ague: so that I have not yet been able to attend to any business." In a week or more he hoped to be able to resume fundraising. In Boston on May 18, Brown was still sick with a "terrible gathering in my ear; & with the ague." But he had not "had a shake for *nearly* Five days." Despite chronic illness, he continued to raise money and prepare for the attack on Harpers Ferry.[13]

II

If John Brown was suffering from a degenerative mental illness by 1856, the outward evidence of it would likely be a deterioration of personal habits, perhaps disorientation, and surely a loss of cognitive skills, especially memory. As a young man Brown had been a model of pious, orderly living. A strict Congregationalist, he rose early, maintained regular hours, worked hard, lived frugally, rebuked idleness in others, and required his apprentices, like his family, to attend church on Sunday and family worship every morning.[14] He set a "plain and simple" table, avoided "luxuries," and neither smoked nor drank. A neat dresser who despised displays of finery, he was clean-shaven, cut his hair short, and was "particular" about cleanliness.

Later visitors to Brown's homes in North Elba and Springfield provided descriptions of these habits. Frederick Douglass found merchant Brown living in Springfield in a small wooden house in the back street of a working-class neighborhood. The house had neither carpets nor a sofa, and his family was unpretentious. Mary and the girls served a plain supper of potatoes, cabbage, and beef soup, and the boys helped wash dishes.[15]

Although these reminiscent descriptions are from sympathetic observers, the portrait they paint is supported by less flattering recollections of Brown's son Salmon and others. "Father was strongly fixed in his habits," Salmon recalled many years after Harpers Ferry. "It was always difficult for him to fit himself to circumstances." Does such a remark point toward what clinicians today call obsessive-compulsive disorder (OCD)? Was Brown markedly compulsive?

The evidence here suggests that the answer to both questions is no. Brown was not immobilized or noticeably distressed when unable to attend to his daily routines, nor was he so compulsive about cleanliness as to exhibit signs of OCD. When family members were ill, Brown stayed up nights attending to them, often finding no time even to change his clothes. While nursing son Frederick in June 1854, for example, for more than two weeks Brown did not change his clothes "except for washing." Working in his fields, pastures, and barnyards over the years, Brown routinely slogged through mud, shoveled manure, and butchered livestock. Bringing his Saxony sheep back to Ohio from the East in the winter of 1845, he was in mud "up to my knees," he reported to Mary while "weather bound" in Buffalo. "I am just going to try my Seventh night in the mid Ship of a Canal boat, among the sheep, (a Sheperd without doubt)," he joked, "wraped up nice in a Buffalo skin." A man who was compulsively clean should have found little humor in such filth and stench.[16]

His appearance changed conspicuously during his later years. His "good clothes" at home in Akron and Springfield were of snuff-colored broadcloth and white shirts with a plait on each side of the breast, or a dark woolen business suit. Fastidious standards of dress could not be maintained in Kansas. As a guerrilla leader in the field, Brown continued to bathe and shave whenever possible, but he was often unshaven and his hair became "long and wild." In camp he wore coarse linen trousers tucked into high, cowhide boots, a cotton shirt open at the throat, a belt designed "for knives and pistols," a long torn linen duster, and a battered chip straw hat. His son John, Jr., thought he often looked "ragged." When in Kansas towns he wore a heavy white linen suit.

Increasingly, his attire reflected the image he sought to inspire. Sanborn remembered that in Chicago Brown discarded the "faded summer garments" he wore in Kansas in favor of a new suit of brown broadcloth or soft wool "cut in the fashion of a dozen years before" that gave Brown "the air of a respectable deacon in a rural parish." In Boston in his last years, when he was ostensibly hiding from "U.S. hounds," his appearance was so "rural" as to attract notice. The portrait photo advertised by Thaddeus Hyatt in the spring of 1859 shows a full-bearded Brown wearing a starched collar, cravat, and the dark, loose-fitting brass-buttoned coat, matching vest, and rumpled pants of a rural businessman of modest circumstances. Brown's clothing, like his demeanor, by this time reflected his flare for the dramatic and was one reason that his New England patrons referred to him as an "Old Covenanter," a "Roundhead hero," or a "border chieftain." As deliberately as he had begun to refer to himself as "Old Brown," he had altered his appearance. This creative self-fashioning refutes any claim on that score that he suffered from dementia, though it raises questions I shall discuss later about his changing persona.[17]

Brown was as set in his ways as he was in his opinions. Son Salmon insisted in old age that his own reason for refusing to go to Harpers Ferry was concern that his father would be caught because of his passion for order. Salmon warned his brothers, he recalled: "'You know father. You know he will *dally* till he is trapped.' Father had a peculiarity of insisting on *order*. For example, he would let no one pack his trunk; it put him on nettles even to have anyone offer to help him pack." As a joke "we used to egg strangers on to offer to help him, to see how it stirred him up," Salmon remembered. He "had a horror of departing from the order that he fixed in his own mind." Salmon claimed that he knew his father would be captured at Harpers Ferry because he "would insist on getting everything arranged just to suit him before he would consent to make a move."[18]

Salmon was mistaken about having warned his brothers. In fact, he probably did not know his father planned to seize Harpers Ferry before Watson and Oliver left home, because they did not know where Brown intended to strike until he disclosed his plan to the company at the Kennedy farm. And on other occasions Salmon gave other reasons for refusing to join the Virginia expedition.

But Salmon was right that his father took great care in packing his trunks. John Brown squirreled away virtually every letter and document that might

FIGURE 8.1. Last portrait of Brown, taken May 1859, and sold to raise money for his family, suggests his changing image of himself. Photo by Black & Bachelder.

CREDIT: Library of Congress.

be useful, and keeping track of their location was often a problem when he was away from home and wanted his wife or sons to look for particular papers.[19] His directions for locating papers thus tell us something about his orderliness and the quality of his memory. They suggest that Brown was less meticulous than Salmon remembered. In 1846, for example, Brown sent home to Akron from Springfield for a business letter and his "old pocket memorandum book" that he wanted John, Jr., to bring with him "without failure or delay" when John came to work for his father in a week or so. The letter was evidently important, but Brown was unsure just where he had left it. "I think the letter is filed, & with a bundle in one of the cupboards.... The pocket book I think is in your chest." "The letter may possibly be with Mr. Perkins."[20] En route to North Elba in 1855, to give another example, Brown wanted Mary to send him the pedigree and bill of sale for "the Bull Calf Essex." The documents, he thought, were in the red trunk upstairs which contained the "greater part of my private papers," but might be among papers in "my old Desk," although he was "quite sure they are not in it." The desk was locked. "I believe I gave you all my Keys; but if not I think they are in the Pocket of my old pantaloons."[21]

Although Brown was often unsure where he had left particular papers, his memory of the contents of letters and documents was often quite good. In 1852 he sent home for one of countless newspaper articles he had saved. "I want to have Jason & Owen overhaul [search] all the bundles of Papers in my old Desk, Trunk, Old Leather Valice, *& small Tin Trunk if it can be found*; to find a number of the (Burlington Free Press) dated 3rd December 1847 together with the wrapper or Envelope which had been torn off from the paper *but was preserved* along *with it*." He advised Mary to open "but one package at once; *while looking* so as not to get the papers any more *mixed* than they now are." Given this disarray, it was not surprising that in 1858 he could not find the contract between Gerrit Smith and the Thompson brothers that established title to the farm he had purchased from the latter.[22]

Brown was unquestionably absent-minded. Once in 1853 he brought home a letter from John, Jr., to son Jason, but forgot it for so long that he "carried it in his pocket till the envelope had come very near letting [the] letter out." His hectic life in Kansas aggravated his problems in keeping track of things. In order to draft a "treaty" between free state and proslavery irregular forces, Brown asked Mary in July 1858 to "search a package of papers" he had left with her and look in his "old Pine Desk" for copies of the resolutions the National Kansas Committee had adopted in January. If Mary could not find the papers, she should have daughter Ruth copy his letter and send it to son John, Jr., in Ashtabula County, Ohio, in hopes the papers were there. Brown was not sure where he had left this critical evidence of his right to the cash and large quantities of weapons that the National Kansas Committee had granted him.

Increasingly, as arms and equipment accumulated, Brown had to rely on the help of others. He was sometimes "at a loss" to know how to transport things to remote locations. Things inevitably got lost. On his way home to North Elba in April 1859, Brown wrote Kagi, "If you have found my writing case and papers, please send them, without delay."[23] The task of arranging the movement and safe storage of wagon loads of supplies and weapons as well as stabling teams of horses overwhelmed his intuitive methods of recall.

Of course citing only letters in which Brown asked for documents or other misplaced items risks overstating lapses of memory. His letters also reveal a continued interest in and mastery of details of day-to-day living. Even during long absences, Brown regularly gave careful instructions about work schedules, hiring laborers, paying bills, even the smallest details of family life. "It will be best for Owen to take the 2nd thickest Calf skins to the Shoemakers, so that the little boys may have their boots made up early," he wrote to Mary in 1846, "& be sure to have the boots made uncommon large to meet the growth of their feet."[24] It was only on the eve of his execution that Brown finally conceded he could no longer advise Mary and son Salmon about the management of the farm or the education of his three youngest daughters.[25]

Brown's recall of events and knowledge of books and public affairs is also relevant here. On these things too Brown's memory in old age remained substantially intact. In his last weeks, he demonstrated a variety of ways in which, if Harpers Ferry suggested flaws in his judgment, his memory processes were still sound. His letters show him to be fully aware of public responses to his raid and able to marshal effective arguments in support of his cause. Despite repeated bouts of malaria and the physical hardships he had endured, his memory of his life was in some respects exceptional. When questioned after his capture at Harpers Ferry, Brown had not slept for forty-eight hours or had the cuts on his head and neck attended to. At one point he conceded, understandably, "I may answer incorrectly, but not intentionally. My head is a little confused by wounds, and my memory of dates and such like is somewhat confused."[26]

But he remembered both distant and recent events accurately, recalling the name of the father of a counterfeiter he had known as a child whose Irish family Brown thought "very low." He recalled correctly a recent trip through Pittsburgh and the speech he had given during the trial of the Oberlin slave rescuers on the Fugitive Slave Act and his own rescue of eleven slaves from Missouri. He recalled meeting Jeb Stuart in Kansas and referred to him by name. To be sure, Brown withheld sensitive information and lied about his role in the Kansas border war. "I killed no man except in fair fight," he declared. But he recalled names and events promptly and his mind never drifted during the lengthy interview.

Brown knew accurately much that happened during the raid. He quarreled with his questioners about the sequence of events, claiming that in the final moments of the raid he and his men had tried to surrender. He recalled the number and manufacturer of the rifles and revolvers he brought to the Kennedy farm, and corrected a questioner about his largest weapon: "It is not properly a swivel," he said, "it is a very large rifle on a pivot. The ball is larger than a musket ball; it is intended for a slug." He recalled orders he had given, actions he had taken, and hostages he had "arrested." He admitted, "We did kill some when defending ourselves," but insisted that he "saw no one fire except directly in self-defense. Our orders were strict not to harm any one not in arms against us." However self-serving these remarks may be or have seemed, they reveal no confusion about what he had done and failed to do at Harpers Ferry.[27]

In sum, Brown's memory evidenced no "deficits" that suggest dementia. Nor did other cognitive functions. He expressed himself ably in speech and his motor skills, at least his writing skills, were functioning. Writing to friends from prison, he marshaled his tiny phalanxes of runic-like characters into words with the same discipline and idiosyncratic spelling, punctuation, and underscoring that his pages had long shown. No tremor or haste was evident in those eloquent, spare epistles. During the session with Governor Wise, a local physician asked Brown if he had "lanced" the neck of a neighbor while at the Kennedy. When Brown admitted that he had, the physician told him it was "done very well and scientifically."[28]

His self-possession and rhetorical displays are equally impressive evidence of the vitality of his cognitive functions in those last weeks. During questioning after the raid, Brown explained his position on slavery and staked out a claim to speak for radical abolitionism. He had come to Harpers Ferry to free the slaves, not to "gratify any personal animosity, revenge or vindictive spirit." "We expected no reward; we expected the satisfaction of endeavoring to do for them in distress – the greatly oppressed – as we would be done by," he declared. He lectured Virginians on the Golden Rule, insisting that "you are guilty of a great wrong against God and humanity." It would be "perfectly right for anyone to interfere with you so far as to free those you wilfully and wickedly hold in bondage." "I wish to say further that you had better, all you people of the South, prepare yourselves for a settlement of this question.... You may dispose of me very easily. I am nearly disposed of now; but this question is still to be settled – this negro question, I mean. The end is not yet." It was with some justice that Wise concluded Brown was fit to hang.[29]

III

Still, something seemed strange about Brown's performance. His explanation of his "disaster" at Harpers Ferry explained little. His insistence that the Virginians "overrated" their strength in thinking they could have captured him if he "had not allowed it," like his claim that he had a "right" to expect 3,000–5,000 men from the region to join him, seemed wildly unrealistic. His eagerness to have his interrogators study his Provisional Constitution and his hints that he had had a vision of the future course of events showed, in his circumstance, unwarranted hubris. Such boastfulness seemed bizarre in a self-styled soldier who had just suffered ignominy and now faced the gallows. Despite this and not having slept for two days, Brown was remarkably eager. Asked if he was well enough to talk, he replied that he would "rather like it." Queried later if the questioning annoyed him, Brown replied, "Not in the least." Despite his apparent composure, his claim to be acting as God's "instrument" seemed to some a confession of derangement.[30]

Was this behavior evidence of mania? That elevated mood, when acute, produces not only exaltation but confusion, unwillingness to abide criticism, and impatience with details. If mania was driving Brown, it could explain his lapses during the raid, his failure to bring adequate provisions for his men, and his apparent misreading of how local residents would respond to his raid. In ignoring Kagi's warnings to leave and in becoming, by his own account, too concerned with the safety of his hostages, Brown seemingly demonstrated distractability. The sheer scale of his project suggested manic grandiosity.

It is typical of manics, moreover, to overindulge in pleasurable activities that risk painful consequences. Brown's speculative ventures in the 1830s brought him bankruptcy and brief imprisonment, his foray at Pottawatomie made him and his sons fugitives, and Harpers Ferry squandered their lives.

But mania involves other, quite distinct symptoms and signs not apparent in Brown during or after the raid. Manic speech is pressured, loud, rapid, difficult to interrupt. During episodes manics may talk nonstop, become theatrical, gesture wildly, even sing as they banter or rant. Their thoughts may race from topic to topic without logical connection. They may be easily distracted by irrelevant details, irritable when thwarted or disappointed, sometimes erupting in "affective storms" or "manic rages." They gesture too rapidly, require little sleep, and remain hyper-alert, misinterpreting the actions of those about them. In extreme cases, they may experience delusions and hallucinations.

Of course some of these features of mania are inapplicable or meaningless in Brown's case. His life as a guerrilla chieftain was a perfect "cover" for bizarre or reckless behavior. Among his inner circle, his obsession with slavery became devotion to the cause. On the other hand, the assumption of his Ohio acquaintances and business associates that anyone who thinks he is at war during peacetime must be mad led to overdiagnosis: To them, as we have seen, Brown was a "monomaniac."

But mania is an expression of disturbed brain chemistry and its symptoms are not confined to particular contexts. If John Brown was manic during or after Harpers Ferry, signs of it would have been conspicuous. Yet so far as the record shows Brown betrayed none of the signs of mania beyond elevated mood and braggadocio. On the first day of the raid, he assured the armory workers he arrested that they would be unharmed, gave them an "abolition speech," and then ignored them. During the long night before the marines' assault, he spoke to his hostages and his men only briefly and intermittently.

During the interview after capture, his talk was neither persistent nor erratic. No one had trouble interrupting him, and he gestured scarcely at all. If he seemed oddly upbeat, he was not "high as a kite," "racing," or notably irritable. He showed respect for his captors and claimed that he did not mean to be "insulting" or "offensive." The Richmond *Enquirer* reported that Brown met Governor Wise with "utmost composure" and was "dignified and respectful."[31] If attorney Andrew Hunter thought Brown "garrulous," the Old Man was not so forthcoming as to give information that might implicate others or betray the fact that several of his raiders were then fleeing through the mountains toward Pennsylvania.[32]

Brown's mood seemed no more elevated three days later, when Hoyt, the young attorney sent to spy out the situation for Boston abolitionists, found him "*desperately* cool & *calm*." During the trial, Brown himself questioned witnesses, but Judge Richard Parker never thought it necessary to rule him out of order or otherwise restrain him. Parker remembered years later that Brown was "always alert & self-poised, much of the time on his feet, guiding his case and watching it closely, and apparently possessed of a vigorous mind and an abundance of strong hard sense.... [H]e was in no sense a fanatic." At the end of the trial, a reporter found Brown "perfectly resigned to his fate and ... unconscious of having committed any crime." In short, outwardly Brown evidenced nothing of that "fever" that had burned in his son Frederick. As an explanation of Brown's behavior during and after Harpers Ferry, we must rule out full-blown mania.[33]

But such fevers may burn low. In hypomanic (mild or less severe) episodes, many of the symptoms of mania may be absent. The hypomanic's mood is euphoric or unusually cheerful, it exhibits conceit and uncritical self-confidence rather than grandiosity. To strangers, hypomanics appear to be sociable, witty, inventive people who command attention by chattering and spouting ideas prolifically. They talk rapidly but not as persistently as manics and are easier to interrupt. They rarely show "flight of ideas" or psychomotor agitation, although a buoyant mood may shift abruptly to irritability. The hypomanic mood not only boosts self-assurance, it increases fluency with words and ideas. It may also boost intelligence and problem-solving skills, evoke a greater variety of ideas and encourage the juxtaposition of widely varied sorts of information and imagery. Hypomanics are divergent, rather than convergent thinkers.[34] Subjectively, they feel themselves lifted out of their ordinary selves, become someone different, even "foreign" and very special.[35]

If Brown's mood was as "cheerful" as he insisted during his last weeks, he may indeed have been mildly hypomanic. His flow of "perfect words" in messages to the "great congregation" and his unwonted eloquence at his sentencing underscore that possibility. If he was not notably talkative, he certainly busied himself writing letters. Eager to defend his cause and having no distractions, he was unusually productive during his last days. But it is doubtful that a flood tide of bipolar illness buoyed that effort. Brown's letters were testimonies to his faith, evidence of a refinement and codification of themes he had often articulated liberally sprinkled with biblical adages. His thinking was, if you will, decidedly "convergent," orthodox, and thematically repetitive. He evoked few new images or metaphors. He carefully censored references to his own past and denied flatly to a visitor that he was responsible for the Pottawatomie killings.

If Brown was subject to abnormal elevations of mood, surprisingly little evidence of it appears in the years before his pilgrimage to Kansas. His letters home were concerned primarily with day-to-day matters, not visions of great things to come. He had kind words for the little girls, and on occasion he poked fun at his boys: "You must get some rasins, or something on my account for Anne, & Kitty to make them a small payment," he wrote to Mary in 1846, "& I do not forget that I shall owe Oliver a good deal when he gets done talking loud in the house."[36] But his letters rarely filled more than a page; they never suggest the profusion of ideas and extraneous information we would expect to find if written during a hypomanic mood. Brown's sons even joked among themselves about "father's" parsimony with words and dislike of frivolous talk. "This letter is so lengthy," Owen teased John, Jr., and his father, "that it is not fit to send to Father. If I had been writing to him only, I should not have written one-fourth part as much."[37]

Among scores of letters Brown wrote in the three decades before Harpers Ferry, only one suggests he experienced such fundamental symptoms of hypomania as sleeplessness and hyper-alertness. But that letter evidences no hint of elevated mood and grandiosity. Rather it betrays anxiety and restlessness. Writing to Mary from Springfield in 1847, Brown reported that business was for once encouraging, "not that we are selling higher but we sell some." He was lonely and "homesick," not elated: "I feel it would do me a great deal of good to return to my home, & to my old way of living," he told Mary. "My mind while here is on the alert by night as well as by day, & I really feel the kneed of rest." His thoughts turned to his family and his hope to set out for home in three or four weeks. "I see you all in my imagination a great part of the time & hope the sight will be real soon." He reminded Mary and the children of the plight of slaves "who are forced away from their dearest relatives with little if any hope of ever meeting them again on this side [of] the grave."[38]

Brown's mood was often somber. Even when he "rejoiced" at the prospect of going home to see his family, he was mindful of the precariousness of the soul. Writing to seventeen-year-old Ruth, Brown reported that he was in "midling health" and very busy, but hoped to "go home if our lives & health are spared next month.... Sometimes my immagination [sic] follows those of my family who have passed behind the scenes," he reflected, "& I would almost rejoice to receive permission to make them a personal visit. I have outlived nearly half of all my numerous family, & I ought to realize that a large proportion of my journey is traveled over." As he so often did, Brown concluded his letter to Ruth with expressions of concern about her and "all at home." Like Job, Brown said, adding "(not that I would ever think to compare myself with Job)," he hoped that "ye *sin* not; that you form no foolish attachments; & that you be not a companion of Fools."[39]

IV

Were such dark musings evidence of depression? By the mid-nineteenth century, the term "depression" had begun to replace the older "melancholia" to describe a form of partial insanity affecting the emotions which was marked by a slowing of mental and physical functions.

Clinicians today recognize several degrees of depression. Severely depressed individuals feel hopeless, discouraged, miserable, fearful, and beyond help; their thinking, speech, and motor skills are slowed and they consider their past lives to be failed and past accomplishments to be meaningless. Their days are colorless, their food and their own bodies repulsive to them. They lack energy. Their lives appear "vegetative." Their sadness is often evident in flat speaking tones and a decreased volume and variety of speech. They are despairing and "do not care anymore." They withdraw from family and give up hobbies and recreations. Their bodily functions slow, they get "tight" headaches, muscle aches, and other maladies.

Less serious "agitated" depressives, on the other hand, often respond to events, even minor frustrations, with angry outbursts. Their image of themselves is negative, they blame themselves for trivial mistakes and may feel responsible for disasters with which they had nothing to do. Preoccupied with guilt and feelings of worthlessness, they may develop delusions about their own impending ruin and of being a burden to others. Their unjustifiable self-reproach may become obsessive, in contrast to the grandiose delusions of manics. Plans to commit suicide or attempts at suicide may be a way to end the pain of depression or to escape from perceived insurmountable obstacles. Death is the only escape.[40]

For the mildest forms of depression, psychiatrists use the term *dysthymia* to denote individuals once described as "neurotic." Dysthymics often complain of lifelong depression. Other symptoms may include poor appetite or overeating, insomnia or hypersomnia, low energy or fatigue, low self-esteem, poor concentration or difficulty making decisions, and feelings of hopelessness. They suffer from chronic feelings of inadequacy and self-denigration and express these feelings in a dramatic manner that defies attempts to remedy them. Dysthymics become depressed over the demands of everyday life and they tend to blame others for their failures as much as themselves. They typically lead narrow lives and have unstable relationships, and they often abuse alcohol or drugs.[41]

John Brown was genuinely depressed from time to time. He saw evil and suffering as the lot of mankind. "This life is intended as a season of training, chastisement, temptation, affliction, and trial; and the 'righteous shall come out of' it all," he wrote his children from prison. He was often discouraged and "gloomy." Business setbacks, the deaths of loved ones, and the threat of deadly diseases were frequent concerns. Repeated bereavements resonated with his tragic reading of human existence. Whenever sickness or death struck, he admonished his adult children to remember that this world is "not the Home of man." "I hope all of you will bear in mind the shortness, & the great uncertainty of life," he wrote to Mary and the children during their first winter in North Elba.[42] Death was very much a part of everyday life.[43] Like an early frost, mourning withered even sanguine spirits.

Psychiatrists today distinguish normal grief and mourning from pathological depression, although symptoms of mourning at times mimic those of severe depression. Bereavement produces a predictable, if somewhat varied, sequence of responses, including an initial numbness or emotional flatness that protects the mourner from pain, a period of pining and preoccupation with thoughts of the deceased, perhaps the development of a set of fixed images and reminders of him or her. This stage is followed by intense grief, free-floating anxiety, loss of interest in the world, loss of the capacity to adopt a new love object, and the disorganization of old habits. Letting go is not only painful but profoundly confusing.

Mourners may feel anger directed toward the deceased or blame fate or God for their loss. They often wonder whether they could have done something to save the loved one or to ease his or her pain; they may also feel guilt about their own ambivalent feelings toward the deceased or simply about surviving a loved one. Their heightened awareness of their own mortality and feelings of abandonment may awaken fear. Mourning may last from six to eighteen months in adults and they may require as long as six months or more before they are ready to resume work and face everyday life. Feelings of loneliness, sadness, anger, despair, and "reactive depression" are normal and appropriate in bereavement. Detachment from the loved one and a reintegration of life can be achieved if these emotions are confronted and resolved. But mourners who deny or ignore their grief may suffer prolonged periods of depression and a diffuse hostility that may be displaced onto friends and relations. They may carry their sense of loss, their anger, and their despondency with them for years. If mourning itself is a normal healing process, unsuccessful mourning may deepen into something more dangerous.[44]

John Brown's seasons of mourning lingered long and his losses at times shook his faith and his hopes for happiness. The first such period for which we have contemporary evidence marked the end of a hopeful time, when in August 1832, his wife Dianthe died of "child bed fever" sixteen months after the Browns' four-year-old son Frederick had died. Perhaps there was bitterness toward God in Brown's letter informing his father of Dianthe's death, but he told the story calmly. "We are again smarting under the rod of our Heavenly Father," he began. "Last night about eleven o'clock my affectionate, dutiful and faithful Dianthe (to use her own words) bade 'farewell to Earth.' My own health is so poor," he went on, "that I have barely strength to give you a short history of what passed since I last wrote you." He reminded his father that Dianthe's health had recently been "very poor." "Tomorrow she is to lay [sic] beside our little son."[45]

Three days after Dianthe's death Brown was still numb with grief. For hours he sat motionless; for days he did not leave his house. He ceased to care about his tannery and felt he would never work again. He lost interest in everything. He was bewildered and distressed by his inability to grieve, ascribing his lack of feeling to his own illness. "Such is the state of my health (& of my mind in consequence), for I am unwilling to ascribe it to any other cause, that I have felt my loss but verry little & can think or write about her, or about disposing of my little children, with as little emotion as of the most common subject. This is a matter of surprise to myself," he added, "for I loved my wife & had lived very agreeably with her.... I supposed & have always supposed my feelings to be as warm & tender as those of other men." Brown's mind was "in a dead calm. I have been pretty much confined to my house for a number of weeks.... I find I am still getting more & more unfit for every thing." He was not "overcome in my feelings but ... I have been growing numb for a good while."[46]

Not long after this, Brown moved out of his house. He and his children boarded with his former apprentice, James Foreman, and for several weeks more Brown could not bring himself to go to the tannery. Not until December did he return to work. When Foreman's wife could no longer manage to care for Brown's family, he took his children home and hired a housekeeper. In the summer of 1833 he married sixteen-year-old Mary Ann Day, the younger sister of his housekeeper, after a brief acquaintanceship in which few words were exchanged and without the formality of courtship.

Dianthe's death long darkened Brown's outlook. In the revealing autobiographical letter that Brown wrote years later, he paid a curious tribute to her. Writing about himself in the third person, he said: "At a little past twenty years led by his own inclination *& prompted also* by his Father, he married a *remarkably plain*; but neat industrious, & economical girl; of excellent character; earnest piety; & good practical common sence; about one year younger than himself. This woman by her mild, frank, *& more than all else*: by her very consistent conduct, acquired; & ever while she lived maintained a most powerful; & good influence over him. Her plain but kind admonitions generally had the right effect; without arousing his haughty obstinate temper."[47]

This rare reference to Dianthe is one of a string of recurring references in his writing to a perhaps unintended theme: personal loss. Brown was ordinarily reticent about his personal life. But in the tale of his childhood Brown made the point about loss repeatedly. Little John at age six had lost "beyond recovery" a treasured yellow marble given him by a poor Indian boy. "*It took years to heal the wound*; & I *think* he cried at times about it." Five months later, John tamed a "*little bob* tail *Squirrel*" that he "almost idolized." "*This too he lost*; by its wandering away; or by getting killed; & for a year or two John was *in mourning*; and looking at all the Squirrels he could see to try & discover Bobtail, *if possible*." Shortly thereafter, Brown turned briefly to the loss of his mother. "At Eight years old, John was left a Motherless boy which loss was complete & pearmanent [sic] for notwithstanding his Father again married to a sensible, intelligent, and on many accounts a very estimable woman; yet he never *adopted her in feeling;* but continued to pine after his own Mother for years." In a meaningful sense, Brown's autobiographical letter was a lamentation about separation and mourning.[48]

This reflected in part Brown's own dark mood at the time. When he wrote this letter, he was recovering from a long bout of malaria that had upset his plans for months. He was en route to Iowa, where he planned to join his recruits. A shortage of funds had forced him to drive one of the wagons loaded with weapons, and he had developed back pain in doing so. He also lacked funds to pay his freight bills, and "together with being much of the time quite unwell; & depressed with disapointments [sic], & delays," he was "exceedingly mortifyed" by his inability to pay his debts on his farm.[49] The resulting depression had cast a shadow over Brown's story of the boy named John.

The likelihood that Brown at times brooded over the loss of loved ones – perhaps a legacy of unresolved mourning – may explain the one striking admission in his life that for a time he had wished to die. Oddly, this confession was offered in a mood of apparent jubilation. In February 1858 at the home of wealthy benefactor Gerrit Smith, who had just reaffirmed his support for Brown's war against slavery,[50] Brown wrote Franklin B. Sanborn, "I felt for a number of years in earlier life: a steady, strong, desire: to die: but since I saw my prospect of becoming a 'reaper' in the great harvest I have not only felt quite willing to live: but have enjoyed life much & am now rather anxious to live for a few years more."[51]

Some scholars have taken this passage as evidence that Brown was a "depressive."[52] But it is not an admission of mental disorder; it is a confession of religious vastation or spiritual blight, of having once felt alienation from God's grace and a readiness to reject a sinning world. It is evidently included in the letter to Sanborn as a kind of emotional counterpoint to dramatize Brown's ecstatic embrace of his role as a "reaper" in God's harvest.

The letter was an effort to recruit the idealistic young Concord school teacher to Brown's "service." "What an inconceivable amount of good you might so effect; by your *counsel, your example, your encouragement, your natural, & acquired ability* for active service," Brown flattered Sanborn. "And then how *very little* can we possibly lose? Certainly the cause is enough to live for: if not to [blank] for…. God has honored but comparatively a very small part of mankind with my possible chance for such mighty & soul satisfying rewards." Brown urged Sanborn to make his own decision "after having *thoroughly counted* the cost. I would flatter no man into such a measure if I could do it ever so easily. I expect to 'endure hardness,'" Brown avowed, "but I expect to effect a mighty conquest even though it be like the last victory of Samson."[53]

In the letter Brown's confession of black thoughts follows his reference to Samson. Christians knew well the story of the ordeal of Samson before he achieved the strength that enabled him to crush the Philistines even as he buried himself under fallen pillars. The reference to Brown's own dark experience invited comparison of Brown's own troubled preparation against slavery with Samson's trials.[54]

The letter to Sanborn was not the first occasion on which Brown had revealed low spirits. In fact, Brown had written Sanborn the previous August that he felt "mortification and depression of feelings" for not having repaid Gerrit Smith and others money they had advanced to him. "My health has been much better of late," Brown declared. "I believe my anxiety and discouragements had something to do with repeated returns of fever and ague I have had, as it tended to deprive me of sleep and to debilitate me."[55]

In these confessions Brown used his "disappointments" and "depression" to justify delays in paying his debts as well as solicitations for financial help. Confession presumably underscored his sincerity and good intent. But in his many appeals to contributors or creditors he never admitted discouragement in his mission to free the slaves. He invariably coupled his recitations of troubles with affirmations of renewed resolve on that score.

Indeed, low spirits seem on occasion to have spurred him to action. A fundraising drive in New England had proved so disappointing, he wrote to John, Jr., in April 1857, that "I have had a good deal of discouragement; & *have often* felt quite depressed: but 'hitherto God hath helped me.' About the *last of* last Week, I gave vent to those feelings in a short piece…headed Old Browns, Farewell. to the Plymouth Rocks; Bunker Hill, Monuments; Charter Oaks; & Uncle Toms Cabbins." But, Brown reported cheerfully, the essay had finally touched the conscience of "this Heaven exalted," this "extravagant" people. It prompted one admiring Bostonian to write Brown "authorizing me to draw on him at sight for $7000, & others were also moved to be in earnest." Brown was now as adept at shaming Yankees into contributing to his war as he was at flattering them for doing so.[56]

Brown's professions of low spirits did not foster mistrust among his benefactors. But admissions of disheartenment were not simply stratagems to wheedle money. Brown was moody. All his children recognized that he bore responsibilities heavily at times and needed encouragement. His long struggle with textile manufacturers over the price of wool had oppressed him and evoked sympathy from his sons. "There seems to be a blue vein running throughout the letter you sent to Jason," John, Jr., wrote in 1850. "Well, I do not wonder at it. My surprise is rather that you can bear up under such a complication of misfortunes with anything like the fortitude you do."[57]

Brown took inspiration from his antislavery work. In Springfield, he had urged "colored friends to 'trust in God & keep their powder dry' at a Thanksgiving public meeting today," he wrote Mary in November 1850. Five weeks later, Brown expressed satisfaction in helping blacks defy slaveholders' agents seeking to return runaways to the South. "I want all my family to imagine themselves in the same dreadful condition," he wrote his children in North Elba. "My only spare time being taken up (often till late hours at night) in the way I speak of, has prevented me from the gloomy homesick feelings which had before so much oppressed me; not that I forget my family at all."[58] He had conquered his depression by throwing himself into his cause and sharing his triumphs with his family.

Even in good times he reflected ruefully on his failings. With the happy conclusion of his new business arrangement with Perkins in January 1844, he praised Mary as "the partner of my own choice, & the sharer of my poverty, trials, discredit, & sore afflictions; as well as of what comfort, & seeming prosperity has fallen to my lot; for quite a number of years." Despite his "habitual neglect" of his family, Brown pleaded, "I am verry much of the time present in spirit. I do not forget the firm attachment of her who has remained my fast, & faithful affectionate friend, when others said of me (now that he lieth he shall rise up no more.)" Noting the "verry [sic] considerable difference in our age, as well as all the follies, & faults with which I am justly chargeable, I really admire at your constancy; & I really feel notwithstanding I sometimes chide you severely that you are *really* my better half."[59]

The threat of a death in the family evoked Brown's memories of past bereavements, which he took to be "afflictively" providential. Ruth recalled her father carrying a dying eleven-month-old Ellen in his arms, singing to her, and crying openly when she was gone. Whenever the family moved, Brown or one of his sons dutifully unearthed all the children's coffins, digging new graves for them behind their next home.[60]

Brown was away from home when his one-year-old daughter Amelia, "little Kitty," was scalded to death. He was "unable to give expression" to his grief on learning of the accident. "I feel assured that notwithstanding God has chastised us *often, & sore*; yet he has not *himself* entirely withdrawn from us, nor forsaken us *utterly*," Brown pleaded with Mary. "The sudden, & dreadful manner in which he has seen fit to call *our dear little Kitty* to take her leave of us, is I kneed not tell you how much on mind; but before *Him*; I will bow my head in submission, & hold my peace." Brown declared that "any ideas that to me the separa[tion] [from the family] is not a painful one are wholly mistaken ones. I have sailed over a somewhat stormy sea for nearly half a century, & have experienced enough to teach me thoroughly that I may most reasonabl[y] buckle up & be prepared for the tempest. Mary," he exhorted her, "let us try to maintain a cheerfull self command while we are tossing up & down, & let our motto still be Action, Action; as we have but one life to live."[61]

Writing in January 1852 to express sympathy to Ruth and her husband Henry, whose infant son was ill, Brown reminded them how often he had lost loved ones. "My attachments to this world have been very strong, & Divine Providence has been cutting me loose one Cord after another ... but notwithstanding I have so much to remind me that all ties must *soon* be severed; I am still clinging like those who have hardly taken a single lesson." He repeated his hope that his sons would yet "understand that this world is not the *home* of man; and act accordingly." For Brown the deepest reality of life was suffering and death.[62]

That last admonition betrayed what was preying on his mind. As he wrote that grim warning, Brown was with John, Jr., who had just told him the painful truth about his children's heretical beliefs. Brown's despair was evident. In contemplating the "religious prospects of my numerous family," he said, he had "*very little* to cheer. That this should be so, is I perfectly understand the legitimate fruit of my own planting; and that only increases my punishment." Once he had been "cheered with the belief that my elder children had chosen the *Lord*, to be their *God*; and I valued much on their influence, & example in atoning for my deficiency, & bad exampel with the younger children." But the latter – Mary's children – were far less thoughtful, & disposed to reflection than were my older children at their age. I will not dwell on this distressing subject but only say that so far as I have gone; it is from no disposition to reflect on any one but myself. I think I can clearly discover where I wandered from the Road. How to get on it with my family is beyond my ability to *see*; or my courage to *hope*."[63] As Brown learned on the eve of Harpers Ferry, even his fifteen-year-old daughter Annie rejected his faith.[64] Ruth was his only child to experience a religious conversion and embrace her father's God.

V

There is, then, ample evidence that Brown was subject to brief periods of profound discouragement and "depression of feelings." The events just reviewed were among what must have been Brown's bleakest moments. Despite those moments, he certainly was not perpetually discouraged or anxious. Nor was he paralyzed by guilt or self-doubt. His admissions of "faults" and "foibles" and of neglecting his family were sometimes coupled with suggestions that the

boys might want to emulate anything "good" they found in his example.⁶⁵ His
self-esteem was not shattered by the tragedies that plagued him nor did he ever
imply that his lot in life was uniquely burdened. Ultimately, he believed, everyone had to face such desolation; the only refuge was God.

The religious apostasy of his children did not lead him to despair for long
or to distance himself from them. He met routine disappointments with initiative, determination, even fervor. Brown was unshaken by the breakup of his
partnership with Perkins in 1853. "Father has just got home and was here
today in very good spirits, we thought, after all his ill success," Jason reported
at the time. "I am really glad to see that Father stands his troubles so well."
After celebrating his fifty-third birthday, Brown was "surprised that one guilty
of such an incredible amount of sin & folly should be spared so long," but
characteristically added that he "still keeps hopeing to do better hereafter."⁶⁶
Failure did not crush him.

John Brown's admissions of feeling "depressed" did not mean quite what
that word implies today. To be "depressed," "anxious," "disheartened," or "discouraged" was not then to be mentally unbalanced or deficient in manhood. To
genteel Northerners, such expressions of feeling may even have been evidence
of moral sensibility. The popular term for what we today call serious depression, as noted earlier, was then *melancholia*. And in his many moments of self-
revelation and despair, Brown never uttered that word in reference to himself.
Nor did anyone in his family suggest that he was melancholic. Even the affiants who sought a commutation of his sentence on grounds of insanity never
claimed he suffered from melancholia; it was his "mania" they complained of.
No one said that he suffered from the "vapours," "hypochondria," or "nervous
disorder" either. No one urged him to enter an asylum, as many people did
when deeply saddened or distressed. If at times his sons described Brown as
"blue" or "disheartened," they also took heart from his repeated charge to meet
disappointment with action. Except for the period following Dianthe's death,
Brown never gave in to "anxiety and discouragement." And except when felled
by the "ague" or other recognizable disease, he was always striving, scheming,
"adoing." Even while bedridden with malaria and so "lame" in the back he
could scarcely walk, Brown kept up his correspondence, his fundraising, and
his efforts to gather men and arms to attack slavery.

It seems clear that Brown's moods fail to meet criteria of clinical depression
or manic-depressive illness, although during his bereavement over Dianthe he
confessed to symptoms we recognize as common to the former. Unresolved
mourning from the loss of his mother in childhood and his first wife as a
young man may have reinforced his vision of life as a season of testing. If he
sometimes hinted that his war against slavery might end in his own death, he
was fully engaged in the realities of his struggle and determined to fulfill his
"mighty purpose."

As some of his contemporaries recognized, his imagination was essentially
religious. His outlook shared something with the religious type William James
later called the "sick soul," for whom the vanity of mortal things, the sense of

sin, and the perception that the natural world was "double-faced and unhome-like" could produce despondency. Sick souls like Tolstoy, James said, reached a point of "absolute disenchantment with ordinary life" and found its "habit-ual values" a ghastly "mockery." Sick souls did not necessarily exhibit "intel-lectual insanity" or delusion about matters of fact; they remained in contact with reality. Only in extreme cases were they disposed to "insane melancholia, with hallucinations and delusions." For these cases, James said, the consola-tion of scriptural texts no longer sufficed to overcome their desperation. The sick soul's "deliverance" had to come in as strong a form as his "grisly blood-freezing heart-palsying sensation" of evil.

Unlike the "healthy-minded" way of viewing life, which dismisses evil and suffering as transitory and affirms the metaphysical wholeness of the universe, the sick soul is "morbid minded." He or she sees failure at every turn and experi-ences melancholia as "passive joylessness and dreariness" or as "active anguish" that brings loathing, irritation, suspicion, anxiety, fear, and self-mistrust. A twice-born sick soul, however, knows the "complex ecstasies" that Christian, Buddhist, and other mystics may gain from renunciation of this world.

Brown was no religious melancholic. Only briefly did he consider something like a retreat from the struggles of this life, when he contracted with philan-thropist Gerrit Smith to move to North Elba to teach black homesteaders how to farm. But just days after his arrival there, his sons called him to send weap-ons to Kansas, and he did not hesitate to enter the fray. As a prisoner after Harpers Ferry, he cited the journey of Paul Bunyan's Christian in *Pilgrim's Progress* from the City of Destruction through the slough of despond to the Celestial City as a metaphor for his "work."[67]

Like James's "twice-born sick soul," Brown overcame depression by affirm-ing his belief that pain, suffering and evil are parts of God's plan of salvation. Late in life Annie Brown remembered that her father had been greatly dis-couraged before his attack on Harpers Ferry as his money was running out and recruits he expected failed to arrive. But if his mood may have influenced the timing of the raid or his defeat and capture, his long journey to reach that triumphant defeat was a measure of his conquest of spiritual darkness. In Kansas he found a calling that reconciled his ambitions, healed his psyche, and renewed his purpose. At Harpers Ferry he was Sisyphus at last atop the summit. Determined to "make the most of a defeat," he lifted his cause to the heights by embracing death as a martyr.

VI

No discussion of Brown's mental condition would be credible without taking account of the gruesome killings at Pottawatomie. To address that subject, it is necessary to consider whether or not Brown suffered from Antisocial Personality Disorder, familiarly known as psychopathy or sociopathy. Out of context, Brown's authorship of Pottawatomie is at least suggestive of that disorder. His secretiveness, disregard for the rights and feelings of others, apparent unconcern about harm to friends and relations that retaliation might bring, readiness to blame the victims for his action – all fit the diagnostic criteria. But *DSM–IV* requires a persistent pattern of antisocial behavior and indifference to others dating from childhood to make a diagnosis of Antisocial Personality Disorder. Brown had no such history. He had strong attachments to family and friends and willingly expended himself working for their welfare. *DSM–IV* specifically warns, moreover, that "seeming antisocial behavior may be part of a protective survival strategy." Thus we must examine the context of the murders to determine whether Brown in ordering them may be considered to have suffered from Antisocial Personality Disorder.[68]

Contexts shape perceptions in everyday life, and perceptions in turn are influenced by cognitive schemata and unnumbered preconceptions. As we have seen, Brown had come to Kansas determined to save his sons from the grasp of a "bogus" proslavery government. En route he had been charged by the Radical Abolitionist convention to help save Kansas for freedom. Abolitionists had even given him the broadswords his sons wielded at Pottawatomie. On that bloody Sabbath, Brown and his assassins were convinced that they and their free-state friends were under attack by proslavery forces who had just "sacked" Lawrence and were roving in armed bands across eastern Kansas. To Brown, he and his party were striking a "retaliatory blow" against the Slave Power, which had perverted territorial courts and poisoned territorial elections. They were at war, making a preemptive strike against men who, they were sure, had threatened the Brown clan and its friends.[69]

The men in the killing party shared the Northern abolitionist political culture that had turned increasingly toward acceptance of violence in the 1850s. Pottawatomie "was all that saved the territory from being over run with drunken land pirates from the Southern States," Salmon Brown insisted after his father's execution.[70] In old age, Henry Thompson still insisted, "It was the best act that was ever done for Kansas"; it had stopped the killing by the "other side." "It was the first thing that made them think there was a little grit left in the Free State men."[71]

But endorsing violence in theory and actually killing people are quite different things. After Pottawatomie three of Brown's boys were deeply distressed about their part in the killings, and two of them were unwilling to fight again. Salmon and Henry Thompson never did. Owen was hysterical with remorse, and guilt haunted him long afterwards, although he and Oliver finally rejoined their father's "army." Brown himself apparently had no such second thoughts. When son Jason, who learned of the killings only afterwards, told him that Pottawatomie was a "wicked act," Brown replied, "God is my judge."[72] Even as he awaited execution after Harpers Ferry, Brown remained silent on the subject. If he even had regrets, he left no evidence of it.

The moral armor that protected Brown from remorse or self-doubt was his belief in his mission to fight slavery and his biblical sense of justice. Conviction sanctioned the horrors he inflicted at Pottawatomie. He was doing the Lord's work to defeat proslavery evil. He saw himself at war not just with menacing neighbors, but with the Slave Power itself. That power resisted the coming of God's Kingdom to the American republic. At Pottawatomie Brown represented his party to his victims as the Northern army. He claimed no divine authority. But if religious belief did not compel him to strike his enemy, it reinforced his Manichaean perspective on the nature of the struggle for Kansas and energized and validated his fanaticism.

If Brown suffered from mental illness or personality disorder, it eludes classification. He was not psychotic. In Kansas, to be sure, he found a new sense of vocation and a new persona. What old friends in Ohio saw in him as obsession, Brown saw as mission. In the guerrilla warfare that exploded in 1856, "Captain Brown" played a conspicuous part. He gained a bankable notoriety. After leaving Kansas in 1857, Brown summarized the sacrifices he and his family had made. The Browns had all "endured great hardships, exposure ... & other privations," he wrote. All six of his sons, his son-in-law, and Brown himself had been ill, two sons had been "subjected to most barbarous treatment" while imprisoned, "two were severely wounded; and One murdered."

Brown was proud of his service in Kansas. "During this time," he said immodestly, he had "figured with some success under the familiar title of Old B[rown] often periling his life in company with his Sons: & Son in law." He was "an *earnest & steady minded* man: & a true descendant of Peter B[rowne] of the Mayflower pilgrims"; and he commended himself to "all who love liberty; & equal rights."[73] This dedication validated his character and warranted his claim to respect and support. He was now one of God's "reapers" in the "great harvest" of souls that would come from the fall of slavery.

That boastful self-assessment raises a final question about Brown's mental balance. If his "secret service" in the cause did not seem bizarre in the world from which he returned in 1857, it may nonetheless have betrayed delusional thinking. Nonbizarre delusions may occur without other signs of mental disorder. Individuals suffering what psychiatrists call Delusional Disorder may appear normal when their delusional ideas are not discussed or challenged. Delusions of inflated self-worth, of having power, knowledge, an implausible identity, or, in Brown's case, a special relationship to God, constitute the Grandiose subtype of Delusional Disorder.[74] Brown's grasp on reality may be assessed only in context. Was his attack on Harpers Ferry inspired by grandiose or paranoid delusions – "phantoms," as Rev. Beecher surmised?[75] To answer that question, it is necessary to reconstruct his "great plan," to examine its coherence, to understand the texture of Brown's thinking it incorporated, and to do so in terms of contemporary understandings of the conflict over slavery.

PART IV

STRATEGIES

9

Propagandist

Nature is mourning for its Murdered and Afflicted Children. Hung be the Heavens in Scarlet.

John Brown, "The Declaration of Liberty"[1]

Well, he fired one gun, and has had the use of the New York Herald and Tribune to repeat its echoes for a fortnight. Has any man ever used types better?

Wendell Phillips[2]

In his unschooled way, John Brown was a master of the printed word. To raise money and arms, he used the press to appeal to readers across the Northeast and Midwest. Although he had little schooling and often wrote ungrammatically, he effectively exploited the "types" or "prints," as newspapers were then called, to create a public persona and further his cause. The penny dailies that emerged in the antebellum era did not routinely commission reporters to interview public figures, but after Harpers Ferry every reporter on the scene wanted to interview him. For weeks thereafter, Brown commanded the news as no one had before.[3] He was not the first "insurrectionist" or adventurer to claim national attention. But he was the first to use the national press to plead a cause and shape his martyrdom. He relished notoriety and exploited it shrewdly. Though a failed revolutionary, he was a strikingly successful propagandist.

What is less often recognized is that Brown's moving speeches in court and eloquent letters from prison were the fruit of years of pleading his cause in writing, much of it for the prints. Admirers thought of Brown as a man of deeds not words. Yet it is surprising how many of his brief writings found their way into print as Brown struggled to identify his audience and craft his message. Those pieces constitute a kind of early skirmishing in his war on slavery. To understand that war, it is necessary to know the disjointed, idiosyncratic body of writing that was its earliest statement.

I

Brown's success as a propagandist was possible because of the conjunction of developments in newspaper publication and his role in the crisis in "Bleeding Kansas." Kansas made Brown famous as a free-state guerrilla leader, and the revolution in newspaper publishing and circulation splashed news of his exploits across the country to a new reading public.[4]

In the 1850s neither newspapers nor reporters were committed to disinterested reporting. Newspapers were openly partisan, often serving as the "organ" or advocate of powerful politicians. Reporters slanted their reports toward the convictions of their editors and spurred events toward their papers' predilections. Steam-driven rotary presses had vastly increased circulation – Horace Greeley's New York *Daily Tribune* reached 170,000 readers. By 1860 the largest papers printed daily local editions but also weekly or semiweekly editions and regional editions for distant readers. The speed of telegraphic reporting whetted appetites for breaking news. Increased productivity and reduced costs resulted in the appearance of "penny papers,"[5] cheap newspapers that relied on sales and advertising rather than patronage and subscriptions for profit. The result was not only an increase in news of recent events from remote scenes but a growth in sensational, partisan reporting of those events.[6]

Even the largest dailies still lacked resources to send staff reporters to distant scenes of breaking news. Instead, they hired reporters already at the scene or men traveling to the scene, and paid them by the column inches of publishable copy they sent in.[7] Dispatches sold by the New York Associated Press, founded in 1846, appeared word for word in scores of subscribing newspapers.[8]

During Brown's time in Kansas the most influential correspondents were young abolitionists swept up by the events they reported to their Northern readers. They took liberties with "lesser truths in pursuit of larger ones," historian Bernard Weisberger has observed, and passed "unrepresented partisan judgments upon affairs with considerable *elan*."[9] In Kansas radical abolitionism among reporters was said to come in two varieties: political and armed. The eastern correspondents, however, were often both. Through their reporting, they sought to awaken concern about the antislavery cause back home; through their martial and political activities in the Territory they furthered the free-state cause. To call the roll of abolitionist correspondents in Kansas is to compile a list of John Brown's admirers and disciples: James Redpath, Thomas Wentworth Higginson, William Addison Williams, Richard J. Hinton, Richard Realf, John Henry Kagi, and others.

Just twenty in 1855 when he came to Kansas, Scottish-born James Redpath was a correspondent for three Republican papers, including Greeley's New-York *Tribune*. He was also a delegate to the first two free-state conventions, a major in the Free State Army, an "adjutant" to James Lane, a "revolutionary" in his passion for abolition, and a Brown idolater. He dedicated his 1859 book, *The Roving Editor: Or, Talks with Slaves in the Southern States*, to Brown, his "Old Hero," whose "dauntless bravery on the field," "religious integrity," and "resolute energy of anti-slavery zeal" had "put the brave young men of Kansas to shame" and "rendered insignificant the puerile programmes of anti-slavery politicians." Redpath urged "the friends of the slave to incite insurrections, and encourage, in the North, a spirit which shall ultimate in civil and servile wars."[10]

William Addison Phillips, another of Greeley's reporters, was in the words of a proslavery critic, "sent out here for the special purpose of manufacturing a new supply of *raw-head-and-bloody-bones* outrages for the New York *Tribune*" in order "to secure the election of Fremont."[11] As if to give credence to that charge, Phillips published his dispatches to the *Tribune* as *The Conquest of Kansas by Missouri and Her Allies*, dedicating it to freeing Kansas from the "iron grasp" of slavery. A colonel in the free-state army, Phillips was later thrice elected to Congress from Kansas. His admiring 1879 article on Brown in *Atlantic Monthly* became a principal source of the Brown legend.[12]

Thomas Wentworth Higginson went to the Territory at the behest of the Massachusetts Kansas Aid Committee and was soon deeply immersed in the antislavery cause there. Lane appointed him a brigadier general in the free-state army. His "letters from Kansas" ran in several Eastern and Midwestern papers over the signature "Worcester."[13] "And if I wanted a genuine warrior of the Revolution," he told a Faneuil Hall audience after returning from Kansas in January 1857, "where could I find him better than in the old Vermonter [sic], Captain John Brown, the defender of Osawatomie…who swallows a Missourian whole, and says grace after the meat."[14]

Englishman Richard J. Hinton, another reporter for Eastern newspapers, arrived in Kansas in June 1856. He soon joined Brown's "army" and later claimed he would have been at Harpers Ferry had he been properly informed of the date of the attack. Richard Realf reported for eastern papers and rode with Lane before volunteering to serve under Brown. John H. Kagi, Brown's second-in-command at Harpers Ferry, reported on Kansas for the *Washington National Era* and abolitionist editor William Cullen Bryant's *New-York Post*.[15] Kagi was the associate editor of the Topeka *Tribune* and a member of the free-state "Topeka boys" militia before joining Brown's company.[16] When Brown left Kansas for the last time, these "armed abolitionists" regarded him as the best hope to continue the antislavery struggle.

II

In the months that followed his flight from Kansas in October 1856, Brown made contact with the Massachusetts Kansas Committee. He met and beguiled its young secretary, Franklin B. Sanborn, who introduced him to the Boston abolitionists who would soon fund his endeavors in Kansas and then in Virginia. With a newly burnished reputation as a guerrilla chieftain and the sponsorship of substantial men, Brown now made public appeals for assistance, speaking to meetings with reformers and "capitalists" as he traveled about the East in the spring of 1857. On March 4, he placed an appeal for funds in Greeley's *Tribune* and other papers. "I ask all honest lovers of *Liberty and Human Rights, both male and female,* to hold up my hands by contributions...either as counties, cities, towns, villages, societies, churches or individuals," Brown wrote. He promised to visit "as many places *as I can* during my stay in the States," but only where he might find contributors. Brown asked "editors of newspapers friendly to the cause kindly to take up the business," and pleaded that such public begging required "*no little sacrifice of personal feeling.*"[17]

When contributions lagged, Brown exploited his celebrity to contact men prominent in the Kansas struggle. On April 1, he sought support from former territorial Governor Andrew H. Reeder, who had been driven from the territory for allying himself with the free-state faction. "As I find...that your ideas of the true course to be pursued by the Free State men in Kansas are almost exactly like my own," Brown told him, "I take the liberty of sending you the enclosed appeal &c: hoping that you may find it in your way to afford me some aid in securing the means of an outfit [a wagon and team]." Neither he nor the men under him received any "pay" for their services. Brown thought Reeder would agree with him that the "kind of persons collected to invade Kansas [i.e., Border Ruffians]; are next to no men at all." Free-staters by contrast had "*every principle to sustain them*; in an hour of trial." Brown closed by urging the "necessity" of Reeder himself returning to the territory in the spring.[18]

Still in Massachusetts two weeks later, Brown wrote Eli Thayer, founder of the New England Emigrant Aid Society and the man chiefly responsible for sending antislavery families to Kansas. Brown asked Thayer's help in getting a small arms shipment to Ohio and in purchasing "two sample Navy sized Revolvers" of the sort he wanted to purchase in large quantity. "I am advised that One of [the]'U S Hounds Is on my track,'" Brown told Thayer to impress him with the urgency of matters, "& I have Kept myself hid for a few days to let my track get cold. I have no idea of being taken," Brown boasted, "*& I intend (if 'God will;')* to go back with Irons *in* rather than *uppon* my hands."[19] Brown was finding his voice.

Such bravado mixed with solemn piety marked Brown's demeanor in his pursuit of money. Contributions thus far had been disappointing. "I have had a good deal of discouragement; & *have often* felt quite depressed: *but hitherto God hath helped me,*" he wrote to John, Jr. from Boston. In early March, he "vented" his frustrations in a "short piece" which he headed "Old Browns, Farewell to the Plymouth Rocks; Bunker Hill Monuments; Charter Oaks; & Uncle Toms Cabbins." The immediate effect of the appearance of this piece was to open a cornucopia of gifts from wealthy New Englanders. The pipe manufacturer George Luther Stearns, pressed by his wife, pledged $7,000, and soon became one of the Secret Six who provided most of the money and weapons for Brown's war on slavery. It was at this time too that the textile manufacturer Amos Lawrence and his brother started the subscription to support Brown's family in case of his death or disability.

Brown was now "quite sanguine" of success, having raised $13,000 in pledges, and was hopeful "his collections" would "soon reach $30,000."[20] The following day he asked Eli Thayer to "have Allen & Co send me by Express" the large revolvers he had requested "as *soon as may be*; together with his best cash terms … by the Hundred." He also ordered rifles and pistols he had already purchased at Allen & Co. packed in a "suitable strong box" and sent to Cleveland.[21] Stearns soon let him know that he would himself pay for 200 revolvers Brown wanted to buy. Stearns urged Brown to go back to Kansas and give the free-state leadership "some Backbone."[22]

The "piece" that had prompted this outpouring of support from New Englanders – "Old Brown's "Farewell," as it became known – was perhaps Brown's most successful exercise in propaganda. It was a brief torrent of words designed to tweak the consciences of reformers. It mixed a compelling account of Brown's struggles in Kansas with the pathos of his disappointment trying to raise money amid the "wealth, luxury, extravagance of this *'Heaven exalted'* people," where he could not find the "necessary supplies for a common Soldier." Referring to himself in the third person, Brown said he had tried "since he had come out of the territory to secure an outfit; or in other words *the means of arming and equiping* thoroughly; his regular minuet men." He was leaving "*the States*; with a *deep feeling of sadness*," having "exhausted" his own money. His family and his "*brave men*" alike had suffered hunger, nakedness, cold, sickness, and "(some of them) imprisonment, with most barbarous, and cruel treatment: *wounds, and death*" as payment for their sacrifice. They had slept on the ground, relied on the care of friendly Indians, and been "hunted like Wolves." All of this they did to sustain a cause "which *every Citizen* of this 'Glorious Republic,' is under equal Moral obligation to do: and for the neglect of which he will be held accountable to God."[23]

Brown had written his "Farewell" for Theodore Parker; but to show his appreciation to Mrs. Stearns, he made a copy for her. In comparing the two drafts, we can see that, for all his misspellings and peculiar punctuation, Brown was meticulous about his style. The copy of the "Farewell" has numerous differences from the original, but the differences are of phraseology not substance. The phrase, a "deep feeling of sadness," in the first draft becomes "a feeling of deepest sadness" in the second, both underlined twice for emphasis. In the second version, Brown drops altogether the final line: "'How are the mighty fallen?'"[24]

What is noteworthy in both versions is the formula he had hit upon in making his appeals for assistance. He establishes his credentials by reminding readers he has just "come out of Kansas" and already "left" to return. He underscores his worthiness by pointing to the suffering his cause requires of his family and his "brave men." He appeals to the historical heritage of those he hopes to tap for funds. His "Farewell" is addressed not to Bostonians or New Englanders but to the "Plymouth Rocks; Bunker Hill Monuments, Charter Oaks, and Uncle Toms Cabbins" that all of them presumably cherish. "Every Man, Woman, and Child of the entire human family; has a deep and awful interest" in his business and is bound by a moral obligation equal to his own. Thus Brown appealed not only to symbols of liberty familiar to

New Englanders, but to the sense of guilt in men too comfortable in their material lives to be at ease with their consciences in a slaveholding nation.

Brown's effectiveness as a propagandist thus rested in part on his ability to touch the sympathy of those to whom he appealed. His own sense of personal loss and having been wronged fueled this inclination.[25] He often recounted in public the horrors he and his sons endured in Kansas. In February 1857, he told a committee of the Massachusetts Legislature considering an appropriation of $100,000 for the relief of Kansas free-staters of his and others' sacrifices. He had been "called out" at night to "try to save Lawrence." In the resulting difficulties, "hundreds of men like ourselves lost their whole time, & entirely failed of securing any kind of crop whatever." Perhaps 500 men had lost 120 days of work and all that that meant to the well-being of their families. Two of his sons were imprisoned "without other crime than opposition to Bogus Legislation; *& most barbarously treated*," he continued. "Both of them were burned out," and their families lost everything they had. Brown himself had seen the body of a man "murdered" for his support of the free-state cause during the "Wakarusa War."[26]

Evidently the immediate emotional appeal of Brown's effort exceeded the sober second thoughts of practical New Englanders. It was one thing to get promises of large contributions; it was another to get cash in hand. Just nine days after boasting of his successes, Brown was forced to sell a saber taken from an officer at the "Black Jack surrender" because he was "literally driven to beg: which is very humiliating."[27] In June he was soliciting funds from friends in New Haven, this time to enable him to ship his crates of arms to Iowa. "It is a severe mortification to be compelled to say, that I am utterly unable to proceed on my way West; for want of means to pay for freights; and traveling expences. Of the $1000, the friends at New Haven voted to raise for me; I have received…$25. Since then I am not informed as any[thing] further has been done."[28]

III

Brown's propaganda initiatives led to an effort to enlist the services of Rev. Theodore Parker, an ardent abolitionist, in his cause. And though that effort was unsuccessful, it shows Brown's skills as a propagandist. As he waited in Iowa during the winter of 1857–8 to see whether Kansas would explode again in violence, he revived an earlier plan to intervene there with the written word. Toward that end, he wanted his new friend Parker to craft an address to men in the U.S. military in Kansas who had become, he believed, unthinking tools of the proslavery government. A year earlier he had hired Hugh Forbes, "a distinguished Scotch officer; & author quite popular *in this country*," to write a similar pamphlet. But Brown had broken with him and did not like what Forbes wrote in "The Duty of the Soldier."

Brown now wanted Parker's help in "composing a substitute" for the "address you saw last season, directed to the officers and soldiers of the United

States Army." He knew what he wanted to say, he told Parker, but "I never had the ability to clothe those ideas in language at all to satisfy myself, and I was by no means satisfied with the style of that address." "I do not know as I can give any correct idea of what I want," he added before proceeding to elaborate his ideas.[29]

The appeal had to be brief enough to be "generally read" and written "in the simplest or plainest language, without the least affectation of the scholar about it, and yet worded with great clearness and power." In an effort at ethnic humor, he added: "The anonymous writer must (in the language of the Paddy) be 'afther others,' and not 'afther himself at all, at all.'" It might be written in the "spirit" of Benjamin Franklin's Poor Richard, but must be "appropriate" and "particularly adapted" to the situation in Kansas and "look to an actual change of service from that of Satan to that of God. It should be, in short, a most earnest and powerful appeal to men's sense of right and to their feelings of humanity."[30]

Warming to his proposal as he continued to describe it, Brown asked Parker to draft a second address to be "sent out broadcast over the entire nation." He hoped it would be such as to reach "all persons, old and young, male and female, slaveholding and non-slaveholding." It should appeal especially to "prisoners" of proslavery thought upon whom "kindness and plain dealing" would have a powerful and lasting effect. "Females," he suggested, "are susceptible of being carried away entirely by the kindness of an intrepid and magnanimous soldier, even when his brave name was but a terror the previous day." This cryptic reminder of his own self-image may not have been lost on Parker, and Brown may not have expected his friend to write the two addresses. Brown was by then deeply committed to his Virginia project, and Kansas was no longer in peril of falling to slavery. Perhaps Brown believed that asking the favor would bind Parker to him in friendship.[31] In any case, Parker declined Brown's request, though he did remain a member of the Secret Six and a supporter of Brown's scheme to attack slavery.[32] When Brown was hanged, Parker, who was dying of tuberculosis, remarked that the distance from the scaffold to heaven was as short as that from a throne.

IV

"Our family interest in Kansas affairs is so often misstated by those who do not know and oftener do not care to tell the truth," Brown complained to John, Jr., in August 1858, that he took up the suggestion of Augustus Wattles, editor at the *Herald of Freedom*, that he write the story himself.[33] He never finished his oddly titled "brief history of John Brown, otherwise (old B) and his family: *as connected with Kansas; by one who knows.*" But the five closely written pages he drafted show that he was indeed finding his voice.[34]

Like Brown's other writings, the "narrative" dwells on his and his sons' hardships and sacrifices. En route to Kansas sons Owen and Frederick endured "great exposure" and "no little suffering." Nearing their destination, they learned of the "wrath & vengeance" of Border Ruffians "then; & there gathering for Free State Men; & abolitionists gone or going to Kansas." His sons were warned "in no very mild language to stop before it should be 'too late.'" When the oldest sons and their wives finally reached Kansas, they were unable to "supply their many absolute wants."

Brown was not shy about his own contributions to the family migration. Some of the "valuable" livestock thieves stole from his sons were bred from his own prize-winning cattle. When his sons asked for his help, he was "fully resolved" to go to Kansas. "He had been somewhat accustomed to border life for over Fifty years…& had been for Thirty Six years a practiceing Surveyor. With the exposures; privations, hardships, & wants of pioneer life he was familiar; & thought he could benefit his Children, & the new beginners from the older parts of the country." But the Border Ruffians allowed them no peace. The territorial government arrested his oldest sons and "burned [them] out" while they were imprisoned. As the Browns left Kansas, two of his sons were ill, another "perfectly insane," and still another "dreadfully wounded," and Brown himself was being "hunted like a Wolf."

In recounting deeds of the Ruffians, Brown was relentlessly disparaging. "Companies of armed men" in Missouri were "continually boasting of what feats of patriotism; & chivalry they had performed in Kansas; & of the still more mighty deeds they were yet to do. No man of them," he ventured, "would blush when telling of their cruel treadings down and terrifying of defenseless Free State men: they seemed to take peculiar satisfaction in telling of the fine horses, & mules they had many of them Killed in their numerous expeditions against the d – d abolitionists." Brown objectified the Ruffians in terms familiar to New Englanders: "The coarse, vulgar, profane, jests, & the bloodthirsty brutal feelings to which they were giving vent (continually) would have been a most exquisite treat to [the] Ears; & their general appearance to the Eyes of the past; & the present Administration." "There cannot be the slightest doubt of a similarly refined feeling amongst their truly *Democratic supporters & the Doughfaces.*"[35]

These political jabs as well as the larger theme of suffering for a cause resonated with the genteel readers he addressed. For them as for Brown, to suffer for one's faith was a mark of godliness. But something more was at work in these appeals. Brown had long thought of himself as a person who learned hard lessons as a child and had often suffered under God's chastisement. Now, after all his sacrifices, his whole project seemed to hang in the balance. Whether his solemn yet hopeful posture here was consciously contrived or reflected a lingering sense of loss and anxiety is open to question. What seems clear is that Brown had learned to exploit that posture for his war on slavery.

V

It was during a final visit to Lawrence, Kansas, in January 1859, that Brown wrote the most widely circulated statement of his exploits. In doing so he was responding to criticism of his December 20 raid into Missouri during a truce in the border fighting. During that raid, Brown rescued eleven slaves and the fallout from it focused national attention on Brown as well as jeopardized the truce in the border war.

The raid itself was occasioned by a direct appeal for help. Jim Daniels, a Missouri slave who expected to be sold away from his family, asked Brown for his help. Despite being a party to the truce, Brown rode into Missouri, liberated Daniels and ten other slaves, and fled with them back to Kansas. In the course of this "dash," Aaron Stevens, leading one party of Brown's raiders, had killed a planter who, Stevens said, had drawn a revolver on him. The raiders had also taken oxen, mules, horses, and provisions during the raid. For a month thereafter, Brown sheltered the freed slaves from irate Missourians searching for them. On Christmas eve, his sister Florella hid them in her back kitchen overnight.

In the days that followed, Brown held a "war council" in the presence of William Hutchinson, the Kansas correspondent of the New York *Times*, who helped spread news of the raid. Thereafter, Brown's story would make news regularly for two months. On January 20, he set out for Lawrence with the fugitives in a cumbersome ox-drawn wagon. There he obtained provisions and lighter, horse-drawn wagons to make the run to the Iowa border. For seven weeks he and his men escorted the fugitives eastward, fighting blizzards, heavy rains, muddy back roads and swollen streams, narrowly evading federal troops, and finally routing a panicky Missouri posse at the so-called Battle of the Spurs. Crossing Iowa, the fugitives found refuge in towns and homes known to be safe for runaways and free-state emigrants. At Springdale, Quakers guarded them until they were concealed in a box car bound for Chicago. There, with Kagi and Stevens beside him, Brown awakened the famous detective Allan Pinkerton at 4:30 in the morning of March 11 asking for his help. Pinkerton raised nearly $600 for Brown during the day and obtained the use of a car on the Michigan Central Railway to carry Brown's party to Detroit, where they took a ferryboat to Windsor. Adding a new-born infant, christened John Brown, along the way, the fugitives had come 1,100 miles in the teeth of winter to reach freedom.

The publicity given this raid and flight created a national sensation. Though it was only one of eight recent incursions across the troubled border, Missouri newspapers condemned Brown's "infamous deed" and threatened that further northern emigration across Missouri to Kansas would be blocked. Even free-state newspapers in Lawrence condemned the raid; both the Governor of Kansas, a Pennsylvania Democrat, and President Buchanan offered rewards for Brown's arrest.

Seizing the opportunity created by the furor, Brown once again exploited the prints personally. At the January meeting at Wattles's home attended by William Hutchinson, he presented a draft of what he called "Parallels" between the summary shooting of eleven free-state men in Linn County by one Charles Hamilton the previous May – the infamous Marais des Cygnes massacre – and his own rescue of the eleven Missouri slaves.[36]

At the Marais des Cynes shooting, all the victims had been "left for dead," but a survivor later identified Charles Hamilton, a Georgian, as the perpetrator, and Hamilton threatened to kill all free-staters in Linn County. Free-staters in turn mounted a company of 200 men to patrol an agreed-upon "line" against another incursion, and agreed in writing not to carry the fighting into Missouri. In the meantime, Brown purchased the land claim on which the murders had occurred, fortified it, and announced that Old Brown was ready "to fight or be peaceable," as the likes of Hamilton might choose. Hamilton soon disappeared.

In his "Parallels," Brown pointed out that the proslavery territorial government never investigated Hamilton or anyone else for the Marais des Cygnes massacre. By contrast, his own raiding party into Missouri had released two hostages unhurt and returned property mistakenly taken from a man who did not own slaves. "Now for the parallel: Eleven persons are forcibly restored to their *natural; & inalienable rights*, with but one man killed; & all 'Hell is stirred from beneath.'" The governor of Missouri demanded Brown's extradition while the marshal of Kansas gathered a posse to pursue Brown and the rescuers, while in Kansas "dough-faced men & Administration tools are filled with holy horror." The double standard, Brown thought, was obvious. The publication of "Parallels" in the New-York *Tribune* and elsewhere created a stir of its own.[37]

It was soon after this that Brown and his ex-slaves had fled from Kansas with federal troops in pursuit. Before leaving, Brown told Augustus Wattles Kansas was now safe from the Border Ruffians, and he felt it his duty to "draw the scene of excitement to some other part of the country."[38] Brown rejoiced that free-state men had rejected the "*foul and loathsome* embrace of the *old rotten whore*," slavery, and that he and his *fellow-sufferers* had held their "*high and holy ground*."[39]

The Missouri raid had served a purpose. At one stroke, Brown recouped his lost credibility among Eastern supporters over the long delay in his attack on slavery caused by Forbes' betrayal of his plans. Back in Iowa, on March 1, Brown wrote to Dr. Samuel Gridley Howe, one of his chief financial backers, with renewed confidence. "What in your opinion can & will be done (now that 'next spring' *has come*) towards furnishing me with the small cash capital promised me about One year ago in a letter written by our Concord friend [Sanborn]," he asked Howe. To effect a good seasons work," Brown urged, "we ought to begin early: & all that I Know of to hinder our doing so is the want of a trifling sum for an outfit." Referring to the Missouri raid, he added, "The entire success of our experiments ought (I think) to convince every *capitalist*."[40]

In Eastern abolitionist circles, Brown was now lionized as an old covenanter, a Cromwell come again to life to destroy evil. Once again promoting his cause in New England, he donned a suit that made him look like a "deacon." He told anew of his fight to save Osawatomie and of his conquest of Henry Clay Pate at Black Jack Creek on the Sante Fe Trail. No one in the East yet knew of his role at Pottawatomie or that free-state Kansans no longer wanted him among them.

VI

Given Brown's success in promoting himself and his cause in the prints, it is ironic that the most revealing document he wrote in his quest to free the slaves – his "Declaration of Liberty" on behalf of "the Slave Population of the United States of America" – was never published. In May 1858, with the aid of Dr. Martin Delaney and others, Brown organized a two-day convention of free blacks in the Canadian town of Chatham, a terminus of the underground railroad not far from Detroit.[41] The purposes of the convention were to adopt an organic document for the political entity Brown expected to create in territory he hoped to liberate in the slaveholding South and to organize and elect officers for a provisional government of that entity. The convention duly chose Brown as commander-in-chief of the as yet unformed "provisional army" of the newly proclaimed but still unrealized entity. As such, Brown would lead the war against the American South. Assisted perhaps by Delaney or the aspiring poet Richard Realf, one of twelve recruits who accompanied him to Chatham, Brown crafted a stirring "Declaration of Liberty" which set forth the principles to which his political entity would be committed.

The document paralleled Jefferson's Declaration of Independence in purpose as well as language.[42] "'When in the course of Human events, it becomes necessary' for an Oppressed People to Rise, and assert their Natural Rights, as Human Beings," Brown began, amending to his purpose words imprinted on Americans' souls. A "long train of abuses & usurpations" committed by slaveholders had "evinced a design to perpetrate an absolute Despotism: and most cruel bondage" upon American slaves. The slaves were by right entitled to "crush this foul system of oppression." Brown's Declaration then called upon the signatories to pledge "Our Lives, and Our Sacred Honor" to achieve freedom for the slaves. "Indeed; I tremble for my Country, when I reflect; that God is Just; And that his Justice; will not sleep forever, &c. &c.," Brown continued, borrowing further from Jefferson. "Nature is mourning for its Murdered and Afflicted Children," he added in peroration. "Hung be the Heavens in Scarlet."

The inclusion of the "et ceteras" suggests that the document was unfinished. Unlike the Provisional Constitution of Brown's political entity, which was published in pamphlet form soon after adoption by the Chatham convention, the Declaration of Liberty was not presented to the convention, perhaps because it was unfinished or because not all of the thirty-four delegates were willing to sign their names to it.[43] Though the only surviving original copy is unsigned, it is clearly Brown's handiwork as evidenced by its characteristic punctuation and misspellings.[44]

Unlike Brown's Provisional Constitution, the Declaration of Liberty did not come to public attention after Brown's capture at Harpers Ferry or during his trial, and historians have ignored it.[45] It had no discernible impact on events. Its wordiness, repetition, and lapses of political taste forbade its celebration as a literary achievement.[46] Its significance lies in its revelation of Brown's thinking

as he matured his conspiracy. By 1858 he had perfected his formula for raising money, but he had had far less success in recruiting men. He knew what
he wanted his Declaration of Liberty to say, but he could not yet effectively
voice the perspective of the slaves and fugitives for whom he wished to speak.
In listing the failings of government, for example, he swiped at the "Members
of Congress; & other servants of the People, who receive exorbitant wages,"
and at the president for dissolving "Representative houses for opposing with
Manly firmness their invasions of the rights of the people." Clearly, in such passages, the "oppressed" people are not slaves but Kansas free-staters, most of
whom had voted to exclude free blacks from the territory. Brown complained
too that the government had made "Judges ['Taney' is penciled in] dependent
upon [its] will alone, for the tenure of their office and the amount and payment
of their salaries." That concern would not seem to have been the focus of black
abolitionists' rage at the author of the Dred Scott decision, which held that
blacks were not citizens and could not bring suits in the courts.

To these complaints, which reflected Brown's own populist concerns and
experiences, he added wrongs suffered by slaves. He condemned the government for keeping slaves in "total darkness and Ignorance," for excluding them
from protections of the law and from dealing equally with their "fellow Men."
He excoriated the government for protecting "base Men, Pirates, (engaged in
a most Inhuman traffic; The "Foreign; & Domestic slave trade.) by mock trials, from punishment, for unprovoked murders which they have committed
upon us, & free Citizens of the States." The "facts ... of the enormous sin of
Slavery, may be found in the General History of American Slavery, which is a
history of repeated injuries, of base hypocracy; & cursed treasonable usurpa-
tion." Such enormities were perpetrated by "Idle, haughty, tyranical Arrogant
Land Monopolists." In spite of them, slaves would soon obtain their natural
rights "or Die in the Struggle to obtain them. We make war upon oppression."

Despite a certain parochialism, this Declaration speaks to us today. It
appealed to the rhetoric of the American Revolution in calling upon slaves to
"Rise, and assert their Natural Rights, as Human Beings, as Native and mutual
Citizens of a free Republic, and break that odious Yoke of oppression, which
is so unjustly laid upon them." "Nature hath freely given to all Men, a full supply of Air, Water, & Land; for their sustinance & mutual happiness," Brown
continued, warning of God's "certain & fearful retribution" for the nation's
sins. Blending disinterested benevolence with natural rights, he declared "self
evident" the "truth" that it is the "highest Privilege, & Plain duty of Man; to
strive in every reasonable way, to promote the Happiness, Mental, Moral, &
Physical elevation of his fellow Man." It called for "equal rights, privileges, &
justice to all; Irrespective of Sex; or Nation."[47] Here, as in his prison letters
later, Brown strives for moving metaphors. Nature mourns her "Murdered and
Afflicted Children"; the scarlet hue of the sky betokens revolution.

The Declaration is thus a failed call to arms. At Chatham Brown sought not
merely publicity but recruits for his "army" among fugitives and free blacks.
Martin Delaney later remembered Brown admitting as much. "It is men I want,

and not money; money I can get plentiful enough, but no men," Brown reputedly told Delany. "Money can come without being seen, but men are afraid of identification with me, though they favor my measures."[48] Brown hoped to renew his war against slavery immediately after the convention and to do so with recruits black leaders would help him enlist at Chatham. That is why he was so disappointed at his failure to persuade Frederick Douglass and Harriet Tubman to attend the Chatham meeting.[49] For more than a year he had explored every means to raise and arm volunteers. In fact, the Declaration culminated a lengthy campaign to legitimate the use of force against slavery. Its rhetorical excesses evidenced Brown's impatience.[50]

But the Declaration apparently resonated less well among fugitives and free blacks in Chatham than it did among white abolitionists, whose rhetoric it reflected. In any case, shortly after the Chatham convention, Hugh Forbes's betrayal of Brown's movement broke the momentum of his campaign. Fearing exposure, Brown took the counsel of his unnerved supporters to lie low until the following spring. By then many of those who might have volunteered had made other commitments or lost confidence in Brown. He learned from painful experience the costliness of delay.

Brown's propaganda depended heavily on its appeal to the republican tradition. The Declaration reminds us how strong Brown believed the tradition of dissent against arbitrary authority to be in 1858. The classical republicanism of the Revolution pervaded the rhetoric of reformers and the larger political culture.[51] If republicanism's attenuated meaning in antebellum America has impaired its analytical usefulness to historians, its very amorphousness enabled it to appeal to Brown as to philosophically minded slaveholders.[52] They no less than Brown put republicanism in the service of "forcible means."

VII

If Brown's biographers have ignored the Declaration of Liberty, they have dismissed his "Provisional Constitution and Ordinances" as "insane" or, at best, "impractical, if not impossible" to implement.[53] As a frame of government, to be sure, it is woefully deficient. But those who dismiss it misconstrue its purpose, and thus what it reveals about Brown's mind. It was a device to obtain the consent of the oppressed to fight a war in their name. It was less a frame of civil government than an explication of rules for governing armed men in the field. Indeed, the Provisional Government was to be more immediately concerned with recruiting volunteers and facilitating military discipline than with peacetime governance of communities of liberated slaves. It provided for a house of representatives but no senate, and included no provisions for structuring or election to the legislative branch. Only two members of the Congress were elected at Chatham, and, since no black leader was willing to be president, the delegates left the task of filling that office to a committee that never met. Terms of office were to be three years, but no mechanism was provided for electing or convening the government. The Congress was empowered to make laws and appropriate money for the "general good," and even to establish schools and churches, but no more members were chosen after Chatham.

Most of the forty-eight provisions of the document were concerned with discipline in the provisional army during the imminent war to overthrow slavery. Power was concentrated in the commander-in-chief, Brown himself. The first duties of the president and the secretary of state, positions never filled, were to identify "the real friends...as well as enemies of this organization" and to inform the commander-in-chief about them. Acting with the Congress, the Supreme Court could remove the president, vice-president, and members of Congress, but not the commander-in-chief. Vacancies in the government were to be filled through the "united action" of the executive and the commander-in-chief. But the latter and his secretary of war acting together were the sole "appointing power of the army." Men in the field could by tried by courts martial duly elected by the "chief officer" of the appropriate command. But the chain of command itself was truncated: After Brown himself and Secretary of War John Henry Kagi, no officer held a commission higher than captain.[54] Only the commander-in-chief might draw on a "safety and intelligence fund" generated from confiscated property, with the concurrence of the secretary of war, who oversaw its books. In short, the Provisional Constitution created a shadow government that would support the war against slavery but interfere little with Brown.

The Preamble of the Provisional Constitution declared that slavery was "none other than the most barbarous, unprovoked, and unjustifiable war" upon blacks whom it condemned to "perpetual imprisonment and hopeless servitude or absolute extermination." Racial discrimination was likewise said to "degrade" blacks in the North, who faced daily humiliation and exclusion from civil society, a circumstance recently validated in the Dred Scott ruling that black Americans had "no rights which the White Man is bound to respect." The delegates at Chatham adopted the Provisional Constitution unanimously.

VIII

The secrecy required during the months between Chatham and the Harpers Ferry raid offered Brown few opportunities for self-promotion. But the documents found at his hideaway after the raid included a small, unfinished, yet noteworthy statement in Brown's handwriting entitled "Vindication of the Invasion, Etc."

The purpose of the "Vindication" is unclear. It began with an obscure reference to the "peace agreement" between free-state and proslavery parties in Kansas that Brown himself had drafted a year earlier. That document restored a previous one in which free-state forces under Brown and James Montgomery and their proslavery counterparts agreed to a cease-fire and an amnesty that prohibited proslavery "criminals" from returning to Kansas.[55] This truce had been broken, Brown noted at the beginning of his "Vindication," evidently implying that that fact somehow gave him permission or justification to renew his war against slavery in Virginia. Brown then listed four reasons for his "invasion":

1st It was in accordance with my settled *policy*
2d It was intended as a discriminating blow at *Slavery*
3 It was calculated to lessen the value of Slaves
4th It was (over and above all other motives) *Right*[.]

Then Brown added several notes, apparently points to be fleshed out later. "Duty of all persons in regard to this *matter*, Criminality of neglect in this *matter*. Suppose a case. Ask for further *support*."[56]

Some have suggested that the "Vindication" was Brown's effort to explain himself in case he was captured or killed at Harpers Ferry.[57] But the notes appended to it repeat a familiar pattern in his writings. The Vindication was not a hedge against disaster; it was to be instead an appeal for support of the war against slavery. The reference to "further support" in the last note suggests clearly that Brown did not expect to be trapped at Harpers Ferry. As his last letters to John, Jr., before the raid confirm, he anticipated a long campaign.[58]

The Vindication raises a further issue: If Brown was planning to publicize his raid by sending a finished version of his Vindication to newspapers, he must not have expected to offend public sentiment in the North in the execution of the raid. The seizure of Harpers Ferry had to have a moral purpose with which Northern reformers could identify. The raid had to be a "discriminating blow," as he said. If members of the Secret Six, whose contributions kept Brown in the field, had no qualms about bloodshed, the wider audience Brown hoped to reach would be shocked by wanton killing. The raid could not be a bloodbath. Like many radical abolitionists, Brown believed killing was morally permissible in defense of freedom. But Brown would keep his army under control; he was not driven by visions of carnage.

The question why Brown left so many "important papers" at his rented farmhouse in Maryland is crucial. It baffled Brown's most diligent biographer, Oswald Garrison Villard. "Had he succeeded ... in gaining the hills and beginning his guerrilla raids," Villard observed, "his enemy would have been in full possession of his purposes and of the names of his confederates in the North."[59] In the weeks before the raid, Brown himself made numerous trips to Chambersburg, where Kagi was stationed, and could easily have sent his papers to John, Jr., on one of those trips. He gave his son Owen, who remained at the farmhouse during the raid under orders to move crates of weapons closer to Harpers Ferry, no directions for the disposition of his papers either before the raid or after it began to go awry. After the raid collapsed and Owen fled, the documents were soon found. Until that point, Brown could easily have had them removed.

What is equally puzzling is that, when asked after his capture whether he "had any correspondence with parties at the North on the subject of the movement," Brown promptly admitted that he had. Asked if he were with the party living at the Kennedy farmhouse, Brown replied: "I was the head of that party. I occupied the house to mature my plans."[60]

Thus Brown virtually insured that his captors would find his papers. A diary listing his correspondents during the six months before the raid and a list of "men to call upon for assistance," which turned up in Brown's carpet bag, soon appeared in the New-York *Herald*.[61] As the "roll of conspirators" grew, Virginia Governor Henry A. Wise issued warrants for the arrest of dozens. In January a Senate Committee investigating the raid obtained many of the letters and began subpoenaing Brown allies.

It is highly unlikely that Brown simply forgot his papers. Why then did he leave them? In light of Brown's hope to create an impression that his "army" was the vanguard of a vast conspiracy, an obvious answer suggests itself: Brown deliberately left his papers for the Virginians to find in case the raid failed. If, as his Vindication also implied, Brown knew he might be defeated or killed at Harpers Ferry, he could magnify the impact of what he had done and sought to do and thereby keep his movement before the public only by leaving a record of it. His papers would bear silent witness to the breadth of his movement and the importance of his mission to many Northerners.[62] As Wendell Phillips later remarked of Brown, "Well, he fired one gun, and has had the use of the New York *Herald* and *Tribune* to repeat its echoes for a fortnight. Has any man ever used types better?"[63]

If Brown hoped Virginians would interpret his papers as evidence of a widespread conspiracy, he was not disappointed. Nothing so tempted them to make political capital out of the "invasion" as the prospect of tying it to the Republican Party. Brown's papers provided that opportunity. Although Governor Wise was tired from "haranguing an impatient crowd" in the aftermath of the raid, he huddled with his staff into the night, and a "motley crowd" gathered to hear Brown's captured papers read aloud. "The purpose of all this was plain enough," a vacationing railroad director remembered. "It was meant to serve as proof of a knowledge and instigation of the raid by prominent persons and party leaders in the North.... The most innocent notes and letters, commonplace newspaper paragraphs and printed cuttings were distorted and twisted by the reading and by the talking into clear instructions and positive plots."[64] Outraged Virginians recognized in Brown's papers weapons they might turn against their enemies.

IX

If Virginians thought they had found evidence of a widespread abolitionist conspiracy, they were mistaken. Most of the men to whom Brown had written knew him as a champion of the free-state cause in Kansas, not as the author of a plan to attack slavery in the South. Those who helped him buy an "outfit" thought he was going back to the territory. One of them, Ohio Congressman Joshua Giddings, who had given Brown $3, denied he ever heard Brown speak of "forcible emancipation" or "inciting insurrection." He had heard only of Brown's intention to devote himself to the underground railroad.[65] Even the Secret Six, who knew Brown intended to carry his war "into Egypt," asked not to be told incriminating details.

But the papers Virginians found revealed that a conspiracy of sorts had been afoot for some time. A disinterested reader would have concluded that Brown had a disappointingly small handful of men in his "army" and had failed to win a similar commitment from a single prominent correspondent, white or black. The Virginians saw what they wanted to see in Brown's papers. But for all Brown's labors, those papers attested only to an undermanned, shoestring, mostly paper conspiracy that he desperately hoped to magnify.

Conspirator

On the whole, the language of Providence to me would certainly seem to say, "Try on."

John Brown[1]

By every military test John Brown's raid on Harpers Ferry was a disaster. Within fifteen hours after he seized the town, local militia companies had trapped him in the armory's fire engine house. There his military pretensions ended when marines assaulted him after dawn on the second day. Officially at least, not a single slave had joined him. Except for five raiders who escaped, Brown's men were either killed or captured, tried, and hanged. Like two of his volunteers, Brown himself might easily have been skewered on a marine bayonet. Chance spared his life. Authorities seized not only his store of weapons but his correspondence, seemingly implicating dozens of people in the raid. Brown himself soon confessed it was a "disaster."[2] Were it not for his subsequent success in portraying himself as a martyr to the "higher-lawism" of abolitionists, history might remember Brown only as Hawthorne's "blood-stained fanatic."[3] Robert E. Lee, who captured Brown, reported officially: "The result proves that the plan was the attempt of a fanatic or madman, which could only end in failure."[4]

Was Lee right? Or did Brown have a plausible blueprint for destroying slavery? What was his strategic purpose in attacking Harpers Ferry?

I

Discussion of Brown's plan generally focuses on its military aspects. By military standards, he violated "every … principle in the book." Brown cut himself off from his supply base, failed to protect his paths of retreat, scattered his men, and allowed himself and most of his men to be trapped in the armory. More than that, he attacked a site surrounded by heights and cut off from retreat by mountains and the confluence of two treacherous rivers. He failed to scout surrounding mountains and prepare a place of refuge, failed to carry food for his men during the raid, and neglected to inform nearby slaves of his plan to free them.

But is the raid best understood in conventional military terms? Was it a guerrilla strike that misfired or an attempt to inspire a slave uprising?[5] Did Brown intend to move south with his captured weapons and an army of slave recruits, to retreat to his base in Maryland, or to funnel his fugitives north through a "subterranean pass way"? If Brown was making what was then called a "dash" – a raid or quick strike – why did he fail to leave before he was trapped and to baffle pursuers by burning or blowing up the Maryland and Shenandoah bridges as he left? Was Harpers Ferry really a "raid" at all, or, as Virginians insisted, a failed insurrection?[6]

The raid, I shall argue, is better understood as a political than as a military act. Thus two strategic questions are logically prior to those asked by military analysts: How did the raid figure in Brown's larger scheme to overthrow slavery? And why did he strike at Harpers Ferry rather than elsewhere? The answers to those questions suggest that Harpers Ferry was the desperate culmination of an unrealized conspiracy.

Brown's strategy is still disputed because evidence of his intentions is variously unclear, incomplete, or unreliable. Brown himself acknowledged a "seeming confliction" between what he told authorities after the raid and what he said at his sentencing two weeks later.[7] Although many people knew of his proposed "incursion" into the South, Brown shared details of his strategy with only a few trusted allies whose recollections later conflicted and were often deliberately misleading. Some of Brown's collaborators were anxious to disavow responsibility for the raid. A few sought to enhance the "old hero's" legend, while others, infatuated with unaccustomed fame, inflated their knowledge of or role in the plot. What we know otherwise of Brown's strategy must thus be inferred from ambiguous circumstantial evidence, Brown's actions during the raid, his incomplete and self-exculpatory comments in the weeks after his capture, and accounts by survivors or witnesses of the raid.

These last sources have weighed heavily in traditional accounts. Indeed, much of the dispute about Brown's intentions stems from uncritical readings of reminiscent evidence. This evidence is heavily colored by awareness of subsequent events, including the Civil War itself, and most of it was generated decades after the raid when the political climate was very different and Americans North and South were writing slavery out of the story of the Civil War. Students of autobiographical memory find that memories of personal experience are altered not only by passing years but by the circumstances in which memories are summoned up and by the rememberer's need to understand his own relationship to events or the times recalled. Stories mutate with retelling, losing detail and often gaining a symmetry and significance that invite skepticism. Indeed, rescripted and false memories may say more of their author's changing sense of self than about the events they relate.[8]

GEORGE L. STEARNS   GERRIT SMITH

FRANK B. SANBORN   T. W. HIGGINSON

THEODORE PARKER   SAMUEL G. HOWE

JOHN BROWN'S NORTHERN SUPPORTERS

FIGURE 10.1. The "Secret Committee of Six," Brown's chief financial backers.
CREDIT: West Virginia State Archives, Boyd B. Stutler Collection.

In light of such concerns, a reappraisal of the evidence about Brown's plans is in order. That reappraisal reveals a Brown shrewder, more thoughtful, more engaged with abolitionist political culture, and more embattled than the religious fanatic of our literature.

II

The swift collapse of Brown's war on slavery seemed to vindicate his naysayers and critics. The "manifest folly" of his raid on Harpers Ferry soon became virtually everyone's settled conviction. Future Massachusetts governor John A. Andrew, who helped secure lawyers for Brown, was sure that the "outbreak at Harper's Ferry…and the circumstances attending it" demonstrated that Brown had become insane.[9] However worthy Brown's cause, an elderly kinsman wrote Brown soon after the raid, "what you intended was an impossibility; and all your friends are amazed that you did not see it."[10] Much of the evidence scholars have used to understand Brown's plans is shaped by such post hoc assessments.

But how did the raid look beforehand to those who knew of it? Did they doubt Brown's sanity? In fact, later claims of some of these men to have been skeptical of Brown's "business" were a gift of hindsight. Thomas Wentworth Higginson never lost his admiration for the "sly old veteran," but his once favorable opinion of Brown's judgment changed sharply after the raid. He did not repudiate Brown. When authorities found Brown's trunk of letters from men implicated in his operation, Higginson alone refused to flee or to destroy papers linking him to the conspiracy, and he condemned the "extreme baseness" of those erstwhile Brown supporters who did.

But his loyalty did not prevent him years later from criticizing what he came to see as Brown's belatedly manifest shortcomings. Fifty years after Harpers Ferry, Higginson blamed himself for failing to see that Brown did not possess "the wit, the capacity, or the penchant for sane, shrewd, pragmatic planning" that might have made the enterprise succeed. "I should have been the one," he now confessed, "to make my brave, mad, noble friend step back from martyrdom. I should have acted to force the sane decision toward reasonableness and safety he had not the ability to make for himself." Though the raid had indirectly hastened emancipation, Higginson believed, he and the other members of the Secret Six had used Brown as "bait on a hook."[11]

Higginson's remorse was unwarranted. Before the raid he had encouraged Brown and had himself advocated insurrection.[12] Though he had questioned Brown's belief that the slaves would rise, he welcomed the first news of the raid with, in his biographer's word, "ecstacy." The raid was the "most formidable insurrection" in history, he believed, a product of "great capacity and skill." Determined men might "hold their own for a long time against all the force likely to be brought against them, and can at last retreat to the mountains and establish a Maroon colony there, like those in Jamaica and Guiana." As that happens, he exulted, "the effect will be to frighten and weaken the slave power everywhere and discourage the slave trade.... In Missouri especially this single alarm will shorten slavery by ten years."[13]

Soon disillusioned by the swift collapse and seeming futility of the raid, Higginson tried unsuccessfully to persuade Brown through intermediaries to cooperate in a plan to rescue him, and agreed to lead an attempt to save two of Brown's condemned raiders, a plan of greater folly than the raid itself, given the troops guarding the prisoners. It was soon abandoned.[14]

Higginson's later certainty that he knew all along that Brown was doomed profited much from retroactive interference. Just months after Brown's execution, he learned that Brown's volunteers had feared the outcome of the raid. In early 1860, a "refugee" from the raid, Charles Plummer Tidd, had told Higginson that Brown's men had threatened "mutiny" over the prospect of the raid. Tidd was a credible witness. Originally from Maine, he was recruited in 1856 to help save Kansas from the Slave Power. A year later he was a trusted Brown associate, one of the men on the Missouri raid, and an aide at the Chatham Convention.[15]

"All the boys opposed Harper's Ferry," Tidd told Higginson, "the younger Browns most of all." The disagreement "nearly broke up the camp"; Tidd himself left the Maryland farmhouse Brown had rented to cool off after "nearly" quarreling with Brown. Tidd similarly told Franklin B. Sanborn early in 1860 that Brown had been "inflexible" in his "rash purpose."[16] Years later Annie Brown Adams, who kept house for the raiders at the time of the quarrel Tidd described and heard details of it from the boys, contradicted Tidd on the essential point of the men's unanimity of opposition to taking Harpers Ferry. According to Adams, John E. Cook, who knew the townspeople and their routines, and John Henry Kagi, argued that the plan could work if the raiders made a quick exit from the town. Though a "half dozen" of the men were prepared to follow Brown wherever he led, because of the majority's opposition, in Adams' telling, Brown had resigned as commander-in-chief only to be reappointed within minutes when his sons dropped their protest and the others followed suit.[17] Reminiscent testimony thus imbues Brown's sons with foresight and heroism.

The real story was less simple. Tidd himself had not actually opposed the plan in principle. When the company finally "consented" to Brown's plan, Tidd reported to Higginson, "it was with the agreement that men should be sent in each direction to burn the bridges."[18] Despite the raid's collapse and his own harrowing escape, Tidd thought Brown's only mistake was to attack before he had enough men to ensure success. With twenty-five men, Tidd believed, Brown could have "paralyzed the whole business of the South, & nobody could take them." Nothing in the notes Higginson made of his discussion with Tidd supported Higginson's later claim in his 1900 memoir, *Cheerful Yesterdays*, that Tidd thought Brown had lost his "mental balance from overbrooding on one idea."[19]

What seems clear is that two months before the raid, intense discussions among the raiders had prompted a meeting at which Brown was absent. One piece of evidence of the meeting survives: a one-sentence, equivocal statement of support for Brown after the meeting that suggests the men's doubts had not been silenced. Dated August 18, addressed to Brown, and signed by son Owen ("Your Friend Owen Smith"), it reads: "We have all agreed to sustain your decisions, untill you have *proved incompetent*, & many of us will adhere to your decisions as long as you will."[20] The men's loyalty had outweighed their fears.

Years later Owen insisted that he too had been among the skeptics. But his father had become depressed because of the opposition, and Owen had stifled his skepticism and finally persuaded Brown not to give up his mission. When his father talked of abandoning the raid, Owen later claimed to have said: "We have gone too far for that, – we must go ahead." His father had replied, 'We have here only one life to live, and once to die; and if we lost our lives it will perhaps do more for the cause than our lives could be worth in any other way.'"[21]

That story may well have been an aphoristic memory. Its validity is certainly questionable. For one thing, Owen thought the conversations he reported and his father's resignation and reappointment had occurred in September, three weeks after the discussion of the raid by Brown's men. Also Owen remembered that a new recruit, Francis Jackson Meriam, was one of those favoring the raid. But Meriam arrived at the Kennedy farm on October 10, seven weeks after the crisis.[22] In attributing the sentiments his father expressed in his memorable October letters from Charlestown jail to his father at this earlier date, more-over, Owen's reminiscence may betray retroactive interference.[23] But if the gist of his story is true – if Brown was ready for a moment to abandon his plan and give up his leadership – the men may have "sustained" Brown not because he had persuaded or intimidated them, but because they loved and respected him.[24] If Owen remembered at all rightly, his father was less obsessed than many later supposed. In any case, we may conclude from surviving contemporary evidence that Brown's men compelled him to rethink tactical issues, notably the planned withdrawal from Harpers Ferry. Presumably, Brown then had an exit strategy.

III

Owen Brown and Higginson were not the only conspirators who later confused the story. Whenever one looks behind reminiscent accounts of Brown's supporters, one finds forgotten passion for his project. Hindsight bestows a specious skepticism on them. Franklin B. Sanborn, secretary to the Secret Six, also later denied the faith he had once placed in "Old Brown." In old age Sanborn still treasured the letter from Brown praising his abilities and judgment, but his faded memories robbed him of reexperiencing the ardor with which he championed Brown's cause among his Boston friends. Fifty years after Harpers Ferry, Sanborn wrote that the Six had agreed to finance Brown's "desperate" proposition in spite of their belief that it was "wholly inadequate in its provision of means, and of most certain result." Despite their fears, Brown was determined to go ahead, leaving his friends "only the alternatives of betrayal, desertion, or support," Sanborn remembered. Their financial aid flowed more from "regard for the man than from hopes of immediate success."[25]

But before Harpers Ferry Sanborn had worked tirelessly to raise money for Brown and had defended his project against the doubters. Two weeks before the raid, he had put Brown in touch with frail, partially blind, guileless Francis Jackson Meriam, who was eager to invest "some money in the speculation." A week later Sanborn was jubilant at the outcome. "Out of the mouths of babes and sucklings come dollars by the hundred, and what is wisdom compared to that?" he mused. "I have a letter from him [Meriam], – he has seen Hawkins [Brown], given him his money, and is to join in the business operation, to be commence[d] next Saturday." After all the delays, Sanborn was upbeat at the news. "Have we seen so little fruit from [Brown's] labors that we should distrust his Fabian valor? Who saved Kansas in '56 and invaded Missouri in '58? ... I have seen no reason yet to doubt our agent, and I bear in mind that 'Though the mills of *John* grind slowly, yet they grind exceeding small.'"[26]

Other Brown intimates had similarly belated changes of mind. The memories of two of them, Frederick Douglass and Richard Realf, the latter the only survivor of Brown's "army" to testify under oath, are worth close scrutiny. Their recollections decisively influenced contemporaries as well as historians and, despite lapses of memory, the two men provide important clues to Brown's thinking before the raid.

Just days after the threatened revolt among his men, Brown received another blow, news that his friend Douglass declined to go along on Brown's perilous raid. Ever since their first meeting in 1847 the two abolitionists had been "friendly and confidential." Douglass claimed that while visiting Brown's home in Springfield, Massachusetts, just days after they met, Brown had outlined a scheme to use the Allegheny mountains as a "pathway for ... a grand exodus" of slaves to the Free States and Canada, and hoped to enlist Douglass's support.[27]

As Douglass remembered this meeting thirty-four years later, Brown had "denounced slavery in look and language fierce and bitter" as he laid out a plan to free the slaves. Brown "did not, as some suppose, contemplate a general rising among the slaves and a general slaughter of the slave-masters," Douglass recalled in 1881. But Brown was "not averse to the shedding of blood," and thought bearing arms would give blacks a "sense of their manhood." Spreading out a map of the United States on his table, Brown had traced the Allegheny Mountains from New York into the South and declared, "God has given the strength of the hills to freedom." The mountains contained "natural forts" and hideaways for safeguarding a body of men acting against slavery "despite all the efforts of Virginia to dislodge them." His object was to "destroy the money value of slave property" by running off slaves "in large numbers." Brown hoped to begin with perhaps twenty-five "picked" men who would operate in squads of five. The "most persuasive and conscientious" of these men would "go down to the fields from time to time" and induce restless or daring slaves to join

Frederick Douglass

FIGURE 10.2. An 1860 portrait of Frederick Douglass, who warned Brown against attacking Harpers Ferry.

CREDIT: Yale Collection of American Literature, Beinecke Rare Book and Manuscript Library.

them. Gradually expanding the force and operating in multiple localities, the squads would sustain themselves through foraging, evade or defeat pursuers, and eventually compel Virginians to sell their slaves south, in which direction Brown would then carry his war.[28]

In later meetings Brown elaborated. His men would feed and shelter runaways and forward them from station to station through the Alleghenies along a line through Pennsylvania and beyond. Even if the plan failed and he was driven from the mountains, Brown told Douglass, the enterprise would keep the slavery question before the nation. Brown showed Douglass plans to construct "forts" so arranged as to connect with one another by "secret passages" (i.e., tunnels). Hence," Douglass remembered, "I assented to...John Brown's scheme or plan for running off slaves."[29]

Brown, a white man who hated slavery with such passion, fascinated Douglass. In subsequent encounters, Douglass's views "became more and more tinged by the color of this man's strong impressions." Douglass was as intrigued by Brown's plan as he was impressed by the man he later came to regard as one of the "greatest heroes known to American fame." In 1847 Douglass had wondered how blacks could win their rights in a new civil order after a bloody race war. In the decade that followed, his pessimism deepened and he drew closer to advocates of slave insurrection like David Walker, Henry Highland Garnet, and John Brown.[30] By August of 1859, when Brown and Douglass met for the last time, Douglass had publicly declared that a "day of reckoning" was at hand and had summoned "black armies of the South" to deliver themselves from slavery. If he still believed that liberation through the federal government was the only way that African Americans could hope for citizenship and equality, he also yearned to strike fear into the hearts of slaveholders. Thus he encouraged Brown.

On January 18, 1858, Brown began a month's stay at Douglass's home in Rochester, New York, during which time Brown wrote his provisional constitution to govern his anticipated army of volunteers and fugitives. Douglass "seems to appreciate my theories, & my labors," he wrote John, Jr. On March 15 Douglass was present at a meeting in Philadelphia with four prominent black leaders during which Brown explained his plan, appealed for money, and urged the leaders to "talk to every family of the right stripe" about how he would ignite the greatest slave uprising in American history. He also urged them to come to Chatham on May 8 to endorse his cause and help him win recruits. But none of the leaders came.[31]

A year later, on April 10, 1859, after a delay occasioned by Forbes's threatened betrayal of his movement to the Buchanan administration, Brown visited Douglass again. This time Brown apparently won Douglass's commitment to support his plan. At least Brown's men were convinced thereafter that Douglass was with them. After a visit with Douglass, Jeremiah G. Anderson, a white volunteer and Kansas veteran, told his brother that Douglass "is to be one of us," and John Henry Kagi wrote Douglass from St. Catherine's in Canada West (Ontario) a hitherto undisclosed letter dated June 23 to "congratulate" him on his "determination to engage '*more earnestly*' in the cause [of] '*Constitutional Liberty.*'...I could scarcely contain myself," Kagi told Douglass, "when I learned of your intention to cooperate in a movement which I can not doubt will prove of more benefit to the African race than all others which have preceded it." Kagi had a "particular reason for rejoicing," he said. "Whenever I have been laboring to induce prospects [recruits] to act in the matter," he continued, "I have almost always been asked '*Has [Douglass] Confidence – will he act.*' – And you can not but know that with many not possessed of an independence of judgment, the reply of 'No' (which it must be to some forms of the interrogation) would utterly annihilate all argument that had been, or might be, offered." It was for the magic of Douglass's name among Canadian fugitives and presumably Virginia slaves that Brown would soon beg him to help "hive the bees."[32]

Just how far Douglass had offered to "cooperate" with Brown is unclear. Perhaps he saw himself chiefly as a conduit to black contributors; he had arranged such introductions before and he brought a check for $10 from a well-to-do black couple to his last meeting with Brown. But Brown and his followers later complained bitterly of Douglass's "defection." When authorities apprehended John E. Cook, whom Brown had planted in Harpers Ferry as a spy a year before the raid, Cook blamed Douglass for the failure of the raid, suggesting implausibly that Douglass had been assigned to bring a large body of reinforcements to the schoolhouse where arms were stored but had failed to do so through "cowardice."[33]

On September 23 Brown had asked Douglass to join him at Chambersburg. "We think you are the man of all others to represent us," Brown said, "and we severally pledge ourselves that in case you will come right on we will see your family well provided for during your absence, or until your safe return to them." Since the letter was found among the papers recovered by authorities at Harpers Ferry, it is unclear whether Douglass ever received that summons.[34] It shows only how passionately Brown hoped Douglass would join him in the raid. If Douglass's memory of the meeting in the stone quarry was accurate, Brown should have known such an appeal would be futile. Brown himself seems to have complained about Douglass to visitors after his trial. In 1909 surviving members of Brown's family claimed that Douglass had failed the old man, but no contemporary evidence supports the claim.[35]

Nonetheless, Cook's public charge after the raid that Douglass had abandoned Brown implicated Douglass in the failed conspiracy. Virginia authorities demanded the extradition of Brown's collaborators, including Douglass, two of whose letters to Brown they found at the Kennedy farm. Warned of the danger, Douglass telegraphed his son in Rochester to burn any letters and documents in his "high desk" written by Brown, and fled to Canada. From Canada, Douglass refuted Cook's charge, denying that he ever pledged "to be present in person at the Harper's Ferry insurrection.... I have never made a promise so rash and wild as this." Furthermore, he had never encouraged "the taking of Harper's Ferry ... by my word or by my vote.... I desire to be quite emphatic here, for of all guilty men, he is the guiltiest who lures his fellow-men to an undertaking of this sort, under promise of assistance which he afterwards fails to render."[36]

Douglass admitted that he knew in advance of Brown's "desperate but sublimely disinterested effort to emancipate the slaves of Maryland and Virginia," and boldly asserted that "it can never be wrong for the imbruted and

FIGURE 10.3. In old age Frederick Douglass still championed Brown's memory.

CREDIT: U.S. National Archives.

whip-scarred slaves, or their friends, to hunt, harass, and even strike down the traffickers in human flesh." Douglass defended his refusal to "assume the base and detestable character of an informer," and explained his refusal to join the "noble old hero" by saying, "'The tools to those who can use them!' Let every man work for the abolition of slavery in his own way."[37]

Through the decades Douglass remained a passionate defender of Brown. "If John Brown did not end the war that ended slavery, he did at least begin the war that ended slavery," Douglass told rapt audiences.[38] But Douglass told the story of his last meeting with Brown only in 1881, when he devoted most of a chapter to it in the last version of his autobiography. That story merits examination because in it Douglass claimed that Brown had changed his earlier plans and become obsessed with taking Harpers Ferry only a short time before the raid itself.

Brown's objective in 1859 was still to destroy the value of slave property by making it insecure, Douglass remembered. "Men do not like to buy runaway horses, or to invest their money in a species of property likely to take legs and walk off with itself." But Brown's plan to run off slaves had involved no insurrection or taking of Harpers Ferry. "Once in a while he would say he could, with a few resolute men, capture Harper's Ferry, and supply himself with arms belonging to the government... but he never announced his intention to do so." The Kansas strife and then Forbes's betrayal postponed the implementation of the plan. Finally, after Brown assembled his men at the Kennedy farm, he "summoned" Douglass to a meeting near Chambersburg, where Douglass found him "disguised" as a fishermen and accompanied by Kagi.[39]

There, in an abandoned rock quarry, Brown first declared it as his settled purpose to take Harpers Ferry, Douglass reported. Douglass opposed the idea as potentially "fatal to running off slaves" and "fatal to all engaged in doing so. It would be an attack upon the federal government, and would array the whole country against us." Brown was not worried about "rousing the nation," insisting that "something startling was just what the nation needed. He had completely renounced his old plan, and thought that the capture of Harper's Ferry would serve as notice to the slaves that their friends had come, and as a trumpet to rally them to his standard."

According to Douglass, Brown thought Harpers Ferry, the town, so easily defensible that it would be impossible to drive him out once he possessed it. Douglass countered that the town was a "perfect steel-trap, and that once in he would never get out alive; that he would be surrounded at once and escape would be impossible." Brown insisted that even if surrounded, he could cut his way out because he would hold hostage a number of the "best citizens of the neighborhood" and could therefore "dictate terms to egress from the town." Douglass warned Brown that "Virginia would blow him and his hostages sky-high, rather than that he should hold Harper's Ferry an hour."

Brown and Douglass spent most of Saturday and part of Sunday debating earnestly, Douglass remembered, Brown for "striking a blow that would rouse the country instantly, and I for the policy of gradually and unaccountably drawing off the slaves to the mountains," as Brown had long ago proposed. Douglass feared a rash act would "rivet the fetters more firmly than ever on the limbs of the enslaved." In a last effort to win over Douglass, Brown put his arms around him and said: "Come with me, Douglass; I will defend you with my life. I want you for a special purpose. When I strike, the bees will begin to swarm, and I shall want you to help hive them.'" Either "discretion or cowardice" made Douglass refuse. But Shields Green, who had accompanied Douglass to Chambersburg and listened to the dispute, did not. When Douglass asked Green to return home with him, Green said, "in his broken way, 'I b'leve I'll go wid de ole man.'"[40]

Since Douglass had often told this story in briefer form on the lecture circuit, it probably benefited from retroactive interference. But the gist of his reminiscence was doubtless true. It vindicated his wisdom in refusing to join Brown's ill-fated expedition. But there is a curious omission in the story: Douglass said nothing about the plan's reliance on attracting the slaves. The latter's restiveness was an article of faith with Brown, and Douglass had for years rejected the charge that slaves were subservients who cared too little "for liberty to fight for it." The history of slave rebellions demonstrated otherwise, he thought.[41]

Whether or not this issue came up in his meeting with Brown, Douglass surely remembered the vengeance visited upon blacks in past uprisings or suspected uprisings. He agreed with Brown and other radicals that slavery was a perpetual state of war against bondsmen, and slaves had every right to rebel. But he knew that flight more than fighting appealed to border state slaves, where, by the 1850s, as Merton Dillon has noted, they were running away "in droves." The increasing tempo of "nullifying flights" held out hope to those left behind and presumably made any invitations to insurrection seem all the more problematic. Among his fugitive friends, Douglass found only Shields Green willing to accompany Brown. Yet in 1881, Douglass did not recall warning Brown that the slaves would mistrust any white man claiming to be their savior. Hence, despite Brown's plea to him to help "hive the bees," Douglass apparently permitted Brown to go to his doom without contesting a crucial assumption on which Douglass's opinion would have been unchallengeable: that the slaves would rise at Brown's appearance.[42]

In public statements after the raid, Douglass never second-guessed Brown, and did his best to turn Brown's defeat to advantage for the cause. His argument in so doing was highly suggestive. Again and again, he observed, Brown had struck fear in the hearts of slaveholders. A veritable Samson shaking the pillars of "this great national temple of cruelty and blood," Brown had "initiated a new mode of carrying on the crusade of freedom, and his blow has sent dread and terror throughout the entire ranks of the piratical army of slavery." In January 1860 Douglass told a cheering audience in Edinburgh, Scotland, that Brown's plan was "not so crazy ... as upon the first sight it appeared. His mistake was that he remained a few hours too long in the arsenal. Had he succeeded in reaching the mountains," Brown "might have ... defied all the power of the United States' army to have dislodged him."[43]

Brown's idea had taken root among the slaves and would grow, Douglass insisted. "Let once the slaves of the South find that, by running up from the plains they could lodge in the mountains, and descend upon the plains as opportunity might offer, and it would be the beginning of the end." Writing to James Redpath, Douglass declared that "American slaves and their friends" now view the "innumerable glens, caves, ravines and rocks" in the Alleghenies as the "hiding-places of hunted liberty. The forty-eight hours [sic] of Brown's school in Virginia taught the slaves more than they could have otherwise learned in a half-century. Even the mistake of remaining in the arsenal after the first blow was struck may prove the key to future successes." Slaveholders were "beyond the reach of moral and humane considerations," Douglass continued. "They have neither ears nor hearts for the appeals of justice and humanity.... The only penetrable point of a tyrant is the *fear of death*.... The efforts of John Brown and his brave associates...have done more to upset the logic and shake the security of slavery, than all other efforts in that direction for twenty years."[44] One measure of Brown's ultimate success was the terror his raid had created.

IV

Historians have relied heavily on the testimony of Richard Realf before the Senate committee appointed to investigate the raid to understand Brown's purpose at Harpers Ferry. Realf was one of Brown's soldiers and was presumed to be well acquainted with his plans. But, perhaps because he feared prosecution, Realf's testimony was self-serving and far from candid. In fact, partisan purposes on the part of committee members as well as witnesses such as Realf tainted much of the evidence gathered in six-months of investigation and hearings. Though Chairman James M. Mason of Virginia assured witnesses they would not be prosecuted for anything they said in their testimony, Brown's accomplices knew that unguarded words could implicate their friends as well as prominent supporters of Brown's cause. The committee failed notably to get to the bottom of what Brown was up to at Harpers Ferry.[45]

A twenty-five-year old Englishman, Realf was the son of a rural constable and blacksmith, a "peasant," he told the committee. An aspiring poet who had once moved among the English "aristocracy" and "literati," Realf had quarreled with his "proteges" and decided to seek his fortune elsewhere. A self-professed "democrat or republican, or, at least, anti-monarchical," he told the committee, "I came to America." A "radical abolitionist," he had joined Brown's company in Kansas in 1857, trudged with other volunteers across Iowa behind the old man's wagonload of rifles, and drilled with them at Springdale. Brown rewarded his loyalty by having him elected secretary of state in the provisional government at the Chatham Convention in 1858.

Soon after that, Brown had dispatched Realf to New York City in a failed effort to "ingratiate himself" with Brown's former confidant, Hugh Forbes, who had betrayed Brown's conspiracy to Republican lawmakers, and to learn what Forbes was up to.[46] Forbes was a shadowy figure whom federal marshals, acting on behalf of the Senate committee, never found, but his published disclosures of Brown's plan significantly affected the hearings.

Realf admitted to the committee his assignment to find Forbes, but did not reveal a second "mission" he had undertaken. Discovering that Forbes was no longer in New York and promising to raise money for Brown in England, Realf asked for and received $250 to pay for his return to England to "forward the interests of the Association" there.[47] That was the last the "Association" or Brown saw of Realf. When Realf returned to the United States in April 1859, he told the Committee, he had repudiated abolitionism and hoped to found a Democratic and proslavery newspaper in New Orleans.

Realf's testimony was neither forthcoming nor generally truthful. He was careful to protect himself and others from possible prosecution. He distanced himself from Brown's movement by insisting that Brown had misled him and that none of the money he raised in England ever reached Brown or anyone in his movement. Indeed, Realf had "finished" with Brown weeks after Chatham, and "never had, directly or indirectly, any acquaintance or connection, in the most remote degree, with the party after my departure from Cleveland."[48]

In fact, just days before giving his testimony, Realf had met several times in Boston with other Brown supporters who had been summoned to testify before the committee. The purpose of these meetings was to coordinate their stories, to agree on what Realf himself suggested as their basic strategy: the claim that Brown was so "secretive" that he told none of his partisans details of his plans. Realf repeated that point over and over in his testimony. Asked about Brown's funding, he replied: "Here I ought to state...that John Brown was a man who would never state more than it was absolutely necessary for him to do. None of his most intimate associates, and I was one of the most intimate," Realf boasted, "was possessed of more than barely sufficient information to enable Brown to attach such companions to him; and none of us were cognizant of more than the general plan of his design until the time we reached Chatham, Canada West."[49] Realf denied flatly that men like Samuel Gridley Howe, Franklin Sanborn, or Gerrit Smith, who were known to the committee to be contributors, knew anything of the planned "invasion."[50] Indeed, throughout his testimony, Realf never mentioned Harpers Ferry. And he flatly denied Cook's charge that he had gone back to England to make money to aid Brown.

The significance of Realf's testimony for present purposes is in what he had to say about Brown and his plan to act against slavery. Richard Realf did not conceal a certain admiration for Brown. Brown had "from the time he went to Kansas, devoted his whole being, mental, moral, and physical, all that he had and was, to the extinction of slavery," Realf volunteered. At Chatham, Brown told him the idea of using the mountains to free the slaves "arose spontaneously in his own mind," and "through...twenty to thirty years it had gradually formed and developed itself into shape and plan." The temporary state he hoped to create in the mountains would be a haven for runaway slaves, who would be taught "useful and mechanical arts" and learn "all the business of life. Schools were also to be established, and so on." Brown's men would serve out of "philanthropy – love for the slave"; Brown himself was wholly disinterested and unselfish." If Realf had in fact repudiated Brown's plan, as he professed, he had not renounced Brown himself.[51]

It had been "during our passage across Iowa," Realf testified, that "Brown's plan in regard to an incursion into Virginia gradually manifested itself." The company had debated whether determined men could make a "successful insurrection" in mountainous country. Realf had argued in the affirmative, "but the men did not learn details of Brown's project until he addressed the Chatham delegates in May 1858. Realf could remember only "certain salient points and leading ideas" of the project, but much of what he remembered was similar to what Douglass later recollected. Brown would base his operation in the mountains that cut through the slave states and raid plantations that lay below them, retreating to "fastnesses" where he could defeat pursuing state militia or federal troops. Brown had spoken of his "passion" to free the slaves, his long study of "insurrectionary warfare," and the history of guerrilla combat from Roman times to "the wars of Toussaint L'Ouverture." "Upon the first intimation" of his presence as a raider or insurrectionary, nearby slaves "would immediately rise all over the Southern States."

Realf's Brown told the assembled blacks at Chatham that once word of his plan and his presence spread, "all the free negroes" in the northern states, "all the slaves in the Southern States," and "as many of the free negroes in Canada" as could accompany him "would immediately flock to his standard." Recalcitrant slaveholders would be taken as "hostages for the safe treatment" of Brown's men captured by the enemy. Nonslaveholding whites would be "protected" if they remained neutral, but otherwise treated as enemies. Brown expected to finance the effort with funds raised from the many "rich people" of the North. In response to Brown's speech laying out this program, Dr. Martin Delaney had pledged that Brown might rely on "all the colored people of Canada" to follow him.[52]

Clearly, Realf was blustering. Brown would scarcely have made such wild claims to an audience of fugitives. But Realf's testimony contributed to the belief that Brown was blinded by hubris and grandiosity. Inadvertently, Realf pictured Brown as monomaniacal.

V

The story of Hugh Forbes's troubled dealings with Brown was well known. Briefly a confidant, he was the only man who had talked at length with Brown about his strategy to destroy slavery. But in a continuing effort to discredit Brown and his wealthy supporters, Forbes had published his correspondence with them in James Gordon Bennett's proslavery New-York *Herald*. In letters to various of those supporters, Forbes had first told his story of his relationship with Brown more than a year before the raid.[53] According to that story, Forbes tendered his services to Brown in March 1857 through his connection with the reformer and editor, Rev. Joshua Leavitt. Brown hired Forbes, who had fought for Giuseppe Garibaldi in the republican struggle to unify Italy, to drill his men and to write a training manual for them and a propaganda tract for his cause.

The two men soon had a falling out, and Forbes began telling Brown's financial backers that Brown lacked the "capacity to direct such an enterprise" as he proposed. Brown had to be stopped, Forbes concluded, if only because he was leagued with Amos Lawrence in a putative plot to drive the price of cotton up and make a financial killing at the expense of the cause of freedom.[54] In disclosing this elaborate scheme by publishing his letters to the "bogus humanitarians," Forbes had presumably found an honorable motive for his betrayal of Brown. Forbes's letters are of interest chiefly because of his knowledge of Brown's plan and because for a time he hoped to win Brown's backers over to his own plan to free the slaves. Indeed, Realf testified that Forbes himself "at one point purposed to conduct the movement."[55]

Forbes's plan, developed after hearing Brown's, was premised on exploiting the penetrable borders between slavery and freedom. He proposed to launch a series of nighttime slave "stampedes" along the "northern slave frontier," each designed to "carry off" twenty to fifty slaves.[56] Forbes apparently believed the slaves were ready to run to their freedom, if not to fight for it. Striking once or twice a month at first, and then weekly along "non-contiguous parts of the line," Forbes's men would resort to force only if attacked. The fugitives they rescued or enticed would be dispatched to Canada so quickly that pursuit would be hopeless. Successful forays would soon make slave property "untenable" along the northern frontier of the institution, which would be pushed continually southward as the frontier crumbled, leading "proslaveryites to commit some stupid blunders."[57]

Forbes failed to say just what the "stupid blunders" might be or how abolitionists might exploit them. He left many questions unanswered about how his plan would work in practice. But his summary of Brown's scheme reveals that seventeen months before Harpers Ferry, Brown had indeed abandoned his Subterranean Passage Way for something bolder. If Forbes reported correctly, Brown too was thinking of coordinated hit-and-run raids in many places. Forbes's Brown insisted that he could "get on the first night from 200 to 500" to flee and would mount about 100 of these on horses to make a "dash" at the Harpers Ferry "manufactory, destroying what they could not carry off." Other recruits would be divided into similar raiding parties who would "beat up other slave quarters whence more men would be sent to join him."[58]

Despite Forbes's skepticism about Brown's plan, he shared many of Brown's basic assumptions about how to free the slaves. He too believed that Virginia slaves might be ready to strike for freedom. But he worried that "slave insurrections" were unpredictable. A "feeble" response by the slaves would compromise the whole effort; a "great rising" would leap beyond Brown's "unskilled direction, sweeping like a prairie fire from Mason and Dixon's line to the Gulf of Mexico."

Forbes may well have distorted as well as oversimplified Brown's plan in his effort to discredit him. After the raid, no one was prepared to dispute Forbes's claims about Brown's scheme. But several of Brown's own comments to reporters about his plans may have been an effort to refute Forbes's widely publicized disclosures.[59] Like other Brown associates following the raid, Forbes too may have unconsciously reassessed Brown. A week after the *Herald* published his letters to Howe and Sanborn, Forbes remembered that Brown was "very pious and had been deeply impressed for years with the story of Gideon, believing that he with a handful of men could strike down slavery." Forbes concluded that Brown had taken Harpers Ferry to draw attention to himself and suggested facetiously that Brown might better have descended upon the White House and "carried off the president."[60]

Forbes and Brown had talked of the political consequences they hoped their raids would induce as they subverted the slave economy. If U.S. troops pressed him in the Alleghenies, Forbes's Brown expected his New England "partisans" to call a northern convention to "restore tranquility and overthrow the pro-slavery administration." As implausible as that seems in retrospect, many militant abolitionists had come to believe that even an unsuccessful slave rebellion might rouse the North to intervene on the slaves' behalf. Douglass himself made such a claim in 1857.[61] Brown hoped for more, in Forbes's words, to effect a "rupture between the free and the slave States."[62] Forbes's disclosures thus suggested that Brown may have intended his guerrilla campaign to bring about disunion and a war to end slavery.

VI

Judge William Arny, who described himself as a railroad president, had seen Brown often in Kansas in 1858 in his capacity as agent of the National Kansas Committee, which provided Brown with weapons and other material support. In testimony before the Senate committee, Arny confirmed the thrust of Realf's account of Brown's plan. At Arny's home, Brown had disclosed his plan to "stampede slaves" or "carry slaves off to Canada," using "just the same language that Realf had used" when he and Arny had met recently in New York City. Brown would "situate a company of men somewhere in the mountains in the slave States ... to assist slaves in escaping, so as to make the system of slavery insecure – make that species of property insecure." In 1858, then, Arny's assumption was that Brown intended something like the Subterranean Pass Way scheme, not a slave rebellion. Arny also added facts about Brown no other witness provided. He had known Brown in Virginia twenty years before, when Brown was a nonresistant, an "ultra" who disavowed violence even in self-defense. When in 1858 Arny demanded to know why Brown had abandoned his former principles, the "old man" had blamed the Border Ruffians for taking his sons' cattle and other "aggressions of slavery."[63]

The testimony of Charles Robinson, the leader of free-state forces in Kansas, greatly strengthens the inference that Brown hoped to embroil the nation in civil war. The committee excluded much of his story of Kansas intrigue from its journal as "hearsay" and as irrelevant to its mandate to investigate Harpers Ferry. But the committee's unstated reason for its doing so may have been that in the inflammatory atmosphere surrounding the hearings, Robinson's story was politically combustible.[64]

When Congress opened the Kansas territory to settlement in 1854, Robinson was in Massachusetts practicing medicine part time and editing a small newspaper. Inspired by Eli Thayer's crusade to make Kansas a free state and by the prospect of becoming wealthy through land sales, Robinson agreed to head the Massachusetts Emigrant Aid Company's first colony of settlers, and in September he situated the company headquarters in Lawrence. Elected "governor" of the free-state territorial government in 1855,[65] Robinson had negotiated the truce that prevented a bloodletting during the Wakarusa War. It was during that December 1855 confrontation with the proslavery authority that Robinson commissioned John Brown as a captain of the free-state militia.[66]

After the burning of Osawatomie, Robinson praised Brown's attempt to defend the town and summoned him to a meeting.[67]

That 1856 Lawrence meeting was the focus of the Mason Committee's questioning. Robinson recalled Brown saying that he intended to "create difficulties and disturbances" rather than to establish a free-state government in Kansas, as Robinson himself hoped to do. Brown said "he did not come to Kansas for the purpose of settling at all. He would never have come there...had he not expected those difficulties would result in a general disturbance in the country, and he hoped that the two sections would get into a conflict which would result in abolishing slavery." Prompted by the Committee, Robinson explained that Brown expected this "collision between the North and the South" to result from public "sympathy with the different parties" in Kansas. Robinson then revealed voluntarily that a small group of "foreigners" working as correspondents of the great metropolitan newspapers in the East, together with radical Kansas politicians, had been conspirators within the free-state movement who shared Brown's hope for a general conflagration and supported him. At one point, he claimed, the conspirators "got up" a movement "to massacre all the pro-slavery men in the Territory" and then to assassinate proslavery leaders in Missouri as well. But as soon as the scheme became known beyond the conspirators themselves, Robinson assured the Committee, it "fell still-born." Although Brown himself was not one of these plotters, they considered Brown and "General" Lane to be their "most efficient" allies "in the field."[68]

Robinson's suppressed revelations to the committee must be read cautiously. Like others who testified, he protected his own reputation by distancing himself from Brown and his chief Kansas rival, Lane. Those who knew Brown best claimed that he had "no idea of fighting" until the Missourians again interfered in territorial elections.[69] In any case, no hint of Robinson's story of a conspiracy to perpetuate the Kansas fighting, much of which was excluded from the published report of the Senate committee, found its way into either the majority or minority reports. Nor did the committee suggest that Brown's ultimate purpose might be to embroil the nation in civil war. But Mason's majority report concluded that Brown had hoped to lead Kansas free-staters into Missouri to incite "servile war," and, when fighting ended in Kansas, into other slaveholding states, using slaves "as his soldiery." Prominent men such as George Stearns and Samuel Gridley Howe, the report said, had failed in their duty to prevent Brown from diverting weapons intended for the defense of Kansas to his own nefarious purposes. Although Congress could not prevent such wanton acts by legislation, Mason warned that the free states must guard against such future attacks by "appropriate legislation," lest the "peace between the States of the Union" be jeopardized.[70]

Vermont Senator Jacob Collamer's minority report concurred that Brown's "object" had been to raise a "slave insurrection in the slaveholding States" and to "subvert" their governments. Collamer insisted that the raid was the work of an isolated band of "young men and boys" entirely under Brown's sway, "many of them foreigners," and included no one of "substance or position in the country." Harpers Ferry was "but an offshoot" of the "outrages and lawlessness in Kansas" triggered by "armed invasions" from the slaveholding states. Collamer said that the inquiry had proved the people of the North had no part in Brown's movement. He accused the majority of taking "great latitude" to call witnesses "suspected of ultra abolition sentiments" even though they were not "implicated" in the raid. Ironically, Collamer accused the majority of doing precisely what Robinson said Brown hoped to accomplish: to stir the waters and keep the slavery controversy alive.[71]

VII

As Frederick Douglass grasped during his 1859 meeting with Brown at the stone quarry, Brown's decision to attack Harpers Ferry rather than to raid plantations and run off slaves was calculated to create widespread panic. And so for a time it did.[72] Even the Mason Committee's Republican minority report, which argued that the raid was an isolated event, conceded that "The place and the boldness of this outbreak, the purpose it entertained, the deaths it involved, and the amount of arms and munitions with which it was supplied, combined to produce not only great alarm, but also a strong suspicion of extensive complicity."[73] Initially, at least, the seizing of Harpers Ferry met one of Brown's principal objectives – to inspire fear – despite his failure to rally the slaves.

Thus our first question is answered. Two years before Harpers Ferry Brown began to envision spreading the war against slavery beyond Kansas and perhaps inciting civil war. The panic Brown's raid into Missouri generated in 1858 created his new celebrity and strengthened his resolve to renew the fighting. By the time he attacked Harpers Ferry, he hoped not only to weaken the peculiar institution economically, but to embroil the nation in civil war. And among Brown's chosen instruments was terror.

With that in mind, Brown abandoned the idea of a subterranean railway to "run off" slaves through the mountains. Slave rescues had enraged slaveholders, but occasional forays did not startle them from their beds. Something more dramatic was required to produce panic. Sometime after Brown left Kansas, therefore, he adopted the plan he discussed with Forbes to attack plantations at night in swift "dashes" and gather a large force before striking Harpers Ferry to confiscate weapons stored there. Moving southward, he would establish maroons, bases in the Appalachian Mountains, from which to continue his raids on the plains. Why, then, had he discarded that plan and struck directly at the Ferry without a larger force?

Part of the answer to that question lies in Brown's failure to recruit volunteers in the northeast and Canada. Despite his effort at the Chatham convention in May 1858, no prominent American black except Martin Delaney attended the convention, and Brown gained only one Canadian recruit there. Brown had come to Chatham after a series of meetings with black activists in which he received only modest financial support and no volunteers. As one of his black supporter had warned him: "The *masses* suffer for the want of intelligence [information] and it is difficult to reach them in a matter like you propose."[74]

Brown had gotten at best mixed responses from blacks in the weeks leading up to the Chatham meeting. On March 2 he wrote Mary that he was experiencing "both great encouragements and discouragements.... I find a much more earnest feeling among the colored people than ever before; but this is by no means unusual. On the whole, the language of Providence to me would certainly seem to say, 'Try on.'"[75] Early in April Brown and Jermain Wesley Loguen, a runaway-turned-clergyman, met with the famous "abductor," Harriet Tubman, at St. Catherines in what is now Ontario to get her help in his enterprise.[76] The meeting went well. "I am succeeding *to all appearances* beyond my expectation," Brown reported. Impressed with the diminutive one-time fieldhand's toughness and audacity, Brown exulted that "Harriet Tubman hooked on *his* whole team at once. *He* is the most of a man, naturally; that I ever met with."[77] Brown began calling her "General Tubman." Tubman liked Brown and embraced his project. She was raising money for him as late as June 1859. But she was bedridden when Brown struck Harpers Ferry,[78] and her absence deprived Brown of her use of the slave "grapevine" to win the trust of local slaves.

In April 1858 Brown was buoyed by the prospect of recruiting men in St. Catherines. "There is the most abundant material; & of the right quality in this quarter beyond all doubt," he declared. Yet no one volunteered. Neither Loguen, Douglass, Garnet, nor any of the militants he had hoped to recruit threw in with his movement. Although such men were cordial, they did not believe that slaves would rise up and join Brown. Even the fiery Garnet, an advocate of rebellion, had earlier warned that the time was not ripe. Blacks in the South were insufficiently aware of their situation and of Northern whites' sympathy with their plight, and those in the North were unprepared because of the "prejudice that shuts them out from both the means and the intelligence necessary."[79]

Despite his disappointments at Chatham, Brown put the best face he could on the outcome. According to the brief Minutes of the Convention, Delaney did rise to encourage Brown as Realf had told the committee, and the "project and the plan" were "agreed to by general consent." But delegate James Monroe Jones told Brown from the floor of the convention that he doubted slaves could be relied upon to rally around an invading force, since American slaves were less impetuous than West Indian slaves.[80] If Harpers Ferry was a "trumpet blast," as Douglass later called it, Brown had ample warning that Virginia slaves would not hear the blast nor rise in response to it.

Despite this outcome at Chatham, Brown left believing he had pledges from a number of Canadian recruits, only one of which was ever fulfilled. He attributed their failure to join him later to the long delay in summoning them occasioned by Forbes' betrayal and the resulting postponement. Indeed, his decision to begin the Virginia project by taking Harpers Ferry may have been determined in part by his wish to restore his credibility among hesitating supporters.

In fact, since Kansas, Brown had found it increasingly difficult to persuade anyone to join his war on slavery. Two months after his sons had renounced war, only thirty-four-year-old Owen encouraged Brown to think he would again "go on with me" back to Kansas.[81] In the end his sons Watson and Oliver and two of Henry Thompson's younger brothers also agreed to serve, but Henry himself and Salmon Brown, two of the Pottawatomie assassins, and all the other North Elba neighbors, refused.[82]

By spring 1859, Brown was in jeopardy of losing even the small nucleus of his army.[83] In March he had left the men at camp in Springdale, Iowa, to raise funds once again in Boston. But he fell ill for weeks and won only modest contributions.[84] Kagi soon wrote Brown that one of their prospective recruits, Luke Parsons, had left. Despite this setback and his own continuing problems, Brown asked Kagi to tell "our folks *all as soon as may be*; that there is *scarce a doubt* but that all will be set right in a very few days more, so that I can be on my way back. They must none of them think I have been slack to *try*: & urge forward a delicate, & very difficult matter." He was worried about keeping his Springdale volunteers committed.[85]

Later that summer, when Brown set up headquarters in his rented Maryland farmhouse, some of his staunchest Kansas fighters failed to show up when summoned.[86] Two months later, Charles H. Langdon, a black leader of the Oberlin rescuers, had become "clear discouraged" because he "thinks the hands too few," John, Jr. wrote.[87] Even among Brown loyalists at the Kennedy farm, skepticism about Harpers Ferry was rampant. Douglass thought the plan too dangerous, and Harriet Tubman was bedridden at home. Without a bold stroke to restore faith in his leadership, Brown saw his prospects eroding away.

VIII

But Brown could not have brought his war plan to antislavery circles at a more propitious time. Opinion about how to fight slavery was changing. Nonresistance was losing support in favor of political intervention and direct action. The growing demand to face down the Slave Power found expression in the rise of the Liberty Party, the Free Soil Party, even the Know-Nothing Party, as well as in various efforts to build antislavery political coalitions, including the emergence in 1854 of the Republican Party.[88] Direct action to obstruct slave catchers became common in New England. Radical abolitionists of both races openly endorsed violence in self-defense. Since the 1840s, rescue attempts in the Upper South had shown the readiness of slaves in increasing numbers to flee and if necessary to seize their freedom by violence. Brown's well-publicized Missouri raid was actually the eighth such incursion from Kansas.[89] The fear of direct abolitionist assaults in exposed border regions had intensified southern sectionalism.[90]

For decades abolitionists had warned the South of slave uprisings, and by the 1840s, immediatists began to see the slaves themselves as allies in the effort to end slavery. They also increasingly endorsed the doctrine that slavery was a state of war in which the slave had the right to resist, if necessary violently. Brown's appearance in antislavery circles in 1857 helped to affect this sea change in abolitionist thinking about how to end slavery.

The question of slaves' willingness to fight had been debated among abolitionists for years before Harpers Ferry. Black abolitionists especially denounced the Southern stereotype of the contented, childlike slave. But racial stereotypes were also widespread among Northerners, including abolitionists, and they functioned to sustain ideas that the slaves would not act boldly against slavery. Theodore Parker had called the African race the "most docile and pliant" of human races. In their "barbarous state," Africans were not, like whites, "addicted" to revenge, they were "prone to mercy," Parker said in January 1859.[91] Prodded in part by Brown's insistence that slaves would rise if provided weapons and leadership, Parker and others had finally begun to overcome these doubts. To find support for his views, Brown queried two moderate black Boston abolitionists who had researched the question of black military exploits, William C. Nell, who had written on the valor of black soldiers in the American Revolution, and William Wells Brown, who had published *St. Domingo: Its Revolution and Its Aftermath* in 1855. The latter believed that American slaves were only awaiting the right moment to wipe out "the wrongs of their oppressors" and "reenact" the Haitian revolution in South Carolina and Louisiana.[92]

Among Brown's associates such thinking was increasingly appealing. Parker had long held that destroying slavery by force would reinvigorate Northern white manhood. By his own admission, he had come to hate slavery not just in the abstract. "I hate *Slave-hunters, Slave-breeders, Slave-steelers,* and *Slave-holders* ... and shall seek to rid the world of such a nuisance," Parker told a friend. "A few years ago it did not seem difficult ... to end [slavery] without any bloodshed," Parker said, voicing a darker sentiment that Brown would echo before he was hanged. "I think this cannot be done now, nor ever in the future." After Harpers Ferry, Parker reaffirmed not just his support for Brown, but the necessity for slaves to kill "all such as oppose their natural freedom."[93]

To refute the idea that mulattoes might have courage only because they were half white, Wendell Phillips began lecturing on Toussaint L'Ouverture, "an unmixed negro – his father stolen from Africa."[94] Thomas Wentworth Higginson also challenged the popular idea of innate black passivity. Slaves had only to witness heroic moral leadership to awaken their "courage of emulation," he wrote in the *Atlantic Monthly*. Parker and Higginson helped convince other members of the Secret Six that only by seizing their freedom could blacks achieve the manhood slavery had denied them. As Jeffery Rossbach has shown, the Six supported Brown ultimately in order to test the possibility of sparking slave militance as a necessary step in transforming blacks into prospective citizens of a democratic, enterprising, competitive society, and to disabuse Northerners of the notion of slave submissiveness. But the Six still had doubts themselves. George Stearns spoke for the others when he assured John Brown, Jr., somewhat equivocally in August, 1859, "that we have the *fullest confidence in his [Brown's] endeavor*, whatever may be the result."[95]

If Brown found few volunteers among blacks, he took heart at signs of growing black militancy. Black radicals called increasingly for the slaves to rise, while repeated triumphs of the "Slave Power" in the 1850s drove Garrisonians to reassess their faith in the efficacy of moral suasion. As the latter saw it, Southerners had become increasingly militant, and even many Garrisonians yearned for forceful revenge against the Slave Power. Lawrence J. Friedman demonstrates that acceptance of Brown's doctrine of righteous violence helped many immediatists feel their efforts were not unavailing. Ultimately, Brown helped vitalize the immediatists' sense of mission and confidence that they could influence the course of events.[96]

By 1859 abolitionist talk of insurrection was in the air. Phillips was proclaiming his conviction that every plantation had its own Toussaint conspiring to rebel.[97] In 1858 the quixotic Boston attorney, Lysander Spooner, had begun to circulate privately his own "Plan for the Abolition of Slavery," in which he sought to exploit the economic and social antagonism between southern small farmers and the planter elite and the restiveness of slaves. Spooner's sweeping objectives were to drive the slaveholders from the federal government, to destroy the "security and value of Slave property, to annihilate the commercial credit of the Slaveholders; and finally to accomplish the extinction of Slavery." Although he hoped to do all this without "blood," he confessed that his "scheme" implied war – in fact "revolution."[98] But unlike Brown, Spooner was a theorist not a warrior. He wished to show that it was possible to imagine the downfall of slavery without federal intervention. "My plan is to have the paper distributed [as] extensively as possible throughout the South," he wrote Higginson.[99]

Though Spooner's "Manifesto" was dismissed by some as *"immature – impractical – impolitic,"* Parker, Higginson, and other militants recognized it would "excite terror among the slave holders." Richard J. Hinton, the Kansas firebrand who was fascinated by Brown and the idea of a slave uprising, assured Spooner that Wendell Phillips, who had found the plan unrealistic, would nonetheless fund the printing of 500 handbills to "help spread the panic."[100] But Brown's supporters urged Spooner to withhold further publication temporarily so as not to alert authorities to Brown's impending incursion. By then Spooner's plan had already appeared in the *Boston Courant,* and nearly 200 copies had been mailed not to abolitionists, but to slaveholders.

Brown himself knew nothing about Spooner's "Manifesto to Nonslaveholders" until sometime after its publication in 1858. But in May 1859, a year after Brown's Chatham convention, Spooner and Brown actually met in Boston, and at Brown's request the attorney agreed to suspend further publication of his Manifesto.[101] It evidently did not frighten slaveholders into strengthening patrols or establishing guards over strategic points such as arsenals; those who received it apparently ignored it.[102] Indeed, it drew scorn as the "howlings of a maniac" in conservative circles in the North.[103] But its wide circulation to slave owners may have led Brown to reassess his own plan which then called for a series of "dashes" at plantations as a prelude to striking Harpers Ferry. Brown had no way of assessing Spooner's impact. Thus the distribution of Spooner's call for forcible resistance may have encouraged Brown to decide on a swift strike at Harpers Ferry instead of hit-and-run raids on plantations.

IX

In Brown's effort to persuade doubtful abolitionists of the slave's courage, he had a potent ally in James Redpath. More than a year before he met John Brown, Redpath advanced a plan to incite "A GENERAL STAMPEDE OF THE SLAVES." In his unsystematic canvass of slave and free black sentiment in the South, he had found widespread discontent, and in Charlestown and other Southern cities he discovered nonslaveholding artisans and small merchants, many from abroad, whom he believed were "secret abolitionists." During his second tour of the South in 1855, he found among the slaves "bold and resolute men who are ready to fly" if they knew the way and could defend themselves from pursuers and their bloodhounds. He urged Northern abolitionists to work for the repeal of the Fugitive Slave Law, to circulate antislavery writings to wavering slaveholders, and to send evidence to nonslaveholders that slavery was driving commerce, manufacturing, and capital from the South. Long before Spooner circulated his plan, Redpath had begun to advocate organizing secret societies to assist slaves to escape. Redpath declared that a "small band of bold but cautious men" could engage the assistance of many free blacks in the border slave states in spreading discontent and distributing supplies to runaways. Working clandestinely, he claimed, "Ten or twelve such Apostles of Freedom could easily, in one year, induce five thousand slaves, at least, to fly to the North."[104]

Like Brown, Spooner, and other radicals, Redpath believed in the efficacy of terror and financial ruin as weapons against slavery. He warned abolitionists that "The South will *never* liberate her slaves, unless compelled by FEAR to do so; or unless the activity of the abolitionists renders human property so insecure a possession as to be comparatively worthless to its owner." In 1857 he became a friend and champion of Brown, who shared with Redpath his plan to seize a federal arsenal and establish a base deep in the Appalachians from which to liberate slaves on the neighboring plains. After leaving Kansas, Redpath became a John the Baptist to Brown among Eastern abolitionists and politicians, attesting to the feasibility of Brown's plan and his mettle as a guerrilla leader. Redpath's admiring posthumous biography of Brown, which appeared less than five weeks after Brown's execution, and a second volume of tributes to Brown, helped make Brown in death the saint-like warrior that Garrisonians required to conquer their ambivalence about whether moral principle could be reconciled with the warrior's virtues.[105]

X

By summer 1859, then, radical abolitionist sentiment and talk of plans to end slavery gave Brown a new sense of urgency. He knew his plan might be betrayed by any of scores of people with whom he had discussed it or to whom he had appealed for help.[106] He would have to strike soon to be sure of surprise. His recruiting efforts had been very disappointing, and not a single African-American leader had pledged to join him in carrying his war into the South. Their warnings that the slaves might not rise were troublesome but were balanced to some degree by the hopefulness of white reformers who insisted the slaves were restive and eager to be free. The emerging abolitionist consensus that violence was permissible, that slavery itself was war, had raised Brown's hopes of inspiring abolitionists to endorse his effort. But as the weeks and months passed, the confidence of his financial backers waned.

Like so many of his radical friends and allies from Kansas, Brown understood the effectiveness of terror. Thus he decided to attack Harpers Ferry instead of waiting until he had made a series of less spectacular forays. That would gain him and his cause national attention and spread confusion, even panic, among slaveholders. Success would be measured not by how many slaves or recruits rallied to his side but by the magnitude and fury of the Slave Power's response. But as soon as Brown opened his attack, these larger political objectives would jeopardize the swift execution of his plan. To succeed politically, he would risk failing militarily.

Insurrectionist

[The insurgents] then dispatched six men ... to arrest the principal citizens in the neighborhood and incite the negroes to join in the insurrection.

Col. Robert E. Lee[1]

His eyes are of a pale blue, or perhaps a sharp gray – much such an eye as I remember his brother filibuster, Walker, to have.

C. W. Tayleure[2]

News reports of the Harpers Ferry raid sometimes referred to John Brown and his men as "filibusters,"[3] a term that in the nineteenth century referred to military adventurers who led or joined expeditions to take over a foreign country. Although the Neutrality Act of 1818 forbad U.S. citizens from undertaking filibustering expeditions, by mid-century the statute was widely flouted. The most conspicuous filibusters were champions of the expansion of slavery like William Walker, who in 1853 invaded La Paz, Mexico, with just forty-five men, proclaimed the "Republic of Lower California," and promptly decreed that Louisiana's legal code would govern his new nation, thus insuring the lawfulness of slavery. Driven from Mexico the following year, in 1856 Walker briefly established himself as dictator of Nicaragua, where he decreed the repeal of Nicaragua's law against slavery, a "key," he announced, to his policy of securing a "permanent presence of the white race in that region." Even in the North, many acclaimed Walker a hero. Later that year an admiring book about his exploits appeared, and a musical entitled *Nicaragua, or, General Walker's Victories* opened on Broadway.[4] Three years later, Walker was planning yet another filibustering expedition to Latin America when John Brown struck Harpers Ferry.[5]

It is not surprising, as Robert May observes, that many Americans had come to associate filibustering with slavery.[6] Lending substance to the suspicion that Walker was a tool of the Slave Power, President Pierce had hastily recognized his Nicaragua regime.[7] Abolitionists accused the South of "filibustering" into Kansas to impose slavery on the territory.[8] Throughout the late 1850s Garrison's *Liberator* denounced the "great scoundrel" Walker and "the perfidious, lawless, and filibustering South." In December 1860 concern over Southern filibustering even impacted the secession crisis. Lincoln warned fellow Republicans that the Crittenden Compromise would open both existing territories and those "hereafter acquired" below the old Missouri Compromise line to slavery. If the Republicans surrendered on that question, he said, "filibustering for all South of us, and making slave states of it, would follow in spite of us."[9]

Thus it was ironic to Brown supporters that Virginians condemned him as a filibuster. To opponents of slavery an *abolitionist* filibuster was an oxymoron. In the North Republicans distinguished Brown from Southern filibusters because Brown, as Richard Sewell points out, "worked to free, not to enslave or oppress."[10] Nor did Brown think of himself in such terms. Asked in 1857 whether he would "invade Missouri or any slave territory" if given the National Kansas Committee's rifles, Brown replied indignantly, "I am no adventurer." Brown believed that his great purpose elevated his schemes morally above those of filibusters, and, unlike the filibusters, he sought neither wealth nor dominion. But the fear of the committee's secretary, H. B. Hurd, that Brown would carry the fighting beyond Kansas was warranted. Like the Secret Six, who encouraged Brown, Hurd recognized in him the boldness of a Walker. The committee voted to deny Brown the weapons, but gave him $5000 for strictly "defensive measures."[11] Brown's foray into Missouri two years later confirmed the committee's fears and his reputation in the South as a freebooter and military adventurer.

Brown's own men saw parallels between their project and Walker's exploits. When Kagi, Brown's second-in-command, wrote to Richard Hinton in March 1859 asking to meet him in Boston, Walker was on Kagi's mind. "I have to-day written to Redpath and Meriam respecting our proposed Nicaragua emigration," he said in a coded reference to their Virginia project. Kagi added that their own expedition offered them "advantages never possessed by Walker."[12] Even Frederick Douglass obliquely acknowledged a parallel between Brown and Walker. If the South seceded, he predicted early in 1860, "men could be found at least as brave as Walker, and more skillful than any other filibusterer, who would venture into those States and raise the standard of liberty" among the slaves.[13] To Douglass such daring had marked Brown's crusade.

With filibustering so much in the air, Virginians easily saw in Brown a "Grey eyed man of destiny" like Walker.[14] And just as Kansas free-staters viewed Southern expeditions into the territory as "foreign forces" seeking to impose a "bogus" government, Governor Wise condemned Brown as "the Border Ruffian of Virginia" sent by Northern abolitionists to overthrow lawful government.[15] In calling Brown a filibuster, some Virginians were voicing their sense that, culturally, he was an alien who had "invaded" their world. Yet their treatment of him after his capture betrayed a kind of admiration perhaps owing to the likeness they fancied between him and Walker. But soon they would call Brown an incendiary and insurrectionist as well.

Brown was no filibuster, but he shared two unstated assumptions of those who were. First, Brown believed he could displace an established political regime, at least in sparsely populated areas, with one of his own devising. Men fighting for a cause, Brown insisted, always prevailed over any adversaries fighting only out of duty. At Harpers Ferry, he expected, at least initially, to face poorly trained militia armed with muskets notably inferior to his Sharps breech-loading carbines. The federal government had only small garrisons of troops scattered among coastal fortifications and outposts on the Indian frontier, and relied on state and local militias to put down disturbances elsewhere. Brown knew of the impotence of federal marshals in the face of mobs protecting fugitive slaves in Northern cities and of the escapes of slave rescuers in Southern border states. After his own Missouri rescue mission, he had taken the slaves he liberated all the way to Canada with federal marshals and others in sporadic, ineffectual pursuit.[16] He had led a guerrilla force in Kansas for months without being captured or defeated. He shared Walker's fatal hubris.

Second, Brown had only contempt for the nation's political leadership. He therefore believed it would be possible to graft a new political order on the old one, at least in the Border South where slavery was more precarious than in the Deep South. There at least he expected to be able to establish his "Provisional Government" with an army of rescued slaves and antislavery whites and to supplant "man-stealing" governments over an ever-widening area.

By the time of Harpers Ferry, Brown's concern was governance not merely rescuing slaves. His purpose "was not the expatriation of one or a thousand slaves," one of his loyalists claimed weeks after the raid, "but their liberation in the States wherein they were born and … held in bondage."[17] Brown would conquer and hold pockets of territory as long as needed to strike a blow fatal to slavery. He thus saw himself as acting in the interest of the nation. Though he expected to confront state and federal forces, his constitution declared that his effort should "not be construed so as in any way to encourage the overthrow of any State government or of the general government." He envisioned no "dissolution of the Union, but simply amendment and repeal." He would accomplish his revolution without treason.[18]

In other words, Brown sought not to sweep away the old regime, but to limit its reach and eventually to extinguish its authority to legalize slavery. His constitution would be in force only where he settled fugitive slaves. The settlements would have more in common with slave maroons in Latin America than with the filibuster regime Walker proclaimed in Nicaragua. How long such arrangements would continue and how the fugitive communities would be integrated into the states in which they were located were uncertainties that Brown never had time to resolve. Thus if Virginians were mistaken to call Brown a filibuster, he was, as Col. Lee recognized, an "insurgent" or "insurrectionist."[19] At Harpers Ferry Brown expected to launch a serial insurrection.

Brown thought even a momentary triumph might achieve much for his purposes, but he failed to establish his quasi-government even for a day. He attacked not an unstable regime with limited resources, but the Old Dominion, a secure state whose citizenry was proud of its history and martial traditions.[20] But since his strategic purpose was primarily political rather than military, Brown could claim a measure of success if his mission only briefly panicked slaveholders and seized the imagination of the nation.

To achieve that end, no hit-and-run attack that might be mistaken for a robbery or a slave rescue would suffice. Brown needed a wide audience to succeed as a "terroriser." He would have to remain in Harpers Ferry long enough to draw attention to his purpose. Yet he would have to withdraw before he was trapped. To command the attention he needed in the press, Brown might thus have to accept the risk of capture. He knew the potential to shape public "sentiment" that his venture offered. His attack might succeed in some measure if it failed spectacularly. To rally the slaves and electrify the nation, Brown's attack and withdrawal required precise timing. This chapter explores how that goal shaped the preparation for, and the execution of, the John Brown raid.

I

Brown knew the federal government had limited military resources immediately available to it. Even in the nation's capital President Buchanan could muster only eighty-six marines in response to initial reports of an insurrection at Harpers Ferry. The Virginia militia likewise was poorly armed, and, as events proved, reluctant to risk men in an assault, however prompt they were in responding to what was at first believed to be a slave uprising. Moreover, the federal arsenal and armory had only token protection. Contrary to most later accounts of this venture, Brown had prepared carefully and weighed his risks. In the end, the outcome owed as much to chance and Clausewitz's "fog of war" as to "bad planning" and strategic misjudgment.[21]

Historians have long recognized Brown's hope to make the raid a political "trumpet blast," but have not always realized the extent to which that objective influenced the course and outcome of the raid. It created an ambiguity in Brown's military thinking and divided his attention. During the raid Brown the guerrilla leader was also Brown the propagandist and would-be terroriser. These roles were not always complementary. Brown hoped to achieve notoriety by capturing a vital federal facility, attracting restive slaves, rounding-up prominent hostages, and lecturing those gentlemen on the evils of slavery before releasing them to bear witness to his purpose. He then hoped to flee the scene safely to continue to spread the panic he had instilled. To some extent, then, Brown was working at cross purposes. In light of his determination to make his presence known and his name feared, his military "blunders" begin to make sense. Brown was not so much a blind fanatic and military incompetent as he was an audacious propagandist and political strategist. But the tactical success of his raid depended upon separating roles at crucial moments.

II

The failure of the raid is sometimes attributed to its supposed premature launching. Bad timing, the critics say, doomed it from the start: Had Brown waited longer, he would have had more men to deploy, and the outcome might have been different. James Redpath thought Brown advanced the date of the raid because he feared that his men's presence at the Kennedy farm had been compromised. A survivor of the raid, Osborne Perry Anderson, Brown's sole black Canadian recruit, believed reinforcements would have reached Maryland in one to three weeks had Brown waited. At the Kennedy farm Brown's men, some of them virtually confined for weeks to avoid detection, had been seen too many times for Brown to account much longer for their presence.[22]

Later reminiscences speak of volunteers on the way to join Brown. One of those who never made it, Richard J. Hinton, claimed that Brown and John Henry Kagi had both written him that the "mining operations" would begin in mid-October. Hinton started for the rendezvous point, Chambersburg, from Leavenworth, Kansas, too late. Perhaps a dozen others might have joined Brown, Hinton thought, if the raid had been delayed. But nosy neighbors had seen a "colored man" in the farmhouse and become suspicious, and local authorities were curious about Isaac Smith & Sons, miners and cattle buyers who did not mine or buy cattle. Estimates of the number of absent volunteers grew with the passing years. By 1908 Salmon Brown was convinced that "about forty more men might have joined [father], had they been informed of the date of the raid accurately."[23]

Blame for misinforming volunteers fell on John, Jr., who himself failed to become one of the "immortal twenty one" because he too reportedly misunderstood when the raid was to begin. In the period between Kansas and Harpers Ferry, Brown had John, Jr., seeking sympathetic families in western Pennsylvania in whose homes fugitive blacks might find temporary refuge. Brown also had John, Jr., raising money, recruiting volunteers, and shipping weapons and other equipment from Ohio to Chambersburg for overland haul to the Maryland farm. John, Jr.'s later plea of ignorance about the timing of the raid rings false, though he was busy with tasks for his father in the months before the raid. Like Kagi, John, Jr., expected a long campaign affording other opportunities to fight.[24]

The story that additional men were en route to Brown's farm on the eve of the raid gains credibility, however, in light of a hitherto unnoticed piece of evidence printed in the *Baltimore American* after the raid. When Brown was captured, authorities found in his pocket an unsigned, undated note addressed to "Captain Brown." "Dear sir," it began:

I have been disappointed in in [sic] not seeing you here ere this to take charge of your freight [i. e., men]. They have been here now two weeks, and as I have had to superintend the providing for them it has imposed on me no small task. Besides they are getting discontented, and if not soon taken on some of them will go back to Missouri. I wish to know definitely what you propose doing.
They cannot be kept here much longer without risk to themselves, and if any of them conclude to go back to the State it will be a bad termination for your enterprise.[25]

The original of this note has been lost, but several conclusions may be drawn from it. It must have reached Brown shortly before the raid, since it was still in his pocket. But where was it from? The writer expected Brown to claim his "freight" in person. Since keeping the men at their present location entailed risk, they were likely not far from the Virginia border. But they were probably not with Kagi in Chambersburg, for Kagi would surely have sent them or brought them from there to the Kennedy farm himself. Oliver Brown had returned to the Kennedy farm via Chambersburg on October 5,[26] and Brown himself was in Chambersburg on October 8. Kagi left Chambersburg after posting a last letter to John, Jr., on October 10, warning that "anyone arriving here after to-day and trying to join us, would be trying a very hazardous and foolish experiment." He then urged John, Jr., to keep recruits "off the border" until the "road" could be safely reopened some weeks or months hence. Kagi himself arrived at the farm with one companion, who returned to Chambersburg the following day.[27]

It seems apparent, too, that Brown's unidentified agent was hosting more than a couple of men, since he warned that "some of them" might return to "Missouri" if Brown did not promptly claim them. It is unlikely that Brown himself had recruited volunteers in Missouri, as Brown had made his notorious raid into that state only the previous December and was sought by the law there. All parties to the conspiracy used code words and false names to avoid betraying their plans, which makes understanding their messages sometimes difficult.

So where were the stranded men from? John, Jr., had organized recruiting efforts ("Liberty Leagues," Osborne Anderson called them) in Ohio and Canada. Two black volunteers from Oberlin, Lewis Sheridan Leary and John Anthony Copeland, Jr., arrived at Brown's farm on October 12, but further volunteers from Oberlin or Cleveland seemed unlikely. Brown's black loyalist, J. H. Harris, a Chatham delegate, wrote from Cleveland in late August that he was disgusted with himself and "the whole negro set" there for failing to volunteer.[28]

Since nothing concrete can be established about the identity of the recruits discussed in the anonymous note, one may speculate about an intriguing possibility. Since the men's presence entailed risk to their host, could they have been the long-awaited contingent from Canada? Even in Chambersburg the presence of unfamiliar black men would have raised suspicions. Osborne Anderson's friend James M. Bell, with whom Brown had lodged during the Chatham convention, had written from Chatham on September 14 that "more laborers may be looked for shortly. 'Slow but sure.'"[29] Harry Watson, a black Chambersburg agent of the underground railroad who had arranged Brown's recent meeting there with Frederick Douglass, could have hosted the men without knowing that Kagi was in Chambersburg to forward recruits to Brown. Blacks going from Canada to join Brown might also have stayed in Philadelphia with William Still, a Brown confidant and leader of the underground railroad. But Brown himself had made a hasty trip to Philadelphia to meet an important late recruit on October 10 or 11, and Kagi's diary shows that he had written to Still as recently as October 12.[30]

Speculation aside, the mysterious note found on Brown does give some weight to later claims that more men were on the way when Brown struck. But by mid-October the raid had been delayed for months, and the additional men who might have joined Brown had had ample notice to present themselves. In any case, the further claim that additional men might have affected the outcome of the raid is dubious. Even a score more would not have enabled Brown to hold the bridges for long once the countryside was aroused and militia companies arrived. Brown's fate hinged not on the numbers he had but when, and how swiftly, he moved after seizing the town. Everything depended on timing.

If the raid was arguably launched too soon, it was also in some respects too late. For many months, Brown had been unable to bring together the elements necessary for success. Forbes's betrayal of Brown's plans had cost Brown a year and perhaps also his prospects of winning black recruits in the aftermath of the Chatham convention. In early 1859 preparations were again hampered by Brown's ill health.[31]

But in May, Brown received from Gerrit Smith and George Stearns the $2,000 he needed to move his weapons and men to Chambersburg, a town of 4,000 forty miles north of Harpers Ferry and an ideal staging area for the raid. Though many residents were sympathetic to slavery, the town had over the years attracted hundreds of free blacks, and its South Ward harbored the largest black community in Franklin County. The railroad provided facilities for shipping the "mining equipment" that John, Jr., forwarded from Ohio and that Kagi secreted before forwarding it to Brown. The forested corridor through which Brown hauled his crates to the Kennedy farm had long been exploited by agents of the underground railroad, and after Harpers Ferry, his son Owen and other fugitives used it to reach allies in Franklin County who helped them escape.[32]

Brown arrived in Harpers Ferry on July 3 with his sons Owen and Oliver and a Kansas veteran, Jeremiah Anderson, eager to find a hideaway at which he could store his weapons and conceal his men. The next day he ran into a local landowner, John C. Unseld, to whom Brown identified himself as Isaac Smith, a cattle grower who was looking for a farm to rent. Unseld told Brown he might be interested in the unoccupied farmhouse belonging to heirs of Dr. Booth Kennedy four and a half miles from Harpers Ferry on the Maryland side of the Potomac.[33] Brown rented the dilapidated two-story wood and stucco building in part because it was 300 feet from the road and from the sight of curious passers-by. For the next three months Brown's men, traveling at night in small groups, arrived at the Kennedy farm unnoticed. Brown himself, riding a mule, guided some of them.

From the start, Brown was plagued by the fear of exposure. Here, too, as Brown recognized, timing was important. Once his men arrived, he could not hire them out without fear of betraying his purpose. Feeding them would be costly. The danger of attracting notice grew as new men arrived. "It will be distressing *in many ways,*" he wrote Kagi on July 10, "to have a lot of hands for many days out of employ. We must have time to get on our freight; & also to get on some who are at a distance; before calling on those who are ready, & waiting. We must make up our lot of hands as nearly *at once, & the same time*; as possible."[34] "If our friends can find some Kind of employment about or near

FIGURE 11.1. The run-down Maryland farmhouse belonging to the heirs of Dr. Booth Kennedy where Brown hid his men before the raid, shown in 1930 with a tour guide.

CREDIT: West Virginia State Archives, Boyd B. Stutler Collection.

you; so as to pay for their board, & washing *untill the freight gets on*," Brown wrote to Kagi on August 2, "it will save a good *deal of expense & some exposure. We can take care of them here*; but they will be compelled to be perfectly idle; & *must not be seen* about us. Everything is *exactly right*; if we can only avoid suspicion; but we shall be *obliged* [to] conceal any increace of numbers; as we cannot find a good excuse for having a larger company. People are very curious about our business."[35]

Meanwhile, in drought-plagued Ohio John, Jr., found it "almost impossible" to hire teams to haul the heavy crates from his home in Ashtabula County to the railroad depot in Akron. It was July 27 before fifteen crates containing ten Sharps carbines each and labeled "hardware & castings" were en route to Chambersburg; another six plus a "chest of household goods" soon followed.[36] Delays also resulted from the fact that the railroad from Harrisburg to Chambersburg carried no freight itself. Kagi thus had to hire forwarding companies to handle to crates, making arrival dates uncertain.[37] Although "disappointed" at the delays, Brown hoped on August 6 to "get hands collected; & *freight on*: as near *together* as possible; & I hope that may yet be brought about in some good measure. I want to know *at once* as soon as Johns *first shipment arives*: as *about* that time we shall need to collect hands here."[38] Despite a promised delivery date of July 1, 1857, 950 pikes from blacksmith Charles Blair, their eight-inch iron blades unattached, did not arrive in Chambersburg until late September.

To conceal his purpose at the Kennedy farm, John dispatched Oliver to North Elba to fetch his wife Mary to keep house for the men. "I don't see how we can get along without [you]," John pleaded with Mary, pledging that she would face "no more exposure here than at North Elba."³⁹ Mary, who had three little girls to care for and privately opposed the dangerous Virginia project, refused his plea. Instead, Oliver returned with his fifteen-year-old sister Annie and his sixteen-year-old wife Martha. Their presence helped the men to pass the time and improved morale. While Martha cooked, Annie watched from the window to catch sight of anyone approaching the house.

Neighbors came by to "chat" from time to time while the men crowded into the loft or retreated to a small cabin away from the house to avoid detection. One afternoon "good, motherly old Mrs. Nichols" came for a visit. Annie signaled her "invisibles" to vanish upstairs, though a tardy one had to scramble out a back window to avoid being seen.⁴⁰ One nosy neighbor, Annie remembered, was "worse than a plague of flees." When John Unseld rode up to visit Brown, he talked to the two "ladies" on the raised porch while he sat on his horse never thinking it odd that no one invited him to come in or that the Brown men were rarely at home.⁴¹ In late September Brown sent the girls home, signaling that he could wait no longer to strike.⁴²

As the weeks passed, Brown worried about the increasing danger of exposure. He and his conspirators adopted code words in their correspondence: the farm was the "boarding house," their occupation farming, mining, or "business"; their weapons crates were labeled "tools" or "hardware and castings," or, covered with tablecloths at the farmhouse, called "furniture." Their enterprise itself was variously the "business," the "purchase," the "mining operation," the "mountain enterprise," the "opening of the coal banks." "All allusions to our business," one of the raiders wrote later, "were made in such a blind way, that they would not have been understood by any outside parties, even should they have been miscarried."⁴³

Some problems could not be managed by correspondence. On August 2 Brown sent son Owen to Chambersburg to brief Kagi on problems at the Kennedy farm and urge him to find a place to hold the men then with him, because Brown could find no excuse for having so many at the farm. "Please notify all to move [to the farmhouse]: if they are impatient but to wait a few days more if not extremely so," Brown pleaded. "*We must not fail* of the purchase now."⁴⁴

The danger that a volunteer might leak his plans also plagued Brown. He urged Kagi to persuade the men to write no unnecessary letters. "If every one must write some *girl*; or some other *extra* friend telling... our location; & telling (*as some have done*) all about our matters," Brown cautioned, "we might as well get the whole published *at once*, in the New York Herald.... Any person is [a] *stupid fool* who expects his *friends* to keep *for him*; that which he cannot keep himself."⁴⁵ It may have seemed that providence enabled Brown to conceal his scheme; at least eighty people by some accounts knew "the secret of the raid," and one of them had written a letter to Secretary of War John B. Floyd on August 20 naming "old John Brown" and betraying his plan to "arm the negroes and strike a blow in a few weeks" at Harpers Ferry. Because the letter was unsigned and mistakenly mentioned an armory in "Maryland," Floyd concluded that "there was nothing in it" and "laid it away."[46]

By August money was running out. Brown's freight bill for the first ship- ment of arms alone was $85. Other freight, hauling, rail fare, and boarding costs were rapidly draining his cash.[47] He instructed John, Jr., whose "northern recruiting tour" was itself budgeted at $200, to intensify fundraising efforts. "It is terribly humiliating to me to begin soliciting of friends again," Brown confided, "but as the harvest opens before me with increasing encouragements, I may not allow a feeling of delicacy to deter me from asking the little further aid I expect to need."[48]

The delays created a credibility problem even among his closest support- ers, who had expected him to act by July 4. Even Higginson lost confidence in the enterprise. In response to a plea from Brown, on August 30 Sanborn was able to send $50 cash from Samuel Gridley Howe, a bank draft for $50 from Mrs. Thomas Russell, and a pledge from Gerrit Smith for another $100. But the remainder of the $300 Brown asked for would "come more slowly."[49]

Expenses continued to mount. Sending Annie and Martha back to North Elba with four pairs of blankets for his three daughters-in-law and Annie, Brown promised to send his wife $50 "to get you through the winter." He added lamely that "I shall certainly do *all* in my power for you." He urged Mary and Salmon to feed the livestock with potatoes, which were "much cheaper than any other food."[50] Days before the raid, Brown had to buy a large new wagon and a team of horses to draw it,[51] but was now so desperate that he apparently borrowed $40 from Edwin Coppoc,[52] one of his volunteers. When Kagi informed John, Jr., on October 10 that he was leaving Chambersburg "for good" that afternoon, he observed that "we have not $5 left, and the men must be given work or they will find it themselves.... We couldn't get along much longer without being exposed."[53] On the eve of the raid, Brown would have been penniless had not a new recruit, Francis Jackson Meriam, arrived with the considerable sum of $600 in gold.

Meriam was a twenty-one-year-old Bostonian whose antislavery zeal rivaled Brown's own. The grandson of Francis Jackson, a leading nonresistant aboli- tionist, Meriam had spurned moral suasion in favor of direct action. In 1858, armed with a letter of introduction from Wendell Phillips, he had first tried, unsuccessfully, to locate Brown in Kansas and then agreed to work for the cause in Haiti with Redpath. "In case you should accept my services," he wrote Brown, "I would return at any time you might wish me to.... I already consider this the whole present business of my life."[54]

In September 1859, once more in Boston, Meriam ran into Lewis Hayden, a fugitive and slave rescuer, who told him of Brown's financial straits. From Sanborn and Stearns, just ten days before the raid, Meriam learned more of Brown's project. He soon met Brown himself in Philadelphia, and promptly left for Baltimore to purchase primers and percussion caps for Brown's rifles. The merchant who sold Meriam his entire supply of 25,000 caps suspected the caps were intended for "some filibustering expedition" and remembered that Meriam seemed "rather excited" at the time of the purchase.[55] Meriam arrived in Harpers Ferry on the night before the raid with a heavy trunk, registered at the Wager House, where he ate dinner and furtively wrote a number of letters, and sent a dispatch to Hayden before two of Brown's men arrived to drive him to the Kennedy farm.[56]

Meriam's $600 in gold coin freed Brown to strike immediately. With it, Brown could purchase food for his considerable force for the weeks and perhaps months of moving and hiding that lay ahead. The raiders could thus launch the war against slavery without carrying provisions with them. When captured after the raid, Brown had $300 of Meriam's gold in his pocket, enough to feed an army for some time.[57] Meriam's arrival ended the waiting.

In a sense, then, circumstances established the timing of the raid, but the day and hour were the result of careful deliberation.

By October 1 Brown had determined to strike soon. The season was growing late. The mountains would soon be barren of foliage, the ground hardened by frost, campfires increasingly risky. Prying neighbors were growing suspicious. One of them had seen Shields Green about the house. Confined to the farmhouse during the day, Brown's men had begun to quarrel and take risks; two of them had hiked to Harpers Ferry and back during daylight. When a thunderstorm passed overhead, the boys took advantage of the noise to "jump about and play" like children to relieve the tension.[58] Time was running out.

The time was also right to strike. "The year's crops have been great, and they are now perfectly housed, and in the best condition for use," Kagi wrote John, Jr. Brown's army could live by foraging as they moved through the Blue Ridge Mountains after the raid.[59] This also partly explains why Brown took no provisions to Harpers Ferry. His men would have to flee across mountainous country with unpredictable numbers of liberated slaves. Laden wagons and bulky knapsacks would hinder their flight, as would livestock brought along for slaughter. Brown was quite prepared to steal from adversaries what he needed for the cause.

There were other promising signs. Brown and his men were close observers of the local slave population. "The moon is just right," Kagi observed. "Slaves are discontented at this season more than at any other, the reasons for which reflection will show you.... A great religious revival is going on, and has its advantages. Under its influence, people who are commonly barely unfavorable to Slavery under religious excitement in meetings speak boldly against it." Local slaves also had other reasons for discontentment. "A fine Slave man near our head-quarters hung himself a few days ago," Kagi continued, "because his master sold his wife away from him. This also arouses the slaves. There are more reasons, ... but I have not time."[60] Watson Brown was also hopeful. "We are all eager for the work and confident of success. There was another slave murdered near our place the other day, making in all five murdered and one committed suicide near our place since we [have] lived here."[61]

Whether these rumors were true is uncertain.[62]

III

The widespread belief that Brown failed to inform himself about the environs of Harpers Ferry is also misleading at best. In June 1858 Brown had dispatched John E. Cook to take up residence in Harpers Ferry and scout the region. A Kansas veteran, Cook was to provide information about security arrangements at the armory, the people Brown might take as hostages, and the habits of the community. While spying for Brown, he worked as a lock tender on the C&O canal, a schoolmaster, and a book agent. He even married a local girl and fathered a child. His affability and marksmanship won him a local reputation.[63] (Shortly before the raid Brown took Cook's wife and child to Chambersburg where his pursuers afterward found her.)[64]

After Brown himself arrived at Harpers Ferry in the summer of 1859, he asked Cook to survey the number of adult "male slaves on or near the roads leading from the Ferry" for a distance of eight to ten miles and to summarize his findings in coded "memoranda." Cook's services were vital to Brown. During the first night of the raid, Cook guided the two parties of raiders who made hostages of three slave owners and liberated such of their slaves as could be found. Then Cook guarded the weapons Brown ordered moved from the Kennedy farm to a schoolhouse nearer Harpers Ferry. But the following day, finding Brown "hemmed in" at the Ferry, Cook, Charles Tidd, Owen Brown, Francis Meriam, and Barclay Coppoc fled to Pennsylvania. Governor Wise offered a $1,000 reward for his capture, and after an intensive search, on October 25 Cook was finally caught near Chambersburg, though his companions escaped. After a week hiding in the mountains, he looked "very rough and shabby." Among the incriminating papers found on him was a pocket notebook containing "drawings of roads, &c., about Harper's Ferry."[65]

Cook soon became a subject of widespread interest. Just twenty-nine at the time, he was from a well-to-do Connecticut family and had studied law at Yale and in New York. After his arrest, he wrote an account of his role in Brown's movement in the hope of winning a pardon.[66] The "confession" was published in pamphlet form and reprinted in newspapers in the East and Midwest. In it, Cook denied that he knew Brown was planning an attack in the South when he joined Brown in Kansas, and claimed that he had quarreled with Brown once he learned of the plan in Iowa in November 1857. However, he and two other recruits had "consented to go on, as we had not the means to return [to Kansas], and the rest of the party were so anxious that we should go with them." If comradery or peer pressure presumably accounted for Cook's staying with Brown in Iowa, it did not explain why he agreed to serve as Brown's agent at Harpers Ferry and accepted a captain's commission in the Provisional Army.[67]

Cook's "confession," published for the financial benefit of a wounded resident of Harpers Ferry, failed to move Governor Wise, who concluded privately that "Cook is the worst of all those villains."[68] But Cook's loyalty to Brown and the other raiders was questionable. While he was in Charlestown jail, raider Albert Hazlett was apprehended and sent to jail.[69] There Cook identified him to authorities though Brown and the others, hoping Hazlett might not be recognized, insisted they did not know him. Brown refused to speak to Cook when he bade farewell to the Charlestown prisoners at the time of his execution, and some of Brown's followers referred to Cook as "Judas."[70] Cook was hanged on December 16.

IV

Harpers Ferry was an unlikely point from which to launch an attack on slavery. By mid-century, about 3,000 people resided in the town. Many of its gunsmiths and machine operators were transplanted Northerners whom locals viewed as outsiders. Other resident whites were employed at the iron foundry, flour mill, cotton mill, and machine shop on Virgilius Island, which lay next to Hall's Island in the Shenandoah, as well as at the hotels, taverns, saloons, shops, and stables in the village proper. The surrounding region was unsuited to staple agriculture, and its residents resented the domination of the state by planter interests in eastern Virginia. Local farmers relied less on slaves than did low-country planters, but nearly 5,000 of the 18,000 slaves in the six-county area around Harpers Ferry were adult males. In Harpers Ferry itself about 1,250 of the 3,000 residents were "free coloreds" and 88 were slaves.[71]

In 1859 Harpers Ferry was a sleepy industrial town a one-day coach ride from Washington and several hours from Baltimore by train. Troops from Baltimore, Washington, or Richmond, once alerted, could reach the town by rail and road in a matter of hours. But local roads made a rapid withdrawal of Brown's men easy, so long as they held the bridges. As the pursuit of five of Brown's fleeing raiders later revealed, tracking guerrillas through surrounding mountains would be difficult. Armed with weapons from the arsenal, Brown would have been able to move swiftly, using the mountains as an ally against pursuing troops.

Security at the armory was light. Because of recent budget cuts, Superintendent Alfred M. Barbour had fired more than one hundred armorers and cut wages for the remainder by 10 percent. He had also reinstituted strict work rules and improved discipline. But after work hours, just two men, both civilians, stationed at opposite ends of the three hundred-yard armory grounds, guarded the facility. Their chief duties were to insure that the fires in the forges were out and to prevent theft.[72] These "fire watchmen" had two old muskets in the watch house, and were otherwise unarmed except for the light sword each carried.[73] At the time of Brown's raid, the two brick arsenal buildings contained hundreds of muskets manufactured at the armory and at the rifle works on Lower Hall's Island a half mile upstream.[74] As Cook reported, the arsenal was unguarded. Towns in the region had volunteer militias that might be summoned in case of trouble, but Harpers Ferry was unprotected from a sudden, brief attack.

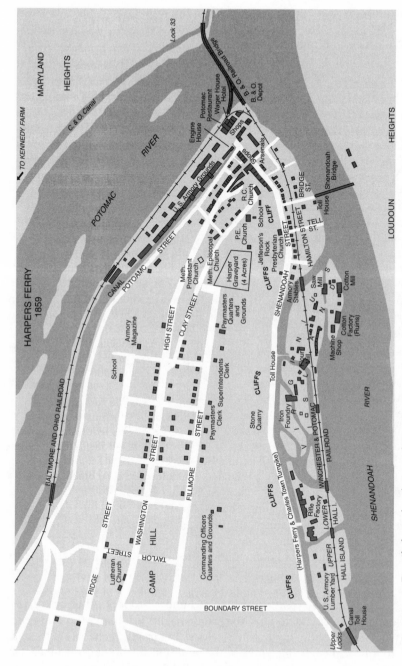

FIGURE 11.2. Detailed overhead map of Harpers Ferry [1859], framed by Loudoun and Maryland Heights.

CREDIT: National Park Service.

Brown's decision to seize Harpers Ferry on Sunday night offered the prospect of finding the road to the Potomac bridge deserted and the town itself protected only by watchmen at the bridges, the armory, and the rifle works. Brown's plan was to the cut telegraph lines and extinguish the gas-lit street lights. With luck, the raiders' presence would remain undetected outside the town until daylight Monday morning. Shielded by darkness, Brown hoped to take the town, the armory, the arsenal, and the rifle works without any incident that would disturb the sleep of residents.

V

According to the incomplete evidence available,[75] on Sunday morning, October 16, Brown called his men together to pray, read his constitution, and administer the oath to recently arrived recruits. Kagi signed their commissions, and Brown issued orders giving the men their assignments. Three of them – Owen Brown, Francis Meriam, and Barclay Coppoc – were to remain at the farmhouse as a rearguard to protect supplies and weapons, which had been boxed up for removal to the schoolhouse on the County Road, three-quarters of a mile from Harpers Ferry. Brown himself would drive a horse-drawn wagon with Cook and Charles P. Tidd walking ahead to cut the telegraph line that ran along the track of the Baltimore and Ohio Railroad as it entered the bridge on the Maryland side of the Potomac. After securing the town, these two were also to cut the wires leading west from Harpers Ferry.

Once in control of the Potomac bridge, Brown's men were to cross into the town, where Brown had assigned them in twos and threes to guard the bridges and occupy and hold the armory, the arsenal, and the rifle works. Captain Aaron Dwight Stevens, the most experienced soldier in Brown's army, would lead the men assigned to take hostages and bring them and their liberated male slaves to the armory. On Monday morning, as workers began to appear at the armory, Brown would redeploy his men. At 8 P.M. on Sunday, Brown ordered, "Men, get on your arms; we will proceed to the Ferry."[76]

The fall chill and light rain betokened the fate of the eighteen men who tramped silently along the dark, unpaved County Road toward the Potomac bridge and the town. Concealing Sharps carbines under long gray shawls, they walked in pairs, each sufficiently distant from the next that, should anyone be encountered, the other raiders could conceal themselves in the woods before being seen. They met no one during the nearly five-mile march. As they approached the Potomac bridge, they halted to fix cartridge boxes outside their shawls.

Constructed in the 1830s, the nearly nine hundred-foot B&O bridge carried the railroad track from the foot of Maryland Heights just above the confluence of the two rivers into the tiny business center of Harpers Ferry before the rails divided to follow the parting banks to the west. On the bridge, a planked surface also carried wagon and foot traffic. On the "town" end, iron trestlework extended beyond the tunnel-like structure of the bridge itself to the railroad platform. The armory grounds lay just past the B&O depot some sixty yards beyond the bridge.

Entering the bridge silently about 9 P.M., the raiders surprised William Williams, the watchman on the Maryland side as he walked across the bridge toward his post. Kagi and Stevens grabbed him as he emerged, lantern in hand, from the dark tunnel. Recognizing Cook and Brown, Williams initially thought his arrest a joke. But he was promptly ordered to be silent and taken to the armory, where he was held prisoner.[77] A half mile away on Lower Hall's Island, Stevens and three others arrested "old Mr. Williams," the watchman at the rifle works, who was also marched to the armory and held prisoner. Kagi and the two free black recruits from Ohio – Lewis Sheridan Leary, and John Anthony Copeland, Jr. – were left to guard the rifle works.

Just minutes after the raiders seized the bridge, the watchman at the armory gate, Daniel Whelan, was also taken by surprise. He had emerged from the watch house carrying his sword when he heard the sound of Brown's approaching wagon on the macadam street. Whelan found two men trying to open the padlock on the heavy chain that secured the iron-bar gate against vehicles entering the armory yard. Thinking that the men might be the head watchman and a companion, Whelan approached, only to discover his error. By then one of the raiders had jumped on one of the masonry piers supporting the gate and stood above him demanding that he open it to admit Brown's wagon. Another man caught Whelan by his coat and others "clapped their guns against my breast." Cook, whom he knew "well," took the sword from his hand.

Although Whelan refused to give up the key to the padlock, the raiders twisted the lock open with a crowbar and drove the wagon into the armory yard to the superintendent's office. There Brown dispatched them to their posts. Brown and two other men remained at the "big gate," where Brown warned Whelan and Williams, as Whelan remembered, "I came here from Kansas.... I want to free all the negroes in this state; I have possession now of the United States armory, and if the citizens interfere with me, I must only burn the town and have blood." The following morning Brown took the keys to the armory gates from Whelan when Stevens returned to the yard with his hostages.[78]

Things had gone as planned. But about midnight two raiders bungled the arrest of Williams's replacement, Patrick Higgins. A watchman assigned to the "out of town" end of the bridge, Higgins crossed through the darkened tunnel, lantern in hand, to find out why Williams had failed to make his half-hourly report. As Higgins emerged onto the railroad platform near the gas-lit intersection of Potomac and Shenandoah streets, Watson Brown and Stewart Taylor, both armed with pikes and carbines, demanded to know where he was going. Higgins replied, "Not far; I am at my station." When one raider said, "I take you prisoner," Higgins asked, "What for? I don't suppose that I have done any man a wrong." Watson Brown grabbed Higgins's left hand, and Higgins hit him in the face with his right.

At this point, in one version of the incident, Higgins was subdued by a thrust of Taylor's pike, but shortly afterwards escaped through a window of

FIGURE 11.3. The gateway to the federal armory showing the fire engine/guardhouse at the left.

CREDIT: West Virginia State Archives, Boyd B. Stutler Collection.

the guard house at the end of the bridge in which Watson had locked him. Higgins then sprinted toward the Wager House, a combination train depot and hotel, a rifle shot passing through his hat and grazing his scalp as he fled. In a second version, Higgins was not taken at all, but dodged Taylor's spear, ran, and, "having ... reached the hotel, burst in at the window, two shots whistling in my wake."[79]

Whatever the details of his escape, Higgins did indeed sound the alarm at the hotel. One of the people there was the clerk, W. W. Throckmorton, who had earlier noticed Brown's wagon creaking by, trailed by a group of men. Initially untroubled, he thought "some gypsies were going by." "All was quiet after this except some men walking the streets," he later told a reporter. About midnight, as Throckmorton went upstairs to awaken several guests who intended to catch the east-bound train for Baltimore, he heard the shots fired at Higgins, who burst into the hotel crying, "Lock your doors, there are robbers on the bridge – several men." Throckmorton assumed that "rowdies from the canal locks" on the other side of the bridge had fired at "the Irishman" to frighten him. But concerned by the incident, Throckmorton tried unsuccessfully to borrow a revolver from the hotel guests, then went to the railroad office where he

FIGURE 11.4. Later photo of the Gerard B. Wager House at the center of Harpers Ferry where B&O passengers took refuge during the raid.

CREDIT: National Park Service, Historic American Buildings Survey.

knew Hayward Shepherd, the free black man who had charge of baggage at the depot, had one. But Shepherd's revolver was not loaded, and Throckmorton, seeing two men with guns on the bridge, decided to warn the conductor of the east-bound train about the danger on the bridge.[80]

At 12:40 A.M., Higgins stopped the train and warned the conductor, Andrew J. Phelps, "You cannot go over; the bridge is taken by a lot of murderers."

Throckmorton also told Phelps the town was in "serious trouble." Presently Phelps and his baggage master, Jacob Cromwell, decided to walk up the track and onto the bridge to investigate. On his own initiative, Shepherd, the baggage handler at the depot, removed his shoes and walked ahead of Phelps. Midway through the tunnel, Watson Brown and Stewart Taylor, now joined by a third raider, commanded Phelps and Cromwell to halt. The trainmen turned and ran amid a volley of rifle balls. Phelps and Cromwell were uninjured, but Shepherd was hit in the back, the ball passing through his body just below the heart. He staggered off the bridge, and from there Throckmorton and the trainmen carried him into the ticket office, where he died the following day.[81] The first casualty in Brown's campaign to free the slaves was a free black man.

As Throckmorton ran to get a doctor to help Shepherd, he encountered two men in the street who threatened him and then fired at him. A passenger had lent Throckmorton his revolver, and as the two raiders ran toward the armory, he fired "all the shots in my revolver at them." By this time hysteria was gripping the passengers, many of whom were "running about in excitement" while women and children were "screaming in the cars." With Phelps's help, Throckmorton got the passengers off the street and into the hotel and turned off the lights to see what was happening outside. Presently the raiders released an elderly man with instructions to tell the hotel keeper and the railroad agent that everyone who offered no resistance would be unharmed. Phelps decided not to take the train across the bridge, "supposing its arches and timbers might have been cut." Brown summoned Phelps to the armory and told him no train would be permitted to pass through Harpers Ferry in either direction.[82] According to one report of that meeting, Brown warned Phelps that, if he were resisted or interfered with, he would "burn down the railroad bridge and cut off all communications."[83]

Hours passed. A light rain continued to fall. The town was in darkness as raiders in the armory yard and arsenal went about their business. About 3 A.M. Brown sent word through a prisoner that the train could go forward. Not persuaded that was safe, Phelps waited. At daylight, he went to see Brown and pleaded that the "women and children on the train were frightened nearly to death." Brown told Phelps he would go to the bridge personally to guarantee the train's safe passage. According to one witness, Brown asked for a guarantee that Phelps "would hold his peace and say nothing along the route that anything was going on here." Brown later denied that emphatically, but he did walk up to the bridge as "the passengers got on as fast as possible." Nearly seven hours behind schedule, the train rumbled across the Potomac bridge.[84]

As soon as Phelps reached Monocacy on the Maryland side, he telegraphed Baltimore the news of his ordeal. His dispatch included a message from Brown: "The leader of those men requested me to say to you that this is the last train that shall pass the bridge either East or West. If it is attempted it will be at the peril of the lives of those having them in charge.... It has been suggested you had better notify the Secretary of War at once."[85]

It took two messages to persuade the incredulous master of transportation at Baltimore that Phelps's alarm was serious. Once persuaded, however, he alerted John W. Garrett, president of the B&O, who lost no time in telegraphing President Buchanan, Governor Wise, and Major General George H. Stewart of the Maryland Volunteers that an insurrection was in progress at Harpers Ferry. "A large band of men said to be abolitionists but thought to be armory men," Garrett told Secretary of War Floyd, had taken guns from the arsenal "for offensive use." Their leaders "notified our men that no trains shall pass the armory and bridge." Garrett wanted Floyd to authorize "government officers and military from Washington to go on our train at three twenty this afternoon."[86] John Brown had blown his trumpet; the nation would soon hear its echoes.

VI

Not everyone awakened by the clamor in Harpers Ferry that night was as alarmed as Andrew Phelps. The sense of present danger awoke only slowly. The clerk of the master armorer, W. B. Downer, who roomed at the Wager House, was awakened at midnight by gunfire and Throckmorton's pounding on his door asking if he had a revolver. Shepherd had been shot for trying to cross the bridge, Throckmorton told him. Downer, who had no revolver, went back to sleep. "Towards morning I got up and found they [the raiders] had taken possession of the town, and were doing everything as if they had a perfectly overwhelming force," he later recounted. "[T]he sentinels marched up and down the streets, and whenever they saw a man outside they would go up to him and say, 'Here, they want you over at the armory,' and if the citizen refused, would give him the choice to go or be shot."[87] George W. Chambers, the liquor merchant who owned the Potomac Restaurant, which was behind the Wager House, was also awakened by the shooting of "the negro on the bridge ... [by] a party of armed men." Passengers who soon crowded into the depot believed that "it was a railroad strike," Chambers recalled. He went home and back to bed. Awakening about dawn, he saw from his window "armed negroes walking about the street." John Cook, whom he knew, was leading a party in a four-horse wagon out of the armory yard. Not long afterward, Chambers was cradling the head of a friend shot to death just a few feet from the depot office.[88]

Events outside the armory yard had thus taken an unexpected turn after the shooting erupted on the Potomac bridge. Brown had planned to arrest the watchmen and people on the streets to prevent them from interfering with his plans or spreading word of his presence. His men had instructions to fire only if attacked. But what were they to do when people ignored their order to surrender? Brown may have directed his men to fire over the heads of uncooperative residents to intimidate them. If so, the shooting of Shepherd in the darkness of the tunnel may have been accidental. But Higgins too had run, narrowly escaping the fire of the raiders on the Potomac bridge. Perhaps Brown simply had not anticipated resistance in the face of armed men shouting orders.

Yet if only a handful of residents offered resistance, Brown would have to take casualties and risk losing possession of the bridges. After the shooting during the night, Brown reasserted his command of the situation. He gave Throckmorton a speech he repeated to others through the next morning. He told Throckmorton, "I am a military man, and I came here to free the slaves of your surrounding country, and I take possession of this government property and arms to assist me in doing so. I can have five thousand men here in less than twenty four hours at my call." Then, Throckmorton remembered, Brown "gave me leave to pass backwards and forwards if I would keep quiet, and if not he would take possession of the hotel. Everyone supposed of course that he had a large force at hand." Shortly after the train left, Brown sent Throckmorton a note: "You will furnish forty-five men with a good breakfast."[89]

Brown wanted to remain in Harpers Ferry until word of his presence and purpose spread across the slave "grapevine" and the story of his invasion hit the "wires." In permitting the train to pass, Brown had set the latter objective in motion. But to tell his story properly, to ensure that he would not be dismissed as an "incendiary" or "filibuster," he needed to impress his purpose in coming to Harpers Ferry on credible local witnesses. For this purpose, he needed hostages from among prominent men in and around the town, preferably slaveholders. Keeping such hostages close to him, he assumed, would insure him and his men from attack and guarantee that the outside world would know that his purpose was to free the slaves.

Toward that end, once his men had secured the armory, arsenal, and rifle factory, Brown set in motion his plan to make hostages of prominent slaveholders who would witness his liberating their slaves. The symbolism of taking such hostages and releasing their slaves would be difficult to ignore. Drawing upon Cook's knowledge of the community, Brown had determined to seize two of its leading citizens, Lewis Washington and John Allstadt. Washington, a wealthy slave owner and military advisor to Governor Wise, was also a great-grandnephew of George Washington and possessed several Washington heirlooms that impressed Brown, notably a pistol from Lafayette and a sword from the Prussian King Frederick the Great. Brown resolved to wear the sword and brandish the pistol as symbols of the kinship of his cause with that of the American revolutionaries.

Surprising Washington at 1:30 A.M. in the bedchamber of his Greek revival country house, Cook, who had once enjoyed a shooting contest with Washington on his lawn, ordered him to dress and to turn over the sword of Frederick the Great. In the meantime, Shields Green had harnessed Washington's team and brought his carriage to the front door. Guarded by Cook, Tidd, and Green, Washington rode in his carriage with his "house servant" driving, while his large, four-horse "farm wagon" carrying another "servant" and a visiting black rumbled along behind. ("Almost all" of his slaves were away visiting, as it was Sunday night.) Once the party reached the armory, Brown asked Washington to stand by the fire in the watch room and warm himself. Presently Brown said, "I will require you to write to some of your friends to send a stout, able-bodied negro; I think after a while, possibly, I shall be enabled to release you, but on condition of getting your friends to send in a negro man as a ransom." If Brown "got the worst" of his encounter with the militia, he added, however, "your life is worth as much as mine."

According to Washington, Brown explained, "I wanted you particularly for the moral effect it would give our cause, having one of your name as a prisoner." Several times during the night, Washington remembered, Brown "made remarks to the effect that he came for the purpose of freeing the slaves, and that he meant to carry it out." He also promised to "take special care" of Washington's sword, and to "endeavor to return it to you after you are released."[90] He carried it in his hand "all day Monday" as fighting erupted, but

FIGURE 11.5. Brown's hostage, Lewis W. Washington, a "leading citizen" and great grandnephew of President George Washington.

CREDIT: West Virginia State Archives, Boyd B. Stutler Collection.

finally lay it on one of the small fire engines where, after the raid, Washington "rescued it."[91]

Brown's raiders also seized two other prominent slaveholders, John Allstadt and Terence Byrne. Returning with Washington and his slaves to Harpers Ferry, Stevens' party forced an entry at the home of Allstadt using a rail from a "Virginia worm fence" to batter in the door. Despite the cries of Allstadt's wife and daughters, he and his eighteen-year-old son and seven male slaves were taken prisoner and delivered to the armory at about 4 A.M. Brown said nothing directly to Allstadt on his arrival, but Brown's men promptly armed his slaves with pikes and told them to guard the slave owners.

Luck played a part in taking the next hostage. At about 4 A.M. Brown sent a party with Cook and Tidd back over the bridge in Washington's four-horse wagon to move the boxes of arms and supplies from the Kennedy farm to a schoolhouse on the County Road. On their way to the farm they passed Terence Byrne, who had risen early to ride into Harpers Ferry on business. Cook recognized him and told him, "'I am very sorry to inform you that you are my prisoner,'" Seeing the barrel of Cook's rifle protruding from under his coat, Byrne agreed to ride back to his own home where Cook made "what we term a higher-law speech" and Byrne's indignant female cousin demanded that he "cowhide these scoundrels out of the house." Though the raiders demanded two male slaves belonging to Byrne and his brother, both servants were away visiting. Later, Cook sent Byrne to the armory guarded by twenty-year-old William Leeman, the youngest of the raiders.[92]

As a gray, rainy dawn began to outline the scene in the armory yard on Monday morning, everything seemed to be going as planned. During the night Brown had questioned watchman Daniel Whelan about the officers of the armory and boasted that he "would have all those gentlemen in the morning."[93] Clearly, Brown had not planned to leave under cover of darkness, and he soon began arresting workers as they arrived at the armory. Alerted by Dr. John Starry, Archibald Kitzmiller, acting superintendent of the armory, came early to the yard and was promptly seized. So was Armistead Ball, the master machinist, and John Daingerfield, the paymaster's clerk. By eight o'clock Brown had at least twenty-five hostages, and the number continued to grow.[94]

VII

As Brown established his hold on the armory and the arsenal, he believed that at least some local slaves might rally to him. The first of his liberated slaves, brought in after Stevens's party arrested their owners, included several who were bolder during the raid than authorities later acknowledged. At least two of them joined Brown eagerly, while others aided the raiders or served as sentinels beyond the armory grounds. Still others voiced support of Brown and fled only when he lost control of things. Because Virginia authorities suppressed evidence of such disloyalty, the story of these men has not been told.

As Brown's fortunes faded on Monday afternoon, the five slaves assisting Cook disappeared. Those in the watch house with Brown's hostages dropped their pikes as the firing from outside intensified. Later, Brown's gentlemen hostages pictured the latter group as cowards or dupes. "About a dozen black men were there," John Daingerfield later testified, "armed with pieces which they carried most awkwardly and unwillingly. During the firing they were lying about asleep, some of them having crawled under the engines."[95]

According to Virginia officials, the liberated slaves saw themselves, like their hostage masters, as captives. It was a "consolation" to Governor Wise that with one exception, "the faithful slaves refused to take up arms against their masters, and those which were taken by force from their happy homes deserted their liberators as soon as they could dare to make the attempt." Brown was "ignorant" of the "patriarchal relations" in which "our slaves everywhere are held by their masters," Wise believed, and of the "bonds of affection and common interest" that united the two.[96]

Senator James Mason, who lived less than twenty miles from Harpers Ferry, was on the scene hours before Wise arrived from Richmond. "The fact is undoubted that *not a man, black or white, joined* [Brown's force] after they came into Virginia, or gave them aid or assistance in any form," Mason later wrote. Besides the slaves of Washington and Allstadt, the "miscreants" had "some five or six other slaves belonging to residents at Harper's Ferry, and found in the streets." At the first assault, these blacks "threw away their pikes and escaped to their homes for refuge. Not a slave escaped or attempted to escape [to the North] during the tumult."[97] In November, as Judge Richard Parker sentenced four of Brown's men to hang, he intoned the same message: "Not a slave united himself to your party, but, so soon as he could get without the range of your rifles, or as night gave him opportunity, made his escape from men who had come to give him freedom, and hurried to place himself once more beneath the care and protection of his owner."[98] The majority report of Mason's Senate Committee concluded that "not one of the captured slaves, although arms were placed in their hands, attempted to use them; but... as soon as their safety would admit, in the absence of their captors, their arms were thrown away and they hastened back to their homes."[99]

Such reassurances did not altogether calm Virginians. Though panic at Harpers Ferry abated after the raid, whites continued to feel insecure. Jefferson and neighboring counties "continue in a state of excitement," reported the Richmond *Enquirer* on November 4. "The inhabitants are not by any means easy in their minds as to the temper of the slaves and the free negroes among them. It has been ascertained, reports to the contrary notwithstanding, that many negroes in the neighborhood, who had been tampered with by Cook and others of Brown's gang, had at least cognizance of the plans of the marauders, if they did not sympathise with them." Slaves who might have warned authorities had kept silent.[100] Weeks later, residents feared that several fires in and around Harpers Ferry were caused by arsonists loyal to Brown.

In their effort to allay panic and to discount Brown's initial success in seizing the armory, authorities overlooked or suppressed evidence of slave collaboration with Brown. The roles slaves played during the raid were known to few. But several slaves were sufficiently defiant to be mentioned in surviving records.

Such is the case of Lewis Washington's hired coachman, Jim, who drowned during the raid. Governor Wise suggested that Jim may have been shot by Cook, but Jim's body was found in the Shenandoah River near Hall's Rifle Works more than a mile distant from Cook, who was on the Maryland side of the Potomac all day Monday and never rejoined Brown at Harpers Ferry.

Jim did not belong to Lewis Washington, and was not on Washington's estate when the raiders took Washington hostage. Returning to the estate soon thereafter and learning that armed men had seized Washington and driven off with him and three of his male slaves, Jim ran after the wagon to join the party. As Washington later explained opaquely to the Mason Committee, "One other heard something was wrong, and got in the wagon at Allstadt's.... He was hired at my house."[101]

The possibility that Jim ran after the raiders to rescue Washington must be dismissed in light of his later actions. At the request of the raider Stevens, Jim drove the four-horse wagon from Allstadt's farm to Harpers Ferry. What Jim said to Brown when he climbed down from Washington's wagon at the armory is unknown, but at that point Brown gave Jim an Ames revolver and cartridges. Washington acknowledged that Jim was "the servant that was drowned at Hall's works," but gave no explanation why Jim was so far from the armory. A report in the Richmond *Enquirer* suggests an explanation: "There is no doubt that Washington's negro coachman Jim, who was chased into the river by citizens and drowned, had joined the rebels with a good will. A pistol was found on him, and he had his pockets filled with ball cartridges when he was fished out of the river."[102] Jim had drowned while fleeing.

Two of Washington's slaves reacted quite differently to the kidnapping of their master. His "house-servant" remained ostentatiously loyal. When Washington was taken to the Ferry, this servant eagerly replaced Shields Green as driver of Washington's carriage, and at the armory, refused to take one of the pikes offered to the liberated slaves. "In a short time after they first appeared with these pikes in their hands," Washington remembered, "I saw my house-servant walking about without one." This servant remained with his owner throughout the ordeal in the watch house.[103] According to a story in the *Shepherdstown Register*, when told that he was free and should join Brown, the servant replied that he was "free enough before you took me. I am not going to fight until I see Massa Lewis fighting, and then I fights for him."[104]

Another of Washington's liberated slaves was also in the end eager to show his loyalty. But he may have flirted with the idea of siding with Brown. When Washington was "arrested" at his home, his horses were misaligned and refused to draw his carriage. "I got down and put my foot on the wheel, and one of my servants came to help shift the horses," Washington later explained, "the servant whom they afterwards had in Maryland and who returned." At the armory Brown chose this man to accompany the party of raiders he sent back into Maryland to move his Sharps rifles to the schoolhouse. Indeed, Brown presented him with Washington's double-barreled shotgun and an Ames pistol. The slave carried the shotgun Sunday night and all day Monday. Terence Byrne remembered that one of the slaves in the party that arrested him was carrying Washington's "fowling piece,"[105] and had worked with the raiders moving the crated rifles. As Cook related in his "Confession," "About four o'clock in the evening C. P. Tidd came [from the Kennedy farm] with the second load. I then took one of the negroes with me and started for the ferry.... The negro who was with me on Monday evening, when I left the schoolhouse for the Ferry, was armed with a double-barreled shotgun, and, I think, a revolving pistol of the Massachusetts arms manufacture.... He was under my control till I sent him back to report to Tidd that the troops were coming up. He obeyed orders while with me." That slave vanished Monday evening with other slaves Tidd had hidden in the trees behind the schoolhouse.[106]

After Brown's capture the following morning, Cook's armed assistant turned up at Harpers Ferry with no weapons at all, telling authorities that Cook had been across the river Monday evening "only three miles off."[107] By Tuesday night, Washington thought, his "boy" was back "home." Two days later when the raid was over, Washington rode into the hills to recover a stray horse, taking with him "the negro boy who showed me where he had hidden my gun that they had given him to arm himself when he escaped." Washington did not explain what his "boy" had done between Monday evening and mid-morning Tuesday.[108]

But on Monday as this slave and Cook had approached the Potomac bridge, they learned that the raiders were trapped. It is unclear whether this slave had willingly aided Cook during the raid and returned to his master only when that became dangerous, or whether he was biding his time on Monday until he could escape from Cook. The slave did, however, provide helpful information to Cook and Stevens, as the schoolmaster later testified.[109] Perhaps, as Tidd speculated, all of the five slaves who helped move Brown's weapons to the schoolhouse "were ready & glad to be armed against the masters.... But when they heard firing & then the rumor that all [had been] killed, they slipped back & joined their masters."[110]

None of the seven slaves of John Allstadt "liberated" by Stevens's party offered comfort to Allstadt during the raid. On the contrary, one of them, twenty-year-old Phil Lucker, who belonged to Allstadt's wife, openly cooperated with Brown in his master's presence. Trapped in the engine house with Brown and the hostages on Monday afternoon, Lucker at Brown's request chiseled "loop-holes" through the brick wall with tools supplied by Brown. According to Armistead Ball, the master machinist at the armory, Lucker "continued until a brisk fire commenced outside, when he said, 'this is getting too hot for Phil' .... Brown then took up the tools and finished the hole."[111]

That was not the whole story. On November 4, the Richmond *Enquirer* reported that "Phil...who was compelled by Capt. Brown to assist in making the loop-holes through the walls of the engine-house, was arrested and conveyed to jail, on the charge of sympathizing with the insurgents. He has since been lying very ill, and died yesterday of pneumonia, though it is said his sickness was caused by fright."[112] Allstadt claimed he had no idea why Lucker had been held in jail. After the raid while the seriously ill Lucker was in jail, Allstadt "did not go to Charlestown for some few days; I do not know how long; I saw the negro there when I went; he was very sick when I went there, so much so that I could not move him home." Whether a physician had seen Phil Lucker during the two weeks he languished in jail is uncertain. After Lucker's death, Allstadt regretted the loss because "he was a very valuable fellow; the most valuable one I had."[113]

Allstadt left much unsaid: Lucker had forfeited his master's protection – and attention while he was ill – by throwing in with Brown. He had been captured on the armory grounds with a pistol in his possession. "One of our colored men was caught at the armory with a gun and was taken to Charlestown jail," Allstadt later told the Springfield *Republican*. "He got typhoid fever in the jail and died there."[114] Whatever occasioned Allstadt's neglect of his slave, there is no doubt that Lucker cut loopholes for Brown and accepted a pistol from him.

Other slaves helped Brown by patrolling the streets and the Potomac bridge. During the first night of the raid, the train's conductor, Andrew Phelps, saw several black men with pikes in the streets. He also saw a group of Brown's men, among them a "short, stout negro walking with a staff," arrest a citizen on Shenandoah Street. Another black sentinel arrested a white man and marched him to the armory. When this slave's act of rebellion became public, it was dismissed as an aberration resulting from resentment at an act of harsh treatment. "A negro who had been sharply used by one of the town people, when he found that he had a pike in his hand," a dispatch read, "used his brief authority to arrest the citizen, and have him taken to the armory."[115]

Still other evidence shows blacks cooperating with Brown. At about six o'clock Monday morning, W. B. Downer, the master armorer's clerk, saw a "negro man" shot while trying to arrest a storekeeper named Baldwin.[116] A passenger on the B&O train named Logan decided to cross the bridge at about 2:30 A.M. Midway across, four men, "one a negro," seized him, while a white raider warned him sharply: "'D – n you, if you attempt to move an inch further I will blow your brains out,' at the same time placing a pistol to [Logan's] head." They marched Logan to the far end of the bridge and put him under guard by a slave armed with a rifle. Logan asked his guard why they were detaining him and "shooting people." "The guard, who was a negro, replied that they wanted nothing but their freedom, that he had been in bondage long enough, and was now bound to be free."[117]

There were other instances of slave collaboration. W. W. Throckmorton, the clerk at the Wager House, remembered his "servant" Charles Williams talking for "a long time" with John Cook days before the raid. During the night of the raid, the same "boy" showed a keen interest in what turned out to be Brown's wagon as it rumbled past the Wager House toward the armory. Throckmorton concluded in retrospect that Cook had told Williams about the upcoming raid.

Early Monday morning, when Brown ordered breakfast from the Wager House for his prisoners, Charles Williams alone among Throckmorton's servants was eager to carry it to the armory. When Throckmorton, accompanied by Williams, delivered the breakfast to Brown, Throckmorton noticed that Williams "appeared to know [Brown] very well, and had conversation with him in the engine house. He had gone with me to carry the breakfast very willingly, though the other servants hung back, and when I ordered him to take the breakfast things and go back to the hotel, he said he would when he got ready, and I must understand he was as much boss as I was. This amused Old Brown, who laughed at me, and I told him there was no nigger blood in me, at all events." Williams's defiance, of course, invited a heavy penalty once Brown was defeated. "This boy was a slave, belonging to some heirs," Throckmorton said of Williams, "but has been doing for himself and counted free for some time." Williams ran away the day after the raid "and has not been seen since," Throckmorton later told a reporter. "He went away because he knew, I suppose, that there were plenty around who would take a crack at him if they got a chance."[118]

Charles Williams's acceptance of Brown and rebuff to Throckmorton had culminated a surprisingly successful Sunday night. Without firing a shot, Brown had gained control of the arsenal, the armory grounds, and the rifle works. Though his men had mistakenly killed a free black man on the Potomac bridge, the shooting had not brought armed residents into the streets. Brown had his hostages and eleven of their slaves under his control, and only one of those slaves had refused to carry a weapon when offered one. Three slaves had accepted firearms, a decision that would invite certain retaliation against them if Brown were defeated.

If the slaves in the engine house with their masters appeared to local whites to carry their pikes "most awkwardly and unwillingly," and when the firing became fierce, seemed to be asleep or "crawled under the engines," that may suggest that the slaves had become more afraid of retaliation than confident that Brown would prevail.[119] Other slaves chose a bolder course. The slaves and perhaps free blacks who had acted as Brown's sentinels, had patrolled the streets armed only with pikes, and had participated in several arrests, were not captured with the raiders. Their fates are unexplained. They may have set off through the Great Valley to freedom; at least authorities pursued unnamed missing slaves for days following the raid. A dispatch from Frederick, Maryland, on Tuesday – the day Brown was captured – related that "Nothing has been seen of the negroes in this section yet, but they are supposed to be either in the mountains or on their way to Pennsylvania, through the range of mountains near Hagerstown." Dispatches from Chambersburg and Bedford the following day reported "no signs of the fugitives."[120] At 11 P.M. that same night the fugitives had not been located, and Governor Wise himself had set out "with some armed men, to search a cave, where, it is said, fugitive slaves are concealed."[121]

After the raid, rumors begat rumors. According to a news report from Harpers Ferry three days after the raid, a dozen slaves were still missing and presumed to be fleeing across the mountains with John Cook. "A number of persons who knew Cook are still in pursuit of him, impelled by the hope of gaining the $1,000 reward," the dispatch read, "as well as by the desire to recover the negroes, of whom about a dozen are still missing."[122] After his capture, Cook said that the slaves assigned to him at the armory, who belonged to Washington and Allstadt, had fled Monday night, and, according to Col. Lee's report on Brown's raid, those slaves were all accounted for by the 19th.[123] The missing fugitives did not belong to Brown's hostages. But once they had publicly committed to Brown by wielding a pike in the streets, like Charles Williams, the coachman Jim, and Phil Lucker, they could not have gone back to their masters.

VIII

In any case, Brown was confident all was well as daylight arrived on Monday. If he could establish himself in Harpers Ferry long enough, other slaves might rally to him. But once daylight revealed how few men he had, Brown had to calculate how long he could wait before he was hemmed in.

We know, of course, he stayed too long, for which he has been variously criticized, denounced, or dismissed as mad or incompetent. A resourceful scholar, Craig Simpson, has suggested a more interesting explanation, arguing that Brown failed to leave because he harbored uncertainties about the morality of the raid and the possibility of its success. These "ambivalences fatally inhibited him from extricating himself and his followers" from Harpers Ferry "before their position grew untenable." Brown had "an obvious aversion to the shedding of innocent blood," Simpson believes, dismissing the butchery at Pottawatomie by claiming that Brown the guerrilla leader of 1856 "was not the same man who materialized in Virginia three years later." By failing at Harpers Ferry, Simpson suggests, Brown might in some way have hoped to absolve himself of guilt about Pottawatomie.[124]

To be sure, Brown was a complex man and his behavior during the raid seemed inconsistent. But he was not confused or uncertain about his mission. I will address the question of his delay in leaving in Chapter 12. Here I will observe that throughout Sunday night, Brown had acted decisively, and he was evidently confident and self-possessed Monday morning. He was also at that point in no evident hurry to leave. When Throckmorton asked him to pay for the breakfasts he had delivered, Brown replied that "he should want dinner at three o'clock for perhaps 200 men, and he would pay for the whole then."[125]

The purport of this remark is unclear. For all his bravado and later claims of imminent support, Brown had to know that troops from Richmond and Baltimore and perhaps from Washington would soon be on their way to Harpers Ferry. He had urged conductor Phelps to notify authorities of his occupation of Harpers Ferry, and knew that Phelps would sound the alarm. Did Brown really suppose at daybreak that he could still safely be in Harpers Ferry eight hours later? Had the euphoria of his initial success blinded him to danger?

Brown's assessment of the immediate danger from distant troops was not altogether unreasonable. Consider what actually happened after he permitted the train to pass across the Potomac at daybreak. At 7:05 Phelps telegraphed the B&O office in Baltimore, frantically claiming that 150 insurrectionists were trying to free the slaves at Harpers Ferry and would not permit any more trains to pass across the Potomac bridge. By 10:30, B&O President John W. Garrett had telegraphed President Buchanan, Governor Wise, and the commanding general of the Maryland militia in Baltimore.

But in that era before direct means of reaching busy people at scattered workplaces, even alarm bells and galloping riders took longer to roust the militia than authorities hoped. Few militiamen were prepared for the kind of emergency Harpers Ferry might have been. When word reached nearby Martinsburg about 1 P.M., for example, volunteers had to be summoned and assembled to elect a captain before they set out. On the road they met a company from Shepherdstown, and both arrived at 3 P.M. It was not until after sunset that troops arrived by train from Winchester and from Frederick City, Maryland, both less than twenty-five miles away.

In Baltimore troops assembled speedily at their company armories but had to await the train, which did not leave the depot, where an "immense assemblage" had come to see them off, until 4 P.M.[126] In Washington, it was three o'clock before three companies of artillery at Old Point and the marines at Washington barracks, supported by two twelve-pound howitzers, boarded the train.[127] Late that night the troops from Baltimore and eighty-six marines from Washington reached Sandy Hook, a mile and a half east of Harpers Ferry, where the marines waited until Col. Lee, their commander, arrived from Washington on a special train.[128] Governor Wise and the Richmond Grays reached Harpers Ferry early Tuesday afternoon.

Brown was right if he believed a formidable force would not arrive before 3 P.M. Unfortunately for Brown, Harpers Ferry and neighboring towns were not without martial ardor of their own, and Harpers Ferry, as one historian has noted, had its own Paul Revere.[129]

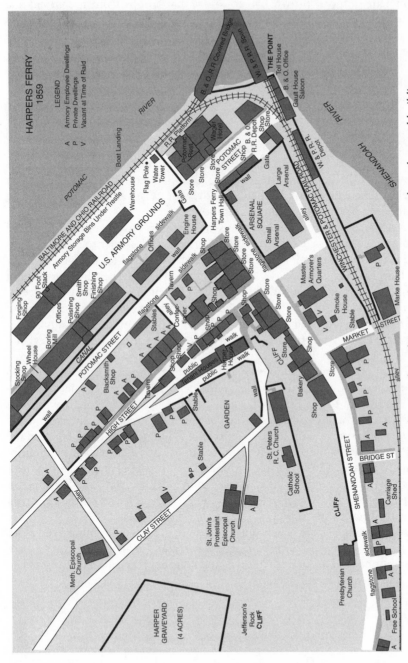

FIGURE 12.1. Map of lower Harpers Ferry showing the railway junction, armory grounds, and arsenal buildings.

CREDIT: National Park Service.

Witness

And the night following the Lord stood by him, and said, Be of good cheer, Paul: for as thou hast testified of me in Jerusalem, so must thou bear witness also at Rome.

King James Bible, Acts 23:11

Remember them that are in bonds, as bound with them; and them which suffer adversity, as being yourselves also in the body.

King James Bible, Hebrews 13:3

In taking Harpers Ferry, John Brown had moved decisively. By 5 A.M. Monday morning his sentinels had herded perhaps twenty men into the guard room of the engine house;[1] soon the number of prisoners swelled to forty as Brown arrested armory officers and workmen reporting to work. Brown seemed confident, even exhilarated as he gave his prisoners brief "abolition speeches."[2] Had he gathered his scattered men at that early hour and withdrawn into the mountains, he might have done so unopposed by any organized force. But as crucial hours passed, he seemed paralyzed by indecision. He tarried far too long and was finally trapped. This chapter explains in part why. Paradoxically, I shall argue, Brown's very dedication to the cause, the "monomania" that finally enabled him to launch his raid, would also undermine it. As hours slipped away, the Harpers Ferry raid would become as much an unthinking witness against slavery as an attack upon it.

Questioned after his capture, Brown conceded that he did not follow his own plan to "remain here but a few hours."[3] When asked whether he stayed expecting a "general rising of the slaves," he replied evasively. "Well, probably I had quite a different idea. I do not know that I ought to reveal my plans. I am here a prisoner and wounded because I foolishly allowed myself to be so. You overrate your strength when you suppose I could have been taken if I had not allowed it. I was too tardy after commencing the open attack in delaying my movements through Monday night and up to the time I was attacked by the Government troops."[4] Later that afternoon Governor Wise asked Brown whether it was not "foolish to calculate on holding the place for any length of time." Brown shot back: "Well, Governor, you must admit that I did hold it for twenty-four hours."[5]

It was an odd boast. It revealed that for Brown just being in possession of the armory was a kind of triumph. But of course by remaining there Brown had insured his own defeat. And conceding that he delayed too long by not leaving Monday night begged the key question, since he was effectively trapped by mid-afternoon on Monday. That question was, why had he not left before – or soon after – daylight on Monday?

The simple answer is that he had not finished what he set out to do. During the night, he waited to let word of his coming spread on the slave "grapevine." As he accumulated hostages after daylight, he told them his raid was the first "demonstration" of a formidable movement, hoping their stories would later spread panic. Then he waited for evidence that his presence was causing a stir. To capture national attention, win new recruits from the North, and keep the wavering allegiance of contributors like those in the Secret Six, he needed visibility.[6] He had already roughed out an appeal for "further *support*" that he intended to publish after the raid.[7] To achieve sufficient public attention, he concluded he had to wait.[8]

But the simple answers do not tell the whole story. Brown himself later had difficulty accounting for his "tardiness" in pulling out. Yet his behavior in the fateful hours around the time he could have safely withdrawn reveals a pattern that clarifies much he left unsaid about his intentions.

I

After the raid Brown tried mightily to explain that "tardiness" and in so doing turn away speculation that his raid was a fiasco. At every opportunity he magnified the support he "expected" to receive after he commenced the raid. He told his captors that he should have held Phelps's train longer, perhaps indefinitely, and fortified the Potomac bridge rather than occupy the armory as he awaited a large relief force. "From my visits and associations and inquiries about here," he told a reporter, "I have the right to expect the aid of from three to five thousand men." Had he "been able to hold the place long enough to inspire confidence in him and his plans," the reporter wrote, summarizing what he took to be Brown's thinking, "then his promised support would have come up."[9] Brown told another correspondent that "he only intended to make the first demonstration at this point, when he expected to receive a rapid increase through Maryland and Virginia, sufficient to take possession of both States, with all of the negroes he could capture."[10]

When Governor Wise asked Brown just hours after the raid what support he expected, prosecutor Andrew Hunter reported later, Brown had replied "promptly" and "distinctly" that he could have called upon "three thousand to five thousand if he wanted them." But Aaron Stevens, lying wounded beside Brown in the posture "dying men usually assume," offered a clarification.

Brown was not sure of any aid, Stevens explained, he only "expected it; 'you do not understand him.'" Brown then said, "'Yes, I merely expected it; I was not certain of any support." But Brown then promptly asserted that he expected both slaves and non-slaveholding whites to join his force "from all quarters."[11]

Brown had evidently persuaded some of his men that reinforcements were actually on the way. Edwin Coppoc, who survived the raid, seemed bitter at having been misled about promised support. Brown's "whole company was opposed to making the first demonstration at Harper's Ferry," he told a reporter after the raid (with some exaggeration), "but Capt. Brown would have it his own way, and we had orders to obey; he promised large reinforcements as soon as we made a demonstration."[12] Stevens told reporters after his capture that once they seized the armory he and other raiders expected blacks to "flock to them by thousands," and they would soon have "force enough for their purpose – one for which he would sacrifice his life." But in this, Stevens remarked, he thought Brown himself had been "greatly deceived."[13]

Of course there was no "promised support" of any significance. And it was not Phelps's warnings that resulted in Brown's entrapment on Monday morning. It was also absurd for Brown to suggest he might have left the armory unoccupied. Had he done so, workmen and townsmen might have armed themselves Monday morning, as townsmen who found arms Brown's men had overlooked eventually did.

If slaves were in fact going to join Brown, he did not have to wait at Harpers Ferry for them. He could have enlisted the handful of daring slaves who joined him during the first night to fan out in surrounding neighborhoods and guide other runaways to him in the mountains had he made his escape.[14] He did not have to reach a self-imposed quota to claim success. But he knew that if he gathered a formidable number of slaves at the armory, news of that fact would emblazon the penny dailies across the nation. His initial success in winning the support of several slaves taken from Washington and Allstadt and others encountered on the streets encouraged him to wait.

If Brown's repeated claim to significant military support was partly face-saving bravado, it was also consistent with his political strategy. He made such claims during as well as after the raid. He had told Phelps the same thing while arranging for the train to pass over the Potomac bridge at dawn on Monday. Magnifying his strength and repeating his intent to carry off slaves, Brown hoped to provoke Southerners into making a political issue of his "invasion." Nothing would have pleased him more than the Senate investigation that made news and magnified his fame for months after his execution. He had hoped to provoke widespread hysteria, and did indeed cause concern in Washington, D.C., and elsewhere. Rumors persisted for weeks of armed bands of escaped slaves in the mountains and of an abolitionist army on the Pennsylvania border preparing to invade Virginia to free Brown.[15]

As the raid began, Brown intimidated the watchmen with a show of force and very tough talk. He told Daniel Whelan that "if the citizens interfere with me, I must only burn the town and have blood," Whelan later recalled.[16] During the first night of the raid, Brown boasted to his hostages and others of the strength of his movement.[17] Hostage Lewis Washington, the governor's military aide, was persuaded at the time that Brown was "very strong. I supposed from his actions," Washington later testified, that Brown's "force was a very large one. Some one asked him the number of his force," Washington remembered, "and he made an evasive answer. Said he, 'I cannot exactly say. I have four companies – one stationed' at such a place, and so on. He used the term 'companies.'"[18] An armory official heard Brown say he had it "in his power to lay the town in ashes and [carry] off the women and children, but that he had refrained from doing so."[19] In seizing the town in the name of the slaves, Brown wanted to personify the danger many Southern whites feared above all else: the prospect of a slave insurrection.

Brown's wish to present himself as a formidable adversary helps account for the choice of Harpers Ferry as the point of attack. His weaponry was daunting in that setting, and if slaves or sympathetic whites had indeed joined Brown, his men at the schoolhouse could have distributed 200 Sharps rifles to them before they entered the town. For those who lacked experience in handling firearms, he had pikes. He also had access to the weapons in the armory. As he told armory officials after arresting them on Monday morning, he was determined to "seize the arms and munitions of the Government, to arm the blacks to defend themselves against their masters." When Brown asked the officers to "deliver into his possession the munitions of war belonging to the Government," master armorer Armistead Ball replied, he later testified, that "they already were in his possession, as we were."[20]

During the night Brown's men had broken into the arsenal buildings but took neither the money in the paymaster's office nor arms. If carrying off government arms rather than merely denying them to townsmen during the raid were his intent, Brown made poor use of the hours before dawn. Whatever he planned to do with the weapons, he chose Harpers Ferry as his target because it contained the only federal armory in the South. Its capture would be big news, the spread of which would encourage the specter of a large force of armed slaves and the memory of Nat Turner and Toussaint L'Ouverture.[21]

This was not the full extent of Brown's weaponry. If, as I believe, inspiring terror was the primary goal of Brown's raid, he had other things that were ideal for that purpose: nearly 100 fagots, about 250 pounds of gunpowder, and a piece of "punk." Each fagot was a bundle of pine and hickory sticks designed to ignite easily and burn slowly. Fagots could be used as torches or for setting fire to such structures as wooden bridges or buildings. The "punk" was dry material that smoldered and was commonly used to light fireworks and fuses. The armory's acting superintendent, Archibald M. Kitzmiller, testified two months after the raid that these potential torches were not recovered at Brown's farm after the raid but "were in the wagon...that Brown came over with."[22] Kitzmiller, who supervised the itemizing of Brown's captured weapons, agreed that the fagots would blaze when lighted and that the hickory would "retain the fire." No one ever asked Brown what he intended to do with so much flammable material, perhaps fearing to create public apprehension at such potentially dangerous torches in the hands of abolitionist "invaders." But during the raid, Brown more than once suggested one use for his fagots: to "burn the town."[23] And as noted earlier, to allay the fears of his men, Brown had agreed weeks before to burn the planking on both bridges when he withdrew from Harpers Ferry after the raid.

What is most surprising about the postmortems of Brown's raid, perhaps, is that no one discussed the potential implications of the ten large kegs of gunpowder, each weighing twenty-five pounds, also found in his wagon. Like the fagots, the explosives arrived at the armory on the night of the raid with Brown himself.[24] A Maryland slaveholder who "piloted" the troops Lee sent to both the schoolhouse and the Kennedy farm found no gunpowder in either place.[25] Lee's summary in his report to the adjutant general of the weapons, tools, and equipment captured on those forays mentioned neither the fagots nor the gunpowder.[26] Kitzmiller found them in the armory yard.

What had Brown intended to do with all that gunpowder? Small amounts of it might have been used for firing muskets and some types of pistols. If Brown had escaped with a supply of such muzzle loaders, he would have needed kegs of gunpowder to use them over a long campaign. Like musket balls and bullets, some observers classified his "abundance of powder" as "other ammunition."[27] But the Sharps carbines Brown's men carried were breech-loaders, which fired cartridges already containing gunpowder and a lead bullet ignited by a percussion cap. It was these "hard cartridges" and caps that Meriam had bought in Baltimore five days before the raid; and Brown's wagon contained no less that 1,300 such cartridges for Sharps rifles and 23,000 percussion caps.[28]

Clearly Brown would have had no need for so much gunpowder for weapons use for a long time.[29] In a long campaign, to be sure, he might have distributed the arsenal's supply of muskets to volunteers, but that prospect was distant. Volunteers who joined him at Harpers Ferry would doubtless have been armed with his Sharps carbines.[30] Brown thus had enough gunpowder in his wagon to make one or more large explosions. Perhaps he planned to blow up one of the bridges after the raid to foil pursuit. Brown's critics notwithstanding, the gunpowder is further evidence that he had made provision for a safe retreat or that he planned to do something spectacular.[31] With 250 pounds of gunpowder he could have exploded shops and mills in the armory as well as the turbines beneath it that drove its machinery or even one of the arsenal buildings. Such an explosion in so small yet politically sensitive a place would indeed have been a trumpet blast.

Brown never made use of his fagots or his gunpowder. Events moved too rapidly for him to do so. Just fourteen hours after taking possession the armory, he was cut off from his base and trapped in the fire engine house.

II

Events in and around Harpers Ferry soon blasted all of Brown's plans. Dr. John D. Starry, a thirty-five-year-old physician who roomed near the Wager House just "fifty steps" from the railroad bridge, was awakened about 1:30 A.M. by shooting and "confusion" around the train halted on the track "just opposite the hotel." Starry bolted from his bed and saw through his window two "low fellows" and a "tall man" exchange shots with the "railroad party." Dressing hastily, Starry hurried to the B&O office where Hayward Shepherd told him how he had been shot. Starry examined the baggage master's wound briefly and then went outside to see what was happening. He then returned to the station, where he told the frightened passengers that he would go to the armory and find out what was going on.[32]

Starry followed three of Brown's men to the armory yard to ask why some people were allowed to pass in and out of the gate while the intruders were

FIGURE 12.2. John D. Starry, the local physician who rallied militia from nearby towns to fight the raiders.

CREDIT: West Virginia State Archives, Boyd B. Stutler Collection.

shooting others "in the street." Starry was ordered to halt, but no effort was made to arrest him. Perhaps because he asked for the watchmen by name, Brown's sentinels thought he was the proprietor of the Wager House or a railroad official. "The fellow told me that there were no watchmen there," Starry recalled, and that he did not know the men Starry was asking for, but "'There are a few of us here.'"[33]

As Starry circled back to the railroad platform about 3 A.M., Oliver Brown, evidently mistaking him for a trainman, asked him from the bridge if the train was going to pass over. Starry asked what the men on the bridge were doing, but got only evasive replies. These raiders did not arrest him either.

At daybreak Starry got his horse from a nearby stable and rode to warn Acting Superintendent Archibald Kitzmiller that an "armed band" held the armory. En route, he awakened officials at Virginius Island and then residents of Bolivar Heights. At Hall's Rifle Works, he saw three heavily armed men patrolling the fence and street. Climbing up Camp Hill again, he learned about 7 o'clock that "an Irishman" he knew, Thomas Boerly, had been killed by the intruders. Starry ordered the ringing of the bell at the Lutheran Church to rouse people and get them together "to see what sort of arms they had." He found among those who gathered "one or two squirrel rifles and a few shot guns" but "no guns fit for use." When he learned that the guns in the arsenal were apparently in the hands of the intruders, he realized he had to get help from neighboring communities. He sent messengers to Shepherdstown and Charlestown and to the nearest office of the B&O urging officials "to stop the trains coming east."

Finally he galloped over to Charlestown to rouse Captain J. W. Rowan, who hastily called together the Jefferson Guards to march against the insurgents. Back in Harpers Ferry about 11 o'clock, Starry helped organize an improvised company of men with weapons Brown's men had overlooked in one of the twenty workshops of the armory. He then helped to guide the militia to what he considered the "best place of attack."[34]

Had Brown's men taken Starry into custody hours before, the course of the raid might have been different.[35] Their failure to do so was a costly mistake, greatly accelerating the military response to Brown's "invasion."

As a result of Starry's effort, Jefferson County was soon alive with armed men. At Charlestown, eight miles west of Harpers Ferry, Starry's warning prompted Col. John Thomas Gibson to call out the Jefferson Guards, a hundred men strong. A new company of Charlestown citizens also mustered in before the courthouse, and quickly chose officers. The two companies then boarded the train for Harpers Ferry. Warned that the insurgents had "taken up" the tracks ahead, the Charlestown men left the train at Halltown, midway between Charlestown and Harpers Ferry. Gibson and Col. Robert W. Baylor of the Third Cavalry, who had joined the men at Charlestown, heard that "large numbers" of insurgents controlled the lower part of Harpers Ferry and promptly asked for reinforcements from Frederick County and Shepherdstown, ten miles west of Harpers Ferry.

Proceeding on foot, the Charlestown companies reached Camp Hill over-looking Harpers Ferry about 11:30 A.M. Leading the untested company him-self, Gibson sent the Jefferson Guards under Captain Rowan, a Mexican War veteran, a mile or so up the Potomac on a flanking maneuver. There Rowan's men crossed into Maryland by boat and marched down the route Brown him-self had taken the previous night. Their orders were to wrest the Potomac bridge from the insurgents. Gibson then sent the new Charlestown company under Lawson Botts to descend from Camp Hill below Jefferson Rock, cross the Winchester and Potomac Railroad tracks, and take possession of the Gault House, a saloon at the rear of the arsenal. From there, Botts could direct fire at the entrance to the armory yard. Gibson then sent two of his officers with a "handful of men" to occupy houses overlooking the arsenal yard. He stationed a small detachment at the west end of the trestle work near the Shenandoah bridge, evidently already abandoned by the raiders, and others on Shenandoah Street, which ran west toward the rifle factory.[36] Altogether, he had 300 to 500 men armed with "Sharps Rifles and revolvers" and prepared to fight.[37] These maneuvers gave Gibson the initiative against Brown.

III

Until the arrival of Gibson's men, Brown could easily have fought his way out of Harpers Ferry and back into Maryland. But Brown still seemed at ease with his growing crowd of prisoners. During the early daylight hours when there was no shooting, Brown's treatment of the prisoners was relaxed, even hospitable. During the night he had "dismissed" an elderly prisoner to go home after delivering a message to Phelps.[38] He permitted the wife and daughter of armorer Benjamin Mills to visit him,[39] and allowed Armistead Ball, accompanied by two raiders, to "return to my family, to assure them of my safety and get my breakfast." The raiders obligingly "stopped at the door" when Ball went into his house, and since his breakfast was not ready, he was allowed to "return home again, under escort, at a later hour."[40] In fact, several prisoners were permitted to go home "several times."[41] Finally, Brown ordered breakfast from the Wager House for the others. The prisoners who testified at Brown's trial agreed that he treated them considerately and was "kind and respectful."[42]

Sporadic shots from street corners and windows soon made outside visits unsafe. Presently George Chambers, the proprietor of the Gault House Saloon, opened for business. But before 9 o'clock, Brown faced only ineffectual opposi-tion. Instead of recalling his men and withdrawing at this point, he began try-ing to engineer a cease-fire. He sent prisoner Joseph A. Brua outside the armory grounds several times to "request the citizens not to shoot as the lives of the prisoners were endangered." Brua returned to the armory each time until, later that day, the firing became too thick for him to do so.[43] At one point, as Lewis Washington later recalled, Brua actually succeeded in bringing in a "promise that the people would not fire while negotiations were pending."[44] But at this early hour no one outside was in overall command, and at about 10 o'clock, the firing became more intense.

At this point, Brown undertook to persuade Col. Washington and the armory officials, whose word he thought the citizens outside would respect, to agree to terms of a cease-fire he would present to representatives of the townspeople. As Armistead Ball explained later, "When the firing commenced, all felt we were in danger," so Ball and other hostages were willing to sign "almost any proposition that was made…to secure our safety." As the morning passed, Brown busied himself with this effort.

But the hostile forces outside the armory gathered momentum. Around noon the Jefferson Guards, firing wildly, drove Oliver Brown, Will Thompson, a young kinsman of Brown, and Dangerfield Newby, a free black, off the Potomac bridge. As the raiders returned fire while falling back across Potomac Street toward the armory, John Avis's detachment had them in a cross-fire. Newby, a Virginia-born "light mulatto" who had joined Brown hoping to free his wife and seven children from bondage, became the first raider to die. After Newby's death, angry citizens cut off his ears as souvenirs and dragged his body into a culvert where, according to a local journalist, they permitted pigs to root at it.[45]

The loss of the Potomac bridge cut Brown off from the men he had left at the Kennedy farm and the party of slaves under Cook who had moved the weapons to the schoolhouse. But the guards too suffered casualties and ended their assault after securing the bridge and taking up positions at the Wager House.

In response to the appearance of the militia, Brown took ten of his prisoners from the guard quarters of the engine house into the engine room next to it, leaving the others unattended. The ten were the "most prominent" of the prisoners, who were now "closely confined," because, in Lewis Washington's words, "in case he got the worst of it in the fight," they "would be of service in procuring good terms." As prisoner Terence Byrne later explained, Brown "did not think any attack would be made upon the Engine-House while the hostages were there."[46]

Shortly after the Jefferson Guard drove his men from the Potomac bridge, Brown asked prisoner Reason Cross to draft a "proposition" to the effect "that Brown should retain possession of the Armory, that he should release us, and that the firing should stop."[47] Armistead Ball remembered that Brown would have kept "what he held, including the armory and negroes." "Col. Washington and the others seemed to acquiesce in this arrangement."[48]

No wonder. If Brown had released his hostages, what would have restrained the angry townsmen from firing as they pleased? Brown evidently withdrew this proposal without attempting to act on it, asking Kitzmiller to draft another. Then Brown sent Cross, accompanied by Will Thompson, out of the armory yard under a flag of truce "to stop the firing." Cross was to confer with Mayor Fontaine Beckham, who had been the town's B&O agent for twenty-five years. But the residents ignored the flag of truce, fired on Thompson, then seized and

FIGURE 12.3. The engine house as it appeared in 1865.

CREDIT: Collection of The New York Historical Society, 065-815-8.

bound him, and took him prisoner. Brown blustered angrily that "he had it in his power to destroy that place in half an hour, but would not do so unless resisted."[49]

A little later he tried once more to halt the firing. This time he sent his son Watson and Aaron Stevens with Kitzmiller to talk with the Jefferson Guards. Kitzmiller had spoken with Brown "several times" and found him open to suggestions. Kitzmiller finally told Brown that the situation was "getting hot work, and if you will allow me to interfere, I can possibly accommodate matters." Brown agreed to send Kitzmiller out with instructions to "use his influence" with the "company of riflemen on the bridge" and to ask one or more of the officers to return with him to the armory to parley with Brown. Perhaps Brown also planned to demand the release of Will Thompson or to "ransom" him by freeing one or more of his prisoners. Shortly after noon, then, he still hoped to affect a cease fire.

Accompanied by Watson and Stevens, who were armed, Kitzmiller discovered that the men holding the bridge were "our own men," and "waved [his] handkerchief" to them as a signal not to shoot. He asked Watson and Stevens to "remain" behind while "he went forward," but "soon heard firing very close." A shot hit Stevens as the three men passed the B&O depot. Stevens fired back and was shot again. Also hit, Watson Brown staggered back to the engine house, gravely wounded and vomiting blood.[50] Kitzmiller did not return to Brown.[51]

When Stevens fell, he appeared to be dead, but his groaning led Joseph Brua to ask Brown to send a man out to help him. But Brown had learned his lesson; the militiamen and residents were not playing by the "rules of war." He would not risk another man to drag Stevens back into the engine house. At this point, Brua offered to go to Stevens's aid himself, and with Brown's consent he found help to carry the badly wounded raider to the hotel. Brua then honored his pledge to return to the armory.[52]

Meantime, the men from Charlestown had cut Brown off from his raiders holding the Rifle Works – John Henry Kagi, John Anthony Copeland, Jr., and Lewis Sheridan Leary. Twenty-four years old, Copeland had been a student preparing to attend Oberlin College before he and Leary, his uncle, an Oberlin saddler and harness maker, had joined Brown in September. As armed men began to appear on the road early in the morning, Kagi had sent Jeremiah Anderson to the armory to warn Brown that the situation was becoming desperate. Brown evidently responded by sending Anderson back to the rifle works by way of the arsenal with instructions to wait a little longer.[53] Hours passed as Kagi awaited orders that never came to abandon the rifle works.

At about 2:30, the tireless Starry urged an angry crowd of "citizens and neighbors of the Ferry" to "show their bravery" by freeing the Rifle Works. He organized an armed party and dispatched it up Shenandoah Street with orders to "commence the fight" as soon as they were in firing range. On receiving the party's fire, Kagi, Copeland, Leary, and an unidentified man dashed out the "back way" toward the raised tracks of the Winchester and Potomac. Scrambling over the railway, they waded into the river only to be greeted by fire from men on the opposite bank. Kagi, Brown's faithful adjutant, was shot trying to reach a flat rock in the river and "died in the water."[54] Leary was also mortally wounded and Copeland captured. We can only speculate that the third man killed, who was not one of Brown's raiders, was Washington's coachman Jim, whose body, as previously noted, was retrieved from the Shenandoah near the rifle works with a revolver in his pocket.[55] Lewis Washington later admitted it was his "servant" who "was drowned at Hall's works."[56] Copeland was captured in the river by James Holt after Holt's pistol misfired at close range because the wet powder failed to ignite. Once Copeland was pulled from the river, a crowd anxious to hang him dragged him toward the armory until Starry rescued him by sheltering the "yellow fellow" with the body of his horse until an officer took Copeland into custody.[57]

Raiders

Jeremiah Anderson

Oliver Brown

Watson Brown

John Cook

John Copeland

Shields Green

William Leeman

Aaron Stevens

Dauphin Thompson

FIGURE 12.4. Nine of Brown's ill-fated raiders, four of whom (Cook, Copeland, Green, and Stevens) survived the raid to face the hangman.

CREDIT: West Virginia State Archives, Boyd B. Stutler Collection.

IV

Brown's deteriorating situation undercut his efforts to "negotiate" a cease-fire. As scores of armed men gathered about the armory, it became clear that he was no longer a threat to the town. Any disposition they may have had to with-hold fire ceased after a third Harpers Ferrian was killed by fire from Brown's men. Shortly after 7 A.M., someone in the arsenal yard shot Thomas Boerly, a grocer, who was firing at the raiders from the corner of High and Shenandoah Streets.[58] A lull followed. As armed citizens gathered during the morning, word of Boerly's death spread. During the early afternoon, as Brown sought to end the firing, his volunteers continued to return fire, and about two o'clock, George W. Turner, a well-to-do farmer and slaveholder, was shot as he rode into town.[59] News of Turner's death circulated rapidly among the hundreds of armed men now ringing Brown's position.

Finally, about four o'clock the raiders killed Mayor Fontaine Beckham, who appeared to be unarmed.[60] Beckham had been distressed by the fatal shoot-ing during the night of his baggage assistant, Shepherd, whose wife and three children Beckham had recently purchased intending one day to set them free. Ignoring the warnings to stay out of the line of fire, Beckham ventured several times onto the B&O platform and peered around the water tower to see what was going on at the armory. Brown had "more than once" cautioned his men "not to fire on any unarmed man,"[61] but they had exchanged many shots with men firing from the water tower.[62] Beckham died almost instantly of a chest wound.

The death of Mayor Beckham in plain view of men who knew and respected him drove the crowd into a frenzy. Chambers the saloon keeper and Harry Hunter, a nephew of Beckham, decided at once to seek vengeance. They led perhaps a dozen furious men who had gathered at Chambers' bar into the Wager House to shoot Will Thompson on the spot. Confronting Thompson, Hunter, Chambers, and others had leveled their weapons, but their purpose was momentarily frustrated when Christine Fouke, a relative of the hotel owner, "threw herself" before Thompson and begged that his life be spared so the law could take its course and the Wager House might be spared from becoming the scene of a killing.

Thompson was saved only for the moment. "We then caught hold of him," Hunter recalled, "and dragged him out by the throat, he saying: 'Though you may take my life, 80,000 will rise up to avenge me, and carry out my purpose of giving liberty to the slaves.'" Hunter and others carried Thompson "out on the bridge, and two of us, leveling our guns in this moment of wild exaspera-tion, fired, and before he fell, a dozen or more balls were buried in him." They then "threw his body off the trestle work" and into the Potomac where it was riddled with balls and bullets for hours. Then they "returned to the bridge to bring out the prisoner, Stephens [sic], and serve him in the same way." But since Stevens appeared near death, "we concluded to spare him and start after oth-ers, and shoot all we could find. I had seen my loved uncle and best friend I ever had, shot down by those villainous Abolitionists, and felt justified in shooting any that I could find; I felt it my duty, and I have no regrets."[63] No one was ever prosecuted for Thompson's death.

William Leeman, at twenty the youngest of Brown's volunteers, met a fate similar to Thompson's. During the first night of the raid, Leeman brought hostage Terence Byrne to Harpers Ferry. Shortly after Stevens and Watson Brown were wounded early Monday afternoon, Leeman tried to escape from the armory, hoping to swim across the Potomac a short distance upstream from the bridge. But he was spotted scrambling through a culvert beneath the yard and came under heavy fire as he emerged at the river bank. Throwing away his rifle and drawing his Bowie knife, he cut off his heavy accoutrements and plunged into the river with a militiaman close behind. When he reached a tiny islet where he paused to catch his breath, Leeman threw up his hands and cried, "Don't shoot." But his pursuer fired and Leeman fell into the water "with his face blown away."[64] Lying for a time on a narrow islet, his body remained a target for scores of militiamen and citizens until the river finally floated it away.[65] The following day, as reporters flocked to Harpers Ferry, the "established order of sight-seeing," one remarked, began with a visit to the places where "the corpses of the insurrectionists" lay "stark and bloody."[66]

Later Monday afternoon, Oliver Brown, Brown's youngest son, was shot in the chest while kneeling in the engine-house doorway to fire. "He fell back exclaiming, 'It is all up with me,'" and died moments later, a prisoner recalled.[67] When soon after, raider Stewart Taylor was shot, Brown had only four effective volunteers and his wounded son Watson left in the armory. On Monday afternoon Watson was able to fire his rifle "frequently" until "his sufferings compelled him to retire," Lewis Washington remembered.[68] Fearing that Watson had "exerted himself too much," that evening Brown persuaded his adversaries to send a doctor to the engine house to treat him. During the night, Terence Byrne remembered, Watson "seemed to suffer intensely, and complained very much."

He asked to be dispatched, or killed, or put out of his misery, or something of that kind, I think [Byrne recalled ten weeks later], and Brown remarked to him, "No, my son, have patience; I think you will get well; if you die, you die in a glorious cause, fighting for liberty, or "freedom," or something like that.[69]

After Brown himself was carried wounded from the engine house early Tuesday morning, his first questions to bystanders were about whether Watson was still alive. Brown's plea for "kind treatment" of his "noble-hearted" son, David Hunter Strother recalled, was the first "show of feeling in the old felon."[70] Watson died about 3 A.M. Wednesday morning.

V

As Brown's desperation grew during Monday afternoon, events outside the engine house moved swiftly. Just after 3 P.M. two companies from

Shepherdstown, the Hamtramck Guards and a mounted company, arrived outside the armory. At about the same time a company from Martinsburg composed chiefly of B&O employees also reached Harpers Ferry.

Colonel Baylor, who commanded the two units from Shepherdstown, now had sufficient men to close Brown's last avenue of escape, the armory yard. He ordered Captain Ephraim Alburtis of the Martinsburg contingent to march his company down Potomac Street and through the armory yard from the upper end. Alburtis divided his men, one contingent moving down the "main avenue" while two others proceeded along the rear of the yard and through the shops as best they could. As his men approached the front of the armory yard, where Brown's men had taken positions in and about the engine house, Alburtis met a "brisk fire." Taking heavy fire themselves, Brown's remaining soldiers withdrew into the engine house and "kept up a continual fire" through one of its heavy wooden doors, which was "four or five inches ajar."[71]

According to Baylor, other companies "near at hand" joined the firefight to relieve pressure on Alburtis, eight of whose men were wounded. According to Alburtis, he received no such help and drew off to tend his wounded. But before he did so he broke the windows of the watch room, enabling Brown's unguarded hostages there to escape.[72]

Soon afterward, Brown raised a "white flag" at the door of the engine house. He wanted to talk. He still held eight hostages and hoped to bargain his way across the Potomac Bridge. Baylor ordered a cease fire and withdrew his troops to positions in front of the arsenal. "Immediately after the troops were withdrawn," Baylor reported, Brown sent a prisoner out with a "verbal communication, stating, if I would permit him to cross the Bridge with his prisoners, to some point beyond, he would set them at liberty." Baylor replied in writing, "If you will set at liberty our citizens, we will leave the government to deal with you concerning their property as it may think most advisable." This brought a further demand from Brown:

In consideration of all my men, whether living or dead, or wounded, being soon safely in, and delivered up to me at this point, with all their arms and ammunition, we will then take our prisoners and cross the Potomac bridge, a little beyond which we will set them at liberty; after which we can negotiate about the government property as may be best. We also require the delivery of our horse and harness at the hotel.[73]

Baylor replied he would under "no consideration consent to a removal of our citizens across the river," and insisted on his previous demand. Brown declined it, thus bringing to an apparent end his attempts to evacuate his men unmolested.[74]

By this time it was dusk and raining hard. Not wishing to endanger Brown's hostages, Baylor posted guards around the armory and called a halt to further action. As dark descended, militia companies continued to arrive, including three from Frederick, Maryland, the first uniformed troops on the scene. Later a Winchester company reported and during the night five Baltimore militia companies further swelled the number of troops.

Shortly before dusk Captain Thomas Sinn of the United Guards of Frederick City ventured close to the engine house, where Brown hailed him from the doorway. Despite the recent fire from that doorway, Sinn boldly went in. He and Brown talked earnestly. Brown again asked to be "allowed to go over the bridge unmolested," after which, Sinn recalled, Brown said "we might then take him if we could." Brown "had fought Uncle Sam before, and he was willing to do it again." But he appealed for consideration on grounds that he had exercised forbearance when he had held the town at his mercy only to see his men "shot down like dogs while bearing a flag of truce." He felt "entitled to some terms." Sinn replied that Brown should have expected his men to be shot down like dogs since he "took up arms" against the town. Brown said he well understood what he would have to endure before he came to Harpers Ferry and that "he had weighed the responsibility and would not shrink from it."[75]

When Sinn told Brown that no compromise could be reached, Brown replied that he held hostages "for his own safety." Sinn observed, however, that the hostages showed no fear of Brown or his men, but feared the undisciplined gunmen outside. "Every man had a gun, and four fifths of them were under no command." The militia "had ceased firing" while Sinn and Brown were talking, "but men who were intoxicated were firing their guns in the air, and others at the engine house."[76]

Sinn left Brown to his fate. Entering the Wager House afterward, he found several men taunting Aaron Stevens, and "shamed" them into leaving the wounded raider alone. If this man "could stand on his feet with a pistol in his hand," Sinn told Stevens's tormentors, they "would all jump out of the window." Remembering a promise to Brown, Sinn persuaded a physician to go to the engine room to see if he could do anything to help Watson Brown.[77]

If Sinn had no sympathy for Brown's mission, he evidently felt some respect for the defiant posture of an old soldier. Called as a defense witness at Brown's trial, he expressed "no sympathy" for Brown's acts or his "movement," and he was eager to see Brown "punished." But he "regarded Capt. Brown as a brave man," and had no hesitancy in saying so. As a "Southern man," he explained, he wanted his testimony to show Northerners that Southerners were not "unwilling to appear as witnesses in behalf of one whose principles [they] abhorred."[78] After his testimony, Sinn and men from his company visited Brown in his jail cell where they were cordially received. Brown thanked Sinn for his "manly and truthful" testimony and told Sinn "he would always remember him for his many noble traits of character." During the Frederick men's visit, Brown played with the "little children of the jailor." Stevens shook "all the company by the hand," and Sinn promised to testify at Coppoc's trial. The event had something of the atmosphere of a reunion.[79]

VI

The familiarity that Brown and Sinn enjoyed is symptomatic of a little noticed aspect of the raid: the curious relationships that Brown developed with a number of his hostages and other men of influence with whom he came in contact. From the first, Brown strove to make a connection with these men, to convey to them his understanding of his intentions, and to win their acknowledgment of his leniency toward them. But once he had won their grudging respect, he and his cause became invested in their survival. When freed, they would be witnesses to his noble purpose. And after his withdrawal – or defeat or death – they alone could spread his story. Brown thus courted their trust in his integrity even as he endangered their lives. To understand Brown's failure to withdraw early Monday morning, the dynamic of that paradox must be recognized.

At the armory he greeted the most prestigious of his prisoners, Lewis Washington, warmly. "Brown came out and invited me in, saying there was a comfortable fire," Washington told reporters later, and urging Washington and John Allstadt "to make ourselves comfortable."[80] "You will find a fire in here, sir; it is rather cool this morning," Washington later remembered Brown saying. "I shall be very attentive to you, sir, for I may get the worst of it in my first encounter, and if so, your life is worth as much as mine. I shall be very particular to pay attention to you."

Brown was deferential. He had taken Washington hostage because, "as the aid to the governor of Virginia, you would endeavor to perform your duty, and perhaps you would have been a troublesome customer to me." Brown also wanted Washington in his custody for the "moral effect" it would give his cause to have "one of your name as a prisoner."[81] Brown said he would later "ransom" Washington for a "stout" negro, and would in the meantime take "special care" of Washington's heirloom sword and return it when he released him. When the militia first arrived, Washington recalled, Brown had picked the ten hostages "he supposed to be the most prominent men" in case he "got the worst of it in this fight" in order to help him "procure good terms."[82]

Brown also gave safety assurances to the men his sentinels arrested during the night and to the armory officials he took into custody. As a result, the men he had "imprisoned," according to a widely reported story, "all testify to their lenient treatment; they were neither tied nor insulted, and beyond the outrage of restricting their liberty, were not ill-used. Captain Brown was always courteous to them and at all times assured them that they should not be injured."[83] To be sure, this treatment may have been calculated to make the prisoners easier to hold or less vindictive toward him should he be captured and they freed.[84]

But even while Brown's prospects still seemed bright, he was surprisingly generous toward his captives. As noted previously, he let some of them go home for breakfast under guard and permitted others to receive food brought to them at the armory.[85] And as townsmen began shooting at him and his men, he asked his hostages to help "negotiate" a cease-fire. More than once he let one of them, Joseph Brua, go out to talk to citizens outside the yard on a pledge to return. Brown even asked the prisoners to vote on his proposal that he and his men be permitted to cross the Potomac bridge with them still in custody.[86]

Nor did he threaten to use the hostages to take reprisals for the shooting of his son Watson and Stevens under a flag of truce. He seemed solicitous of the prisoners' safety throughout the ordeal, permitting them to remain at the back of the engine room safe from the random fire from townsmen outside.[87] Nor did he use them to shield his raiders. Even during the marines' assault, "We were kept in the rear of the engine-house and allowed to keep a safe position," Lewis Washington testified, "so that there was no effort to endanger us."[88] It might even be said that Brown showed more concern for his prisoners than for his own men.

Brown was eager to explain his presence at Harpers Ferry to his adversaries. As he walked with Andrew Phelps across the Potomac bridge ahead of Phelps's train, Brown said, "'You doubtless wonder that a man of my age should be here with a band of armed men, but if you knew my past history you would not wonder at it so much."[89] Or as a bystander recalled the remark, Brown reasoned, "'[I]f you knew my heart and history, you would not blame me.'"[90]

Whatever Brown said, it was evidently an attempt at self-justification based at least partly on his experience in Kansas. Just why he linked his incentive to seize Harpers Ferry with past wrongs he felt he had suffered elsewhere is unclear. But Brown had often alluded to such wrongs in his efforts to raise funds; they testified to his devotion to the cause and he apparently felt deeply about them. If his comment to Phelps seemed an appeal for understanding, Brown was quick to disavow it when Phelps saw him again with Governor Wise after the raid. Brown "asked no sympathy, and had no apologies to make; he knew exactly what he was about," he told Governor Wise after his capture. Moments later, however, Brown "said something about a battle in Kansas," Phelps recalled, "and having one of his sons shot." He said "if his life were forfeited he was prepared to suffer."[91]

For Brown reaffirming his readiness to suffer for the slave heightened his confidence in God's call. During the raid Brown alluded to his sacrifices repeatedly. "'We are Abolitionists from the North," Brown told one of his prisoners; "we come to take and release your slaves; our organization is large and must succeed; I suffered much in Kansas, and expect to suffer here in the cause of human freedom.'"[92] Terence Byrne recalled Brown saying, "'Gentlemen, if you knew my past history, you would not blame me for being here' ...." He had gone to Kansas "a peaceable man," only to be "hunted down like a wolf by the pro-slavery men" who killed one of his sons. "'[A]nd now,' he said, 'I am here.'" As Brown spoke, Watson lay wounded beside the Maryland slave owner "suffering intensely."[93]

Brown wanted to be understood as a man inspired by his compassion for the slaves, not as an instrument of vengeance. He based his defense at his trial on the concern he had shown for his prisoners and his reluctance to take innocent lives. After the raid compassion was his explanation for his misjudgments. Should he have held the train longer? "I wanted to allay the fears of those who believed we came here to burn and kill," Brown insisted. "For that reason

I allowed the train to cross the bridge, and gave them full liberty to pass on. I did it only to spare the feelings of those passengers and their families, and to allay the apprehensions that you had got a band of men who had no regard for life and property, nor any feeling of humanity."[94] Why had he stayed too long in the armory? "It was all occasioned by my desire to spare the feelings of my prisoners and their families, and the community at large." "I should have gone away," Brown admitted to Senator Mason, "but I had thirty odd prisoners, whose wives and daughters were in tears for their safety, and I felt for them."[95]

By Monday morning the implacable filibuster who had intimidated the watchmen Sunday night had given way to a more approachable figure. Brown had gained a human face. By now he was engaged in a running exchange with his "prominent men." Terence Byrne, who reached the armory under guard at about 9 A.M., soon found Brown talking so much with his prisoners that Byrne could not recollect "one fifth part" of what Brown said.[96] In "repeated interviews" with Acting Superintendent Kitzmiller, Brown explained that his intention was to free the slaves, and "if necessary to fight the Pro Slavery men for that purpose." "I was first surprised, then indignant, and finally disgusted" with Brown's endless negotiations, Kitzmiller told the court at Brown's trial.[97] During the long hours of the prisoners' confinement, Brown's rifle was cocked all the time.

The implicit threat of force and the continued firing of Brown's men from the engine house may help explain why none of Brown's prominent prisoners took any overt action during their imprisonment to interfere with him. They showed none of the boldness that marked Virginians' conduct during the Civil War. It is too much to say that they developed any of the positive feelings toward their captors that modern researchers have documented in psychological studies of hostages. At Harpers Ferry, conditions did not favor the development of psychological malaise or the Stockholm syndrome.[98] Even the first hostages – the slaveholders – were not alone with their captors, they did not long fear Brown personally, and their ordeal lasted only about thirty-one hours. Brown unexpectedly evidenced consideration for them even as he used their slaves to help prevent them from fleeing. His behavior encouraged them to converse freely with him, and their reaction to their ordeal owes something to that tendency of hostages to placate their captor and affect outward friendliness toward him. "I was disposed to assume a character that I did not have at the time, that of cheerfulness," Terence Byrne recalled of his capture. "My mind was busy with the future. I was fearful of a bloody civil war."[99] Even during the last hours of the raid, Brown evidenced no mistrust of his hostages.

VII

By dusk Monday evening, every window, doorway, and rooftop commanding a view of the engine house harbored men firing as they pleased. Col. Baylor's Virginia militia guarded every avenue of escape, but it was the random rifle fire of townsmen and local farmers that pinned the raiders inside the engine house. After sunset, when volunteers from Winchester and Fredericktown arrived, perhaps 1,500 men encircled the remnant of Brown's band. Later that night the Baltimore militia reached Sandy Hook by train and the detachment of U.S. marines sent by President Buchanan marched across the B&O bridge to the scene of the "insurrection." Fearing that a nighttime assault might sacrifice the lives of Brown's hostages, their commander, Lee, waited until daylight to demand the "insurgents'" surrender.[100]

During the long night, Brown did not sleep. His mood was sober. Occasionally he spoke to one or another of his eight remaining prisoners, but most of those words were soon forgotten following their rescue. During the night one of the raiders, probably Jeremiah Anderson or Dauphin Thompson, asked Brown if it was treason to resist the marines, to which Brown reportedly replied yes. Protesting he was there just "to liberate the slaves," the raider declared, "'I will fight no longer.'"[101]

The situation was desperate. Shields Green and Edwin Coppoc were Brown's only other able-bodied men, and none of his loyal boys had any heart to fight against the new, overwhelming odds.

The prisoners too worried that Brown would bring their destruction by refusing to surrender. During the skirmishes late Monday afternoon, they had sought shelter behind the armory's two hand-drawn fire engines and hose cart and hugged the cold brick floor at the back of the engine room. But it would be difficult for the marines to distinguish prisoners from raiders in the dimness and smoke of an early morning assault, their bayonets at the ready. As dawn approached, Brown warned the hostages he could not guarantee their lives. "If they were not dear enough to their fellow citizens to accept the terms he had proposed to secure their safety," Brown reportedly said, the armed men outside "must be barbarians."[102]

A crucial part of the story of the final assault has never been told. The original definitive account of that assault, Oswald Garrison Villard's *John Brown, 1800–1859: A Biography Fifty Years After* (1910), was so persuasive that few historians have since reviewed the primary sources. Villard privileged Col. Lee's report of the assault and dismissed out of hand Brown's own version of what he did and did not do in it.[103]

The story of the assault, then, has been told from Lee's point of view. His report of what happened was focused, concise, factual. But Lee was not omniscient or wholly disinterested. He omitted important details concerning the assault, and he could not see what happened inside the engine house. He did not yet recognize the implications of the movement he had crushed, but he was careful to note its apparent parameters. He accounted for all the men on the roster of the Provisional Army that his aid, Jeb Stuart, found at the Kennedy farm and identified the bodies of the dead. On October 19, the day after Brown's capture, Lee himself took the night train from Harpers Ferry with the marines back to Washington, where he finished the report the following day.[104]

FIGURE 12.5. Army Col. Robert E. Lee, later the Confederacy's most honored general, ordered the marines to storm the engine house at daybreak.

CREDIT: Library of Congress.

Lee was eager to set minds at ease. "The blacks whom [Brown] forced from their homes in this neighborhood, as far as I could learn, gave him no voluntary assistance," he wrote. The "servants" of Washington and Allstadt "took no part in the conflict"; those taken into Maryland "returned to their homes as soon as released." "The result proves that the plan was the attempt of a fanatic or madman, which could only end in failure." Brown's "temporary success was owing to the panic and confusion [Brown] succeeded in creating by magnifying his numbers." Lee's tale of the marines' assault and the delivery of the "insurgents" to Charlestown jail was factually correct, but omitted discordant details that reveal something of the purposes, determination, and calculation of his defeated adversary.

After dawn, through his staff officer Stuart, Lee had the volunteer companies "paraded" on lines outside the armory enclosure, cleared the streets, and issued orders to prepare for the attack. Worried about the lives of Brown's hostages, Lee sent Stuart under a flag of truce to demand Brown's surrender. Stuart presented a written summons calling on the "persons in the armory buildings" to "peaceably surrender themselves" and relinquish the "pillaged property." If they did so, they would be "kept in safety to await the orders of the President." "In all frankness," the summons concluded, it was "impossible for them to escape; ... the armory is surrounded on all sides by troops; and ... if [Colonel Lee] is compelled to take [the insurgents] by force he cannot answer for their safety."[105]

Lee expected the insurgents to reject his terms and instructed Stuart not to consider counterproposals from them. Stuart's talk with Brown would be brief and pointed. But Stuart's "parley" with Brown was "a long one." With perhaps 2,000 spectators watching, he approached the engine house accompanied only by Samuel Strider, an elderly citizen of Harpers Ferry, who carried the flag of truce. Brown opened one of the double doors "about four inches, and placed his body against the crack, with a cocked carbine in his hand." Brown rejected Lee's terms, "presented his [own] propositions in every possible Shape with admirable tact, but all, amounting to the only condition he would surrender upon [was] to be allowed to escape with his party."

As the two men spoke, Stuart heard urgent voices from the engine room. "Many of his prisoners begged me with tears to ask Col Lee to come & see him," Stuart remembered. "I told them he never would I knew accede to any terms but those he had offered, and as soon as I could tear myself away from the importunities of the prisoners – I left & waved my cap." That was the signal for the assault.[106] During their importunings, one of the prisoners, Armistead Ball, pleaded with Brown "on the ground of humanity to the prisoners as well as to the men who appeared so bound to him, not to persist in spilling more blood." But the plea had failed to move Brown.[107] This last-minute effort was not without significance.

Stepping abruptly away from the engine-house door and waving an ostrich-plumed hat, Stuart positioned himself a few steps away against the abutment framing the watch-house door. From there he could call out to Lt. Israel Green during the assault. In his "parley" with Brown, he learned that the hostages were in the farthest corner of the engine house and thus out of the line of fire.[108] That information was crucial to Green as he forced an entry into the building in the face of fire from within.

Stuart had also recognized his adversary. "When Smith first came to the door – I immediately recognized Old Ossawattomie [sic] Brown who had given us so much trouble out here in Kansas," Stuart wrote later, "and not until he was knocked down & dragged out *pretending* to be dead, and I proclaimed it – did the vast multitude and the world find out that John Brown was Old Brown. No one else could have done that there but myself."[109] In thus revealing Brown's identity, Stuart had done a great service for the old man; he had sounded Brown's trumpet. Newsmen now had a compelling figure on whom to hook their stories of the "uprising." Whether or not Brown survived, they knew that readers throughout the country would recognize him as the daredevil free-state guerrilla from Kansas.[110]

Events now moved swiftly. Green had picked a storming party of twelve men and stationed them near the engine house out of the line of fire. Lee ordered them forward in two lines, one on each side of the doors: "My object was, with a view of saving our citizens, to have as short an interval as possible between the summons and attack." The marines were to attack with bayonets not gunfire. When once inside, they were to distinguish "our citizens" from the insurgents and not to "injure the blacks detained in custody unless they resisted."[111] To force an entry, three additional marines had sledgehammers to break in the doors.

Brown had barricaded the doors by pushing the fire engines against them and had tied the double doors together with ropes. The spring that the ropes gave the doors as the sledgehammers struck cushioned the blows; the doors swayed but held, and Green quickly abandoned the hammers. As the hammering began, Brown and his men took up positions behind the doors and "commenced firing."[112] Outside the doors, by chance, lay a heavy, forty-foot ladder. Green ordered the storming party aside and had a second detail of marines drop their muskets, hoist the ladder, and at a full run of perhaps twenty-five feet, crash it into the door as a battering ram. The second or third run splintered a leaf in the lower half of the door, which slanted inward, and moments later the storming party slipped inside.

"The fire of the insurgents up to this time had been harmless," Lee reported of the entry. "At the threshold one marine fell mortally wounded. The rest, led by Lieutenant Green and Major Russell, quickly ended the contest. The insurgents that resisted were bayoneted. Their leader, John Brown, was cut down by the sword of Lieutenant Green, and our citizens were protected by both officers and men. The whole was over in a few minutes."[113]

But Lee omitted a crucial fact. After the door was "shattered sufficiently to obtain an entrance," Col. Baylor reported, "immediately, a heavy volley was fired in by the marines, and an entrance effected."[114] Capt. Alburtis saw the volley as well and deduced its purpose. After a "third blow" of the ladder "took the door in," Alburtis reported, "the men inside fired full upon the outsiders, killing Luke Quinn, a marine, and wounding Nicholas Rupert, the ball taking off a part of his lower lip." The marines "returned" the raiders' fire, Alburtis said.[115] A report wired to the conservative New-York *Journal of Commerce* a half hour after the assault noted: "The rioters fired briskly…the marines firing in turn."[116]

Perhaps this volley was an instinctive response of inexperienced troops to seeing a comrade fall. That assumption gains credence in light of later admissions. During the questioning of Brown just hours after the raid, a marine officer explained that "orders were not to shoot anybody; but when [the storm-ers] were fired upon by Brown's men and one of them killed, they were obliged to return the compliment." Brown insisted the marines fired first. Lee and Stuart, both present, said nothing of the incident.[117]

There is a second possibility. If, as Brown claimed, the marines had fired first, Green may have ordered the volley to suppress the insurgents' fire and drive them from the entrance. Whoever shot first, there is no question that the marines shot into the doors before wedging themselves through the opening. Lewis Washington later told the Mason Committee that "both sides" had fired. "Was there firing upon the engine-house also?" Washington was asked. "There was firing upon it and from it."[118]

The timing of this exchange of shots is crucial. It establishes that the two marines hit by the raiders' fire were outside the engine house and that their officers had not yet entered the room.[119] John Allstadt, who testified eagerly against Brown, conceded that he could not say who had shot the marine who died. "He might have been killed by shots fired before the door was broken open," said Allstadt, who was "much confused and excited at the time."[120]

What actually happened before the first marines entered the engine house can be only partially reconstructed. "We first heard a hammering at the door, and then the Brown party commenced firing at the door," hostage Terence Byrne later testified. "There was a cessation for a moment or two, and during this time one of Brown's men turned round to him and said, 'Captain, I believe I will surrender.' [Brown's] answer was, 'Sir, you can do as you please.'" "This man," probably Dauphin Thompson, "was then down on his knees, and he got upon his feet, and turned round to me and said, 'Hallo 'surrender' for me.'" Byrne and hostage John E. P. Daingerfield both cried, "'One man surrenders,'" but they "could not make ourselves heard on the outside." At this point Edwin Coppoc urged Thompson to get down "or your head will be shot off."[121] A second man, Jeremiah Anderson, then joined Thompson in crying for "quar-ter" and both lay down their weapons, Daingerfield recalled. But "after the marines burst open the door they picked them up again and renewed the fight." Both were bayoneted and died almost instantly. Brown's two other effectives, Shields Green and Edwin Coppoc, surrendered moments later.[122]

Just before the marines burst open the door, Brown dropped his carbine and joined his boys in calling for quarter. After the "first attack," hostage Daingerfield recalled days later, "Capt. Brown cried out to surrender, but he was not heard." Daingerfield "did not see him fire afterwards"; but he did see Brown "wounded on the hip by a thrust from [Green's] saber, and several saber cuts on his head. When the latter wounds were given, Capt. Brown appeared to be shielding himself, with his head down, but making no resistance."[123]

Just hours after the assault, Brown, his hair matted with blood and his face and hands still "begrimed" from gunpowder smoke, told a similar story at his questioning. "These wounds were inflicted upon me, both the saber cut on my

FIGURE 12.6. Hostage John E. P. Daingerfield, the armory paymaster who testified at Brown's trial but later confused the story of Brown's capture in memory.

CREDIT: West Virginia State Archives, Boyd B. Stutler Collection.

head and the bayonet stabs in the different parts of my body," he insisted to the reporters present, "some minutes after I had ceased fighting, and had consented to surrender for the benefit of others, and not for my own benefit." He could have killed "the major here" just as easily "as I could kill a mosquito" when he had entered the engine room, Brown claimed, referring to Major W. W. Russell, but "I supposed that he came in only to receive our surrender."[124] "There had been long and loud calls of surrender from us – as loud as men could yell – but in the confusion and excitement I suppose we were not heard." Brown did not believe "the Major, or anyone else, wanted to butcher us after we had surrendered."[125] Although he was mistaken about who had assaulted him and in referring to "bayonet stabs," in later public statements Brown elaborated his claim to have surrendered.[126]

Lewis Washington had a different recollection of the final moments. Putting on a pair of white gloves and reclaiming his famous heirloom sword, he waited until the raiders were taken into custody and Brown's prisoners had left the engine house to "deafening cheers" to make an appearance. Washington "was the last to show himself, and when he did," a reporter from Baltimore wrote, "the mountainsides reverberated with the shouts of the multitude, who had thronged the railroad platform, crowded the windows of all the houses in the vicinity, and filled the different streets."[127] Almost immediately Washington reported that "all the insurgents wished to surrender but Brown; that he never quailed, but exhibited coolness and courage seldom equaled.... During the firing," Washington said, Brown "never faltered."[128]

After conferring with Governor Wise and his aides, Washington talked to reporters the following day, emphasizing Brown's stubborn refusal to surrender.[129] To Lee's offer of protection, he had replied "that he could expect no leniency, and he would sell his life as dearly as possible," Washington said. "There was no cry of 'surrender' on his part except from one young man, and then Brown said – 'Only one surrenders.'" As the doors were being battered in, Washington recalled, one of Brown's men had shouted, "'I surrender.' The Captain immediately cried out, 'There's one surrenders – give him quarter,' and at the same moment fired his own rifle at the door."[130]

But that was not Washington's final word. At Brown's trial he initially testified that he had heard no "general cry of 'surrender.'" But Washington changed his story when cross-examined. He conceded that he and the other hostages "were kept in the rear [of the] engine-house and allowed to keep a safe position." Thus he was not well placed to see and hear Brown throughout. He could not even say for sure whether the marines had fired "after they broke into the Engine House." In the end, he admitted that "The noise was great, and several shouted from inside that someone had surrendered the prisoners."[131] It was a crucial concession. Only Brown himself could have released the hostages. In effect, Washington had repudiated his earlier public statements.

If Brown had indeed tried to surrender as the marines burst into the engine house, that might explain why Anderson and Thompson first surrendered and then reportedly picked up their rifles again, only to be bayoneted. If Brown too had finally thrown down his carbine and called for quarter, they might have sought to protect him when Green lunged at him with his saber. Also, if some of the marines came into the engine house firing, as several accounts had it, Anderson and Thompson might have resumed the fight in self defense. If Brown had not surrendered, why had he failed to shoot Green as he scrambled through the splintered door and paused to scan the engine room to locate the hostages?

The answer is that Green was not the first officer to enter the room. The actions of Major Russell, attached as a staff officer to the marines, point persuasively to a frantic, last moment surrender as well. Russell was a key player. Commanding the second detachment of marines but armed only with a rattan cane, according to observers Russell entered the engine house before Green.

J. E. B. Stuart thought that Russell, "feeling great pride in his Corps, and his southern blood being up a little too, jumped in I believe foremost through" the opening in the splintered door.[132] Reporters on the scene confirmed Stuart's recollection: "A third blow shivered the door, and the order was given to enter. Major Russell in the most cool and gallant manner entered first, without weapons, with his right hand raised, demanding a surrender."[133] "The cool bravery displayed by Maj. Russell in entering the engine house in advance of his men, was the subject of special praise," writes the reporter for the New York *Tribune*. In this reporter's surprising, neglected account, Russell actually ends the fighting himself!

While the gallant Major thus risked his own life, he was aiming to prevent unnecessary bloodshed. A number of shots had been fired by both sides when some one in the house cried for quarters. Instantly, Major R. commanded the marines to cease firing; but seeing another volley about to be shot, he snatched a Sharps rifle from one of the insurgents, and turning to his own men declared he would shoot the man who fired another gun. This ended the desperate struggle, which had continued for about two minutes with rifles muzzle to muzzle. Lieut. Green also displayed great coolness and daring during the short but terrible encounter with these desperate men.[134]

This account may owe something to the reporter's imagination. Could someone stationed outside the armory yard have witnessed Russell "snatch" a carbine from one of the insurgents inside the engine house, even if Coppoc or Green had handed their rifle to him? But Russell himself later escorted reporters to the paymaster's office where he had had Brown carried and had ordered a surgeon to attend to him. Thus the *Tribune* reporter, who had interviewed Brown sometime "after his capture," could have heard details of Russell's heroics from Russell himself. At the very least, we know that Brown had seen Russell enter the engine house in the final moments of the assault. In the paymaster's office, "Brown looked up and, recognizing Russell, said, 'You entered first. I could have killed you, but I spared you.' In reply to which the Major bowed and said, 'I thank you.'"[135]

VIII

The erroneous story of Brown's suicidal last stand has long diverted attention from the calls of surrender that punctuated the last moments of the assault. To the usually careful Oswald Garrison Villard it was inconceivable that Lee could have failed to mention that the marines had fired when forcing their entry or that Brown had called for quarter.[136] Villard's story of the assault also drew uncritically upon reminiscent accounts published in popular magazines a quarter century after the raid, notably those of two of the chief witnesses – John Daingerfield and Lt. Israel Green. Daingerfield's brief, theatrical memoir contradicted his own 1859 testimony on numerous points; he now credited himself for aiding the marines' entry by "rigging" the ropes holding the closed doors to slip.[137]

Distressed by the "great many misstatements" in the narratives published by former hostages, Green had refuted Daingerfield's wild story of Green's attack on Brown. But "The whole scene passed so rapidly," Green confessed, "that it hardly made a distinct impression upon my mind." He could "only recall the fleeting picture of an old man kneeling with a carbine in his hand, with a long gray beard falling away from his face, looking quickly and keenly toward the danger that he was aware had come upon him."[138] Even in this description Green was mistaken. Brown's odd, grizzled beard had been cropped close before the raid.[139] Green did not explain why the marines had bayoneted Thompson and Anderson if, as he claimed, Brown was the only one still fighting. More important, Green could not adequately explain why Brown had failed to shoot him and Russell as they stepped through the splintered door just a few feet from the muzzles of Brown's carbine and his Ames pistols.[140] Green's failing memory had rewritten the story.

IX

Daybreak on Tuesday had greeted Brown with unpalatable choices: make a final, suicidal stand or surrender. In the end, he chose both. He continued to stand even after his boys dropped their weapons and called out to surrender, then when it was too late to make a difference, he did the same thing. He could not have managed the situation worse. Why had he failed to accept Lee's offer of protection from Stuart at the engine house door? And why had he surrendered minutes later after it was too late to protect his men?

The first question asks precisely what his captors asked. In a rambling examination by authorities in the afternoon following his capture, someone asked Brown why he did not surrender before the assault. Brown had earlier given a series of faltering answers to questions from reporters, but he was now on message. "I did not think it was my duty or interest to do so," he answered. "We assured the prisoners that we did not wish to harm them, and they should be set at liberty. I exercised my best judgment, not believing the people would wantonly sacrifice their own fellow citizens, when we offered to let them go on condition of being allowed to change our position about a quarter of a mile," Brown said, casting his proposal to Stuart as favorably as he could.

"The prisoners agreed by vote among themselves to pass across the bridge with us," Brown continued, alluding to discussions of the previous day. Without waiting for another question, he explained his purpose in seizing the prisoners: "We wanted them only as a sort of guarantee of our own safety; that we should not be fired into. We took them in the first place as hostages and to keep them from doing any harm." "We did kill some men in defending ourselves, but I saw no one fire except directly in self-defence. Our orders were strict not to harm any one not in arms against us."[141]

But Brown had come to Harpers Ferry breathing fire. He brought a wagon load of weapons and incendiary materials; he talked fiercely to the watchmen he arrested and warned he might have to burn the town. He came, in short, as Osawatomie Brown, the terror of Kansas. Even before the raid, Brown had come to think of himself as a "soldier," a "captain," a warrior at war against slavery. He was proud of his spirited defense of the free state cause in Kansas. As a self-styled warrior, he considered courage in battle a measure of honor and manhood. "[W]e soldiers are not afraid of death," he reputedly told Stuart before the assault. "I would as leave die by a bullet as on the gallows."[142] Thus, when his efforts to negotiate were rebuffed, he had no choice in his own mind but to fight on. Witnessing his brave men die, he could not surrender to save himself. That would have been to admit, among other things, that he had sacrificed his young followers in vain. To surrender was also to give up his dream of liberating the slaves, to admit failure in his mission. He could not act in a way that might be seen as panic, cowardice, or betrayal. Pride did not permit it.

Why, then, was he able to surrender when everything was lost? It was not easy. Even when he excused Anderson or Thompson to call for quarter, he shouted with Daingerfield and Byrne, "One man surrenders!" or "Only one man surrenders!" Thus he withheld permission for Coppoc and Shields Green to surrender too, and in so doing perhaps preserved the fantasy that he was making a stand. But moments later, Green and Coppoc threw down their rifles as marines pounded the door and fired into the engine room. It was only then that Brown called out that the prisoners were released.

Perhaps Brown also shouted "surrender," as he later claimed. But in that moment he found a rationale for surviving the assault to face trial. He was not surrendering; he was releasing his hostages to protect them. "At the moment when the doors were broken in," a reporter noted, "the prisoners, at the suggestion of Col. Washington, threw up their hands, so that it might be seen they were not combatants."[143] Perhaps seeing his prisoners make a gesture of surrender, Brown could reclaim authority for their actions only by ratifying their silent wish to be freed.

That paradox may account for the contradiction in Brown's later testimony: his insistence that he had been attacked after surrendering, and the declaration that he had never called for quarter.[144] In the final moments of the assault, Brown no longer had any claim to control his hostages; it was fatuous to say he was releasing them. But Brown was evidently sincere in doing so. He had declined Stuart's offer of protection and stood his ground until the assault threatened the lives of his hostages. Then he surrendered them. By surrendering to save the hostages, he could deny to himself that he had wantonly sacrificed his own men in further futile resistance. It was for the safety of others, not himself, that he surrendered. Thus, for Brown only recklessness on the part of the marines had caused his injuries and Anderson and Thompson's deaths.

Whatever else happened in those frantic final moments, Brown believed he had surrendered to protect his hostages. It was a counterintuitive belief. Whether saving the hostages was excuse or incentive to surrender – or both – is uncertain. But it is apparent that in Brown's mind his concern for their fate gave him permission to do so. He could tell himself that he did it as a gesture of humanity, but they were not just any men for whom he had accepted a responsibility. They were "leading men" and witnesses to his lofty purpose and to his tale of his life of sacrifice.

In the days after the raid, Brown attempted to press these men into service on his behalf. They would "testify that they heard me continually order my men not to fire into houses, not even when we were fired upon from them, lest we should kill innocent persons.... Your own citizens," he replied hotly to a skeptical reporter, "will testify that such were my orders; that is the fact and you know it.'"[145] Brown would call upon the prisoners to give evidence of his innocence at his trial. He wanted to stand trial "that he might have justice as to the faith of [his and his men's] motives."[146]

The cause of the slave was the mandate that had energized his sense of mission. When he failed as a guerrilla leader and insurrectionist, he grasped that he might still win a propaganda victory over slavery as a man moved solely by compassion for the "downtrodden." Facing certain execution, he determined to bear further witness on behalf of "God and humanity." If God had permitted John Brown to fail as a soldier, He had miraculously permitted him to live to stand trial and given him an unequaled pulpit from which to offer that final testimony.

PART V

MESSAGES

13

God's Emissary

I think I feel as happy as Paul did when he lay in prison. He knew if they killed him it would greatly advance the cause of Christ .... Let them hang me.

John Brown[1]

Has ever such an epistle been written from a condemned cell since the letter "to Timotheus," when Paul "was brought before Nero the second time?"

Rev. L. W. Bacon[2]

And almost all things are by the law purged with blood; and without shedding of blood is no remission.

King James Bible, Hebrews 9:22

In the six weeks between his capture and his hanging, John Brown agonized over why he had met "disaster" doing God's work and struggled to restore his damaged self-esteem. Dismissing critics who charged that his own "infatuation" had led him astray, Brown turned as always to scripture to salve his spiritual wounds and quiet his doubts. There he found answers that made sense of his failure and reconsecrated him to the cause. In prison Brown the failed insurrectionist became Brown the martyred apostle of militant antislavery. That transformation was rooted in an altered sensibility about the uses of righteous violence.

I

At its heart John Brown's war against slavery had been dangerously flawed. He had no model for the war he hoped to wage. His goals were to destroy an institution, not a government, to raise public consciousness of evil, not to lay waste homes and plantations. At the least he hoped to create the impression that he had delivered slavery a devastating blow and thereby rekindle the sectional quarrel over it.

Brown never lost faith in his mission. But his ability to execute his plan was compromised by inconsistencies in his own thinking – by unrecognized cognitive dissonance – that prevented him from matching means and ends. In the end the raid failed not because his force was too small or his plan fool-hardy, but because Brown considered his hostages misguided adversaries rather than implacable foes. In war hostages can be militarily useful. But Brown's first impulse was to lecture his rather than deploy them as cover for his men or use them as bargaining chips. They included, as Col. Lee observed, the "principal citizens in the neighborhood," men Brown regarded as gentlemen. As such, even the slave owners among them were not personally responsible for the peculiar institution, and they had committed no offense against Brown or his men. He could therefore not objectify them as he had his victims at Pottawatomie or needlessly imperil their lives. In that respect, Brown's "war" had no ascribed class of enemies.

Of course he did not renounce violence. His foes in the field he defined as whoever tried to stop him; under his rules of engagement his men were free to target any townsman or militiaman firing at them and to "seize at once" any-one found armed in "occupied territory."[3] But at Harpers Ferry Brown operated under the self-imposed code of honor embodied in his Provisional Constitution, many copies of which he brought with him to distribute. His self-defined man-date in the field was to defend the slaves he freed, not to slay their masters. He did not hesitate to liberate Lewis Washington's slaves, but he obliged himself to treat Washington and other prisoners with "every degree of respect and kindness" that "circumstances" permitted.[4] He held the slaveholders captive, Brown told them, to exchange later for slaves and to insure that his men would not "be fired into." When that failed, he protected the hostages from random fire. Under his code, he could confiscate "real and personal property as needed whenever and wherever it may be found," but could not "needlessly" burn or destroy "useful property," his fagots and gunpowder notwithstanding.[5] Brown could support his "regulars" by foraging, but promised to return Washington's heirloom sword and pistol out of respect for the colonel's name or because they were taken unfairly when Washington was in his nightshirt.

It was an oddly disjointed war, recognized as a war only by Brown and his company. If Brown saw himself as constrained by conventions of warfare, his adversaries were not similarly bound. Discovering armed men holding various points in the town and inexplicably shooting at people in the dark, townsmen felt bound by no such rules as Brown observed. To them, Brown's "army" were variously "rioters," "filibusters," or "insurgents," clandestine "invaders," criminals unlawfully holding private and public property, imprisoning citizens, and stealing slaves. The raiders' victims included the town's black baggage master and its elderly mayor, both shot though apparently unarmed. Whatever Brown's professed motives and code of conduct, incensed Virginians gave his raiders no consideration as soldiers. Brown would complain bitterly that his men had been seized or shot under flags of truce and abused and murdered after capture. But his "claim or expectation" to "have been treated accord-ing to the rules of honorable warfare" was an "absurdity," the state's attor-ney declared at Brown's trial, since he commanded only a "band of murderers and thieves."[6] After the raid, only Lee's marines stood between him and swift retribution by the mob.

If Brown failed to recognize the difficulties in pursuing a one-sided, unrecognized war, he was quick to blame his adversaries for failing to honor his rules of warfare. "I did not intend to stay here so long," Brown told a reporter shortly after his capture, "but they [the citizens] deceived me by proposing compromises which they had no intention of carrying out."[7] "I intended to remain here but a few hours," Brown told another reporter, "but a lenient feeling towards the citizens led me into a parley with them as to compromise, and by prevarication on their part I was delayed until attacked, and then in self-defence was forced to entrench myself."[8] Ten days later, in a private moment, Brown and Stevens, who shared a jail cell, confided to attorney George Hoyt that it had been "a great mistake, chaffering [talking idly], to save the lives & the shedding of the blood of men.... [The raiders] might yet have got away & into the mountains where no body of men could have captured them, had it not been for this mistake," Hoyt reported to the Boston friends.[9] Brown had failed to recognize that even his prestigious prisoners could not hope to bind their angry fellow citizens to a truce with criminals or "insurrectionists."

As a construct in Brown's imagination, his war had mutated over the years. It had originated as a scheme to rescue slaves via a "subterranean passageway," evolved into an amorphous plan for a series of "dashes" against tidewater plantations, and morphed into the formal pledge at Chatham to establish communities of fugitives in the Alleghenies in the aftermath of a series of swift raids. It gained material expression in the waning months of Bleeding Kansas with the recruitment of fighters and the financial support of the Secret Six. It acquired a quasi-legal standing for Brown with the approval of the Chatham Convention. Only late in this evolution did Harpers Ferry itself become its focal point. That development reflected Brown's fear that to keep the idea of his war alive, he had to make a "demonstration" for his supporters. Like Brown's earlier appeals in the penny dailies for money to defend freedom in Kansas, Harpers Ferry was to be a manifesto as well as a military strike.

Though the failed attack proved to be the war's culminating event, it was conceived as the first of a series of ventures. Asked by authorities after the raid whether he expect a "general uprising of the slaves," Brown replied, "No, sir, nor did I wish it. I expected to gather strength from time to time, then I could set them free."[10] Thus the raid was to signal supporters that the war had begun. The initial step had been taken in an invasive campaign to make "slave property" insecure and to terrorize southern whites. As Robert E. Lee grasped immediately, Brown's purpose was to spread "panic and confusion" by "magnifying his numbers"[11] and thereby exaggerating the perceived threat he represented to slavery. Brown was "deeply impressed for years with the Bible story of Gideon," the defector Forbes observed scornfully after the raid, "believing that he with a handful of men could strike down slavery."[12] From the first, Harpers Ferry was to be a Jeremiad, a warning to slaveholders of God's impending vengeance.

The war had always been a personal project. If Brown had loyal followers, he had few close confidants and no independent advisors. In his imagination the war long subsisted as shifting configurations of people, plans, and resources, but throughout its several incarnations Brown saw himself as its originator and "commander-in-chief." He was guided exclusively by his own shifting vision. That was partly why Forbes quit Brown's army and why Brown's friend Douglass could not dissuade him from attacking Harpers Ferry. Because the war was Brown's creation, he felt obligated to justify his actions to his hostages at Harpers Ferry. He was no "incendiary or ruffian," he told them, but an abolitionist doing "God's work." "He explained his purposes to them," a reporter noted, "and whilst he had the workmen in confinement made an abolition speech to them."[13] Recognizing his eagerness to be understood, Brown's hostages played upon his pride, and he permitted himself to trust them to witness to the "purity" of his intentions. If he claimed the war as his own, at Harpers Ferry the war claimed him as well.

Its hold on him failed to end with the fighting. Once captured, he spoke and wrote much of himself, defending his actions while fashioning a new public persona. He was unwilling to appease his captors or to repudiate his cause. But he may briefly have hoped to avoid the gallows. When Brown and his surviving men were moved under heavy guard to Charlestown, he immediately wrote to Boston asking his friend Judge Thomas Russell or "some good man" to serve as counsel for himself and the "young men prisoners" with him. "Do not send an ultra abolitionist," he advised, perhaps fearing to alienate the court or create unnecessary distraction.[14] Four days later, just a week after the raid, he and the other prisoners were indicted and ordered to trial. Manacled at this preliminary hearing to Edwin Coppoc and flanked by Shields Green and the wounded Aaron Stevens, Brown asked not that his life be spared; he insisted instead that he was "ready for [his] fate." But he demanded to be "excused" from a "mockery of a trial" and from being "foolishly insulted only as cowardly barbarians insult those who fall into their power." Given a "fair trial," he declared, he would present "mitigating circumstances … in our favor."[15]

The judge obligingly permitted Brown to dismiss his court-appointed attorneys, name his own counsel, call and question witnesses himself, and make brief speeches, thus providing a national forum through the newspapers during his six-day trial. At the trial, Brown focused his defense on his efforts during the raid to protect his hostages and minimize killing. He used the platform of the trial to reinvent his war and define himself to a widening northern public. Proclaiming his innocence of hostile intent, he claimed the moral high ground in a new salient of the war against slavery.

II

The full extent of the cognitive dissonance Brown experienced during the raid reappeared, largely unnoticed, during his trial. It has not hitherto been explored. Not only had Brown been unable or unwilling to jeopardize his hostages to win safe passage over the Potomac bridge, but his capture obscured the matter of what he would have done with his liberated slaves had he and they escaped. Would he have "run them off" to the free states and Canada, as Frederick Douglass supposed? Established a military base or maroon in the Allegheny Mountains to the south of the Ferry, as Richard Realf testified? Might he have retreated across the Potomac Bridge to rendezvous with other deserting slaves in Maryland? Or did he intend to stand his ground at Harpers Ferry expecting hundreds, perhaps "thousands" of self-liberated slaves and whites to answer his summons, as he boasted after the raid? Was his hope to "incite" slaves "to join in insurrection," as Lee concluded,[16] or to enlist in a guerrilla movement?

The historical confusion about Brown's strategy stems in part from contradictory accounts of his plan he gave after his capture. In fact, he pictured two quite different wars, implicitly projecting different images of himself as well. In the two weeks between his capture and sentencing, Brown the insurrectionist and terroriser gradually became Brown the Christian martyr. And in the month he awaited the hangman, Brown became a self-anointed apostle of abolitionist gospel. The credibility of this new, benign persona turned for many Americans on what he had intended to do with the slaves he might have freed.

FIGURE 13.1. Virginia Governor Henry Wise and other officials question Brown and Aaron Stevens, both wounded, as correspondents record the event in shorthand.

CREDIT: West Virginia State Archives, Boyd B. Stutler Collection.

Brown's first version of his war materialized in the interview with Governor Henry Wise, attorney Andrew Hunter, and others, just hours after his capture on October 18. During the interview Brown seized the moment to urge Wise to read his Provisional Constitution. Asked where he would have put the Constitution into effect, Brown responded, according to Hunter, "Here, in Virginia, where I commenced operations." Also according to Hunter, Brown denied that he planned to "stampede slaves off." Instead, he "intended to put arms into their hands to defend themselves against their masters, and to maintain their position in Virginia and the South." Brown at this point expected that slaves and "non-slaveholding whites would flock to his standard as soon as he got a footing there, at Harper's Ferry; and as his strength increased," Hunter continued. Brown "would gradually enlarge the area under his control," providing a "refuge" for slaves and a "rendezvous for all whites disposed to aid him, until he overrun [sic] the whole South."[17] Rather than "stampeding" slaves northward, Brown told a reporter earlier that day, he expected to adopt "a general southwest course through Virginia, varying as circumstances dictated or required."[18]

This audacious scenario was crucial evidence for Brown's captors. It explained to them why Brown struck at the federal arsenal and why he stayed in town so long. Since the militia would have fought stubbornly alongside slaveholders to recover stolen slaves and retake the town, Brown's plan to arm bondsmen and keep them in Virginia could only have meant bloodshed. To his captors, this amounted to a confession of insurrection. Thus, Hunter added the charge of conspiring to instigate a slave insurrection to the indictment against Brown. Together with the charges of murder and treason, this made three capital counts on which Brown could be convicted.[19] As Hunter put it in his summation at the trial, Brown had tried to "take possession of the Commonwealth and make it another Hayti."[20]

But the ambiguity of Brown's stance toward killing became evident during the trial. Just twelve days after Brown's interview with Wise and Hunter, Jefferson County Circuit Judge Richard Parker prepared to pronounce sentence. Asked if he had anything to say, Brown responded with a riveting speech in which he told a quite different story of his plan. He now professed he had intended only to duplicate his Missouri raid, which he misleadingly claimed he had accomplished "without the snapping of a gun on either side," and after which he had transported his rescued blacks out of the country to Canada. "I designed to have done the same thing again on a larger scale. That was all I intended to do," Brown declared. "I never did intend murder or treason, or the destruction of property, or to excite or incite the slaves to rebellion, or to make insurrection."[21]

This assertion was so palpably at odds with the information on which he had been convicted, including Brown's own previous statement, that Governor Wise went to see Brown in his Charlestown prison cell to seek clarification. Brown later told Hunter that he had tried to correct the "seeming confliction" between what he told Wise after the raid and his remarks in court. He sought to reassure Hunter that his original statement was correct, and asked Hunter to publish his explanation to "vindicate his memory." Hunter later provided Brown's handwritten note to the Mason Committee; in it Brown insisted he had "given Governor Wise a *full and particular* account" of his intentions "respecting the slaves we took *about the Ferry*." But he was completely surprised when asked in court if he had anything to say, because he expected to receive his sentence later with the other prisoners.

In the hurry of the moment [Brown explained] I forgot much that I had before *intended to say*, and did *not* consider the full bearing of what *I then said*. I intended to convey this idea, that it was my object to place the slaves in a condition to defend their liberties, if they would, *without any bloodshed, but not* that I intended *to run them out of the slave States*.... I do not suppose that a man in *my then circumstances* should be *superhuman* in respect to the *exact purport* of every word he might utter. What I said to Governor Wise was spoken with all the deliberation I was master of, *and was intended for truth*; and what I said in court was *equally intended for truth*, but required a more full explanation *than I then gave*.[22]

Wise was satisfied. He had committed himself publicly and politically to Brown's truthfulness about his plans. On returning from Harpers Ferry to Richmond before the trial, Wise had declared that Brown "is a man of clear head, of courage, fortitude and simple ingenuousness. He is cool, collected and indomitable." Brown "inspired me with great trust in his integrity, as a man of truth," Wise continued. "He is a fanatic, vain and garrulous, but firm, and truthful, and intelligent."[23]

That endorsement of Brown's "simple ingenuousness" created a curious, unacknowledged collaboration between Wise and his prisoner. Though Wise was determined to hang Brown, he needed a formidable antagonist to account for Virginia's humiliation in failing promptly to crush Brown's undermanned "insurrection" and to advance his own prospects in his upcoming bid for the presidency.[24] Wise's praise helped Brown save face and imagine that he might yet reclaim his "lost capital."

But in fact Brown's two accounts were contradictory, just as Wise and Hunter believed. The Missouri raid had been a classic slave rescue at the conclusion of which Brown's party quickly fled the scene on horseback. At Harpers Ferry Brown brought sufficient weapons to arm a battalion of slaves and, until he was trapped, seemed bent on holding the armory and remaining for the time being at Harpers Ferry. Brown's efforts to reconcile the two versions were puzzling at best. If he had planned to keep freed slaves at or near Harpers Ferry, how could he have avoided bloodshed as he professed to wish?

His eloquent statement to the court was clearly rehearsed. In it, he denied all three charges against him and adopted the posture of an innocent servant of the Almighty. "I see a book kissed, which I suppose to be the Bible," he said rhetorically,

which teaches me that all things whatsoever I would that men should do to me, I should do even so to them. It teaches me further to remember them that are in bonds as bound with them. I endeavored to act up to that instruction. I believe that to have interfered as I have done, as I have always freely admitted I have done in behalf of His despised poor, is no wrong, but right. Now, if it is deemed necessary that I should forfeit my life for the furtherance of the ends of justice, and mingle my blood further with the blood of my children and with the blood of millions in this slave country whose rights are disregarded by wicked, cruel, and unjust enactments, I say let it be done.

Brown felt "no consciousness of guilt," he said, adding: "I never had any design against the liberty of any person, nor any disposition to commit treason or commit any person to rebel or make any general insurrection. I never encouraged any man to do so, but always discouraged any idea of that kind."[25]

Brown's speech won widespread approval in the North and the admiration of subsequent generations of idealists and reformers beguiled by his courage, "manliness," and high-mindedness.[26] By accepting his sentence – "I say let it be done" – Brown inspired the abolitionist conviction that he "gave his life" for the slave. In capturing Harpers Ferry, Brown had indeed put his life at risk. If his raid was ill-conceived, admirers said, Brown had sacrificed even his own sons in the cause of "God's despised poor." Indeed, he had been trapped by his humanity toward his hostages, further evidence, as a black newspaper enthused, of the "moral grandeur of the man."[27]

But if at sentencing Brown pictured himself as a martyr who had sought to avoid shedding blood, why had he told Wise and Hunter a different story of his intentions? And why then did he repudiate his courtroom stance in trying to persuade Wise and Hunter that he had not changed his story?

Concerning the first of these question, it seems evident that Brown was speaking to different audiences when he gave the conflicting versions of his plan. Immediately after Harpers Ferry, Brown was responding to interrogators, though he made brief speeches to the correspondents in the room whenever opportunity arose. Even after his capture, he may still have hoped to terrorize the South. Or he may simply have hoped not to be dismissed as a deluded fanatic and a "dunce." In effect, he was auditioning as Osawatomie Brown.

Clearly, he could not terrify Virginians if he told them he planned merely to run off slaves to the North or that he had at his command only the handful of men killed or taken at the Ferry. To avow a "stampede" as his aim would have minimized his impact. Clearly, too, he could not betray his hope to provoke southerners into taking his bait to raise the level of the slavery controversy by demanding a national slave code or renewing talk of secession. To be seen as formidable, Brown had to claim that he had a credible plan to broaden his attack and to make use of the 200 rifles, 200 revolvers, and 950 pikes he had assembled. Thus he blustered about imaginary "thousands" he expected to rally to his side.

That version of the war, however, was soon a casualty of new circumstances. In the courtroom two weeks later Brown hoped to speak past his immediate listeners to sympathetic northerners. In citing the Golden Rule and embracing his fate in behalf of God's "despised poor," he touched values widely shared by genteel Northerners. His effort to picture himself as the protector of his hostages and as the victim of needless violence won sympathy in the North if not from his jury. Ralph Waldo Emerson famously announced that Brown's martyrdom would make "the gallows glorious like the cross." Theodore Parker suggested that "the blessing of those that are ready to perish will fall on him.... The road to heaven is as short from the gallows as from the throne."[28] Even cautious Republicans like Lincoln, who believed Brown "insane" and disapproved sternly of his attack, nevertheless conceded Brown's "great courage [and] rare unselfishness."[29] William Lloyd Garrison, the voice of nonresistant abolitionism, concluded that Brown "had no other motive for his conduct at Harper's Ferry, except to break the chains of the oppressed, by the shedding of the least possible amount of human blood..., and ... if he shall be put to death, he will not die ignobly, but as a martyr to his sympathy for a suffering race, and in defence of the sacred and inalienable rights of man."[30]

Of course Brown's speech won few admirers in the white South. He had come, Jefferson Davis declared, "to incite slaves to murder helpless women and children."[31] Edmund Ruffin, the fiery Virginia secessionist, who initially admired Brown's daring and "animal courage," came to see Brown's "whole course" as "one of deception & falsehood except when it best served his purpose to be 'ingenuous.'" Ruffin blamed Wise for furnishing northern abolitionists a "false eulogy" that enabled them to make Brown a martyr. Brown had been "'humane to his prisoners,' taken at Harper's Ferry," Ruffin wrote in his diary, only "because ... his own chances for escape, & for life, depended on preserving them." The sixty-five-year-old Ruffin borrowed a uniform overcoat and arms from Virginia Military Institute to witness Brown's execution in person.[32]

Virginians were profoundly annoyed at Brown's inability to see, as Forbes had warned, that his "invasion" might have flashed out of control and brought unconstrained bloodshed. To them Brown had stirred an insurrection of potentially immense dimensions. To that extent, Brown succeeded in his goal of appearing as a formidable threat. For days, the "outbreak" was seen in the surrounding area as only a "first act," and suspected Brown associates were arrested as far away as Texas. On October 22, a correspondent reported to the New York *Herald*, "The feeling that the attack upon Harper's Ferry was the first of a widespread conspiracy is gaining ground here."[33] Just days before Brown was hanged, Ruffin still feared that 2000 "desperadoes" sworn to obey Brown would attempt his rescue.[34]

But as the days went by, Brown's efforts to hype his failed attack appeared more and more to be hot air. His extravagant claims of having reserves soon came to be dismissed as braggadocio born of humiliation. By the end of his trial on November 2, the modest limits of his actual resources to accomplish so grandiose a scheme were widely known. Rumors that Brown had allies throughout the South had thus far proved false. No phantom abolitionist armies appeared. Panic abated. Virginians spoke less of what they had at first called an "invasion," and Northern newspapers ridiculed Governor Wise's excessive military buildup in response to a mere "emeute." Virginia authorities assured a shaken public that no slaves had heeded Brown's call.

Thus by November 2 Brown confronted a situation quite different from the one he found when captured. Facing the gallows in thirty days, he adopted a new tack. Now the "cause of God and humanity" needed a martyr and Brown determined to fill the need by adopting a posture of Christian resignation and "joyfully" embracing the gallows. Two weeks after acknowledging his hope of inspiring a slave uprising, Brown was refashioning himself as a victim. He was "quite cheerful," he wrote Mary on November 8, "having (as I trust) 'the peace of God which passeth all understanding to rule in my heart;' & the testimony (in some degree) of a good conscience, that I have not lived altogether in vain."[35] In his courtroom speech and a score of letters written thereafter from Charlestown jail he renounced the role of a terroriser and revolutionary in favor of that of a would-be slave rescuer, an inspired Jeremiah to the South and the nation, a martyr to the cause of the "crushed millions who 'have no comforters.'"[36]

Why this about-face? Essentially, Brown knew he could not forfeit Wise's confidence in his truthfulness without jeopardizing his new stance as a religiously inspired crusader.[37] Thus he tried to reconcile his courtroom claim of intending only to rescue slaves to take North with his initial story that he planned to overrun the South with an army of slaves and abolitionists. Writers hostile to Brown have seen his claim that he expected little bloodshed at Harpers Ferry as a blatant lie. Perhaps it was. But, as his rules of engagement implied, Brown had persuaded himself that he felt no malice toward Virginians. Writing to a cousin in late November, he denied as "utterly false" a report that he told Wise he came to avenge "the wrongs of either myself or my family," insisting instead that he had "never yet harbored such a feeling." Wise, he said, "ought to correct that impression" as well as the "impression" that he had intended to spark a "general insurrection."[38] If Wise had indeed fostered this report, he had evidently heard what he wanted to hear in Brown's "clarification." Their collaboration had its limits.

Clearly, Brown's courtroom speech was intended to win Northern approval of his conduct and shift the burden of the killing during the raid to the slave regime. For some it worked. It was slavery and not Old Osawatomie Brown that was barbaric, crowed abolitionists.[39] But something deeper and more personal was also at work in Brown's tortured logic.

III

Seizing the moral high ground after the raid demanded all the courage and discipline Brown could muster. For all his public bluster, privately he was desperately trying to come to terms with his "disaster" – his defeat, the loss of his "two noble boys; & *other friends*,"[40] and his approaching execution. Though the wounds he sustained in the raid were healing, he struggled to keep calm and "firm" in the face of "afflictions." It took him nearly four days to finish his first letter to Mary since the raid. In it he explained tersely how and when their sons and the others had died and noted the "sabre cuts in my head" and, as he supposed, "Bayonet stabs in my body." Despite the "terrible calamities" he had experienced, he assured Mary that a kind jailor was protecting him "whilst thousands are thirsting for my blood." He commended his wife and "Children every one" to "him 'whose mercy endureth forever': to the God of my *fathers* .... whom I serve.'" He asked his eldest daughter, Ruth, to copy and send his letter to "your sorrow stricken brothers" to "comfort them." In a postscript he reported receiving his sentence "to be hanged" on December 2. "Do not grieve on my account," he added. "I am still quite cheerful."[41]

The depth of his actual distress is suggested by his response the following day to news that his wife was en route to see him. By November 3 Thomas Wentworth Higginson had already escorted Mary from North Elba to Boston. Higginson was intent on sending her to Brown in the hope that she could persuade Brown to cooperate with a rescue attempt despite George Hoyt's warnings from Charlestown that any such attempt would be madness. Unaware of Higginson's motive in the matter, Brown opposed Mary's coming. "If my wife were to come here just now it would *only tend* to distract *her mind, Tenfold*; & would *only add* to my affliction," he wrote Higginson on November 4. "Her presence *here* will deepen my afflictions a thousand fold. I beg of her to be *calm & submissive*; & not to go *wild* on my account. I lack *for nothing* & was feeling quite cheerful before I learned she talked of *coming on. I ask her to compose her mind* & to remain quiet till the last of *this month*; out of pity to me."[42] A week later Hoyt wrote a blunt warning to Mary to stay away from Charlestown. "Mr. Brown fears your presence will undo the firm composure of his mind," Hoyt wrote, "& so agitate him as to unman & unfit him for the last great Sacrifice."[43]

These confidential messages contrast with the carefully crafted letters Brown began to send to Mary when she was staying at the homes of abolitionist friends. On November 8 Brown set out more selfless reasons for wishing Mary not to come to Charlestown. She should not waste her "scanty means" on travel, he began. More importantly, their meeting under such "dreadful circumstances would only add to our distress." In Charlestown, Mary would be a "gazing stock ... in all sorts of papers, throughout the whole country," and be compelled to endure a "dreadful sacrifice of feeling." The excitement attendant on the recent visits of "one or two female friends" had been "very annoying."[44]

In subsequent letters, Brown gradually relented. He would be "most glad" to see Mary, he wrote on the 16th. But as she would be "insulted on the road; & perhaps *while here*," and her "wretchedness made complete," he added, "I *shrink* from it. [Her] composure; & fortitude of mind may be *quite equal to it all*, but I am in *dreadful doubt*; of it." She might visit him at the end of the month, he finally conceded, but he would "say *no more* on this *most painful* subject." His mind was "very tranquil, I may say *joyous*," he assured Mary; "I continue to receive every kind attention that I have any possible need of."[45] He explained to Rebecca Spring, with whom Mary stayed briefly in Philadelphia, that Mary failed to realize he left "many things" unsaid in his letters because his mail was examined by the sheriff or state's attorney. Moreover, the jailer sat in on all his visits, which would sharply limit what he and Mary could say to each other if she came.[46]

By November 26, however, Brown had overcome these concerns. "If you *now feel* that you are *equal* to the undertaking," he wrote Mary, "do *exactly as you feel disposed to do* about coming to see me before I suffer. *I am entirely willing*."[47] He had found the courage and the moment to welcome Mary for a final, publicized reunion.[48]

In these last letters Brown said nothing of his early fears of being "unmanned." His effort to maintain his "composure" during his imprisonment was tested further by news that Lydia Maria Child, a celebrated writer and nonresistant abolitionist whom he had never met, had asked Governor Wise for permission to visit Brown in order to "dress his wounds" and "speak soothingly to him." Brown was annoyed at the idea. Hoyt made clear to his Boston sponsors privately that Brown did not want such attention. "Do not allow Mrs. Child to visit B.," he wrote. "... He *don't* want *women* there to unman his heroic determination to maintain a firm and consistent composure. Keep Mrs. Child *away at all hazards. Brown* and *associates* will certainly be lynched, if she goes there."[49] Brown himself wrote to Child on November 4 urging her politely to stay away. She could better show her compassion for him, he suggested, by sending money to his wife and children and by encouraging her friends to do likewise.[50]

Though Brown insisted in his prison letters that he was "cheerful," even "happy" with the "near prospect of the gallows," regrets about his failings as a father and a Christian plagued him. On the eve of Harpers Ferry, Brown had learned that his fifteen-year-old daughter Annie, like his sons before her, had rejected what she understood her father to mean by Christianity. Brown upheld the dissenting covenant faith that linked him to six generations of patriarchal forbears. Owen Brown, a passionate adherent of the New Divinity, had carried that faith along with his family to Ohio when John was a child. In part because of his own wanderings, John had never won the kind of uncontested sway over his children that Owen had. Influenced by a corroding theological liberalism, all Brown's children save Ruth had repudiated belief in a God who predestined man to sin and suffering in this life. That had been a painful blow to Brown, who never ceased trying to win them back to his God. But he had failed. Now, he made repeated appeals to them to return to the "God of our fathers."

Two weeks before the raid, he had admonished Anne, who had just left him after keeping house for his men at the Kennedy farm, "I want you first of all to become; a *sincere, humble, earnest & co[n]sistent, Christian*: & then to acquire good *& efficient business habits*."[51] But although she believed in God and an afterlife, Annie would still not avow herself a Christian just three days before her father's execution: "I have *several reasons* (which are satisfactory to me) for not being what is commonly termed a *Christian*," she wrote to Thomas

Wentworth Higginson, "one of which is, if there is another existence after this, (and I believe there is,) I believe that *all* will finally be forgiven and *saved*. The notion of *eternal damnation* is contrary to all my ideas of justice, mercy, or benevolence. I choose to suffer individually for all the evil deeds done in this world by *me*."[52]

Facing his imminent "public murder," Brown could plead with his children with renewed moral authority. "Nothing" could be more gratifying to him than to know that "you are all 'fully persuaded to be Christians,'" he wrote his daughters in North Elba.[53] To his sons in Ohio, he appealed to the memory of their "own dear mother" whose "calm peace" while awaiting "her last change" now seemed to "fill my mind by day and by night." Nothing would please him more than to know that they were "fully persuaded to be Christians."[54]

In his last letter to all his children he again pressed upon them the "divine inspiration" of the Bible and the necessity for a selfless religious piety.[55] "Circumstances like my own...convince me beyound [sic] *all doubt*; of our great need: of something more to rest our hopes on: than merely our own vague theories framed up, while our *prejudices* are excited; or our *Vanity* worked up to its highest pitch," he admonished. In images reminiscent of Melville, Brown wrote: "Oh do not trust your eternal all uppon the boisterous Ocean, without *even* a *Helm*: or *Compass* to *aid* you in steering. I do *not ask any* of you; to throw *away your reason*: I only *ask* you, to make a candid, & sober *use of your reason*." He begged his "younger children" in North Elba to "listen to this last poor admonition" to "give your whole hearts to God .... Do not be vain; and thoughtless: but *sober minded*." The "purity" of its moral teachings and its promise of eternal life convinced Brown of the Bible's truthfulness. "Be determined to know by experience *as soon as may be*: whether [that] bible instruction is of *Divine origin* or not; *which says; 'Owe no man anything but to love one another.'*"[56] In his last will he left each of his children a copy of the Bible "to be carefully preserved in remembrance of me."

These last pleas to his children underscored Brown's image as a man of faith and kept his larger message to the nation on point. "I charge you all never (in your trials) to forget the grief of 'the poor that cry; & of those that have none to help them,'" he wrote on November 8.[57] His death would "seal my testimony (for God, & humanity) with my blood." It would "do vastly more to advance the cause (I have earnestly endeavored to promote) than all I have done *in my life*." Brown begged all of his children "meekly & quietly to submit to this; not feeling yourselves to be in the least *degraded* on that account.... Jesus of Nazareth," he reminded them, "suffered a most excruciating death on the cross as a fellon;...Think also of the prophets & apostles, & Christians of former days; who went through greater tribulations than you & I; & be reconciled." Searching for historical parallels, in his final letter, he recalled that when facing death the sixteenth-century Protestant martyr John Rogers had written to his children, "'Abhor that arrant whore of Rome.'" Now, in the same circumstance, Brown urged his own children "to abhor with *undiing hatred*, also: that 'sum of all villainies;' Slavery."[58]

The faith he now urged upon his family called likewise for renunciation of worldliness. "I beseech you all," he wrote, "to live in habitual contentment with verry [sic] *moderate* circumstances; & gains, of *worldly store*: & most earnestly to teach this: to your *children; & Childrens, Children*; by *example: as well*; as precept."[59] When he learned that Mrs. Spring and others were taking an interest in the education of his youngest daughters, he reminded Mary that "I have always expressed a decided preference for a very *plain but perfectly practical education* for both *Sons & Daughters*." He wanted them to have enough schooling to be "*useful though poor*; & to meet the *stern realities* of life with a good grace."[60] Writing directly to Mrs. Spring, Brown said he wanted his three youngest daughters to grow up as "strong, intelligent, expert, industrious, Christian housekeepers" and "matter-of-fact women" after the precepts in Frankin's "'Poor Richard.'"[61]

This had hardly been his aim years before in sending John, Jr., and Ruth to a fashionable academy. But in thus finding sanctions for living "plainly," he evinced his own triumph over the lure of wealth and social rank about which he had long felt such deep ambivalence. Facing death, he found a rationale for rejecting not only worldliness but worldly failure. He had been "remarkably prosperous," he wrote a cousin, "having *early learned* to regard the welfare & prosperity of others as *my own*." He could therefore "recount unnumbered *& unmerited* blessings among which would be some very severe afflictions; & those the most needed blessings of all." His victory over the fear of death was, however, fragile and emotionally costly: "Now when I think how easily I might be *left to spoil* all I have done, or suffered in the cause of freedom: I hardly dare risk another voyage; if I even had the opportunity."[62]

In rehearsing the lessons of his faith, Brown affirmed the authority of his own father as well as that of the God of his "fathers." His admonitions to his family echoed those Owen had often made to him. In espousing martyrdom, John Brown aspired to a station higher than any he might have coveted in the struggle for wealth or worldly success. His crusade against slavery linked him with the noblest aspirations and achievements of his forbears.

IV

The war against slavery had always been an outward expression of Brown's search for God's purpose in his life. His sons' appeal for help against the Slave Power in Kansas had come to him as a religious call, and he had hoped "to answer the end of [his] being" in the struggle for Kansas.[63] He found a widely admired avocation in leading a band of free-state fighters in Bleeding Kansas and, as trial Judge Richard Parker discerned, had grown fond of that life. After the Kansas fighting subsided, Brown had decided to carry the war against slavery into "Africa," its southern stronghold, looking at every step in doing so for signs of God's favor. "On the whole, the language of Providence to me would certainly seem to say, 'try on,'" he wrote Mary while raising funds in the East.[64] His successful raid into Missouri confirmed his belief in the providential nature of his mission, as did the appearance of Francis Jackson Meriam with pockets full of gold coin on the eve of the attack at Harpers Ferry.

His capture and the destruction of his force at the Ferry thus necessitated a painful reassessment. They challenged his assurance that he had been doing God's work and deflated his persona as a feared guerrilla chief. If he was not God's "instrument" against slavery, what was God's purpose for him? By ingrained habit, Brown sought answers in bible stories and lessons. He compared his circumstances to those of biblical figures, peppering his letters with references to Samson, Gideon, Peter, and others. Finding apt analogies, he concluded like many evangelicals that his own lifetime might bring the fulfilment of prophecy – not the return of Christ but an event or events that foretold the return, notably the end of slavery.

In the days after his defeat, his waking hours were crowded with unscripted events. But by the eve of his dramatic speech at his sentencing, Brown had found answers to his questing prayers in the New Testament writings attributed to the apostle Paul.[65] While himself in prison in Rome, God's "emissary" Paul had counseled the Ephesians (6:17) to arm themselves with truth and the "breastplate of righteousness" against "rulers of the darkness" and "spiritual wickedness in high places." "Take the helmet of salvation, and the sword of the Spirit, which is the word of God," Paul advised.

Paul's imprisonment and death at the hands of the Romans offered Brown an inspiring model of manly piety and a self-affirming explanation for his worldly failure. God now had a different assignment for him. As Brown searched for meaning in his imminent death, the analogy of his captivity with that of Paul resonated. On November 1, as Brown's trial was drawing to a close, he repeated one of Paul's phrases in a letter to a Quaker sympathizer. "You know that Christ once armed Peter," he wrote. "So also in my case I think he put a sword into my hand, and there continued it so long as he saw best, and then kindly took it from me.... I wish you could know with what cheerfulness I am now wielding the 'sword of the Spirit' on the right hand and on the left."[66] Two weeks later he repeated the metaphor: "Christ, the great captain of liberty; as well as of salvation; ... *saw fit* to take from me a sword of steel after I had carried it for a time, but he has put another in my hand: ('the sword of the Spirit;'), & I pray God to make me a faithful soldier, wherever he may send me."[67]

Warming to the parallels between his and Paul's final days, Brown found a language of renewed strength. "I would readily own my wrong were I in the least convinced of it," he wrote his sons. "I have now been confined over a month, with a good opportunity to look the whole thing as 'fair in the face' as I am capable of doing." He was "grateful that I am counted in the least possible degree worthy to suffer for the truth."[68] "I have no doubt but that our seeming disaster: will ultimately result in the most *glorious success*," Brown wrote in his last letter to his family. "Do not feel ashamed on my account; nor *for one moment* despair of the cause; or grow *weary* of *well doing*. I bless God; I never felt stronger confidence in the certain & near approach of a *bright Morning; & glorious day*."[69]

He could readily acknowledge his "seeming disaster" now that he saw it
as God's will rather the failure of an inept soldier. He could accept his painful losses and embrace his fate knowing God intended them. "I think I feel as
happy as Paul did when he lay in prison," Brown wrote in late November. "He
knew if they killed him it would greatly advance the cause of Christ.... Let
them hang me."[70] God had saved Brown in "battle" through almost "miracu-
lous" deliverances, he wrote cousin Heman Humphrey. The reflection that
God "overrules all things in the best possible manner" had "in some degree
reconciled" Brown to his own "weaknesses and follies even." For years, he
confessed, "I have felt a strong impression that God has given me powers and
faculties, unworthy as I was, that he intended to use" to free the slaves. After
more than a month of reflection he could not find "in my heart. ... any cause
for shame."[71]

Paul's epistles may even have inspired Brown's repeated insistence that
he and his friends and family need feel no shame on his account. Paul had
counseled his "son in the faith" Timothy to "Be not thou therefore ashamed
of the testimony of our Lord, nor of me his prisoner: but be thou partaker of
the afflictions of the gospel according to the power of God" (2 Timothy 1:8).
An explicit renunciation of shame runs through nearly all Brown's last letters.
"I neither feel *mortified, degraded, nor in the least ashamed* of my imprisonment, my chain, or my near prospect *of death by hanging*," he wrote a cousin.[72]
"Nothing could be more grateful to my feelings," he told his "beloved Sisters
Mary A. & Martha," "than to learn, that you do *not* feel *dreadfully mortified & even disgraced* on account of your relation to one who is to *die on the
scaffold*."[73] Brown coupled his religious appeals for his children with denials
that his death sentence carried any stigma. He urged his brother Jeremiah to
tell "my poor boys" in Ohio not to grieve "for one moment on my account,"
suggesting that they would see the time when they would not "blush to own
your relation to Old John Brown."[74]

He admitted he had gone "against the laws of men, it is true; but, 'whether
it be right to obey *God* or *men*, judge ye,'" he wrote to a sympathetic minister.
Citing a familiar passage in Paul's letter to the Hebrews (13:3), Brown asserted
that "Christ told me to remember them that are in bonds, as *bound with them*."
His "conscience," he said, "bade me do that. I tried to do it, but failed. ... I have
no regret on that score."[75]

Brown repeatedly denied feeling guilt or shame. On the contrary, he "felt
astonished that one *so exceedingly vile & unworthy* as *I am*" would be permitted to pay the "'debt of nature' in defence of the *right*: & of Gods *eternal &
immutable truth*." The scaffold held "*no terrors*" for him. He wept not in grief
or sorrow but "for *joy: & gratitude*," and he prayed, "May the God of peace
bring us all again from the dead."[76]

Thus he reconciled himself to death. "The near approach of my great change
is not the occasion of any particular dread," he reassured Mary. "I trust that
God who has sustained me for *so long*; will not *forsake* me when I most
feel my need of *Fatherly aid; & support*." With perhaps a note of doubt, he

added: "Should [God] hide his face; my spirit will droop, & die: *but not otherwise: be assured.*"[77]

In crafting these letters Brown found a purposeful outlet for his energy. "Please let all our friends read all my letters when you can," he begged correspondents, as he had no time to write to every well-wisher.[78] Writing in his cell often far into the night, Brown found an idiom that enabled him to refashion his sense of self. Captivity thus ironically permitted him to resolve much of the cognitive dissonance and emotional anguish that plagued his adult life. The "pulpit" he found in writing letters that he knew would be preserved and published in the newspapers helped save him from despair and maintain his hard-won "composure." He was permitted not just to "suffer affliction," he observed to a "dear stedfast [sic] friend" and former teacher, but to preach "righteousness in the great congregation."[79] Brown even tried to "improve" proslavery visitors to his cell, speaking to them "faithfully, plainly, and kindly." He had hoped to be a minister himself," he wrote a clergyman, "but God had another work for me to do."[80]

In thus reaching out to friends and admirers, Brown found a kind of earthly salvation. Reasoning through familiar biblical parables, he also found a story of his own, one that explained his present situation. God was using him in captivity as He had once used Paul, as an "emissary" to the faithful. His death would advance God's work of ending slavery more than his life before had ever done. Borrowing again from Paul (2nd Timothy 4:7), he concluded: "'I have fought the good fight,' and have, as I trust, 'finished my course.'"[81]

V

In his letters, to be sure, Brown may have sought absolution – to distance himself morally from his failure at Harpers Ferry and the killings at Pottawatomie, his responsibility for which was then little known. He ascribed his sins to God-appointed duties in the service of all he held sacred. If John Brown felt the terrors that his father had felt in his last illness, he gave no hint of it. He remained cheerful before prisoners, jailors, and visitors alike. Holding that "life is intended as a season of training, chastisement, temptation, affliction, and trial" from which only the "righteous" survive, he believed, the human soul was at risk.[82] But this bleak universe was redeemed by a just God. If, like Melville, Brown saw man as a castaway on perilous seas, a compass of faith, not a Tahiti of "peace and joy," promised a respite from spiritual desolation. In the ritual affirmations of faith with which he filled his prison letters, John Brown clung to that compass.

In a sense, then, Brown remained a pilgrim obsessed with destiny. The imminent prospect of meeting his God invited him to plead his cause to the world; it also ripened and mellowed his message. His own worldly ambitions at last suppressed, he had no other avowed goals than to face death as a martyr and win back his children and his countrymen to the faith. Gone was all stridency. Not once during his imprisonment did he exhibit the "furious" agitation once said to manifest his "monomania." Encircled by intensely curious audiences in court and in jail, Brown spoke with deliberation and calm.[83] An incredulous public now avidly awaited and scrutinized his every word. No longer did he have to demand respect or attention or defend his dubious credibility as a warrior. His speeches in court and his carefully crafted letters had won him widespread admiration in the North. Devoting his last days to his correspondence and interviews, he never wavered from his newfound duty as "emissary" of the "God of the oppressed." Collectively, his letters constitute a kind of theological defense of his cause and his sanity. As he awaited the hangman, his compass – the religious "monomania" that had guided him to Harpers Ferry – now charted a campaign for martyrdom that, paradoxically, discredited all allegations of his madness.

VI

On the last morning of his life, Brown struck a final blow for the slave. He turned to prophecy. As his jailers marched him to the open wagon that would bear him, seated on his wooden casket, to the scaffold, Brown handed a note to one of his escorts. Its words were menacing: "I John Brown am now quite *certain* that the crimes of this *guilty, land: will* never be purged *away*;

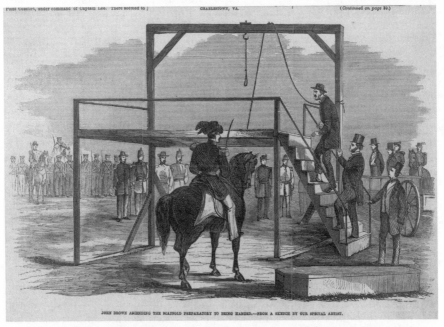

FIGURE 13.2. John Brown's hanging on December 2 inspired demonstrations against the slave regime throughout the North.

CREDIT: Library of Congress.

FIGURE 13.3. View of Harpers Ferry and remnants of the Potomac railroad bridge after the Civil War.

CREDIT: Library of Congress.

but with Blood." This ominous declaration would be long remembered. For knowledgeable observers, it harkened back to the familiar words of Paul: "Almost all things are by the law purged with blood; and without shedding of blood is no remission" (Hebrews 9:22). But Brown's statement was not so much an appeal to biblical authority as a stark warning, a chilling jeremiad. Brown had cautioned the South in the aftermath of his capture that despite his defeat the slavery question would not go away.[84] Now he made that warning a prophecy: slavery, he was saying, would end only with bloodshed.

"I had *as I now think: vainly* flattered myself," his final note continued, "that without *very much* bloodshed; it might be done."[85] That apparent afterthought seemed to admit that he had overreached in his war against slavery, not because God had other plans for him, but because he had failed to see that slavery was too deeply rooted to be defeated by half measures. As if to underscore that insight, Brown refused to have local ministers on the scaffold to pray for him because they supported slavery. Adversaries of every class, he knew at last, had to be acknowledged as enemies. No one could attack slavery, he was now saying, without challenging the polity that upheld it. Brown's prophecy thus resolved any cognitive dissonance he might still have had about the use of violence. Standing motionless and hooded on a scaffold surrounded by 1,500 uniformed soldiers, Brown's silent, "unflinching firmness" as he awaited the fall of the trap door on which he stood spoke louder than the most impassioned screed anyone ever uttered in condemning him.

Four years later, as General William Tecumseh Sherman watched regiments of his army march by him from a hill above Atlanta, flames racing through the city below, a band struck up "John Brown's Body" and the soldiers sang the words lustily. "Never before or since," Sherman remembered years later, "have I heard the chorus of 'Glory, glory, hallelujah!' done with more spirit, or in better harmony of time and place."[86] To be sure, John Brown did not cause the Civil War. But he hastened its coming. His real legacy to his "guilty land" may have been to make war thinkable if subserved to a Godly purpose. For thousands and tens of thousands in the North, John Brown's "martyrdom" sanctified his cause and war itself.

Notes

CHAPTER 1 – AN EXALTED DEFEAT

1. Standard accounts of the raid explain Brown's procrastination by suggesting that he was waiting for slaves from nearby plantations to rally to him as word of the raid passed along the slaves' "grapevine." See, for example, James M. McPherson, *Ordeal By Fire: The Civil War and Reconstruction* (New York: Knopf, 1982), 114–15. Other writers argue that Brown was confused or demented.

2. See, for example, Brown's description of the fighting at Osawatomie. John Brown to "Dear Wife [Mary Ann Brown] & Children every one," Lawrence, 7 Sept. 1856, John Brown Collection, KSHS. For a summary of the Border War, see later in this chapter and in Chapters 3 and 4.

3. But see the discussion in Chapter 11 for evidence of slave support for Brown. On the local slaves' response to the raid, also see Benjamin Quarles, *Allies for Freedom: Blacks and John Brown* (New York: Oxford, 1974), 100–2; Robert E. McGlone, "Forgotten Surrender: John Brown's Raid and the Cult of Martial Virtues," *Civil War History* 40, no. 3 (Sept. 1994): 185–201.

4. On the Armory, see Merritt Roe Smith, *Harpers Ferry Armory and the New Technology: The Challenge of Change* (Ithaca, NY: Cornell University Press, 1977).

5. It was his "painful consideration" for the safety of Brown's hostages that persuaded Lee to "summon the insurgents to surrender" at first light. Lee's Report to Col. S. Cooper, the Adjutant General of the Army, handwritten mss., Oct. 19, 1859, 8 pp., *Letters Received by the Office of the Adjutant General (Main Series), 1822–1860*, MS67, NAR.

6. James Ewell Brown Stuart to Mrs. Elizabeth Stuart [his mother], Jan. 31, 1860, typed copy, Stutler Collection, WVDCH.

7. One of Brown's hostages, John E. P. Daingerfield, who was acting superintendent of the armory at the time of the raid, attributed this reply to Brown. Daingerfield, "John Brown at Harper's Ferry," *The Century Magazine* XXX, no. 2 (June 1885): 267. Daingerfield's memoir, as I shall note elsewhere, is mistaken on several important details of the raid.

8. For a revisionist view of the final moments, see McGlone, "Forgotten Surrender," 185–201.

9. Testimony of Andrew Hunter, January 13, 1860, United States Senate, 36th Congress, 1st Session, *Report of the Select Committee of the Senate appointed to inquire into the late invasion and seizure of the public property at Harper's Ferry*, 2 vols. (Washington, DC, 1860), II: 60. Hereafter cited as *The Mason Committee Report*.

10. Robert A. Ferguson has argued that the trial itself exemplified the "Romance" form. Ferguson, "Story and Transcript in the Trial of John Brown," *Yale Journal of Law & the Humanities* 6, no. 37 (1994): 37–73.

11. James Redpath, "Notes on the Insurrection: Harper's Ferry As a Success," *The Liberator*, 19, no. 44 (Nov. 4, 1859): 1. Reprinted from the *Boston Atlas and Bee*.

12. See C. Vann Woodward, "John Brown's Private War," in *The Burden of Southern History* (rev. ed.; Baton Rouge: Louisiana State University, 1968), Chapter 3; Paul Finkelman, ed., *His Soul Goes Marching On: Responses to John Brown and the Harpers Ferry Raid* (Charlottesville: University Press of Virginia, 1995).

13. Brown did not "bother to work out an escape plan should militia and federal troops come to the town's defense," Oates said, "believing... God would 'guard and shield' him and alone would determine the outcome." Oates credits Brown with recognizing that even if the raid failed, however, it would provoke a violent sectional crisis and possibly civil war. Stephen B. Oates, *To Purge This Land with Blood: A Biography of John Brown* (New York: Harper & Row, 1970), 287–9, 333–4.

14. Louis A. DeCaro, Jr., argues that Brown's determination to destroy slavery was essentially a reflection of his religious training and that we should think of him as a "Protestant saint – a sincere believer, however imperfect." DeCaro, *"Fire from the Midst of You": A Religious Life of John Brown* (New York: New York University Press, 2002), 6–7, Chapter 4, et passim.

15. This injunction appears in five books of the Bible: Matthew 19:19 and 22:39, Mark 12:31 and 33, Romans 13:9, Galatians 5:14, and James 2:8.

16. Evangelicals differed from other Christians chiefly in their greater emphasis on biblical authority in theology and morals, conversion, individualistic engagement in personal and social duties, and devotion to Christ's redeeming work as true religion. See Mark A. Noll, *America's God: From Jonathan Edwards to Abraham Lincoln* (New York: Oxford University Press, 2002), 5. What distinguished the cadre of Garrisonian abolitionists that emerged in the 1830s from missionaries of Brown's earlier generation was that their moral intensity was directed at reforming their own community rather than launching missions to foreign lands. On the religious roots of immediatism, see Lawrence J. Friedman, *Gregarious Saints: Self and Community in American Abolitionism, 1830–1870* (Cambridge: Cambridge University Press, 1982), Chapter 1, esp. 18–21.

17. Admirers sometimes likened Brown to Spartacus or the black revolutionaries Nat Turner and Toussaint L'Ouverture. Horace Greeley, arguably the nation's most influential newspaper editor, compared Brown to Samson and declared that "History would accord an honored niche to Old John Brown." Cited in Glyndon G. Van Deusen, *Horace Greeley: Nineteenth-Century Crusader* (New York: Hill & Wang, 1953), 237–8.

18. James Oliver Horton and Lois E. Horton, *In Hope of Liberty: Culture, Community and Protest Among Northern Free Blacks, 1700–1860* (New York: Oxford, 1997), 232.

19. "No Writ of Error Allowed," Richmond *Enquirer*, Nov. 22, 1859, p. 1.
20. For a recent study reflecting a less sympathetic view of Brown's religious fanaticism, see Edward J. Renehan, *The Secret Six: The True Tale of the Men Who Conspired with John Brown* (New York: Crown Publishers, 1995), 136–9, 143.
21. See, for example, Brown to Rev. McFarland of Wooster, Ohio, Nov. 23, 1859, in Louis Ruchames, *The Making of a Revolutionary* (New York: Grosset & Dunlap, 1969), 153–4. Brown did not know this sympathetic correspondent.
22. See, for example, Brown to Rev. Luther Humphrey, Nov. 19, 1859, Eldridge Collection, HEHL; Brown to Rev. Heman Humphrey, Nov. 25, 1859, in Ruchames, *Making of a Revolutionary*, 157–8. Brown had long used biblical similes and analogies. In 1847, for example, he wrote his children that his deepest worry was that they "sin not ... form no foolish attachments ... and be not a companion of fools." He compared his concern for them to what "we read that Job had about his family," but added, "(Not that I would ever think to compare myself with Job.)" Brown to Miss Ruth Brown, Jan. 5, 1847, copy by Katherine Mayo, Villard Collection, CUL.
23. See James Redpath, *The Public Life of Captain John Brown* (Boston: Thayer and Eldridge, 1860), 112–14. Citing remarks of Franklin B. Sanborn at an 1897 Boston antislavery reunion, Edward J. Renehan, Jr., says that Brown believed God had told him in a "revelation" to incite an insurrection in Virginia. Renehan, *The Secret Six*, 143, 283 n4.
24. Salmon Brown to William E. Connelley, Dec. 2, 1913, Stutler Collection, WVDCH.
25. "Notes for a Sermon," handwritten mss., n.d., Stutler Collection, WVDCH.
26. "Christ the great Captain of liberty ... *saw fit* to take from me a sword of steel after I had carried it for a time," Brown wrote to a friend from Charlestown jail, "but he had put another in my hand: ("the sword of the spirit;") & I pray God to make me a faithful soldier wherever he shall send me. ..." "God's plan, was Infinitely better," Brown now thought, than his own failed plan. John Brown to Rev. H. L. Vaill, Nov. 15, 1859, photocopy, John Brown Miscellaneous Papers, NYPL. Intended for publication, the letter appeared in the New York *Herald* and was widely reprinted. See Ruchames, *The Making of a Revolutionary*, 143–4.
27. See Wendell Phillips Garrison and Francis Jackson Garrison, *William Lloyd Garrison, 1805–1879*, 4 vols. (Boston: Houghton Mifflin, 1894), III: 87–8.
28. The speech, delivered February 18, 1857, was in support of a bill to appropriate $100,000 for relief of free-state men in Kansas. Untitled handwritten mss., 2 pp., n.d., Stutler Collection, WVDCH.
29. "Old Browns [sic] *Farewell*: to the Plymouth Rocks, Bunker Hill, Monuments; Charter Oaks; and Uncle Toms Cabbins [sic]," handwritten mss., Stutler Collection, WVDCH. Brown wrote his "Farewell" for Theodore Parker, kept a copy, and made a second copy for Mrs. George Luther Stearns, who was so moved by the appeal that she persuaded her husband to give Brown a draft for $7,000.
30. John Brown to Franklin B. Sanborn, Feb. 24, 1858, John Brown Jr. Papers, OHS. To Sanborn, Brown likened himself to Samson, who affected a "mighty conquest" that assured his own destruction. Brown seems to have been more sanguine about surviving when motivating his volunteers at the Kennedy farm before the raid, as noted later.
31. On the belief that a conspiracy of Southern planters dominated the Democratic Party and the federal government, see Leonard L. Richards, *The Slave Power: The Free*

North and Southern Domination, 1780–1860 (Baton Rouge: LSU Press, 2000). On the politics of the Kansas trouble, see Mark W. Summers, *The Plundering Generation: Corruption and the Crisis of the Union, 1849–1861* (New York: Oxford University Press, 1987) and Kenneth Stampp, *America in 1857: A Nation on the Brink* (New York: Oxford University Press, 1990). On the Kansas strife, see Nicole Etcheson, *Bleeding Kansas: Contested Liberty in the Civil War Era* (Lawrence: University Press of Kansas, 2004), Paul Wallace Gates, *Fifty Million Acres: Conflicts over Kansas Land Policy, 1854–1900* (Ithaca, NY: Cornell University Press, 1954), James A. Rawley, *Race & Politics: "Bleeding Kansas" and the Coming of the Civil War* (Philadelphia: J. B. Lippincott, 1969). A popular treatment is Thomas Goodrich, *War to the Knife: Bleeding Kansas, 1854–1861* (Mechanicsburg, PA: Stackpole Books, 1998).

32. The quote is from "Sambo's Mistakes," reprinted in Oswald Garrison Villard, *John Brown: A Biography Fifty Years After* (1910; repr., Gloucester, MA: Peter Smith, 1965), Appendix A, 661.

33. Potter, *The Impending Crisis, 1848–1861* (New York: Harper & Row, 1976), 357–62.

34. Brown's widely reprinted speech on sentencing met with acclaim in abolitionist circles. See "Brown's Trial," New-York *Daily Tribune*, Nov. 3, 1859, p. 5.

35. Stephen B. Oates, "John Brown and His Judges: A Critique of the Historical Literature," *Civil War History* 17 (March 1971): 11, 17.

36. Oates, *To Purge This Land with Blood*, 13–14, 37–8, 43, 148, 77, 273, 333–4.

37. Oates, "John Brown and His Judges," 8.

38. In "*Fire from the Midst of You*," Louis A. DeCaro, Jr., reasserts the claim of Brown's early abolitionist biographers that Brown should be considered religiously inspired, but not a "fanatic" (pp. 6–7 et passim).

39. Brown's brother-in-law, Orson Day, and his family remained in Kansas for many years as well. See James Claude Malin, *John Brown and the Legend of Fifty-six* (Philadelphia: American Philosophical Society, 1942), 490.

40. Malin, *John Brown and the Legend of Fifty-six*, 754–5.

41. Oates also stresses cultural determinants of Brown's behavior. "It was not only Brown's angry, measianic mind," Oates declares, "but the racist, slave society in which he lived ... that helped bring John Brown to Harpers Ferry. Oates, *To Purge This Land with Blood*, 333.

42. Daryl J. Bem and Andrea Allen, "On Predicting Some of the People Some of the Time: The Search for Cross-Situational Consistencies in Behavior," *Psychological Review* 81, no. 6 (1974): 508.

43. Douglas T. Kendrick and David O. Stringfield, "Personality Traits and the Eye of the Beholder: Crossing Some Traditional Philosophical Boundaries in the Search for Consistency in All of the People," *Psychological Review* 87, no. 1 (1980): 89–90.

44. For an introduction to the psychology of memory, see Daniel L. Schacter, *Searching for Memory: The Brain, the Mind, and the Past* (New York: Basic Books, 1996). On the inaccuracy of memoirs, see McGlone, "Forgotten Surrender," 185–201.

45. On aphoristic memories, see Robert E. McGlone, "Deciphering Memory: John Adams and the Authorship of the Declaration of Independence," *The Journal of American History*, 85 (Sept. 1998): 411–38.

46. See Vann Woodward, "John Brown's Private War," 56–8.

CHAPTER 2 – THE CONNECTION

1. The literature on Brown's symbolic significance is voluminous. An insightful, comprehensive treatment is the unpublished doctoral dissertation of Vincent Victor Verney, Jr., "John Brown: Cultural Icon in American Mythos," PhD dissertation, State University of New York, Buffalo, 1996. It was directed by Leslie Fiedler. See also Franny Nudelman's intriguing *John Brown's Body: Slavery, Violence, & the Culture of War* (Chapel Hill: University of North Carolina Press, 2004).

2. Statement of John Brown, Dec. 2, 1859, facsimile, John Brown, Jr., Papers, OHS. After four years of "terrible" civil war, Lincoln himself suggested much the same idea in his eloquent Second Inaugural Address. God, he said, may have permitted "this mighty scourge of war" to continue as "the woe" due to both North and South for tolerating the existence of slavery. Quoted in T. Harry Williams, ed., *Selected Writings and Speeches of Abraham Lincoln* (New York: Hendricks House, 1943), 259–61.

3. In a newspaper ad, Hyatt explained that the "*figure* in the picture" was 6 1/2 inches in height and mounted on Bristol board. Purchasers in New York City could "subscribe" to obtain the portrait at the office of the *Tribune*, while those living in the "country" could order the photo by mail. "A Card from Mr. Hyatt," New-York *Weekly Tribune*, Dec. 3, 1859, p. 4.

4. On reactions to Brown's raid and execution, see Paul Finkelman, ed., *His Soul Goes Marching On: Responses to John Brown and the Harpers Ferry Raid* (Charlottesville: University Press of Virginia, 1995).

5. In *The Black Hearts of Men: Radical Abolitionists and the Transformation of Race* (Cambridge, MA: Harvard University Press, 2002), John Stauffer reminds us that, encouraged by his wealthy abolitionist patron, Gerrit Smith, John Brown gave a rousing, unscheduled speech appealing for arms to a convention of the tiny Radical Abolitionist Party meeting in Syracuse in 1855. Smith became the party's presidential candidate, while Brown seems to have had no further involvement with it. On Smith's political odyssey, see Lawrence J. Friedman's indispensable *Gregarious Saints: Self and Community in American Abolitionism, 1830–1870* (Cambridge: Cambridge University Press, 1982), Chapter 4.

6. Quoted in James M. McPherson, *Ordeal by Fire: The Civil War and Reconstruction* (New York: Knopf, 1982), 115.

7. A sample of such eulogies by Wendell Phillips, Ralph Waldo Emerson, and Henry David Thoreau, who are quoted above, is included in Louis Ruchames, ed., *John Brown: The Making of a Revolutionary* (2nd ed.; New York: Grosset & Dunlap, 1969), 266–78. Zoe Trodd and John Stauffer have collected and edited many important documents relating to Brown in *Meteor of War: The John Brown Story* (Maplecrest, NY: Brandywine Press, 2004).

8. Richard O. Boyer, *The Legend of John Brown: A Biography and a History* (New York: Knopf, 1973). Jeffrey Rossbach finds that Brown's closest financial backers, including Gerrit Smith, viewed Brown's war against slavery as something of an experiment to awaken the manhood of the slaves. Despite their admiration for him, he was never one of them. Rossbach, *Ambivalent Conspirators: John Brown, the Secret Six, and a Theory of Slave Violence* (Philadelphia: University of Pennsylvania Press, 1982).

9. See, for example, Bertram Wyatt-Brown's "'A Volcano Beneath a Mountain of Snow': John Brown and the Problem of Interpretation," in Finkelman, *His Soul*

Goes Marching On, Chapter 1, and my own contribution, "John Brown, Henry Wise, and the Politics of Insanity," Chapter 8. As noted in Chapter 1, Stephen B. Oates concludes that the question of Brown's sanity cannot be definitively answered. Oates, *To Purge This Land with Blood: A Biography of John Brown* (New York: Harper & Row, 1970), 329–34.

10. See, for example, McPherson, *Ordeal by Fire* 94, 114–17. As noted in Chapter 1, Allen Nevins was convinced that Brown suffered from "reasoning insanity" or "paranoia." Allan Nevins, *The Emergence of Lincoln*, vol. 2, *Prologue to Civil War, 1859–1861* (New York: Scribner's Sons, 1950), 7–11, 84. Bertram Wyatt-Brown believes Brown was a "depressive." See Wyatt-Brown, in Finkelman, ed, *His Soul Goes Marching On*, 13–16, 21–2, 26–7.

11. A correspondent for the New York *Times* reported during Brown's Virginia trial that Brown was "in a class of one … A fanatic; sui generis," but not so "malignant" in temperament as abolitionists like Wendell Phillips. Quoted in Trodd and Stauffer, *Meteor of War*, 133.

12. See Robert E. McGlone, "Forgotten Surrender: John Brown's Raid and the Cult of Martial Virtues," *Civil War History*, 40 (Sept. 1994), 185–201, esp. 186–8.

13. In a sweeping narrative, David W. Blight brilliantly assesses the dynamics of Americans' collective memory of the Civil War, which for generations privileged sectional reconciliation above racial acceptance. See Blight's *Race and Reunion: The Civil War in American Memory* (Cambridge, MA: Belknap Press, 2001). Even among African Americans, the "culture of reconciliation," Blight recognizes, encouraged forgetting figures like Brown (pp. 315–17). Blight chronicles Frederick Douglass's valiant struggle to preserve the centrality of emancipation to the meaning of the Civil War in *Frederick Douglass' Civil War: Keeping Faith in Jubilee* (Baton Rouge: LSU Press, 1989).

14. The best concise discussion of early Brown biographies is Merrill Peterson's, *John Brown: The Legend Revisited* (Charlottesville: University of Virginia Press, 2002), Chapter 4. See also Stephen B. Oates, "John Brown and His Judges: A Critique of the Historical Literature," *Civil War History*, 17 (March 1971), 5–24. The most comprehensive discussion of Brown scholarship, as noted earlier, is Vincent Victor Verney, Jr., "Cultural Icon in American Mythos."

15. See Robert E. McGlone, "Rescripting a Troubled Past: John Brown's Family and the Harpers Ferry Conspiracy," *Journal of American History*, 75 (March 1989), 1179–1200, esp. 1186–9.

16. John's brother Salmon (1802–33), who is discussed in Chapter 3, was an attorney, briefly the editor of the New Orleans *Bee*, and a Jackson man in politics. Doubtless he did not share his family's hostility toward slavery.

17. Brown first reported directly to his wife the deaths of her sons Watson and Oliver and the Thompson boys, Dauphin and William, together with the status of his own wounds and his trial, on October 31, at the close of his six-day trial. Other letters followed regularly. A convenient collection of his prison letters is included in Louis Ruchames, ed., *A John Brown Reader* (London and New York: Abelard-Schuman, 1959), Part 1, esp. 128–9, 132–3, 137–8, 141–2.

18. John Brown to "Dear Wife; & Children All," Oct. 8, 1859, as quoted in Oswald Garrison Villard, *John Brown: A Biography Fifty Years After* (1910; repr., Gloucester, MA: Peter Smith, 1965), 422.

19. See, for example, Brown's appeals to Lydia Maria Child and E. B. of Rhode Island. "Letters from John Brown," New-York *Weekly Tribune*, Nov. 18, 1859, p. 7.

20. Copies of Brown's wills are included in the Clarence S. Gee Collection, HLHS.
21. The term *connection* had been in popular use since colonial times. It described a variety of step- and blended-family structures and collateral relationships in the eighteenth-century Carolina low country. See: Lori Glover, *All Our Relations: Blood Ties and Emotional Bonds Among the Early South Carolina Gentry* (Urbana: University of Illinois Press, 2001). Sometimes the Browns used the term to include persons or families allied with them or dependent on them.
22. John Brown to Mary Ann Day Brown & children, Feb. 1, 1856, typed copy, Villard Collection, CUL.
23. See, for example, John Brown to "My Dear Wife," Jan. 8, 1847, James William Eldridge Collection, HEHL. Despite comfortable accommodations he enjoyed while a merchant in Springfield, he wrote to Mary in 1850, "It all does not make home. I feel lonely /&/ restless no matter how neat & comfortable my room & bed, nor how richly loaded may be the Table; they have verry [sic] /few/ charms for me, away from home. I can look back to our Log Cabin at the Centre of Richfield with a Supper of Porridge, & Johny [sic] Cake, as to a place of far more interest to me, than the Massasoit [Hotel] in Springfield." JB to "Dear Wife," Nov. 28, 1850, Stutler Collection, WVDCH.
24. John Brown to "Dear Wife, and Children," Dec. 5, 1838, Stutler Collection, WVDCH.
25. For a summary of the collections, see: Boyer, *The Legend of John Brown*, 613–22. The Boyd B. Stutler Collection owned by the West Virginia Department of Culture and History is online as well as on microfilm.
26. John Brown to "My Dear Wife and Children," May 28, 1839, John Brown, Jr., Papers, OHS.
27. John Brown to "My Dear Mary," Oct. 19, 1846, Eldridge Collection, HEHL.
28. John Brown to "Dear Wife & Children every one," Oct. 20, 1857, Logan Collection, CHS.
29. "Do not fail of doing it," he also often urged. See: John Brown to "My Dear Wife and Children," April 3, 1838, Stutler Collection, WVDCH.
30. John Brown to "My Dear Wife & Children," Nov. 26, 1838, Stutler Collection, WVDCH.
31. John Brown to "My Dear Wife and Children," May 28, 1839, John Brown, Jr., Papers, OHS.
32. John Brown to "Dear Wife," Aug. 22, 1850, copy, Sanborn Folder, HU.
33. John Brown to "Dear Ruth [Brown Thompson]," Aug. 10, 1852, Eldridge Collection, HEHL.
34. Owen Brown to John Brown, Dec. 10, 1850, Stutler Collection, WVDCH.
35. I will take a close look at that story in Chapter 3. The chief writers in this tradition were active supporters of the war against slavery and later used interviews with family members as a primary source. Within weeks of Brown's hanging, James Redpath, a self-proclaimed revolutionary who avowed that Brown "did right in invading Virginia," published *The Public Life of Capt. John Brown* (Boston: Thayer & Eldridge, 1860). Brown's chief defender in the late nineteenth century was Franklin B. Sanborn, one of the Secret Six who had helped Brown raise money for his war against slavery. See Sanborn's *The Life and Letters of John Brown, Liberator of Kansas, and Martyr of Virginia* (1885; repr., New York: Negro Universities Press, 1969). One of Brown's absent volunteers, Richard Josiah Hinton, reaffirmed Brown's cause in *John Brown and His Men: With Some Account of the*

Roads They Traveled to Reach Harper's Ferry (New York: Funk and Wagnalls,
1894). Villard's *John Brown Fifty Years After* also relies heavily on reminiscent
sources.

36. This story originated in a memoir of Brown's daughter, Ruth Brown Thompson.
    Ruth Brown Thompson, "Reminiscences of John Brown and Harper's Ferry,"
    unpublished mss., Put-in-Bay, Ohio, Dec. 2, 1882, Rust Collection, HEHL. It
    gained belated support in 1908, when a researcher working for Oswald Garrison
    Villard interviewed the daughter of Brown's adopted brother, Levi Blakesley. Her
    words are quoted earlier. See Villard, *John Brown Fifty Years After*, 18, 592 n19.

37. The questionable claim that a sacred family oath was taken sometime in 1837–9 is
    considered in Robert E. McGlone, "Rescripting a Troubled Past," 1194–8.

38. The primary source for this unflattering assessment of Brown is a statement alleg-
    ing Brown suffered from an "imperial egotism" by a defector Brown had criticized
    for failing to "do his duty," George P. Gill. Statement of George P. Gill, July 7, 1893,
    Richard J. Hinton Papers, KSHS. A newspaper war over Pottawatomie erupted in
    1879. Soon after, a widening controversy about Brown's contribution to Kansas
    history shook loose a roost of accusations against him. In *The Kansas Crusade*, Eli
    Thayer, a founder of the New England Emigrant Aid Society, belittled Brown as
    unwise, untruthful, and an "anarchist." The widow of Territorial Governor Charles
    Robinson, himself once a Brown ally, hired an old Kansan, Hill Peebles Wilson,
    to refute the "fables" of Brown's abolitionist admirers. In *John Brown, Soldier of
    Fortune: A Critique* (1913), Peebles claimed that Brown was motivated by avarice
    and had abandoned the cause of freedom when he disbanded his Liberty Guards
    after only a few days of service to enter upon a "career of crime." The anti-Brown
    tradition culminates in James T. Malin's heavily researched but diffuse *John Brown
    and the Legend of Fifty-Six* (Philadelphia: American Philosophical Society, 1942).
    David M. Potter challenges both Brown's celebrators and debunkers by asking
    "whether a man who sincerely believed himself to be an agent of Jehovah could
    stoop to steal horses, and whether a man with his mind set on running off horses
    could sincerely believe [the Pottawatomie killings] to be Jehovah's work." See
    Potter's classic, *The Impending Crisis, 1848–1861* (New York: Harper & Row,
    1976), 213.

39. Leslie Albert Waardunaar, *John Brown: The Literary Image*, PhD dissertation,
    UCLA, 1974, 462.

40. Robert Penn Warren, *John Brown: The Making of a Martyr* (1993; repr., New
    York: Payson & Clark, 1929), 22, 350. Lusk had allegedly broken with Brown
    before his beloved sister Dianthe married Brown in 1820 and later held Brown
    responsible for her death in childbed. See Milton Lusk's memoir in Franklin B.
    Sanborn, *The Life and Letters of John Brown, Liberator of Kansas, and Martyr of
    Virginia* (1885; repr., New York: Negro University Press, 1969), 33–4, and Villard,
    John Brown Fifty Years After, 19. Yet in 1855 when John was raising money in
    Hudson for the struggle to win Kansas for freedom, Milton came to see him off
    and wish him well. Interview with Benjamin Kent Waite by Katherine Mayo, Dec.
    26, 27, 1908, Villard Collection, CUL.

41. Warren, *Making of a Martyr*, 350.

42. Nevins, *The Emergence of Lincoln*, 2: 5–11, esp. 11, 77. The argument is antici-
    pated by Thomas Dixon's novel, *The Man in Gray* (New York: Appleton, 1921).

43. "For a failed ex-businessman, martyrdom at Harpers Ferry was a form of success in
    the wake of an inglorious string of failures," writes Jeffrey Rossbach in *Ambiguous*

Conspirators, 225. See also McPherson, *Ordeal by Fire*, 94. An influential synthesis indebted to the failure thesis is in Potter, *Impending Crisis*, 357, 361–2, 374, 376. John Stauffer offers a variant of that theme in explaining Brown's conviction that he was God's instrument to destroy slavery. "[H]is material *failures* (rather than his successes) convinced him of his election and his vocation as a prophet," Stauffer claims. "His unquestioning faith in the latter eventually destroyed all sense of humility and led to extreme forms of self-righteousness." Stauffer, *The Black Hearts of Men*, p. 122.

44. Quoted in Williams, *Selected Writings and Speeches of Lincoln*, 83–105, esp. 96, 99. Lincoln was not alone in attributing Brown's attack on slavery to a "brooding temperament." Henry Ward Beecher suggested in a sermon given just after Brown's trial that Brown had been "crazed" by the death of one of his sons in Kansas. See Chapter 8, pp. 2–3.

45. On the "special question of the readiness of slavery to crumble at a blow," Nevins concluded, "his monomania ... or his paranoia, as a modern alienist would define it, rendered him irresponsible." The disease also accounted for Brown's "sense of a God-given mission," Nevins thought. But he conceded that Brown understood that his probable failure would "deepen antislavery sentiment" in the North and bring the struggle over slavery to a "crisis." It would give antislavery men an example of "desperate action." "In so far as he grasped these ideas," Nevins acknowledged, "Brown was making no mad attempt." Nevins, *The Emergence of Lincoln*, 2: 77, 84.

46. John Brown to Frederick Brown (brother), Nov. 21, 1834, cited in Villard, *John Brown Fifty Years After*, 44.

47. John Brown to "Dear Son John," Springfield, Mass., May 15, 1847, The Lee Kohns Memorial Collection, NYPL.

48. John Brown to "Dear Father," Springfield, Mass., Jan. 10, 1849, John Brown Papers, KSHS.

49. In 1847 Brown reportedly confided to Frederick Douglass, a leading black abolitionist and publisher, a sweeping plan to attack slavery in guerrilla raids from Allegheny mountain hideaways throughout the South and then send liberated slaves north on a "Subterranean Pass Way." Douglass's story, first disclosed many years later, is discussed in a later chapter. Frederick Douglass, *The Life and Times of Frederick Douglass, Written By Himself* (1892; repr., London: Collier-Macmillan, 1962), 272–5. The origins of Brown's "war" against slavery are probed in Chapters 4, 5, and 6.

50. Owen Brown to Marian Brown Hand (daughter), n.d. (c. 1850), Gee Collection, HLHS.

51. Reminiscent accounts picture Brown as a stern, if affectionate, sometimes tender patriarch at first exercising an "iron rule" over his large family but softening over the years. See, for example, Stephen B. Oates, *To Purge This Land with Blood*, 17, 22–4. Contemporary evidence suggests that Brown used persuasion more than coercion with his sometimes difficult boys. I will return to this question in Chapter 3.

52. Brown's efforts to develop Franklin by bringing the canal through the village are summarized in Villard, *John Brown Fifty Years After*, 27–8. On the Browns' canal proposal, see Oliver Owen Brown [brother] to H. Wheedon, July 10, 1835, Gee Collection, HLHS. See John Brown to Seth Thompson, Jan. 4, 1836, Gee Collection, HLHS, for the layout of the village as Brown initially envisioned it. Lots and purchasers' names are penciled in. On his relationship with Zena Kent, see "Brown's

and Thompson's Addition to Franklin Village," undated newspaper article, Stutler Collection, WVDHC.

53. See Brown to Seth Thompson, Jan. 4, 1836, Gee Collection, HLHS.

54. Owen Brown to Marian Brown Hand (daughter), n.d. [c. 1850], Gee Collection, HLHS.

55. John Brown to "My Dear Wife and children," June 12, 1839, as quoted in Boyer, *The Legend of John Brown*, 327.

56. John Brown to "My Dear Wife and Children," June 19, 1839, Sanborn Folder, HU. Quoted in Boyer, *The Legend of John Brown*, 327.

57. See Edward J. Balleisen, *Navigating Failure: Bankruptcy and Commercial Society in Antebellum America* (Chapel Hill: University of North Carolina Press, 2001).

58. The Agreement, signed in Federal District Court, Oct. 17, 1842, is reprinted in Louis Ruchames, *Making of a Revolutionary*, 57.

59. John Brown to George Kellogg, Oct. 17, 1842, as quoted in Ruchames, *Making of a Revolutionary*, 57.

60. "Inventory and appraisement of the necessaries ... set off and allowed to John Brown of the Township of Richfield, in the County of Summit, Ohio," Sept. 28, 1842, Stutler Collection, WVDCH.

61. A copy of the agreement is in the Sanborn Folder, HU.

62. John Brown to John Brown, Jr., Jan. 11, 1844, quoted in Villard, *John Brown Fifty Years After*, 34.

63. Manufacturers believed that their "present difficulties" were created by artificially high prices that growers "forced" upon them. Brown argued that "supply and demand" had set wool prices, not a conspiracy of growers. See his letter responding to published articles in the *American Cabinet* and the Boston *Atheneum* on behalf of the manufacturers. Brown to "Messrs. Mason, Dean & Sabine," Sept. 25, 1842, copy, Sanborn Folder, HU.

64. John Brown to Simon Perkins, Dec. 16, 1846, typed copy, Villard Collection, CUL.

65. John Brown to John Brown, Jr., Nov. 4, 1850, as quoted in Villard, *John Brown Fifty Years After*, 64.

66. John Brown, Jr., to "Dear father," Nov. 29, 1850, Sanborn Folder, HU.

67. John Brown to "Dear Sons John, Jason, & Frederick, & Daughters," Dec. 4, 1859, John Brown, Jr., Papers, OHS.

68. John Brown, Jr., to John Brown, Dec. 1, 1850, John Brown, Jr., Papers, OHS.

69. John Brown to "Dear Son John," Dec. 6, 1850, John Brown, Jr., Papers, OHS.

70. John Brown to "Dear Children," Feb. 21, 1853, copy by Katherine Mayo, Villard Collection, CUL.

71. "Mentalite" is a term borrowed from French historians that refers broadly to the attitudes of ordinary people toward everyday life.

72. See Stephen Innes, *Labor in a New Land: Economy and Society in Seventeenth-Century Springfield* (Princeton, NJ: Princeton University Press, 1983).

73. The literature on what social historians call the "microhistory" of early British America is voluminous. See Darrett B. Rutman, "Assessing the Little Communities of Early America," *William and Mary Quarterly*, 3rd Series, 43, no. 2 (April 1986), 165–78.

74. Gregory H. Nobles, *Divisions throughout the Whole: Politics and Society in Hampshire County, Massachusetts, 1740–1775* (New York: Cambridge University Press, 1983), 13.

75. Edwards is quoted in Mark A. Noll, *America's God: From Jonathan Edwards to Abraham Lincoln* (New York: Oxford University Press, 2002), 272–4; and in Sydney E. Ahlstrom, *A Religious History of the American People* (New Haven, CT: Yale University Press, 1972), 309–10.
76. My interpretation follows Noll, *America's God*, 134–5, 274–5, 290–2.
77. See Friedman, *Gregarious Saints*, 48, 64–6.
78. Quoted in Noll, *America's God*, 135.
79. See the discussion in Ahlstrom, *A Religious History*, 408–9.
80. Samuel Hopkins, *A discourse upon the Slave-Trade, and the Slavery of the Africans* (Princeton, 1793), as quoted in Noll, *America's God*, 271.
81. Owen Brown to Sally Marian Brown Hand [daughter], n.d. [c. 1850], Gee Collection, HLHS. The closely written, seven-page mss. on legal size paper cited above is a copy apparently made by one of Owen's granddaughters either from the original or from a copy made by Marian Brown Hand, who faithfully preserved Owen's errors of spelling and grammar because his words seemed "sacred" to her. Hereafter cited as Owen Brown's autobiography.
82. Owen Brown's autobiography, pp. 1–2.
83. Owen Brown's autobiography.
84. John Brown to "Dear Son John," March 12, 1857, Miscellaneous John Brown Manuscripts, YUL.
85. Historian Mark Noll brilliantly traces the convergence of the evangelical movements that swept the new nation with the Revolution's ideology of classical republicanism and Scots commonsense philosophy in *America's God*, previously cited.
86. These values found expression in the partisan discourse of the Whigs, the political party that opposed Andrew Jackson's Democrats. See Lawrence Frederick Kohl, *The Politics of Individualism: Parties and the American Character in the Jacksonian Era* (New York: Oxford University Press, 1989).
87. The Hudson Library and Historical Society in Hudson, Ohio, houses a remarkable Brown family genealogy assembled over many years by Dr. Clarence S. Gee. I am indebted to Thomas Vince, the historian and curator for many years, and his successor, James Caccamo, for their assistance in exploring the Hudson collections and the neighborhoods where the Browns lived.
88. Population Schedules of the Seventh Census of the United States, 1850, National Archives Microfilm Publications, Microcopy No. 432, Roll 732, Summit County, Ohio.
89. I use the Browns' own term, "connection," to describe the family's sense of its parameters because the term is both more inclusive and better suggests internal complexity than such anthropological terms as *kinship group, extended family,* or what historian Philip Greven has called the *modified* extended family – a "kinship group of two or more generations living within a single community in which the children's dependence continues after marriage and they are living under a separate roof." In the Brown connection, the shifting patterns of interdependence muddied the picture. See Philip Greven, Jr., *Four Generations: Population, Land and Family in Colonial Andover, Massachusetts* (Ithaca, NY: Cornell University Press, 1970).
90. Owen Brown's autobiography, undated statement [1850], Grafton, Ohio, Gee Collection, HLHS.
91. Population Schedules of the Seventh Census of the United States, 1850, National Archives Microfilm Publications Microcopy No. 432, Roll 732, Summit County, Ohio.

92. Howard Clark to Clarence S. Gee, Feb. 5, 1962, Gee Collection, HLHS.
93. Historian Philip Greven, Jr., has developed a similar concept, the "modified extended family," which he defines as a kinship group of two or more generations living within a single community in which the dependence of children continues after they have married and are living under a separate roof. See Greven, "Family Structure in Seventeenth-Century Andover, Massachusetts," *William and Mary Quarterly*, 3rd ser., 23 (April 1996), 234–56.
94. Watson Brown and Salmon Brown to "My Dear Grandfather," Springfield, Jan. 23, 1848, Clark-Brown Collection, HLHS.
95. Ruth Brown Thompson to Wealthy Hotchkiss Brown, Feb. 22, 1852, John Brown, Jr., Papers, OHS.
96. Ruth Brown Thompson to Wealthy Hotchkiss Brown, North Elba, Essex County, New York, Feb. 22, 1852, John Brown, Jr., Papers, OHS.
97. Wealthy H. Brown to Ruth & Henry Thompson, Wayne, Ashtabula Co., Ohio, Jan. 4, 1857, Clark-Brown Collection, HLHS.
98. Modern researchers have not been able to substantiate the Browns' connection to Peter of Plymouth. Their indisputable ancestor, one Peter Brown of Windsor (1632-), was probably the son of John Browne, the brother of the Mayflower Peter. No matter. By 1850 several published genealogical treatises confirmed the record of family tombstones in Connecticut and old family Bibles.
99. Heman Humphrey, *Domestic Education* (Amherst, MA: J. S. & C. Adams, 1840).
100. All scholars of the Brown family are indebted to the remarkable family genealogy amassed over many years by Clarence S. Gee and housed at the Hudson Library and Historical Society in Hudson, Ohio. A former curator, Thomas L. Vince, generously made important documents available to me.
101. John Brown to Henry L. Stearns, July 15, 1857, Stutler Collection, WVDCH. This important, oft-cited, ostensibly autobiographical letter will be discussed in Chapter 3. It is worth noting here, however, that it includes a note dated Aug. 8, 1857 to Henry's father, George Luther Stearns, relating news of Brown's ill health and financial difficulties. It was aimed as much at the senior Stearns and his wife as at the boy and was evidently written over a three-week period.
102. John Brown to Luther Humphrey, Nov. 19, 1859, photocopy, Eldridge Collection, HEHL.
103. Ruth Brown Thompson to "Dear Brother & Sister," Akron, Jan. 8, 1853, John Brown, Jr., Papers, OHS.
104. John Brown buried two unborn sons without naming them. A stillborn son, Dianthe's seventh child, was buried with his mother who died shortly after the delivery, August 7, 1832. The twelfth child of John and Mary, born April 26, 1852, contracted measles and "Hooping [sic] Cough" [John Brown to John Brown, Jr., May 14, 1852, John Brown, Jr., Papers, OHS, and died May 17 without receiving a name. Its place of burial was not recorded. See Clarence S. Gee, Brown Family Genealogy, HLHS, pp. 32, 34.
105. Owen Brown's 1850 autobiography, p. 5.
106. "The last thing my grandfather said to me when I left Ohio in March 1855 for Kansas was that he did not want to hear of any of his decentants [sic] ever showing the *white feather* in the coming conflict," Salmon wrote to Franklin B. Sanborn. "I am thankful that I lived up to the hopes of my honored grandfather, a Son of a revolutionary Captin [sic]." Salmon Brown [son] to Franklin B. Sanborn, Nov. 17, 1911, Stutler Collection, WVDCH. See also Salmon Brown to William

E. Connelly, May 28, 1913, typed letter (19 pp.), signed, with handwritten note, pp. 16–17, Stutler Collection, WVDCH; Salmon's interview with Katherine Mayo, Oct. 11–13, 1908, Villard Collection, CUL, and Salmon's statement to K. Mayo, 1908, Villard Collection, CUL.

107. Owen Brown's autobiography, p. 6, Gee Collection, HLHS.

108. John Brown to Owen Brown, quoted in Sanborn, *Life and Letters of John Brown*, 21.

109. Owen Brown [father] to Samuel Lyle Adair "and others," Jan. 26, 1856, Stutler Collection, WVDCH.

110. Jonathan Edwards, for example, actually preached that separation from their parents and misery would be children's lot in death if they did not repent. See David Stannard, *The Puritan Way of Death: A Study of Religion, Culture, and Social Change* (New York: Oxford University Press, 1977), 65–6.

111. The illness may actually have been dysentery or cholera. Grace Goulder [Izant], *Ohio Scenes and Citizens* (Dayton: Landfall Press, 1973), 198.

112. These four children and two infants who died later were all buried in Fairview Cemetery in Richfield, Ohio, although the four may initially have been buried in makeshift coffins on the property Brown was renting. See the Brown Family Genealogy, Gee Collection, HLHS, pp. 34–5.

113. John Brown to "Dear Son" [John, Jr.], Sept. 25, 1843, Ricks Collection, Illinois State Historical Library, Chicago.

114. Although Jason would later repudiate the Calvinist God, he echoed his father at this trying time. "Let us not murmur," he pleaded. "The Judge of all the Earth, has done, and will do right. But let us give glory and honor and power and thanks unto him that Sitteth on the throne forever and ever." Jason Brown to "Dear Brother," Sept. 25, 1843, Ricks Collection, Illinois State Historical Library, Chicago. Jason's brief letter was on the same page as that of his father.

115. Lawrence Lerner, *Angels and Absences: Child Deaths in the Nineteenth Century* (Knoxville, TN: Vanderbilt University Press, 1997).

116. Ruth Brown Thompson, "Reminiscences of John Brown of Kansas and History," unpublished mss., Dec. 2, 1882, Horatio N. Rust Collection, HEHL, 24 pp. The quote is on p. 3.

117. John Brown to "My Dear Afflicted Wife, & Children," Nov. 8, 1946, as quoted in Villard, *John Brown Fifty Years After*, 35–6.

118. John Brown to Mary Brown, March 7, 18[47], Stutler Collection, WVDCH. The letter was misdated.

119. John Brown to Mary Brown, Jan. 7, 1853, copy, Sanborn Folder, HU.

120. John Brown to Ellen Brown, May 13, 1859, Stutler Collection, WVDCH. This child was his second daughter named Ellen, the first having died.

121. John Brown to Mary Brown, Oct. 17, 1845, copy, Sanborn Folder, HU.

122. John Brown to John Brown, Jr., June 25, 1847, John Brown, Jr., Papers, OHS.

123. John Brown to "Dear Daughter Ruth," Sept. 1, 1847, copy, Villard Collection, CUL.

124. John Brown to Ruth Brown, Sept. 16, 1847, Dreer Collection, PHS.

125. In one letter to John, Jr., and Wealthy, Brown refers to getting Jason "clear of the Canaanites that dwell in the land," presumably a disparaging reference to the lifestyle of the Sherbondys. John Brown to John Brown, Jr., June 25, 1847, John Brown, Jr., Papers, OHS.

126. Harvey C. Mansfield and Delba Winthrop, trans., *Democracy in America*, by Alexis de Tocqueville, 2 vols. (Chicago: University of Chicago Press, 2000), II: 558–63.

127. John Brown to "Dear John," Aug. 6, 1852, Gee Collection, HLHS.
128. See Laurel Thatcher Ulrich's fascinating *A Midwife's Tale: The Life of Martha Ballard, Based on Her Diary, 1785–1812* (Vintage ed.; New York: Random House, 1990), 228 et passim.
129. [Salmon Brown] unsigned statement entitled "Memorial Day Address," n.d., Stutler Collection, WVDCH.
130. John Brown to Ruth Brown, Sept. 1, 1847, copy by Katherine Mayo, Villard Collection, CUL.
131. Basing his thinking on the outdated humoral theory of disease, Brown assumed that an excess of bile from Jason's liver accounted for his illness and depression. Brown was sufficiently confident of his prescription to recommend it to his absent son John, Jr.: "Try it if only to gratify me: & report the result to Jason; & to me," John urged. John Brown to John Brown, Jr. [Akron], n.d., 1858, John Brown, Jr., Papers, OHS.
132. Ruth Brown Thompson, "Reminiscences of John Brown and Harper's Ferry," unpublished mss., Put-in-Bay, Ohio, Dec. 2, 1882, Horatio N. Rust Collection, HEHL.
133. John Brown, Jr., to Henry & Ruth Thompson, Troy, New York, Jan. 17, 1852, Villard Collection, CUL.
134. The classic study of the origins of the "separation of spheres" is Nancy F. Cott, *The Bonds of Womanhood: "Woman's Sphere" in New England, 1780–1835* (New Haven, CT: Yale University Press, 1977).
135. John Brown to "Dear Mary," July 28, 1846, copy, Sanborn Folder, HU.
136. John Brown to "Dear Mary," Sept. 3, 1846, copy, Sanborn Folder, HU.
137. John Brown to "My Dear Mary," Oct. 19, 1846, copy, Sanborn Folder, HU.
138. John Brown to "Dear Wife," Dec. 3, 1846, copy, Sanborn Folder, HU.
139. John Brown to Simon Perkins, Springfield, Mass., May 1, 1849, ALS, BPL.
140. Mary A. Brown to John Brown, Jr., Nov. 8, 1849, Stutler Collection, WVDCH.
141. John Brown, Jr., to John Brown, Sept. 18, 1849, John Brown, Jr., Papers, OHS.
142. Ruth Brown Thompson to Wealthy C. Brown, North Elba, March 10, 1859, John Brown, Jr., Papers, OHS.
143. Annie Brown [daughter] to John Brown, Jr., and Wealthy, Dec. 15, 185[7], John Brown, Jr., Papers, OHS; Mary A. Brown to Mrs. George L. Stearns, Aug. 4, 1863, Gee Collection, HLHS; Mary A. Brown to J. Miller McKim, Sept. 2, 1863, Gee Collection, HLHS.
144. See the notation by Dr. Clarence S. Gee on Mary's August 4, 1863, letter to Mrs. George L. Stearns, cited in note 143. L. L. McCoy, "The California History of the Family of John Brown of Harper's Ferry Notoriety," unpublished essay, dated March 12, 1932, Stutler Collection, WVDCH; [Carol Dietz] "John Brown's Family in Tehama County," typed essay in Velma Sykes Collection, KSHS.
145. See McGlone, "Rescripting a Troubled Past," 1188–9.

CHAPTER 3 – FIRST SON

1. The precise origins of Brown's letter to young Harry Stearns are unclear. In 1902, an aged Henry Stearns told the engaging story of giving all his pocket money to Brown one day in January 1857 to "buy something ... for some poor little boy in Kansas" and then asking, "'Captain Brown, will you sometime write me a letter, and tell me what sort of a little boy you were?'" (Statement of Henry L. Stearns,

Oct. 26, 1902, typed copy, Gee Collection, HLHS.) But that story may be a false memory. Brown's immediate motive for writing to young Harry was doubtless to please his father, who had asked Brown to write his son in the course of making a $100 contribution and giving Brown authority to draw on the Massachusetts Kansas Committee for an additional $1,000. "Enclosed please find Thirty cents a gift to you from my eldest son Henry L. Stearns," the senior Stearns explained. "Will you at your leisure write a note to him, acknowledging the receipt of it for Kansas relief. I want him to keep it. It was his own desire to give the money, not prompted by his parents. He is 12 years old." George L. Stearns to John Brown, April 18, 1857, Stutler Collection, WVDCH. One way or the other, in any case, Harry's generosity prompted Brown to pen the story of his childhood. Since the note to Harry's father accompanying the letter is dated August 8, Brown may have worked on the story of his childhood at intervals for three weeks as he drilled a small company of volunteers in Red Rock, Iowa, and tried to raise money for the war against slavery.

2. Eakin argued that "autobiographical truth is not a fixed but an evolving content in an intricate process of self-discovery and self-creation, and, further, that the self that is the center of all autobiographical narrative is necessarily a fictive structure." Paul John Eakin, *Fictions in Autobiography: Studies in the Art of Self-Invention* (Princeton, NJ: Princeton University Press, 1985), 3. For current thinking about autobiography and its relation to fiction, see Jeremy D. Popkin, *History, Historians, & Autobiography* (Chicago: University of Chicago Press, 2005), Chapters 1 and 2.

3. John Brown to Henry L. Stearns, July 15, 1857, photstat, Gee Collection, HLHS. The original is in the Villard Collection, CUL. Hereafter cited as John Brown's autobiography.

4. Brown's letter was so full of implicit and explicit moral lessons that Mrs. Thomas Russell thought it might be published as a children's story. On the literature of advice for parents, see Bernard Wishy, *The Child and the Republic: The Dawn of Modern American Child Nurture* (Philadelphia: University of Pennsylvania Press, 1968).

5. John Brown's autobiography, p. 6.

6. John Brown's autobiography, p. 4.

7. John Brown's autobiography, p. 3.

8. *Aphoristic memories* are false or distorted memories that are retold often in old age because they convey important meanings about the life of the rememberer. Typically, the stories change somewhat with each retelling. See McGlone, "Deciphering Memory: John Adams and the Authorship of the Declaration of Independence," *The Journal of American History*, 85, no. 2 (Sept. 1998): 411–38.

9. On the persistence of slavery in the Old Northwest, see Paul Finkelman, *Slavery and the Founders: Race and Liberty in the Age of Jefferson* (Armonk, NY: M. E. Sharpe, 1996), Chapter 2.

10. Even Brown admirers have had difficulty crediting this story. Benjamin Quarles suggests that it may have been "an example of sentiment playing a trick on memory. It reads like a wishful reconstruction, however well intended and honestly held." Benjamin Quarles, *Allies for Freedom: Blacks and John Brown* (New York: Oxford University Press, 1974), 16. Louis DeCaro, Jr., suggests that the black youth may have been an "abused worker," and Brown may have used the boy's story to bring his own "life story into harmony with" the slavery controversy. DeCaro also notes that careful scholars concede "the possibility that the story was something of a moral tale" or that Brown's memory "may have 'colored' the tale

a bit.'" DeCaro, *"Fire from the Midst of You": A Religious Life of John Brown* (New York: New York University Press, 2002), 56, 298 n10.

11. Writing to his wife from Springfield in 1847, for example, Brown reflected that the "prospect" of coming home "is really a consolation, & ought to make me feel the more for vast numbers who are forced away from their dearest relatives with little if any hope of ever meeting them again on this side the grave." John Brown to "My Dear Wife," Jan. 8, 1847, Eldridge Collection, HEHL.

12. See James West Davidson and Mark H. Lytle, *After the Fact: The Art of Historical Detection*, 2 vols. (5th ed.; Boston: McGraw Hill, 2005), 166. In a resourceful "psychoanalytical" interpretation of Brown's letter, they conclude that his memory of his inability to keep "title" to pets and other property as a child evidenced an unconscious conflict with his father's authority. "This ambivalent father-son relationship suggests that Brown's intense lifelong identification with black slaves might have sprung from the struggle he experienced with paternal discipline" (p. 172). In a later chapter, I shall offer a different reading of the Stearns letter's theme of loss. It must suffice here to note that Calvinists routinely taught children to be wary of attachments to worldly possessions.

13. On the problem of false memories, see Robert E. McGlone, "Rescripting a Troubled Past: John Brown's Family and the Harpers Ferry Conspiracy," *The Journal of American History*, 75, no. 4 (March 1989): 1179–1200.

14. John Brown's autobiography, pp. 1–2.

15. Scott Casper identifies an emerging biographical genre in this period that "championed *individualism*, the entrepreneurial ethos of the new middle class." Ben Franklin was a transitional figure, the archetype of both republican civic virtue and "liberal self-made manhood." See Scott E. Casper, *Constructing American Lives: Biography and Culture in Nineteenth-Century America* (Chapel Hill: University of North Carolina Press, 1999), p. 90.

16. Jeffery Rossbach argues that although the letter to Harry Stearns is "revealing," it is also a "carefully constructed tactical device designed… to cultivate confidence in his character and, ultimately, support for insurrection." Rossbach, *Ambivalent Conspirators: John Brown, the Secret Six, and a Theory of Slave Violence* (Philadelphia: University of Pennsylvania Press, 1982), 122–4.

17. Owen Brown to "Dear Son John an[d] other Children," Sept. 30, 1855, Gee Collection, HLHS.

18. Owen Brown to "Dear Son John and Others," Jan. 26, 1855, Stutler Collection, WVDCH.

19. Owen Brown to "Dear Son John an[d] other Children," Sept. 30, typed copy, Gee Collection, HLHS.

20. Reminiscence of Lydia Brown Crowthers, June 12, 1928, copy, Gee Collection, HLHS.

21. Remark of Prof. B. A. Hinsdale as reported by Wendell Phillips Garrison, "The Preludes of Harper's Ferry," *Andover Review*, 14 (Dec. 1890): 587. See also Sarah Brown, interview with Katherine Mayo, Sept. 16–20, 1908, Villard Collection, CUL.

22. The classic study is Philip J. Greven, Jr., *Four Generations: Population, Land, and Family in Colonial Andover, Massachusetts* (Ithaca, NY: Cornell University Press, 1970). On the impact of inheritance in perpetuating extended families, see John Demos, *A Little Commonwealth: Family Life in Plymouth Colony* (New York: Oxford University Press, 1970), 118–20 et passim.

23. Copies of all three wills, as well as documents relating to the settlement of Owen Brown's estate, are in the Gee Collection, HLHS. On the Puritan tradition of inheritance, see Greven, *Four Generations.*
24. Owen Brown's autobiography, p. 1.
25. Even in the twentieth century, oldest sons in large families continued to feel a special responsibility as namesakes and presumptive family leaders. For an overview of the literature, see Monica McGoldrick, Randy Gerson, and Sylvia Shellenberger, *Genograms: Assessment and Intervention* (2nd ed.; New York: Norton, 1999), 65–89. See also Cecile Ernst and Jules Angst, *Birth Order: Its Influence on Personality* (Berlin, New York: Springer Verlag, 1983) and L. Forer, *The Birth Order Factor* (New York: Simon & Schuster, 1976).
26. Owen Brown's 1841 Memoir, p. 2, Gee Collection, HLHS.
27. Owen Brown's autobiography, p. 4, Gee Collection, HLHS.
28. Owen Brown's 1841 Memoir, p. 1, Gee Collection, HLHS.
29. John Brown to Henry L. Stearns [Brown's Autobiography], July 15–Aug. 8, 1857, photostat, Gee Collection, HLHS.
30. On Nov. 4, 1824, Samuel Murdock of Washington County, Pennsylvania, deeded about 41 acres to Levi Blakeslee for $100.00 paid for Balkeslee by Owen Brown. Medina County Deed Records, Vol. C, page 301. Cited in the Gee Collection, HLHS.
31. Levi Blakeslee to Oliver Owen Brown, Feb. 21, 1858, Jones Donation, Gee Collection, HLHS.
32. Owen Brown to John Brown, Nov. 16, 1855, copy, Franklin B. Sanborn Folder, HUL.
33. Owen Brown's 1841 memoir, p. 3, Gee Collection, HLHS.
34. See Davidson and Lytle, *After the Fact,* Chapter 7.
35. John Brown's autobiography, July 15–Aug. 8, 1857, Gee Collection, HLHS.
36. Franklin B. Sanborn, *The Life and Letters of John Brown, Liberator of Kansas, and Martyr of Virginia* (1885; repr., New York: Negro University Press, 1969) 31, note.
37. James Foreman to James Redpath, Dec. 28, 1859, Hinton Collection, KSHS.
38. John Brown's autobiography, p. 5.
39. Owen Brown's 1850 Memoir, p. 6, Gee Collection, HLHS
40. Salmon Brown to "Honored Father," Feb. 28, 1829, as quoted in Sanborn, *Life and Letters of John Brown,* 27.
41. Salmon Brown [brother] to Owen Brown, Apr. 17, 1827, Gee Collection, HLHS.
42. Owen Brown's 1850 Memoir, p. 6, Gee Collection, HLHS.
43. Oliver Owen Brown to Owen Brown, Feb. 16, 1853, Logan Collection, CHS.
44. Oliver Owen Brown to "Dear Father" [Owen Brown], Aug. 19, 1855, Logan Collection, CHS.
45. See Owen's wills and the records of his executors in the Gee Collection, HLHS.
46. Court records obtained in 1908 by Katherine Mayo showed that John Brown filed an appeal of a judgment against him in the amount of $1202.28 and court costs. His brothers Oliver Owen and Frederick were securities on the appeal bond. Notes by Katherine Mayo, Villard Collection, CUL.
47. John Brown, Jr., to "My Dear Friend" [Franklin B. Sanborn], Jan. 8. 1884, Stutler Collection, WVDCH.
48. Salmon Brown [son] to "Dear Folks One and all," Jan. 2, 1857, Stutler Collection, WVDCH.

49. Oliver Owen Brown to "Dear Friends" [Salmon (his son)], Feb. 11, 1858, James W. Eldridge Collection, HEHL.
50. Oliver Owen Brown to "Dear Friends" [Salmon (his son)], Feb. 11, 1858, Eldridge Collection, HEHL.
51. John Brown, Jr., to "My dear Friend" [Franklin B. Sanborn?], Jan. 8, 1884, Stutler Collection, WVDCH.
52. John Brown to Frederick Brown [brother], Oct. 26, 1833, as cited in Sanborn, *The Life and Letters of John Brown*, p. 27.
53. See the *Cleveland Weekly Plain Dealer*, Nov. 23, 1859, copy, Villard Collection, CUL.
54. John Brown to "Dear Brothers Frederick & Jeremiah," Oct. 11, 1856, typed copy, Villard Collection, CUL. By this time Frederick had moved to Rockford, Illinois, where he opened a law office and was elected marshal of the city. Oliver [John's son] to "Dear Father and Brothers," June 16, 1855, copy, Franklin B. Sanborn Folder, HU; Oliver [son] to "Dear Mother Brother & Sisters," July 4, [1857], Stutler Collection, WVDCH.
55. Quoted in *The Liberator*, Dec. 2, 1859, p. 191.
56. Francis Jackson to John Brown, Jr., Boston, Feb. 12, 1860, Stutler Collection, WVDCH; Samuel May, Jr., to Thomas Wentworth Higginson, Feb. 16, 1860, Higginson Papers, BPL, 175; Lydia Maria Child to Mary Ann Brown [wife], Mar. 12, 1860, Huxtable Donation, KSHS.
57. See, for example, Frederick Brown to "Jerymiah [sic]," Sept. 20, 1858, Gee Collection, HLHS.
58. Frederick Brown to Jeremiah Root Brown, Feb. 1, 1873, Clark-Brown Collection, HLHS. Frederick would outlive Jeremiah, who died a year later (Feb. 22, 1874) of tuberculosis in Santa Barbara, by some three years (July 15, 1877).
59. John Brown to "Dear Father," Apr. 9, 1839, copy, Villard Collection, CUL.
60. John Brown to John Brown, Jr., Apr. 25, 1850, John Brown, Jr., Papers, OHS.
61. Owen Brown to "Dear Son John," Dec. 10, 1850, Stutler Collection, WVDCH.
62. Jeremiah Root Brown to Samuel Lyle Adair, Oct. 11, 1855, Adair Family Collection, KSHS.
63. John Brown to Owen Brown, Mar. 26, 1856, Gee Collection, HLHS.
64. Wealthy Hotchkiss to Ruth & Henry Thompson, Jan. 4, 1857, Clark-Brown Collection, HLHS.
65. Jeremiah Root Brown to Samuel Lyle and Florella Adair, Feb. 8, 1857, Adair Family Collection, KSHS.
66. In 1856 Edward and Samantha had a son, Lucien, named after Edward's brother, who had died of tuberculosis in 1847, and a daughter Florilla Eva Brown. Both children married and had long lives. If Edward was a "hard case," he outlived all Owen's other children except two of his sisters to reach age sixty.
67. The trust between Owen and John was evident. In 1838, fearful he would fail to obtain a loan he desperately needed, for example, John cautioned Mary that "You may show this [letter] to my father, but to no one else." (John to "My dear wife and children," June 12, 1838, copy, Sanborn Folder, HU.) He was proud that he could help "Father" to resolve "old difficulties" so that Owen might "die somewhat in peace." John to John, Jr., Aug. 3, 1854, James W. Eldridge Collection, HEHL.
68. On the Browns' work on the Underground Railroad, see Richard O. Boyer, *Legend of John Brown: A Biography and a History* (New York: Alfred Knopf, 1973), esp. 401–5; Stephen B. Oates, *"To Purge This Land with Blood": A Biography of John Brown* (New York: Harper & Row, 1970), 64–5.

69. In 1849 Owen returned to his old church for reasons that are unclear. Clarence S. Gee, "Owen and His Wife Ruth Mills Brown, Church Affiliation," unpublished report, Gee Collection, HLHS.
70. John Brown, Jr., reminiscent account, reprinted in Louis Ruchames, *A John Brown Reader* (London: Abelard-Schuman, 1959), 181–2. See also Ruth Brown Thompson, "Reminiscences of John Brown of Kansas & Harper's Ferry," Gibraltar, Put-in-Bay, Dec. 2, 1882, unpublished mss., Rust Collection, HEHL.
71. Letter from Owen Brown, Apr. 24, 1837, in "Report of the Second Anniversary of the Ohio Anti-Slavery Society, held in Mount Pleasant, Ohio, April 27, 1837," Stutler Collection, WVDCH.
72. Owen Brown to John Brown, Sept. 30, 1855, copy, Sanborn Folder, HU.
73. In Boston's Faneuil Hall Wendell Phillips condemned Lovejoy's killers and defended the slain man as a republican hero, thus launching Phillips's career as a leading abolitionist. James Brewer Stewart, *Wendell Phillips: Liberty's Hero* (Baton Rouge: Louisiana State University Press, 1986), 58–63.
74. Lora Case, *Hudson of Long Ago: Personal Reminiscences of an Aged Pioneer* (Hudson: The Hudson Library & Historical Society, 1963), 53–4. A second reminiscent account by the Rev. Edward Brown, John's cousin, differing in detail, is related by J. Newton Brown, editor of the *Northwestern Congregationalist*, where the former's memoirs first appeared in 1892. Newton Brown's letter relating the story of John Brown's pledge as Edward Brown remembered it appeared in the Feb. 12, 1914, issue of *The Nation*, and is reprinted in Louis Ruchames, ed., *A John Brown Reader* (London, New York: Abelard-Schuman, 1959), 179–81.
75. See, for example, Brown's "Words of Advice" to the United States League of Gileadites, an organization of black Springfield residents Brown founded in response to the adoption of the national Fugitive Slave Law of 1850. The text is reproduced in Louis Ruchames, ed., *John Brown: The Making of a Revolutionary* (2nd ed.; New York: Grosset & Dunlap, 1969), 84–6.
76. John Brown to Owen Brown, March 26, 1856, Gee Collection, HLHS.
77. Both wrote occasional sermons or screeds on public questions. See John's undated Notes for a Sermon [on the character of the true God], Stutler Collection, WVDCH, and Owen Brown on Intemperance, unpublished, untitled essay, typed copy, Clarence S. Gee Collection, HLHS.
78. John Brown to "Dear wife and children," June 12, 1839, as quoted in Ruchames, *A John Brown Reader*, 44–5.
79. Owen Brown to "Dear Son John," Nov. 16, 1855, copy, Franklin B. Sanborn Folder, HU.
80. Statement of John Brown, Dec. 2, 1859, facsimile, John Brown, Jr., Papers, OHS.
81. John's fourth son, Frederick, had developed symptoms of mental illness at age sixteen. John Brown to Owen Brown, May 23, 1850, copy, Villard Collection, CUL.
82. Owen Brown's 1850 memoir, p. 5.
83. John Brown's autobiography, July 15, 1857, photstat, Gee Collection, HLHS.
84. Henry Thompson, statement to Katherine Mayo, Aug. 22–Sept. 1, 1908, Villard Collection, CUL.
85. E. Shuman was a litigant in a suit with a "man at Monroe" about the ownership of some of Owen's sheep. Jason Brown to John Brown, Jr., Feb. 15, 1853, John Brown, Jr., Papers, OHS.
86. In 1956 maverick anthropologist Gregory Bateson and collaborators from several other disciplines enunciated the theory of the double bind as a partial explanation

for schizophrenia. The theory was based on the assumption that the illness resulted from failed communications between a parent and the schizophrenic child, who was unable to distinguish "messages" of different levels of abstraction from one another. (The levels were indebted to Bertrand Russell's Theory of Logical Types.) Thus the "victim" might mistake jokes or kidding for literal comments. Although Bateson later elaborated the theory, no controlled studies were done, and Bateson himself admitted that his "hypothesis" was never statistically tested. More recently psychiatric research on schizophrenia has turned away from family interaction theories such as the double bind in favor of neurobiological explanations. Schizophrenia is a brain disease with genetic roots. But Bateson's double bind remains a suggestive metaphor for understanding stressful parent–child interaction. See Gregory Bateson, *Steps to an Ecology of Mind* (New York: Ballantine Books, 1972), 201–27, et passim. For a review of theories written for the general reader, see E. Fuller Torrey, *Surviving Schizophrenia: A Family Manual* (rev. ed., New York: Harper & Row, 1988), Chapter 6.

87. John Brown to "Dear Father," Apr. 2, 1847, Stutler Collection, WVDCH.
88. John Brown to Owen Brown, Dec. 2, 1847, Rust Collection, HEHL. By contrast, John was exhilarated when he could assist his father in business matters. "This is the Second very burthensome truble I have assisted him in disposing of comfortably; within a short time," John wrote to John, Jr. "When another with (J R) is got over; he will feel that he may die somewhat in peace." John Brown to John Brown, Jr., Aug. 3, 1854, Eldridge Collection, HEHL.
89. John Brown to "Dear Father," June 12, 1830 Gee Collection, HLHS.
90. John began the letter asking his father to "excuse [him] for writing you again so soon," and concluded, "affectionately, your unworthy son." John Brown to "Dear Father," Dec. 13, 1838, Sanborn Folder, HU.
91. In a remarkable study of historical figures who in various fields have overturned existing intellectual, social, and political orders, historian Frank J. Sulloway has argued that *younger* sons account for the great innovations and revolutions of the past several centuries. Thus, on the face of it, Brown would not seem to have been a likely revolutionary. But in the context of territorial disorder, I shall argue, and in the name of a biblically inspired world view, he proved explosive. See Frank J. Sulloway, *Born to Rebel: Birth Order, Family Dynamics, and Creative Lives* (New York: Vintage Books, 1996).

CHAPTER 4 – PILGRIM

1. In a fundraising speech in Cleveland on March 18, 1859, Brown is reported to have said that he never killed anyone, but to have admitted that "on some occasions he had *shown his young men with him*, how some things might be done as well as others, and they had done the business." Quoted from the Cleveland *Leader* of March 22 by Oswald Garrison Villard, *John Brown, 1800–1859: A Biography Fifty Years After* (1910; repr., Gloucester, MA: Peter Smith, 1965), 391–3. [Italics in text.] Several old Kansas allies later claimed that Brown had admitted privately he was responsible for Pottawatomie. The most candid of these alleged statements is reported by James Hanway, a local amateur historian, who quotes Brown as saying: "'If that was murder, I am not innocent,' repeating the remark several times while walking up and down the room." "The Pottawatomie Tragedy: Was John Brown Present? Testimony of Judge James Hanway, who was a Member of John

Brown Jr.'s Company at the Time," Lawrence (Kansas) *Daily Journal*, Nov. 27, 1879, p. 2, cols. 2–3.

2. See the affidavits of James Harris and Mrs. Louisa Jane Wilkinson, the wife of one of the slain, in Thirty-Fourth Congress, First Session, *U. S. House Reports*, No. 200 (Serial 869), "Report of the Special Committee Appointed to Investigate the Troubles in the Territory of Kansas" (3 vols., 1855–6), vol. II, pp. 1177–9, 1179–81. Hereafter cited as the *Howard Committee Report*.

3. Brown was never indicted for Pottawatomie. But his reputation as a free-state guerrilla leader soon brought him to national attention. In February 1859, when Brown left Kansas for the last time, he proudly escorted eleven slaves he had "liberated" from their owners in Missouri the previous December to freedom in Canada. President Buchanan offered a reward of $250 and the governor of Missouri $3000 to anyone who would deliver Brown to Missouri authorities. On the rewards, see Villard, *John Brown Fifty Years After*, 393.

4. James Redpath, *The Public Life of Capt. John Brown* (Boston: Thayer and Eldridge, 1860), 118–19, 239.

5. While John Brown was awaiting the hangman, a half-brother, Jeremiah Root Brown, though he suspected the truth, responded to accusations from free-state opponents of Brown by stating flatly the family's position: "My brother, at the time William [sic] Doyle and others were killed, was not present, did not assent to the act, nor had [he] any knowledge of it, and [he] was eighteen miles distant at the time of the occurrence." Letter to the Editor of the Cleveland *Plain Dealer*, Nov. 22, 1859, as quoted (from the Cleveland *Herald*) in the New York *Daily Tribune*, Nov. 30, 1859, p. 6, col. 4. In a letter to an abolitionist in Vermont, Salmon declared in 1859 that his father was not a "participator" in the Pottawatomie killings. Salmon asserted nonetheless that the deed was "all that saved the territory from being over run with drunken land pirates from the Southern States." Salmon Brown to Rev. Joshua Young, Dec. 27, 1859, in James T. Malin, *John Brown and the Legend of Fifty-six* (Philadelphia: American Philosophical Society, 1942), 267. After the Browns' responsibility for the killings had been established, Salmon tried to save his credibility. "Because I denied that father had any part in the Pottowamie [sic] massacre at the time of the Congressional investigation of Harper's Ferry affairs," he wrote Franklin Sanborn, "it does not follow that I have misstated other matters. At the time I did not propose to give anybody away, certainly not myself." Salmon Brown to Franklin B. Sanborn, Aug. 8, 1909, Stutler Collection, WVDCH. John Brown, Jr., who was not one of the Pottawatomie assassins, claimed to have been misinformed about his family's role until July 1860, when, presumably, his brother Owen told him the truth. See Franklin B. Sanborn, *The Life and Letters of John Brown, Liberator of Kansas, and Martyr of Virginia* (1885; repr., New York: Negro University Press, 1969), 260–1.

6. Townsley's "confession" first appeared in the Lawrence *Daily Journal*, Dec. 10, 1879, p. 2, under the heading "The Potawatomie [sic] Tragedy, John Brown's Connection With It, Statement of James Townsley, an Eye-Witness." It is reprinted in Louis Ruchames, *A John Brown Reader* (New York: Abelard-Schuman, 1959), 197–203. Eli Thayer, the founder of the New England Emigrant Aid Society and once a Brown ally, considered Brown an "anarchist." "If we admit his sanity, we must then regard him as a felon or a fiend," Thayer wrote in the New York *Sun* in 1887. "If any butcher... should hack and slash to death his own hogs and steers as John Brown hacked and slashed to death these men and boys in Kansas,"

Thayer insisted, "he would be arrested and imprisoned without delay." Quoted in Eli Thayer, *A History of the Kansas Crusade: Its Friends and Its Foes* (1889; repr., New York: Books for Libraries Press, 1971), 195–6.

7. On abolitionist direct-action schemes, see Merton L. Dillon, *Slavery Attacked: Southern Slaves and Their Allies, 1619–1865* (Baton Rouge: Louisiana State University Press, 1990), Chapters 10–11.

8. In early April, 1859, Brown told an old acquaintance in Ohio, David King, that he was God's chosen instrument to free the slaves. King concluded Brown lacked a "balance wheel." Affidavit of David L. King, Nov. 15, 1859, Wise Papers, LOC. A correspondent reported from Kansas that Brown suffered from the "religious hallucination" that he had been appointed an "instrument of the Almighty" to destroy slavery. New York *Weekly Tribune*, Oct. 29, 1859, p. 3, cols. 1–2.

9. See the discussion in Chapter 2 of Allan Nevins's thesis that Brown suffered from "reasoning insanity," a form of "paranoia." See also James Claude Malin, *John Brown and the Legend of Fifty-Six*, 308–9.

10. The story of the messenger seems to have originated in the reminiscences of Salmon Brown. See Salmon Brown to "Friend F. B. Sanborn," Nov. 17, 1911, Stutler Collection, WVDCH, and Salmon Brown to William E. Connelly, May 18, 1913, typed copy, signed, Stutler Collection, WVDCH. It has been widely repeated. See Oswald Garrison Villard, *John Brown Fifty Years After,* 154; Stephen B. Oates, *To Purge This Land with Blood: A Biography of John Brown* (New York: Harper & Row, 1970), 129; James McPherson, *Ordeal by Fire: The Civil War and Reconstruction* (New York: Knopf, 1982), 94.

11. Brown may have heard the news of Sumner's beating on his return to the free-state camp three or four days after the event. I am indebted to the late Michael Johnson of Kansas City for establishing that the Missouri & Western Telegraph Company line up the Missouri River (from St. Louis to Omaha) had not reached western Missouri by the summer of 1856. News to and from Kansas to the East traveled slowly. For example, Thomas Wentworth Higginson's report, dated July 2 at St. Louis, to the New York *Daily Tribune*, took five days even with access to the telegraph. (Higginson, "Late Outrages on the Missouri," New York *Daily Tribune*, July 7, 1856, p. 5.) A rider leaving Lawrence at midnight on May 15 arrived in Leavenworth the following morning bringing word of the siege of Lawrence, but that story, dated May 16, did not appear in the *Daily Tribune* until May 23, almost eight days later. On the building of the telegraph and the expansion of Western Union, see Robert Luther Thompson, *Wiring a Continent: The History of the Telegraph Industry in the United States, 1832–1866* (Princeton, NJ: Princeton University Press, 1947), Chapter 18, esp. p. 297, and James D. Reid, *The Telegraph in America: Its Founders, Promoters, and Noted Men* (1879; repr., New York: Arno Press, 1974). The celebrated Pony Express, established in 1860, ended with the opening of the transcontinental telegraph in 1861. Because of the commencement of the Civil War, it bypassed the Missouri route. On "Bully Brooks's" attack on Sumner, see David Herbert Donald, *Charles Sumner and the Coming of the Civil War* (New York: Alfred Knopf, 1960), 288–97. A convenient collection of documents relating to the incident is T. Lloyd Benson, *The Caning of Senator Sumner* (Belmont, CA: Wadsworth/Thompson Learning, 2004).

12. An astute assessment of the role of abolitionist "propaganda" in the creation of Brown's reputation is David Potter's "Two Wars in Kansas," chapter 9 of *The Impending Crisis, 1848–1861* (Torchbook ed.; New York: Harper & Row, 1976), esp. 218–23.

13. Some Brown defenders claimed that Dr. Charles Robinson, who had been chosen as governor by the free-state settlers, and Jim Lane had asked Brown to undertake the Pottawatomie mission, only to renounce the action later. See, for example, Sam Walker to Judge James Hanway, Feb. 5, 1875, John Brown Collection, KSHS.

14. Franklin B. Sanborn was the Browns' chief defender. See his *The Life and Letters of John Brown*, Chapter 9, esp. 257–69.

15. George B. Gill, who had been a trusted member of Brown's "Provisional Government" in 1858, "defected" shortly before Harpers Ferry. "I hope," Brown wrote to his second-in-command, that "George G. will so far *redeem himself* as to try: & do his duty after all." (John Brown to John Henry Kagi, Aug. 6, 1859, Ferdinand J. Dreer Collection, PHS.) Still bitter in 1893, Gill said Brown was "essentially vindictive in his nature" and had "neither sympathy [n]or feeling for the timid or weak of will." Gill to Richard J. Hinton, July 7,1893, as quoted in Louis Ruchames, ed., *John Brown: The Making of a Revolutionary* (New York: Grosset & Dunlap, 1969), 239–42.

16. In 1879 the editor of the Lawrence *Daily Journal* had published a series of articles relating to Pottawatomie, and he finally solicited Townsley's statement with the help of James Hanway, among others, to resolve disputed points. See Ruchames, *The Making of a Revolutionary*, 205–11.

17. See, for example, Malin, *John Brown and the Legend of Fifty-six*, Part 2.

18. Malin cited statements in which Salmon explicitly claimed that Brown returned to Pottawatomie to "break up Cato's court." (Sterling G. Cato was Judge of the 2nd [of two] Judicial Districts in the territory and Associate Justice of its Supreme Court). Salmon even argued that because the Browns had warned Cato "against trying any-one under that [territorial] code, ... Cato was responsible for the killing of those five men – Cato and nobody else." (Malin, *John Brown and the Legend of Fifty-six*, 753–56. Salmon repeated essentially this explanation of the killings to Franklin B. Sanborn in 1911. "It was believed by our people that if the officers of Catos [sic] Court were cut off no one else would dare take there [sic] places and that would break up the Court altogether." Salmon also claimed that Judge Henry H. Williams of Osawatomie, then living on Pottawatomie Creek, had personally selected the victims in the camp of the Rifles. Williams, who was "acquainted with all the men that had been appointed by Judge Cato[,] put down the names in my presence ... [of] the men that would have to be put out of the way to save the lives of the free state men.... This was a clear case of who would steal the march on the other or be anhialated [sic] or driven out of the country." Williams, of course, denied that he had endorsed the killings, let alone chosen the victims. (Salmon Brown to "Friend F. B. Sanborn," Nov. 17, 1911, Stutler Collection, WVDCH). It is important to note, however, that the first hint of the theory that Pottawatomie was a blow at Cato's court came only after many years. In 1880 Brown's son Owen, one of the assassins, remarked: "I reflected that these men [the Pottawatomie victims] are influential persons, leading men and among the worst holding office", but he said nothing directly about Cato's court. Owen Brown interview by Franklin B. Sanborn, June 27, 1880, Sanborn Folder, HU.

19. Pottawatomie was, Malin speculated, "the explosive self-assertion of a frustrated old man, defeated on all points relative to the expedition under the command of his son – a means by which he might enjoy untrammeled authority and restore his confidence in himself." Malin, *John Brown and the Legend of Fifty-Six*, 563. Malin wrote a heavily documented, 764-page book about Brown to prove he was insig-nificant in Kansas history.

20. Potter, *The Impending Crisis, 1848–1861* (Torchbook ed.; New York: Harper & Row, 1976), 213.

21. A useful summary of these events is James A. Rawley, *Race & Politics: "Bleeding Kansas" and the Coming of the Civil War* (Philadelphia, 1969). Oates's summary is reliable. Oates, *To Purge This Land with Blood,* Chapter 10.

22. On the postmillenialism of Hopkins, see E. Brooks Holifield, *Theology in America: Christian Thought from the Age of the Puritans to the Civil War* (New Haven, CT: Yale University Press, 2003), 148–9. See also George M. Marsden, *The Evangelical Mind and the New School Presbyterian Experience: A Case Study of Thought and Theology in Nineteenth-Century America* (New Haven and London: Yale University Press, 1970), Chapters 1–4, 9. Taking issue with Perry Miller, Marsden argued that the concept of the nation's covenant with God lingered in American Protestantism in New School theology until the Civil War (pp. 200–1).

23. "Our admonitions have been very frequent," he wrote in 1842, "but I cannot say the affects have been very good [W]e are yet stupid and sinfull." God's "admonitions" here referred to the deaths of several relations and Hudson friends of scarlet fever. Owen Brown to Samuel Lyle Adair "and family," Jan. 20, 1842, Box 3, folder 11, Samuel Lyle & Florella Brown Adair Family Collection, KSHS.

24. See David Brion Davis's classic, *The Slave Power Conspiracy and the Paranoid Style* (Baton Rouge: LSU Press, 1969), 71–84.

25. Owen Brown to "Dear Brethren" (Ohio Anti-Slavery Society), April 24, 1837, typed copy, Gee Collection, HLHS. Owen Brown, statement, 1850, as quoted in Sanborn, *Life and Letters of John Brown,* 10–11.

26. John Brown, Jr., confirmed his father's initial dislike as a child for Sally Root, his new stepmother, but denied knowing anything about the story that little John had tried to blow up Sally in a "small-sized Gun-powder plot." John Brown, Jr., to "My Dear Friend" [Franklin B. Sanborn], Jan. 8, 1884, Stutler Collection, WVDCH.

27. See John Brown's autobiography, in John Brown to Henry L. Stearns, July 15, 1857, Photostat, Gee Collection, HLHS.

28. Quoted in Sanborn, *Life and Letters of John Brown,* 142–3.

29. John to John, Jr., May 23, 1845, as quoted in Sanborn, *Life and Letters of John Brown,* 140.

30. John Brown to "Dear Father," Oct. 19, 1855, Gee Collection, HLHS.

31. John Brown to Owen Brown, Dec. 2, 1847, Rust Collection, HEHL. See the discussion in Chapter 3 of Brown's perceived conflict over his piety – his "double bind" – in his relationship with Owen.

32. John Brown, Jr., to "Dear Grandparents," March 20, 1856, Gee Collection, HLHS.

33. Wealthy Hotchkiss Brown to "My Dear Aged Grandfather," March 19, 1856, Gee Collection, HLHS.

34. Perkins regularly sent what Brown viewed as "kind hints" about business while Brown often sought his advice and approval of his decisions. See, for example, John Brown to Simon Perkins, July 23, 1846, ALS, Miscellaneous John Brown Manuscripts, YUL; Brown to Perkins, May 1, 1849, BPL; Brown to Perkins, Oct. 29, 1849, Gee Collection, HLHS; and Brown to Perkins, Dec. 3, 1852, Manuscript Vault, YUL.

35. Salmon Brown, interview with Katherine Mayo, Oct. 11–13, 1908, Villard Collection, CUL.

36. John Brown to "Dear Son John, & Wife," April 12, 1850, as quoted in Villard, *John Brown Fifty Years After,* 64.

37. John Brown to John Brown, Jr., Nov. 4, 1850, as quoted in Villard, *John Brown Fifty Years After*, 64.
38. See Brown's letter to Ruth and Henry Thompson, April 14, 1854, as quoted in Franklin B. Sanborn, *Life and Letters of John Brown*, 110. Perkins's deference may have reflected concern for harmony in light of the marriage in March of his daughter, Samantha, to Brown's half-brother, Edward. Brown and Perkins had become in-laws.
39. John Brown to John Brown, Jr., August 21, 1854, Sanborn Folder, HU.
40. John Brown to Ruth and Henry Thompson, Sept. 30, 1854, Dreer Collection, PHS. On November 2, Brown was "still pretty much determined to go back to North Elba" even though his sons Owen and Frederick were setting out for Kansas the following week. Gerrit Smith had urged him to settle at North Elba, but his black friends, Douglass and Dr. James McCune Smith, had not replied. Brown to "Dear Children" [Ruth and Henry Thompson], Nov. 2, 1854, as quoted in Sanborn, *Life and Letters of John Brown*, 110–11.
41. Ruth Brown Thompson to Mary Brown, North Elba, Nov. 15, 1854, copy by Katherine Mayo, Villard Collection, CUL.
42. Malin insists that Brown had decided to join his sons in Kansas in February, 1855, before the "difficulties," as Brown later put it, had begun, and had gathered weapons en route as "an afterthought." Malin, *John Brown and the Legend of Fifty-six*, 8–15. Stephen B. Oates concludes with Malin that Brown initially planned to follow his sons to Kansas to do surveying and "investigate business prospects" before bringing Mary and his younger children there. Oates, "John Brown and His Judges: A Critique of the Historical Literature," *Civil War History*, 17 (March 1971), 5–24, esp. 10.
43. Villard, *John Brown Fifty Years After*, 77. See also Sanborn, *Life and Letters of John Brown*, 166, 203; Sanborn, *Recollections of Seventy Years* (Boston: Richard G. Badger, 1909), I, 77–8.
44. John Brown to John W. Cook, February 13, 1855, as quoted in Villard, *John Brown Fifty Years After*, 84. This correspondent should not be confused with John E. Cook, later one of Brown's men at Harpers Ferry.
45. On the doubtful story that Brown pledged his sons to fight slavery long before the passage of the Fugitive Slave Act of 1850, see Robert E. McGlone, "Rescripting a Troubled Past: John Brown's Family and the Harpers Ferry Conspiracy," *The Journal of American History*, 75 (March 1989), 1179–1200, esp. 1194–8.
46. John Brown to "Dear Children" [Ruth and Henry Thompson], Akron, Jan. 23, 1855, Logan Collection, CHS.
47. Owen rejoiced at "all the blessings" God granted the newlyweds, but characteristically reminded them that "Earthly happyness" was fleeting unless they had "an eye to things that are spiritual and eternal." Owen Brown to Samuel Adair "and family," Jan. 20, 1842, Adair Family Collection, Box 3, Folder 11, KSHS.
48. John Brown, Jr., to John Brown, May 6, 1855, copy, Sanborn Folder, HU.
49. John Brown, Jr., to John Brown, May 20, 24, and 26, 1855, ALS, Dreer Collection, PHS.
50. John Brown, Jr., to John Brown, May 20, 24, and 26, 1855, Dreer Collection, PHS.
51. Franklin B. Sanborn reprints a series of Brown family letters during this period in *The Life and Letters of John Brown*, chapter 8.
52. Salmon Brown to John Brown, May 21, 1855, copy, Sanborn Folder, HU.

53. John, Jr., Jason, Owen, Frederick, and Salmon Brown to John Brown, June 29, July 2, 1855, Sanborn Folder, HU.

54. John Brown to "Dear Wife, & Children All," Sept. 4, 1855, John Brown Collection KSHS. On receiving his sons' appeal for help, Brown later wrote, "the elder Brown was fully resolved to proceed at once to Kansas, & join his children." Quoted from Brown's unfinished narrative, "A brief history of John Brown otherwise (old B) & his family: *as connected with Kansas*; by one who Knows," handwritten mss., n.d. [August 1858] 5 pp., Dreer Collection, PHS, p 2.

55. The claim that Brown went to Kansas to open the war against slavery rests on scant contemporary evidence. Richard Realf testified after Harpers Ferry that Brown's purpose in Kansas was "to gain a footing" for a broader attack on slavery. But Realf was a late recruit to Brown's "army," joining in July 1857, by which time Brown had indeed begun to prepare to carry the war beyond Kansas. "Report of the Senate Select Committee appointed to inquire into the late invasion and seizure of the public property at Harper's Ferry," *U. S. Senate Committee Reports*, No. 278, 2 vols. (36th Cong., 1st sess., 1859–60), 2: 99. (Hereafter cited as the *Mason Committee Report*.) In 1889 Eli Thayer, a Brown debunker who thought Brown had done "great injury" to the free-state cause, alleged Brown had said to him: "I have not come to make Kansas free, but to get a shot at the South." Eli Thayer, *A History of the Kansas Crusade: Its Friends and Its Foes* (New York: Harper & Brothers, 1889), 195. Villard quotes an 1886 letter from Annie Brown Adams, a teenager when her father left for Kansas, to the effect that Brown and Henry Thompson went "only to fight, not to settle." As noted previously, Villard declares Brown went to "test himself as a guerrilla leader ... for no other purpose." Villard, *John Brown Fifty Years After*, 77, 81. On the other hand, Malin suggests that Brown went to Kansas to make a "business deal" – John, Jr.'s letter and the wagon load of weapons notwithstanding. Stephen Oates is closer to the truth in suggesting that Brown went because of his sons' appeal, and as he told his interrogators after Harpers Ferry, "because of the difficulties." Oates, *To Purge This Land with Blood*, 376, note 15. But in those trying circumstances, Brown himself had no doubt forgotten how favorably he was at first impressed with Kansas as a place to settle.

56. Augustus Wattles, testimony of Feb. 17, 1860, *Mason Committee Report*, 2:225.

57. Henry Thompson to Ruth Brown Thompson, Oct. 19, 1855, copy, Villard Collection, CUL. Although John Brown did not take a claim, Henry did. He abandoned it when he and the others left Kansas not long after Pottawatomie.

58. Owen Brown and John Brown to "Samuel Adair and Family," Aug. 8, 1855, Adair Family Collection, Box 3, Folder 11, KSHS.

59. Owen Brown to "Dear Son John," Nov. 16, 1855, copy, Sanborn Folder, HU.

60. Owen Brown to "Samuel Adair and Family," Munroe Falls, Ohio, Aug. 8, 1855, Adair Family Collection, KSHS.

61. Owen Brown to "Dear Son John and other children," Sept. 5, 1855, typed copy, Gee Collection, HLHS.

62. Owen Brown to John Brown, Nov. 26, 1855, Stutler Collection, WVDCH.

63. Owen Brown to John Brown, Nov. 16, 1855, copy, Sanborn Folder, HU.

64. Owen Brown to "Dear son John and other children," Sept. 30, Oct. 1, Oct. 4, 1855, ALS, Sanborn Folder. HU.

65. Salmon Brown to "Friend F. B. Sanborn," Nov. 17, 1911, Stutler Collection, WVDCH; Salmon to William E. Connelly, May 28, 1913, typed copy, signed with

handwritten note, Stutler Collection, WVDCH. On the widespread celebration of martial virtues and John Brown's adherence to the code, see Robert E. McGlone, "Forgotten Surrender: John Brown's Raid and the Cult of Martial Virtues," *Civil War History*, 40 (Sept. 1994), 185–201.

66. John Brown to Owen Brown, Nov. 9, 1855, Gee Collection, HLHS.
67. Owen Brown to John Brown, Nov. 16, 1855, copy, Sanborn Folder, HU.
68. John Brown to "Dear Wife & Children every one," Oct. 14, 1855, typed copy, Villard Collection, CUL.
69. John Brown to "Dear Wife & Children every one," Nov. 2, 1855, John Brown Collection, KSHS.
70. Mary A. Brown to John Brown, May 20, 1856, typed copy, Gee Collection, HLHS.
71. Watson Brown to "Dear Father and Brothers," Dec. 4, 1855, Sanborn Folder, HU.
72. Oliver Brown to "Dear Mother, Brother, & Sisters," Feb. 4, 1856, Villard Collection, CUL.
73. Oliver Brown to "Dear Mother, Brother, & Sisters," Feb. 4, 1856, Villard Collection, CUL.
74. Samuel Lyle Adair to "Dear Father Brown," Mar. 4, 1856, typed copy, Gee Collection, HLHS.
75. Copies of all these documents can be found in the Gee Collection, HLHS. I am indebted to the former Librarian and Curator, Thomas Vince, and his successor, James Caccamo, for valuable assistance.
76. The first of these autobiographical statements was written in 1841 while Owen was traveling alone on a canal boat and feeling "rather lonesome." He had lost his first wife and at seventy may have had a premonition of his own death. The memoir was evidently written for his children, but the account ends in 1813. (Hereafter cited as Owen Brown's 1841 Memoir.) The second, longer manuscript, was written at the request of his eldest daughter, Sally Marian Brown Hand, while Owen was visiting her home in Grafton, Ohio, probably in 1850. (Hereafter cited as Owen Brown's autobiography.) Owen Brown to "My Dear Daughter Marian," undated mss [1850], Gee Collection, HLHS.
77. Owen Brown to John Brown and family, Jan. 26, 1856, Gee Collection, HLHS.
78. Owen Brown to John Brown and family, Jan. 26, 1856, Gee Collection, HLHS.
79. Jeremiah Root Brown to Brother John, Adair and Others," Hudson, May 14, 1856, Adair Family Collection, KSHS.
80. Owen Brown to Charles Storrs Adair, Feb. 23, 1856, Adair Family Collection, KSHS.
81. Owen Brown to John Brown, Hudson, March 27, 1856, ALS, KSHS.
82. Jeremiah Root Brown to "Brother John, Adair and Others," May 14, 1856, Adair Family Collection, KSHS.
83. John Brown to "Dear Father," Oct. 19, 1855, Gee Collection, HLHS.
84. John Brown to "Dear Father," Oct. 21, 1855, Gee Collection, HLHS.
85. John Brown to "Dear Father," March 26, 1856, Gee Collection, HLHS.
86. John Brown to "Dear Father," May 8, 1856, Gee Collection, HLHS.
87. The Brown family genealogy compiled by the Rev. Clarence S. Gee gives the date of Owen's death as May 8. But both Brown's brother Jeremiah and sister Florella place it on Saturday, the third. Services were conducted the following day. See Jeremiah to "Brother John Adair, & Others," Hudson, Ohio, May 14, 1856, Adair Family Collection, KSHS, and Sally Marian Hand to "Dear Brother and Sister"

[Samuel Lyle and Florella Brown Adair], May 6, 1856, Adair Family Collection, KSHS.

88. Owen's February 11 letter to Adair arrived March 4. Samuel Lyle Adair to Owen Brown, March 4, 6, 1856, Gee Collection, HLHS.

89. Samuel Lyle Adair to "Dear Father Brown," May 16, 1856, typed copy, Gee Collection, HLHS.

90. In April 1856 the stage left Osawatomie for the return trip to Kansas City on Thursdays. See Samuel Lyle Adair to "Dear Father Brown," Apr. 28, 1855, Gee Collection, HLHS; John Brown, Jr., to "Dear Grandparents," March 20, 1856, Gee Collection, HLHS. Someone from Brown's station, usually Frederick, hiked over to Osawatomie to pick up and post letters only on Saturdays, occasioning further delays. John Brown to "Dear Father," Nov. 9, 1855, Gee Collection, HLHS.

91. Florella dated her letter on the 19th and 21st. Sally Marian Hand [and Titus S. Hand] to "Dear Sister," [June 10], Adair Family Collection, KSHS.

92. John Brown to "Dear Father," Nov. 9, 1855, Gee Collection, HLHS.

93. Jeremiah to "Brother John Adair, & Others," Hudson, Ohio, May 14, 1856, Adair Family Collection, KSHS.

94. Samuel Lyle Adair to "Sister Hand & Other Friends," May 23, 1856 [sic. May 28], Gee Collection, HLHS.

95. Hebrews 11:13, King James Bible.

CHAPTER 5 – STEWARD

1. Cited in John Brown's unfinished memoir, "A brief history of John Brown otherwise (old B) & his family: *as connected with Kansas*; by one who Knows," handwritten mss., n.d. [August 1858], 5 pp., Ferdinand J. Dreer Collection, PHS, p. 2.

2. John Brown to "Dear Wife, & Children All," Sept. 4, 1855, John Brown Collection, KSHS.

3. Like most newspapers of the time, the territorial papers were avowedly partisan. The Leavenworth City *Weekly Herald*, for example, proclaimed itself "devoted to Southern Principles." On the local press, see James Claude Malin, *John Brown and the Legend of Fifty-six* (Philadelphia: American Philosophical Society, 1942), Chapters 3 and 4.

4. On the Pierce administration's Kansas policy, see: Larry Gara, *The Presidency of Franklin Pierce* (Lawrence: University Press of Kansas, 1991), Chapter 5, esp. p. 104.

5. John Brown to "Dear Wife & Children every one," Oct. 13, 14, 1855, typed copy, Villard Collection, CUL.

6. John Brown to "Dear Father," Nov. 9, 1855, Gee Collection, HLHS.

7. Jason Brown to "Dear Grandfather" [Owen], June 14, 1855, Gee Collection, HLHS.

8. Jason Brown to "Dear Grandfather," Jan. 23, 1856, Gee Collection, HLHS.

9. John Brown to "Dear Wife & Children every one," Oct. 13, 14, 1855, typed copy, Villard Papers, CUL.

10. James A. Rawley, *Race and Politics: "Bleeding Kansas" and the Coming of the Civil War* (Philadelphia: J. B. Lippincott, 1969), 92–7. A standard treatment is Alice Nichols, *Bleeding Kansas* (New York: Oxford University Press, 1954). A concise introduction to Bleeding Kansas is Robert W. Richmond, *Kansas: A Land of Contrasts* (St. Charles, MO: Forum Press, 1974), Chapter 5. On the role of Charles

Robinson, see Don W. Wilson, *Governor Charles Robinson of Kansas* (Lawrence: University of Kansas Press, 1975).

11. In 1859 G. W. Brown charged that Old Brown "commenced fomenting difficulties in camp, disregarding the commands of superior officers, and trying to induce the men to ... make an attack" on the proslavery forces encamped nearby. In this version, G. W. Brown claimed, the committee "several times" headed off Brown's "wild projects." *Herald of Freedom*, Oct. 29, 1859, as quoted in Malin, *John Brown and the Legend of Fifty-six*, pp. 20–1. His later version differs in essential respects. Brown makes only one inflammatory speech, but that is after the treaty has been announced, and G. W. Brown himself is responsible for having Old Brown arrested. Like most reminiscent accounts, the story has become more self-centered and pointed, probably from frequent repetition. G. W. Brown's "Reminiscences of Old John Brown, No. IV: John Brown in Kansas," Lawrence *Daily Journal*, Nov. 9, 1879, p. 6, cols. 1–2.

12. See Daniel L. Schacter, ed., *Memory Distortion: How Minds, Brains, and Societies Reconstruct the Past* (Cambridge, MA: Harvard University Press, 1995).

13. Of course, Malin also observes, G. W. Brown was attempting to expose John Brown and "was giving the worst possible interpretation of his record." Malin, *John Brown and the Legend of Fifty-six*, pp. 20–1.

14. Salmon Brown to William E. Connelly, May 18, 1913, typed draft, signed, Stutler Collection, WVDCH. Jason Brown and Henry Thompson both mentioned the incident in old age, but both had been ill during the Wakarusa War and were not with Brown at Lawrence. They might have known of the incident, presumably, because Owen or Salmon had told them of it. But it is more likely that they were merely trying to put a better spin on G. W. Brown's stories about their father. See Jason Brown, interview with Katherine Mayo, Dec. 13–14, 1908, pp. 2–3, Villard Collection, CUL, and Henry Thompson's statement dictated to his daughter, Mary, December 1900, as quoted in Franklin B. Sanborn, *Recollections of Seventy Years*, 2 vols. (Boston: Richard G. Badger [The Gorham Press], 1909), 129. Also compare the discussions in Malin, *John Brown and the Legend of Fifty-six*, 16–23 with Stephen B. Oates, *To Purge This Land with Blood: A Biography of John Brown* (New York, Harper & Row, 1970) 108–10. For Robinson's role in the Wakarusa War, see Wilson, *Governor Charles Robinson*, 33–5.

15. John Brown to "Dear Wife & Children every One," Dec. 16, 1855, John Brown Collection, KSHS.

16. John Brown to Orson Day, Dec. 14, 1855, photocopy, John Brown Collection, KSHS. Brown to Day, February 21, 1856, photocopy, John Brown Collection, KSHS.

17. John Brown to "Dear Wife & Children every One," Dec. 16, 1855, John Brown Collection, KSHS.

18. Quoted in Wilson, *Governor Charles Robinson*, 34.

19. John Brown to "Dear Wife & Children every One," Dec. 16, 17, 1855, John Brown Collection, KSHS.

20. John Brown to "Dear Wife & Children every One," Dec. 16, 1855, John Brown Collection, KSHS.

21. John Brown to Owen Brown, Jan. 19, 1856, copy, Villard Collection, CUL.

22. John Brown to "Dear Wife, & Children every one," Jan. 9, 1856, John Brown Collection, CHS.

23. "The Crisis Approaching," *Herald of Freedom*, Jan. 26, 1856, p. 2, col. 2. On the *Herald of Freedom*, see: Malin, *John Brown and the Legend of Fifty-six*, 32–3, 63–8.

24. Quoted in Villard, *John Brown, 1800–1879: A Biography Fifty Years After* (1910; repr., Gloucester, MA: Peter Smith, 1965), 129. In a brilliant assessment of the role of the antislavery press in Kansas, David Potter has suggested that abolitionists won the "propaganda war" in Kansas. Potter contends that Bleeding Kansas was an anomaly because the slavery issue "reached a condition of intolerable tension and violence" even though a majority of the inhabitants "did not care very much one way or the other about slavery." Slavery was not a "basic source of tension," but it was "certainly crucial in structuring and intensifying the friction." David Potter, *The Impending Crisis, 1848–1861* (New York: Harper & Row, 1976), 218–24, 202–3.

25. Testimony of George A. Taylor, Leavenworth City, May 15, 1856, 34th Cong., 1st Session, *U.S. House Reports*, No. 200 (Serial 869), "Report of the Special Committee Appointed to Investigate the Troubles in the Territory of Kansas" (3 vols., 1855–6), Vol. II, 1002–4. Hereafter cited as the *Howard Committee Report*.

26. Testimony of Joseph H. Bird, Leavenworth City, May 16, 1856, *Howard Committee Report*, 980–5, and Henry J. Adams, Leavenworth City, May 15, 1856, *Howard Committee Report*, 985–9.

27. Testimony of David Brown (no relation to R. P. Brown), Leavenworth City, May 15, 1856, *Howard Committee Report*, 996–8.

28. See the testimony of Dr. James Davis, May 16, and Dr. J. G. Park and Dr. Samuel F. Ferr (or Fee), May 17, all of whom had run their forefinger(s) into the dead man's head to assess the wound. *Howard Committee Report*, II: 1004–6. For a detailed account of the murder of Reese Brown, see Nicole Etcheson, *Bleeding Kansas: Contested Liberty in the Civil War Era* (Lawrence: University Press of Kansas, 2004), 89–91.

29. Potter, *The Impending Crisis*, Chapter 9, esp. 218–22.

30. "The Storm Rising," *Herald of Freedom*, January 19, 1856, p. 2, col. 2.

31. Samuel Lyle Adair to Owen Brown, Jan. 31, 1856, Gee Collection, HLHS.

32. John Brown to "Dear Wife & children every one," Feb. 1, 1856, typed copy, Villard Collection, CUL.

33. Villard, *John Brown Fifty Years After*, 132–3.

34. See Michael Fellman, *Inside War: The Guerrilla Conflict in Missouri during the American Civil War* (New York: Oxford, 1989), 11–22, v; and Fellman, "Rehearsal for the Civil War: Antislavery and Proslavery at the Fighting Point in Kansas, 1854–1856," in Lewis Perry and Michael Fellman, eds., *Antislavery Reconsidered: New Perspectives on the Abolitionists* (Baton Rouge: LSU Press, 1979), 287–307. On the stereotyping of rural Southwesterners by Eastern writers, see Fellman, "Alligator Men and Card Sharpers: Deadly Southeastern Humor," *Huntington Library Quarterly*, 49 (1986): 227–42.

35. Nicole Etcheson speculates that Pierce's motives for his belated condemnation of the free-state movement may have been to discredit H. H. Reeder, the former governor allied with the Topeka government. Etcheson, *Bleeding Kansas*, 91–2. See also Villard, *John Brown Fifty Years After*, 130–1.

36. Jason Brown to "Dear Grandfather," Jan. 23, 1856, Gee Collection, HLHS.

37. Quoted in Villard, *John Brown Fifty Years After*, 131.

38. Joshua Giddings to John Brown, March 17, 1856, John Brown Collection, KSHS.

39. John Brown to "Dear Father," March 26, 1856, Gee Collection, HLHS.

40. Adair to "Father Brown," Mar. 4, 6, 1856, Gee Collection, HLHS.

41. John Brown, Jr., to "Dear Grandparents," March 20, 1856, Gee Collection, HLHS.

42. Don W. Wilson, *Governor Charles Robinson of Kansas* (Lawrence: University of Kansas Press, 1975), 38.

43. Samuel Lyle Adair to "Father Brown," Mar. 4, 6, 1856, Gee Collection, HLHS.

44. John Brown, Jr., to [no salutation], Apr. 4, 1856, John Brown, Jr., Papers, OHS. The letter appeared in *Frederick Douglass' Paper* on May 2, 1856.

45. For a discussion of McRae's case, see Villard, *John Brown Fifty Years After*, 109–10.

46. Stephen B. Oates notes that the minutes of the Osawatomie settlers' meeting do not reflect the moderates' walkout or mention the speeches of Brown and White. See Oates, *To Purge This Land with Blood*, 118–19.

47. John Brown, Jr.'s letter, written at Pottawatomie on April 29, included the resolutions adopted by the free-state members of the Osawatomie settlers' meeting of April 16 repudiating the authority of the "foreign" legislators at Shawnee Mission, and detailing the actions of the Pottawatomie Rifles at the opening session of "Cato's" court. See "The Right Spirit" in the "Original Correspondence" of the *Herald of Freedom*, May 10, 1856, p. 2.

48. Salmon Brown to William E. Connelly, May 18, 1913, typed copy signed [and edited], Stutler Collection, WVDCH. Portions of this nineteen-page typed letter, which Salmon evidently dictated to his daughter, Ethel Brown Chamberlain, were later published under the title "John Brown and Sons in Kansas Territory" in the *Indiana Magazine of History*, 31 (June 1935), 142–50, and are reprinted in Louis Ruchames, ed., *A John Brown Reader* (London: Abelard-Schuman, 1959), 189–97, esp. 190–1.

49. "Statement of Henry Thompson Concerning His Kansas Experiences, 1855–56," dictated to Mary Thompson, December, 1900, as quoted in Franklin B. Sanborn, *Recollections of Seventy Years*, 2 vols. (Boston: Richard G. Badger [The Gorham Press], 1909), I: 129.

50. John Brown to "Dear Brother Adair," April 22, 1856, as quoted in Villard, *John Brown Fifty Years After*, 136.

51. John, Jr., observed that although Cato did not respond directly to the question whether he would enforce territorial law, the judge spoke of "our laws" and placed his hand on the statute book while swearing the jurors. Letter to the editor dated April 29, 1856, in *The Herald of Freedom*, May 10, p. 2, cols. 3–4.

52. Brown to Adair, April 22, 1856, as quoted in Villard, *John Brown Fifty Years After*, 136.

53. In a 1911 reminiscence, Salmon Brown wrote that John, Jr., and his father "served [the] warning on Judge Cato. I and some others went along." Salmon Brown to Franklin B. Sanborn, Nov. 17, 1911, ALS, Stutler Collection, WVDCH. But Salmon's memory was mistaken on several points. He recalled, for example, that the settlers' meeting had "selected" his father and brother John "to serve the warning on Judge Cato," telescoping events. In fact, it was John's company that decided to deliver the resolutions to Cato, whoever actually did so. Salmon also mistakenly says that Cato "got out warrants for all the Browns and the members of the Free State Legislature that were in his district." In this scenario, Salmon wrongly makes Doyle a "constable" and his two eldest sons "deputies" to serve warrants on "the whole Brown crowd and Henry Thompson." Salmon Brown to William E. Connelly, May 18, 1913, typed letter signed, 19 pp., Stutler Collection, WVDCH.

54. John Brown to "Dear Father," May 8, 1856, Gee Collection, HLHS.

55. In fact, in his letter to the *Herald of Freedom*, John Brown, Jr., was careful to mention no names apart from members of the court. Acknowledging himself a witness

to the events, he refers only to the "Captain of the Company" in recounting his own call to assemble the Rifles in order to adopt the Osawatomie resolutions. Doubtless, John, Jr., wished to invite no future court to indict him for publicly disavowing territorial law. Letter to the editor dated April 29, 1856, in the *Herald of Freedom*, May 10, p. 2, cols. 3–4.

56. John Brown to "Brother Adair," April 22, 1856, John Brown Collection, HLHS.

57. This summary concurs with John, Jr.'s, report. Letter to the editor dated April 29, 1856, in the *Herald of Freedom*, May 10, p. 2, cols. 3–4.

58. Only weeks before the bound volumes of law enacted the previous summer by the first session of the Territorial Legislature had been shipped up the Missouri River from St. Louis at the opening of navigation. The territorial courts had had little time to study the laws they were to enforce. See Malin, *John Brown and the Legend of Fifty-six*, 537–59.

59. Cato indicted Brown with nine others at the Lykins County session for conspiracy to resist the tax laws in consequence of signing the Osawatomie resolutions. (Ironically, he had no property to assess.) John Brown, Jr., was arrested and held several months on other charges but the tax cases against him and his father were dismissed in 1857. After Cato interviewed James Harris and obtained affidavits from Joseph B. Higgins and George W. Grant on May 31, however, he issued a warrant for the arrest of Brown and seven others for the Pottawatomie killings. See Malin, *John Brown and the Legend of Fifty-six*, 570–9.

60. Salmon Brown to Franklin B. Sanborn, Nov. 17, 1911, Stutler Collection, WVDCH.

61. Malin, *John Brown and the Legend of Fifty-six*, 754–5.

62. Affidavit of James Harris, 34th Cong., 1st Sess., *U.S. House Reports*, No. 200 (Serial 869), "Report of the Special Committee Appointed to Investigate the Troubles in the Territory of Kansas" (3 vols., 1855–65), II, 1179–81. Hereafter cited as the *Howard Committee Report*. Also see Malin, *John Brown and the Legend of Fifty-six*, 754–5.

63. Oates, *To Purge This Land with Blood*, 387–8 n7.

64. Adair to "Father Brown," May 16, 1856, John Brown Collection, HLHS.

65. John Brown to Frederick Douglass, Jan. 9, 1854, as quoted in Ruchames, *A John Brown Reader*, pp. 84–5.

66. "Exciting Times in Lawrence," the *Herald of Freedom*, April 26, 1856, p. 2, cols. 1–3.

67. "Another War Threatening Us," the *Herald of Freedom*, May 10, 1856, p. 2, cols. 1–2.

68. On April 12 the Free State Hotel, whose foundations had been excavated a year earlier at the instance of agents of the New England Emigrant Aid Company, was finished. With its stables and outhouses, it occupied four lots. During the Wakarusa War, the unfinished three-story stone structure had served as headquarters for the free-state volunteer army. Now the walls rose above the hotel's flat roof sufficiently to permit port holes, temporarily plugged with stones, from which riflemen could command a view of the surrounding area. It was to the hotel that the wounded Sheriff Jones had been taken for medical aid. But to Missourians the Free State Hotel was an abolitionist fortress, and it was destroyed by cannon fire during the "invasion." The *Herald of Freedom*, April 12, 1856, p. 2, col. 2.

69. Samuel Lyle Adair to "Father [Owen] Brown," May 16, 1856, John Brown Collection, HLHS.

70. Malin, *John Brown and the Legend of Fifty-six*, 320; Oates, *To Purge This Land with Blood*, 126; Villard, *John Brown Fifty Years After*, 170–88, esp. 172.
71. Florella Brown Adair to Martha Lucretia Brown Davis, May 16, 1856, Villard Collection, CUL.
72. Oates finds the evidence that the "Wilkinson-Sherman-Doyle faction flung threats and insults" at the Browns "quite convincing." Oates also stresses the "hysteria" and frustration created by the sack of Lawrence as a determining factor in Brown's decision to strike a "retaliatory blow." See Oates, *To Purge This Land with Blood*, 122, 382, note 24, 128, 384, note 3, 387–8, note 7.

CHAPTER 6 – TERRORISER

1. Lincoln's assassin, the actor John Wilkes Booth, referred thus of Brown in recounting Brown's hanging to a friend. Booth to John Clark, Apr. 20, 1865, Stutler Collection, WVDCH.
2. For a discussion, see Robert E. McGlone, "Rescripting a Troubled Past: John Brown's Family and the Harpers Ferry Conspiracy," *Journal of American History*, 75 (March 1989): 1179–1200.
3. "The Potawatomie [sic] Tragedy, John Brown's Connection With It, Statement of James Townsley, an Eye-Witness," Lawrence *Daily Journal*, December 10, 1879, p. 2. Townsley's statement was actually drafted by an attorney, John Hutchings; others drafted two later versions. How much the advice of Hutchings influenced Townsley's account raises yet another question about its accuracy. See Oswald Garrison Villard, *John Brown, 1800–1879: A Biography Fifty Years After* (1910; repr., Gloucester, MA: Peter Smith, 1965), 609 n17.
4. See Johnson Clark's statement in the Lawrence *Daily Journal*, Nov. 18, 1879, p. 2, cols. 2–4.
5. Samuel Lyle Adair to "Brother & Sister Hand & Other Friends," typed copy, May 28, 1856, John Brown Collection, HLHS.
6. Adair to "Father Brown," May 16, 1856, John Brown Collection, HLHS.
7. Owen Brown, interview with Franklin B. Sanborn, June 27, 1880, Sanborn Folder, HU.
8. Villard insists six free-state men had been murdered and that Brown's defenders later fudged the figure to give significance to the number he killed. But Adair and others did not include Samuel Collins, who died on October 25, 1855, perhaps because Collins was shot in a fair fight and it was debatable whether Collins or his adversary, as Villard admits, "assumed the offensive." Villard, *John Brown Fifty Years After*, 112–13, 180.
9. "The Potawatomie [sic] Tragedy, John Brown's Connection With It, Statement of James Townsley, an Eye-Witness." Lawrence *Daily Journal*, Dec. 10, 1879, p. 2.
10. Quoted in Villard, *John Brown Fifty Years After*, 158. In addition to the statement he made to Villard's research assistant in 1908, Salmon Brown wrote two accounts of his Kansas experience that touched on the Pottawatomie raid: Salmon to Franklin B. Sanborn, Aug. 8, 1909, typed draft, Stutler Collection, WVDHC; Salmon to William E. Connelly, May 28, 1913, typed draft, signed, 19 pp., Stutler Collection, WVDHC.
11. If Brown had sought only to ask directions at that first cabin, Townsley's claim to a thorough knowledge of the neighborhood must be questioned. In his 1879

statement, he conceded, "I have forgotten whose cabin it was if I knew at the time." Townsley's "Confession."

12. Affidavit of Mahala Doyle, June 7, 1856, Jackson County, Missouri, in the *Howard Report*, 1175–6; statement of John Doyle, June 7, 1856, Jackson County, in Ibid., 1176–7.

13. Salmon Brown claimed that Brown had divided his men into two parties, Henry Thompson and August Weiner in one and the Brown boys in the other, with old Brown "running back and forth between the two parties." But Salmon mistakenly says that Henry Thompson killed *Henry* Sherman, who was not slain. Although Villard regarded Salmon as the sanest of the surviving Browns, Salmon's reminiscent testimony is often badly muddled and tenaciously partisan. Salmon Brown, "John Brown and Sons in Kansas Territory," as reprinted from the *Indiana Magazine of History*, 31 (June 1935): 142–50, in Louis Ruchames, ed., *A John Brown Reader* (London: Abelard-Schuman, 1959), 194.

14. Affidavit of Mrs. Louisa Jane Wilkinson, June 13, 1856, Jackson County, Missouri, in *Howard Committee Report*, 1179–81.

15. Affidavit of James Harris, June 6, 1856, Jackson County, Missouri, in the *Howard Committee Report*, 1177–79.

16. Affidavit of Louisa Jane Wilkinson, June 13, 1856, *Howard Committee Report*, 1179–81.

17. As previously noted, "Judge H. H. Williams [was] ... at the time living on Pottowattomie [sic] Creek and was acquainted with all the men that had been appointed by Judge Cato put down the names in my presence of ... the men that would have to be put out of the way." Salmon Brown to "Friend F. B. Sanborn," Nov. 17, 1911, Stutler Collection, WVDCH.

18. See especially G. W. Brown's letters of April 12 and 13. in the *Herald of Freedom*, April 26, 1856, p. 4, cols. 2–4.

19. "Fate of Murderers of Lovejoy," *The Herald of Freedom*, April 12, 1856, p. 2, col. 7. In the issue of the *Herald of Freedom* that carried an extensive account of the public meeting at Lawrence, which had been called to repudiate the assault on Sheriff Jones, G. W. Brown, back from his holiday, ran a story on the Lovejoy murder, which was "still fresh in the minds of our readers." In May the editor himself fell into the hands of a mob in Kansas City and was made prisoner by proslavery officials. "The Murder of Lovejoy," *Herald of Freedom*, April 26, 1856, p. 3, col. 2.

20. Oswald Garrison Villard to Franklin B. Sanborn, June 25, 1909, ALS, John Brown Papers, KSHS; Villard, *John Brown Fifty Years After*, 172–3.

21. Oates agrees, however, that John Brown himself had grown to "fear" and "detest" the proslavery men on the Pottawatomie. Stephen B. Oates, *To Purge This Land with Blood: A Biography of John Brown* (New York: Harper & Row, 1970), 122–3, 382–3, notes 25 and 26.

22. Salmon Brown to Franklin B. Sanborn, Nov. 11, 1917, ALS, Stutler Collection, WVDCH.

23. Quoted in Franklin B. Sanborn, *The Life and Letters of John Brown, Liberator of Kansas, and Martyr of Virginia* (1885; repr., New York Negro University, 1969), 260, 258–9.

24. Quoted in Sanborn, *Life and Letters of John Brown*, 250.

25. Quoted in Malin, *John Brown and the Legend of Fifty-six*, 317.

26. Malin's land key map shows that John G. Morse's claim was upstream from that of John T. Grant and that Henry Sherman's crossing did lie athwart the path. The

map also reveals that "old" Squire Morse's claim was adjacent to that of Simeon B. Morse, whose relationship to the Squire, if any, is unknown. Also a Samuel Morse lived a short walk away. If these Morses were relatives, Squire Morse might presumably have found protection with them rather than the Grants. Clearly, a number of unanswered questions surround the story of his demise. The maps are in Malin, *John Brown and the Legend of Fifty-six*, 764.

27. Interview with George W. Grant (and Henry C. Grant) in the Lawrence (Kansas) *Daily Journal*, December 5, 1879, p. 2, cols. 1–3. Compare the story drawn from this interview by Sanborn in *Life and Letters of John Brown*, 255–6, with George Grant's 1908 statement, quoted in Villard, *John Brown Fifty Years After*, 174–5.

28. Hinton's article appeared in the Boston *Traveler*, Dec. 3, 1859. It is here quoted in G. W. Brown's "Reminiscences of Old John Brown," Lawrence *Daily Journal*, Nov. 23, 1879, p. 6, cols. 1–5.

29. Redpath, *Public Life of Capt. John Brown* (Boston: Thayer and Eldridge, 1960), 372–5.

30. Quoted in Sanborn, *Life and Letters of John Brown*, 256.

31. Quoted in Villard, *John Brown Fifty Years After*, 172–3.

32. Franklin Sanborn, Brown's chief defender, included two versions of the story in his *Life and Letters of John Brown*. An "old Kansas settler," E. A. Coleman, reported that Brown himself told him of the surveying incident and claimed, "'I heard that these men were coming to the cabin that my son and I were staying in ... to set fire to it and shoot us as we ran out." John, Jr.'s, version differed somewhat, Sanborn noted, and was "doubtless the correct one." Sanborn, *Life and Letters of John Brown*, 258–60.

33. Interview with George W. Grant (and Henry C. Grant) in the Lawrence (Kansas) *Daily Journal*, December 5, 1879, p. 2, cols. 1–3.

34. John Brown to E. B. Whitman, undated handwritten memo, signed, John Brown Collection, HLHS. Salmon Brown credited Mills with saving the lives of Owen Brown and Henry Thompson, both of whom had been wounded by gunshot in Kansas. Salmon Brown interview with Katherine Mayo, Oct. 11–13, 1908, Villard Papers, CUL.

35. Statements of Mrs. Orson [Mary] Day, Francis Morse, John T. Grant, and William Grant to Dr. Lucius Mills, June 12, 14, 1856, Adair Family Collection, KSHS.

36. Ibid.

37. See, for example, Villard, *John Brown Fifty Years After*, 176.

38. Franklin Sanborn's handwritten notes of a conversation with Owen Brown, June 17, 1880, Sanborn Folder, HU.

39. Owen's recollection also had the Brown party leaving the Rifles' camp in the morning rather than the afternoon. When Owen rode up to the Adair cabin soon after the raid, Adair turned him away, saying, as Owen recalled, "You are a marked man – you see what a terrible calamity you have brought upon your friends, and the sooner you go away the better." To this Owen replied, "I intend to be a marked man." He never saw his Uncle Adair again. Sanborn's notes of a conversation with Owen Brown, June 27, 1880, Sanborn Folder, HU.

40. James Hanway to James Redpath, March 12, 1860, as quoted in Malin, *John Brown and the Legend of Fifty-six*, 314–15.

41. Adair to "Father [Owen] Brown," May 16, 1856, John Brown Collection, HLHS.

42. Oswald Garrison Villard, who was determined to vindicate the idea that moral suasion alone was the proper response to slavery, uses this letter to show that the Brown women were "never harmed." The threats, he says, were a later "fabrication."

The more salient point illustrated by Jason's letter is that the expectation that women might be harmed was real enough. See Villard, *John Brown Fifty Years After*, 172–3.

43. John Brown to Mary Brown, June [26] 1856, quoted in Sanborn, *Life and Letters of John Brown*, 236–7. Jason remembered that "our cabins were empty" and his and John's families "had gone to Osawatomie for safety while we were at Palmyra" (near Prairie City on the Sante Fe Road – i.e., on the march to Lawrence). "Pottawatomie: Statement By Jason, Second Son of John Brown," Akron Ohio *Beacon*, Jan. 21, 1880, as quoted in the Lawrence (Kansas) *Daily Journal*, Feb. 8, 1880, p. 2, cols. 3–4.

44. Townsley also mentions Probate Judge George Wilson of Anderson County as one of Brown's intended victims, allegedly because Wilson had been notifying free-state men to leave the territory. Townsley himself recalled receiving such a notice. The claim is doubtful, however, since it is not clear why Brown should have expected to find Wilson at Dutch Henry's Crossing. Townsley's "Confession," Lawrence *Daily Journal*, Dec. 10, 1879, p. 2, col. 2.

45. On the survivors' struggle to cope with Brown's legacy, see Robert E. McGlone, "Rescripting a Troubled Past: John Brown's Family and the Harpers Ferry Conspiracy," *The Journal of American History*, 75 (March 1989): 1179–1200.

46. Jason told the story of his confrontation with his father often in later years. In an 1880 version, however, he showed uncertainty about what his father had said. Confronting the Old Man near his brother's cabin after first learning of the massacre, Jason asked John whether he had had anything to do with the killings. "I think he said (but cannot be certain), that he denied it," Jason admitted. Then he ventured what has become an oft-quoted exchange, John Brown asserting: "'I did not do it, but I approved of it.' I told him that whoever did it, I thought it was an uncalled for, wicked act. He answered: 'God is my judge; and the people of Kansas will yet justify my course.'" In later versions, Jason would drop the disclaimer; historians would do well not to take such memories as literal accounts. "'Pottawatomie': Statement By Jason, Second Son of John Brown," Akron (Ohio) *Beacon*, Jan. 21, 1880, as quoted in the Lawrence (Kansas) *Daily Journal*, Jan. ?, 1880, p. 2, cols. 2–4.

47. See, for example, John Brown, Jr., to Sanborn, Apr. 8, 1885, Stutler Collection, WVDCH.

48. Henry Thompson interview by Katherine Mayo, Aug. 22–Sept. 1, 1908, Villard Collection, CUL.

49. See the discussion in Chapter 1 of Allan Nevins's contention that Brown suffered from "reasoning insanity," which he declared was a form of "paranoia." Nevins, *The Emergence of Lincoln*, 2 vols. (New York: Scribner, 1950), II: 77, 81–4. For a vigorous dissent, see Louis A. DeCaro, Jr., *"Fire from the Midst of You": A Religious Life of John Brown* (New York: New York University Press, 2002), 1–4. The question whether Brown may have suffered from mental illness is the subject of Chapters 7 and 8.

50. We have only reminiscent evidence to substantiate this warning. Interview with George and Henry C. Grant, *The Daily Journal* (Lawrence, Kansas), Dec. 5, 1879, p. 2, cols. 1–3. In 1868 James Hanway, who had been with the Rifles at Prairie City, claimed that an older member of the Rifles had asked Brown what he planned to do as his men prepared to return to the Pottawatomie. When Brown replied that he was "going to regulate matters on the Potawatomie," the old gentleman

urged Brown to "act with caution." According to Hanway, Brown replied curtly,
"'Caution! Caution! – These are always the words of cowardice." Hanway's several
accounts are published in full in Malin, *John Brown and the Legend of Fifty-six*,
Chapter 12, esp. 328–30. On John, Jr.'s alleged quarrel with his father, see Oates,
To Purge This Land with Blood, 129.

51. Townsley claimed that he and Weiner and Frederick Brown took no part in the
killing. Owen also acknowledged that Weiner killed no one and "acted as a guard"
around the houses of the victims. Salmon, on the other hand, insisted that Weiner
was spoiling for revenge against the Shermans, who had warned him to leave the
territory. Salmon remembered Weiner as a "big, savage, bloodthirsty Austrian"
who "could not be kept out of any accessible fight." "Henry Thompson and Weiner
killed Wilkinson and Sherman," Salmon testified. (Quoted in Villard, *John Brown
Fifty Years After*, 162 n39.) Townsley may well have exonerated Weiner because
that gentleman was still living near Lawrence. Townsley may even have hoped that
Weiner would testify in support of his statement about the killings, but Weiner
remained silent to the end.

52. Frederick Brown's illness is discussed in Chapter 7. Both Owen and Salmon agreed
that Frederick, who was later killed by a proslavery posse, took no part in the
killings. Owen claimed that Frederick had opposed the project from the outset.
Owen Brown interview by Franklin B. Sanborn, June 27, 1880, Sanborn Folder,
HU; Salmon Brown to William E. Connelly, May 28, 1913, typed copy, Stutler
Collection, WVDCH; Salmon Brown interview by Sanborn, Nov. 17, 1911, Stutler
Collection, WVDCH; Salmon Brown to Sanborn, Aug. 8, 1909, Stutler Collection,
WVDCH.

53. In a statement to Franklin B. Sanborn, Owen admitted obliquely that he had been
one of those to wield a bloody broadsword. Unlike his father, Owen had seen
the Doyles "two or three times" and presumably knew them to be supporters of
the Ruffians. Owen agreed that Townsley had opposed the plan and had not participated in the killing. He remembered that Weiner acted as a "guard around the
house" of one victim, but Weiner did not to his knowledge kill anyone. (Owen
Brown interview by Franklin B. Sanborn, June 27, 1880, Sanborn Folder, HU.)
Implicitly, Salmon acknowledged his own role. "Owen Brown cut down one of
them and another son cut down the other and the old man Doyle.... Henry [sic,
William] Sherman was killed by Henry Thompson, and also Wilkinson, about the
same time that the Doyles were killed." After dispatching the Doyles, the party
had divided, Weiner accompanying Thompson and "old man Townsley" accom-
panying the four Brown boys. John Brown ran "back and forth between the parties." Salmon Brown to William E. Connelly, May 28, 1913, typed copy, Stutler
Collection, WVDCH; Salmon Brown interview by Sanborn, Nov. 17, 1911, Stutler
Collection, WVDCH; Salmon Brown to Sanborn, Aug. 8, 1909, Stutler Collection,
WVDCH.

54. In 1910 the pacifist, Oswald Garrison Villard, assuming that Brown's sons necessarily had to be opposed to the killing, suggested lamely: "Whether it was the compelling personality of their father, whose dominating manner and will-power later
led men willingly to their death ... or whether there was in the sons a sufficient
touch of an inherited mental disturbance to make them less than rational in their
reasoning, there was no attempt at a filial revolt against a parental decision, even
when they went unwillingly." Villard, *John Brown Fifty Years After*, 158. Villard's
argument here is an interesting reversal of the view other writers would take: For

him Old Brown was sane, but his sons had to be mentally disturbed to aid him in
so brutal an act. In fact, neither Salmon, Owen, nor Henry Thompson, who did
the killing, showed signs of mental disorder in later years. As I note in Chapter 7,
however, John, Jr., who did not accompany his father to Pottawatomie; Frederick,
who would not kill but went along; and their sister Ruth all evidenced symptoms
of mental disorder at one time or another.

55. John Brown to "Dear Son John," Aug. 26, 1853, Stutler Collection, WVDCH.
56. John Brown to "Dear Children," Sept. 24, 1853, as quoted in Sanborn, *Life and
    Letters of John Brown*, 154–5.
57. James M. McPherson generalizes Oates's thesis, claiming that Brown had "an
    almost mesmeric influence over many of his associates." *Battle Cry of Freedom:
    The Civil War Era* (New York: Ballantine Books, 1988), 152.
58. Oates, *To Purge This Land with Blood*, 130–4.
59. Salmon Brown to William E. Connelly, May 28, 1913, Stutler Collection,
    WVDCH.
60. It is worth noting that Townsley returned with Brown after the raid to the camp of
    the Rifles. Evidently, he was not then eager to dissociate himself from the killings.
    Townsley's "Confession," Lawrence *Daily Journal*, Dec. 10, 1879, p. 2.
61. Owen Brown interview by Franklin B. Sanborn, June 27, 1880, Sanborn Folder,
    HU.
62. In Salmon's first account, he remembered that Townsley "killed Doyle's hounds
    and bulldogs." In the second, Salmon claims Townsley was with one of the two
    groups of assassins and "worked with all his might, not as a prisoner, as he has
    since claimed." Salmon to Friend Franklin B. Sanborn, Nov. 17, 1911, Stutler
    Collection, WCDCH; Salmon Brown to William E. Connelly, May 28, 1913, typed
    letter, signed and with a handwritten note, Stutler Collection, WVDCH.
63. Henry Thompson interview by Katherine Mayo, Aug. 22–Sept. 1, 1908, Villard
    Collection, CUL.
64. John Brown to "Dear Son John," Apr. 3, 1854, John Brown, Jr., Papers, OHS.
65. Quoted in John Anthony Scott and Robert Alan Scott, *John Brown of Harper's
    Ferry* (New York: Facts on File, 1988), 97–8.
66. Salmon's account of the younger boys' pranks and defiance of their father are
    instructive. After a particularly severe thrashing during which Salmon refused to
    cry out, his father allegedly said at last: "'You are a very bad boy' and left me. He
    never tried to punish me again." While such reminiscences are doubtless much
    rescripted, Salmon's pride in his manliness and early independence, judging from
    his letters, is probably warranted. (Salmon Brown interview with Katherine Mayo,
    Oct. 11–13, 1908, Villard Collection, CUL, pp. 4–5.) Even Jason, who branded
    himself the family coward, denied that he had ever feared his father. See the notes
    of his interview with Katherine Mayo, Dec. 13–14, 1908, Villard Collection, CUL,
    pp. 1, 24.
67. A year after returning to North Elba from Kansas, Oliver left home to work in
    the axe factory of Charles Blair, whom his father had commissioned to make
    pikes. Oliver's gracious apology to his family reveals another side of the youth.
    "Unpleasant word" had passed between himself and his brother Watson, for which,
    Oliver wrote, "I hold myself entirely balmable. Nothing has troubled me so much
    since I left home as the foolish and reckless manner in which I trampled upon and
    robbed myself of the good feeling of my family: Anna in particular has received
    a double dose of my abuse, and mother, too ... to whom I owe a greater debt of

gratitude than to any other person in the world. For these offenses I would humbly beg the pardon of the family, and hope to mend my ways hereafter." Oliver Brown to "Mother, Brother[s] and Sisters," July 28, 1857, hand copy, Sanborn Folder, HU.

68. Brown briefly considered sending Oliver to a military school. Sarah Brown, interview with Katherine Mayo, Sept. 16–20, 1908, Villard Collection, CUL.

69. Salmon Brown interview with Katherine Mayo, Oct. 11–13, 1908, Villard Collection, CUL. Also see Villard, *John Brown Fifty Years After*, 223.

70. Oates, *To Purge This Land with Blood*, 128–33.

71. Interview with George W. Grant (and Henry C. Grant) in the Lawrence (Kansas) *Daily Journal*, Dec. 5, 1879, p. 2, cols. 1–3.

72. Salmon Brown, "John Brown and Sons in Kansas Territory," in Ruchames, *A John Brown Reader*, 194.

73. Owen's 1885 statement as quoted in Sanborn, *Life and Letters of John Brown*, 270–1.

74. On the theft of the horses, see Salmon Brown to William E. Connelly, May 28, 1913, typed letter signed, Stutler Collection, WVDCH, and Salmon to "Friend F. B. Sanborn," Nov. 17, 1911, Stutler Collection, WVDCH. Also see the affidavit of James Harris, June 6, 1856, Jackson County, Missouri, in the *Howard Committee Report*, 1177–9 and the testimony given before U.S. Commissioner Edward Hoogland on June 20, 1856 at Tecumseh, Kansas, to determine if there was sufficient evidence to hold John Brown, Jr., and others for a grand jury scheduled to meet in September on charges of treason. Commissioner Hoogland concluded to ask Judge Sterling Cato to issue warrants for John, Jr., and H. H. Williams. See James C. Malin, "The Hoogland Examination: The United States v. John Brown, Jr., et al," *Kansas Historical Quarterly*, 7 (May 1938): 133–53, esp. 139–42.

75. Brown was deeply disappointed. "I have only to say as regards the resolution of the boys to 'learn and practice war no more' that it was not at my solicitation that they engaged in it at the first," he told Mary somewhat disingenuously. John Brown to Mary A. Brown, March 31, 1857, Villard Collection, CUL. "My wife wrote me as follows," he wrote to Franklin B. Sanborn, "'The boys have all determined both to practise and learn war no more.' This I said nothing about [to New England supporters]," Brown added, "lest it should prevent my getting any further supplies." Brown to Sanborn, May 27, 1857, as quoted in Ruchames, *The Making of a Revolutionary*, 115–17. It was more than a year before Brown was able to persuade one of his sons, Owen, to join his company; even then Owen disputed his father "in any & everything." Owen Brown Diary, Rust Collection, HEHL. See McGlone, "Rescripting a Troubled Past," *The Journal of American History*, 75 (March 1989), 1186–7.

76. Salmon Brown to John Brown, May 21, 1855, handwritten copy, Sanborn Folder, HU.

77. Salmon to "Mother, Brothers, Sisters," Aug. 20, 1855, Stutler Collection, WVDCH.

78. John Brown, Jr., to Mary Brown, Sept. 16, 1855, hand copy, Sanborn Folder, HU.

79. Frederick Brown to "Dear Brother Watkin [Watson]," Nov. 10, 1855, John Brown, Jr., Papers, OHS.

80. Oliver Brown to "Dear Mother, Brother, & Sisters," Feb. 4, 1856, Villard Collection, CUL.

81. Henry Thompson to Ruth Brown Thompson, April 16, 1856, copy by Katherine Mayo, Villard Collection, CUL.

82. Jason Brown reported that Thompson wrote his story of Pottawatomie because he "owed it to posterity to reveal the truth," but that his daughter burned it. Jason Brown interview with Katherine Mayo, Aug. 22–Sept. 1, 1908, Villard Collection, CUL.

83. Henry Thompson, interview with Katherine Mayo, Aug 22–Sept. 1, 1908, Villard Collection, CUL.

84. Henry Thompson to Ruth Brown Thompson, Jan. 26, 1856, copy by Katherine Mayo, Villard Collection, CUL.

85. James H. Holmes, undated notes of interview with Henry Thompson, copy by Katherine Mayo, Villard Collection, CUL.

86. Albert Bandura, "Mechanisms of Moral Disengagement," in Walter Reich, ed., *Origins of Terrorism: Psychologies, Ideologies, Theologies, States of Mind* (New York: Cambridge University Press, 1990), 162.

87. Samuel Lyle Adair to "Dear Father Brown," May 16, 1856, typed copy, Gee Collection, HLHS.

88. "The Potawatomie [sic] Tragedy, John Brown's Connection With It, Statement of James Townsley, an Eye-Witness," Lawrence *Daily Journal*, Dec. 10, 1879, p. 2.

89. See Judges 7: 8–20.

90. John Brown, "Words of Advice," a statement to the Springfield "Branch of the United States League of Gileadites," adopted January 15, 1851, as quoted in Ruchames, *A John Brown Reader*, 76–8.

91. The word "terrorism" is not indexed in Richard Maxwell Brown's classic 1975 study of vigilantism in American history. Brown, *Strain of Violence: Historical Studies of American Violence and Vigilantism* (New York: Oxford University Press, 1975). Other precursors of terrorism were not long in appearing on the American scene, notably the Molly Maguires in 1865 and the Ku Klux Klan during Reconstruction. The German anarchist Johann Most migrated to America in 1882, and Mikhail Bakunin himself visited the United States in 1861 en route to Europe after his escape from Siberia, too late to have inspired John Brown. Albert Parry, *Terrorism: From Robespierre to Arafat* (New York: Vanguard Press, 1976), 91–6, passim.

92. Despite the flood of books about international terrorism published since 9/11, Anthony J. Marsella concludes that defining terrorism may be possible only in broad terms: For him it is the use of force or violence by individuals or groups that is directed toward civilian populations and intended to instill fear as a means of coercing individuals or groups to change their political or social positions. See Marsella, "Reflections on International Terrorism: Issues, Concepts, and Directions," in Fathali M. Moghaddam and Anthony J. Marsella, eds., *Understanding Terrrorism: Psychosocial Roots, Consequences, and Interventions* (Washington, DC: American Psychological Association, 2004), Chapter 1. An excellent discussion of this issue is Yonah Alexander and Alan O'Day, "Introduction: Dimensions of Irish Terrorism," in Alexander and Day, *The Irish Terrorism Experience* (Aldershot, England: Dartmouth Press, 1991), 1–7. David E. Long concludes that the characteristics of political terrorism include a profound sense of injustice that presumably cannot be assuaged in any other way. Hence terrorism is often called the "tactic of last resort." A further characteristic of twentieth-century terrorist organizations has been their appeal to "universal truths" or holy causes, such as a crusade against evil or the fulfillment of national destiny, to justify their actions. Despite the claims of such organizations and the popularity of the term "sacred

terror," among religions, only Wahabist and radical versions of Islam are believed to espouse or justify the practice of terrorism. See David E. Long, *The Anatomy of Terrorism* (New York: The Free Press, 1990), 1–13. Although Albert Parry devoted a chapter of his 1976 history of terrorism to America, he did not mention John Brown in *Terrorism*, Chapter 8 et passim. See also Walter Laquer, *A History of Terrorism* (New Brunswick, NJ: Transaction, 2001).

93. Affidavit of Louisa Jane Wilkinson, June 13, 1856, cited in the *Howard Committee Report*, 1179–81.

94. A founder of social behaviorism, Bandura assesses the origins and prevention of terrorism in "The Role of Selective Moral Disengagement in Terrorism and Counter-terrorism," in Moghaddam and Marsella, *Understanding Terrorism*, Chapter 6.

95. Albert Bandura, "Mechanisms of Moral Disengagement," in Reich, *Origins of Terrorism*, 161–91. Bandura also uses the term "moral disinhibition," implicitly implying that the impulse to violence is logically prior to constraints of conscience. See Bandura, "The Role of Selective Moral Disengagement."

96. Indeed, even scientists exhibit "confirmation bias," often failing to seek discon-firmatory evidence, to use it when available, to test alternative hypotheses, or to consider whether evidence supporting a favored hypothesis supports alternative hypotheses as well. See the discussion in Ryan D. Tweney, Michael E. Doherty, and Clifford R. Mynatt, *On Scientific Thinking* (New York: Columbia University Press, 1981), part IV.

97. Bandura, "Mechanisms of Moral Disengagement," 188–91.

98. John Brown to "Dear Wife & Children, every one," April 7, 1856, John Brown Collection, KSHS.

99. When Virginia authorities interrogated Brown after Harpers Ferry, a bystander asked Brown: "Do you consider yourself an instrument in the hands of Providence?" Brown answered simply, "I do." He also insisted that he had seized Harpers Ferry in obedience to the golden rule, "not to gratify any personal ani-mosity, revenge or vindictive spirit. It is my sympathy with the oppressed and the wronged, that are as good as you and as precious in the sight of God." Clearly, such a claim to moral justification for the deaths at Pottawatomie would have been difficult to sustain. Brown's interview is quoted in the Richmond *Enquirer*, Oct. 21, p. 1, cols. 7–8.

100. See Brown's letter to Congressman Joshua Giddings, Feb. 20, 1856, cited in Villard, *John Brown Fifty Years After*, 131. The migrants from Alabama and Georgia, Adair thought, were "hard cases" – drunken, profane, and restless. They were "threaten-ing to drive off free state men from their claims and take possession of them," caus-ing "great insecurity" and "much alarm." Adair to "Father Brown," May 16, 1856, typed copy, Gee Collection, HLHS.

101. Townsley's "Confession," Lawrence *Daily Journal*, Dec. 10, 1879, p. 2, col. 2.

102. Salmon Brown, "John Brown and Sons in Kansas Territory," as quoted in Ruchames, *A John Brown Reader*, 194.

103. Owen Brown, interview with Franklin Sanborn, June 27, 1880, Sanborn Folder, HU. Even at so late a date Owen was unsure whether it was safe to "tell all these particulars" to his father's most trusted biographer.

104. Affidavit of Mahala Doyle, June 7, 1856, as quoted in the *Howard Committee Report*, 1175–6.

105. Affidavit of James Harris, June 6, 1856, as quoted in the *Howard Committee Report*, 1178–9.

106. Oates, *To Purge This Land with Blood*, 135.
107. Salmon Brown to William E. Connelly, May 28, 1913, typed letter signed, Stutler Collection, WVDCH.
108. Affidavit of Louisa Jane Wilkinson, June 13, 1856, as quoted in the *Howard Committee Report*, 1179–81.
109. Brown had written of the revolutions in Europe that "God is carrying out his eternal purpose in them all." John Brown to "Dear Mary," Dec. 22, 1851, as quoted in Ruchames, *A John Brown Reader*, 78–9.
110. As we have seen, G. W. Brown originated the story that Brown had tried to undermine the Wakarusa settlement by calling for war. Long after, Brown's sons made a similar claim based on Salmon's dubious account, but contemporary evidence conflicts with the story. Jason was not a witness and he claimed only that he had heard the story from his brothers Owen and Salmon. Jason Brown interview with Katherine Mayo, Dec. 13–14, 1908, Villard Collection, CUL. Salmon Brown to William E. Connelly, May 28, 1913, Stutler Collection, WVDCH.
111. The first attribution to John Brown of this biblical quote from the Epistle of Paul to the Hebrews (9:22) appeared in G. W. Brown's debunking "Reminiscences of Old John Brown." The former editor first charged that Brown had affirmed it as doctrine at a convention of "Ultra Abolitionists" meeting "somewhere" in central New York in 1855, where Brown appealed for arms and money to transport them to Kansas ("Reminiscences of Old John Brown," Lawrence *Daily Journal*, Nov. 6, 1879, p. 2, col. 3). Later G. W. Brown claimed to have himself heard Brown cite the damning passage of scripture while "haranguing" a crowd during the Wakarusa War (Lawrence *Daily Journal*, Nov. 9, 1879, p. 6, cols. 1–2). Paul's "Epistle" refers to the ancient Mosaic custom of sprinkling the blood of goats and calves about the tabernacle to sanctify it. But the import of the text is that Christ "by his own blood ... [had] obtained eternal redemption for us" (Hebrews 9:12–28). A reviewer who knew John Brown personally argued that to "assert that John Brown so used the phrase is to make a gibbering idiot of him" ("John Speer: G. W. Brown Reviewed," letter to the editor of the Lawrence *Daily Journal*, Nov. 25, 1879, p. 2, col. 2). I can find no contemporary evidence that John Brown repeated the text in question or alluded to blood sacrifice before the final "prophecy" he wrote just before being hanged, suggesting that civil war might "purge" the "this guilty land" of its sin of slavery.
112. Salmon Brown told an interviewer that his father did not like their cousin Lucian Mills, who refused to fight, because Mills was "too pious for Father. 'But was not your father pious, too,'" asked the interviewer. Laughing, Salmon agreed: 'Why yes – with a cranky sort of piety'!" Salmon Brown interview with Katherine Mayo, Oct. 11–13, 1908, Villard Collection, CUL.
113. John Brown to his wife and children, March 12, 1857, John Brown Collection, KSHS.
114. Brown claimed the sobriquet as his own despite its earlier attribution to a founder of that ill-fated town, Orville C. Brown, who had publicly repudiated the Pottawatomie killings. On the origins of the name "Osawatomie Brown," see, for example, Col. James Blood to G. W. Brown, Nov. 29, 1879, as published in the Lawrence *Daily Journal*, Dec. 3, 1879, p. 3, col. 2. Also see Villard, *John Brown Fifty Years After*, 167, 230. At Harpers Ferry, Brown acknowledged himself to be "old Osawatomie Brown." See his interview with authorities following the raid, Cincinnati *Daily Gazette*, Oct. 21, 1859, p. 3, col. 2.

115. John Brown to John, Jr., Apr. 15, 1857, Stutler Collection, WVDCH.
116. Brown was Shubel Morgan, Nelson Hawkins, Isaac Smith, or simply "Old Hundred." See, for example, John Brown to Mary Ann Brown "and children every one," Aug. 17, 1857, typed copy, Villard Collection, CUL; John Brown to John Brown, Jr., Feb. 4, 1858, Stutler Collection, WVDCH.

CHAPTER 7 – MONOMANIAC

1. Jim Bishop, *The Day Lincoln Was Shot* (New York: Harper, 1955), 57.
2. Three reporters using the new system of shorthand were at the authorities' interrogation of Brown. Two report the quote as shown here. See C. W. Taleure's version in the *Baltimore American*, Oct. 21, 1859, p. 1, and the Cincinnati *Daily Gazette*, Oct. 21, 1859, p. 3. But in the New York Morning *Herald*, Oct. 21, 1859, p. 1, Brown adds the words "and you are mad."

   The idea that God or the gods make a person mad to destroy him dates from antiquity. In *Antigone*, Sophocles wrote: "Whenever God prepares evil for a man, he first damages his mind." Sophocles' great rival, Euripides, put it thus: "When God would work evil to a man, first he deprives him of his senses." Adam Lindsay Gordon (1833–70), an Australian poet, popularized another version in *Ye Weary Wayfarer*:

   > So rashness can hope for but one result.
   > We are heedless when fate draws nigh us.
   > And the maxim holds good
   > Quen Perdere Bult, Deus dementat Prius.

   (Cited in *Putnam's Complete Book of Quotations* [New York, 1927], 150a, 476a, et passim.) James Duport (1606–79) penned still another variant of the saying in *Homeri Gnomologia* (1660). The form of the maxim familiar to Americans – the form Brown used – appears again in Longfellow's *The Masque of Pandora* (1875). I am indebted to Prof. Michael Speidel for the translation of Euripides and to him and the staff at the Center for Biographical Studies at the University of Hawai'i for tracking down the above sources.
3. Cited in the *Cincinnati Daily Gazette*, Friday, Oct. 28, 1859, p. 3; also see *Life, Trial, and Execution of John Brown Known as Old Brown of "Ossawatomie"* (1859; repr. New York: Robert M. De Witt, 1859), 64–65. Brown did permit his attorneys to submit a petition for a writ of error on the grounds that only a resident of Virginia owed the state allegiance and could therefore commit treason against it. The Richmond *Enquirer* published the petition and the decision of the Court of Appeals rejecting it. "No Writ of Error Allowed," Richmond *Enquirer*, Nov. 22, 1859, p. 1. At this writing no transcript of the trial itself has been found, but the University of West Virginia at Morgantown has a complete file of court documents.
4. Nineteenth-century usage of terms such as "lunacy," "madness," and "insanity" is discussed briefly in Lynn Gamwell and Nancy Tomes's excellent illustrated introduction, *Madness in America: Cultural and Medical Perceptions of Mental Illness before 1914* (Ithaca, NY: Cornell University Press, 1995), 9. *Lunacy* originated in the traditional belief that episodic mental illness was linked to the phases of the moon and implied severe impairment, while *madness* implied wild, irrational, emotionally uncontrolled behavior. A less emotionally charged term then preferred by physicians, *insanity* meant literally not "sane" (clean or healthy).

5. John Brown to "Dear Wife & children *every one*," Nov. 8, 1859, Stutler Collection, WVDCH; John Brown to Rev. Luther Humphrey, Nov. 19, 1859, Eldridge Collection, HEHL.

6. Brown to "My Dearly beloved Sisters Mary A. and Martha," Nov. 27, 1859 (sabbath), facsimile, Gee Collection, HLHS. The original is in the Chicago Historical Society. Heman Humphrey to "Mr. John Brown," Nov. 20, 1859, as quoted in Franklin B. Sanborn, *The Life and Letters of John Brown, Liberator of Kansas, and Martyr of Virginia* (1885; repr., New York: Negro University Press, 1969), 602–603. The two were acquainted. Some years before Heman Humphrey had called on his cousin when Brown lived in Springfield. Brown to "Dear Father," Jan. 10, 1849, as cited in Louis Ruchames, ed., *A John Brown Reader* (London: Abelard-Schuman, 1959), 67.

7. Brown to "Rev. Heman Humphrey, D. D.," Nov. 25, 1859, as quoted in Sanborn, *Life and Letters of John Brown*, 603–04.

8. John Brown to Daniel R. Tilden, Nov. 28, 1859, as quoted in Ruchames, *A John Brown Reader*, 154–55. A slightly altered version appears in Sanborn, ed., *Life and Letters of John Brown*, 609–10. Tilden found the letter "full of thanks ... and great heroism," and promptly determined to have it published and to read it "at our meeting tomorrow evening." Tilden then informed Brown's half brother, Jeremiah, that he wanted Henry Ward Beecher to "officiate at the funeral." It is doubtful that Tilden believed for a minute that Brown was really insane. Daniel R. Tilden to Jeremiah Root Brown, Dec. 1, 1859, Gee Collection, HLHS.

9. The term "mental illness" is not without problems. As the authors of the American Psychiatric Association's *Diagnostic and Statistical Manual of Mental Disorders, IV* point out, the distinction between "mental" and "physical" disorders is a "reductionist anachronism of mind/body dualism." There is much "physical" in "mental" disorders and conversely. But at present we have no better term for the psychiatric illnesses. I choose the term "illness" rather than "disorder" for two reasons: First, the major illnesses germane to my discussion were perceived as such by Brown and his contemporaries; they were "diseases" requiring medical attention, treatment, and sometimes commitment to an asylum. They brought pain, distress, disability, and social stigma to those affected. Second, the major cluster of conditions explored here falls under the heading of affective or mood disorders. Unlike many psychiatric disorders (such as personality disorders), they are known to be biological in origin and run in families. As the authors of the most comprehensive study of the scientific literature relating to affective disorders maintain, the prevailing view is that manic-depressive illness is a "medical condition, an illness to be diagnosed, treated, studied and understood within a medical context." They see bipolar disorder as a major form of manic-depressive illness, linked with unipolar (major depressive) disorder by a common pattern of recurrence – cyclicity. See the discussion in Frederick K. Goodwin and Kay Redfield Jamison, *Manic-Depressive Illness* (New York: Oxford, 1990), Chapter 1, esp. 2–5.

   In the 1970s critics of psychiatry such as Ronald David Laing challenged the medical model on the grounds that, unlike infectious diseases, psychiatric illnesses reveal no organic structural changes over the course of an illness and no pathological anatomical findings post mortem. Other critics argued that the syndromes of psychiatric illnesses are illusory. The claim of the antipsychiatry movement was that even schizophrenia and manic-depressive illness were "myths" having no biological substrate. Since that time, however, evidence of the heritability of both conditions has become overwhelming, and the use of lithium and other medications has made differential diagnosis far more reliable. As twin and family studies show, moreover, a vulnerability to manic-depressive illness and schizophrenia is part of the genetic heritage of the human species.

I do not deny, of course, that in the name of medicine psychiatrists have wrongly incarcerated, medicated, given electroconvulsive (shock) therapy to, even lobotomized "patients" whose "illnesses" are cultural constructs without any identified organic substrate. Culture influences both the definitions of mental illness and the frequency with which persons in a given age cohort suffer from them. Illnesses have a history beyond medicine. For an introduction to the issue, see Seymour S. Kety, "From Rationalization to Reason," *American Journal of Psychiatry*, 131 (1974), 957–63, reprinted in Ronald B. Miller, ed., *The Restoration of Dialogue: Readings in the Philosophy of Clinical Psychology* (Washington, DC: American Psychological Association, 1992), Chapter 13. See M. Siegler and H. Osmond, *Models of Madness, Models of Medicine* (New York: Macmillan, 1974). For a summary of the history of specific mental diseases, see German E. Berrios and Roy Porter, eds., *History of Clinical Psychiatry: The Origins and History of Psychiatric Disorders* (New York: Washington Square Press, 1995). In 1983 a leading authority on schizophrenia, E. Fuller Torrey, dismissed Laing's theories as "romantic nonsense." See E. Fuller Torrey, *Surviving Schizophrenia: A Family Manual*, rev. ed. (New York: Harper & Row, 1988), 165–6.

10. See, for example, C. Vann Woodward, "John Brown's Private War," in *The Burden of Southern History* (rev. ed.; Baton Rouge: LSU Press, 1968), 41–68, esp. 46. Despite his remark about Brown's "close association with insanity" and Woodward's negative assessment of Brown's character, Woodward stops short of saying he suffered from mental disorder.

11. Since 1952 the American Psychiatric Association has used the term "mental disorder" rather than the more stigmatizing term "mental illness" to describe "clinically significant behavioral or psychological syndromes" that entail "distress" (such as pain), "disability," or a "significant risk" of suffering death, pain, or disability, or "a loss of freedom." See the American Psychiatric Association, *Diagnostic and Statistical Manual of Mental Disorders, IV* (Washington, DC: American Psychiatric Association, 1994), xxi–xxii. Further complicating the issue, some illnesses have been redefined or renamed; *manic-depressive illness*, for example, has become *bipolar disorder*. For a discussion of the problems entailed in such labeling, see Johns Hopkins Professor of Psychiatry Kay Redfield Jamison's *An Unquiet Mind: A Memoir of Moods and Madness* (New York: Vintage Books, 1995), 179–84. I use the terms interchangeably.

12. The Henry A. Wise Collection in the Library of Congress contains documents Wise received from persons alleging that Brown was insane and urging clemency.

13. Allan Nevins, *The Emergence of Lincoln, Vol. 2, Prologue to Civil War, 1859–1861* (New York: Scribner's, 1950) II, 5–11, 70–84, esp. 11, 77. This view was anticipated by the novelist Thomas Dixon, *The Torch: A Story of the Paranoiac Who Caused a Great War* (New York: The Author, 1927).

14. Allan Nevins, *The Statesmanship of the Civil War* (rev. ed. 1962; New York: Collier-Macmillan, 1953), 29–30. For a concise discussion of Nevins's affinities with revisionists, see David Potter, "The Literature on the Background of the Civil War," in *The South and the Sectional Crisis* (Baton Rouge: LSU Press, 1968), Chapter IV, esp. 104–05. The literature on the coming of the Civil War is too

voluminous to summarize, but Thomas J. Pressly's *Americans Interpret Their Civil War* (1954; repr., New York: The Free Press, 1962) remains a valuable introduction. A recent discussion is Gary J. Kornblith, "Rethinking the Coming of the Civil War: A Counterfactual Exercise," *The Journal of American History*, 90 (June 2003), 76–105. The "crazy" John Brown to whom Nevins gave academic credibility had appeared on movie screens for years in films such as the fictionalized 1940 Warner Brothers production, "The Santa Fe Trail." The film so offended sixty-three-year-old Nellie Brown Groves, a granddaughter of Brown, that she tried unsuccessfully to bring suit against Warner Brothers for picturing Brown as a "revengeful and ruthless killer and murderer ... a madman, an enemy of the human race, and a foe of the Union." See "John Brown Distorted in Film," typed copy of a 1941 article by Nellie Brown Groves, Stutler Collection, WVDCH.

15. In a monograph dedicated to Nevins, James A. Rawley softens Nevins's view, remarking that the Pottawatomie massacre was "the act of a man with insanity in his ancestry and failure in his own past." Rawley, *Race & Politics: "Bleeding Kansas" and the Coming of the Civil War* (Philadelphia: Lippincott, 1969), 133. See also Joseph Chamberlain Furnas, *The Road to Harpers Ferry* (New York: William Sloane Associates, 1959), 11; William R. Brock, *Conflict and Transformation: The United States, 1844–1877* (Middlesex, England: Penguin Books, 1973), 174–75.

16. James G. Randall and David Donald, *The Civil War and Reconstruction* (2nd ed.; Boston: D. C. Heath, 1961), 100, 124. As recently as 1983, in the fifth edition of his popular text, John A. Garraty let stand the assertion that Brown should have been committed to an asylum. *The American Nation: A History of the United States to 1877* (5th ed.; New York: Harper & Row, 1983), 345, 353–55. Doubts about Brown's sanity have long concerned scholars. Writing in 1929 for the prestigious *Dictionary of American Biography*, Allen Johnson, Dumas Malone's coeditor, anticipated Nevins's thesis that Brown's "inability to earn a livelihood" led him to think more about those in bondage. Brown's "obsession" to free the slaves and his "unaccountableness to anybody but his Maker" created doubts as to his sanity, Johnson remarked. The affidavits of Brown's "erratic behavior" were "unimpeachable testimony" and "prima facie evidence" that "no modern court of law could ignore." *Dictionary of American Biography* (New York: Scribner's, 1928–58), II, 131–34. Although Johnson says the raid was "inexplicable on any rational grounds," Nevins acknowledges him only to claim that Johnson "suggests" Brown "might have fared better in an area containing more slaves." Nevins, *Emergence of Lincoln*, II: 84.

17. Among the brief partisan biographies, Barry Stavis, *John Brown: The Sword and the Word* (South Brunswick: A. S. Barnes, 1970), defends Brown's attack on Harpers Ferry as a "brilliant commando raid" that went awry and sees his martyrdom as a victory. Truman Nelson portrays Brown as a hard-nosed, quite rational revolutionary in *The Old Man: John Brown at Harper's Ferry* (New York: Hold, Rinehart, & Winston, 1973). Black historians' tributes to Brown include, Benjamin Quarles, *Black Abolitionists* (New York: Oxford, 1969), 235–45, and *Allies for Freedom: Blacks and John Brown* (New York: Oxford, 1974), 118–19. Louis Ruchames reissued his edited volume, *A John Brown Reader* (London: Abelard-Schuman, 1959) as *John Brown: The Making of a Revolutionary* (New York: Grosset & Dunlap, 1969), declaring that the new title better reflected Ruchames's purpose to "portray John Brown, in life and death, as one of the great revolutionaries in American history" (p. 8).

18. Ruchames, *A John Brown Reader*, 30–31, n17.

19. Jules Abels, *Man on Fire: John Brown and the Cause of Liberty* (New York: Macmillan, 1971), 249–52, esp. 252.

20. James Redpath, *The Public Life of Capt. John Brown* (Boston: Thayer & Eldridge, 1860), pp. 308–309.

21. From the *Journal of Ralph Waldo Emerson*, as quoted in Richard Seidenbaum, ed., *The Response to John Brown* (Belmont, CA: Wadsworth Publishing, 1972), 81–82.

22. Ruchames, *A John Brown Reader*, 30.

23. Villard, *John Brown, 1800–1859: A Biography Fifty Years After* (1910; repr., Gloucester, MA: Peter Smith, 1965), 506–10.

24. Furnas, *Road to Harper's Ferry*, Chapter 6.

25. Abels, *Man on Fire*, 249–54, esp. 249.

26. Quoted in Potter, "John Brown and the Paradox of Leadership among American Negroes," in *The South and the Sectional Conflict* (Baton Rouge: LSU Press, 1968), 212–13. Don Fehrenbacher has drawn on this essay in piecing together the discussion of Brown in Potter's unfinished classic, *The Impending Crisis, 1848–1861* (Torchbook ed.; New York: Harper & Row, 1976), 372–74, 357, 359.

27. Stephen B. Oates, *To Purge This Land with Blood: A Biography of John Brown* (Torchbook ed.; New York: Harper & Row, 1970), viii, xi, 331–32, 133. Similarly, Edward J. Renehan, Jr., says Brown is a "puzzle to remain forever unsolved." Renehan, *The Secret Six* (New York: Crown, 1995), 274. Both cite approvingly the words of William A. Phillips, a reporter who accompanied Brown to Kansas, interviewed him at length, and concluded: "He was always an enigma." But Phillips's comment suggests something more. He saw Brown's personality as "a strange compound of enthusiasm, and cold, methodical stolidity, – a volcano beneath a mountain of snow." William A. Phillips, "Three Interviews with Old John Brown," *The Atlantic Monthly*, 44 (Dec. 1879), 738–44, esp. 739. If his sense of Brown's potential for explosive action benefited from hindsight, his articles provide one of the few explorations of Brown's political philosophy. In *The Conquest of Kansas, by Missouri and Her Allies* (Boston, 1856), Phillips portrayed Brown as a "strange, resolute, repulsive, iron-willed, inexorable old man." Quoted in Oates, *To Purge This Land with Blood*, 159.

28. Reflecting Oates's agnosticism and the new sympathy for abolitionism, recent surveys of the Civil War era have been similarly circumspect. David Herbert Donald's balanced narrative in *Liberty and Union* (Lexington, MA: D. C. Heath, 1978), 64, 73–75, offers no opinion of Brown's mental condition. Although James M. McPherson refers to Brown's raid as a "wild scheme" and his tactics as "incredibly amateurish," he makes no judgments about Brown's sanity. McPherson speculates that, in failing, Brown may have realized that his martyrdom could provoke a "final showdown" between North and South. *Ordeal by Fire: The Civil War and Reconstruction* (New York: Knopf, 1982), 114–17. Richard P. Sewell refers to Brown's raid as a "reckless foray" but says little of Brown himself in assessing his impact on the sectional crisis. *A House Divided: Sectionalism and Civil War, 1848–1865* (Baltimore: Johns Hopkins Press, 1988), 68–72. Charles P. Roland is equally circumspect in his lively *An American Iliad: The Story of the Civil War* (New York: McGraw-Hill, 1991), 12–13, 18–19.

29. Bertram Wyatt-Brown, "'A Volcano Beneath a Mountain of Snow': John Brown and the Problem of Interpretation," in Paul Finkelman, ed., *His Soul Goes Marching*

On: Responses to John Brown and the Harpers Ferry Raid (Charlottesville: University of Virginia Press, 1995), chapter 1. In this introduction to the Finkelman volume, Wyatt-Brown acknowledges my own earlier speculations about whether Brown suffered from bipolar disorder. See McGlone, "John Brown, Henry Wise, and the Politics of Insanity," in Finkelman, *His Soul Goes Marching On,* Chapter 8, esp. 236–43.

30. In 1999 psychologist Kenneth R. Carroll asked three Brown scholars to take the *Minnesota Multi-Phasic Personality Inventory, Second Edition* as if they were answering for Brown. In my view (as one of the three Browns), the exercise was seriously flawed. However useful the MMPI has proved with patients in the latter twentieth century, it presuppose a world Brown never knew. Carroll's three historians had to guess how their imagined Brown might have responded to questions and situations he did not encounter. The historians' images of Brown, moreover, were shaped by a highly partisan and reductionist Brown biographical tradition and their own readings of the pronouncements of Brown's contemporaries, largely predetermining the conclusion. The anecdotal evidence Carroll reviews in support of his claim that the test results are confirmed by historical evidence largely ignores its historical context. Carroll postulates a charismatic, bipolar Brown who succeeded in recruiting volunteers and raising money despite being "obviously delusional," having "highly disruptive interpersonal relationships," and "poor impulse control," as his composite "symptomatic profile" concludes. See Carroll, "A Psychological Examination of John Brown," in Paul Finkelman, ed., *Terrible Swift Sword* (Athens: Ohio University Press, 2005), Chapter 8.

31. The recent discovery of schizoaffective disorder further complicates efforts at diagnosis. For my purposes, identifying a cluster of symptoms that major illnesses share would be sufficient to establish whether Brown was mentally ill, however a modern diagnostician might classify that syndrome in a patient who can be examined and tested.

32. American Psychiatric Association, *Diagnostic and Statistical Manual of Mental Disorders, IV,* xv.

33. See the summary of research on manic-depressive illness by Elliot S. Gershon in Frederick K. Goodwin and Kay Redfield Jamison, *Manic-Depressive Illness* (New York: Oxford, 1990), Chapter 15, esp. 373. I follow Goodwin and Jamison in preferring the term mental "illness" to "mental disorder" in part because pathophysiological mechanisms involved in the transmission of manic-depressive illness have been identified.

34. Elliott Gershon observes that several alleged genetic markers for manic-depressive illness have been refuted by recent research, leaving at present only the reported linkage to the color blindness region of the X chromosome as a likely candidate. Gershon, "Genetics," in Goodman and Jamison, Ibid., 399.

35. On the incidence and creative as well as destructive impact of manic-depressive illness, see Kay Redfield Jamison, *Touched with Fire: Manic-Depressive Illness and the Artistic Temperament* (New York: The Free Press, 1993). Jamison, who is associate professor of psychiatry at the Johns Hopkins School of Medicine, chronicles her own thirty-year contest with the disease in *An Unquiet Mind.* In the 1970s a number of public figures and psychiatrists launched a campaign to remove the stigma from manic-depressive illness and popularize the use of lithium. Psychiatrist Ronald R. Fieve recruited Abraham Lincoln, Theodore Roosevelt, and Winston Churchill to his cause as case studies of "great men" who suffered from the illness:

Fieve, *Moodswing: The Third Revolution in Psychiatry* (Toronto: Bantam Books, 1975), Chapter 7. His slapdash arguments did little, however, to persuade historians of the utility of such inquiries. Indeed, popularizers have pressed some historical figures (such as Vincent Van Gogh) into service as a sufferer of both schizophrenia and manic-depressive illness – take your pick. But recent scholarship has demonstrated the necessity to confront such issues and the possibility to do so responsibly. Literary scholars in particular have written convincingly about mood disorders. See, for example, Thomas C. Caramagno, *The Flight of the Mind: Virginia Woolf's Art and Manic-Depressive Illness* (Berkeley: University of California Press, 1992).

36. Dix was addresssing the state legislature. Quoted in E. Fuller Torrey, *Surviving Schizophrenia: A Family Manual* (rev. ed.; New York: Harper & Row, 1983), 1.

37. See James C. Mohr, *Doctors and the Law: Medical Jurisprudence in Nineteenth-Century America* (New York: Oxford University Press, 1993), 164–70.

38. Lynn Gamwell and Nancy Tomes, *Madness in America: Cultural and Medical Perceptions of Mental Illness before 1914* (Ithaca, NY: Cornell University Press, 1995), 35.

39. Gideon Mills describes himself as an "uncle" in his affidavit but says, oddly, that his mother was a sister of John Brown's mother. That of course would make Gideon John's cousin, not his uncle. Affidavit of Gideon Mills, Nov. 11, 1859, Wise and Family Collection, LOC. References to him in other affidavits, however, make it clear that Gideon Mills was a brother of Ruth Mills.

40. The affidavits are in the Henry A. Wise and Family Collection, LOC. Kendrick complicates the picture by noting that Florilla Brown Edwards, a half-sister to Brown and daughter of Owen's second wife, Sally Root, had been committed to his asylum twice. Affidavit of O. C. Kendrick, Nov. 12, 1859, Wise and Family Collection, LOC.

41. Affidavit of Sylvester H. and Mills Thompson, Nov. 11, 1859, Wise and Family Collection, LOC; affidavit of Salmon Thompson, fragment, Nov. 1859, Wise and Family Collection, LOC.

42. Mohr, *Doctors and the Law*, Chapter 10; Gerald Grob, *Mental Institutions in America: Social Policy to 1875* (New York: Free Press, 1973).

43. The 1875 sanity trial and confinement of Mary Todd Lincoln requested by her son Robert and her subsequent confinement to an asylum reveals just how uncertain the evidence of mental instability might be and how wide the leeway of courts was in making such determinations in Illinois. Historians' judgments of the mental condition of the troubled Mary have been equally conflicting. Compare Mark E. Neely, Jr., and R. Gerald McMurtry, *The Insanity File: The Case of Mary Todd Lincoln* (Carbondale: Southern Illinois University Press, 1986), 11, 31–33, et passim, who concede that Mary suffered "hallucinations" and other symptoms, with Jean Baker's more charitable evaluation in *Mary Todd Lincoln: A Biography* (New York: W. W. Norton, 1987), Chapter XI.

44. In some states people rightly or wrongly confined had no means of release except through habeas corpus. At age forty-eight, John Brown's cousin, Julia Brown, returned home from an asylum, but as one of her nieces wrote, Julia "rather laughs at the idea of their calling her crazy and thinks she has never been so." Wealthy Hotchkiss Brown to Ruth Brown Thompson and Henry Thompson, Jan. 4, 1857, Clark-Brown Collection, HLHS. An excellent, illustrated overview of life in nineteenth-century asylums is presented by Lynn Gamwell and Nancy Tomes in *Madness in America: Cultural and Medical Perceptions of Mental Illness before 1914* (Ithaca, NY: Cornell University Press, 1995).

45. Salmon Brown to Owen Brown, Apr. 17, 1827, Gee Collection, HLHS; Owen Brown, Sr., to Marian Brown Hand, n.d., typed copy, Stutler Collection, WVCH.
46. Salmon Brown to Owen Brown, Aug. 22, 1830, John Brown, Jr., Collection, OHS.
47. New Orleans *Bee*, Sept. 4, 1833, p. 2, col. 3.
48. John Brown to Ruth Brown, Sept. 1, 1847, copy by Katherine Mayo, Oswald Garrison Villard Collection, CUL; Jason Brown to John Brown, Jr., July 30, 1850, John Brown, Jr., Collection, OHS; Ruth Brown to Wealthy Hotchkiss Brown, Aug. 8, 1850, John Brown, Jr., Collection, OHS; John Brown to Mary Brown, Aug. 22, 1850, handwritten copy, Sanborn Folder, HU.
49. John Brown to "Dear Son John," Dec. 1, 1851, John Brown, Jr., Collection, OHS; John Brown to "Dear Children," March 20, 1852, copy by Katherine Mayo, Villard Collection, CUL; Jason Brown to John Brown, Jr., and Wealthy Hotchkiss Brown, Jan. 23, 1854, John Brown, Jr., Collection, OHS.
50. John Brown to Mary Brown and children, March 6, 1856, typed copy, Villard Collection, CUL; Samuel Lyle Adair to Owen Brown, Sr., March 26, 1856, Clark-Brown Collection, HLHS; Adair to Owen Brown, Sr., May 16, Clark-Brown Collection; Samuel Adair, "Frederick Brown," handwritten manuscript, n. d. [1857], typed copy, Gee Collection, HLHS.
51. Notes of Samuel Lyle Adair, n.d., typed copy, Stutler Collection, WVDCH.
52. Frederick Brown to "Brother Watkin" (Watson, a pun), Nov. 10, 1855, John Brown, Jr., Collection, OHS.
53. Frederick to John Brown, Jr., Nov. 3, 1853, John Brown, Jr., Collection, OHS; Annie Brown to Thomas Wentworth Higginson, Nov. 29, 1859, Higginson Papers, BPL; Jason Brown, interview with Katherine Mayo, Dec. 13–14, 1908, Villard Collection, CUL. (See also the discussion of Frederick's relation to Mary Grant in Chapter 6.) Annie Brown Adams, handwritten statement, n.d., John Brown Collection, KSHS.
54. Frederick Brown to John Brown, Jr., Nov. 3, 1853, John Brown, Jr. Collection, OHS; Salmon Brown, interview with Katherine Mayo, Oct. 11–13, 1908, Villard Collection, CUL.
55. James Hanway to Richard J. Hinton, Dec. 5, 1859, Richard J. Hinton Collection,; Samuel Lyle Adair, notes on Frederick Brown, n.d. [1856], typed copy, Stutler Collection, WVDCH; Salmon Brown, interview with Katherine Mayo, Oct. 11–13, 1908, Villard Collection, CUL.
56. John Brown to Owen Brown (father), May 23, 1850, copy by Katherine Mayo, Villard Collection, Columbia; John Brown, "A brief history of John Brown otherwise (Old Brown) & his family: *as connected with Kansas*; by one who knows," unfinished manuscript, Dreer Collection, PHS; John Brown to John Brown, Jr., Aug. 3, 1854, William J. Eldridge Collection, HEHL. In one reference to Frederick, Brown refers to "a most terrible opperation for his breach." As Brown spells this term, it could be a reference to a rupture or muscular tear. But if Brown meant breech, he may have referred to Frederick's the lower back or buttocks. Samuel Johnson, *Dictionary of the English Language* (1818), I, part 1. (no pagination, title page missing). See also Robert A. Dutch, ed., *The Original Roget's Thesaurus of English Words and Phrases* (1852; new rev. ed., New York: St. Martin's Press, 1965), 141.
57. Frederick's body actually lay in the road until "some time in the afternoon" of the day on which he was shot. He and two others were buried the next day. Adair, "Frederick Brown," Gee Collection, HLHS.

58. John Brown to John Brown, Jr., Jan. 27, 1846, John Brown, Jr., Papers, OHS.
59. On the criteria for a major manic episode, see American Psychiatric Association, *DSM–IV*, pp. 328–32; Goodwin and Jamison, *Manic-Depressive Illness*, Chapter 5, esp. 120–21. The problem is made more complex by the possibility to diagnose differing degrees of bipolar disorder and such less marked conditions as cyclothymic disorder, in which less severe manic (hypomanic) and depressive episodes alternate frequently. The issue may be clouded further because of recently identified disorders such as schizoaffective illness, which may be a distinct disorder or a subtype of either affective illness or schizophrenia. The boundaries of manic-depressive illness also overlap with personality disorders, especially borderline disorders, inviting researchers to think of a continuum or spectrum of illnesses. See Goodwin and Jamison, *Manic-Depressive Illness*, pp. 96–103.
60. J[ason] L. Brown to "Dear Brother [Watson], Sister [Ruth], and all Dear Friends," June 28, 1856, Villard Collection, CUL; Jason Brown interview with Katherine Mayo, Dec. 13–14, 1908, esp. 3, 14–15, Villard Collection, CUL. (In Kansas Jason began adding a middle initial to his name [either O or L], evidently to distinguish his initials from those of his brother John and his father. John, Jr., to Franklin B. Sanborn, March 24, 1885, Stutler Collection, WVDCH. It may be symbolic of his brief estrangement from his father that the "L" first appears soon after Pottawatomie and Jason's arrest.
61. J[ason] L. Brown to "Dear Brother [Watson], Sister [Ruth], and all dear Friends," June 28, 1856, Villard Collection, CUL; also Jason Brown interview with Katherine Mayo, Dec. 13–14, 1908, esp. 3, 14–15, Villard Collection, CUL.
62. John Brown, Jr., to Frederick Brown, Aug. 13, 1856, copy, Sanborn Folder, HU.
63. John Brown to "Dear Brothers Frederick & Jeremiah," Oct. 11, 1856, typed copy, Villard Collection, CUL; John Brown, Jr., to "My Dear General [Edmund B.] Whitman," Feb. 26, 1858, John Brown Collection, KSHS; John Brown to "Dear Wife: & Children, *All*," June 16, 1858, Stutler Collection, WVDCH.
64. John Brown, Jr., to Franklin B. Sanborn, Apr. 8, 1885, Stutler Collection, WVDCH.
65. John Brown, Jr., to Jason Brown, March 25, 1862, Eldridge Collection, HEHL.
66. The concept of "soldier's heart" achieved scholarly recognition only in 1918. Like other formulations of post-trauma illness such as "shell shock," it was superseded by the general term PTSD, or posttraumatic stress disorder. The diagnosis of the disorder has long been entangled with public policy issues, such as liability for accidents and, in Britain, army authorities' fear during the First World War that recognizing "shell shock" as a disorder would encourage malingering. Modern authorities recommend treatment of PTSD with antidepressants and therapy that may emphasize reliving the traumatic events in imagination. The medical literature on PTSD is substantial, and recently scholars in the humanities and social sciences have given it considerable attention. See Eric Dean, *Shook Over Hell: Post Traumatic Stress Disorder, Vietnam and the Civil War* (Cambridge, MA: Harvard University Press, 1999). In 1984 Congress mandated the creation of a National Center for Post Traumatic Stress Disorder to carry out multidisciplinary research. Since 1990 the center has published the *PTSD Quarterly*. For a concise introduction to posttraumatic stress disorder, see Harold I. Kaplan and Benjamin J. Sadock, *Synopsis of Psychiatry: Behavioral Sciences, Clinical Psychiatry* (5th ed.; Baltimore: Williams and Wilkins, 1988), 329–32.
67. Salmon Brown to "Dear Folks one and All [Mary A. Brown, Watson, Annie, Sarah, Ellen Brown]," Dec. 28, 1856, Stutler Collection, WVDCH. Details of Jason's later life may be tracked in Pasadena newspapers. See for example, "Abolitionist Auld

Lang Syne: John Brown's Sons Found Haven Here During 80's," Pasadena *Star Bulletin*, June 12, 1955. A sometimes inaccurate summary is: Salmon Brown, typed statement, n.d. [1912], Stutler Collection, WVDCH. At one time Pasadena residents raised $100 for Jason and Owen who were apparently "destitute," but the Browns sent the money to victims of an earthquake in Charleston, South Carolina. Elizabeth Roberts Townsend, "Ruth Born Brown Thompson: Anniversary of Her Wedding Was Celebrated at Pasadena, Cal., Wednesday P. M., September 20, 1900," *The Western Home* [Pasadena], (July 1901), 4–5.

68. Ruth Brown Thompson to James H. Holmes, Sept. 25, 1899, Villard Collection, CUL. We know little of the lives of Ruth's five children. Three (John Henry, Ella Jane, and Grace R. Thompson) married and the first two had children. A son named Dauphin died at age sixteen. The last, Mary E. Thompson, a school teacher who supported her parents and cared for her invalid father after Ruth's death in 1904, suffered a "collapse" in July 1909 at age thirty-eight. She had recovered sufficiently by September that, with the help of a "housekeeper-nurse," she could care once again for her "helpless" father and return to work despite fears that she would have to quit. Henry died in February 1911; Mary in 1938. Mary E. Thompson to Franklin B. Sanborn, Jan. 24, 1910, Villard Collection, CUL.

69. Franklin B. Sanborn, *Life and Letters of John Brown*, 36; Mrs. Dianthe Lusk Pettingill [Milton Lusk's daughter] interview with Katherine Mayo, Dec. 20, 1908, Villard Collection, CUL; Mrs. Nelson Waite, interview with Katherine Mayo, Dec. 20, 1908, Villard Collection, CUL. Mrs. Waite was the daughter of Brown's old friend, Zina Post, who was once an apprentice to Brown's brother, Oliver Owen Brown. She told Mayo that her parents often spoke of Brown's "unkindness" to Dianthe. She never heard that he beat her, but some unspecified unkindness was allegedly "common talk" because Dianthe had so many relatives that their influence created feeling against Brown in the community on that account. Another witness said that she was "shocked" at the accusations related by Mrs. Waite, and that she had heard "much to the contrary." Ms. Claibourne interview with Katherine Mayo, Dec. 20, 1908, Villard Collection, CUL. Milton Lusk allegedly refused to attend either Dianthe's wedding or, despite his abolitionist convictions, the memorial service in Hudson held in Brown's honor on the day of his execution. But see his statement to Sanborn in note 71 in this chapter.

70. After John Brown, Jr., fled from Kansas, he and his wife Wealthy and their son stayed at the homes of relations until they could get settled. Wealthy reported having had "quite a good visit at … Uncle Milton Lusks." Wealthy Hotchkiss Brown to Ruth and Henry Thompson, Jan. 4, 1857, Gee Collection, HLHS. Brown's son Frederick thought Milton's son, James W. Lusk, "one of the finest men I have seen lately[,] a perfect Gentleman in every sense of the word." The close relations between Milton and his nephews are confirmed by Milton's daughter, Lucy Lusk, who stayed with John, Jr., at his home in Ashtabula before Harpers Ferry and said that John, Jr. was "very attached" to Milton. Lucy Lusk interview with Katherine Mayo, Dec. 21, 1908, Villard Collection, Columbia.

71. Annie alleged that Dianthe had thrown one of her babies "into the fire" one night and that Brown had rescued the baby with its clothes "in flames." Sanborn, *Life and Letters of John Brown*, 33–34; Anne Brown Adams to Franklin B. Sanborn, Jan. 29, 1896, as cited by Sanborn in a letter to "Dear Friend [Oswald Garrison Villard]," Feb. 29, 1896, carbon copy of typed draft, Sanborn Folder, HU; Anne Brown Adams, interview with Katherine Mayo, Oct. 2 & 3, 1908, Villard Collection, CUL.

72. John Brown to Owen Brown (father), Aug. 11, 1832, typed copy, Velma Sykes Collection, KSHS. Another copy is in the Clarence Gee Collection, HLHS.

73. Miss [?] Claibourne, interview with Katherine Mayo, Dec. 20, 1908, Villard Collection, CUL.

74. On neurosyphilis and its heritability, see "Treponema Pallidum [Syphilis]," in Gerald L. Mandell, R. Gordon Douglas, Jr., and John E. Bennett, eds., *Principles and Practices of Infectious Diseases* (New York: John Wiley & Sons, 1979), 1820–37, esp. 1829; James R. Rundell and Michael G. Wise, "Neurosyphilis: A Psychiatric Perspective," *Psychodynamics*, 26 (Apr. 1985), 287–95; Brian F. Hoffman, "Reversible Neurosyphilis Presenting as Chronic Mania," *Journal of Clinical Psychiatry*, 43 (Aug. 1982), 338–39; Renee L. Binder and William A. Dickman, "Psychiatric Manifestations of Neurosyphilis in Middle-Aged Patients," *American Journal of Psychiatry*, 137 (June 1980), 741–43.

75. The nineteen affidavits, written in longhand on legal-sized paper by notary publics or probate judges, vary from about 150 to 300 words in length and are located in the Wise and Family Collection, LOC.

76. For a discussion of the problem of false memory as it affects historical research, see Robert E. McGlone, "Deciphering Memory: Schema Theory, Identity, and the Historian's Craft," paper presented to the 89th Annual Meeting of the Organization of American Historians, March 28–31, 1996, Chicago, Illinois.

77. See, for example, the affidavit of Brown's old schoolmate, Captain Orson Oviatt, a Cleveland merchant and former business partner of Brown, who endorsed other affiants as among "our most reputable citizens." U.S. District Judge H. O. William affirms that Oviatt and others with him, in turn, are "gentlemen of high standing" in the community. Also see the character testimonials of Brown's half brother, Jeremiah. Henry Alexander Wise and Family Collection, LOC.

78. With few exceptions, the similarity of many of the statements suggests the possibility that affiants may have been coached about what to say. Johnathan Metcalf, seventy-two, for example, illustrates the model. He had "ever estimated [Brown] a strictly conscientious man but ... of peculiar organization ... [and] subject to fits of insanity." At times Metcalf had seen Brown "when I was well convinced he was positively insane." When Brown first went to Kansas, Metcalf had found him insane on "matters relative to Kansas."

79. The strategy of establishing Brown's praiseworthy character and then claiming that "wrongs" he suffered in Kansas or a hereditary vulnerability to monomania drove him to madness also marks an earlier, independent appeal for clemency. One of Brown's uncles, the Rev. Edward Brown of La Crose, Wisconsin, had known Brown "intimately" since his "earliest recollection," and he assured Wise that no "more high minded honorable honest truthful benevolent or peaceable man" could be found. But the "unhappy" war occasioned by the Kansas-Nebraska Act had brought a train of misfortunes alike to proslavery and antislavery settlers in Kansas. Edward concluded that the tragedies to his family had unbalanced Brown and "changed him from a peaceful, Christian citizen, to a shrewd plotter of a wild scheme that upon its very face shows the marks of insanity." Although Edward had not seen John in three years, he knew that the "troubles" had made the "old gentleman" a "wreck of what he once was." Edward thought that the "principles of humanity" called for "such a commutation of his sentence as shall be both merciful and at the same time for the public safety." Wise could hold out the olive branch to the North and achieve a "chivalrous disarming of northern prejudice" by sparing

the "old gentleman." Edward Brown to Gov. Henry A. Wise, Nov. 5, 1859, Wise and Family Collection, LOC.

80. Occasionally Brown spoke when not invited. One of his uncles, Rev. Leonard Bacon of New Haven, Connecticut, recalled that when he himself had spoken at the semicentennial celebration of the settlement of the town of Talmadge, Ohio, Brown had asked to speak about Kansas, a subject "entirely inconsistent with the character of the occasion." Gentlemen seated near Bacon remarked that Brown's mind was "evidently deranged on that subject." Bacon's own impression was that his nephew's mind "had become diseased and unbalanced in the conflicts and sorrows through which he had passed." Rev. Leonard Bacon to Henry A. Wise, Nov. 14, 1859, Dreer Collection, PHS.

81. John Brown, Jr., to "My Dear Friend" [Franklin B. Sanborn]. Jan. 8, 1884, Stutler Collection, WVDCH.

82. See *The Liberator*, Dec. 2, 1859, p. 191. Frederick and John were both ardent abolitionists, but Frederick tried his hand at law and even held public office in Rockford, Illinois. Oliver Brown to "Dear Mother Brother & Sisters," July 4, 1856, Stutler Collection, WVDCH. Lydia Child met Frederick in Boston in January and "judged him to be a chip from the strong-hearted old family-tree." Lydia Maria Child to Mary Ann Brown, March 12, 1860, Huxtable Collection, KSHS. Frederick's relationship to John was a ticket to momentary fame. He addressed the Annual Meeting of the Massachusetts Anti-Slavery Society and spoke in numerous towns near Boston. Francis Jackson found his "honest countenance & sensible talk" likely to draw audiences. Francis Jackson to John Brown, Jr., Feb. 12, 1860, Stutler Collection, WVDCH. Also see Samuel May to Thomas Wentworth Higginson, Feb. 16, 1860, Higginson-Brown Collection, BPL. Brown's brother, Oliver Owen, was as ardent an enemy of slavery as John. In February 1858 Oliver Owen wrote to Brown's family at North Elba that he "rejoiced because the end of this manstealing government is at hand. I am more & more satisfied there is no hope for the slave but in the disolutions [sic] of the American union." Oliver Owen Brown to "Dear Friends," Feb. 11, 1858, Eldridge Collection, HEHL.

83. See Daniel R. Tilden to Jeremiah Root Brown, Dec. 1, 1859, Gee Collection, HLHS.

84. Frederick had learned that Jeremiah was dying of tuberculosis and wanted to "bury" old grudges. He denied he had "ever said that I was the only brother of John Brown or that I lost my property in aiding him in Kansas or … in any raid … that he was engaged in." See Frederick Brown (brother) to Jeremiah Brown, Feb. 1, 1873, Clark-Brown Collection, HLHS.

85. The Secret Six arranged to give money and arms belonging to the National Kansas Committee to Brown before it went out of business in 1857 for lack of contributions. Copies of resolutions of the National Kansas Committee affecting Brown and related correspondence are in the John Brown Collection at the Kansas State Historical Society.

86. See Jeffery Rossbach's important study, *Ambivalent Conspirators: John Brown, the Secret Six, and a Theory of Slave Violence* (Philadelphia: University of Pennsylvania Press, 1982), Chapter 3, esp. 80.

87. See Douglass's address commemorating the fourteenth anniversary of the founding of Storer College at Harpers Ferry, May 30, 1881, as reprinted in Ruchames, *Making of a Revolutionary*, 278–99, esp. 290.

88. Lawrence's journal entries are here cited in William Lawrence, *Life of Amos A. Lawrence* (Boston: Houghton Mifflin, 1899), 123, 131–32. Amos A. Lawrence to "My Dear Sir" [Brown], Feb. 19, 1857, John Brown Collection, KSHS. A month later Lawrence again pledged: "The family of Capt. John Brown of Osawatomie will not be turned out to starve in this country until liberty herself is driven out." Lawrence to John Brown, March 20, 1857, John Brown Collection, KSHS.

89. Lawrence, *Life of Amos A. Lawrence*, 131–32; Brown to Sanborn, May 27, 1857, in Ruchames, *The Making of a Revolutionary*, 116–17. Though Lawrence helped to pay for Brown's counsel after Harpers Ferry, his letter to Governor Wise informing him of Brown's "monomania" was consistent with views expressed in his diary. Amos A. Lawrence to Henry A. Wise, Oct. 25, 1859, Wise and Family Collection, LOC.

90. Jeremiah Root Brown to "Dear Brother & Sister Adair," Hudson, Nov. 1, 1856, Adair & Family Papers, Box 3, Folder 8, KSHS. Jerry and Samuel Adair had a frank exchange on "the question of war" in their letters. (Samuel Lyle Adair to Jeremiah Brown, Feb. 8, 1857, Gee Collection, HLHS.) By July 1857, Adair fore-saw only peace: "As to Bro. John's preparations for war; I do not think they will likely be needed here," he concluded. "The day of fighting to make Kansas a pro slavery state has passed by." Adair thought that sectional feeling had "recently given way before the mighty dollar." Adair to Jeremiah Brown, June 26–July 2, 1857, Gee Collection, HLHS.

91. Jeremiah Root Brown to "Dear Brother & Sister Adair," Hudson, Nov. 1, 1856, Adair & Family Papers, Box 3, Folder 8, KSHS.

92. JRB to "Dear Brother & Sister Adair & Family," Hudson, Dec. 7, 1856, ALS, Box 3, Folder 8, Adair & Family Papers, KSHS; Florilla Brown Adair to Jeremiah and Abigail Brown, Nov. 9, [1856], typed copy, Brown-Clark Collection, HLHS; JRB to "Dear Brother Sister & Family," Feb. 8, 1857, ALS, Adair & Family Papers, Box 3, Folder 8; Samuel Lyle Adair to "Dear Brother Jeremiah," March 12, 1857, typed copy, Clark-Brown Collection, HLAS.

93. Of course, King might have been unwittingly reconstructing his own memory of Brown from newspaper reports of Brown's interview with authorities at Harpers Ferry three weeks earlier. At that time a bystander had asked the wounded Brown if he thought himself an "instrument in the hands of Providence?" and Brown replied, "I do." Baltimore *American*, Oct. 21, 1859, p. 1.

94. Affidavit of Jeremiah Root Brown, Wise & Family Collection, LOC.

95. John Brown to "Dear Brother J. R.," Apr. 15, 1857, Gee Collection, HLHS. Jeremiah helped to raise money in Connecticut for the relief of the Brown and Adair families in Kansas in September 1857, and he assisted John, Jr., in the ship-ment of Brown's weapons and supplies to Chambersburg.

96. See Weld's affidavit, Wise and Family Collection, LOC.

97. James H. Lane to "Dear Genl" [Brown], Sept. 28, 1857, John Brown Collection, KSHS. Lane awarded numerous commissions as generals in the free-state army.

98. John Brown to "Dear Wife & Children every one," June 1856, cited in Ruchames, *A John Brown Reader*, 94–7. Wise is quoted in Rawley, *Race & Politics*, 162.

99. On Wise's decision not to have an expert examine Brown or to hold a sanity trial, see: Robert E. McGlone, "John Brown, Henry Wise, and the Politics of Insanity," in Finkelman, *His Soul Goes Marching On*, Chapter 8, esp. 220–2.

100. Isaac Ray, *Treatise on the Medical Jurisprudence of Insanity* (3rd ed.; Boston: Little, Brown & Co., 1853). Ray served as superintendent of the Maine Insane Hospital and Butler Hospital for the Insane in Providence.

101. Gerald Grob, *Mental Institutions in America: Social Policy to 1875* (New York: Free Press, 1973), 146; Norman Dain, *Concepts of Insanity in the United States, 1789–1865* (New Brunswick, NJ: Rutgers University Press, 1964), 56.
102. Ray, *Treatise*, 159–65.
103. *Treatise on Insanity and Other Disorders Affecting the Mind* (London: Sherwood, Gilbert, & Piper, 1835).
104. Ray, *Treatise*, 170–71, 201–33. Like Esquirol, Ray described the symptoms of an as yet nameless and little noticed but "very common and well marked form of insanity ... chiefly confined to the moral sentiments." Its defining feature was "excitement alternating with depression," the "two conditions" varying in "intensity" and duration, separated by "lucid intervals" between them. Ray's unnamed syndrome bore a striking resemblance to what we today call bipolar or manic-depressive illness. In 1854 two French physicians independently named Ray's still nameless bipolar illness. Jean Pierre Fairet called it "La Folie a Double Forme," and Jules Baillarger, "La Folie Circulaire." But it was not until 1896 that Kraepelin, as mentioned previously, named it "manic-depressive psychosis" and distinguished it from "dementia praecox." A brief summary of major advances in the history of psychiatry is Kaplan and Sadock, *Synopsis of Psychiatry*, 1–18. A more comprehensive discussion is German E. Berrios & Roy Porter, *A History of Clinical Psychiatry: The Origin and History of Psychiatric Disorders* (New York: NYU Press, 1995).
105. Ray, *Treatise*, 1.
106. In the 1790s medical writers had emphasized excessive mental effort, especially prolonged or intense study, as well as strong passions such as "immoderate terror," joy, fear, passionate love, and jealousy as major contributors to "mental alienation." To an extent, then, "lunatics" and "maniacs" brought on their own woes. In the young, masturbation could trigger an attack of mania. "Inordinate desires, ambitious vices and grand projects" often caused madness. The American physician and reformer, Benjamin Rush, whose landmark treatise on mental illness appeared in 1812, explained that excessive study and intense emotion created hypertension in the vascular system, which was the chief somatic or bodily cause of madness. Consequently, Rush used periodic bleeding and compression of the arteries to relieve pressure. He also favored purging, dunking in cold water, dosing with opium, and physical restraints such as straight-waistcoats and restraining chairs for manic patients. Benjamin Rush, *Medical Inquiries and Observations Upon the Diseases of the Mind* (Philadelphia, 1812), 50, as quoted in Mary Ann Jimenez, "Madness in Early American History: Insanity in Massachusetts from 1700 to 1830," *Journal of Social History*, 20 (Fall 1986), 25–44, esp. 33.
107. Edward Jarvis, "Causes of Insanity," *Boston Medical and Surgical Journal*, 45 (Nov. 12, 1851), 294, as quoted in Grob, *Mental Institutions in America,* 155.
108. Edward Jarvis, "Report of the Trustees of the Massachusetts General Hospital for the Year 1858," *North American Review*, 185 (Oct. 1859), 316–39, esp. 323, 318, 322–3.
109. Grob, *Mental Institutions in America,* 156. Lynn Gamwell and Nancy Tomes point out that American asylums were a "mirror image" of the customs, social stratification, and prejudices of society. Differences in rank determined the daily routines of patients, with farmers and laborers doing heavy labor to help offset the asylum's cost, while more affluent patients read and played games. Genteel women did lighter household chores than working-class women. In the North African American patients were housed in separate wards or buildings that had

fewer amenities, while in the South some institutions refused to admit blacks while others would accept only free blacks. Gamwell and Tomes, *Madness in America*, 56–58.

110. Ray, *Treatise*, 135.

111. Dain, *Concepts of Insanity in the United States*, 72–77.

112. Joseph Workman, "Case of Moral Mania," *American Journal of Insanity*, 19 (Apr. 1863), 406–16; "Monomania," *American Journal of Insanity*, 13 (July 1856), 51–54.

113. Mohr, *Doctors and the Law*, 143.

114. "Commonwealth vs. Abner Rogers, Jr.," in Theron Metcalf, ed., *Reports of Cases Argued and Determined in the Supreme Judicial Court of Massachusetts* (Boston, 1851), vol. 48, p. 502, as quoted in Henry Nash Smith, *Democracy and the Novel: Popular Resistance to Classic American Writers* (New York: Oxford University Press, 1978), 38.

115. Mohr, *Doctors and the Law*, 147–8.

116. Jarvis inveighed against the assumption that the spirit supplied the mind with limitless energy. The mind, he insisted, is fused with the "animal body by means of the brain.... So long as the immaterial spirit is inseparably associated with material substance, all its powers of action and endurance are in exact correspondence with those of the physical organ." Jarvis, "Report of the Trustees," 318.

117. See, for example, Berrios and Porter, *History of Clinical Psychiatry*, 360–63, 620, 633–34, 576, 633–35. No aetiological foundation for antisocial personality disorder has been established, and it is not clear whether it constitutes a "disease" in the sense defined earlier.

118. Gamwell and Tomes, *Madness in America*, 79.

119. Although Junius Brutus Booth's wife burned all his papers, Stephen M. Archer has painstakingly reconstructed his career and provides an annual list of places where he performed. See the Appendix to Archer's *Junius Brutus Booth: Theatrical Prometheus* (Carbondale: Southern Illinois University Press, 1992), esp. 271–75.

120. On the impact of Spartacus, see Joseph Chamberlain Furnas, *The Road to Harpers Ferry* (New York: William Sloan Associates, 1959), 235–6. Furnas identified a "Spartacus Complex" among abolitionists. An intriguing parallel is drawn between the imagination and careers of Edwin and John Wilkes Booth in Albert Furtwangler's *Assassin on Stage: Brutus, Hamlet, and the Death of Lincoln* (Urbana, IL.: University of Chicago Press, 1991).

121. "On Monomania Induced through Imitation," *American Journal of Insanity*, 1 (Oct. 1844), 116–21. Like many articles in the early issues of the *American Journal of Insanity*, this one was a translation of a portion of a French text on insanity. See Jean Etienne Dominique Esquirol, *Mental Maladies: A Treatise on Insanity*, trans. E. K. Hunt (Philadelphia: Lea & Blanchard, 1845).

122. David Meredith Reese, *Humbugs of New-York: Being a Remonstrance Against Popular Delusion; Whether in Science, Philosophy, or Religion* (2nd ed.; New York: John S. Taylor, 1838), 180–4.

123. "The Autobiography of a Monomaniac," *Southern Literary Messenger*, 7 (Oct. 1841): 665–85. The anonymous author warned especially about the dangers of introspection. A commentator expressed doubt about the author's claim to be a monomaniac on the grounds that an afflicted person could not talk "common sense" about his own illness. Also see anonymous, "The Confessions of a Monomaniac," *Lyttell's Living Age*, 4 (Feb. 1, 1845): 293–9. It is reprinted from *Hunt's London Journal*.

124. I. Edwards, "Insanity – How Far a Legal Defense," *American Whig Review*, 8 (Sept. 1848): 269–75. British tales of monomania appeared regularly in genteel American magazines. A reviewer for *The Spectator* thought a volume of stories of monomania showed the "utter dreariness" of the malady, which in any case, he or she concluded, afflicted chiefly those of below average intelligence. "Stories of Monomania," review of *Shirley Hall Asylum; or, the Memoirs of a Monomaniac* (London: W. Freeman, 1863), in *Lyttell's Living Age*, 79 (Dec. 26, 1863), 613–15.

125. Frederick Law Olmsted, *A Journey in the Back Country* (1860; repr., New York: Shocken Books, 1970), 125.

126. Jim Bishop, *The Day Lincoln Was Shot*, 57.

127. In *American Assassins*, James C. Clarke rejects the notion that Booth may have been disturbed and rejects efforts to diagnose assassins because the terms have "very little conceptual or diagnostic clarity." As the title implies, Clarke sees several distinct types of assassins. But he fails to consider the possibility that mood disorders may have fostered the deep emotional commitments of his type 1 subjects. Clarke says flatly that neither Booth nor Leon Czolgosz were "mentally deranged," but his discussion of the latter's "breakdown" invites questions Clarke has ruled out of order. James C. Clarke, *American Assassins: The Darker Side of Politics* (Princeton, NJ: Princeton University Press, 1982), 5–6, 14, 18, 51.

128. Harry Levin, *The Power of Blackness: Hawthorne, Poe, Melville* (Vintage ed.; New York: Random House, 1958), 145.

129. George Stade, "Horror and Dissociation, with examples from Edgar Allan Poe," in Jacques M. Quen, ed., *Split Minds/Split Brains: Historical and Current Perspectives* (New York: NYU Press, 1986), 149–70, esp. 151, 152, 158. The scientific study of multiple personality lagged a generation behind. It was not until 1890 that William James met Ansel Bourne, whose split personality became a classic case in psychiatry. See Michael G. Kenny, *The Passion of Ansel Bourne* (Washington, DC: Smithsonian Institution Press, 1986), 68.

130. This is not to deny, of course, that Ahab's monomania, as Henry Nash Smith observed, raises him to a "mythical level." Acknowledging that Ishmael's explanations of that madness were inconsistent, nonetheless Smith sees the essence of it as a "*gran rifiuto:* an utterance of NO! in thunder." But determining the target of Ahab's "ferocious hostility" – just what the White Whale represents – has long been a central issue in Melville scholarship. Smith argues that Melville does not give the reader enough "fictional substance" to account for the "nameless, inscrutable, unearthly" madness that is, in Melville's words, Ahab's "cozening, hidden lord and master, and cruel, remorseless emporer." Ahab is not merely alienated from society. Smith argues that Melville invests Ahab with a "scope and grandeur that warrant comparing him with Shakespearian tragic heroes." Henry Nash Smith, "The Madness of Ahab," in *Democracy and the Novel: Popular Resistance to Classic American Writers* (New York: Oxford University Press, 1978), Chapter 3, esp. 52–54.

I am suggesting that Melville may see madness – or a predisposition to madness – as a given, a heritable condition, defining human nature. The medical literature of the time supported the notion that insanity was inherited and his own experience confirmed it. His father, who suffered from manic episodes, was obsessed with business and died with a "deranged" mind, or so his family believed. Mental illness ravaged several other close relations and Melville's own son Malcolm killed himself with a pistol at age eighteen. Melville himself suffered from severe mood swings and at times talked of suicide, although he was never hospitalized.

Edwin H. Miller argued that Melville was a "man of silences" who revealed himself only in the pages of his novels. "He dared to peer into the abyss of his own troubled, sensitive nature.... What he discovered at great pain and suffering he transmuted into an art which throbs and reverberates with the inner drama in an almost manic depressive rhythm." If mood swings informed Ahab's character, Melville's Ahab may thus be a creature of the author's imagination in unsuspected ways. Edwin Haviland Miller, *Melville* (New York: Persea Books, 1975), 16.

131. Herman Melville, *Moby-Dick or, The Whale*, ed. Charles Feidelson, Jr. (Indianapolis: Bobbs-Merrill, 1964), 272, 170, 168–9.

CHAPTER 8 – GOD'S REAPER

1. Brown to Franklin B. Sanborn, February 24, 1858, John Brown, Jr., Papers, OHS.
2. George H. Hoyt to Mary Brown, Nov. 11, 1859, Stutler Collection, WVDCH. Eventually, of course, Brown and his wife had a final, tearful goodbye in Charlestown jail.
3. Beecher's sermon is reproduced in Henry Ward Beecher, *Patriotic Addresses* (New York: Fords, Howard, and Hurlbert, 1887), 206–7. An abbreviated version is in Richard Warch and Jonathan F. Fanton, eds., *John Brown* (Englewood Cliffs, NJ: Prentice-Hall, 1973), 105–6. Hinton relates Brown's comments on the sermon in *John Brown and His Men* (1968; repr., New York: Funk and Wagnalls, 1894), 433–7. Whether Brown took his cue from earlier newspaper reports of abolitionist speeches urging that his hanging could make him a "heroic success," as Paul Finkelman suggests, or he fashioned his martyrdom on his own initiative, is uncertain. His determination to die for his cause is certainly evident in his historic courtroom speech at sentencing and in his October 31 letter to his wife and his November 1 letter to the mysterious "E. B." But Brown may have discussed his role with Hoyt and his other new attorneys, all of whom were in touch with leading abolitionists, before making his speech. Finkelman argues that abolitionists "manufactured" Brown's martyrdom and early recognized the potential victory the movement might gain from his death. See Paul Finkelman, "Manufacturing Martyrdom: The Antislavery Response to John Brown's Raid," in Paul Finkelman, ed., *His Soul Goes Marching On: Responses to John Brown and the Harpers Ferry Raid* (Charlottesville: University of Virginia Press, 1995), Chapter 2, esp. 42.
4. Hinton, *John Brown and His Men*, 433–4.
5. Quoted in the Cincinnati *Daily Gazette*, Oct. 21, 1859, p. 3. In a bogus report published by the Baltimore *Exchange*, Brown allegedly told an interviewer earlier that afternoon that he conceived his plan in Kansas to gain revenge. "After my property was destroyed, one of my sons killed, and my happiness destroyed by the slave party of Kansas, I determined to be revenged. I also was moved in this matter by a hope to benefit the negroes." The story also claimed that Brown's young officer, Aaron Stevens, badly wounded and surrounded by enraged Virginians, stated that Brown had "deceived" his men and that he, Stevens, regretted he had come. This whole "interview" was fabricated. The interviewer claims that Brown gave his age as 63, and of course Brown himself had not taken a claim in Kansas. During Brown's lengthy interview with officials and reporters later that same day, moreover, no one representing the Baltimore *Exchange* was present.

6. Compelling proof of this point is psychiatrist Kay Redfield Jamison's account of her own struggle with bipolar disorder (manic-depressive illness). *An Unquiet Mind: A Memoir of Moods and Madness* (Vintage ed.; New York: Random House, 1995).

7. Allan Nevins, *Emergence of Lincoln, II, Prologue to Civil War, 1859–1861* (New York: Scribner's Sons, 1950), 9–11.

8. In a standard survey of psychiatric interviewing, Doctors Ekkehard and Sieglinde Othmer distinguish between insight-oriented interviewing, in which the interviewer or clinician attempts to identify "unconscious conflicts," and descriptive interviewing, whose purpose is simply to "collect a set of symptoms and signs that fit diagnostic criteria for categorical disorders." My contention in this chapter is that the historian may gather data that permits him or her to approximate many of the conclusions of the latter sort of interview. I am not trying to "psychoanalyze" Brown. Granted, my method differs in important respects from that employed in conducting an interview with a live patient. The Othmers stress the need for the interviewer to establish rapport, eventually trust with his/her patient. Transference, wherein the interviewee projects emotions from other relationships onto the interviewer, may then occur, enabling the therapist to uncover the unconscious roots of symptoms. A reading of Brown's correspondence with close relations invites the same sort of unprovable inferences. What is surprising in Brown's letters to family members and key supporters – and in their replies to him – is the degree of confidence, trust, and affection that many of the parties are able to take for granted. Of course Brown also often wrote with unstated purposes and could be less than truthful, but the historian has numerous opportunities to check out specious claims and misrepresentations of fact; interviewers may not be so fortunate with new patients. Interviewers may of course introduce tests and ask probing questions that find no analogue in Brown's letters, but Brown left a number of unguarded reflections in his notebooks, and his political statements are quite revealing of his patterns of thought. Finally, the interviewer must probe his or her subject in a relatively short span of time to unearth what the biographer may seek in a lifetime of Brown's correspondence, notebooks, and assorted documents. See Ekkehard Othmer and Sieglinde C. Othmer, *The Clinical Interview Using DSM–IV*, 2 vols. (2nd ed.; Washington, DC: American Psychiatric Press, 1994), I, Chapter 1 et passim.

9. Perhaps it was his early years he remembered when he claimed that he had "generally enjoyed remarkably good health" among the "unnumbered and unmerited blessings" that God had bestowed on him. Brown to Rev. Luther Humphrey, Nov. 19, 1859, Eldridge Collection, HEHL.

10. John Brown to Ruth Brown, Aug. 10, 1852, Eldridge Collection, HEHL; Brown to "Dear Son John," Aug. 26, 1853, Stutler Collection, WVDCH; John Brown to "Dear Wife, & Children All," Sept. 15, 19, 1855, Stutler Collection, WVDCH; Wealthy Hotchkiss Brown to "My Dear Aged Grandfather," March 17, 1856, Gee Collection, HLHS.

11. John Brown to "Dear Mary & Children 'every one,'" May 27, 1857, copy, Villard Collection, CUL; Brown to "Dear Wife & Children every one," June 3, 1857, Stutler Collection, WVDCH; Brown to "Dear Wife: & Children; every one," Sept. 26, 1857, Stutler Collection; Brown to E. B. Whitman, Oct. 5, 1857, John Brown Collection, KSHS.

12. John Brown to "Dear Wife & Children *all*," Sept. 9, 1858, Stutler Collection, WVDCH; Brown to "Dear Wife," Sept. 13, 1858, Stutler Collection, WVDCH; John Henri Kagi to "My Dear Sister, and Father," Sept. 23, 1858, Richard J. Hinton

Papers, KSHS; Brown to ?, Aug. 3, 1858, John Brown Collection, KSHS; Brown to "Dear Friend" [Franklin B. Sanborn?], Sept. 9, 1858, copy, Sanborn Folder, HU; Brown to "Dear Wife, & Children; All," Oct. 11, 1858, Stutler Collection, WVDCH; Brown to "Dear Friend" [John Brown, Jr.], Nov. 1, 1858, John Brown, Jr., Papers, OHS; Brown to "Dear Wife & Children All," Dec. 2, 1858, Stutler Collection, WVDCH; Brown to "Dear Wife & Children *all*," March 2, 1859, John Brown Collection, KSHS.

13. John Brown to John Henri Kagi, Apr. 16, 1859, Dreer Collection, PHS; Brown to Kagi, May 16, 1859, Dreer Collection, PHS; Edwin Morton to Franklin B. Sanborn, Apr. 13 and April 18, 1959, as quoted in Franklin Benjamin Sanborn, *Recollections of Seventy Years*, 2 vols. (Boston: Richard G. Badger/The Forham Press, 1909), I, 161; Brown to Kagi, Apr. 25, 1859, typed copy, Dreer Collection, PHS; Brown to Augustus Wattles, May 18, 1859, Hinton Papers, KSHS; Brown to "Dear Mary & Children *All*," Aug. 7, 1859, copy, Villard Collection, CUL.

14. Contemporary sources confirm that Brown preached these values to his children long after they had grown to adulthood. See, for example, his remark on the value of *"early rising."* John Brown to "Dear Sons John, Jason & Frederick, & daughters," Dec. 4, 1854, John Brown, Jr., Papers, OHS.

15. James Foreman to James Redpath, Dec. 28, 1859, ALS, Hinton Collection, KSHS; Journal of Richard Henry Dana, June 28–29, 1849, as quoted in Richard O. Boyer, *The Legend of John Brown: A Biography and a History* (New York: Knopf, 1973), 146–8; Frederick Douglass, *The Life and Times of Frederick Douglass*, as quoted in William S. McFeely, *Frederick Douglass* (New York: Norton, 1991), 186.

16. Salmon Brown, "My Father, John Brown," n.d., as quoted by Louis Ruchames, ed., *John Brown: The Making of a Revolutionary* (New York: Grosset & Dunlap, 1969), 195; John Brown to John Brown, Jr., June 28, 1854, copy, Sanborn Folder, HU; John Brown to "Dear Mary," Nov. 23, 1845, Eldridge Collection, HEHL.

17. Numerous photos and descriptions of Brown survive. Thaddeus Hyatt raised about $2,000 by selling the 1859 three-quarter length portrait showing Brown with a full beard. A copy with a note on the back is in the Frank W. Logan Collection of the Chicago Historical Society. On his appearance, see Franklin B. Sanborn, *Life and Letters of John Brown, Liberator of Kansas, and Martyr of Virginia* (1885; repr., New York: Negro University Press, 1969), 428–9; Hinton, *John Brown and His Men*, 201–5; Frederick Douglass, *The Life and Times of Fredrick Douglass, Written by Himself* (rev. ed.; Boston: DeWolfe, Fiske, & Co., 1892), 272–3; "Nora Marks," pseud., "Old John Brown's Story [an interview with John Brown, Jr.]," *Sandusky Daily Register*, May 31, 1889, p. 2; Salmon Brown, "My Father, John Brown," n.d., cited in Ruchames, *Making of a Revolutionary*, 192–3; Salmon Brown to Sanborn, Aug. 8, 1909, Stutler Collection, WVDCH; Osborn Perry Anderson, *A Voice from Harper's Ferry*, 9.

18. Salmon Brown interview with Katherine Mayo, Oct. 11–13, 1908, Villard Collection, CUL.

19. As memory experts have known since antiquity, carefully noting the physical arrangements in which documents are placed can be an essential device for remembering how to find them. See the classic study by Frances A. Yates, *The Art of Memory* (Chicago: University of Chicago Press, 1966).

20. Brown to "Dear Mary," June 29, 1846, Eldridge Collection, HEHL.

21. Brown to "Dear Wife," Apr. 26, 1855, ALS, Anthony Collection, NYPL.

22. Brown to "Dear Wife," Dec. 31, 1852, Ricks Collection, Illinois State Historical Library, Springfield; Brown to "Dear Wife & Children every One," Apr. 16, 1858, Logan Collection, CHS.

23. Jason Brown to John Brown, Jr., March 13, 1853, John Brown, Jr. Papers, OHS; John Brown to "Dear Wife: & Children *All*," July 9, 1858, Stutler Collection, WVDCH; Brown to John Brown, Jr., Dec. 1, 1858, John Brown, Jr., Papers, OHS; Brown to John Henri Kagi, April 16, 1859, reprinted in the New York *Journal of Commerce*, Oct. 30, 1859, p. 3.

24. See for example John Brown to "Dear Mary," Oct. 19, 1846, Eldridge Collection, HEHL; Brown to "Dear Mary," June 29, 1846, Eldridge Collection, HEHL.

25. "I. Smith" [Brown] to John Brown, Jr., July 27, 1859, John Brown, Jr. Papers, OHS; Brown to Lora Case, Dec. 2, 1859, Eldridge Collection, HEHL.

26. Unless otherwise noted all the quotes from the interview noted below are from the version in the Baltimore *American*, Oct. 21, 1859, p. 1. The New York *Herald* gives this statement as follows: "My head is a little confused by wounds, and my memory obscure on dates, &c." New York *Herald* (Morning Edition), Oct. 21, 1859, p. 1.

27. During his trial, moreover, Brown himself questioned witnesses closely about his actions and remarks during the raid. On the final moments and the trial, see: Robert E. McGlone, "Forgotten Surrender: John Brown's Raid and the Cult of Martial Virtues," *Civil War History*, 40 (Sept. 1994), 185–201.

28. Quoted in the Baltimore *American and Commercial Advertiser*, Oct. 21, 1859, p. 1.

29. Cited in the *Baltimore American*, Oct. 21, 1859, p. 1. The report is by C. W. Tayleure. Compare his shorthand version with those of two other reporters present during Brown's interview. New York *Herald*, Oct. 21, 1859, p. 1; *Cincinnati Daily Gazette*, Oct. 21, 1859, p. 3.

30. *Baltimore American*, Oct. 21, 1859, p. 1.

31. "Insurrection at Harper's Ferry: Authentic Details," Richmond *Enquirer*, Oct. 21, p. 2. Aaron Stevens, who lay wounded beside Brown, continued to show his "captain" the loyalty that Brown's men had evidenced in following him despite what they regarded as his flawed plan, suggesting that self-preoccupation had not isolated Brown from his followers. After the raid, of course, prominent people who had helped to finance him in Kansas and some who knew that he intended to strike in the South distanced themselves from Brown. Fearing federal indictment, Franklin Sanborn destroyed documents connecting him to Brown, and he, Samuel Gridley Howe, and George Luther Stearns fled to Canada. Gerrit Smith entered an insane asylum. Of the Secret Six, only Theodore Parker, who was dying in Italy, and Thomas Wentworth Higginson, openly acknowledged their support of Brown.

32. A vivid account of manic-depressive illness is psychiatrist Kay Redfield Jamison's extraordinary memoir, *An Unquiet Mind*.

33. George H. Hoyt to John W. Le Barnes, Oct. 21, 1859, Hinton Papers, KSHS; Judge Richard Parker, "Trial of John Brown," undated memoir, Miscellaneous Manuscripts Collections, LOC, 17–18.

34. For a discussion of mania and creativity, see: Kay Redfield Jamison, *Touched with Fire: Manic-Depressive Illness and the Artistic Temperament* (New York: The Free Press, 1993), esp. 105–8; also Goodman and Jamison, *Manic-Depressive Illness*, Chapter 14. Recent research is summarized in Ruth Richards, et al., "Creativity in Manic-Depressives, Cyclothymes, Their Normal Relatives, and Control Subjects,"

Journal of Abnormal Psychology, 97, no. 3 (1988): 281–8, esp. 287. An intriguing finding that echoes a favorite theory of Edward Jarvis and other mid-nineteenth-century pioneer psychiatrists is that "work-oriented temperament" may be associated with risk for manic-depressive illness. In *Moodswing: The Third Revolution in Psychiatry* (Toronto: Bantam Books, 1975), Ronald R. Fieve cites a host of prominent, accomplished people he believes suffer or suffered from mood disorders. Of John Brown Fieve says only that he "was able to attract a large following precisely because of the grandiosity of his ideas (137)."

35. See the brilliant study of Virginia Woolf by Thomas C. Caramagno, *The Flight of the Mind: Virginia Woolf's Art and Manic-Depressive Illness* (Berkeley: University of California Press, 1992), esp. 68–74.

36. John Brown to "My Dear Mary," Oct. 19, 1846, Eldridge Collection, HEHL. Annie was not yet three, "Kitty" (Amelia), was one, and Oliver was seven.

37. Owen Brown (son) to "Dear Father and Brother [John, Jr.]," Feb. 28, 1858, & March 18, 1858, typed copy, Rust Collection, HEHL.

38. John Brown to "My Dear Wife," Jan. 8, 1847, Eldridge Collection, HEHL.

39. John Brown to Ruth Brown, Jan. 5, 1847, copy, Villard Papers, CUL. It is true that others in Brown's family conventionally added the phrase, "if life continues" or "if our lives are spared" to their news of an impending visit. But like his father, Brown himself regularly coupled his reports with admonitions about the "precariousness of life." Ruth Brown Thompson to Wealthy Hotchkiss Brown, Sept. 27, 1852, John Brown, Jr., Papers, OHS.

40. As biographer Thomas Caramagno points out, "Depressives habitually look on the gloomy side of any question. They come to believe that their very existence bodes ill for themselves and their families." Caramagno, *Flight of the Mind*, 44–8.

41. A recent field study confirms the usefulness of distinguishing between major depression and dysthymia, on the one hand, and depressive personality disorder, on the other. Over the course of the twentieth century, labels similar to the latter have described gloomy, joyless, anxious, and despairing persons who are typically guilt-ridden, duty-bound, and lacking in self-confidence. They are brooding, self-denigrating, unable to feel pleasure, and lethargic. They exhibit a depressive temperament, constitutional moodiness, and neurotic depression. But personality disorders may be differentiated from mood disorders. They have an early (often insidious) onset, have cognitive and interpersonal features, are characteristic of a person's mode of functioning, and are persistent. In contrast, mood disorders can begin at any time, are usually episodic, and their composite symptoms tend to reflect disturbances of mood, drive, and soma. Mood disorders tend to be predominantly ego-dystonic (not in harmony with the ego and its standards) and distressful to the patient. The core problem in depressive personality disorder is excessive negative, pessimistic beliefs about oneself and other people. Depressive personality disorder may be viewed as a subset of mood disorder or at least as overlapping substantially with the latter, but it is not congruent with any of them. Clearly, the symptoms of neither dysthymia nor depressive personality disorder describe John Brown. See *DSM–IV*, 345–9, 732–3.

42. Brown to Ruth and Henry Thompson, Jan. 23, 1852, John Brown Collection, CHS; Brown to Mary Brown, Aug. 22, 1850, Eldridge Collection, HEHL.

43. Women were especially at risk. In the first half of the nineteenth century, only 20 percent of American married women survived to see their youngest child reach maturity. Joseph Kett, *Rites of Passage: Adolescence in America, 1790 to the Present* (New York: Basic Books, 1977), 15.

44. See, for example, John E. Ruark and Thomas A. Gonda, "Grief and Mourning," in Anastasios Georgotas and Robert Cancro, eds., *Depression and Mania* (New York: Elsevier, 1988), chapter 38; Charles Binger and Dennis Malinak, "Death & Bereavement," in Howard H. Goodman, ed., *Review of General Psychiatry* (2nd ed.; Norwalk, CT: Appleton & Lange, 1988), Chapter 9.

45. John Brown to "Dear Father," Aug. 11, 1832, as quoted in Ruchames, *Making of a Revolutionary*, 49–50.

46. Quoted in Boyer, *Legend of John Brown*, 249–50.

47. John Brown to "Mr. Henry L. Stearns," July 15, 1857, Stutler Collection, WVDCH. A photo copy is in the John Brown Collection, KSHS. As noted in Chapter 3, assessments of the letter have run the gamut. Villard begins his narrative with the complete text of this "simple, straightforward, yet remarkable narrative." Oswald Garrison Villard, *John Brown, 1800–1959: A Biography Fifty Years After* (1910; Gloucester, MA: Peter Smith, 1965), 1–7. Biographer Jules Abels concludes, on the other hand, that the "autobiography" was a sales pitch to young Henry's father. Jules Abels, *Man on Fire: John Brown and His Cause of Liberty* (New York: Macmillan, 1971), 7.

48. To be sure, Brown may have been drawing a lesson; a few lines later Brown spoke of the "wretched, hopeless condition, of *Fatherless & Motherless* slave *children*: for such children have neither Fathers [n]or Mothers; to protect, & provide for them." But in so doing he drew attention to his own remembered grief. Brown to Henry L. Stearns, July 15, 1857, Stutler Collection, WVDCH.

49. Ibid.

50. Brown to John Brown, Jr., Feb. 20, 1858, John Brown, Jr., Papers, OHS.

51. Brown to Franklin B. Sanborn, Feb. 24, 1858, John Brown, Jr., Papers, OHS.

52. The most persuasive is Bertram Wyatt-Brown, who credits an earlier paper of my own for raising the possibility that Brown may have suffered from bipolar disorder. See Wyatt-Brown, "A Volcano Beneath a Mountain of Snow': John Brown and the Problem of Interpretation," in Paul Finkelman, ed., *His Soul Goes Marching On: Responses to John Brown and the Harpers Ferry Raid* (Charlottesville: University Press of Virginia, 1995), 10–38, esp 13.

53. Brown to Sanborn, Feb. 24, 1858, John Brown, Jr., Papers, OHS.

54. Sanborn took the letter as evidence of Brown's trust in him. And that trust was seductive. Sanborn remembered that he had concluded that "no confidence could be too great, no trust nor affection too extreme, towards this aged poor man whom the Lord had chosen as his champion." Sanborn, *Life and Letters of John Brown*, 445.

55. Brown to Franklin B. Sanborn, Aug. 13, 1857, quoted in Ruchames, *A John Brown Reader*, 107–9. See also Brown to E. B. Whitman, Oct. 5, 1857, copy, John Brown Papers, KSHS.

56. John Brown to John Brown, Jr., April 15, 1857, Stutler Collection, WVDCH. The text of "Old Brown's Farewell" is in the John Brown Collection, KSHS, and is reprinted in Ruchames, *A John Brown Reader*, 106. In March Brown had written Amos Lawrence pleading his poverty. "I have never hinted to any one else that I had a thought of asking for any help to provide in any such way for my family; & *should not to you*: but for your own suggestion." Brown to Amos Lawrence, March 19, 1857, ALS, John Brown Collection, MHS.

57. John Brown, Jr., to John Brown, Nov. 29, 1850, copy, Sanborn Folder, HU; John Brown to John Brown, Jr., Dec. 6, 1850, John Brown, Jr., Papers, OHS.

58. In drafting his "Words of Advice" to the assembly of blacks he called the League of Gileadites on January 15, Brown hoped to help "revive their broken spirits." John Brown to "Dear Wife," Jan. 17, 1851, as quoted in Ruchames, *A John Brown Reader*, 75. Brown's covenant for the League is reprinted in Ruchames, *A John Brown Reader*, 76–9.

59. Brown to John Brown, Jr., Sept. 25, 1843, as quoted in Ruchames, *A John Brown Reader*, 50–1. At this sorrowful time Mary was six months pregnant. Brown's fear for her life and that his children would not survive the respiratory infections that plagued the family was perennial. See Brown to Simon Perkins, May 1, 1849, John Brown Collection, BPL; Brown to Owen Brown [father], Jan. 10, 1849, reprinted in Ruchames, *A John Brown Reader*, 67.

60. Salmon's reflections were reported in the Portland *Star* in 1906 and reprinted in *True West*, Nov.–Dec. 19, 1975, pp. 32–3, a copy of which is in the Jones Donation, Hudson Library and Historical Society. Ruth remembered that her father "had a wonderfuly [sic] sweet silvery voice when he sang," and that he cried after little Ellen died. Ruth Brown Thompson to James H. Holmes, March 30, 1899, Villard Collection, CUL.

61. Brown to Mary, Nov. 29, 1846, Stutler Collection, WVDCH. Brown seems to have been untouched by the culture of sentimentality that enabled many contemporary middle-class women to cope with the loss of a child by "transforming their grief into restorative mourning" through a hitherto forgotten genre of popular poetry. See Mary Louise Kete, *Sentimental Collaborations: Mourning and Middle Class Identity in Nineteenth-Century America* (Durham, NC: Duke University Press, 2000), 7.

62. Brown to Ruth Brown Thompson and Henry Thompson, Jan. 23, 1852, ALS, Brown Collection, CHS.

63. Ibid. When Ruth and her husband Henry were converted during a revival in Essex County, Ruth found herself at odds with her brothers John, Jr., Jason, and Owen. See her reproachful letter to John, Jr., and his wife Wealthy, protesting what they called their "soul cheering views," belief in the "sufficiency of our natural faculties," and denial of future torments and the infallibility of scripture. Ruth Brown Thompson to John Brown, Jr., April 19, 1853, John Brown, Jr., Papers, OHS. See also Frederick Brown [son] to John Brown, Jr., May 25, 1853, John Brown, Jr., Papers, OHS.

64. "Anne I want you first of all to become; a *sincere, humble, earnest, & consistent, Christian*. Save this letter to remember your Father by Anne." Brown to "Dear Wife; & Children *all*, Oct. 1, 1859, Eldridge Collection, HEHL.

65. When John, Jr., was seventeen, his father suggested that "the older boys read and coppy [sic] my old Letters as I proposed to them, I want to have them all preserved with care." Brown to his wife and children, Dec. 5, 1838, Stutler Collection, WVDCH.

66. Jason Brown to "Dear Brothers, Sisters & *Nephew*," Feb. 8, 1853, John Brown, Jr. Papers, OHS; Brown to Ruth and Henry Thompson, May 10, 1853, Stutler Collection, WVDCH. By October Jason and his brothers Owen and Frederick planned to move to a large farm near Akron and were encouraging John, Jr., and Wealthy to move there. "I can do well there John, (as Father says) 'I know it.'" Jason Brown to John Brown, Jr. October 2, 1853, John Brown, Jr. Papers, OHS.

67. Brown also likened himself to that "erring servant" Samson and the sixteenth-century Protestant martyr John Rogers, who had "perished at the stake" in 1555 for preaching against Catholicism. Rogers had written to his children, Brown noted,

urging them to "abhor that arrant whore of Rome." In similar fashion, Brown asked his children to "abhor with undiing hatred, also: that 'sum of all vilanies' [sic]; Slavery." John Brown to "My dear steadfast friend," [Rev. Henry Vaill], Charlestown, Va., Nov. 15, 1859, in New-York *Weekly Tribune*, Dec. 3, 1859, p. 3.

68. A diagnosis of Antisocial Personality Disorder also requires a history of crimes and physical assaults (such as spouse beating or child beating), chronic deceitfulness and manipulation, and impulsivity and failure to plan ahead. Typically such people have a long history of unwillingness to work even when jobs are available and they look out only for "number one." Although some of Brown's more hostile biographers have suggested that he was profoundly dishonest and that his raid lacked forethought, Brown's abandonment of his farm to the care of his adult sons to fight slavery was surely no indication of unwillingness to work. See American Psychiatric Association, *Diagnostic and Statistical Manual of Mental Disorders*, 4th ed., (Washington, DC: American Psychiatric Association, 2005) *DSM–IV*, 645–50.

69. The essential difference between a delusional and a rational fear of attack, according to one authority, is not to be found in the plausibility of the belief or even in the lack of subsequent proof of its truthfulness, but in the conviction that a threat is imminent when evidence of it is lacking. Whether the Browns had sufficient evidence that the Pottawatomie victims were going to act on their threats, as I note in chapter 6, has long been matter of controversy. See David Schlager, "Evolutionary Perspectives on Paranoid Disorders," in *Delusional Disorders*, Mark J. Sedler, ed., *The Psychiatric Clinics of North America*, 18, No. 2 (June 1995): 263–79, esp. 272.

70. Salmon Brown to Rev. Joshua Young, Dec. 27, 1859, in James Claude Malin, *John Brown and the Legend of Fifty-Six* (Philadelphia: American Philosophical Society, 1942), 267.

71. Henry Thompson, interview with Katherine Mayo, Pasadena, California, Aug. 22–Sept 1, 1908, Villard Collection, CUL.

72. Eventually Jason came to agree with his brothers that the killings were "necessary" as a "defensive measure." Reminiscences of Jason Brown, as told to F. G. Adams, College Hill, Topeka, Kansas, typed draft, John Brown Collection, KSHS. On Brown's family's efforts to come to terms with his deeds and growing legend, see Robert E. McGlone, "Rescripting a Troubled Past: John Brown's Family and the Harper's Ferry Conspiracy," *The Journal of American History*, 75 (March 1989): 1179–1200.

73. Handwritten statement of John Brown, n.d., Stutler Collection, WVDCH, reel 1.

74. See *DSM–IV*, 296–301; Mark J. Sedler, ed., *The Psychiatric Clinics of North America: Delusional Disorders*, 18, no. 2 (June 1995), 199–425, is comprehensive.

75. Brown did not have persecutory delusions; it was not himself but the slaves who he believed were oppressed by the Slave Power. On Delusional Disorder and Paranoia, see Sedler, ed., *Delusional Disorders*, and *DSM–IV*, 296–301.

CHAPTER 9 – PROPAGANDIST

1. Brown's line is evidently indebted to Shakespeare's "Hung be the heavens with black, yield, day, to night!" from *King Henry VI (1591), Part I, Act I, sc. l*, 1. Although the Declaration of Liberty is unquestionably Brown's work, the lines quoted from it above may have been suggested by one of his associates.

2. Quoted in Lawrence J. Friedman, *Gregarious Saints: Self and Community in American Abolitionism, 1830–1870* (Cambridge: Cambridge University Press, 1982), 210.

3. Some papers even printed false interviews. See "Interviews with Three Rebels: Special Report to the Baltimore *Exchange*," quoted in the *New York Times*, Oct. 20, 1859, p. 1. Some papers added the phrase, "Authentic Details," to their stories. See "Insurrection at Harper's Ferry: Treatment of Prisoners, Authentic Details," Richmond *Enquirer*, Oct. 21, p. 2. Rivalry among the new weekly illustrated newspapers led to accusations that *Harper's Weekly* had published fraudulent pictures of the raid. "Bogus Illustrations," *Frank Leslie's Illustrated Newspaper*, No. 206, Vol. VIII, Nov. 12, 1859, pp. 367–8.

4. David Potter develops the notion that events in Kansas were misrepresented in the East as a sectional quarrel. See Potter's classic *The Impending Crisis, 1848–1861*, compiled and edited by Don Fehrenbacher (New York: Harper & Row, 1976), Chapter 9. For the view that Brown was in fact an insignificant figure in Kansas history, see James Claude Malin, *John Brown and the Legend of Fifty-six* (Philadelphia: American Philosophical Society, 1942).

5. Actually selling for two cents an issue, the New-York *Daily Tribune* also carried price listings for semi-annual and annual subscriptions. New-York *Daily Tribune*, Oct. 18, 1859, p. 1.

6. On the emergence of the penny dailies, see William E. Huntzicker, *The Popular Press, 1833–1865* (Westport, CT: Greenwood Press, 1999) and Thomas C. Leonard, *The Power of the Press: The Birth of American Political Reporting* (New York: Oxford University Press, 1986), 63–96. Still useful is Michael Schudson, *Discovering the News: A Social History of American Newspapers* (New York: Basic Books, 1978), Chapter 1.

7. Bernard A. Weisberger, *Reporters for the Union* (Boston: Little Brown, 1953), chapter 1. See also Louis M. Starr, *Reporting the Civil War: The Bohemian Brigade in Action, 1861–65* (New York: Collier Books, 1962).

8. Historian Menahem Blondheim has shown that during the Civil War President Lincoln learned how to exploit the New York Associated Press to control news from the battlefield. See Menahem Blondheim, "'Public Sentiment Is Everything': The Union's Public Communications Strategy and the Bogus Proclamation of 1864," *The Journal of American History*, 89 (Dec. 2002): 869–99.

9. Weisberger, *Reporters for the Union*, 21–2.

10. James Redpath, *The Roving Editor: Or, Talks With Slaves in the Southern States* (1859; repr., New York: Negro University Press, 1968), Dedication.

11. "Arrival of 'Raw-Head-And-Bloody-Bones,'" Leavenworth City *Kansas Weekly Herald*, Oct. 4, 1856, p. 1.

12. William Addison Phillips, "Three Interviews With Old John Brown," *Atlantic Monthly*, 44 (Dec. 1879): 738–44.

13. A leader in the famous 1854 attempt to rescue fugitive slave Anthony Burns from authorities in Boston, Higginson sought to perpetuate the guerrilla fighting in Kansas but denied that antislavery agitators were prolonging the fight there to elect Fremont. New-York *Daily Tribune*, Oct. 6, 1856, Oct. 21, 1856. Tilden G. Edelstein, *Strange Enthusiasm: A Life of Thomas Wentworth Higginson* (New Haven, CT: Yale, 1968), 184, 191–2.

14. Quoted in Edelstein, *Strange Enthusiasm*, 195–6.

15. See the summary in Weisberger, *Reporters for the Union*, 23–30.

16. Kagi's scornful editorial reference to a former Pierce appointee to the territorial bench led to a gun fight in which Kagi and his attacker were both wounded. See James Redpath's "Reminiscences of the Insurrectionists, Number IV," in the Boston *Atlas and Daily Bee*, Oct. 26, 1859, p. 1.

17. Quoted in Oswald Garrison Villard, *John Brown, 1800–1859: Fifty Years After* (1910; Gloucester, MA: Peter Smith, 1965), 279.

18. John Brown to "Hon. A[ndrew] H. Reeder," April 1, 1857, John Brown Collection, CHS. Brown had met Reeder just days before in company with Sanborn and a free-state leader, Martin Conway. See Villard's "Chronology of Brown's Movements," *John Brown Fifty Years After*, Appendix, 674.

19. John Brown to Hon. Eli Thayer, April 16, 1857, Eldridge Collection, HEHL.

20. John Brown to John Brown, Jr., April 15, 1857, Stutler Collection (West Virginia Department of Culture and History).

21. John Brown to "Hon Eli Thayer," April 16, 1857, Eldridge Collection, HEHL. His enthusiasm restored, Brown added his boast about being pursued by one of the "'U S Hounds."

22. Stearns's letter to Brown is quoted without citation in Villard, *John Brown Fifty Years After*, 288–9.

23. "Old Browns [sic] *Farewell*; to the Plymouth Rocks, Bunker Hill Monuments, Charter Oaks, and Uncle Thoms [sic] Cabbins," unpublished essay, April, 1857, Stutler Collection, WVDCH.

24. "Old Browns [sic] Farewell; to the Plymouth Rocks, Bunker Hill Monuments, Charter Oaks, and Uncle Thoms [sic] Cabbins," unpublished essay, April, 1857, John Brown Collection, CHS. A copy of this version, slightly edited, is in Louis Ruchames, ed., *John Brown: The Making of a Revolutionary* (New York: Grosset & Dunlap, 1969), 114.

25. Brown restates this theme in his interview with Senator Mason and other officials after his capture even as he denies he sought vengeance in coming to Harpers Ferry. New York *Herald*, Oct. 21, 1859, p. 1.

26. Notes for a speech to the Massachusetts Legislative Committee, n.d., Stutler Collection, WVDCH.

27. John Brown to Horatio N. Rust, April 25, 1857, CHS.

28. John Brown to S. G[ilbert] Hubbard, June 1, 1857, John Brown Collection, CHS. Original in possession of the University of Chicago Library.

29. John Brown to Theodore Parker, March 7, 1858, in Franklin B. Sanborn, *The Life and Letters of John Brown, Liberator of Kansas, and Martyr of Virginia*, (1885; repr., New York: Negro University Press, 1969), 448–9. Caution is required in citing from Sanborn's affectionate tribute to his hero: Sanborn edited many of Brown's letters for style. In this instance, his version differs slightly from that in Villard, *John Brown Fifty Years After*, 324–5. Neither quotation preserves Brown's unusual habit of underlining and his eccentric punctuation, and neither author cites the original.

30. Brown to Parker, March 7, 1858, in Sanborn, *Life and Letters of John Brown*, 448–9. Brown also made a joking reference to spiritualism (the "dear sister spirits").

31. Ibid.

32. It is not clear whether Parker ever knew of the location of Brown's proposed invasion. See Jeffery Rossbach, *Ambivalent Conspirators: John Brown, the Secret Six,*

and a Theory of Slave Violence (Philadelphia: University of Pennsylvania Press, 1982), 144–50.

33. Quoted in Villard, *John Brown Fifty Years After*, pp. 355–6.
34. "A brief history of John Brown otherwise (old B) & his family: *as connected with Kansas*; by one who Knows," handwritten mss., n.d. [Aug. 1858], 5 pp., Dreer Collection, PHS, p. 2.
35. "A brief history of John Brown otherwise (old B) & his family: *as connected with Kansas*; by one who Knows," Dreer Collection, PHS, p. 4.
36. On the meeting, see Wattles's testimony to the Mason Committee, Feb. 17, 1860, United States Senate, 36th Congress, 1st Session, *Report of the Select Committee of the Senate appointed to inquire into the late invasion and seizure of the public property at Harper's Ferry*, 2 vols. (Washington, 1860), II, 213–25, esp. 216–17. Hereafter cited as *The Mason Committee Report. Marais des Cygnes* means "Marsh or Marshland" of Swans in French.
37. The original document, dated Trading Post, January 1859, is in the John Brown Collection, KSHS. On the response to Brown's "Parallels," see Villard, *John Brown Fifty Years After*, 375–6.
38. Wattles's testimony in the *Mason Committee Report*, II, 223.
39. Nelson Hawkins [John Brown] to Augustus Wattles, April 8, 1857, reprinted in Wattles's testimony, *Mason Committee Report*, II, 220.
40. John Brown to Dr. Samuel Gridley Howe, March 1, 1859, Sanborn Folder, HU.
41. Chatham was in Canada West, now Ontario, close to Lake Erie. Martin Delaney was the chief rival of Frederick Douglass as a "redeemer of his race." Instead of signing up with Brown, in July 1859, Delaney left for West Africa, where he hoped to establish an African American colony in the Yoruba region near Lagos. On Delaney and Brown, see Robert S. Levine, *Martin Delaney, Frederick Douglass, and the Politics of Representative Identity* (Chapel Hill: University of North Carolina Press, 1997), 178–83.
42. On the vogue for such declarations, see Pauline Maier, *American Scripture: Making the Declaration of Independence* (New York: Knopf, 1997). The Declaration of Sentiments adopted by the Seneca Falls convention in 1848 to raise women's consciousness of their exploitation by "man" may have been a precedent for Brown's Declaration.
43. The journal of the convention, kept by its elected secretary, John Henry Kagi, a trusted Brown volunteer, is reprinted in the *Mason Committee Report*.
44. Richard J. Hinton, a Brown loyalist, reprinted the Declaration, slightly edited, among the documents in the 150-page appendix to his celebratory *John Brown and His Men* (1968; repr., New York: Funk and Wagnalls, 1894), 637–43. The elegant handwritten draft of Brown's Declaration in the Dreer Collection at the Pennsylvania Historical Society may be the only copy to survive.
45. Oswald Garrison Villard, Stephen B. Oates, and Louis DeCaro, Brown's most thorough biographers, fail to mention the Declaration of Liberty even in their discussions of the Chatham convention. Published collections of documents relating to Brown also omit it. See Quarles, ed., *John Brown: The Making of a Revolutionary* and Zoe Trodd and John Stauffer, eds., *Meteor of War: The John Brown Story* (Maplecrest, NY: Brandywine Press, 2004). David S. Reynolds is an exception. See his *John Brown Abolitionist: The Man Who Killed Slavery, Sparked the Civil War, and Seeded Civil Rights* (New York: Knopf, 2005), 300–3.

46. Brown refers to the United States president and other officials, for example, as "Leeches," to lesser officeholders as "Blood Suckers and Moths," and to the Southern plantation master as a "vile Thief, Rober, Libertine, Pirate; & Woman killing Slave Holder."

47. Brown's Provisional Constitution, however, provided for women only insofar as it required soldiers to protect and respect their virtue.

48. The quote is from Frank A. Rollins, *Life and Public Services of Martin R. Delaney, Sub-Assistant Commissioner, Bureau of Refugees, Freedmen, and Abandoned Lands, and Late Major 104th United States Colored Troops* (Boston: Lee & Sheppard, 1868), 85–90, as reprinted in Hinton, *John Brown and His Men*, Appendix, pp. 714–18.

49. Brown expected "General" Tubman to be on the same train that had brought him to Canada. On arriving, he wrote to a mutual friend, "I did not find my friend Harriet as I expected; but believed she would certainly be on every moment until the train left.... I came on believing she would be on by the next train.... May I trouble you to see her at once; & if she is well: by all means have her come on immediately." John Brown to William H. Day, April 16, 1858, photocopy, John Brown Collection, HLHS. Though she did not attend the Chatham meeting, Tubman soon after took up residence in St. Catherines, Canada, and in June Brown was helping Tubman raise money to buy a house for her "aged Father; & Mother." At her suggestion, he urged Frederick Douglass to let her go on tour with him. "Could you not manage to *make* as much as you would *loose* [sic] by her presence?" Brown asked. "Any thing you *can do* for Gen Tubman the *man of deeds* will be fully appreciated by your Sincere Friend, Old Hundred." Brown to "Fred[e]rick Douglas[s], Esqr.," June 22, 1858, John Brown Collection, HLHS.

50. On belief in the Slave Power Conspiracy, see Leonard L. Richard's important reinterpretation of the issue, *The Slave Power: The Free North and Southern Domination, 1780–1860* (Baton Rouge: LSU Press, 2000). Delaney did not remember that Brown proposed to attack Harpers Ferry. Rather he thought Brown had planned to move the terminus of the underground railroad from Canada to Kansas in the hope that the question of black rights would be tested and won there. If that was the impression Brown conveyed at the Chatham meeting, it is apparent why no one was eager to sign onto such a dangerous scheme. See Delaney's remarks quoted indirectly in Hinton, *John Brown and His Men*, 714–16.

51. The literature on the political culture of antebellum parties is extensive. See especially Jean H. Baker, *Affairs of Party: The Political Culture of Northern Democrats in the Mid-Nineteenth Century* (Ithaca, NY: Cornell University Press, 1983) and Eric Foner, *Free Soil, Free Labor, Free Men: The Ideology of the Republican Party Before the Civil War* (Oxford: Oxford University Press, 1970). On the political abolitionists, see Richard H. Sewell, *Ballots for Freedom: Antislavery Politics in the United States, 1837–1860* (New York: Norton, 1976).

52. On the "republican synthesis," see Daniel T. Rodgers's perhaps premature epitaph: "Republicanism: The Career of a Concept," *The Journal of American History*, 79 (June 1991): 11–38.

53. The "Provisional Constitution and Ordinances for the people of the United States" is reprinted as document No. 3 in the *Mason Committee Report*, I, 48–59. Oswald Garrison Villard concluded that, despite its "admirable" spirit, the document was an "indictment of Brown's saneness of judgment." Villard, *John Brown Fifty Years After*, 334–6. Brown's latest biographer, David Reynolds, focuses on its egalitarian

promise but concedes the document was "hardly unproblematic." David Reynolds, *John Brown, Abolitionist*, 8, 249–53.

54. On October 20, just a week before the raid on Harpers Ferry, Brown set forth the "organization" of the provisional army in General Order No. 1. A company was to consist of fifty-six privates, twelve noncommissioned officers (eight corporals and four sergeants), two lieutenants, a captain, and a surgeon, and would comprise two platoons. A battalion consisted of four companies, a regiment of four battalions, and a brigade of four regiments. Privates were to elect their own non-commissioned officers and the "War Department" (Brown and Kagi) would name the commissioned officers above them. The document is in Kagi's handwriting. General Order No. 1 is reprinted as document No. 4, *Mason Committee Report*, I, 59–60.

55. Brown's ally, James Montgomery, presented Brown's Peace Agreement to a meeting at Sugar Mound, Linn County, on December 6, 1858. A copy is included as Appendix D in Villard, *John Brown Fifty Years After*, pp. 665–6. Within ten days of its signing, however, Brown's "treaty" was violated by Montgomery. See Villard's discussion, pp. 364–5.

56. Brown's "Vindication of the Invasion, etc." is in the Dreer Collection, PHS. It was widely published. See "The Virginia Rebellion," *New York Times*, Oct. 22, 1859, p. 1.

57. See, for example, Stephen B. Oates, *To Purge This Land with Blood: A Biography of John Brown* (Torchbook ed.; New York: Harper & Row, 1970), 283–4; Reynolds, *John Brown Abolitionist*, 303.

58. Early in October Brown urged John, Jr., that forming "associations to *hinder, delay* and *prevent* our *adversaries* might perhaps effect much. Our *active enemies* should be spotted to a man, and some shrewd person should be on the border to look after that matter somewhat *extensively*. Can you dig up a *good and true* man, to communicate with us on the border [between Pennsylvania and Maryland], *or close to it* where we may name places from time to time." Isaac [John Brown] to "Dear Friend" [John Brown, Jr.], n.d., copy included in letter, John, Jr., to Lysander Spooner, Esq., October 17, 1859, Brown Documents, BPL.

59. Villard, *John Brown Fifty Years After*, 467.

60. Quoted in the New York *Herald*, Oct. 21, 1859, p. 1.

61. Republican papers like Greeley's *Tribune*, on the other hand, chided the *Herald* for suggesting that the letters were evidence of the "complicity" of "important persons at the North" and pronounced the letters "of very little consequence." See "John Brown's Invasion, Correspondence of the Conspirators," New-York *Daily Tribune*, Oct. 26, 1859, p. 6.

62. Although counting the loss of Brown's "incriminating documents" among his errors at Harpers Ferry, historian Bertram Wyatt-Brown notes that their publication "did much to terrorize the slaveholding population." See Bertram Wyatt-Brown, "'A Volcano Beneath a Mountain of Snow': John Brown and the Problem of Interpretation," in Paul Finkelman, ed., *His Soul Goes Marching On: Responses to John Brown and the Harpers Ferry Raid* (Charlottesville: University Press of Virginia, 1995), p. 25.

63. Quoted in Friedman, *Gregarious Saints*, 210.

64. John G. Rosengarten, "John Brown's Raid: How I got Into It, and How I Got Out of It," *Atlantic Monthly*, 15 (June 1865): 716–17.

65. See "Mr. Gidding and Mr. Brown," New-York *Daily Tribune*, Oct. 27, 1859, p. 5.

CHAPTER 10 – CONSPIRATOR

1. John Brown to Mary A. Brown, March 2, 1858, as quoted in Franklin B. Sanborn, ed., *The Life and Letters of John Brown, Liberator of Kansas, and Martyr of Virginia* (1885; repr., New York: Negro Universities Press, 1969), 442–3.

2. Brown to "My Dear Friend E. B. of R. I.," Nov. 1, 1859, as quoted in the New-York *Weekly Tribune*, Nov. 17, 1859, p. 7; Brown to "My Dear Young Friend," Nov. 17, 1859, in the New-York *Weekly Tribune*, Dec. 3, 1859, p. 3.

3. Several recent writers have emphasized Brown's conscious self-creation. He was a "consummate spin doctor," writes Lacy Baldwin Smith. In committing treason and dying for man's political and social well-being, as well as his soul, she suggests, Brown broadened the idea of martyrdom. Smith, *Fools, Martyrs, Traitors: The Story of Martyrdom in the Western World* (New York: Knopf, 1997), 231, 249–50. Brown recreated himself in "mythic terms," writes Victor Vincent Verney, Jr., John Brown: Cultural Icon in American Mythos, PhD dissertation, University of New York at Buffalo, p. 1, 7. The Hawthorne quote is on page 63. On trial for his life, observes Robert A. Ferguson, Brown "achieved a special imaginative power by mixing legal artifice with religious understanding." Ferguson, "Story and Transcription in the Trial of John Brown," *Yale Journal of Law & the Humanities*, 6, 37 (1994): 38–73. Paul Finkelman shows that Brown's beatification was very much a collaborative effort. See "Manufacturing Martyrdom: The Antislavery Response to John Brown's Raid," in Paul Finkelman, ed., *His Soul Goes Marching On: Responses to John Brown and the Harpers Ferry Raid* (Charlottesville: University Press of Virginia, 1995), Chapter 2.

4. Col. Robert E. Lee to Adjutant General S. Cooper, Oct. 19, 1859, in United States Senate, 36th Congress, 1st Session, *Report of the Select Committee of the Senate appointed to inquire into the late invasion and seizure of the public property at Harper's Ferry*, Rep. Com. No. 278, 2 vols. (Washington, 1860), I, Appendix, 40–3. Hereafter cited as the *Mason Committee Report*.

5. The term "guerrillas" was widely but imprecisely used in the mid-nineteenth century. Roughly, it stood for unorganized, irregular troops not attached to an army, who carried on, in Robert Mackey's words, "petty war chiefly by raids, extortion, destruction, and massacre" and were unable to "encumber themselves with many prisoners." During the Civil War, irregular warfare augmented the field armies. The Confederacy distinguished guerrillas from partisans ("elite conventional forces given an unconventional role," such as reconnaissance, raiding, and counter guerrilla actions), and conventional cavalry used as raiders. See Robert R. Mackey, *The Uncivil War: Irregular Warfare in the Upper South, 1861–1865* (Norman: University of Oklahoma Press, 2004), Chapter 1.

6. Allan Nevins, *The Emergence of Lincoln*, II, *Prologue to Civil War, 1859–1861* (New York: Scribner's Sons, 1950), 74–8; David Potter, *The Impending Crisis, 1848–1861*, ed. and completed by Don E. Fehrenbacher (1960; Torchbook ed.; Harper & Row, 1976), 367–71. For a sympathetic popular assessment of the raid as a "commando attack," see: Barrie Stavis, *John Brown: The Sword and the Word* (South Brunswick: A. S. Barnes, 1970).

7. See the discussion of these disparities in Chapter 13 and Brown to [Prosecutor] Andrew Hunter, Nov. 22, 1859, reprinted in Louis Ruchames, *John Brown: The Making of a Revolutionary* (2nd ed.; New York: Grosset & Dunlap, 1969), 152.

8. On the problem of false memories, see Robert E. McGlone, "Deciphering Memory: John Adams and the Authorship of the Declaration of Independence," *The Journal*

of American History, 85 (Sept. 1998): 411–38; McGlone, "Forgotten Surrender: John Brown's Raid and the Cult of Martial Virtues," *Civil War History*, 40 (Sept. 1994): 185–201; David Thelen, ed., *Memory and American History* (Bloomington: Indiana University Press, 1990). For an introduction to recent thinking about memory, see Daniel L. Schacter, *Searching for Memory: The Brain, the Mind, and the Past* (New York: HarperCollins, 1996).

9. Asked by Senate investigators whether Brown was reputed to be insane in Massachusetts before Harpers Ferry, Andrew said: "I am not aware that I had ever heard it suggested by any man that Captain Brown was insane." See Andrew's testimony before the Mason Committee, Thursday, Feb. 9, 1860, *Mason Committee Report*, II, 186–95, esp. 190.

10. Rev. Heman Humphrey to Brown, Nov. 20, 1859, quoted in Sanborn, *Life and Letters*, 602–3.

11. Higginson to Oswald Garrison Villard, Boston, Nov. 12, 1909, Villard Papers, CUL. On the Secret Six, see Jeffery Rossbach, *Ambivalent Conspirators: John Brown, the Secret Six, and a Theory of Slave Violence* (Philadelphia: University of Pennsylvania Press, 1982), 216–35, and Edward Renehan, Jr., *The Secret Six: The True Tale of the Men Who Conspired with John Brown* (New York: Crown Publishers, 1995).

12. As early as February 1858, Higginson learned from his trusted friend, Franklin B. Sanborn, that Brown "expects to overthrow slavery in a large part of the country.… I should not wonder if his plan contemplated an uprising of slaves – though he has not said as much to me." Sanborn added that E. B. Whitman, the Kansas Committee's representative, reported that "some say he is insane." Franklin B. Sanborn to Thomas Wentworth Higginson, Feb. 11, 1858, Higginson Collection, BPL.

13. Higginson to "Dearest Mother," Nov. 5, 1859, in Mary Thacher Higginson, ed., *Letters and Journals of Thomas Wentworth Higginson, 1846–1906* (New York: Houghton Mifflin, 1921), 86–7.

14. Tilden G. Edelstein, *Strange Enthusiasm: A Life of Thomas Wentworth Higginson* (New Haven, CT: Yale University Press, 1968), 212–36, esp. 221. See also Rossbach, *Ambivalent Conspirators*, 146–8, 217–20.

15. Tidd had introduced himself to Higginson in hopes of learning the fate of a fellow survivor of the raid. Tidd to Higginson, Dec. 18 [Nov. 18?], 1859, Higginson Papers, BPL; Tidd to Higginson, Dec. 8, 1859, Higginson Papers, BPL. The first letter is clearly misdated.

16. Owen's statement to Franklin Sanborn, May 5, 1885, in Sanborn, *Life and Letters of John Brown*, 541–2. Sanborn's colorful version of the mutiny cast Brown's sons as heroes for refusing to let their father die alone despite their presumed conviction that they were all going to their deaths at Harpers Ferry.

17. Annie's own statements conflicted on some details. Her 1886 account had Tidd leaving the Kennedy farmhouse for several days to stay with Cook in Harpers Ferry in protest of the plan, while she later told Hinton that Tidd was gone for more than a week. More important, she first said that Owen had as always supported her father, only to have him contradict her. Compare Annie Brown Adams's 1886 statement, Logan Collection, CHS, with Annie Brown Adams as quoted in Hinton, *John Brown and His Men*, 258–9. Perhaps to excuse his own participation in the raid, Edwin Coppoc told Virginia authorities before his trial that "The whole company was opposed to making the first demonstration at Harper's Ferry, but Captain Brown would have his own way, and we had to obey orders." Statement

to the correspondent of The New-York *Times*, as quoted in the New-York *Tribune*, Oct. 20, 1859, p. 6. Also see Sanborn, *Life and Letters of John Brown*, 424–5.

18. Tidd apparently did not tell Higginson whether the men wanted to burn the bridges before leaving Harpers Ferry to buy time or afterwards to prevent pursuit.

19. Thomas Wentworth Higginson, conversation with Charles Plummer Tidd, Feb. 10, 1860, Higginson Papers, BPL. Compare Higginson's notes with his summary in *Cheerful Yesterdays* (Boston: Houghton, Mifflin & Co., 1900), 229.

20. Owen Smith [Owen Brown] to Dear Sir [John Brown], Harpers Ferry, Aug. 18, 1859, Dreer Collection, PHS.

21. Quoted in Sanborn, *Life and Letters of John Brown*, 542.

22. Oswald Garrison Villard, *John Brown, 1800–1859: A Biography Fifty Years After* (1910; Gloucester, MA: Peter Smith, 1965), 420–1.

23. Quoted in Sanborn, *Life and Letters of John Brown*, 542. Compare, for example, that quote with "I am fully persuaded that I am worth inconceivably more to *hang* than for any other purpose" (John Brown to Jeremiah Root Brown, Nov. 12, 1859, in Villard, *John Brown Fifty Years After*, 496) or "I am worth infinitely more to die than to live." Villard, *John Brown Fifty Years After,* 546, citing S. C. Pomeroy's letter to the *Christian Cynosure* of March 31, 1887.

24. Owen [Brown] "Smith" to John Brown, Aug. 18, 1859, Dreer Collection, PHS. Owen's statement, May 5, 1885, in Sanborn, *Life and Letters of John Brown*, 541–2. (Same in *Recollections*, I, 175, 182–4.) Also see Sanborn, "Oliver Brown," *Kansas History,* I (n.d.), 68, handwritten copy in Villard Collection, CUL. On aphoristic memory, see Robert E. McGlone, "Deciphering Memory: John Adams and the Authorship of the Declaration of Independence," *Journal of American History*, 85 (Sept. 1998): 411–38. For a different interpretation of Brown's conduct, see Stephen B. Oates, *To Purge This Land with Blood: A Biography of John Brown* (Torchbook ed.; New York: Harper & Row, 1970), 279–80. Memory inevitably rewrites our life stories.

25. Franklin Benjamin Sanborn, *Recollections of Seventy Years*, 2 vols. (Boston: Richard G. Badger/The Gorham Press, 1909), I, 145–7.

26. Sanborn to Thomas Wentworth Higginson, Oct. 6, 1859, Higginson Papers, BPL; Sanborn to Higginson, Oct. 13, 1859, Higginson Papers, BPL.

27. Douglass had become famous as a public speaker on the abolitionist circuit, had lectured widely in England, and had published an influential account of his own harrowing escape from slavery. His elegant hilltop home in Rochester was a station on the underground route of runaways to freedom across the Canadian border, and in December 1847 he was to launch his antislavery newspaper, *The North Star*, beginning a distinguished editorial career. On Douglass's early years and rhetorical skills, see Gregory P. Lampe, *Frederick Douglass: Freedom's Voice, 1818–1845* (East Lansing: Michigan State University Press, 1998).

28. *Life and Times of Frederick Douglass, Written by Himself* (rev. ed.; Boston: De Wolfe, Fiske, & Co., 1892), 339–42.

29. *Life and Times of Frederick Douglass*, 339–42.

30. On Douglass's thought, see David W. Blight, *Frederick Douglass' Civil War: Keeping Faith in Jubilee* (Baton Rouge: LSU Press, 1989). Douglass, *Life and Times*, 370–2, 374–7.

31. Also attending was Douglass's sometime adversary, the radical Rev. Henry Highland Garnet; William Still, a key figure in the underground railroad; and host the Rev. Stephen Smith. John Brown to John Brown, Jr., Rochester, NY, Feb. 4, 1858, John

Brown, Jr. Papers, OHS. Martin B. Pasternak, *Rise Now and Fly to Arms: The Life of Henry Highland Garnet* (New York: Garland, 1995), 94; Benjamin Quarles, *Allies for Freedom: Blacks and John Brown* (New York: Oxford, 1974), 40–41; Villard, *John Brown Fifty Years After*, 323, 627, n31.

32. Jeremiah Goldsmith Anderson to Dr. John B. Anderson, January 17, 1859, in Hinton, *John Brown and His Men*, 238–9 n1. John Henry Kagi to "Friend [Douglass]," St. Catherine's, Ontario, Thursday, June 23, 185[9], Miscellaneous Brown Papers, PHS. Douglass's name is blacked out in the salutation and the text, but internal evidence establishes him as the recipient. The year is confirmed by Kagi's reference to the recent death of Dr. Gamaliel Bailey, editor of a widely read antislavery newspaper, the Washington *National Era*.

   A political abolitionist fearful that direct attacks on slavery would injure the Republican Party, Bailey, on learning in 1858 of Brown's plan to attack slavery militarily, had warned Massachusetts Senator Henry Wilson cryptically to advise Samuel Gridley Howe and other Brown supporters "to get those arms out of Brown's hands." On Bailey, see Stanley Harrold, *Gamaliel Bailey and Antislavery Union* (Kent, Ohio: Kent State University Press, 1986), 125–7, 141, 192, 202–3, and Richard H. Sewell, *Ballots for Freedom: Antislavery Politics in the United States, 1837–1860* (New York: W. W. Norton, 1976), 132–3.

33. But for the failure of Douglass to show up early Monday morning, Cook claimed, Brown might have succeeded even though he waited too long to retreat to the mountains. See "Fred. Douglass' Treachery," New York *Herald*, Nov. 1, 1859, p. 1.

34. The envelope was addressed to John Henri, the alias of John Henry Kagi, who was evidently instructed to forward it. [John Brown] to "F. D.," September 23, 1859, as reprinted in the New-York *Daily Tribune*, Oct. 26, 1859, p. 6.

35. Villard, *John Brown Fifty Years After*, 323, 627 n33; Mrs. Thomas Russell, interview with Katherine Mayo, New York *Evening Post*, Oct. 23, 1909, as quoted in Louis Ruchames, ed., *A John Brown Reader* (London: Abelard-Schuman, 1959), 234–41, esp. 239. Some even suggested that Douglass had sent twenty-two-year-old Shields Green "in his place" because Green was an unwanted suitor for Douglass's twenty-year-old daughter, Rosetta. Although no contemporary evidence supports this supposition or impugns Douglass's conduct, such stories often gain a life of their own in the politics of memory. On the substitute theory, see Hinton, *John Brown and His Men*, 260–3, and Quarles, *Allies for Freedom*, 79. On Douglass's ambition for his bright, proud, oldest daughter, see William S. McFeely, *Frederick Douglass* (New York: W. W. Norton, 1991), 218–23.

36. Frederick Douglass to the Editor, Rochester *Democrat and American*, Canada West, Oct. 31, 1859, reprinted in Douglass, *Life and Times*, 380–1.

37. Douglass was willing to face an impartial jury in New York state, he said, but he objected to "being caught by the hounds of Mr. Buchanan, and '*bagged*' by Gov. Wise." Frederick Douglass to the Editor, Rochester *Democrat and American*, Canada West, Oct. 31, 1859, reprinted in Douglass, *Life and Times*, 380–1.

38. Frederick Douglass, address delivered at Storer College, Harper's Ferry, May 30, 1881, in Louis Ruchames, ed., *John Brown: The Making of a Revolutionary* (New York: Grosset & Dunlap, 1969), 278–99, esp. 298.

39. John Brown, Jr., later questioned whether the stone quarry meeting had ever taken place but conceded that he had no evidence that it did not and that he did not know how far Douglass had been committed to help his father. Quarles, *Allies for Freedom*, 78–9.

40. Douglass, *Life and Times*, 383–91.

41. Quoted in Quarles, *Allies for Freedom*, 67. During the Civil War Douglass would raise recruits, including his sons Lewis and Charles, for the famous Massachusetts 54th regiment.

42. Maria Diedrich speculates that Douglass and other black leaders may have spurned Brown's appeals to join him because under Brown's plan black liberation would be achieved by a "white mastermind" with blacks in subordinate roles. Maria Diedrich, *Love Across Color Lines: Ottilie Assing & Frederick Douglass* (New York: Hill and Wang, 1999), 212–16. See Douglass's 1843 rebuttal to Henry Highland Garnet's call for insurrection, cited in Merton L. Dillon, *Slavery Attacked: Southern Slaves and Their Allies, 1619–1865* (Baton Rouge: LSU Press, 1990), 214.

43. Douglass to Gerrit Smith, Aug. 9, 1867, Frederick Douglass Mss., Frederick Douglass Memorial Home, Anacostia, D. C., as quoted in Philip S. Foner, ed., *The Life and Writings of Frederick Douglass*, 5 vols. (New York: International Publishers, 1950–5), 2: 552–3 n11. Douglass's 1860 speech is quoted in John W. Blassingame, ed., *The Frederick Douglass Papers, Series One: Speeches, Debates, and Interviews*, 3 vols. (New Haven, CT: Yale University Press, 1979–92), 3: 317–18.

44. Foner, II, 485–6. Brown failed only in being sufficiently ruthless, Douglass suggested. "The tender regard which the dear old man evinced for the life of the tyrants – and which should have secured him his life – will not be imitated by future insurgents. Slaveholders are as insensible to magnanimity as to justice, and the measure they mete must be meted to them again." Douglass to James Redpath, as quoted in Philip S. Foner, ed., *The Life and Writings of Frederick Douglass*, 5 vols. (New York: International Publishers, 1950–5), 2: 485–6.

45. The Committee consisted of Democrats Mason of Virginia (chair), Jefferson Davis of Mississippi, and Graham Fitch of Indiana, and Republican members Jacob Collamer of Vermont and James R. Doolittle of Wisconsin.

46. Testimony of Richard Realf, *Mason Committee Report*, II, 90–113. If possible, Realf was to retrieve incriminating letters Brown had written to Forbes when Forbes was a trusted ally.

47. Richard Realf to George Luther Stearns, Franklin B. Sanborn, Theodore Parker, and others, May 29, 1858, typed copy, as quoted in Renehan, *The Secret Six*, 167.

48. Realf's failure to keep in contact with the "association," he said cheerily, was "evidence that I was not collecting money for them in England, or that if I did, they did not get it; which, so far as implicating me is concerned, amounts to about the same thing. ..." Testimony of Richard Realf, *Mason Committee Report*, II, 104–6.

49. Rossbach, *Ambivalent Conspirators*, 248. Testimony of Richard Realf, January 21, 1860, *Mason Committee Report*, II, 100, 107–8.

50. Testimony of Richard Realf *Mason Committee Report*, II, 100–1, 108–9.

51. Testimony of Richard Realf, *Mason Committee Report*, II, 96–8, 113.

52. Testimony of Richard Realf, *Mason Committee Report*, II, 97–98, 99.

53. See "Most Important Disclosures," New-York *Herald*, Oct. 27, 1859, pp. 3–4, 8; "More Evidence About the Harper's Ferry Conspiracy – Another Letter from Forbes," New-York *Herald*, Nov. 1, 1859, pp. 6, 10. Horace Greeley and James Redpath each published a "card" in the *Herald* to refute Forbes's charges against them. See "The Forbes Correspondence: Cards from Horace Greeley and James Redpath," New-York *Herald*, Oct. 29, p. 10.

54. Forbes to Howe, May 14, 1858, as quoted in the New-York *Herald*, Oct. 27, 1859, p. 4. Mark Summers mentions neither Brown, Hugh Forbes, nor any member of

the Secret Six in his important study of political corruption in the sectional crisis. See Mark W. Summers, *The Plundering Generation: Corruption and the Crisis of the Union, 1849–1861* (New York: Oxford, 1987).

55. Testimony of Richard Realf, *Mason Committee Report*, II, 113.

56. Renehan, *The Secret Six,* 128. Attorney Andrew Hunter, who prosecuted Brown, recalled having asked Brown during his trial whether he intended to "stampede slaves" near Harpers Ferry, to which Brown had replied he did not. Testimony of Andrew Hunter, *Mason Committee Report*, II, 62.

57. Forbes to Howe, May 14, 1859, in the New-York *Herald*, Oct. 27, 1859, p. 4.

58. Forbes to Howe, May 14, 1858, in the New-York *Herald*, Oct. 27, 1859, p. 4. Forbes's suggestion that Brown would await a moment when the slaves were restive to strike helps explain, as I note in Chapter 11, why he chose October 18 to launch his raid on Harpers Ferry.

59. See, for example, the remarks attributed to Brown in Horace Greeley's rival New-York *Tribune* explaining his "real plan." "What Brown's Plan Really Was," New York *Weekly Tribune*, Nov. 12, 1859, p. 6.

60. In his Oct. 27, 1859, letter to the *Herald*, Forbes included a letter to Howe in which he recounted a meeting with Senator William Seward during which Forbes told him about the "whole matter in all its bearings." The staunchly Democratic *Herald* was only too happy to accuse Seward of failing to alert the government of the conspiracy. See "The Harper's Ferry Invasion: Seward Clearly Implicated," the New-York *Herald*, Nov. 1, 1859, p. 10.

61. See Stanley Harrold, *The Abolitionists and the South, 1817–1914* (New York: Harper & Row, 1971), 54.

62. Testimony of Richard Realf, *Mason Committee Report*, II, 102.

63. Testimony of William F. M. Arny, Jan. 16–17, 1860, *Mason Committee Report*, II, 68–90.

64. *Mason Committee Report*, II, 201.

65. See Don W. Wilson, *Governor Charles Robinson of Kansas* (Lawrence: University Press of Kansas, 1975), Chapter 3; Homer Socolofsky, *Kansas Governors* (Lawrence: University Press of Kansas, 1990), 59–64.

66. After a proslavery posse burned Osawatomie to the ground on August 30, 1856, Robinson had written Brown that he deserved "the highest praise from every patriot," and "posterity would pay homage" to his "heroism." Years later, Robinson's widow hired a writer to debunk Brown. Charles Robinson to "Capt. John Brown," Sept. 15, 1856, as quoted in Villard, *John Brown Fifty Years After*, 262–3.

67. Robinson to Brown, Sept. 13, 1856, quoted in Villard, *John Brown Fifty Years After*, 263; Testimony of Charles Robinson, Feb. 10, 1860, *Mason Committee Report*, II, 196.

68. Testimony of Charles Robinson, Feb. 10, 1860, *Mason Committee Report*, II, 196–201.

69. Testimony of Augustus Wattles, Feb. 17, 1860, *Mason Committee Report*, II, 213–25, esp. 225.

70. Majority Report in *Mason Committee Report*, I, 2, 7, 10, 17.

71. Minority Report, *Mason Committee Report*, I, 21–5.

72. C. Vann Woodward saw the raid as decisive in poisoning the political climate. "Paranoia continued to induce counterparanoia, each antagonist infecting the other reciprocally, until the vicious spiral ended in war." C. Vann Woodward, "John

Brown's Private War," in *The Burden of Southern History* (rev. ed.; Baton Rouge: LSU Press, 1968), 41–68. On the consequences of the raid, see Paul Finkelman, ed., *His Soul Goes Marching On: Responses to John Brown and the Harpers Ferry Raid* (Charlottesville: University Press of Virginia, 1995).

73. Minority Report, *Mason Committee Report*, I, 23.

74. Rev. James Gloucester to John Brown, Feb. 19, 1858, John Brown Collection, KSHS.

75. John Brown to Mary A. Brown, March 2, 1858, as quoted in Sanborn, *Life and Letters of John Brown*, 442–3.

76. Catherine Clinton, *Harriet Tubman: The Road to Freedom* (New York: Little, Brown, & Co., 2004), 98.

77. Brown to John Brown, Jr., April 8, 1858, John Brown, Jr. Papers, OHS. Brown had paid her expenses to St. Catherines and soon after sent her an additional $25.

78. Clinton, *Harriet Tubman: The Road to Freedom*, Chapter 9, esp. 128–33.

79. During the seventeen-month delay between the Chatham meeting and the raid, Brown lost credibility with his Canadian supporters and at the critical time a number of potential recruits were out of the country or otherwise occupied. See the summary in Quarles, *Allies for Freedom*, 72–80. On Loguen, see Carol M. Hunter, *To Set the Captives Free: Reverend Jermain Wesley Loguen and the Struggle for Freedom in Central New York, 1835–1872* (New York: Garland, 1993). The authority for Garnet's statement is John S. Rock, the first black attorney admitted to practice before the Supreme Court, who spoke on the occasion of Brown's hanging. See *The Liberator*, Dec. 15, 1859, and Martin D. Pasternak, *Rise Now and Fly To Arms*, 94. The talented Rock called upon blacks to "elevate" themselves through education and hard work, but in 1858 he, like Brown, had believed that "Sooner or later, the clashing of arms will be heard in this country" and the military capacities of blacks would be needed and respected. See James and Lois Horton, *In Hope of Liberty: Culture, Community, and Protest Among Northern Free Blacks, 1700–1860* (New York: Oxford University Press, 1997), 121, 124, 266.

80. Brown asked "Friend Jones" to keep such views to himself, as Brown expected to find plenty of others equally as skeptical. Minutes of the Convention, in Horton, *In Hope of Liberty*, 10–13; also see the copy entitled Journal of the Provisional Constitutional Convention, held on Saturday, May 8, 1858, Chatham, Canada West, appended to the majority report in *Mason Committee Report*, I, 45–7. James C. Hamilton, "John Brown in Canada," *The Canadian Magazine* (Dec. 1894): 132, as quoted in Quarles, *Allies for Freedom*, 47.

81. John Brown to "Dear Wife and Children, Every One," May 27, 1857, quoted in Ruchames, *The Making of a Revolutionary*, 114–15.

82. On Brown's hopes that others "would take hold," see John Brown to "Dear Wife; & Children every one," St. Catherines, Canada West, April 6, 185[8], photocopy, Gee Collection, HLHS, and Robert E. McGlone, "Rescripting a Troubled Past: John Brown's Family and the Harpers Ferry Conspiracy," *Journal of American History*, 75 (March 1989): esp. 1186–90.

83. Despite the rigors of an Iowa winter that drove snow into their bunks and numerous "hot discussions" among the man, Brown's contingent was closely bonded and committed to the cause. But things did not always go smoothly. On February 11, 1859, for example, Owen Brown noted in his diary that "ugly words" had passed between "Moffit, Cook, and Leeman, much swearing and giving each other the lie; many of the settlers threaten to raise a crowd, driving all the rest of us away saying

that we are all as bad as runaways." Owen's diary was found among Brown's papers after the raid and published in the newspapers. "Diary of one of the Harper's Ferry Conspirators," Richmond *Daily Whig*, Oct. 29, 1859, Villard Collection, CUL.

84. John Brown to "J. H. Kagi," April 16, 1859, Dreer Collection, PHS.
85. Brown to "J. H. Kagi," May 16, 1859, Dreer Collection, PHS.
86. See Villard, *John Brown Fifty Years After*, 413–15.
87. Found among Brown's papers after the raid, the letter appeared in the New-York *Herald*, October 25. Here cited in the New-York *Daily Tribune*, Oct. 26, 1859, p. 6.
88. On antislavery politics, see the classic studies by Richard Sewell, *Ballots for Freedom*; Frederick J. Blue, *The Free Soilers: Third Party Politics, 1848–54* (Urbana: University of Illinois Press, 1973); and Eric Foner, *Free Soil, Free Labor, Free Men: The Ideology of the Republican Party Before the Civil War* (New York: Oxford, 1970). Tyler Anbinder has shown that the rapid rise of the northern Know Nothings in the mid-1850s was indebted primarily to intense antislavery sentiment. Anbinder, *Nativism and Slavery: The Northern Know Nothings and the Politics of the 1850s* (New York: Oxford, 1992). Daniel J. McInerney shows that abolitionism was deeply indebted to the spirit of 1776: McInerney, *The Fortunate Heirs of Freedom: Abolitionism & American Thought* (Lincoln: University of Nebraska Press, 1994), and Leonard Richards grounds abolitionist fears of the dominance of the "Slave Power" in political reality. Richards, *The Slave Power: The Free North and Southern Domination, 1789–1860* (Baton Rouge: Louisiana State University Press, 2000).
89. Villard, *Brown Fifty Years After*, 373.
90. On the impact of slave rescue attempts on southern public opinion, see Stanley Harrold, *The Abolitionists and the South, 1831–1861* (Lexington: University Press of Kentucky, 1995).
91. George M. Fredrickson, *The Black Image in the White Mind: The Debate on Afro-American Character and Destiny, 1817–1914* (New York: Harper & Row, 1971), Chapter 4; Theodore Parker, as quoted in Rossbach, *Ambivalent Conspirators*, 148–52.
92. Parker was also impressed with courageous Anthony Burns, whose freedom abolitionists had purchased, and Bostonian Lewis Hayden, who led the successful attempt in 1852 to free the fugitive Shadrach and who later helped to recruit Francis Meriam to Brown's company. Rossbach, *Ambivalent Conspirators*, 4, 18, 148–54.
93. Michael Fellman, "Theodore Parker and the Abolitionist Role in the 1850s," *Journal of American History*, 61 (December 1974): 666–84.
94. James Brewer Stewart, *Wendell Phillips, Liberty's Hero* (Baton Rouge: Louisiana State University Press, 1986), 199–208.
95. Irving H. Bartlett, *Wendell & Ann Phillips: The Community of Reform, 1840–1880* (New York: W. W. Norton, 1979), 61–6; Fredrickson, *The Black Image in the White Mind*, 119; Rossbach, *Ambivalent Conspirators*, 148–59, 182–3, 268; John Brown, Jr., to "Friend Henri [Kagi]," Syracuse, Aug. 17, 1859, quoted in the *Mason Committee Report*, I, 69–70.
96. Quoted in Benjamin Quarles, *Black Abolitionists* (New York: Oxford University Press, 1969), 234–5; Lawrence J. Friedman, *Gregarious Saints: Self and Community in American Abolitionism, 1830–1870* (London: Cambridge University Press, 1982), Chapter 7, esp. 208–16.
97. James Brewer Stewart, *Wendell Phillips, Liberty's Hero* (Baton Rouge: Louisiana State University Press, 1986), 199–208.

408 Notes to pages 243–246

98. Lysander Spooner, "A Plan for the Abolition of Slavery (and) To the Non-Slave-Holders of the South," in Charles Shively, ed., *The Collected Works of Lysander Spooner*, 4 vols. (Weston, MA: M & S Press, 1971), IV, n.p., following a seven-page introduction. A copy of Spooner's plan is in the Spooner Papers at the Boston Public Library and another in the Spooner Papers at the New York Historical Society.

99. Lysander Spooner to Thomas Wentworth Higginson, Nov. 28, 1858, Higginson Papers, BPL.

100. Stewart, *Wendell Phillips: Liberty's Hero*, 200.

101. Spooner was so taken with Brown that after the Harpers Ferry raid he conceived a daring plan to kidnap Virginia Governor Henry Wise and spirit him away from Richmond as a hostage to insure that Brown would not be executed. Phillips and several others briefly supported the idea but were unable to raise the money necessary for the operation before Brown's execution. Renehan, *The Secret Six*, 173–5; Rossbach, *Ambivalent Conspirators*, 185–9.

102. Shively, Introduction to "A Plan for the Abolition of Slavery," in Shively, *Collected Works of Lysander Spooner*, IV, part 3, p. 4.

103. The quote is from the *Boston Courier*, which noted how damaging Spooner's plan would be to Boston's commercial interests if put into effect. See Shively, *Collected Works of Lysander Spooner*, IV, part 4, p. 4.

104. James Redpath, *The Roving Editor; Or, Talks with Slaves* (1859; reprint, New York: Negro University Press, 1968), 129–32.

105. See Redpath's *The Roving Editor*, iii–iv, and Redpath, ed., *Echoes of Harper's Ferry* (Boston: Thayer and Eldridge, 1860).

106. Brown could not be sure Forbes would remain silent, though rumor placed Forbes back in Italy, where he had fought with republican forces. John Brown, Jr., to "Friend J. Henrie" [John Henry Kagi], Aug. 11, 1859, Dreer Collection, PHS.

CHAPTER 11 – INSURRECTIONIST

1. Lee's "Report to the Adjutant General," as cited in United States Senate, 36th Congress, 1st Session, *Report of the Select Committee of the Senate appointed to inquire into the late invasion and seizure of the public property at Harper's Ferry*, Rep. Com. No. 278, 2 vols. (Washington, 1860), I, 40. Hereafter cited as the *Mason Committee Report*.

2. Reporter C. W. Tayleure, *The Baltimore American and Commercial Advertiser*, Oct. 21, 1859, p. 1. Eyes were thought to be the "window" of the soul, but it seems that eye color was in the eye of the beholder. A previous dispatch to the same paper said Brown had "blue eyes." *The Baltimore American*, Oct. 20, 1859, p. 1. In other reports, Brown's eyes were variously described as light grey, blue, and "black or very dark grey." "His eyes were sharp, penetrating, and steady," writes another observer. See, for example, the instant book of news clippings assembled by Robert M. DeWitt, *The Life, Trial and Execution of Captain John Brown, known as "Old Brown of Ossatatomie"* (1859; repr., New York: Da Capo Press, 1969), 8, 14. Much of DeWitt's text is borrowed without acknowledgment from articles by Brown's self-appointed champion, James Redpath, and wire stories.

3. See, for example, the New-York *Weekly Tribune*, Oct. 29, 1859, p. 1, the statement by W. B. Downer, the Master Armorer's clerk, in the New York *Herald*, Oct. 24, 1859, p. 2, and in the same issue of the *Herald*, "The Insurrection in Virginia," p. 2. Broadly, a filibuster is a freebooter or soldier of fortune who engages in

unauthorized warfare against a foreign country with which his own country is at peace in order to enrich himself. *Webster's New Twentieth Century Dictionary of the English Language* (unabridged, 2nd ed.; Cleveland, OH: William Collins, 1979), 685. Of course, as the story of Harpers Ferry unfolded, the raiders were also called by other names: "insurrectionists," "insurgents," "conspirators," "rioters," "incendiaries," "banditti," "ruffians," and so forth.

4. The book was William V. Wells's *Walker's Expedition to Nicaragua*. In 1987, *Walker*, a "postmodernist" film parody of the popular nineteenth-century filibuster, failed to attract moviegoers but intrigued historians. See the essays by Sumiko Higashi and Robert A. Rosenstone, in Rosenstone, ed., *Revisioning History: Film and the Construction of a New Past* (Princeton, NJ: Princeton University Press, 1995), Chapters 12 and 13.

5. On filibustering, see Robert E. May, *Manifest Destiny's Underworld: Filibustering in Antebellum America* (Chapel Hill: University of North Carolina Press, 2002). In a final filibustering expedition, Walker was captured and executed by a Honduran firing squad on September 12, 1860. On William Walker and filibustering, see also May, *The Southern Dream of a Caribbean Empire, 1854–1861* (Baton Rouge: LSU Press, 1981), Kenneth M. Stampp, *America in 1857: A Nation on the Brink* (New York: Oxford University Press, 1990), 189–92, 295–7, and Reginald Horsman, *Race and Manifest Destiny: The Origins of Racial Anglo-Saxonism* (Cambridge, MA: Harvard University Press, 1981), 167–8. Still useful are Charles H. Brown, *Agents of Manifest Destiny: The Lives and Times of the Filibusters* (Chapel Hill: University of North Carolina Press, 1980), and Lawrence Greene, *The Filibuster: The Career of William Walker* (Indianapolis: Bobbs-Merrill, 1937).

6. May, *Manifest Destiny's Underworld*, Chapter 9, esp. 267–72.

7. On the role of the "doughface" presidents, Pierce and Buchanan, see May, "The Slave Power Conspiracy Revisited: United States Presidents and Filibustering, 1848–1861," in David W. Blight, ed., *Union & Emancipation: Essays on Politics and Race in the Civil War Era* (Kent, OH: Kent State University Press, 1997), Chapter 1.

8. May, *Manifest Destiny's Underworld*, 267–72.

9. Quoted in Frederick Merk, *Mission and Manifest Destiny: A Reinterpretation* (New York: Vintage Books, 1963), 212.

10. See Richard Sewell, *Ballots for Freedom: Antislavery Politics in the United States, 1837–1860* (New York: W. W. Norton, 1976), 354–7.

11. Brown's further remarks offered little reassurance. "You all know me. You are acquainted with my history. You know what I have done in Kansas. I do not expose my plans." In 1860 Hurd related his recollection of Brown's remarks at the January 24, 1857, meeting of the National Kansas Committee at the Astor House in New York City to George Luther Stearns. Hurd to Stearns, March 19, 1860, Stearns Papers, KSHS. See Oswald Garrison Villard, *John Brown, 1800–1859: A Biography Fifty Years After* (1910; Gloucester, MA: Peter Smith, 1965), 275–6.

12. John Henry Kagi to Richard J. Hinton, March 18, 1859, as quoted in Hinton, *JB and His Men*, 464–5.

13. Quoted in May, *Manifest Destiny's Underworld*, 79.

14. Hence the significance of C. W. Tayleure's reference to the color of Brown's eyes. See his description of Brown as a prisoner after the raid in *The Baltimore American and Commercial Advertiser*, Oct. 21, 1859, p. 1.

15. Because John Brown misread the temper of the slaves he sought to liberate, declared Virginia Governor Henry Wise, he became "the Border Ruffian of Virginia." See Wise's speech of October 21 on his return to Richmond from Harpers Ferry in the Richmond *Enquirer*, Oct. 25, 1859, p. 2.

16. Brown boasted of his Missouri rescue to authorities during his informal interrogation after Harpers Ferry. See the "despatches" of C. W. Tayleure in the *Baltimore American and Commercial Advertiser*, Oct, 21, 1859, p. 1.

17. Richard J. Hinton's essay was published in James Redpath's 1860 biography and reprinted as "An Interview with John Brown and Kagi," in Hinton, *John Brown and His Men* (repr., 1968; New York: Funk and Wagnalls, 1894), Appendix, pp. 670–6, esp. 673.

18. The complete text of the Provisional Constitution (a preamble and 48 articles) is printed in the *Mason Committee Report*, I, 48–59. On October 10, just a week before the raid, Brown provided his men with an organizational picture of a greatly expanded Provisional Army in General Order 1, drafted at the "Headquarters War Department" at Harpers Ferry. Ibid., 59–60.

19. Lee's "Report to the Adjutant General," in the *Mason Committee Report*, I, 40–3.

20. The literature on Southern honor and martial traditions is rich. A good place to begin is Bertram Wyatt-Brown's classic, *Southern Honor: Ethics and Behavior in the Old South* (New York: Oxford, 1982).

21. First published in 1832, Clausewitz's influential study had not been translated into English in Brown's time. See Carl von Clausewitz, *On War*, Anatol Rapoport, ed. (London: Penguin Books, 1968).

22. Osborne P. Anderson, *A Voice from Harper's Ferry: A Narrative of Events at Harper's Ferry* (Boston: Privately printed, 1861), 26–7.

23. James Redpath, *Public Life of Captain John Brown* (Boston: Thayer and Eldridge, 1860), 238, 243–4; Anderson, *A Voice from Harper's Ferry*, 26–7; Hinton, *John Brown and His Men*, 269–72; Salmon Brown, interview with Katherine Mayo, Oct. 11–13, 1908, Villard Collection, CUL.

24. For John Brown, Jr.'s role in the conspiracy and his defense of it, see Robert E. McGlone, "Rescripting a Trouble Past: John Brown's Family and the Harpers Ferry Conspiracy," *Journal of American History*, 75 (March 1989): 1190–3.

25. Quoted in *The Baltimore American*, Oct. 19, p. 1.

26. John Brown to "Dear Wife; & Children *All*," Oct. 8, 1859, Stutler Collection, WVDCH.

27. Kagi's journal of the week previous to the raid, found on his body, was published in the New-York *Weekly Tribune*, Oct. 29, 1859, p. 1.

28. Quoted in Villard, *John Brown Fifty Years After*, 413. During Reconstruction Harris was elected to Congress from North Carolina.

29. J. M. B. [James M. Bell] to John Brown, Jr., [Sept. 14, 1859] as quoted in Anderson, *A Voice from Harper's Ferry: A narrative of Events at Harper's Ferry* (1861; repr., Freeport, NY: Books for Libraries Press, 1972), 22. On September 24, Anderson met with Brown, his son Watson, and Kagi at Chambersburg. The following day Brown took Anderson to the farm in his wagon (p. 23).

30. Kagi's memorandum book, as quoted in the New-York *Weekly Tribune*, Oct. 29, 1859, p. 3. Kagi's entry for that date also includes the cryptic words: "Wrote to S. Jones, sending men off. Guerrilla operations at Brownsville, Texas."

31. John Brown, Jr., to John Henry Kagi, April 22, 1859, Dreer Collection, PHS; John Brown to Kagi, April 25, 1859, Dreer Collection, PHS.

32. On Chambersburg, see Edward L. Ayers, *In the Presence of Mine Enemies: The Civil War in the Heart of America, 1859–1863* (New York: Norton, 2003), 3–16, 32–3, 34–41.

33. Testimony of John C. Unseld, January 5, 1860, *Mason Committee Report*, II: 1–12.

34. "Isaac Smith" [Brown] to "John Henrie Esqr.," n.d. [July 10?], 1859, Dreer Collection, PHS.

35. Brown to Kagi, August 2, 1859, Dreer Collection, PHS.

36. John Brown, Jr., to "Friend Henrie" [Kagi], July 27, 1859, Dreer Collection, PHS; John, Jr., to "Friend Henrie," Sept. 8, 1859, quoted in the *Mason Committee Report*, I: 65–6.

37. "J. Henrie" [Kagi] to "J. Smith & Sons," July 18, 1859, as quoted in the *Mason Committee Report*, I: 61.

38. "Isaac Smith" [John Brown] to "Dear Friends *all*," Aug. 6, 1859, Dreer Collection, PHS.

39. John Brown to Mary A. Brown, July 5, 1859, as quoted in Villard, *John Brown Fifty Years After*, 404–5. On Mary's opposition to the Virginia expedition, see Annie Brown Adams, statement to Franklin B. Sanborn, November 1886, Logan Collection, CHS. For a discussion of the crafting of Mary Brown's public image, see McGlone, "Rescripting a Troubled Past," 1188–9.

40. Handwritten statement of Anne Brown Adams [for Franklin B. Sanborn], 38 pp, John Brown Collection, CHS.

41. Testimony of John C. Unseld, Jan. 5, 1860, *Mason Committee Report*, II: 4–5.

42. In a note dated Sept. 20, Brown advised Mary, "All well. Girls will probably start for home soon." It accompanied a brief letter he must have held for nearly two weeks before sending it. John Brown to "Dear Wife & Children All," Sept. 8, 1859, Stutler Collection, WVDCH.

43. Statement of John E. Cook, n.d. [Oct. 1859], as quoted in Hinton, *John Brown and His Men*, Appendix, p. 706. Since Kansas Brown had taken the precaution to send his mail home addressed to trustworthy neighbors or his son-in-law, Henry Thompson, with a note to pass it to his family because, he told Mary, "I have fears that my letters are stoped *near you*." Brown's concern in this instance was occasioned by the fact that he had received no reply to his last five letters from Tabor, Iowa, during the preceding seven weeks. The uncertainty of his own movements may have explained the silence from North Elba. John Brown to "Dear Wife & Children every one," Oct. 20, 1857, John Brown Collection, CHS.

44. Brown to Kagi, Aug. 2, 1859, Dreer Collection, PHS.

45. John Brown to John Henry Kagi, August 11, 1859, Dreer Collection, PHS.

46. For the text of the anonymous letter and Floyd's reaction to the warning, see Floyd's testimony in the *Mason Committee Report*, II: 250–2. After the raid, Floyd received numerous similar letters, including one purporting to disclose a rescue attempt. "But of course that was extremely ridiculous, and I paid not the slightest attention to it," he told the Committee. Floyd "did not preserve any of the letters at all." The anonymous letter warning about Brown was apparently written by David J. Gue, a Quaker who knew and liked Brown, with the aid of several other Quakers. Their hope was that Secretary Floyd would strengthen the guard at the Harpers Ferry arsenal sufficiently to persuade Brown to give up his plan to attack it and thus they would save Brown's life. See Villard, *John Brown Fifty Years After*, 410–12.

47. "J. Henrie" [Kagi] to "Messrs. J. Smith & Sons," Aug. 11, 1859, quoted in the *Mason Committee Report*, I: 63.

48. John Brown to John Brown, Jr., August, 1859, as quoted in the New York *Herald*, Oct. 25, 1859, p. 4.

49. "F." [Franklin B. Sanborn] to "Dear Friend" [Brown], Aug. 30, 1859, quoted in the *Mason Committee Report*, I: 68.

50. Brown to "Dear *Wife*, & Children *all*," Chambersburg, Oct. 1, 1859, Eldridge Collection , HEHL.

51. New York *Times*, Oct. 22, 1859, p. 1.

52. Years later Annie Brown Adams told this to Oswald Garrison Villard. See Villard, *John Brown Fifty Years After*, 420–1.

53. "J. Henrie" [Kagi] to John Brown, Jr., Oct. 10, 1859, copy by John Brown, Jr., in letter to Lysander Spooner, Esq., Oct. 17, 1859, MS 986, BPL.

54. Letter from Francis J. Meriam to "Dear Sir," ALS, Boston, Dec. 23, 1858, doc. 27, Dreer Collection, PHS. Escaping Harpers Ferry, Meriam would serve as a captain in the Third South Carolina Colored Infantry during the Civil War.

55. See the testimony of Edward K. Shaeffer, Feb. 2, 1860, in the *Mason Committee Report*, II: 145–7. Shaeffer concluded that such expeditions were generally "got up" in New Orleans or New York, not in Baltimore, and shipped all $45 worth to Meriam's hotel.

56. On Lewis Hayden, see Jeffrey Rossbach, *Ambivalent Conspirators: John Brown, the Secret Six, and a Theory of Slave Violence* (Philadelphia: University of Pennsylvania Press, 1982), 4, 18–19, 30, 151, 211; Stanley J. and Anita W. Robboy, "Lewis Hayden: From Fugitive Slave to Statesman," *New England Quarterly*, 46 (December 1973): 591–613; James Oliver Horton and Lois E. Horton, *In Hope of Liberty: Culture, Community and Protest among Northern Free Blacks, 1700–1860* (New York: Oxford, 1997), 123, 254.

57. New York *Herald*, Oct. 19, 1859, p. 3.

58. Anne Brown Adams, statement to Oswald Garrison Villard, as quoted in Villard, *John Brown Fifty Years After*, 416–20.

59. Ibid. In James Redpath's biography of Brown published just weeks after his execution, Richard J. Hinton claimed that Kagi had told him long before Harpers Ferry that Brown expected to procure "provisions enough for subsistence by forage, as also arms, horses, and ammunition." Richard J. Hinton, *John Brown and His Men*, Appendix, 674.

60. "J. Henrie" [Kagi] to John Brown, Jr., Chambersburg, Pa., Monday, Oct. 10, 1859, copy by John Brown, Jr., in letter to Lysander Spooner, Esq., West Andover, Ashtabula County, Ohio, Monday, Oct. 17, 1859, MS 986, BPL.

61. Quoted in Villard, *John Brown Fifty Years After*, 416.

62. No public documents recorded the death of slaves, and slave owners were not required to notify authorities of slave fatalities. Indeed, even the names of slaves were unlikely to appear in any public record. Census takers recorded only the names of slave owners and the gender, age, and "race" (black or mulatto) of persons held in slavery. The only public records that might list groups of slaves by their names were tax assessments – and this was rare – or probate inventories. Thus if indeed five slaves had been "murdered" in Washington County or nearby during the three and a half months preceding the raid, their deaths would probably not have been recorded anywhere publicly unless scandalous enough to appear in a local newspaper or in a civil suit proceeding. I am indebted to Emily Oland Squires of the Maryland State Archives and especially to Dr. David Taft Terry, Research Specialist in the History of Slavery and African American History, Maryland State Archives, for the information above.

63. The impulsive Cook kept a Sharps rifle at his house to show off his skill. According to local lore, he was able to "twirl the weapon upon his finger, draw a bead at the five of clubs, and at a hundred yards knock out each spot." Quoted in the *Baltimore American and Commercial Advertiser*, Oct. 21, 1859, p. 1.

64. Statement of John E. Cook, November 1859, as quoted in Hinton, *John Brown and His Men*, Appendix, 700–14, esp. 707. Hereafter cited as "Cook's Confession." The authorities did not prosecute Cook's wife as a conspirator.

65. The announcement of Cook's capture quickly drew a crowd of 300 in Chambersburg. See "Details of the Arrest of Capt. John E. Cook in Chambersburg," New York *Journal of Commerce*, Oct. 29, 1859, p. 3. Cook is also described in the New York *Herald*, Oct. 22, 1859, p. 1. "Description of Capt. Cook, the Insurrectionist," Cincinnati *Daily Gazette*, Oct. 21, 1859, p. 3.

66. "Visit of the Frederick City United Guards to the Harper's Ferry Insurrectionists," New York *Journal of Commerce*, Nov. 1, 1859, p. 3. On the possible influence of Cook's brother-in-law, see Salmon Brown to William E. Connelley, Dec. 2, 1913, Stutler Collection, WVDCH.

67. Cook's Confession, in Hinton, *John Brown and His Man*, Appendix, 702.

68. Wise's position had hardened in response to what he perceived to be "an entire social and sectional sympathy" that he thought had incited Brown to attack slavery and to the threatening letters he had received from the raiders' more extreme sympathizers. "I wish you to understand confidentially," Wise wrote to his prosecutor, "that I will not reprieve or pardon one man *now* after the letters I have received from the North." Henry A. Wise to Andrew Hunter, Nov. 6, 1859, Quincy Papers, MHS.

69. "The Arrested Insurgent at Carlisle," New York *Herald*, Oct. 24, 1859, p. 2.

70. See Villard, *John Brown Fifty Years After*, 554.

71. The 1850 U.S. Decennial Census for Jefferson County, in which Harpers Ferry is located, had a white population of 11,016 and 4,341 slaves, while Washington County, Maryland, where the Kennedy farm was located, had 28,754 whites and 2,000 slaves. Extrapolating from the totals of neighboring counties, the *Baltimore Sun* (Oct. 19, 1859) concluded that no fewer than 20,000 slaves, of whom 5,000 were men, were within twenty miles of Harpers Ferry. Quoted in the New York *Times*, Oct. 20, 1859, p. 3. An excellent summary of the population and the history of Harpers Ferry is U. S. Department of the Interior, Office of Publications [William C. Everhart and Arthur L. Sullivan], *John Brown's Raid*, National Park Service History Series (Washington, DC: GPO, 1973), 12–18.

72. Testimony of Armistead M. Ball, January 10, 1860, *Mason Committee Report*, II: 52–3.

73. Testimony of Daniel Whelan, January 6, 1860, *Mason Committee Report*, II: 19–22.

74. Merritt Roe Smith, *Harpers Ferry Armory and the New Technology: The Challenge of Change* (Ithaca, NY: Cornell University Press, 1977), 302–4.

75. In addition to Cook's narrative, in 1861 Osborne P. Anderson, the black Canadian printer and Chatham recruit, published a controversial memoir, *A Voice from Harper's Ferry: A Narrative of Events at Harper's Ferry* (1861; repr., Freeport, NY: Books for Libraries Press, 1972). It was written in part to refute charges by Virginia authorities that the blacks in Brown's company had been cowards during the raid.

76. Anderson, *A Voice from Harper's Ferry*, 28–32.

77. See "A Connected Narrative of the Affair," New York *Herald*, Oct. 19, 1859, p. 3.

78. Testimony of Daniel Whelan, Jan. 6, 1860, *Mason Committee Report*, II: 22. Evidently illiterate, Whelan made his mark at the end of the statement.

79. Filed on Wednesday, Oct. 19, Higgins's first story appeared on Friday. "The 'Servile' Insurrection at Harper's Ferry," Cincinnati *Daily Gazette*, Oct. 21, 1859, p. 2. The second, included among dispatches filed by C. W. Tayleure on Thursday, also appeared on Friday. "Statement of Patrick Higgins," *The Baltimore American and Commercial Advertiser*, Oct. 21, 1859, p. 1.

80. "The Insurrection in Virginia: The Statement of W. W. Throckmorton," New York *Herald*, Oct. 21, p. 2.

81. Shepherd worked under the supervision of a resident B&O agent and had the permission of Jefferson County to remain at Harpers Ferry. Testimony of John D. Starry, Jan. 6, 1860, *Mason Committee Report*, II: 23–7, esp. 24.

82. "Arrival of the Train: Statement of Conductor Phelps and His Officers," *The Baltimore American and Commercial Advertiser*, Oct. 18, 1859, p. 1.

83. "Another Account: Arrival of the Train from Harper's Ferry," *The Baltimore American and Commercial Advertiser*, Oct. 18, 1859, p. 1.

84. Statement of W. W. Throckmorton, New York *Herald*, Oct. 24, 1859, p. 2.

85. Quoted in Villard, *John Brown Fifty Years After*, 434.

86. John W. Garrett, President, Baltimore & Ohio Railroad, to Hon. John B. Floyd, Secretary of War, Oct. 17, 1859, Letters received by the Office of the Adjutant General, NAR, 386W. Received Oct. 19, 1859.

87. "The Insurrection in Virginia: Statement of W. B. Downer," New York *Herald*, Oct. 24, 1859, p. 2.

88. Testimony of George W. Chambers, Jan. 6, 1859, *Mason Committee Report*, II: 28–9.

89. "The Insurrection in Virginia: Statement of W. W. Throckmorton," New York *Herald*, Oct. 24, 1859, p. 2.

90. Lewis Washington's statement in the New York *Herald*, Oct. 24, 1859, p. 1.

91. Testimony of Lewis W. Washington, Jan. 6, 1860, *Mason Committee Report*, II: 29–40. Cook had fled with Washington's historic pistol, but did not have it when captured in Pennsylvania. But sometime after the raid, Owen Brown mailed the Lafayette pistol to its owner.

92. Testimony of Terence Byrne, Jan. 6, 1860, *Mason Committee Report*, II: 13–17.

93. Testimony of Daniel Whelan, January 6, 1860, *Mason Committee Report*, II: 22.

94. Robert E. Lee's report estimates that Brown had forty hostages. Col. Robert E. Lee, Col. Commanding, to Col. S. Cooper, Adjutant General, Oct. 19, 1859, in *The Mason Committee Report*, I, 40. (Hereafter cited as Lee's Report.) Witness Elijah Avey placed the number at "sixty odd" and counting. See *The Capture and Execution of John Brown: An Eyewitness Account* (1906; reprint, New York: Thomas Y. Crowell, 1971), 122–3.

95. Quoted in the New-York *Weekly Tribune*, Nov. 5, 1859, p. 3. In Osborne P. Anderson's account, it is the Virginians who are "cowardly." Anderson, *A Voice from Harper's Ferry*, 38, 40, 42.

96. It is worth noting that this text is billed as a "corrected" version of the Governor's remarks to the troops. The tradition of substituting an approved version for an actual speech was still common in sponsored "organs" like the Richmond *Enquirer*, which was edited by Governor Wise's son, Jennings. See the Richmond *Enquirer*, Oct. 25, 1859, p. 2.

97. Quoted in the Richmond *Enquirer*, Oct. 28, p. 1. The *Enquirer* was published semiweekly on Tuesdays and Fridays.

98. Quoted in the Richmond *Enquirer*, Nov. 15, 1859, p. 1. Brown's raid was "regarded as proving the faithfulness of the slaves, and no fears are entertained of them,"

reported the New York *Journal of Commerce* on October 27. Indeed, the slaves feared Brown more than their masters, the *Journal* stated. "Consternation among the slaves is caused by the fear of being seized as those of Col. Washington were, and they firmly believe the object of the prisoners were [sic] to carry them South and sell them."

99. Majority Report, *Mason Committee Report*, I: 7.

100. "News, Rumors and Gossip from Harper's Ferry," Richmond *Enquirer*, Nov. 4, 1859, p. 4, col. 6. Because small papers seldom hired reporters in the field, the *Enquirer* often published articles like this one "From the New York Herald" or other conservative journals. Slave owner and school teacher Lind Currie also failed to spread the alarm.

101. Quoted in the *Mason Committee Report*, II: 35.

102. "News, Rumors and Gossip from Harper's Ferry," in Richmond *Enquirer*, Friday Morning, Nov. 4, 1859, p. 4, cols. 5–6. The *Enquirer* made no comment on this story from the New York *Herald*.

103. Testimony of Lewis Washington, *Mason Committee Report*, II: 35.

104. *Shepherdstown Register*, Nov. 12, 1859, as quoted in Quarles, *Allies for Freedom*, 100. Washington's slaves taken in the raid were Sam, Mason, and Catesby. Washington referred in his testimony, however, simply to the "boy." A list of slaves taken in the raid is included in Brown's indictment. A copy of a separate list is in the Villard Papers, CUL.

105. Testimony of Terence Byrne, January 6, 1860, *Mason Committee Report*, II: 16.

106. Cook's Confession, in Hinton, *John Brown and His Men*, 709, 713–14.

107. "Harper [sic] Ferry Insurrection, Further Details, Startling Disclosures," Cincinnati *Daily Gazette*, Oct. 20, 1859, p. 3.

108. Testimony of Lewis Washington, *Mason Committee Report*, II: 33–9. We have no way of determining the age of Washington's "boy."

109. Testimony of Lind F. Currie, January 11, 1860, *Mason Committee Report*, II: 57.

110. Thomas Wentworth Higginson, notes of a conversation with Charles Plummer Tidd, Feb. 10, 1860, Higginson Papers, BPL.

111. Testimony of Armistead Ball, as quoted in "Brown's Invasion," New-York *Weekly Tribune*, Nov. 5, 1859, p. 3. Brown had recently purchased a stone drill and other tools useful to masons. Also see the testimony of Lewis Washington, *Mason Committee Report*, II: 35.

112. Quoted in the Richmond *Enquirer*, Friday Morning, Nov. 4, 1859, p. 4.

113. Testimony of John H. Allstadt, January 6, 1860, *Mason Committee Report*, II: 43–44.

114. See the interview of Allstadt by Clifton Johnson, "Harper's Ferry Prisoner," Springfield *Republican*, n.d., Stutler Collection, Scrapbook 2, WVDCH, and the reminiscence of Allstadt's eighteen-year-old son, who was one of Brown's hostages, dated April 15, 1909, typed copy of the original, Harpers Ferry National Park, 8 pp.

115. Quoted in the Richmond *Enquirer*, Oct. 21, 1859, p. 2.

116. Statement of W. B. Downer in the New York *Herald*, Oct. 24, 1859, p. 2.

117. According to a fellow B&O passenger, Logan offered his captors money for his release and later told them that they might count him as "one of them" and "that he sincerely felt for them and hoped they would be successful." His strategy evidently worked. After a while the "leader of the gang" ordered Logan to return to the train and tell conductor Phelps that he might take his train across the bridge if he did so in twenty minutes. Statement of C. W. Armstrong, New York *Herald*, Oct. 19, 1859, p. 2.

118. "The Insurrection in Virginia: The Statement of W. W. Throckmorton," New York *Herald*, Oct. 21, p. 2.
119. See the testimony of John E. P. Daingerfield at Brown's trial, as quoted in the New-York *Weekly Tribune*, Nov. 5, 1859, p. 3. As Bertram Wyatt-Brown has shown, male slaves might respond to unpredictable, dangerous situations by exhibiting shamelessness – thus avoiding the danger while still preserving a sense of personal autonomy by ignoring the restraints and rules of dignity imposed upon their owners by Southern culture. See Bertram Wyatt-Brown, *The Shaping of Southern Culture: Honor, Grace, and War, 1760s–1880s* (Chapel Hill: University of North Carolina Press, 2001), Chapter 1, esp. 17–19.
120. See the dispatches "By Telegraph to the Journal of Commerce," New York *Journal of Commerce*, Oct. 19, 1859, p. 2.
121. Dispatch dated Harper's Ferry, Oct. 19, 11 P.M., Boston [Evening] *Journal*, Oct. 19, 1859, in Sanborn Scrapbook, Stutler Collection, WVDCH.
122. See *The Baltimore American and Commercial Advertiser*, Oct. 22, 1859, p. 1.
123. Col. Lee reported on the 19th that "The servants of Messrs. Washington and Allstadt, retained at the armory, took no part in the conflict, and those carried to Maryland returned to their homes as soon as released." Lee's "Report to the Adjutant General," in the *Mason Committee Report*, I: 42.
124. Craig Simpson, *A Good Southerner: The Life of Henry A. Wise of Virginia* (Chapel Hill: University of North Carolina Press, 1985), 203–18.
125. "The Insurrection in Virginia: The Statement of W. W. Throckmorton," New York *Herald*, Oct. 21, 1859, p. 2.
126. "Movements of the City Military," *The Baltimore American and Commercial Advertiser*, Oct. 18, 1859, p. 1.
127. "Military Movements," *The Baltimore American and Commercial Advertiser*, Oct. 18, 1859, p. 1.
128. According to the marine muster rolls, Lt. Green's actual force was eighty-six, not ninety men. See Bernard C. Nalty, "'At All Times Ready…;' The United States Marines At Harper's Ferry and in the Civil War," Marine Corps Historical Reference Pamphlet, rev. (Washington, DC: Historical Branch, G-3 Division Headquarters, U.S. Marines Corps, 1966), p. 3.
129. The analogy is made by Villard, *John Brown Fifty Years After*, 434.

CHAPTER 12 – WITNESS

1. "Statement of Anthony Nunnamaker," *Baltimore American and Commercial Advertiser*, Oct. 21, 1859, p. 1. Nunnamaker listed the names of twenty-five hostages he knew personally among the number Brown eventually held.
2. "Insurrection at Harper's Ferry: Treatment of Prisoners, Authentic Details," Richmond *Enquirer*, Oct. 21, 1859, p. 2.
3. "The Harper's Ferry Rebellion, Revelations of Captain Brown," the New York *Times*, Oct. 20, 1859, p. 1. In this interview, Brown claimed he had widespread support among "abolitionists" in Maryland and Virginia.
4. "A Conversation with 'Old Brown,'" *Baltimore American and Commercial Advertiser*, Oct. 21, 1859, p. 1. Three correspondents took the "conversation" down "verbatim" in shorthand. See also the New-York *Herald*, Oct. 22, 1859, p. 1, and the *Cincinnati Daily Gazette*, Oct. 20, 1859, p. 3. C. W. Tayleure of the Baltimore paper mentions that two reporters from New York were present with

him during Brown's interrogation, but does not confirm the claim of the *Daily Gazette* to have had a "special reporter" present as well.

5. Quoted in the *Baltimore American and Commercial Advertiser*, Oct. 21, 1859, p. 1.
6. "If I had succeeded in running off slaves this time," Brown reputedly later told a correspondent for the Baltimore *Exchange*, "I could have raised twenty times as many men as I have now for a similar expedition." Quoted in "Interview with the Rebels," the New York *Times*, Oct. 20, 1859, p. 1. Billed as "authentic," this article contained inaccuracies suggesting that the reporter either reconstructed Brown's replies to his questions after the interview or fabricated them.
7. See Brown's "Vindication of the Invasion, etc." Dreer Collection, PHS. See my discussion of it in Chapter 9. It was widely published. See "The Virginia Rebellion," New York *Times*, Oct. 22, 1859, p. 1.
8. W. E. B. Du Bois speculated that Brown was waiting for the arrival of his crated Sharps rifles as the hours passed on Monday morning. He had ordered son Owen and Charles Tidd to take the weapons from the Kennedy farm to the schoolhouse. Cook later claimed that he waited all afternoon for orders to bring the rifles to the armory. Such an order would have made sense if Brown planned to withdraw from Harpers Ferry over the Shenandoah bridge, as Du Bois believed. William Edward Burghardt Du Bois, *John Brown* (1909; New York: International Publishers, 1962), 276.
9. Quoted in the *Baltimore American and Commercial Advertiser*, Oct. 21, 1859, p. 1.
10. Quoted in the New-York *Daily Tribune*, Oct. 20, 1859, p. 6.
11. Statement of Andrew Hunter, January 13, 1860, as cited in United States Senate, 36th Congress, 1st Session, *Report of the Select Committee of the Senate appointed to inquire into the late invasion and seizure of the public property at Harper's Ferry*, Rep. Com. No. 278, 2 vols. (Washington, 1860), II, 61. Hereafter cited as the *Mason Committee Report*.
12. Quoted in the New-York *Daily Tribune*, Oct. 20, 1859, p. 8.
13. Quoted in the New-York *Daily Tribune*, Oct. 19, 1859, p. 5. The reporter of the *Baltimore Exchange* quoted Stevens as putting the blame squarely on his "Captain." "Brown made us believe that we had only to strike the blow, and thousands of negroes would join us. I have found that he deceived us, and if I had known what I know now, I would not have been here." Quoted in "Interviews with the Rebels," New York *Times*, Oct. 20, 1859, p. 1.
14. Although Cook had evidently warned Charles Williams to expect a move to free the slaves and may have alerted several others, Brown seems to have made no provision for getting word to outlying farms. See "The Insurrection in Virginia: The Statement of W. W. Throckmorton," New York *Herald*, Oct. 21, 1859, p. 2.
15. Merritt Roe Smith, *Harpers Ferry Armory and the New Technology: The Challenge of Change* (Ithaca, NY: Cornel University press, 197), 305–7. An insightful overview of Southern responses to the Harpers Ferry raid is Peter Wallenstein, "Incendiaries All: Southern Politics and the Harpers Ferry Raid," in Paul Finkelman, ed., *His Soul Goes Marching On: Responses to John Brown and the Harpers Ferry Raid* (Charlottesville: University of Virginia Press, 1995), Chapter 6.
16. Testimony of Daniel Whelan, January 6, 1860, *Mason Committee Report*, II: 22.
17. "Harper[s] Ferry Insurrection: Further Details," Cincinnati *Daily Gazette*, Oct. 20, 1859, p. 3.
18. Testimony of Lewis Washington, January 6, 1860, *Mason Committee Report*, II: 37.
19. Testimony of John E. P. Daingerfield at Brown's trial, 4th day [Oct. 29, 1859], as reported in the New-York *Weekly Tribune*, Nov. 5, 1859, p. 3.

20. Testimony of Armistead Ball at Brown's trial, 3rd day [Oct. 28, 1859], in New-York *Weekly Tribune*, Nov. 5, 1859, p. 3. At Brown's preliminary hearing on October 25, 1859, Ball said that Brown's "object was to place the United States arms in the hands of the black men, and he proposed to free all the slaves in the vicinity." See "Examination of the Harper's Ferry Conspirators," New-York *Daily Tribune*, Oct. 26, 1859, p. 5.

21. Brown's raid evoked images of Nat Turner's revolt once it was clear that the "outbreak" involved slaves, not railroad workers, as initially supposed. See, for example, "The Virginia Insurrection of 1831 and the Tennessee Outbreak of 1856," New York *Herald*, Oct. 19, 1859, p. 2. On the significance of references to the Haitian revolution in the response to Brown's raid, see William E. Cain, "Angel of Light: Interpreting John Brown," *Reviews in American History*, 23, no. 4 (1995): 606–11. On Haiti's wider influence, see Laurent Dubois, *Avengers of the New World: The Story of the Haitian Revolution* (Cambridge, MA: Harvard University Press, 2004) and David P. Geggus, ed., *The Impact of the Haitian Revolution in the Atlantic World* (Columbia: University of South Carolina Press, 2001).

22. Testimony of Archibald M. Kitzmiller, January 10, 1860, *Mason Committee Report*, II: 50.

23. Testimony of Albert Grist, one of Brown's hostages, at Brown's trial, Oct. 28, 1859, as reported in Robert M. De Witt, ed., *Life, Trial, and Execution of Captain John Brown, Known as Old Brown of Ossawatomie* (1859; repr., New York: Da Capo Press, 1969), 76.

24. See the list compiled by Kitzmiller appended to his testimony, in the *Mason Committee Report*, II: 51–2. Perhaps because Virginia Col. Robert W. Baylor mistakenly assumed that the gunpowder was found with the weapons brought to the armory from the school house by the Baltimore Greys or from the Kennedy farm by the marines on the evening of the 18th, scholars too have ignored it. But Baylor evidently did not witness the troops' arrival himself, because he erred grossly in reporting the numbers of weapons found and those subsequently deposited at the armory. On October 22, four days after Brown's capture, Baylor reported that the Greys "returned about six o'clock, having found two hundred Sharp's rifles." Only 102 of that original number Brown had brought to the school house were deposited, however. Baylor's handwritten report was published in the newspapers later. See Robert W. Baylor, Col. Commanding the Virginia Troops at Harper's Ferry, to Hon. Henry A. Wise, Governor of Virginia, October 22, 1859, Dreer Collection, PHS. It is reproduced in De Witt, *Life, Trial and Execution of Captain John Brown*, 41–4.

25. See the detailed testimony of John C. Unseld, who often visited Brown's rented farm in the months before the raid. *Mason Committee Report*, II: 1–12. Unseld says that Lieutenant Green, not Stuart, headed the detachment sent to the Kennedy farm.

26. Brevet Colonel Robert E. Lee to Adjutant General S. Cooper, Oct. 18, 1859, in the *Mason Committee Report*, Part 1, Appendix, p. 42.

27. "The Virginia Insurrection," New-York *Daily Tribune*, Oct. 20, 1859, p. 4.

28. Brown's wagon also carried fifty-eight powder flasks for use with the Ames's revolvers with which he had armed his men. Testimony of Archibald M. Kitzmiller, January 10, 1860, *Mason Committee Report*, II: 49–51. Kitzmiller's list of Brown's munitions was appended to his testimony, pp. 51–2.

29. See Kitzmiller's testimony in the *Mason Committee Report*, II: 49–51.

30. Because muskets required training to load and fire and slaves would have no such training, in October 1857 he had commissioned the manufacture of 1000 pikes "as a cheap but effectual weapon to place in the [hands] of entirely unskilful, &

unpracticed men; which will not easily get out of order; & require no Amunitions [sic]," he had reported to Franklin Sanborn. John Brown to Franklin B. Sanborn, Oct. 1, 1857, Stutler Collection, WVDCH.

31. I am indebted to Dr. Maxwell D. Cooper, a member of the Hawai'i Historic Arms Association, for sharing his expertise on Civil War era pistols and muskets with me.

32. Starry gave at least two slightly different versions of his actions during the raid. In his neglected testimony at Brown's trial, he said that he told the passengers in the station he would ask the *watchman* at the armory what was going on, not the armed men he had seen in the street. Initially, some passengers thought the "disturbance" may have been a railroad strike. See: "John Brown's Invasion: Trial Hurried Through," New-York *Weekly Tribune*, Nov. 5, 1859, p. 3. For Starry's most complete account, see his testimony before the Mason Committee, see *Mason Committee Report*, Jan. 6, 1860, II: 23–7.

33. Starry's testimony before Senator Mason, *Mason Committee Report*, Jan. 6, 1860, II: 24.

34. Testimony of John D. Starry, *Mason Committee Report*, Jan. 6, 1860, II: 23–7; New-York *Weekly Tribune*, Nov. 5, 1859, p. 3.

35. Their failure to arrest Starry puzzled him, and after the raid he asked Brown why the raiders had not seized him at the armory. Brown replied that he "did not know why [Starry] had not been taken prisoner." Testimony of Dr. John D. Starry, Jan. 6, 1860, *Mason Committee Report*, II: 23–7.

36. Col. John Thomas Gibson, Commandant, 55th Regiment [Volunteers] to Governor Henry A. Wise, Oct. 18, 1859, handwritten report, Dreer Collection, PHS. Although Baylor joined Gibson and his men at Charlestown and formally assumed command at Harpers Ferry only late that afternoon, he takes credit in his report for most of the tactical decisions Gibson represents as his own. See Robert W. Baylor, Col. Commanding the Va. Troops at Harpers Ferry to Hon. Henry A. Wise, Governor of Virginia, Oct. 22, 1859, handwritten report, 10 pp., Dreer Collection, PHS.

37. Baylor's report to Governor Wise, Dreer Collection, PHS, p. 3.

38. Testimony of Albert Griest at Brown's trial, 3rd day [Oct. 28, 1859], New-York *Weekly Tribune*, Nov. 5, 1859, p. 3.

39. Testimony of Benjamin Mills at Brown's trial, 4th day [Oct. 29, 1859], New-York *Weekly Tribune*, Nov. 5, 1859, p. 3.

40. Testimony of Armistead Ball at Brown's trial, 4th day [Oct. 29, 1859], New-York *Weekly Tribune*, Nov. 5, 1859, p. 3.

41. Testimony of Lewis Washington at Brown's trial, 2nd day [Oct. 27, 1859], New-York *Weekly Tribune*, Nov. 5, 1859, p. 3.

42. See, for example, the testimony of Reason Cross during Brown's trial, 3rd day [Oct. 28, 1859], New-York *Weekly Tribune*, Nov. 5, 1859, p. 3.

43. Testimony of Mayor Benjamin Mills at Brown's trial, 3rd day [Oct. 28, 1859], New-York *Weekly Tribune*, Nov. 5, 1859, p. 3.

44. Testimony of Lewis Washington at Brown's trial, 3rd day [Oct. 28, 1859], New-York *Daily Tribune*, Nov. 5. 1859, p. 3.

45. Newby was shot in the neck from a nearby house by an armorer who, having no bullets, had fired a six-inch lead spike. According to news reports, Newby's body, which remained in the street until noon of the following day, met with "every indignity" that could be inflicted upon it. "Additional Particulars of the Insurrection," New-York *Journal of Commerce*, Oct. 20, 1859, p. 2.

46. Testimony of Terence Byrne at Brown's trial, 4th day [Oct. 29, 1859], New-York *Weekly Tribune*, Nov. 5, 1859, p. 3.

47. Testimony of Reason Cross at Brown's trial, 3rd day [Oct. 28, 1859], New-York *Weekly Tribune*, Nov. 5, 1859, p. 3.

48. Testimony of Joseph A. Brua at Brown's trial, 3rd day [Oct. 28, 1859], as reported in the New-York *Daily Tribune*, Nov. 5, 1859, p. 3.

49. Testimony of Joseph A. Brua at Brown's trial, 3rd day [Oct. 28, 1859], as quoted in the New-York *Weekly Tribune*, Nov. 5, 1859, p. 3. Also see DeWitt, *Life, Trial and Execution of John Brown*, 75.

50. Testimony of John E. P. Daingerfield during Brown's trial, 3rd day [Oct. 28, 1859], New-York *Weekly Times*, Nov. 5, 1859, p. 3.

51. Testimony of Alexander M. Kitzmiller at Brown's trial, 3rd day [Oct. 28, 1859], New-York *Daily Tribune*, Nov. 5, 1859, p. 3. Kitzmiller's testimony at Brown's preliminary hearing, Oct. 25, 1859, as quoted in the New-York *Daily Tribune*, Oct. 26, 1859, p. 5.

52. Testimony of Joseph Brua at Brown's trial, 3rd day [Oct. 28, 1859], New-York *Weekly Times*, Nov. 5, 1859, p. 3.

53. Osborne P. Anderson, *A Voice from Harpers Ferry: A Narrative of Events at Harper's Ferry* (1861; repr., Freeport, NY: Books for Libraries Press, 1972), 42. Though Osborne Anderson was a survivor of the raid, his account contains numerous errors. Some writers say that Kagi sent repeated "urgent" warnings to Brown throughout the "early morning," but I can find no contemporary source to confirm additional messages beyond whatever word Jeremiah Anderson carried back to Brown. As noted below, however, the presence of another man at the armory when it was retaken suggests the possibility of a second messenger from Brown. As armed militiamen and townsmen appeared on the streets, it must have been increasingly difficult to send messengers from the rifle works to the armory. See Oswald Garrison Villard, *John Brown, 1800–1859: A Biography Fifty Years After* (1910; repr., Gloucester, MA: Peter Smith, 1965), 438.

54. This detail is supplied by the 1883 memoir of former Jefferson County Congressman Alexander R. Boteler, who also claims that four men fled the Rifle Works with Kagi. That number is either in error or must include at least two slave volunteers, since all the other raiders who came with Brown can be accounted for. See Boteler, "Recollections of the John Brown Raid By a Virginian Who Witnessed the Fight," *Century Magazine*, 26 (July 1883): 399–411, esp. 406–7.

55. Col. Gibson, who witnessed the incident, testified that "three insurgents were killed at the rifle factory, and Copeland captured." Testimony of Col. John Thomas Gibson at Brown's trial, 3rd day [Oct. 28, 1859], in the New-York *Weekly Tribune*, Nov. 5, 1859, p. 3.

56. Testimony of Lewis Washington, Jan. 6, 1860, *Mason Committee Report*, II: 39.

57. Testimony of John D. Starry, Jan. 6, 1860, *Mason Committee Report*, II: 27.

58. Testimony of George Chambers, Jan. 6, 1860, *Mason Committee Report*, II: 28; testimony of Alexander Kelly at Brown's trial, 3rd day [Oct. 28, 1859], cited in New-York *Weekly Tribune*, Nov. 5, 1859, p. 3.

59. Stories of his death conflicted. A B&O passenger returning from holiday claimed to be standing beside Turner on the slope above the Ferry when a rifle bullet fired by an unseen shooter claimed his life. Another version had Turner leveling his gun at two of the raiders when their return fire killed him. John G. Rosengarten, "John

Brown's Raid: How I Got Into It, and How I Got Out of It," *Atlantic Monthly*, 15 (June 1865): 711–17, esp. 712.

60. Two witnesses later conceded that Beckham apparently had a pistol in his pocket, but insisted he had nothing in his hands when shot. Thinking that Beckham was not dead, George Chambers ran across the trussel-work to his aid. Beckham's son-in-law later took the body down to Beckham's house, just "fifteen steps" from where he was killed. Testimony of George W. Chambers, Jan. 6, 1860, *Mason Committee Report*, II: 28–29. See also the testimony of Benjamin T. Bell as quoted in DeWitt, *Life Trial and Execution of John Brown*, 74.

61. Testimony of Lewis Washington at Brown's trial, 2nd day [Oct. 27, 1859], as cited in DeWitt, *Life, Trial and Execution of John Brown*, 71.

62. Testimony of Henry Hunter (the son of prosecutor Andrew Hunter) at Brown's trial, 3rd day [Oct. 28, 1859], in New-York *Weekly Tribune*, Nov. 5, 1859, p. 3. Hunter conceded that Beckham may have had a pistol in his coat pocket, but Beckham was evidently not displaying it when shot.

63. Testimony of Henry Hunter at Brown's trial, 3rd day [Oct. 28, 1859], in New-York *Weekly Tribune*, Nov. 5, 1859, p. 3.

64. See the two dispatches from Harpers Ferry dated Oct. 18, 1859, as quoted in The New-York *Journal of Commerce*, Oct. 20, 1859, p. 2. In another version of Leeman's final moments, a G. A. Schoppert placed his pistol at Leeman's head before pulling the trigger.

65. See Villard, *John Brown Fifty Years After*, 440.

66. "Additional Particulars of the Insurrection," New-York *Journal of Commerce*, Oct. 20, 1859, p. 2.

67. Testimony of John E. P. Daingerfield at Brown's trial, 3rd day [Oct. 28, 1859], cited in New-York *Weekly Tribune*, Nov. 5, 1859, p. 3. In a letter from Charlestown prison to Annie Brown, Aaron D. Stevens confirmed the time of Oliver's death and Watson's shooting on the 17th. Stevens to Annie Brown, Jan. 6, 1860, Higginson Papers, BPL.

68. Statement of Lewis Washington at Brown's trial, quoted in the New-York *Journal of Commerce*, Oct. 29, 1859, p. 3.

69. Testimony of Terence Byrne, Jan. 6, 1860, *Mason Committee Report*, II: 19. A story repeated in numerous biographies depicts a callous Brown indifferent to Watson's suffering. The source of the damning picture of Brown is two inaccurate, much later statements of John Thomas Allstadt, who at age eighteen had been taken prisoner with his father and held in the engine house. The first statement read: "Young Brown lay in a corner. 'O kill me and put me out of this sufferin',' he'd beg his father. But old Brown would tell him to quit his noise and 'die like a man.' Toward mornin' old Brown, who was settin' near the door, called to his son and got no answer. 'I guess he's dead,' the old man said." Quoted in "Harper's Ferry Prisoner Taken in John Brown's Raid Gives Personal Experience: Intimate Story of the Stirring Days in October, 1859," Springfield [Ohio] Sunday *Republican*, n.d., Stutler Collection, WVDCH. Allstadt provided the second statement, dated April 15, 1909, in which he confuses Watson with Oliver, to Oswald Garrison Villard, who included it, somewhat altered, in *John Brown Fifty Years After*, 448. Allstadt's memories conflict with contemporary evidence.

70. Strother promptly reminded himself that the "hoary villain" who "prates about his sons" had plotted "against the lives and happiness of thousands.... And all about this good-humored, good-for-nothing, half monkey race – the negroes,"

he added. Porte Crayon [David Hunter Strother], "The Late Invasion at Harper's Ferry," *Harper's Weekly*, III, No. 149 (Nov. 5, 1859), 714. Strother recorded his observations of the aftermath of the raid in an unpublished essay entitled "The John Brown Raid: Notes by an Eye Witness and Citizen of the Invaded District" sometime between October 18 and November 1, 1859. See Cecil D. Eby, "The Last Hours of the John Brown Raid: The Narrative of David H. Strother," *The Virginia Magazine of History and Biography*, 73 (1965): 169–77, esp. 173.

71. "Capt. Alburtis' Statement," New York *Herald*. Oct. 24, 1859, p. 2.

72. "Capt. Alburtis' Statement," New York *Herald*, Oct. 24, 1859, p. 2. Anthony Nunnamaker, one of Brown's watch room prisoners, made his escape with six other prisoners following the attack of the Martinsburg men. "Statement of Anthony Nunnamaker," *Baltimore American and Commercial Advertiser*, Oct. 21, 1859, p. 1.

73. Baylor's report to Governor Wise, Dreer Collection, PHS, p. 6. Brown's reference in this note to "government property" must be an allusion to weapons he expected his men to have loaded into his wagon at the arsenal.

74. Baylor's report to Governor Wise, Dreer Collection, PHS, p. 7.

75. "Trial of John Brown: The Fourth Day's Proceedings" [Oct. 29, 1859], New-York *Daily Tribune*, Oct. 31, 1859, p. 5.

76. "Trial of John Brown: The Fourth Day's Proceedings" [Oct. 29, 1859], New-York *Daily Tribune*, Oct. 31, 1859, p. 5.

77. Testimony of Captain Thomas Sinn at Brown's trial, 4th day [Oct. 29, 1859], in New-York *Weekly Tribune*, Nov. 5, 1859, p. 3.

78. "Trial of John Brown: The Fourth Day's Proceedings" [Oct. 29, 1859], New-York *Daily Tribune*, Oct. 31, 1859, p. 5.

79. "Trial of John Brown: The Fourth Day's Proceedings" [Oct. 29, 1859], New-York *Daily Tribune*, Oct. 31, 1859, p. 5; "The Frederick City United Guards," New-York *Daily Tribune*, Oct. 31, 1859, p. 5.

80. Quoted in "The Insurrection in Virginia, Statement of John A. [sic] Washington," New York *Herald*, Oct. 24, 1859, p. 1.

81. Testimony of Lewis Washington, January 6, 1860, *Mason Committee Report*, II: 34.

82. Quoted in "The Insurrection in Virginia, Statement of John A. [sic] Washington," New York *Herald*, Oct. 24, 1859, p. 1.

83. Quoted in "Harper[s] Ferry Insurrection, Further Details," Cincinnati *Daily Gazette*, Oct. 20, 1859, p. 3. Their testimony at Brown's trial supported that assessment. Testimony of Archibald Kitzmiller at Brown's trial, Friday, Oct. 28, 1859 [3rd day], in New-York *Weekly Tribune*, Nov. 5, 1859, p. 3.

84. The influential secessionist, Edmund Ruffin, concluded that Brown "was 'humane to his prisoners' taken at Harper's Ferry, because he held them as hostages, & his own chances for escape, & for life, depended on preserving them." William Kaufmann Scarborough, ed., *The Diary of Edmund Ruffin*, 3 vols. (Baton Rouge: Louisiana State University Press, 1972–89) I: 372.

85. "At breakfast time," Anthony Nunnamaker remarked shortly after the raid, Brown's guards "allowed our families to send food in to us, the female members of our families being treated with uniform courtesy and kindliness." "Statement of Anthony Nunnamaker," *Baltimore American and Commercial Advertiser*, Oct. 21, 1859, p. 1. The armory's master machinist, Armistead Ball, was permitted to go home to get his breakfast twice that morning. Also see the Testimony of Armistead Ball at Brown's trial, Thursday, Oct. 27, 1859 [2nd day], quoted in the New-York *Weekly Tribune*, Nov. 5, 1859, p. 3.

86. See the interview conducted by Senator Mason and others after the raid. New York *Herald*, Oct. 21, 1859, p. 1. Brown could hardly have lied about this without Lewis Washington, who was present, rebuking him.

87. Testimony of Joseph A. Brua at Brown's trial, 3rd day [Oct. 28, 1859], quoted in the New-York *Weekly Tribune*, Nov. 5, 1859, p. 3. Even during the marines' assault, Brown made "no attempt to deprive his prisoners of the places they had taken for shelter." Testimony of John E. P. Daingerfield (for the prosecution) at Brown's trial, quoted in the New-York *Daily Tribune*, Nov. 5, 1859, p. 3.

88. Testimony of Lewis Washington at Brown's trial, Thursday, Oct. 27, 1859 [2nd day], quoted in the New-York *Weekly Tribune*, Nov. 5, 1859, p. 3.

89. Testimony of Andrew Phelps at Brown's trial, 2nd day [Oct. 27, 1859], as quoted in the New-York *Weekly Tribune*, Nov. 5, 1859, p. 3.

90. A passenger also overheard Brown's remark, but remembered it differently. "[I]f you knew me and understood my motives," Brown said, "you would not blame me so much." Quoted in the *Baltimore American and Commercial Advertiser*, Oct. 21, 1859, p. 1.

91. Testimony of Andrew Phelps, Oct. 27, 1859 [2nd day], as quoted in the New-York *Daily Tribune*, Oct. 28, 1859, p. 5; Phelps's testimony is quoted more fully in the New-York *Journal of Commerce*, Oct. 28, 1859, p. 3.

92. Quoted in the New York *Times*, Oct. 20, 1859, p. 1.

93. Testimony of Terence Byrne, Jan. 6, 1860, *Mason Committee Report*, II: 19.

94. "The Harper's Ferry Outbreak, Statement to the Herald Reporter," New York *Herald*, Oct. 21, 1859, p. 1.

95. "The 'Servile' Insurrection at Harper's Ferry: Details by Express, The Outbreak and the Suppression," Cincinnati *Daily Gazette*, Oct. 21, 1859, p. 2. The quotation, the *Gazette* announced, was from "our own correspondent" at Harpers Ferry. It had reached Cincinnati by express because the telegraph was not yet operating.

96. Testimony of Terence Byrne, Jan. 6, 1860, *Mason Committee Report*, II: 19.

97. See Kitzmiller's statements at Brown's preliminary hearing, "Examination of the Harper's Ferry Conspirators," New-York *Daily Tribune*, Oct. 26, 1859, p. 5; Testimony of Archibald Kitzmiller at Brown's trial, Friday, Oct. 28, 1859 [3rd day], quoted in the New-York *Weekly Tribune*, Nov. 5, 1859, p. 3.

98. Stockholm Syndrome, according to researchers in clinical psychology, refers to the "paradoxical development of reciprocal feelings between hostages and their terrorist captors, which is said to enhance the hostages' ability to cope with their captivity." In a 1994 study, psychologists attempted to measure the subjective interpersonal impacts of "a highly stressful simulated captivity situation" and to measure hostage adjustment and "emotional distress levels" within that controlled situation. Their findings proved useful in developing interpersonal strategies to manage "fate control" stress situations. See Stephen M. Auerbach, Donald J. Kiesler, Thomas Strentz, James A. Schmidt, and Catherine Devany Serio, "Interpersonal Impacts and Adjustment to the Stress of Simulated Captivity: An Empirical Test of the Stockholm Syndrome," *Journal of Social and Clinical Psychology*, 13, no. 2 (1994): 207–21.

99. Testimony of Terence Byrne, Jan. 6, 1860, *Mason Committee Report*, II: 16–17.

100. Brevet Col. Robert E. Lee to Adjutant General, Col. S. Cooper, Oct. 19, 1859, cited in *Mason Committee Report*, I: Appendix No. 1, 40–3. Hereafter cited as Lee's Report.

101. Testimony of John E. P. Daingerfield at Brown's trial, Saturday, Oct. 29, 1859 [4th day], quoted in the New-York *Weekly Tribune*, Nov. 5, 1859, p. 3.

102. Testimony of Armistead Ball at Brown's preliminary hearing on Oct. 25, 1859, as quoted in "Examination of the Harper's Ferry Conspirators," New-York *Daily Tribune*, Oct. 26, 1859, p. 5.

103. On Lee's steadfast adherence to the code and its personal costs, see Michael Fellman, *The Making of Robert E. Lee* (Baltimore: Johns Hopkins University, 2000), xvi–xx, 7–8, et passim.

104. Testimony of Robert E. Lee, Jan. 10, 1860, *Mason Committee Report*, II: 46–7.

105. The summons was included in Lee's Oct. 19 Report to the Adjutant General, herein cited in *Mason Committee Report*, I: Appendix No. 1, 42–3.

106. Lieutenant J. E. B. Stuart to "Dear Mama" [Elizabeth Stuart], Jan. 31, 1860, typed copy, Stutler Collection, WVDCH.

107. Ball's remarks were reported in the New-York *Journal of Commerce*, Oct. 24, 1859, p. 3.

108. As Washington admitted during cross examination at Brown's trial, the prisoners "were kept in the rear [of the] engine-house and allowed to keep a safe position." Testimony of Lewis Washington at Brown's trial [Thursday, 2nd day], quoted in the New-York *Weekly Tribune*, Saturday, Nov. 5, 1859, p. 3.

109. Lieutenant J. E. B. Stuart to "Dear Mama" [Elizabeth Stuart], Jan. 31, 1860, typed copy, Stutler Collection, WVDCH.

110. "Captain John Brown, the commander and instigator of this most singular project," observed the Richmond *Enquirer*, "has been known by the name of 'Ossawatomie Brown,' in which character he obtained quite a notoriety throughout the country as one of the leaders of the Free State party in Kansas. He was the hero of fifty guerilla [sic] fights in the vicinity of Ossawatomie, in one of which his son Frederick Brown was killed." "Insurrection at Harper's Ferry, Authentic Details," Richmond *Enquirer*, Oct. 21, 1859, p. 2.

111. Lee's Report, quoted in *Mason Committee Report*, I: Appendix No. 1, p. 41.

112. "We were taken in[to] the engine house and pointed to the back part of the room, and told to stand there.... The Brown party occupied the front part, and if we had taken any other position than we did, we should have been in their way." Testimony of Terence Byrne, Jan. 6, 1860, *Mason Committee Report*, II: 18, 20. Also see the testimony of John Thomas Allstadt at Brown's trial, quoted in the New-York *Journal of Commerce*, Oct. 29, 1859, p. 3.

113. Lee's Report, quoted in *Mason Committee Report*, I: Appendix No. 1, p. 41–2.

114. Baylor's report to Governor Wise, Dreer Collection, PHS, p. 9.

115. "The Military Attack on Harper's Ferry, as Described by Captain [Ephraim G.] Alburtis," Richmond *Enquirer* Oct. 25, 1859, p. 1. Other reports of the marines firing during the assault include, "The Virginia Insurrection, Old Brown's Doings," New-York *Daily Tribune*, Oct. 20, 1859, p. 6, and "The Attack on the Armory – Old Brown," New-York *Daily Tribune*, Oct. 20, 1859, p. 6.

116. The Insurrection at Harper's Ferry," New-York *Journal of Commerce*, Oct. 20, 1859, p. 2.

117. "The Harper's Ferry Outbreak, Verbatim Report of the Questioning of Old Brown by Senator Mason, Congressman Vallandigham, and Others," New York *Herald*, Oct. 21, 1859, p. 1. C. W. Tayleure of the Baltimore *American* summarized the exchange as follows: "An officer present here stated that special orders had been given to the marines not to shoot anybody, but when they were fired upon by Brown's men, and one of them had been killed and another wounded, they were obliged to return the compliment. Brown insisted, with some warmth, that the

marines fired first." "Latest from Harper's Ferry, Conversation with Capt. Brown – His Views, Plans and Purposes," *Baltimore American and Commercial Advertiser,* Oct. 21, 1859, p. 1.

118. Testimony of Lewis Washington, Jan. 6, 1860, *Mason Committee Report,* II: 38.

119. For additional evidence that the marines were shot outside the engine house, see C. W. Tayleure's report in the *Baltimore American and Commercial Advertiser,* Oct. 21, 1859, p. 1 and dispatches in the New-York *Journal of Commerce,* Oct. 19, 1859, p. 2. Artists' sketches, drawn after the event from the testimony of witnesses, claimed to show where "every man is placed." *Harper's Weekly,* 3, no. 149 (Nov. 5, 1859), 712; *Frank Leslie's Illustrated Newspaper,* 9, no. 210 (Dec. 10, 1859), 18. Boteler's detailed and accurate account, reconstructed from notes, is particularly convincing. See his "Recollections of the John Brown Raid," 409.

120. Testimony on cross of John Allstadt at Brown's trial, quoted in the New-York *Journal of Commerce,* Oct. 29, 1859, p. 3. Although Allstadt initially claimed that he had seen Brown fire or at least level his gun at the door, Armistead Ball testified several times that "I did not see Captain Brown fire once from the engine house." Ball's testimony, New-York *Journal of Commerce,* Oct. 29, 1859, p. 3.

121. Testimony of Terence Byrne, January 6, 1860, *Mason Committee Report,* II: 20.

122. "After the first attack," Daingerfield told the court during Brown's trial, he saw Coppoc "attempt to fire twice, but the caps exploded." Testimony of John E. P. Daingerfield at Brown's trial, Saturday, Oct. 29, 1859 [4th day], quoted in the New-York *Weekly Tribune,* Nov. 5, 1859, p. 3. "Captain Brown and I were the only ones that fought to the last," Coppoc boasted later. Edwin Coppoc to [Dear Friends], Nov. 22, 1859, as quoted in Richard J. Hinton, *John Brown and His Men, With Some Account of the Roads They Traveled to Reach Harper's Ferry* (1894; repr., New York: Arno Press, 1968), 488.

123. Daingerfield added that "The parties outside appeared to be firing as they pleased." Testimony of John E. P. Daingerfield at Brown's trial, Saturday, Oct. 29, 1859 [4th day], quoted in the New York *Journal of Commerce,* Oct. 30, 1859, p. 3. Also see the New-York *Weekly Tribune,* Nov. 5, 1859, p. 3. Twenty-five years later, Daingerfield, his memories much faded, would tell a quite different and misleading story of the final moments. See John E. P. Daingerfield, "John Brown at Harper's Ferry: The Fight in the Engine House, As Seen By One of His Prisoners," *The Century Magazine,* 30, no. 2 (June 1885), 265–7.

124. Not recognizing Major Russell among Brown's auditors, the reporters supposed Brown was referring to Lt. Stuart. But Brown had reminded Russell that he might have shot him when Russell, who was the marine's paymaster, had Brown carried to the armory paymaster's office. "The Harper's Ferry Rebellion,... Revelations of Captain Brown," the New York *Times,* Oct. 20, 1859, p. 1. The story was filed before Governor Wise began questioning Brown.

125. The unidentified "officer" who responded to Brown's charge was probably Russell, who had moved Brown to the paymaster's office. Quoted from Tayleure's report in the *Baltimore American and Commercial Advertiser,* Oct. 21, 1859, p. 1. See also the New York *Herald,* Oct. 21, 1859, p. 1.

126. After receiving his sentence from the court, Brown wrote his wife, Mary, repeating his accusations against the marines in even more damning terms: "I was taken prisoner immediately after which I received several Sabre-cuts in my head; & Bayonet stabs in my body," he complained. John Brown to Mary Ann Day Brown [wife], Oct. 31, Nov. 3, 1859, Stutler Collection, WVDCH.

127. "The Attack on the Armory – Old Brown," New-York *Daily Tribune*, Oct. 20, 1859, p. 6.

128. "The Virginia Insurrection, Old Brown's Doings," New-York *Daily Tribune*, Oct. 20, 1859, p. 6.

129. John G. Rosengarten, "John Brown's Raid: How I Got Into It, and How I Got Out of It," *Atlantic Monthly*, 92 (June 1865), 716–17.

130. The *Enquirer* duly noted the "discrepancy" between the statements of Washington and Brown. Richmond *Enquirer*, Oct. 21, pp. 1–2. See also "The Insurrection in Virginia: Col. John A. [sic] Washington's Statement," New York *Herald*, Oct. 24, 1859, p. 1.

131. "Trial of Captain Brown," New-York *Journal of Commerce*, Oct. 28, 1859, p. 3.

132. Lieutenant J. E. B. Stuart to "Dear Mama" [Elizabeth Stuart], Jan. 31, 1860, typed copy, Stutler Collection, WVDCH.

133. "The Attack on the Armory – Old Brown," New-York *Daily Tribune*, Oct. 20, 1859, p. 6. This story was from the *Baltimore Exchange* and wrongly dated Oct. 17 rather than Oct. 18. The writer has Quinn and Rupert shot just as Russell enters the engine house.

134. "The Virginia Insurrection, Old Brown's Doings," New-York *Daily Tribune*, Oct. 20, 1859, p. 6. After interviewing Russell, the reporter finished writing his story just a "few moments" after Governor Wise arrived in Harpers Ferry at about 2 P.M.

135. "The Attack on the Armory – Old Brown," New-York *Daily Tribune*, Oct. 20, 1859, p. 6.

136. Even when an unidentified officer (probably Russell) conceded during the interview in the paymaster's office in the presence of Stuart and Lee that the marines "were obliged to return" the fire of the raiders, Villard stated: "This statement is erroneous; the marines fired no shots whatever." To Brown's claim during the interview that he had been attacked after he called "surrender," Villard said, "this portion of the interview is evidently erroneous." Villard, *John Brown Fifty Years After*, 461–2.

137. See John E. P. Daingerfield, "John Brown at Harper's Ferry: The Fight at the Engine House, As Seen By One of His Prisoners," *The Century Magazine*, 30, no. 2 (June 1885): 265–7.

138. Israel Green, "The Capture of John Brown," *The North American Review*, 141 (December 1885): 564–9.

139. Numerous contemporary reports and artists' sketches from Harpers Ferry confirm this point. See, for example, David H. Strother's sketches in "The Late Invasion at Harper's Ferry," *Harper's Weekly*, 3 (Nov. 5, 1859): 712, 713. Green's memory may have been influenced by the popular photo portrait of Brown taken in June, 1859, and distributed by Thaddeus Hyatt, which showed Brown with a full, flowing beard, or by published reproductions of the apocryphal drawing showing Brown kneeling with a carbine in one hand while feeling for the pulse of a dying son with the other. But Green's memory deceived him.

140. See Robert E. McGlone, "Forgotten Surrender: John Brown's Raid and the Cult of Martial Virtues," *Civil War History*, 40 (Sept. 1994): 185–201.

141. Quoted in the New York *Herald*, Oct. 21, 1859, p. 1.

142. Quoted in Alexander R. Boteler, "Recollections of the John Brown Raid," *Century Magazine*, 26 (July 1883): 409.

143. Washington spoke to reporters shortly after he exited the engine house. Quoted in the New-York *Daily Tribune*, Oct. 19, 1859, p. 5.

144. Testimony of Andrew Hunter, January 13, 1860, *Mason Committee Report*, II: 60; Brown's opening remarks to the Virginia Court, Oct. 27, 1859, quoted in Zoe Trodd and John Stauffer, eds., *Meteor of War: The John Brown Story* (Maplecrest, NY: Brandywine Press, 2004), 131.

145. "The Harper's Ferry Outbreak, More Views and Opinions of Old Brown... Special Despatch to the *Herald*," Oct. 21, 1859, New York *Herald*, Oct. 22, 1859, p. 1.

146. Quoted in "The Harper's Ferry Outbreak: ... Special Despatch to the Herald," New York *Herald*, Oct. 22, 1859, p. 1.

CHAPTER 13 – GOD'S EMISSARY

1. John Brown to Rev. James W. McFarland, Nov. 23, 1859, in Louis Ruchames, ed., *John Brown: The Making of a Revolutionary* (New York: Grosset & Dunlap, 1969), 153–4.

2. Rev. L[eonard] W. Bacon to the Editors of The *Independent*, Litchfield, Connecticut, Nov. 21, 1859, as quoted in the New-York *Weekly Tribune*, Dec. 3, 1859, p. 3. Bacon is referring to Brown's "heroic and sublime reply" to his former teacher at Morris Academy. John Brown to Rev. H. L. Vaill, Nov. 15, 1859, photocopy, John Brown Miscellaneous Papers, NYPL. It is reprinted in Ruchames *Making of a Revolutionary*.

3. For Brown's instructions to his men, see Cook's so-called "Confession," Statement of John E. Cook, Nov. 1859, in Hinton, *John Brown and His Men* (1968; repr., New York: Funk and Wagnalls, 1984), Appendix, 700–14, esp. 708. Osborne Anderson also remembered that Brown had presumably even reminded his company before starting out for Harpers Ferry that "the lives of others are as dear to them as yours are to you. Do not, therefore, take the life of any one if you can possibly avoid it, but if it is necessary to take life in order to save your own, then make sure work of it." Osborne Perry Anderson, *A Voice from Harper's Ferry: A Narrative of Events at Harper's Ferry* (Boston: Privately printed, 1861), 29.

4. Article 32, "Provisional Constitution and Ordinances for the People of the United States," as cited in United States Senate, 36th Congress, 1st Session, *The Select Committee of the Senate appointed to inquire into the late invasion and seizure of the public property at Harper's Ferry*, Report No. 278, 2 vols. (Washington, DC, [1860]). Hereafter cited as the *Mason Committee Report*, I: 48–59, esp. 56.

5. Articles 36, 35, "Provisional Constitution and Ordinances," in *Mason Committee Report*, I: 56–7.

6. The opening statement for the Commonwealth of Mr. Harding Oct. 29, 1859 [4th day], 1859, cited in Robert M. De Witt, ed., *The Life, Trial and Execution of Captain John Brown, Known as Old Brown of Ossawatomie* (1859; repr., New York: Da Capo Press, 1969), 84.

7. Quoted in the New York *Times*, Oct. 20, 1859, p. 1; the same wire story is printed in the New-York *Daily Tribune*, Oct. 20, 1859, p. 6.

8. Quoted in "The Harper's Ferry Rebellion, Revelations of Captain Brown," New York *Times*, Oct. 20, 1859, p. 1.

9. "Brown says he doubts not it is all right in the providence of God & is resigned to his fate," Hoyt added. George H. Hoyt to "My Dear [John W.] Le Barnes," Oct 31, 1859, Hinton Papers, KSHS. The letter is reprinted, slightly altered, in Hinton, *John Brown and His Man*, 368.

10. Quoted in the *Baltimore American and Commercial Advertiser*, Oct. 21, 1859, p. 1. A reporter for the New York *Herald* also recorded the interview in shorthand. See the *Herald*, Oct. 21, 1859, p. 1. A third version in the Cincinnati *Daily Gazette*, Oct. 21, 1859, p. 3, is pirated from that of C. W. Tayleur in the *Baltimore American*, cited earlier. Brown's questioner, Ohio Congressman Clement Vallandigham, was a political ally of Governor Wise and a Peace Democrat or "Copperhead" during the Civil War.

11. Colonel Robert E. Lee to Adjutant General S. Cooper, Oct. 18, 1859, in the *Mason Committee Report*, Part 1, Appendix, pp. 40–3. Hereafter cited as Lee's "Report to the Adjutant General."

12. "Another Letter from Forbes," New York *Herald*, Nov. 1, 1859, p. 10.

13. "Insurrection at Harper's Ferry: Treatment of Prisoners. Authentic Details," Richmond *Enquirer*, Oct. 21, 1859, p. 2. cols. 7–8.

14. John Brown to "Hon. Thos. Russell," Oct. 21, 1859, in Zoe Trodd and John Stauffer, eds., *Meteor of War: The John Brown Story* (Maplecrest, NY: Brandywine Press, 2004), 137.

15. "The Harper's Ferry Outbreak... Old Brown's Harangue to the Court," New York *Herald*, October 26, 1859, p. 1. The complete report of the preliminary hearing and trial is reprinted in Robert M. De Witt, ed., *The Life, Trial and Execution of Captain John Brown, Known as Old Brown of Ossawatomie* (1859; repr., New York: Da Capo Press, 1969), 55–95.

16. Lee's "Report to the Adjutant General," in the *Mason Committee Report*, Part 1, Appendix, pp. 40–3.

17. Wise had directed Hunter to make notes of Brown's remarks. Testimony of Andrew Hunter, January 30, 1860, *Mason Committee Report*, II: 60. Wise had also brought a reporter from his political organ, the Richmond *Enquirer*. See "Captain Brown's Interview with Governor Wise [reprinted from the Richmond *Enquirer*]," *Baltimore American*, Oct. 21, 1859, p. 1.

18. See "The Harper's Ferry Rebellion, Revelations of Captain Brown," New York *Times*, Oct. 20, 1859, p. 1.

19. The full text of the grand jury's indictment was widely published. See "The Harper's Ferry Outbreak: The Bill of Indictment Found Against the Prisoners," New York *Herald*, Oct. 30, 1859, p. 1. The court made no transcript of testimony, but reporters taking it down in shorthand published much of it in the dailies. Official documents – indictments, warrants, motions, etc. – are deposited in the Archives and Manuscripts Section of the West Virginia University Library, Morgantown. Brown's attorneys argued, of course, that since officially no slaves responded to Brown's call, he could not have been guilty of conspiring with slaves to rebel.

20. De Witt, *The Life, Trial and Execution of Captain John Brown*, 93. On the significance of references to the Haitian revolution in the response to Brown's raid, see William E. Cain, "Angel of Light: Interpreting John Brown," *Reviews in American History*, 23, no. 4 (1995): 606–11.

21. Quoted in De Witt, *The Life, Trial and Execution of Captain John Brown*, 94–5. A court stenographer took down Brown's speech.

22. Quoted in the *Mason Committee Report*, II: 67–8.

23. "Speech of Governor Wise on his return to Richmond from Harper's Ferry," Richmond *Enquirer*, Oct. 25, 1859, p. 2.

24. On the collaboration of Wise and Brown to cast Brown as a formidable adversary of slavery, see McGlone, "John Brown, Henry Wise, and the Politics of Insanity,"

in Paul Finkelman, ed., *His Soul Goes Marching On: Responses to John Brown and the Harpers Ferry Raid* (Charlottesville: University of Virginia Press, 1995), Chapter 8.

25. Quoted in De Witt, *The Life, Trial and Execution of Captain John Brown*, 94–5. Newspaper reports of this famous speech vary slightly; this is the text as recorded by the court stenographer.

26. See Robert E. McGlone, "Forgotten Surrender: John Brown's Raid and the Cult of Martial Virtues, *Civil War History*, 40 (Sept. 1994): 185–201. On the literary heritage and Brown's impact on American political culture, see Victor Vincent Verney, Jr., John Brown: Cultural Icon in American Mythos, PhD dissertation, State University of New York at Buffalo, 1996. A number of recent books, discussed elsewhere, deal with aspects of Brown's troubled legacy.

27. Quoted from the *Anglo-African* in "Old Brown and Nat Turner, the Colored Men's Heroes," New York *Herald*, Oct. 29, 1859, p. 10.

28. Quoted in Trodd and Stauffer, *Meteor of War*, 136.

29. Quoted in David Herbert Donald, *Lincoln* (New York: Simon & Schuster, 1995), 239. For Lincoln's rebuttal to Democratic charges of Republican complicity in Harpers Ferry, see his Address at Cooper Union, New York, Feb. 27, 1860, reprinted in T. Harry Williams, *Selected Writings and Speeches of Abraham Lincoln* (New York: Hendricks House, 1980), 83–105, esp. 96–9.

30. "Garrison's View of the Harper's Ferry Movement," New York *Herald*, Oct. 29, 1859, p. 10, quoting the Boston *Liberator* of Oct. 28, 1859.

31. Quoted in Oswald Garrison Villard, *John Brown, 1800–1859: A Biography Fifty Years After* (1910; repr., Gloucester, MA: Peter Smith, 1965), 565.

32. William K. Scarborough, ed., *The Diary of Edmund Ruffin* (Baton Rouge: Louisiana State University, 1972), I: 365, 68–72.

33. Despatch from "Our Special Correspondence," New York *Herald*, Oct. 25, 1859, p. 4.

34. Scarborough, *Diary of Edmund Ruffin*, I: 366.

35. John Brown to "Dear wife & children *every one*," Nov. 8, 1859, handwritten copy, Dreer Collection, PHS.

36. The phrase is from Brown's Nov. 8, 1859, letter to Mary, cited above, handwritten copy, Dreer Collection, PHS.

37. See McGlone, "John Brown, Henry Wise, and the Politics of Insanity," Chapter 8.

38. Brown to "Rev. Heman Humphrey, D. D.," Nov. 25, 1859, as quoted in Sanborn, *Life and Letters of John Brown*, 603–4.

39. Even old-line abolitionists like William Lloyd Garrison, who had exalted the principles of moral suasion and nonresistance, nevertheless distinguished Brown's righteous violence from the heathen violence of slaveholders. Garrison likened Brown to the Founding Fathers in taking up arms to vindicate freedom. Lawrence J. Friedman, *Gregarious Saints: Self and Community in American Abolitionism, 1830–1870* (Cambridge: Cambridge University Press, 1982), 210–11.

40. "I have been *a good deal* disappointed as it regards *myself* in not keeping up to *my own plans*," Brown confessed to his old Litchfield teacher. Brown had been "induced to act very contrary to my better judgment: and I have lost my two noble boys; *& other friends, if not* [like Samson] *my two eyes*." Brown to H. L. Vaill, Nov. 15, 1859, photocopy, John Brown Miscellaneous Papers, NYPL.

41. John Brown to "my dear Wife, and Children every one," Oct. 31–Nov. 3, 1859, in Trodd and Stauffer, *Meteor of War*, 137–8.

42. John Brown to Thomas Wentworth Higginson, Charlestown, Jefferson County, Va., Nov. 4, 1859, Sanborn Folder, HU. Later, Brown thanked Higginson for his financial assistance and "kind attentions" to his family, despite his wish that Mary would not "come on when she first set out." Brown to Higginson, Nov. 22, 1859, as quoted in Louis Ruchames, ed., *A John Brown Reader* (London and New York: Abelard-Schuman, 1959), 145.

43. George H. Hoyt to Mary Brown, Nov. 11, 1859, Stutler Collection, WVDCH.

44. Brown to Mary, Nov. 8, 1859, handwritten copy, Dreer Collection, PHS. The visits of two wealthy northern women, Mrs. Rebecca Spring and Mrs. Mary Ellen Russell, wife of Massachusetts Judge Thomas Russell, early in November, had caused indignation as an affront to Southern women. See Wendy Hamand Venet, "'Cry Aloud and Spare Not': Northern Antislavery Women and John Brown's Raid," in Paul Finkelman, ed., *His Soul Goes Marching On: Responses to John Brown and the Harpers Ferry Raid* (Charlottesville: University of Virginia Press, 1995), 104.

45. John Brown to "My Dear Wife," Nov. 16, 1859, Frank G. Logan Collection, CHS.

46. Brown to "My Dear Mrs. [Rebecca] Spring," Nov. 24, 1859, as quoted in Trodd and Stauffer, *Meteor of War*, 150–1.

47. Brown to "My Dear Wife," Nov. 26, 1859, as quoted in Ruchames, *A John Brown Reader*, 151–2.

48. The jailor's account of the meeting between John and Mary, complete with an ostensible conversation between them in quotation marks, was widely published in the newspapers. See, for example, New York *Daily Tribune*, Saturday, Dec. 10, pp. 2–3.

49. George L. Hoyt to J. W. Le Barnes, quoted in Villard, *Brown Fifty Years After*, 479–80n. No date is cited.

50. John Brown to "Mrs. L. Maria Child," Nov. 4, 1859, New York *Weekly Tribune*, Nov. 18, 1859, p. 7. Child's letter to Gov. Henry A. Wise and his lengthy reply were published in the *Tribune* and elsewhere, and subsequently, with Child's exchange of letters with Margaretta Mason, the wife of Virginia Senator James Mason, published as a pamphlet by the American Anti-Slavery Society that sold an astonishing 300,000 copies. See Venet, "'Cry Aloud and Spare Not'," 106–11.

51. John Brown to "Dear *Wife*; & Children *all*," Oct. 1, 1859, Eldridge Collection, HEHL.

52. Annie Brown to Thomas Wentworth Higginson, Nov. 29, 1859, Higginson Papers, BPL.

53. John Brown to "Dear wife & children *every one*," Nov. 8, 1859, handwritten copy, Dreer Collection, PHS.

54. Brown to "Dear Children" [in Ohio], Nov. 22, 1859, copy by Jason Brown, Stutler Collection, WVDCH.

55. Brown's position that knowledge of the Word of God and its acceptance as true were prerequisite to a saving faith was a fundamental Protestant doctrine. See, for example, Virgilius Ferm, ed., *An Encyclopedia of Religion* (New York: The Philosophical Library, 1945), 690.

56. John Brown to My Dearly beloved Wife, Sons: & Daughters, *every one*, Nov. 30, 1859, ALS, photocopy, John Brown Collection, KSHS.

57. John Brown to "Dear wife & children *every one*," Nov. 8, 1859, handwritten copy, Dreer Collection, PHS.

58. John Brown to "My Dearly beloved Wife, Sons: & Daughters, *every one*, Nov. 30, Trodd and Stauffer, eds., *Meteor of War*, 157–9.

59. Brown to "Dear Wife & children *every one*," Nov. 8, 1859, Stutler Collection, WVDCH; Brown to "Dear Children" [in Ohio], Nov. 22, 1859, copy by Jason Brown, Stutler Collection, WVDCH.
60. John Brown to "My Dear Wife," Nov. 16, 1859, Logan Collection, CHS.
61. John Brown to "My Dear Mrs. [Rebecca] Spring," Nov. 24, 1859, in Trodd and Stauffer, *Meteor of War*, 150–1.
62. John Brown to "My Dear Friend" (Rev. Luther Humphrey), Nov. 19, 1859, photocopy, Eldridge Collection, HEHL.
63. John Brown to "Dear Wife, & Children All," Sept. 4, 1855, John Brown Collection, KSHS.
64. John Brown to Mary A. Brown, Mar. 2, 1858, as quoted in Franklin B. Sanborn, *The Life and Letters of John Brown, Liberator of Kansas, and Martyr of Virginia* (1885; repr., New York: Negro Universities Press, 1969), 442–3.
65. Modern scholars have questioned the authorship of at least six of the Pauline letters. In *What Paul Meant* (New York: Viking, 2006), historian Gary Wills accepts only seven "as certainly by him" (p. 15). See also M. Jack Suggs, Katharine Doob Sakenfeld, and James R. Mueller, eds., *The Oxford Study Bible: Revised English Bible with the Apocrypha* (New York: Oxford University Press, 1992). My quotations are from the King James bible.
66. Brown to Dear Friend E. B. of R. I., Nov. 1, 1859, as quoted in the New-York *Weekly Tribune*, Nov. 17, 1859, p. 7.
67. John Brown to Rev. H. L. Vaill, Nov. 15, 1859, photocopy, John Brown Miscellaneous Papers, NYPL. See also the New-York *Weekly Tribune*, Dec. 3, 1859, p. 3.
68. Brown to "Dear Children" [in Ohio], Nov. 22, 1859, copy by Jason Brown, Stutler Collection, WVDCH.
69. Brown to My Dearly beloved Wife, Sons: & Daughters, *every one*, Nov. 30, 1859, ALS, photocopy, John Brown Papers, KSHS.
70. John Brown to Rev. James W. McFarland, Nov. 23, 1859, in Ruchames, *Making of a Revolutionary*, 153–4.
71. John Brown to Rev. Heman Humphrey, D. D., Nov. 25, 1859, Ruchames, *Making of a Revolutionary*, 149.
72. John Brown to "My Dear Friend" [Rev. Luther Humphrey], Nov. 19, 1859, photocopy, Eldridge Collection, HEHL.
73. Brown to "My Dearly beloved Sisters Mary A. and Martha," Nov. 27, 1859 (Sabbath), facsimile, Gee Collection, HLHS. The original is in the Chicago Historical Society.
74. John Brown to Jeremiah Root Brown, Nov. 12, 1859, in Trodd and Stauffer, *Meteor of War*, 142.
75. John Brown to Rev. James W. McFarland, Nov. 23, 1859, in Ruchames, *Making of a Revolutionary*, 153–4.
76. Brown to "My Dearly beloved Sisters Mary A. and Martha," Nov. 27, 1859 (Sabbath), facsimile, Gee Collection, HLHS.
77. John Brown to "My dear Wife," Nov. 26, 1859, in Ruchames, *Making of a Revolutionary*, 151–2.
78. John Brown to "My dear Wife," Nov. 26, 1859, in Ruchames, *Making of a Revolutionary*, 151–2.
79. John Brown to Rev. H. L. Vaill, Nov. 15, 1859, photocopy, John Brown Miscellaneous Papers, NYPL. It is reprinted in Ruchames, *Making of a Revolutionary*.
80. John Brown to Rev. McFarland, Nov. 23, 1859, in Trodd and Stauffer, *Meteor of War*, 150.

81. John Brown to Jeremiah Root Brown [brother], Nov. 12, 1859, in Trodd and Stauffer, *Meteor of War,* 142.
82. Brown to "Dear Children" [in Ohio], Nov. 22, 1859, copy by Jason Brown, Stutler Collection, WVDCH.
83. See for example the report in *The Baltimore American,* Oct. 21, 1859, p. 1.
84. Asked for a statement during his interview with Senator Mason, Brown said he had come only to "aid those suffering great wrong." Then he warned "*that you had better–all you people at the South–prepare yourselves for a settlement....* [T]his question is still to be settled–this negro question I mean; the end of that is not yet." "The Harper's Ferry Outbreak... Statement to the Herald Reporter," New York *Herald,* Oct. 21, 1859, p. 1.
85. Statement of John Brown, Dec. 2, 1859, Dreer Collection, PHS. For convenience, see the fascimile copy in Villard, *John Brown Fifty Years After,* opposite page 554.
86. Sherman's Memoirs, II, 179, cited in James M. McPherson, *Ordeal By Fire: The Civil War,* 3 vols. (3rd ed.; New York: McGraw Hill, 2001), 497.

Index

Note: All illustrations – prints, maps, photographs – are indicated by page numbers in *italics*. The name Brown, standing alone, refers to John Brown throughout.